ELIE NADELMAN
Sculptor of Modern Life

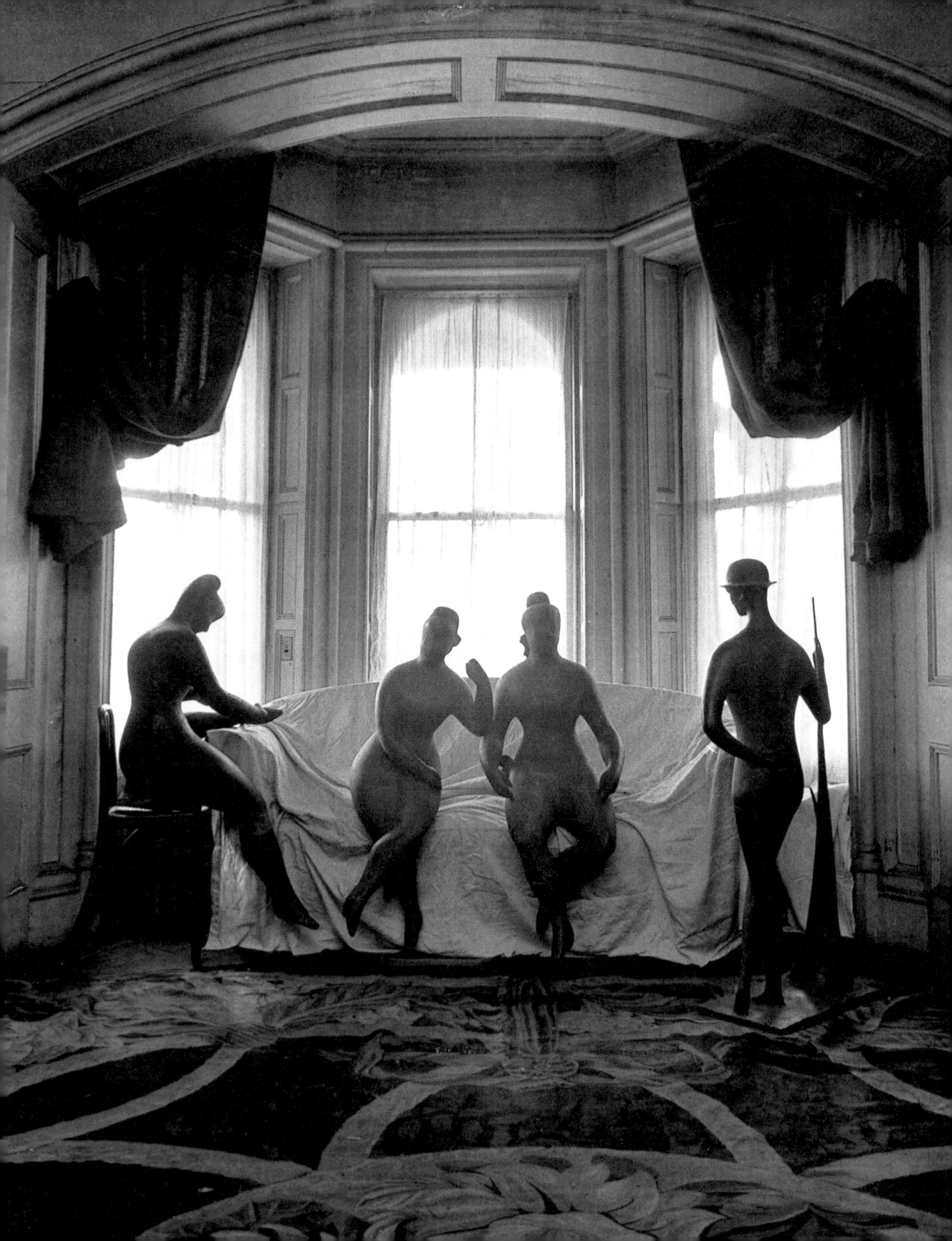

ELIE NADELMAN
Sculptor of Modern Life

Barbara Haskell

WHITNEY MUSEUM OF AMERICAN ART, NEW YORK

DISTRIBUTED BY HARRY N. ABRAMS, INC., NEW YORK

This book was published on the occasion of the exhibition **Elie Nadelman: Sculptor of Modern Life**, at the Whitney Museum of American Art, New York, April 3–July 20, 2003.

Support for **Elie Nadelman: Sculptor of Modern Life** is provided by the National Endowment for the Arts, The Brown Foundation, Inc., Houston, Laurie Tisch Sussman, Susan R. Malloy, Shen Family Foundation, The Lunder Foundation, and the Chairman's Council of the Whitney Museum of American Art.

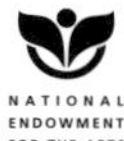

Design and installation of this exhibition has been made possible by the American Fellows of the Whitney Museum of American Art.

The catalogue is supported by Furthermore, a program of the J. M. Kaplan Fund, and the Dedalus Foundation.

Photographs from the Lincoln Kirstein Collection are reproduced by permission of the New York Public Library (Astor, Lenox, and Tilden Foundations).

© 2003 Whitney Museum of American Art
945 Madison Avenue at 75th Street
New York, NY 10021
www.whitney.org

Frontispiece
Sculpture by Elie Nadelman; parlor of Alderbrook, 1948
Photography by W. Eugene Smith/TimePix

Library of Congress Cataloging-in-Publication Data

Haskell, Barbara.
 Elie Nadelman : sculptor of modern life / Barbara Haskell.
    p. cm.
Includes index.
 ISBN 0-87427-130-4 (cloth) -- ISBN 0-87427-132-0 (pbk.)
 1. Nadelman, Elie, 1882-1946. I. Whitney Museum of American Art. II.
Title.
 NB237.N23 A4 2003
 730'.92--dc21
                          2002014478

Distributed in 2003 by

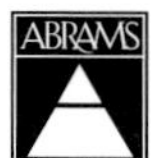
Harry N. Abrams, Inc.
100 Fifth Avenue
New York, N.Y. 10011
www.abramsbooks.com

Abrams is a subsidiary of

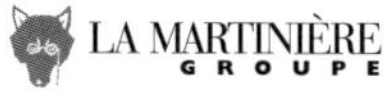

Contents

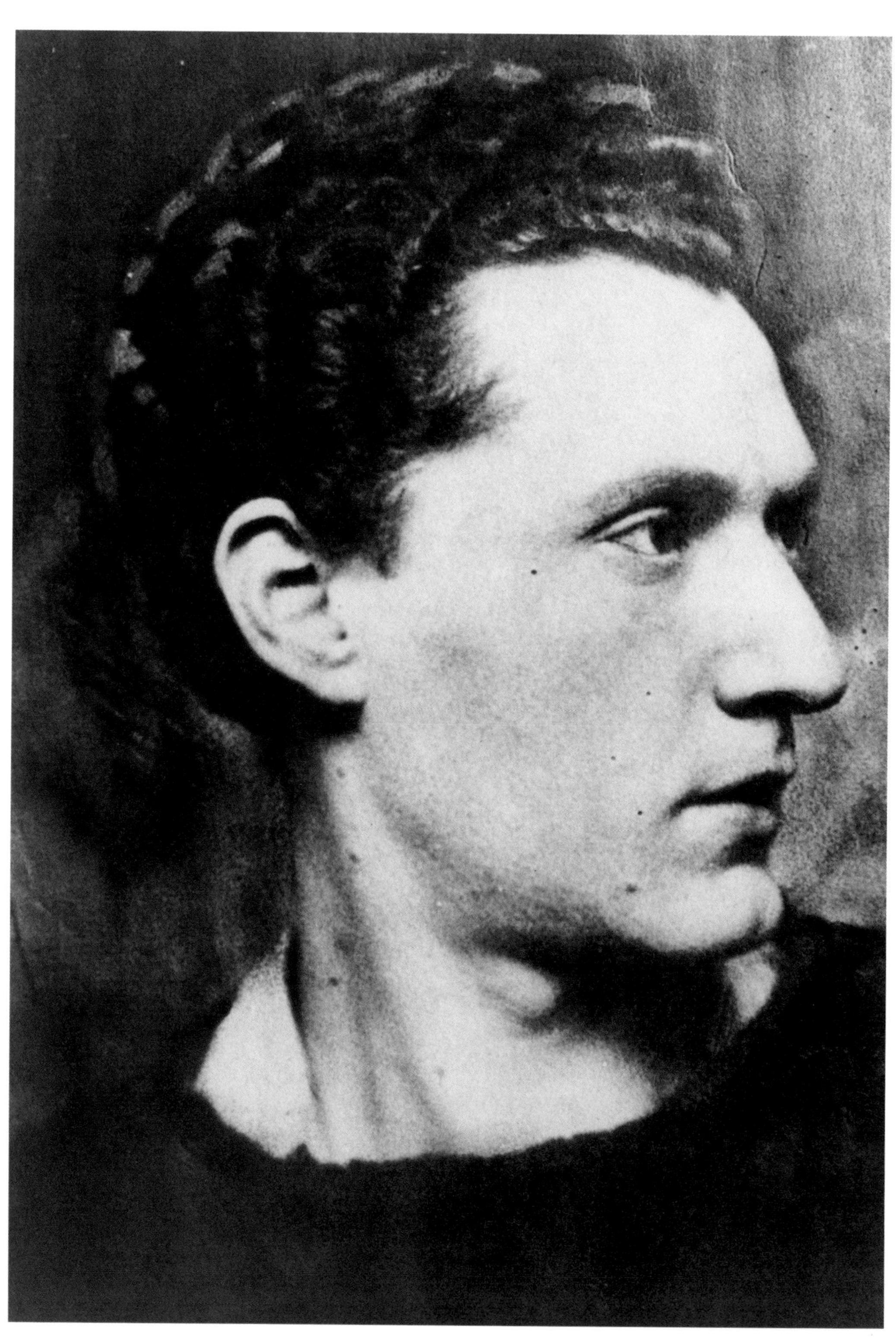

Foreword

When we think of sculpture in the twentieth century, it is the remarkable strides by artists working with abstraction that first come to mind—the allusive forms of Picasso, González, Calder, and Miró, and later David Smith, Mark di Suvero, Donald Judd, and many others who took turns at the manipulation of form without the necessity of an accompanying narrative. But in the first half of the century, a Polish immigrant named Elie Nadelman, having inflected classical style with a sleek attenuation characteristic of Futurists such as Brancusi, ultimately made himself at home in the vernacular of American folk art, replete with narrative, and established himself as one of the century's best sculptors. Barbara Haskell has brought us a thorough analysis of the master's emergence from a conventional visual vocabulary to the unique forms that make his work instantly recognizable. She organized the exhibition with the help of Assistant Curator, Prewar Art and Special Projects, Evelyn Hankins; Senior Curatorial Assistant, Prewar Art, Jennifer Palladino; and Research Assistant Patricia Hughes. The present catalogue was undertaken by Director of Publications and New Media, Garrett White, together with Managing Editor, Rachel de W. Wixom and Senior Graphic Designer Makiko Ushiba.

Our thanks go to Laurie Tisch Sussman, for her financial support of this exhibition and for her co-chairmanship, along with Melanie Shorin, of the American Fellows, the Whitney patrons dedicated to the art of the first half of the twentieth century. We are also grateful to the National Endowment for the Arts, The Brown Foundation, Inc., Houston, Susan R. Malloy, Shen Family Foundation, The Lunder Foundation, and the Chairman's Council of the Whitney Museum of American Art. In addition, our thanks go out for the additional support given by the J. M. Kaplan Fund and the Dedalus Foundation.

It is a privilege to celebrate through this exhibition the Whitney's 1997–99 acquisition of sixty-seven works by Nadelman, which makes us the nation's leading collector of his work. This museum, founded by Gertrude Vanderbilt Whitney, a sculptor of Nadelman's epoch, remains deeply committed to chronicling the achievements of her peers and successors in the medium of sculpture.

Maxwell L. Anderson
Alice Pratt Brown Director

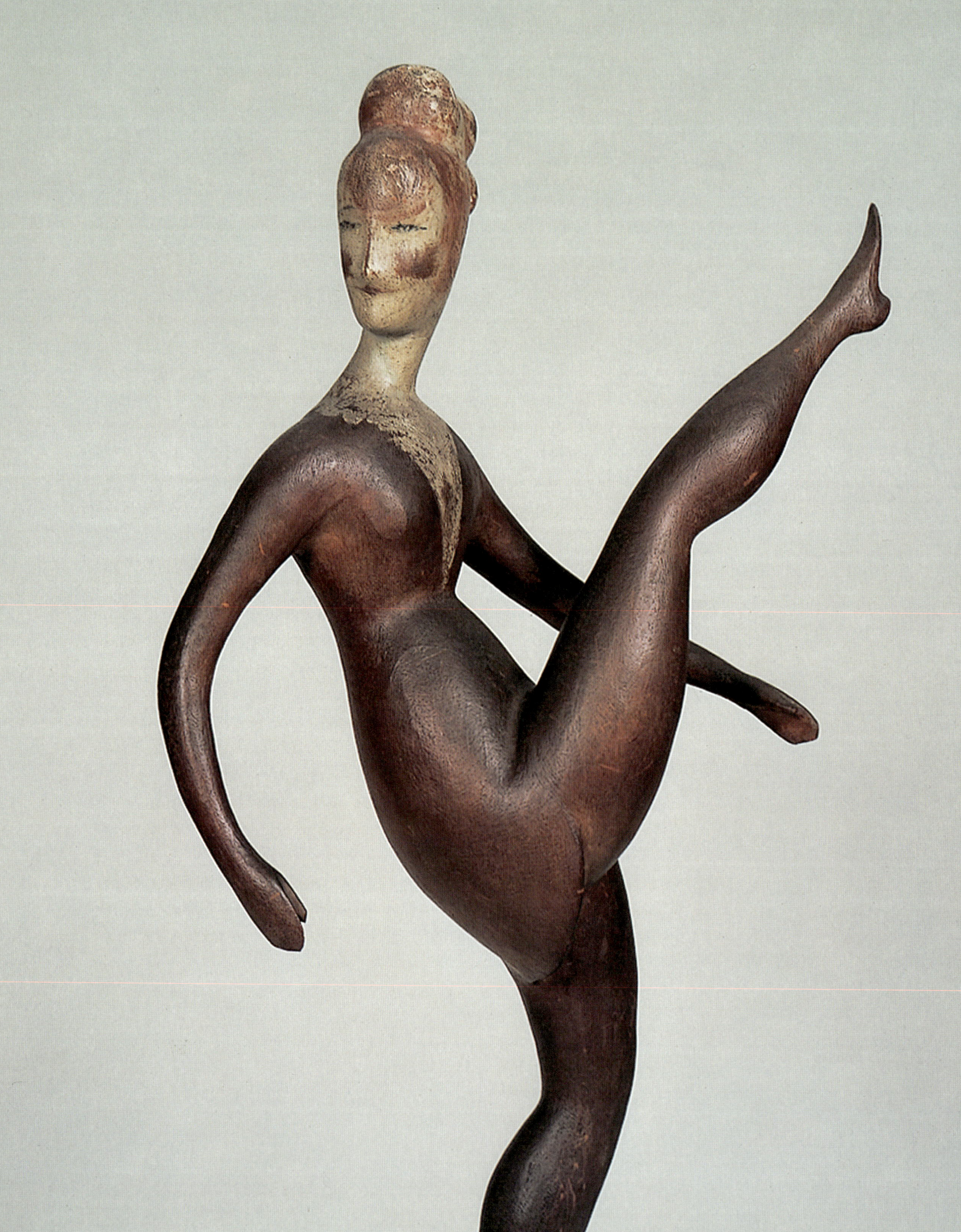

Elie Nadelman: Sculptor of Modern Life
Barbara Haskell

Throughout his career, Elie Nadelman successfully pursued a modern-day classicism by expunging blatantly subjective and biographical references from his art in favor of formal purity and idealized, geometric forms; yet the effect of his life experiences and personality on his aesthetic choices and the critical reception of his art is undeniable. His attraction as a young Jewish artist in Poland to an aesthetic divorced from references to the personal and the particular can be seen as a reaction to the country's predominantly nationalist—and, by extension—largely anti-Semitic art community. Nadelman found in modernism's exclusive emphasis on formal values a license to ignore subject matter and thereby obliterate reminders of the ethnic, religious, and social distinctions upon which nationalism rests. Choosing modernist abstraction over subject matter allowed him to pursue a timeless, universal art based on order, reason, and harmony. At a time when sculptors were seeking an alternative to the hegemony of Auguste Rodin and the Symbolist aesthetic, Nadelman's formulation of a sculptural vocabulary based on the simplified geometric forms of Greek classical art won enthusiastic welcome. At age twenty-seven he captured the attention of the Parisian art world.

Nadelman's immigration to America in 1914 precipitated a shift in his subject matter from classical sources to American popular culture. With an outsider's perspective on American society, he constructed simplified, whimsical genre figures that both celebrated and mocked the high society of which he became a member through his 1919 marriage to American heiress Viola Spiess Flannery. For the remainder of his life, he sought in his art to subvert the distinctions between high and low culture and the gulf between historical and contemporary styles. He sustained the practice of amalgamating motifs from the past and the present and from high and low art even as his imagery became more disquieting in the wake of financial ruin, ill health, and the political and social crises created by World War II. In the last ten years of his life, having refused all offers to exhibit his sculpture and all but forgotten by the art world, he produced hundreds of miniature plaster figurines that embodied both his personal anxieties and the turmoil and uncertainty of a world at war.

Critical assessment of the various stages through which Nadelman's art evolved has shifted dramatically over the last one hundred years. From the time of his first highly acclaimed exhibition in 1909 until after his death, he was lauded almost exclusively for his classically inspired, idealized heads and figures. The stylized painted portraits of subjects from popular culture that he began to produce after his arrival in America earned him mixed reviews and only one sale. In post–World War II America, aesthetically dominated as it was by Abstract Expressionism, neither these works nor any other aspect of Nadelman's output was given more than scant attention. Not until the 1960s, with the ascendancy of Pop and Minimal art, did the bold immediacy and populist appeal of his simplified, elegant genre figures catch the attention of a new generation of artists and critics who hailed him as a precursor of Pop art and a prophet of modernism. Since then, these works have earned universal regard as masterpieces of American sculpture. Yet it was not until the end of the twentieth century that the entire spectrum of Nadelman's work, including his late plaster figurines, gained the art world's respect. In the eclectic climate of postmodernism, in which differences between high and low art are often muted and artists revel in figuration and the recycling of historical art, Nadelman has emerged as a complex and heroic figure whose art anticipated the issues and strategies of the late twentieth and early twenty-first centuries.

Formative Experiences: Poland, 1882—1903

Eliasz Nadelman was born in Warsaw on February 20, 1882, into a Poland that had ceased to exist as a nation eighty-seven years earlier, when Russia, Prussia, and Austria had divided the country among themselves.[1] These powers had abolished Polish schools and institutions and banned the Polish language from public use, but had been unable to diminish Polish patriotism and the dream of Polish reunification. For Polish Jews, occupation engendered an ambivalent response, especially in the Russian zone, of which Warsaw was a part.[2] Here the czar had attempted to avert a united Jewish-Polish rebellion by introducing extensive reforms in the laws affecting Jews, among them emancipation and the elimination of most legal restrictions on Jewish residency and economic activity.[3] The resulting suspicion among Poles about Jewish antagonism to the czar and loyalty to the cause of Polish independence exacerbated an already deep current of anti-Semitism.[4]

Still, despite anti-Jewish pogroms that lasted well into the 1880s, most assimilated Jews in Warsaw regarded themselves as Polish.[5] This was true of Nadelman's parents, Philip and Hannah Nadelman, who chose to live outside the Jewish district, in an apartment above their jewelry shop on Marszałkowska Street, in the city's most beautiful residential and commercial center.[6] Unlike the majority of Polish Jews—who remained religiously observant, spoke only Yiddish, and wore traditional Jewish clothing—the Nadelmans saw themselves as part of an enlightened Polish cultural world.[7] They wrote and spoke Polish at home, wore modern European dress, and gave their children secular names.[8] Only with the youngest of their seven children did they make an exception, Eliasz being the Polonized spelling of Elijah, the name of the Hebrew prophet.

Eliasz Nadelman perpetuated his parents' loyalty to the Polish people throughout his life. Long after becoming an American citizen, he spoke of Poland as "my country."[9] Yet he never taught his son to speak or write Polish and never returned to the country after leaving it at age twenty-two.[10] His ambivalence was understandable. Despite his acculturation, he remained an outsider in the eyes of the Polish public and was denied full equality as a Polish citizen. Not surprisingly, he grew up with a complicated relationship to Polish nationalism and Jewish identity—one that would affect his decisions as an artist in unmistakable ways.

Nadelman graduated in 1899 from a Warsaw gymnasium, a German-style academic high school, fluent in Russian and fully conversant with Russian history and literature, as was required of all gymnasium graduates. His diploma granted him a status few Jews enjoyed. Quotas restricting the education of Jews were strictly enforced, and fewer than 1 percent of Polish Jews received a secular secondary-school education; the formal education of the majority was far more limited, with most Polish Jews attending only Jewish primary schools where Yiddish was exclusively spoken.[11] Even discounting his educational attainments, Nadelman was unusual within the assimilated Jewish community. With his oldest brother in the family jewelry business and the other a dentist, he was encouraged to pursue a career in the arts. He decided against becoming a singer, a profession that his family viewed as too effeminate, and chose instead to become a visual artist—a decision that thrust him into one of the epicenters of Polish cultural nationalism.

Under occupation, discussions of Polish nationalism were censored, and all social, cultural, and economic links among the three occupied zones were suppressed. Visual art became the conduit through which national consciousness was covertly expressed. Artists valorized art as a weapon—and saw themselves as warriors—in the service of the nation.[12] As the country's foremost art group put it after Poland had gained independence, "Never for a moment, one generation after another, was the thought of final victory renounced by Polish warriors."[13] Fueled by this nationalist imperative, Polish artists sought to portray the distinctive character of Polish culture and heritage and to underscore the nobility of the Polish people and the beauty of their country through depictions of Polish history, folk imagery, and landscape.

For Jewish artists this union of art and nationalism was problematic. As Jews they were suspected of being ambivalent about Polish independence and thus were implicitly barred from participation in the nationalist mission of the art world. The introduction of modernist aesthetic theories in the late nineteenth century offered a way to circumvent this exclusion. From the modernist perspective, subject matter and the imitation of nature were unimportant; what mattered were formal values and personal expression. The best way for artists to serve the nation, Polish modernists argued, was through internationally acclaimed art that would gain recognition for Poland as a cultural force worthy of independence. Verisimilitude was thereby vanquished as a measure of aesthetic quality, but expressing the "Polish soul" remained an imperative.

The critic whose aesthetic theories severed this remaining link between art and nationalism was Stanisław Witkiewicz. Witkiewicz had abandoned writing to found an arts commune eight years before Nadelman entered the art world, but his ideas retained currency in the Polish art community through the continued circulation of his 1891 book, *Art and Criticism in Our Country*.[14] Witkiewicz's advocacy of the autonomy of art and his attendant dismissal of subject matter and the imitation of nature as irrelevant to aesthetic quality had led him to deify Greek art and excoriate that of the Renaissance because it imitated nature. For Witkiewicz, formal values alone determined aesthetic quality. "The value of a work of art," he proclaimed, "does not depend on the real-life feelings contained in it or on the perfection achieved in copying the subject matter but is solely based upon the unity of a construction of pure formal elements."[15] This formalistic criterion for aesthetic judgments was difficult for most artists to embrace until later in the century. Few among even Witkiewicz's early supporters accepted his proposition that "true art" was exclusively contingent on "pure form." For Nadelman, however, the idea would prove liberating, becoming central to his ideology by 1910. In the meantime, other theories fired his imagination, namely those of the Symbolist movement.

In the early years of the century, Symbolism was seen in Poland, as elsewhere, as a way to bypass the imitation of observed reality without sacrificing subject matter. The movement's advocacy of inner vision and personal expression took hold among the Polish vanguard after the founding in Kraków in 1897 of the art and literary journal *Życie (Life)*. *Life*'s editor, Stanisław Przybyszewski, promoted Symbolism as a handmaiden of nationalism, a way to embody the Polish soul without relying on demonstrably Polish subject matter.[16] Attracted to the preoccupation with decadence and evil in the art of James Ensor and Edvard Munch, he featured their paintings in *Life*, along with the work of Arnold Böcklin, Edward Burne-Jones, Ludwig Hoffmann, and Auguste Rodin. Przybyszewski's fascination with irrational states of mind and his exploration of satanic rituals ultimately led to his departure from Kraków following the murder of his wife by another member of his circle, but not before he had introduced Poland—and Nadelman—to an art that used nonillusionistic formal elements to evoke feelings that could not be conveyed by naturalism alone.[17]

Przybyszewski's call for an art based on emotion and intuition rather than on objective observation was taken up by the Warsaw-based art journal

Chimera in 1900. Published in Nadelman's hometown and allied, through interlocking friendships, with Warsaw's only commercial contemporary art gallery, Salon Krywult, where Nadelman would first show his art, *Chimera* extended Nadelman's appreciation of Symbolist art through its extensive coverage of the movement's seminal artists.[18] Equally important was the magazine's partiality to ornamental linearity and its attendant promotion of Art Nouveau, which Nadelman would later combine with Symbolism to create his first aesthetic breakthrough.

Life and *Chimera* were portals for Nadelman and his contemporaries into a world of international art that was otherwise unavailable in Poland. This was especially true for art students, most of whom remained in Poland. While many opted to study in Kraków, universally considered Poland's aesthetic and intellectual center, Nadelman chose to remain at home and enroll in Warsaw's School of Drawing, the city's only art training facility. This school was all that remained of the Warsaw School of Fine Arts after the Russian government abolished all formal art instruction in its zone following the January Insurrection of 1863–64.[19] Known unofficially as Gerson's School, after Wojciech Gerson, who served as its chairman from 1872 to 1896, the school offered only limited courses in the fine arts. Its focus was vocational, with the majority of its classes in architecture and industrial drawing. For fine artists it functioned primarily as a preparatory school, laying the groundwork for studies elsewhere.

Nadelman entered the school after graduating from gymnasium in 1899. Primed by his probable encounters with *Life* and *Chimera*, he immediately aligned himself with the school's modernists. By the end of 1900 he had coauthored a satirical drawing with fellow student Witold Wojtkiewicz entitled *Pochód modernizmu*, or *The March of Modernism*, which depicted an army of artists marching unopposed across a field as if in certain victory against academic conservatism (FIG. 1).[20] Two years later the drawing would be included in a group show at Salon Krywult and reproduced in *Tygodnik Ilustrowany (Illustrated Weekly)*.

On his eighteenth birthday, after less than a year at the School of Drawing, Nadelman became eligible for draft in the Russian imperial army.[21] Military service was compulsory, but because the army operated on a quota system, not all eligible males who were drafted were called to serve. Being called meant four or more years of brutal conditions and, for Jews, few restraints on anti-Semitism. An alternative available to the 10 percent of the

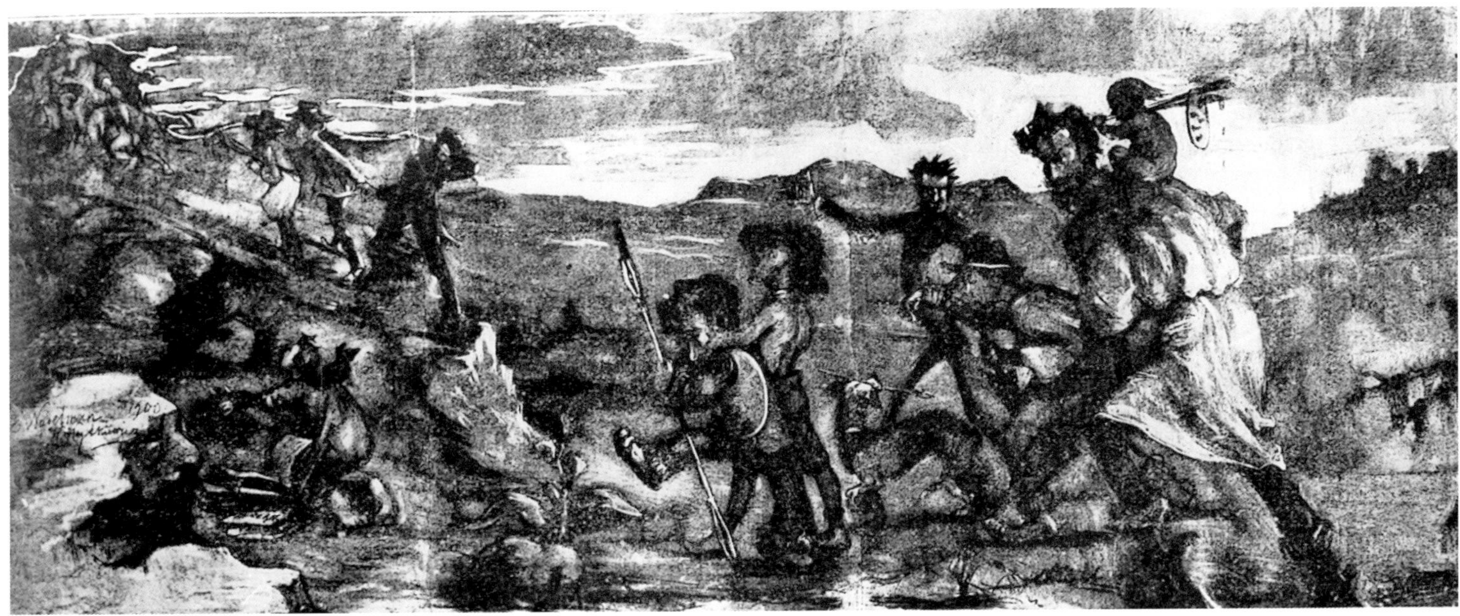

Fig. 1
Elie Nadelman and Witold Wojtkiewicz
The March of Modernism, 1900
Pencil on paper; lost
Reproduced from **Tygodnik illustrawany**
(*Illustrated Weekly*), 1902

male population who had graduated from gymnasium was to volunteer. Doing so meant entering the army as an officer trainee, a status that carried privileges and benefits such as shorter terms of duty, special uniforms, and servants. Jews could not be officers, but if they were gymnasium graduates, they could enter the army as noncommissioned trainees and receive the same benefits that accrued to non-Jewish gymnasium graduates. Given the discriminatory legislation that made Jews more likely to be called for service than non-Jews, Nadelman's chances of being inducted were high. Sensibly, he decided to volunteer. The common prejudice that Jews' artistic proclivities and effeminacy made them unfit for battle worked to his advantage;[22] among his assignments during his term of duty was the teaching of drawing and flute to officers' children. A year later, in 1901, he was discharged as an army corps reservist.

Once back in Warsaw, Nadelman resumed his studies at the School of Drawing and reestablished his friendship with Wojtkiewicz. By 1901 the latter had already embarked on a style of painting later described as the "purest form of early expressionism in Polish painting."[23] Reminiscent of the Symbolism of Ensor, his canvases portrayed children caught in a macabre and decadent world populated by clowns, jugglers, circus performers, masked actors, and marionettes (FIG. 3). While not a direct influence on Nadelman, Wojtkiewicz's work encouraged his friend's Symbolist inclinations and alerted him to the potential of popular entertainment as subject matter.

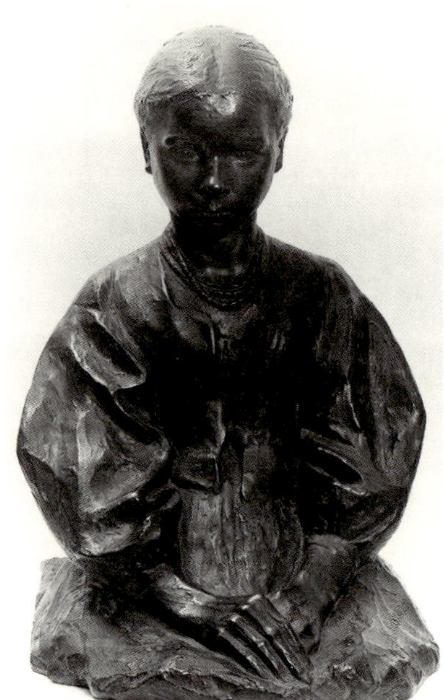

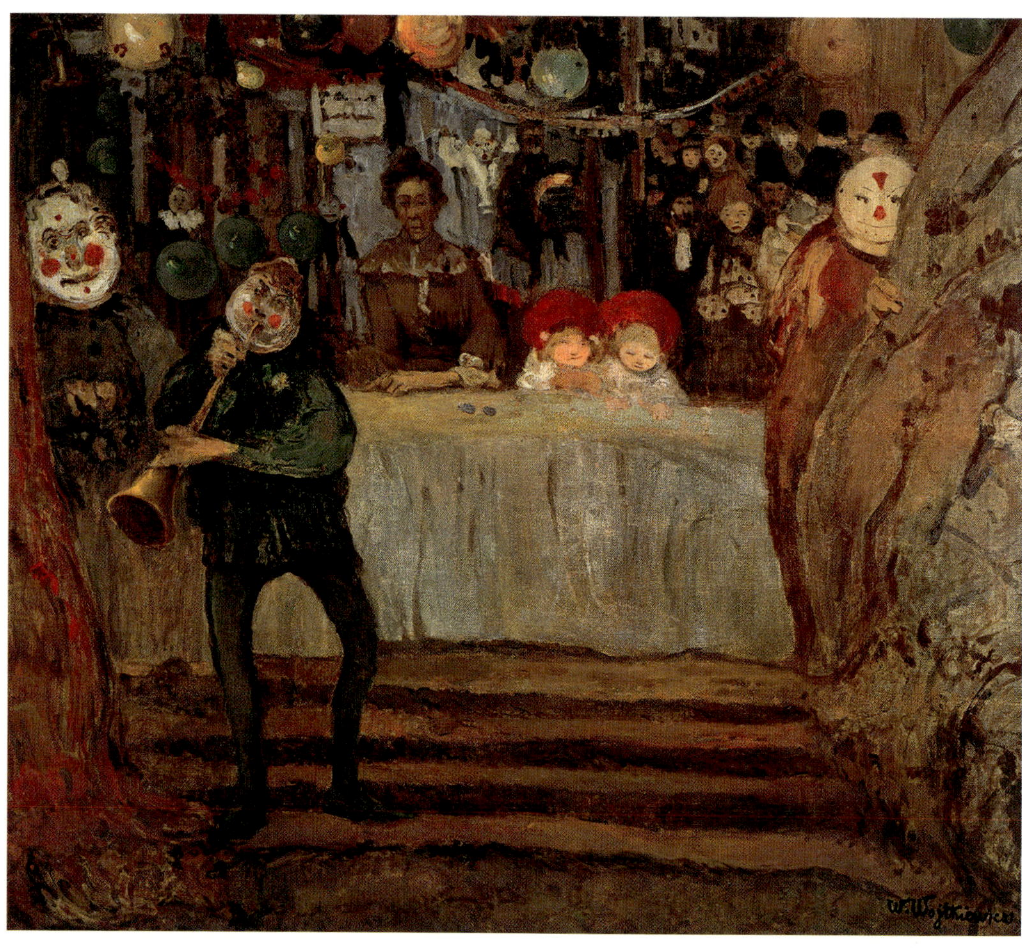

The two artists left Warsaw together in 1902 to enroll in Kraków's
Academy of Fine Arts. Wojtkiewicz remained through 1906; Nadelman left
after two days.[24] His claim that he left because his work was more advanced
than that of his teachers and fellow students is implausible. Unlike Warsaw's
School of Drawing, with its exclusive focus on draftsmanship, the Academy of
Fine Arts offered a full curriculum that included the only formal sculpture
instruction in all of Poland.[25] Reformed in 1895, it was considered one of the
most progressive and important art institutions in all of Central Europe.
Nadelman's later account that he went to Kraków to study with Konstanty
Laszczka, head of the academy's sculpture department, is revealing. Acclaimed
internationally for its expressive realism, Laszczka's work would have been well
known to Nadelman through its frequent reproduction in *Life* and *Chimera*
and its regular exhibition in Warsaw. Laszczka's gesturally modeled surfaces
and psychologically charged iconography linked his sculpture with that of
Rodin, whom he had known in Paris. Not surprisingly, given Laszczka's place

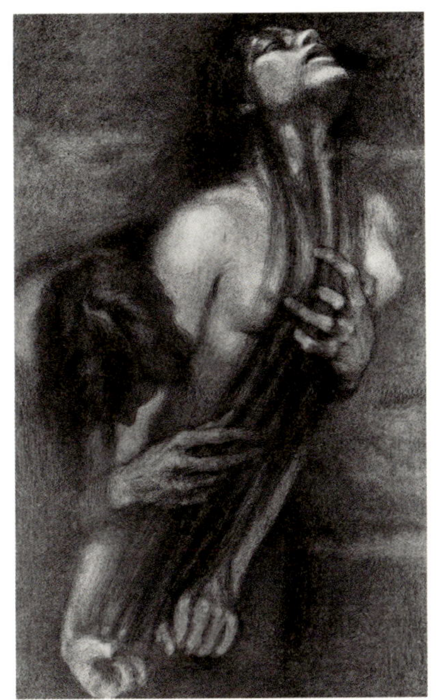

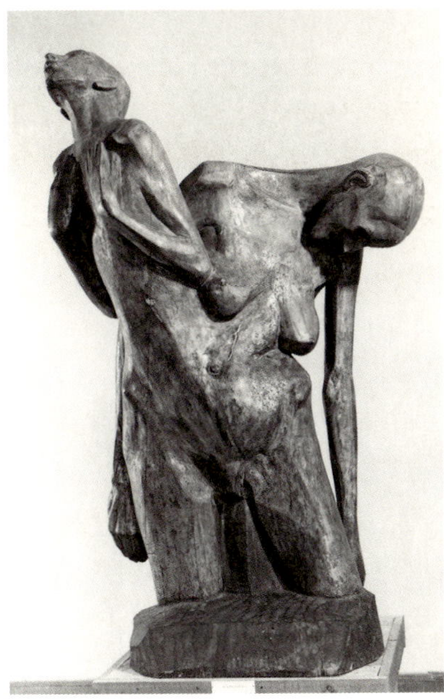

Fig. 4
Elie Nadelman
Bemol (B Minor), 1904
Pencil on paper; lost
Reproduced from *Sztuka* (Paris), no. 7 (1904)

Fig. 5
Xawery Dunikowski
Maternity, c. 1903
Gilded wood, 68 7/8 x 40 3/16 x 28 5/16 in.
(175 x 102 x 72 cm)
National Museum, Warsaw—Dunikowski
Museum

within the ranks of the Polish avant-garde, most progressive Polish sculptors studied with him; that he was Nadelman's reason for going to Kraków suggests that by 1902 Nadelman had already chosen sculpture as his metier.

Laszczka passed on to his students a reverence for Symbolist subjects and expressively handled surfaces. Enrolling in his class would have put Nadelman in contact with these ideas and with sculpture students such as Xawery Dunikowski, who was in his last year at the academy. Later considered Poland's most important twentieth-century sculptor, Dunikowski was already crafting powerful statements on the anguished struggle between life and death (FIG. 5).[26] Nadelman may have been disinclined to compete with him in the classroom out of a wish to resolve in private any lingering uncertainties he had about his sculptural direction, which may not have been as advanced as Dunikowski's in 1902. Indeed, it had been only two years since he had coauthored *The March of Modernism* with Wojtkiewicz. Nothing is known of Nadelman's art between 1900 and 1904. Although he would soon distinguish himself as a Symbolist, it is possible that what prompted him to seek out Laszczka was not the older artist's connection to Symbolism and Rodin, but rather his more conservative busts of folkloric characters in contemporary clothing (FIG. 2). Sometimes these portraits verged on caricature; most often they mirrored Laszczka's affection for the unpretentious honesty of rural subjects. More than a decade and a half later, Nadelman would undertake his own version of Laszczka's clothed quotidian archetypes, avoiding the Polish artist's rural subjects but echoing his would-be mentor's implicit valorization of the premodern and the nonindustrial by choosing to work in a folk medium: painted wood.

Kraków could not have failed to impress Nadelman with its intellectual and artistic vitality and the relatively high level of freedom and autonomy its Austro-Hungarian rulers tolerated there and elsewhere within their zone. Not only was Kraków home to Poland's most revered Gothic masterpiece—Veit Stoss's late-fifteenth-century polychrome wood altarpiece in Saint Mary's Church in the city's center (FIG. 6)—but it was also a magnet for the artists, writers, and theater people in the Young Poland movement, a small, covert organization that had shifted the fight for Polish independence from direct political resistance to the nurturing of a Polish art that would gain recognition inside and outside the country.[27] Allied with the Young Poland movement in this endeavor was the Kraków-based Society of Polish Artists, known as Sztuka (Art). Founded in 1897 as an exhibition association by ten professors from the

Kraków academy, Sztuka was committed to national independence.[28] It aimed to promote the visibility of Polish art by organizing temporary exhibitions in the three occupied zones and abroad. To maintain quality, Sztuka kept its roster small, even though it accepted as members Polish artists living in the three occupied zones as well as those abroad. In 1902, when Nadelman visited Kraków, the group had only twenty-three members—all, however, considered the foremost Polish artists of the day.

Nadelman's flight from such a cultural and political hotbed after only two days is curious. Even acknowledging the possible offense he might have taken at the academy's requirement that first- and second-year sculpture students model from plaster casts rather than work from live models, his departure was inexplicably precipitous. He may have been put off by the city's overt nationalism and the undercurrent of anti-Semitism it inevitably engendered. Dominating both Sztuka and the Kraków academy in those years were artists whose central themes still revolved around Poland—its peasants, its history, and its countryside. Indeed, so strong was Sztuka's valorization of folk culture and folk artifacts that its exhibitions regularly included Polish arts and crafts, and many of its members also belonged to the Kraków-based Polish Applied Art Society. Although Nadelman would eventually join Sztuka in 1913, he did so from the safety of Paris, where émigré status fostered a cohesion within the Polish community that overrode the potentially divisive issue of ethnic identity.

Nadelman returned to Warsaw in time to see *The March of Modernism* exhibited in a group show entitled *Humor in Art* at Salon Krywult. This modest validation of his ability as an artist fueled his instinct for independence, and he opted not to reenroll in the School of Drawing—a decision that caused him to miss the institution's liberalization in 1904 and its appointment of four young modernists as professors, among them Dunikowski. Instead, Nadelman worked independently for two years before going abroad. Like the majority of other young artists who left the country to study, he selected a city within easy reach of Poland. For many Polish art students, the favored choice was Munich, which ranked alongside Paris as one of the great international meccas of the period.[29] Nadelman was no exception. He spent six months in the Bavarian capital, absorbing doctrines and styles that would form the basis of his future art.[30]

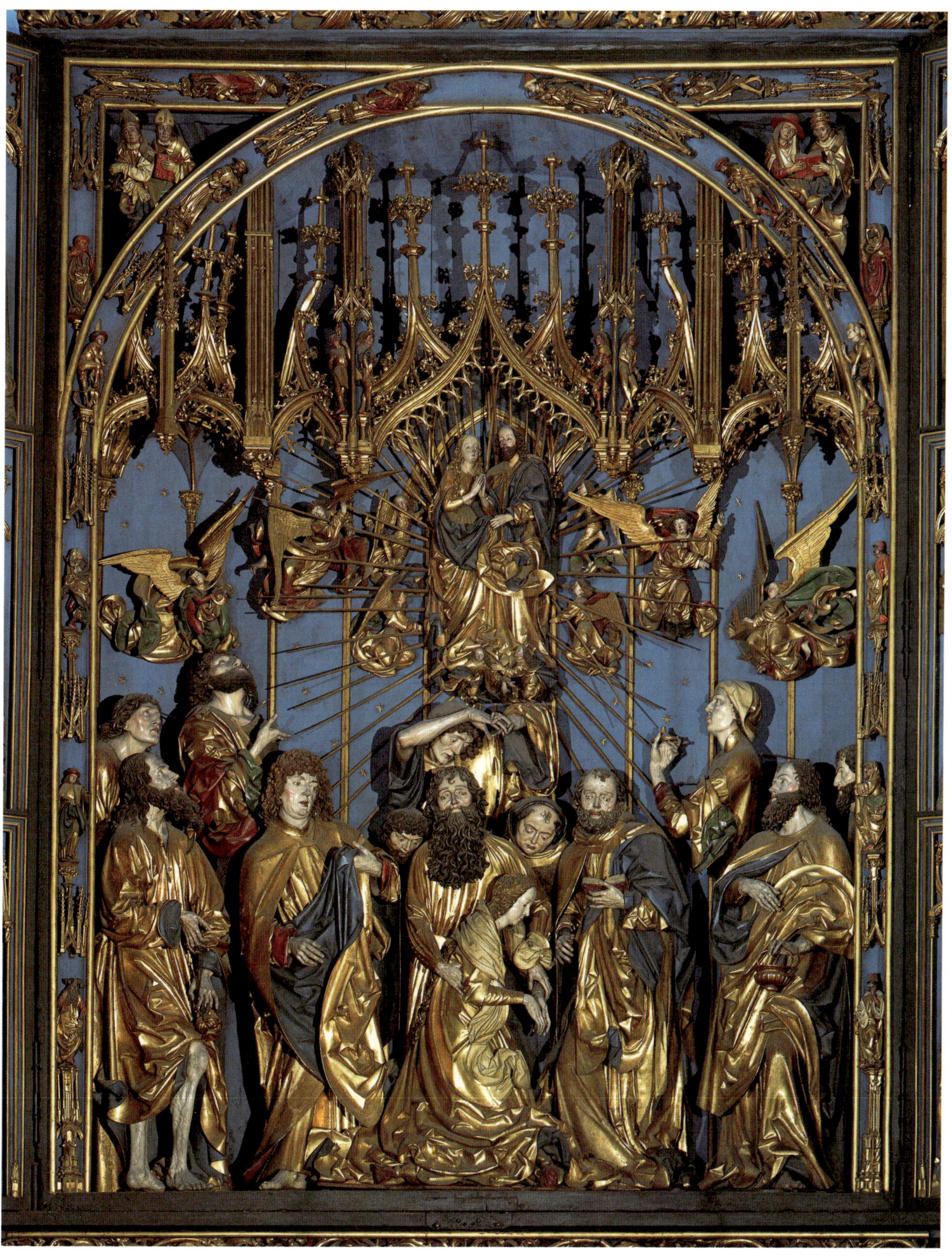

An Aesthetic Emerges: Munich, 1904

For Nadelman, whose residence in Poland had limited his exposure to significant historical art, Munich's aesthetic riches were beyond measure. He took full advantage of the opportunities by seeing everything he could in the hope that it would provide fodder for future work. The Munich he encountered in 1904 was under the spell of a triumvirate of aesthetic currents: Romanticism, Classicism, and Jugendstil. Having been thoroughly steeped in Symbolist ideology in Poland, he was initially attracted to the city's nineteenth-century Romantic artists. Eschewing descriptive realism in favor of the supernatural and the mythological, Romantic artists such as Böcklin and Franz von Stuck tinged their Neoclassical vocabularies with a languid melancholy and wistful nostalgia for a civilization untroubled by industry, poverty, and the threat of change. Nadelman responded enthusiastically to their dreamlike antidotes to ordinary experience. Equally appealing to him was Jugendstil, the style whose mixture of freely curved lines and simple, rectilinear profiles—a result of conflating elements of Art Nouveau and the English Arts and Crafts movement—dominated the Munich-based magazines *Jugend* (*Youth*) and *Simplicissimus*. Graphically, these publications were indistinguishable. Although *Simplicissimus* specialized in social and political satire and *Jugend* restricted itself to the fine arts, the journals' employment of the same artists and promotion of the same curvilinear graphic style ensured Jugendstil's omnipresence in Munich.[31]

Jugendstil's emphasis on essence and idea over narrative and descriptive detail—especially in the branch of it that favored abstract, rectilinear forms over floral ornamentation—struck a responsive chord in Nadelman. Admonishing artists to replace all references to nature with abstract forms, Jugendstil's geometric practitioners called for the arbitrary play of shapes and colors to elicit emotional response. Praising art "which bubbles up out of the human soul through forms that are like nothing known, that represent nothing, and symbolize nothing, that work through freely invented forms," the Jugendstil architect August Endell proclaimed that "there is no greater error than the belief that the painstaking imitation of nature is art."[32] This vision of an art that dispensed with naturalistic references and dealt exclusively with formal elements—line, color, and shape— was the basis of abstraction. Its impact on Nadelman would have been all the more profound since it so closely echoed the theories of Polish critic Witkiewicz.

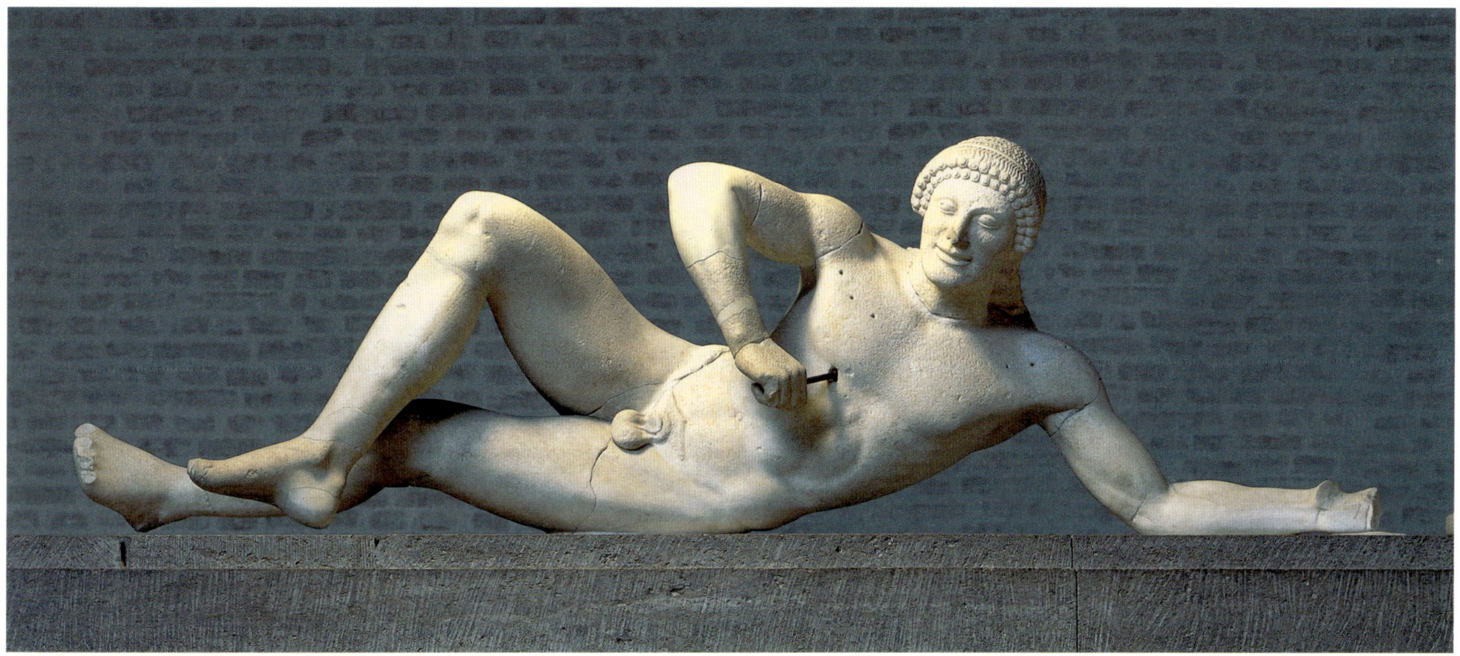

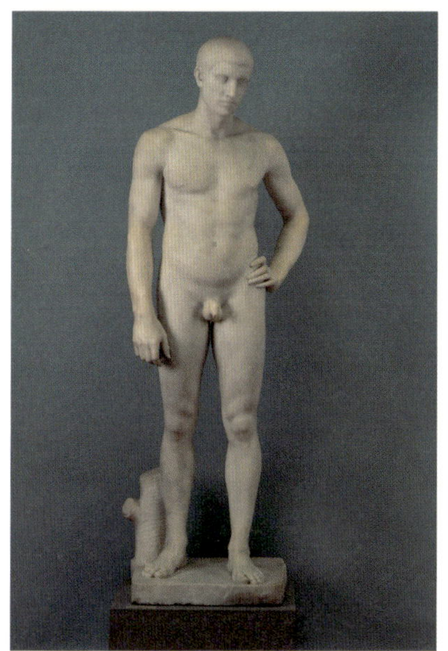

Jugendstil's emphasis on formal qualities found a parallel expression in the ideas of the Munich-based sculptor Adolf von Hildebrand, whose aesthetic formulations Nadelman would adopt almost intact in his later manifestos. In his influential 1892 book *The Problem of Form in Painting and Sculpture*, Hildebrand proposed that true art did not imitate nature—that, indeed, art could not claim self-sufficiency if it was a mere counterfeit of observed reality. Rather, art must obey its own internal structural laws in order to achieve its true content and immutable aim: formal unity. Subject matter and personal expression were irrelevant; what counted was the unity of form, which was attainable only by means of distinct outlines, compact form, and smooth surfaces. For Hildebrand, the art of antiquity epitomized the formal unity necessary for true art. Consequently, he advised contemporary sculptors to use it as a guide for overcoming the "poverty of sculptural art to-day."[33]

Hildebrand's affection for Greek art was shared by many other Munich residents, including Crown Prince Ludwig I, whose urban renewal project gave Munich the sobriquet "Athens on the Isar," and the Munich Secession, whose symbol was a helmeted Athena.[34] The Greek art that Munich prized was not the florid expressionism of the Hellenistic age, but rather the architectonic clarity of its Early Classical predecessors. Hildebrand's severe classicism, devoid of ornament and sensuous effects, was the late-nineteenth-century version of this classical ideal (FIG. 8); the geometrically simplified

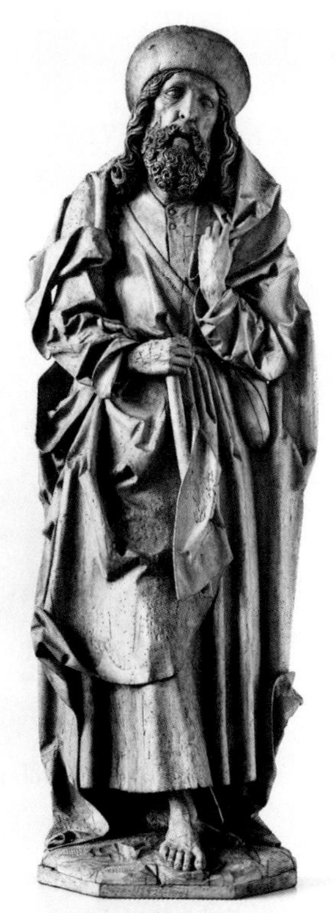

Fig. 9
Tilman Riemenschneider
Saint James the Greater, c. 1505
Lime wood, 58 1/4 x 20 1/2 x 9 in.
(148 x 52 x 23 cm)
Bayerisches Nationalmuseum, Munich

Fig. 10
Unknown artist
The Adoration of the Shepherds (detail),
Naples, 1750–70
Terra-cotta, painted wood, and fabric, 15 in.
(38 cm) high
Bayerisches Nationalmuseum, Munich

utilitarian objects produced under the auspices of Jugendstil's Vereinigte Werkstätten (United Workshops) were its modernist counterparts.

Not coincidentally, Early Classical Greek art dominated the collection of Munich's antiquities museum, the Glyptothek, whose crowning glory was the sculpture from the east and west pediments of the Temple of Aphaia on the island of Aegina.[35] Discovered in 1811, these pedimental sculptures were restored in the nineteenth century by the Danish Neoclassical sculptor Bertel Thorvaldsen. Although their restoration was controversial from the beginning and has since been removed, Nadelman saw the figures intact, their missing and damaged parts replaced and patched in marble by Thorvaldsen. The two sets of figures, executed by the same sculptor but separated by ten years and a changed state of consciousness, visually illustrated the difference between Archaic and Early Classical art. As the first genuine examples of Greek art that Nadelman had ever seen, they exerted a strong impression on him, all the more so because of their similarity to Hildebrand's work. The figures on the two pediments shared with the Munich sculptor's work a compact, volumetric simplicity and the absence of ornamental detail and overt expressions of emotion. What they added was frozen gestures. Like dancers whose bodies are momentarily arrested between steps, the Temple of Aphaia figures had been caught in characteristic "stop" positions (FIG. 7). After Nadelman came to the United States in 1914, these characteristics, particularly the freezing of an iconic gesture, would become central to his work.

In his effort to absorb all that Munich had to offer, Nadelman also spent countless hours in the Bayerisches Nationalmuseum, where he studied the female nudes of sixteenth-century sculptor Giambologna—with their elongated, sinuous linearity and bland, ovoid faces—and the limewood sculptures of Tilman Riemenschneider (FIG. 9). The museum's vast collection of the sculptures of this German Late Gothic artist would have triggered Nadelman's memories of Veit Stoss's painted wood altarpiece in Kraków (FIG. 6), particularly since Stoss, following a practice common among Gothic wood-carvers, had painted the Riemenschneider works on display in the Bayerisches Nationalmuseum's galleries. Both artists exploited calligraphic linearity and the crisp, arcing edges made possible by the straight ridges and raised facets of drapery passages to enliven their spiraling, counterpoised figures. Nadelman never forgot these compositional strategies. In 1920, when he began to sculpt wood totems of the performers and personalities of twentieth-century popular

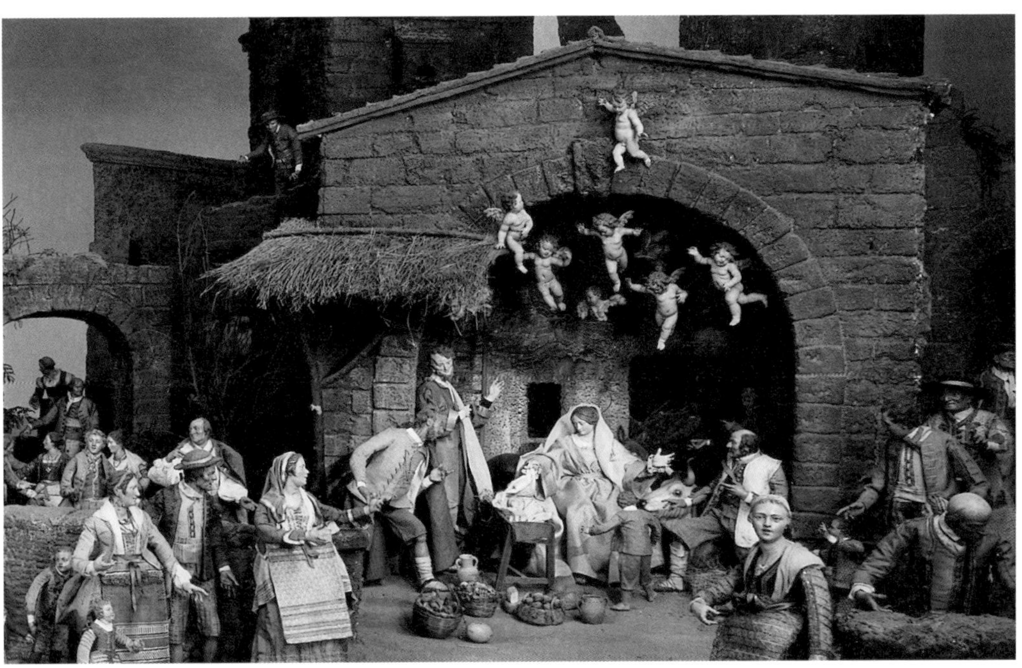

culture, he may have unconsciously enjoyed doing so in the same medium and with the same crisp, calligraphic contours that Riemenschneider and Stoss had employed in their portraits of Christian saints.

These late-fifteenth-century wood sculptures, juxtaposed with the Bayerisches Nationalmuseum's world-famous collection of crèches—or *Krippen* (cribs), as they were called—gave Nadelman his first insight into a theme that would shape his attitude toward art throughout his life: the existence of shared aesthetic conventions among artworks from different times and cultures and on different levels of the aesthetic hierarchy. Crèches were small-scale painted figures that were rearranged throughout the year, along with their accompanying accessories, in tableaux that illustrated different moments in the life of Christ.[36] Mobile and freestanding, they were the "low" art equivalents of Stoss's and Riemenschneider's carved limewood sculptures. Among the most impressive of the museum's holdings were the eighteenth-century Neapolitan crèches, whose iconic gestures and elaborate settings were intended to make the liturgy more tangible and comprehensible to ordinary people (FIG. 10). Dressed in actual fabric costumes and engaged in the activities of everyday life, the figures in these and other crèches in the museum's collection had been part of the religious life of communities throughout Germany and Italy since the fifteenth century. With an outsider's instinct for art that transcended the divisions of social class, Nadelman would have

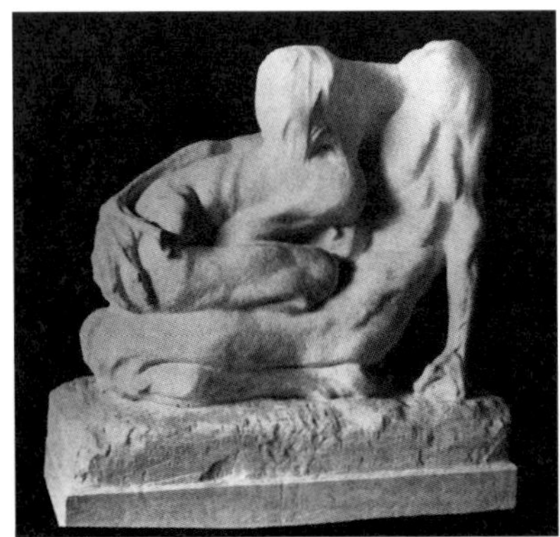

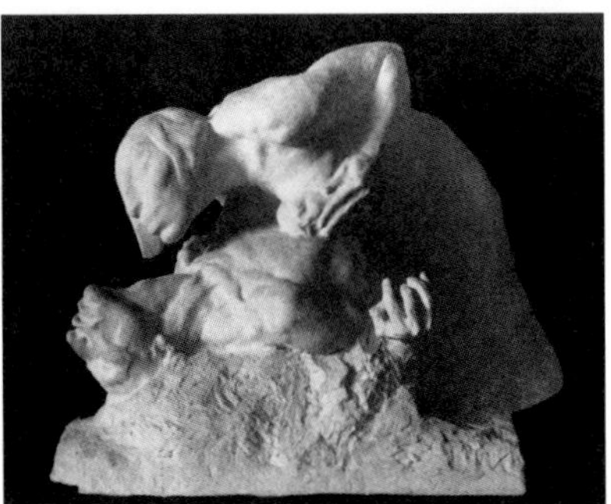

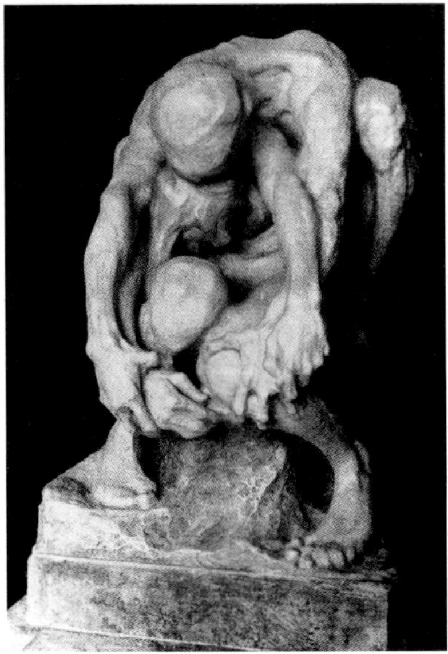

Figs. 11–13
Elie Nadelman
Three Untitled Sculptures, 1903–04
Plaster; lost
Reproduced from *Sztuka* (Paris), nos. 8–9 (1904)

noticed the crèches' stylistic similarity to painted wood altarpieces and their attendant muting of aesthetic distinctions between high and low. Only later, however, would he address cross-fertilizations between high art and popular culture in his own sculpture.

For the moment Nadelman committed his extraordinary manual facility to successfully developing a style that reflected the era's prevailing aesthetic, Symbolism. In April 1904, after only a few months' residence in Munich, he entered a drawing competition sponsored by the monthly Polish-language journal *Sztuka* (Art). Founded in Paris in 1904 by the Polish editor Antoni Potocki for Polish artists living in the French capital, the magazine had no relation to the Kraków-based arts organization with which it shared a name. Its first issue that April announced a competition for drawings inspired by the music of the Polish composer Frédéric (Fryderyk) Chopin which would be suitable for printing in one color. Artists were to present their entries anonymously, along with a sealed envelope containing their names. Owing to the magazine's youth, only seven artists entered the competition. Nadelman was one, along with another Warsaw artist residing in Munich at the time, Gustaw (Gustav) Gwozdecki. Both artists received awards, Gwozdecki winning first prize for *Ballada F-dur* (Ballad in F major), and Nadelman winning second prize for *Bemol* (B minor) (FIG. 4).[37]

Nadelman's drawing, coming as it did from a totally unknown artist, took everyone by surprise. At age twenty-two, with little formal training, he had successfully assimilated the Symbolist vocabulary and themes, which were prevalent in Poland as a result of the proselytizing of *Life*'s charismatic editor, Przybyszewski. *Sztuka*'s Potocki—having earlier fallen under the influence of Przybyszewski's view that art's primary subject was the misery of the artist's "naked soul"—was enraptured by Nadelman's work. Applauding its clear and harmonious expression of psychological and physical anguish, Potocki requested that the artist send photographs of other pieces for use in the magazine's later issues. Based on his stylistic assessment of *Bemol*, Potocki announced in the magazine that Nadelman was a sculptor, a guess borne out by the photographs the artist subsequently sent him—all of sculptures (FIGS. 11–13).[38] Potocki published three of these reproductions in the following two issues of *Sztuka*. All mirrored Symbolism's preoccupation with death and sexual violence by portraying intertwined figures engaged in fierce, anguished struggle. Their melodramatic subjects, violently distorted poses, and tense, tortured surfaces

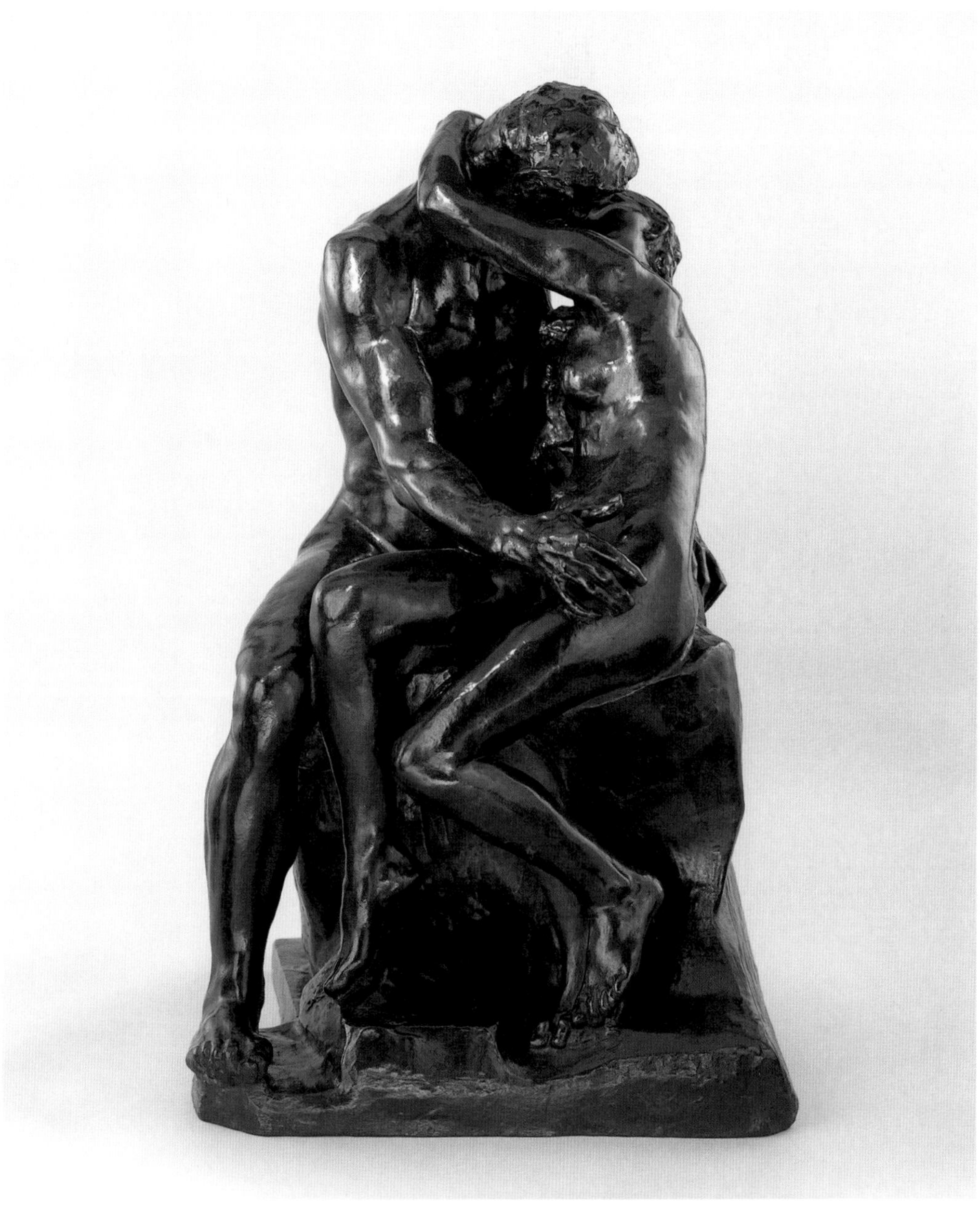

testified to Nadelman's newfound allegiance to Rodin, the symbolist sculptor whose rejection of sentimental, academic idealism and conventional notions of beauty had transformed the discipline (FIG. 14). Most vanguard sculptors began their careers by emulating the French artist's vigorous surfaces and metaphysical themes. That Nadelman did so as well placed his work on sculpture's cutting edge.

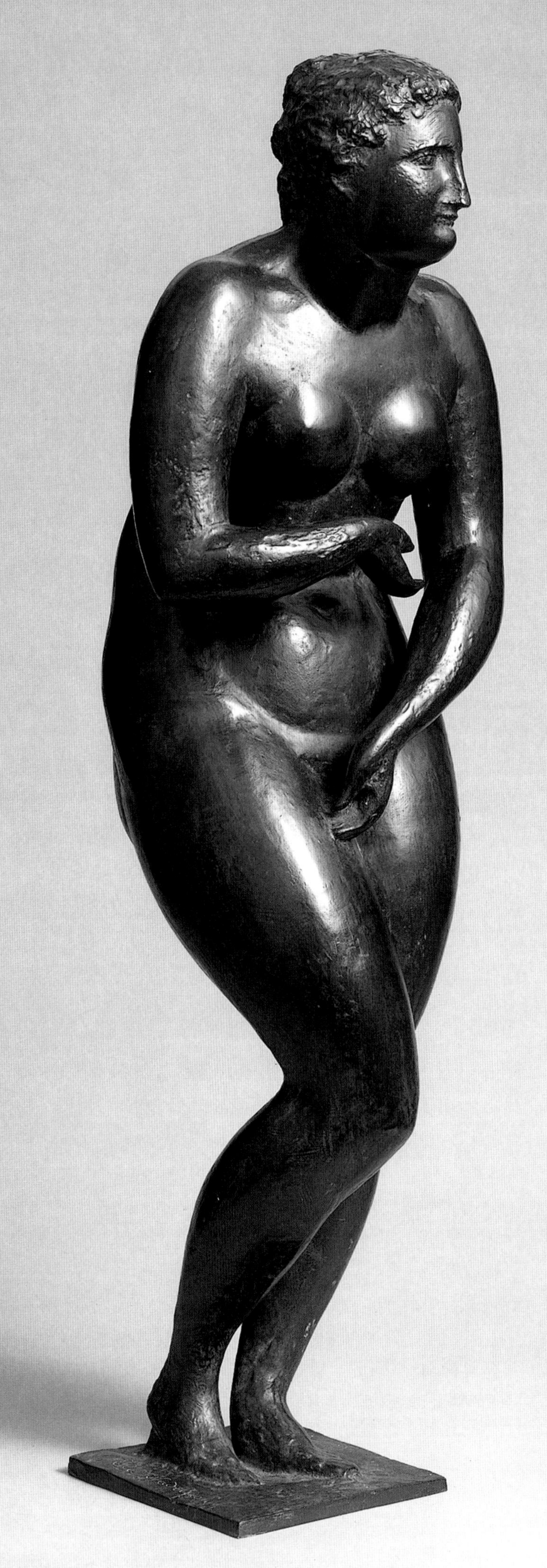

Launching a Career: Paris, 1904—09

Fig. 15
Elie Nadelman
Standing Female Figure (Gertrude Stein),
c. 1908—09 (cast later)
Bronze, 29 1/2 x 10 1/2 x 9 1/2 in.
(74.9 x 26.7 x 24.1 cm) including base
Whitney Museum of American Art, New York;
Gift of the Estate of Elie Nadelman
Photography by Jerry L. Thompson

With the five hundred francs he won in the Chopin competition, Nadelman financed his relocation to Paris—the city to which Munich was widely considered a stepping stone. By November 1904 he was already sufficiently established within the Polish colony there to warrant his inclusion in an article on the colony that Potocki wrote that month for *Sztuka*. Unlike the eighteenth- and nineteenth-century Parisian Polish colonies, which had been composed of political and economic asylum seekers, this Polish colony consisted of well-educated bohemians and students from the urban middle class who traveled freely back and forth between Poland and Paris.[39] Paradoxically, Paris allowed them what had been forbidden at home: the expression of Polish patriotism. They opened Polish schools, established Polish libraries and hospitals, and published Polish journals.

The Polish artists who came to Paris—more than two hundred by 1912—remained a close-knit enclave, frequenting the same cafés (primarily the Café du Dôme and Café de la Rotonde) and living in the same district. By the time Nadelman arrived, this was Montparnasse. The bohemian successor to Montmartre, Montparnasse was home to a vast population of foreigners, many of them from Eastern Europe, especially Poland and Russia. Their concentration in Montparnasse created what Marcel Duchamp called "the first really international colony of artists we ever had."[40] Jewish artists constituted such a large percentage of this group that, to many, the district was synonymous with Jewry.[41] For Jews, Paris offered vertical social mobility and the equality denied them in Eastern Europe. Small wonder that many became French patriots and, as soon as they had the chance, French citizens.

The Polish colony included among its members three of Paris's most important art critics: Guillaume Apollinaire, Adolphe Basler, and André Salmon.[42] All three credited their initiation into modern art to protean aesthetic philosopher and fellow countryman Mecislas Golberg, whose belief in the recurrence throughout art history of formal properties had led to his early appreciation of Fauvism and Cubism. Golberg's numerous contributions to vanguard Parisian art journals, including his own *Cahiers de Mecislas Golberg* (1900–1907), and the extensive quotation by Apollinaire, Basler, and Salmon of his commentaries on the metaphysical correspondence between formal values and universal states of consciousness made it impossible for anyone in the Polish community to be unaware of his theories. After his death in 1908, familiarity with the ideas in his posthumously published collection of essays, *The Morality of the Line* (1908), was essential for participation in café conversation.

Unlike his contemporary Wilhelm Worringer, who postulated that art styles oscillated between abstraction and representation, Golberg believed in the steady reappearance of formal characteristics and motifs. For Golberg, line was the essential ingredient of art. The more simplified and precise it became, the more intense and profound was the art. Because line was the sole determinant of art's quality, no inherent difference existed between art of different styles and different epochs or between art made by trained and untrained craftsmen. The geometric linearity of modern art was analogous, according to Golberg, to that of Greek antiquity. His deification of line found a receptive audience in Nadelman, who had already been seduced by the formalist ideologies of Witkiewicz and Hildebrand. Line, along with Golberg's belief in the concordances between art of widely disparate times and genres, would eventually become key to Nadelman's aesthetic.

For the next three years Nadelman struggled to reconcile the simplified classicism promoted by Hildebrand and Golberg with the melodramatic themes and expressive vocabulary of Rodin. Occasionally he attended the Académie Colarossi, where he could sketch from a live model for the day or a few hours by paying a fee at the door. Otherwise he worked independently, without pause, under conditions of debilitating poverty. One commentator described the hysteria of Nadelman's landlady and her daughter over Nadelman's lack of food and heat during the winter months, while another wrote of his eating horsemeat for dessert because of his lack of money.[43]

Nadelman's perseverance was rewarded. In November 1905 judges for the Salon d'Automne accepted three of his drawings and one plaster figure for exhibition. The salon, inaugurated two years earlier, was an elite alternative to the open, nonjuried Salon des Indépendants, which had started in 1884. With 1,625 works by 397 artists, the 1905 selections represented a large cross-section of artists later associated with the modern movement. Although Nadelman's work went unmentioned in the French press, his inclusion in the exhibition that launched the Fauves testifies to his entry into the art world at a critical juncture in the evolution of modernism.[44]

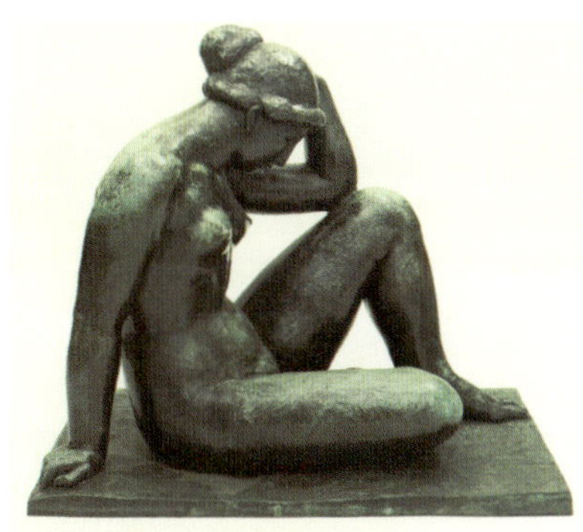

Nadelman's participation in the show also ensured his awareness of Aristide Maillol's *The Mediterranean* (FIG. 16), which attracted widespread popular and critical acclaim in that exhibition. The static, formal purity and self-sufficient repose of this tranquil, self-contained image of the female body were hailed by critics as an alternative to the restless, thrusting energy of Rodin's agitated depictions of the male figure. With his simplification of the body into idealized, geometric forms and of surfaces into smooth, curving volumes, Maillol paid homage to Greek sculpture of the fifth century B.C.

Maillol was not alone in turning to the solid forms and clearly defined volumes of classicism as an antidote to Rodin. The memoirs of many early-twentieth-century modernists testify to their empathy with antiquity.[45] Rejecting the imitation of nature that had prevailed since the Renaissance, they went back to the Greeks in order to start fresh, to recover a simplicity and emotional restraint absent from academic art. As Apollinaire noted, "it was not a question of competing with models of classical antiquity, but of renewing subjects and forms by bringing artistic observation to the first principles of great art."[46] For the huge contingent of foreign sculptors in Paris, ancient art offered a tradition untainted by nationalism. Unlike painting, sculpture at the turn of the century still carried the burden of celebrating national heroes, institutions, and middle-class values. Foreigners were discouraged from participating in this endeavor not only because of their personal history but also because non-French citizens were excluded from the Prix de Rome competitions and subsidies at the Ecole des Beaux-Arts. Denied access to official patronage and alienated from mainstream French society, foreign sculptors searched for a timeless, universal art free of anecdote and temporal specificity. Their aim was not to create a Neoclassical revival, but to find a new classical language appropriate to the modern, international community in which they lived. This return to classicism for inspiration was particularly appealing to Jewish artists because it bypassed the Renaissance and the Christian subject matter in which its art was steeped.

By 1908 Nadelman was well on his way to fashioning a personal vocabulary within this context. Following Hildebrand's prescriptions for plastic unity, he replaced excessively kneaded surfaces and histrionic themes with self-contained subjects and simplified geometric forms. Out-flung limbs and gestural surfaces yielded to immediately perceived subjects with distinct outlines and architectonic volumes. Although the rounded forms, smooth

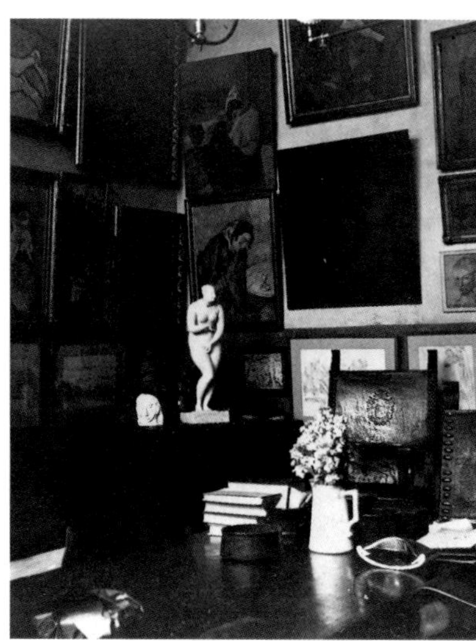

Fig. 17
Gertrude and Leo Stein's apartment,
27, rue de Fleurus, Paris, c. 1912
Photography courtesy Beinecke Rare Book and
Manuscript Library, Yale University

surfaces, and nonnarrative subjects of Nadelman's work allied it with that of others who were turning to ancient art for inspiration, critics found his sculptures particularly reminiscent of the pedimental figures from Aegina's Temple of Aphaia. On one occasion, Salmon noted that Nadelman "look[ed] at the ancients the way people look at them in Munich"; on another, he described the artist's conception of Greek art as being that of Aegina.[47]

Nadelman's mining of classical sources ultimately caught the attention of fellow Pole Thadée Natanson, co-owner, with his brother Alexandre, of *La revue blanche*. Nadelman's graceful contour line drawings of nudes so impressed Thadée that he immediately arranged to visit the artist in his Montparnasse studio. The visit initiated a patronage that went well beyond the purchasing of works. Immensely well connected in the Parisian art world, Natanson introduced Nadelman to important critics and patrons, among whom were André Gide, Octave Mirbeau, Leo Stein, and Nadelman's future dealer, Eugène Druet.[48] Stein became as enraptured by Nadelman's work as was Natanson, buying examples of both drawing and sculpture (FIG. 17) and inviting the artist to attend the vanguard art soirees that he and his sister Gertrude hosted every Saturday evening at their apartment at 27, rue de Fleurus.[49] Here, amid an impressive array of the period's most advanced paintings, Nadelman met the celebrities of Parisian bohemia.

Nadelman's entry into this society was aided by what contemporaries described as his extraordinary charm, charismatic grace, and strikingly handsome appearance. Slender, with deep, intense eyes and an angelic countenance, he exuded "unearthly beauty" and "eternal youth," as Gertrude Stein's companion, Alice B. Toklas, put it.[50] Nadelman was apparently as aware as others that these qualities made him extremely appealing to women. Jacques Lipchitz recalled him speaking of "nothing but women and his manly powers," while Stein, in her word portrait of him, wrote that Nadelman was "one needing to be one completely loving women."[51] The artist's charm and beauty were combined with a polite but self-protective reserve that he dropped only when discussing art. In his pronouncements on aesthetics, he displayed a messianic fervor at once intransigent and dogmatic, expressing his formulations about the "true forms of art" and the kinds of truths they could convey in impassioned and imperious speeches that brooked no disagreement or dialogue.[52] Once he even got into a brawl with Filippo Marinetti after the Italian Futurist denounced the art of the Greeks

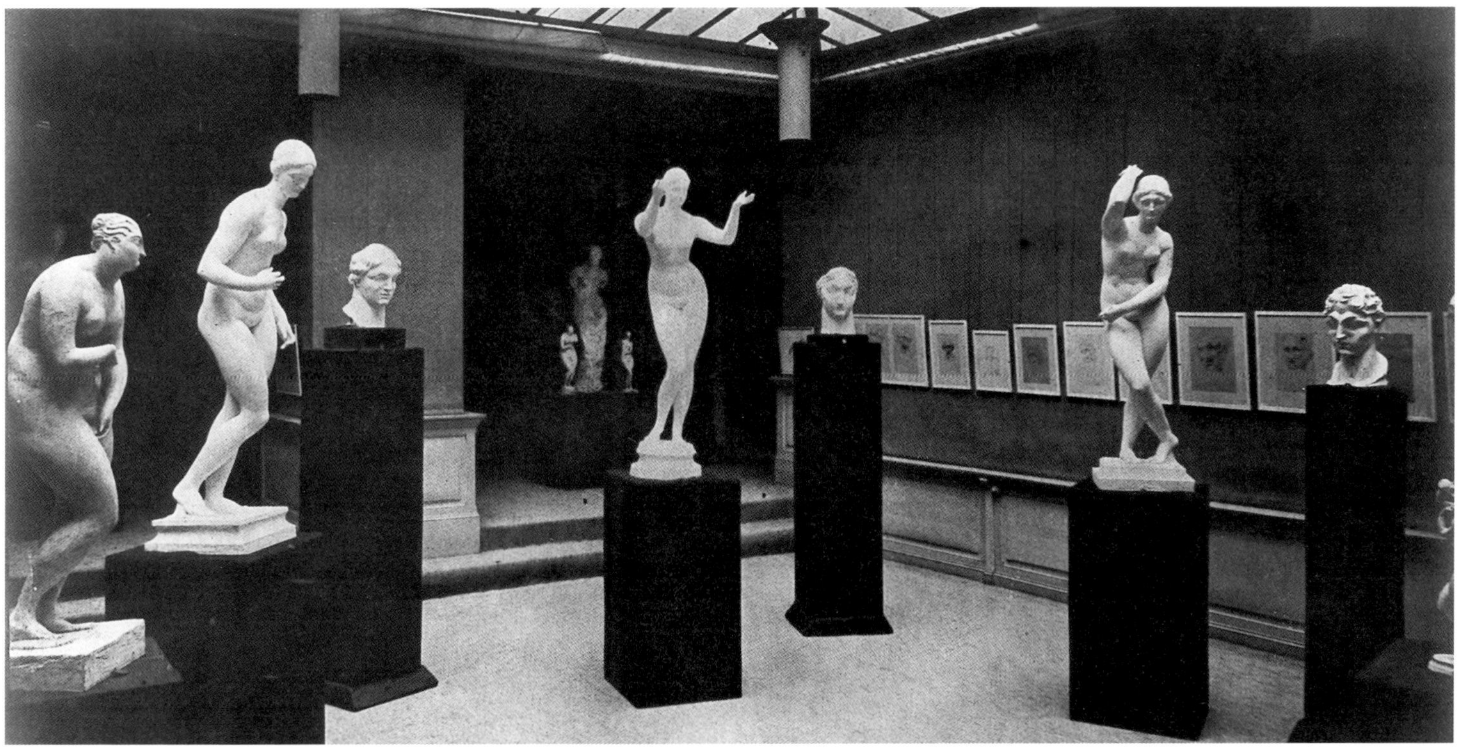

during a lecture in 1912 at the Bernheim-Jeune gallery.[53] Nadelman's intense moralism about aesthetic issues would resurface later and ultimately lose him patronage and critical support.

In April 1909, with the opening of his one-person exhibition at Paris's Galerie E. Druet, Nadelman publicly showcased the full range of his sculpture (FIGS. 18–27). Druet's many years of work as Rodin's photographer no doubt sensitized him to the novelty of Nadelman's sculpture, and he had responded promptly and enthusiastically when Natanson proposed that he show the work. It may also have helped that the gallery had successfully debuted the paintings of Witold Wojtkiewicz, Nadelman's earlier collaborator, two years before. Druet was one of the most important commercial agents for modernist art in Paris; in 1913 he would lend more pieces to America's Armory Show than any other single contributor.[54] Inclusion in his roster thus carried an imprimatur that guaranteed attention. Nevertheless, the thirteen plaster models and one hundred drawings that Nadelman exhibited that April took even Paris by surprise.[55] His radical simplification of form and stylized distortion of shape became a pulse point of debate about the future of sculpture, reportedly disturbing even Picasso and stimulating Amedeo Modigliani to turn temporarily to sculpture.[56]

31

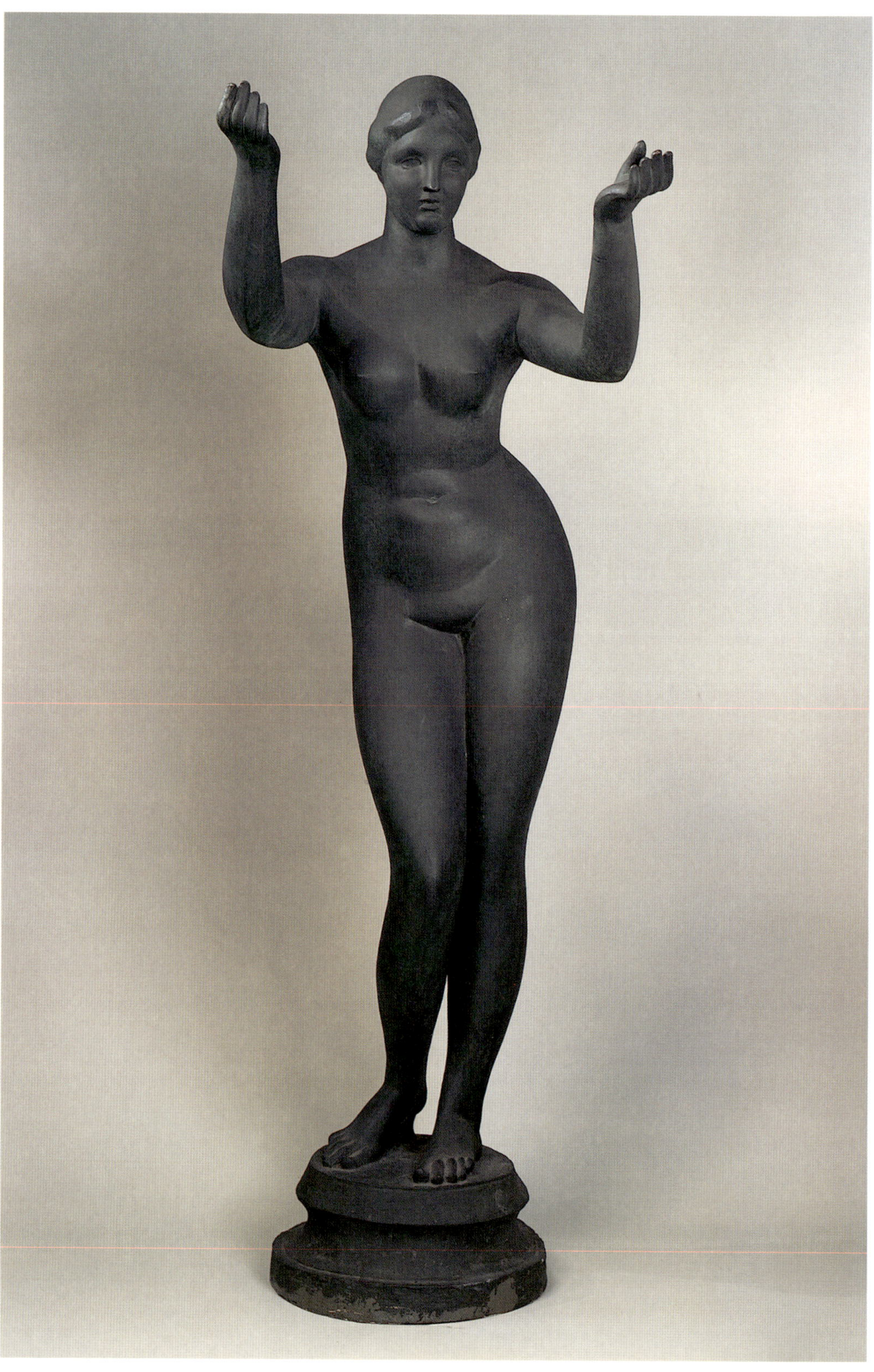

Fig. 19
Elie Nadelman
Suppliant, c. 1908–09
(cast later from plaster original)
Bronze, 56 1/2 x 18 3/4 x 31 1/2 in.
(143.5 x 47.6 x 80 cm)
Estate of Elie Nadelman, courtesy
Salander-O'Reilly Galleries, New York
Photography by Paul Waldman

Fig. 20
Elie Nadelman
Standing Female Nude, c. 1908–09
(carved later from plaster original)
Pear wood, 15 x 3 3/4 x 4 1/2 in.
(38.1 x 9.5 x 11.4 cm)
The Minneapolis Institute of Arts;
Gift of Ruth and Bruce Dayton

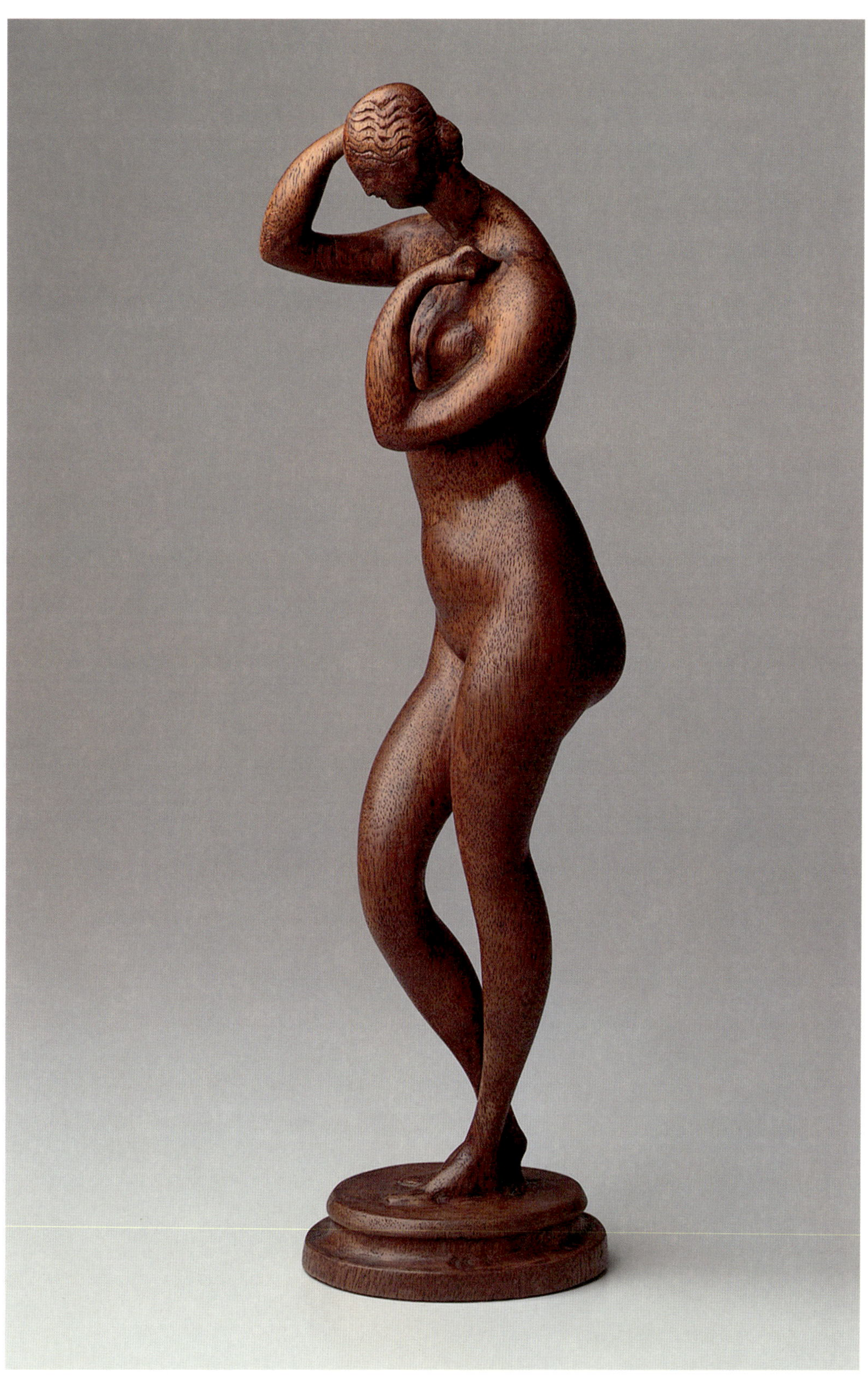

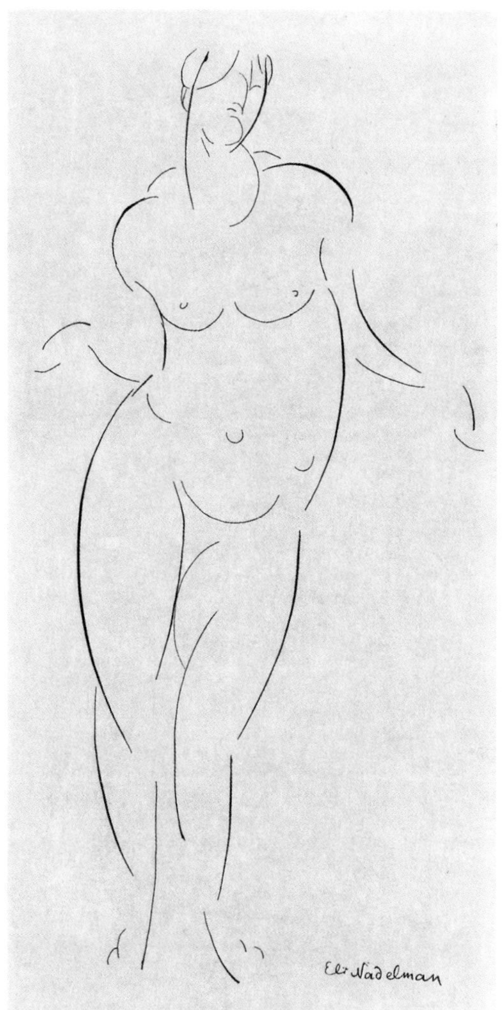 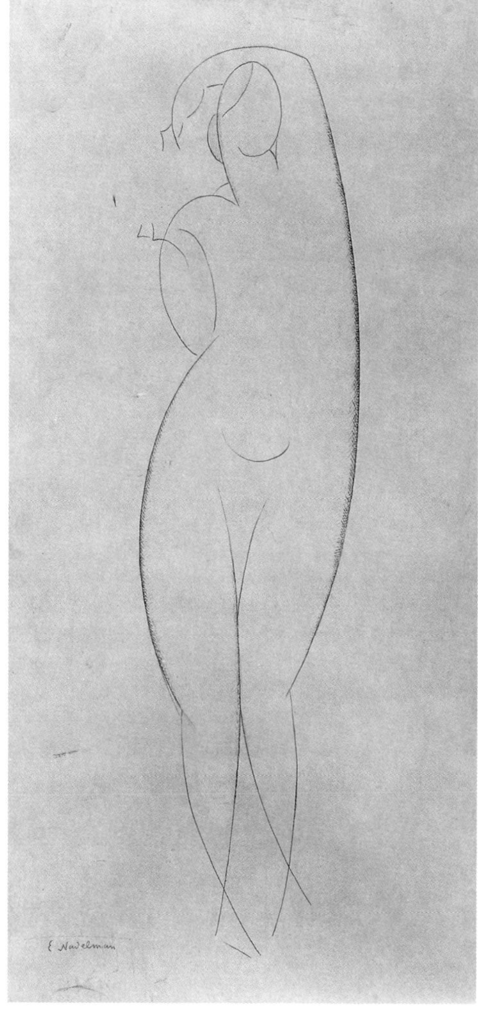 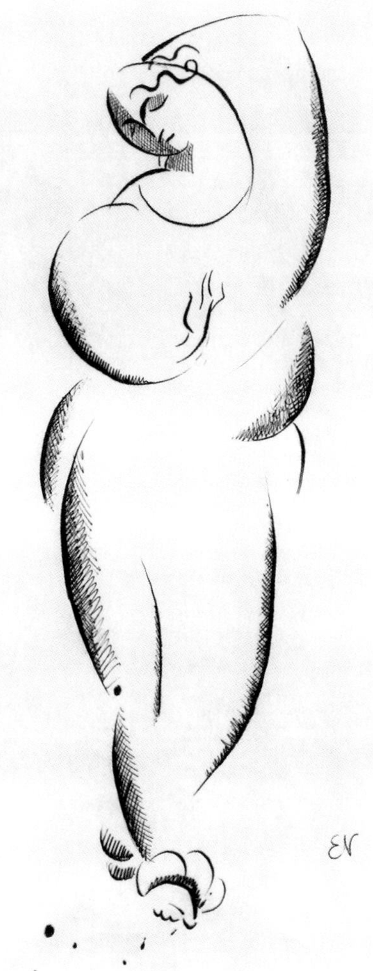

Fig. 21
Elie Nadelman
Standing Female Nude, c. 1907–09
Ink on paper, 11 3/8 x 5 1/4 in. (28.9 x 13.3 cm)
The Baltimore Museum of Art; Gift of Mme.
Helena Rubinstein

Fig. 22
Elie Nadelman
Standing Nude, c. 1907–09
Ink and pencil on paper, 36 1/4 x 16 5/8 in.
(92.1 x 42.2 cm)
The Metropolitan Museum of Art, New York;
Bequest of Schofield Thayer, 1982
©2002 The Metropolitan Museum of Art

Fig. 23
Elie Nadelman
Nude, c. 1907–09
Ink on paper, 22 15/16 x 10 1/2 in. (58.3 x 26.7 cm)
Whitney Museum of American Art, New York;
Purchase, with funds from the Richard and
Dorothy Rodgers Fund
Photography by Sheldon Collins

Fig. 24
Elie Nadelman
Seated Figure, c. 1907–09
Ink on paper, 11 3/4 x 7 3/4 in. (29.8 x 19.7 cm)
Collection of Susan and Herbert Adler

Fig. 25
Elie Nadelman
The Bird, c. 1907–09
Ink on paper, 25 1/4 x 19 3/8 in. (64.1 x 49.2 cm)
Whitney Museum of American Art, New York;
Purchase, with funds from Philip Morris
Incorporated
Photography by Sheldon Collins

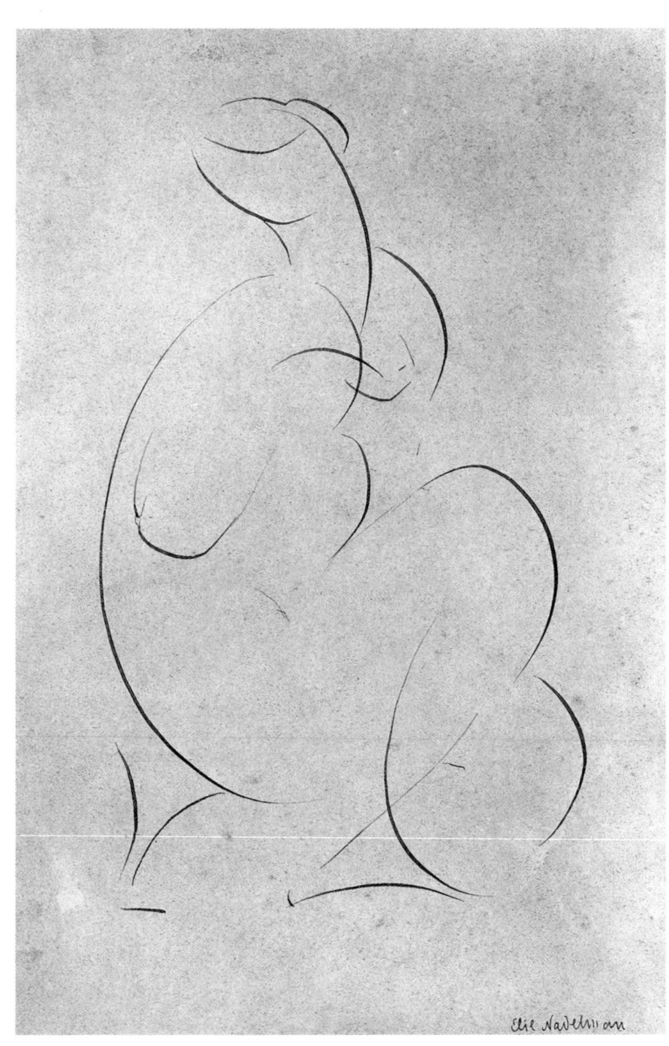

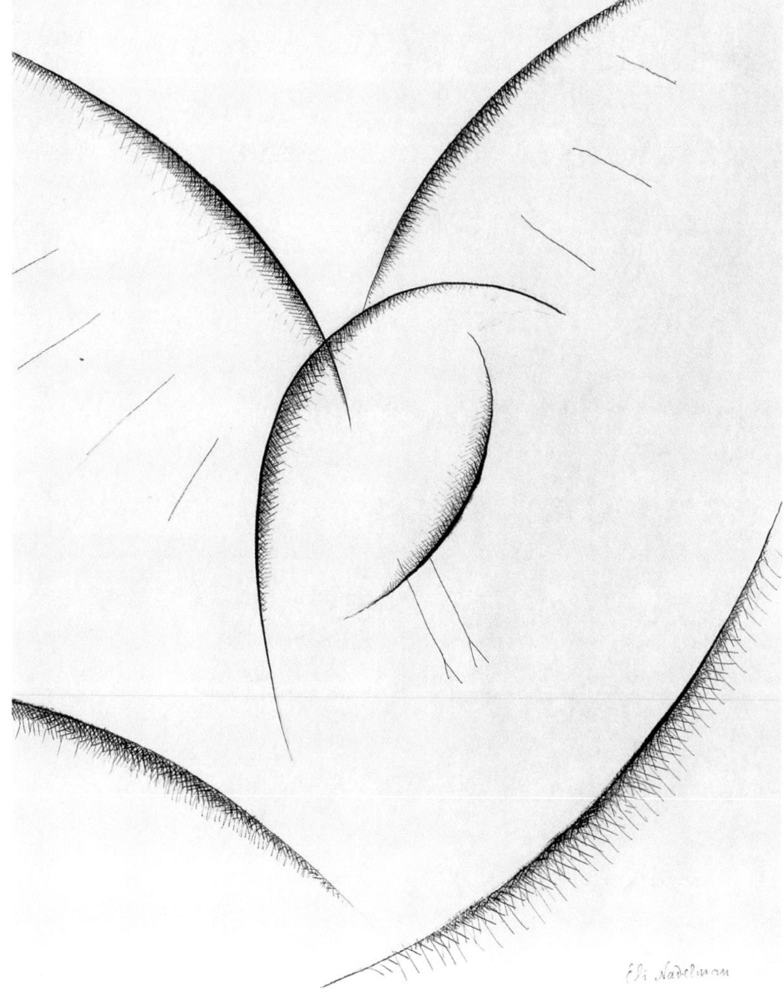

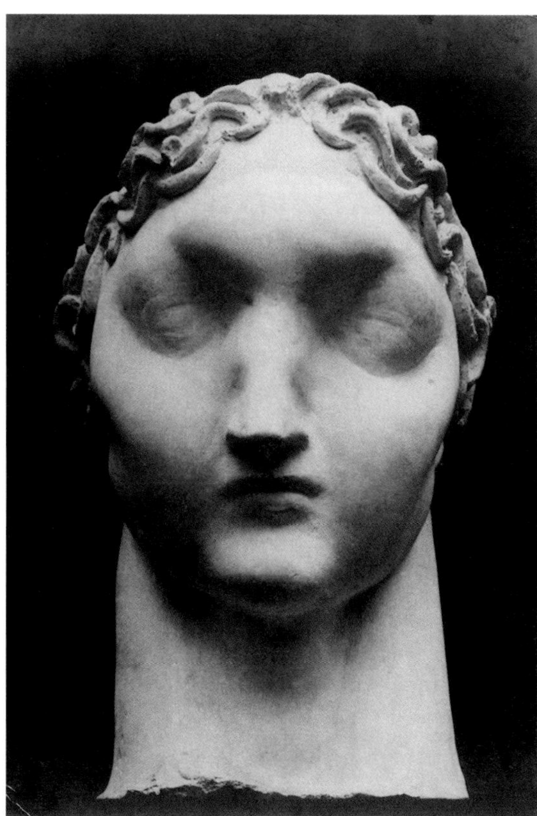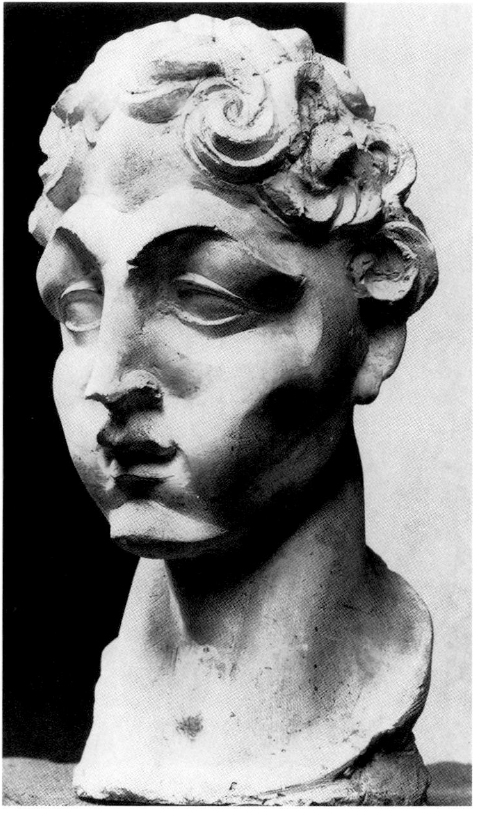

Nadelman attained his role as a leading representative of modernism by going back to the art of fourth-century B.C. Greek sculptor Praxiteles. He adapted the languid, soft grace and dreamy sensuality with which Praxiteles had endowed his female nudes, but he did so in a way that paid homage to the spirit of these Greek antecedents without in any sense copying them. The chaste poses of Nadelman's large standing figures evoke Praxiteles' images of Aphrodite being surprised by an intruder while bathing, but their design and conception are wholly modern. Nadelman had sacrificed fidelity to external reality for the relationship between opposing and corresponding reciprocal curves. He had purged his figures of all detail and particularity and reduced his forms to closed, sinuous volumes. Pushed to the edge of abstraction, they bridge tradition and modernity. Indeed, so simplified were the figures' eyes, mouths, eyebrows, and noses that Gide dismissively characterized one head (FIG. 26) as "about as much formed as a duck of three days' incubation."[57] By logically assembling his formal elements and eliminating anything that would detract from their unity, Nadelman ensured the perceptual immediacy of each piece.

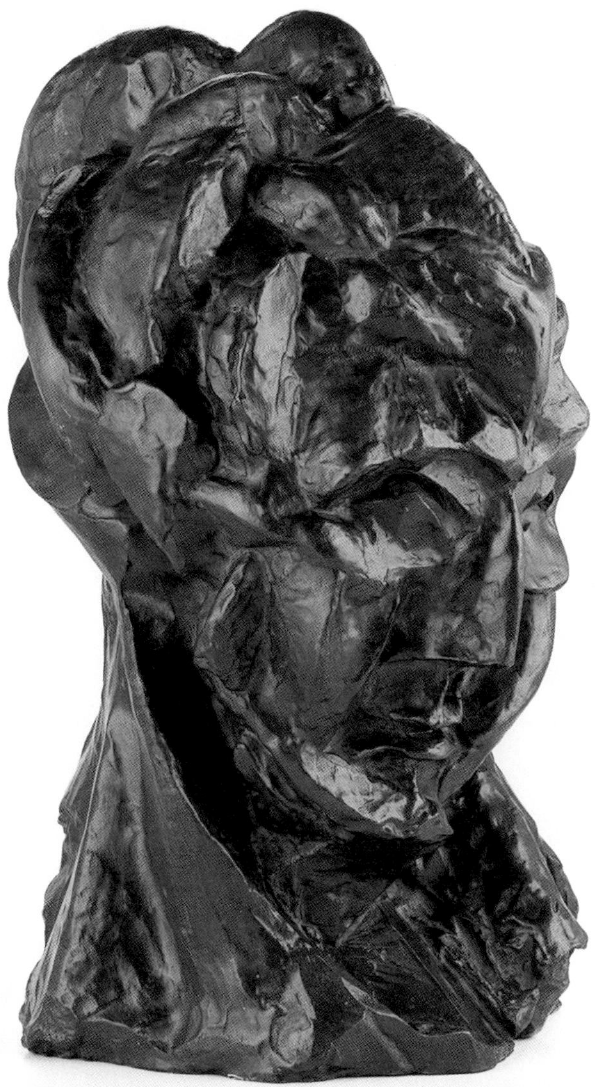

Formal simplification was even more striking in Nadelman's drawings, which were composed of lines so crisp and pure they seemed incised rather than drawn. Fueled by Golberg's vision of the whole sweep of art history as one seamless continuum, Nadelman freely amalgamated elements from the art of different cultures and eras. Some drawings revealed his analytic dissection of form into intersecting curves and concavities; others recalled Buddha and bodhisattva heads from Chinese Turkestan, recently acquired by the Louvre. Still others evoked the linear, lyrical refinement of Francesco Primaticcio.[58] Taken as a whole, the drawings served as a visual treatise on abstraction. The importance of their slender, graceful contours and chiseled, rhomboidal features was appreciated by Leo Stein, who purchased more than sixty-five of them before the close of the exhibition. For Nadelman, the drawings offered compelling visual testimony to aesthetic unity and plastic beauty. In a spirit of pedagogy, he arranged in 1913 with La Belle Edition to publish forty of them in a limited-edition portfolio, which was issued the following year under the title *Vers l'unité plastique*.[59]

These drawings were the basis of Nadelman's claims in 1921 and 1925 that he—not Picasso—had invented "Abstract Form." The controversy arose out of a visit Leo Stein had arranged in late 1908 between Picasso and Nadelman at the latter's studio. There Picasso saw Nadelman's drawings and the plaster head that Nadelman had created exclusively out of convex and concave volumes (FIG. 27). The Spaniard's use of a similar vocabulary several months later in his portrait drawings and sculpted bust *Head of Fernande Olivier* (FIG. 28) outraged Nadelman, who felt that Picasso had purloined his formal breakthrough. In fact, Nadelman's dissection of mass into curved, intersecting planes and his extrapolation of those fractured planes to three dimensions did precede Picasso's—a primacy acknowledged even by contemporary Cubist propagandists. Salmon, for example, cautioned his readers not to forget that Nadelman "sacrificed all to the relativity of volumes," and Basler affirmed that the "principle of spherical decomposition in Nadelman's drawings and sculptures actually preceded later researches of Picasso as a Cubist."[60]

Nevertheless, Nadelman exaggerated when he claimed that his work provided the impetus for Picasso's experiments with ruptured, discontinuous surfaces; by 1908 Picasso had finished *Les demoiselles d'Avignon* (1907) and *Three Women* (1907–08) and had already begun the collaboration with Georges Braque upon which Cubism would be founded.[61] Nadelman's later insistence that he had revolutionized art by being the first to introduce abstract form may have partly reflected his abhorrence of Picasso's fracturing of three-dimensional form into arbitrary kaleidoscopic units that created spatial ambiguity and destroyed focal points. For Nadelman, abstraction was not a license for capriciously arranging form, but a technique for ordering the ambiguity and flux of the world by means of immutable and moral aesthetic laws. He never forgave Picasso and the Cubists for distorting these laws by divorcing art from nature and disregarding logic in the creation of abstract forms. A note found among his papers after his death reads: "Cubism . . . towards external (rather than interior) form . . . feverish changes while unsatisfied."[62]

Statement of Aesthetic Principles
Camera Work, 1910

Alfred Stieglitz, the photographer and founder of New York's Little Galleries of the Photo-Secession, saw Nadelman's drawings on his scouting trip to Paris in the summer of 1909.[63] He apparently needed little encouragement to put him in the company of the other vanguard European and American painters and sculptors who had joined his roster a year earlier, when "291," as the gallery was by then called, expanded its focus to include nonphotographic work. Before returning to America that summer, Stieglitz arranged for a group of Nadelman's drawings to be shipped to "291" for exhibition. By the end of the 1909–10 season, however, he still had not exhibited them; when Nadelman requested that they be returned to Europe for inclusion in another exhibition, Stieglitz obliged.

Stieglitz nevertheless proceeded to publish Nadelman's exhibition statement in the October 1910 issue of his journal *Camera Work*. In this text Nadelman set forth the cornerstone of his aesthetic theory: formal values alone determine artistic quality. Dismissing both imitative description and personal expression as irrelevant, Nadelman avowed that "significant form"—the harmonious playing of one shape against another—was the exclusive agent of pleasure in art.[64] This assertion anticipated a similar theory of "significant form" proposed by English critic Clive Bell several years later and placed Nadelman squarely at odds with Wassily Kandinsky, whose book *On the Spiritual in Art* (1912) Stieglitz would excerpt in *Camera Work* in 1913. Nadelman rejected the claim that art expressed the artist's spiritual consciousness and emotional responses to nature. Instead, building on Golberg's treatise on the morality of line, he declared that he exclusively used curved lines in order to create harmony and significance.

For American audiences, whose exposure to the art and theories of modernism was limited, Nadelman's ideas were revolutionary. Although his proposals would ultimately clash with the tendency within Stieglitz's circle to elevate intuition over reason, his call for logically constructed forms—derived from but not imitative of nature—provided America with its first taste of one of the primary justifications for abstraction in twentieth-century aesthetics.

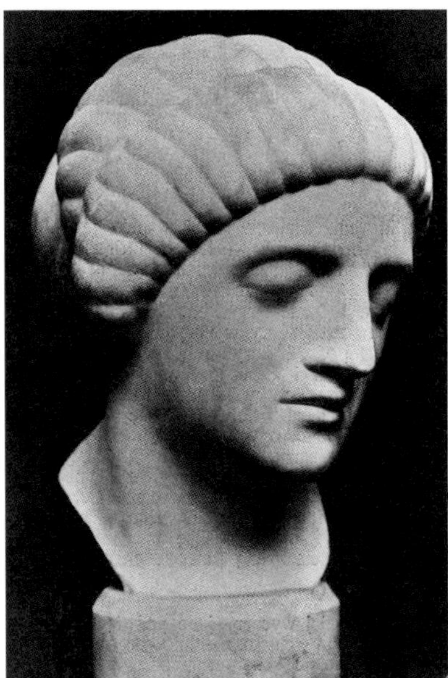

Paterson Gallery and Helena Rubinstein London, 1911

In April 1911 Nadelman was honored with a one-person exhibition at London's William B. Paterson Gallery. In the text that accompanied the show, he extended his theory of significant form to include a corollary requirement for aesthetic quality: compatibility between ambition and means.[65] Art, he asserted, must not try to communicate more information than its formal limitations allow. Plastic beauty was all art could convey; to attempt to express psychological states or to imitate nature doomed art to failure and the artist to frustration. Echoing Hildebrand and Witkiewicz, he declared that only logical relationships of form could engender aesthetic beauty and, by extension, aesthetic satisfaction and significance.

The exhibition that occasioned Nadelman's text consisted of ten female marble heads revealing the artist's increased debt to Praxiteles (FIG. 29).[66] With their chiseled features, schematically patterned coiffures, mysterious smiles, and blank or downcast eyes, heads such as *Nocturne* (FIG. 30) suggested a world of generic rather than individual truth. By extrapolating ideal forms from real life, Nadelman portrayed the elemental and eternal realities underlying multiple, transient sensory perceptions (FIGS. 31–41, 43) and placed his work in relation to that of Neoclassicists Antonio Canova (FIG. 42), Jacques-Louis David, and Jean-Auguste-Dominique Ingres, whose large retrospective Nadelman would have seen at the 1905 Salon d'Automne. For them, as for Nadelman, line was the basis of artistic expression. While Nadelman's vocabulary of crisp outlines, detailed execution, and smooth surfaces allied his art stylistically with that of the Neoclassicists and their Ecole des Beaux-Arts academic successors, he avoided the enervated artificiality and didacticism of the later academicians by adhering to the principle of significant form. It spared him their obligation to express abstract, spiritual values and divine moral truths. Soft, sensuous, and introspective, his marble heads were permeated far less by the spirit of academicism than by that of Praxiteles—a quality his friends in the Society of Polish Artists acknowledged when they cast him as "Eliasz Praksytelman" in a cabaret performance in Paris in 1912.[67]

Nadelman's purity of line and idealized depictions of female beauty attracted the attention of fellow Pole Helena Rubinstein, who had relocated

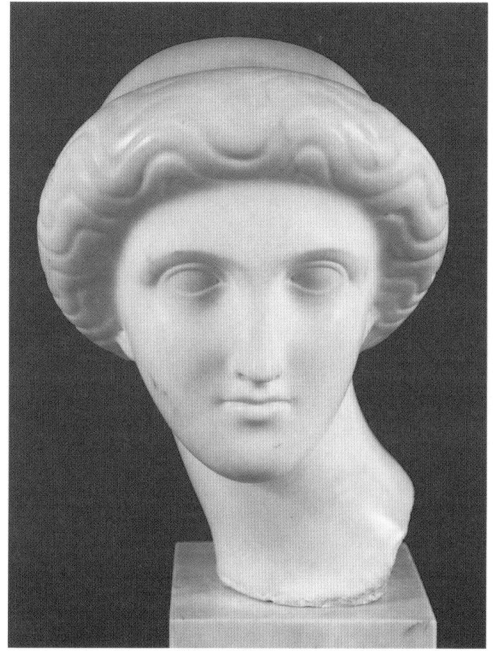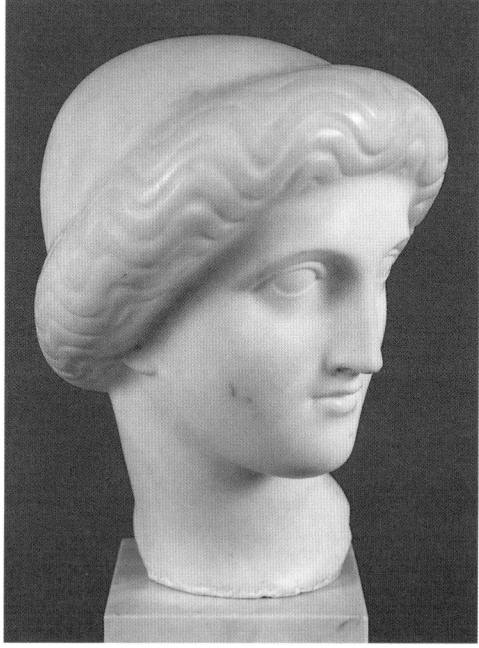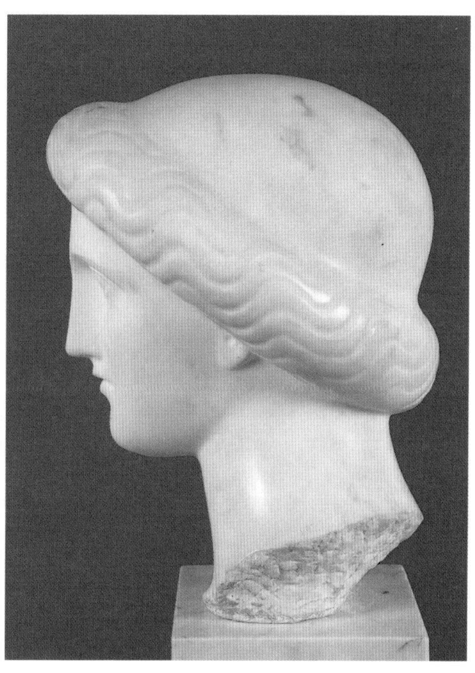

Fig. 31
Elie Nadelman
Classical Head, c. 1910–11 (three views)
Marble, 14 1/8 in. (35.8 cm) high
Allen Memorial Art Museum, Oberlin College,
Oberlin, Ohio; Mrs. F. F. Prentiss Fund, 1968

her cosmetics company from Australia to London in 1907.[68] Already an avid collector of contemporary and African art, Rubinstein purchased the entire contents of Nadelman's London show and commissioned him to execute a quartet of freestanding female figures engaged in the daily activities of bathing, combing their hair, and dressing.[69]

In executing *The Four Seasons* (FIG. 44), as the suite was called, Nadelman shifted his gaze from Early Classical to Hellenistic art. But rather than emulate the restless anatomy, florid drapery, and individualized psychology of the presumed masterpieces of Hellenistic art, he turned to the miniature terra-cotta figurines of the fourth century B.C. named after the Boeotian town of Tanagra, where they were first found.[70] Small in size and mass-produced by means of sectional molds, these early terra-cottas retained the closed, compact forms of their Early Classical antecedents while simultaneously mirroring Hellenism's sympathy for the world of everyday experience and its respect for the nobility of the seemingly ordinary. The most common Tanagra subject was a woman standing in a statuesque but entirely natural pose, wearing the layered, body-concealing costume of the time (FIG. 45). Although held in low esteem in classical times, Tanagra figurines were highly prized and collected by early-twentieth-century artists, among them Picasso, Rodin, and James McNeill Whistler, who owned an album of more than thirty photographs of them.[71] Articles in contemporary Parisian journals

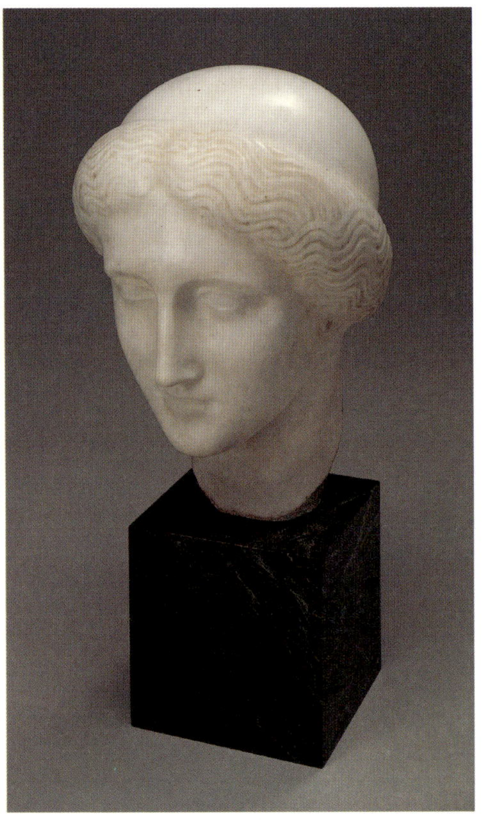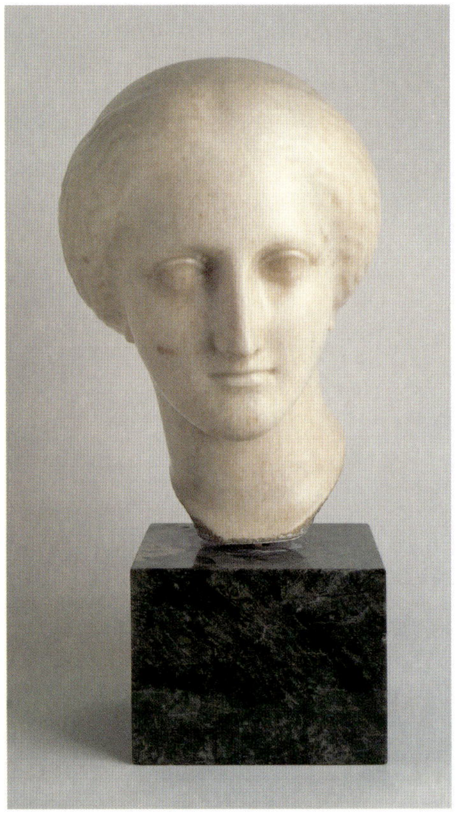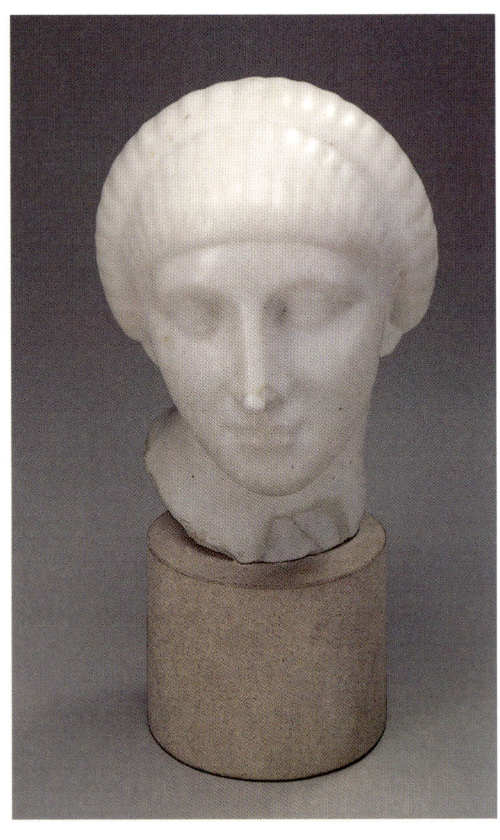

comparing the dancers Isadora Duncan and Loie Fuller with these ancient votive figurines reinforced their contemporaneity and indirectly validated Nadelman's belief in the formal correlations between art of different cultures and epochs.[72] The Louvre boasted a large collection of Tanagras, but it was not until Nadelman visited the British Museum during his stay in London and saw its extensive holdings of these fired-clay figurines that they caught his attention as source material. Their appeal may have been their coy, everyday charm and their unpretentious democratization of the Praxitilean ideal, both of which seemed appropriate for a beauty salon. Nadelman adapted their columnar volumes and channeled folds of drapery to his own purposes. Enlarged in scale and rendered more architectonic than their Tanagra models, this suite of women introduced fluted, formal motifs and domestic subject matter into his repertoire.

In commissioning this work, Rubinstein became Nadelman's most important benefactor, a role that became even more crucial after 1913, when Leo Stein renounced modern art and moved out of the household he and Gertrude had shared. Gertrude retained possession of the first Nadelman sculpture Leo had purchased (FIG. 17), but without her brother's advocacy, Nadelman would become a less visible member of her circle. Rubinstein willingly filled the void. For her, Nadelman's sculptures embodied the image of beauty she felt her products made possible, and she adopted them as emblems of her business by installing them in her salons and using them in her advertisements.[73] After she moved to Paris in early 1914, she became even more friendly with Nadelman through their mutual friendship with fellow countryman Misia Natanson and frequently invited the artist to her "at home" parties, where she introduced him to would-be patrons.[74]

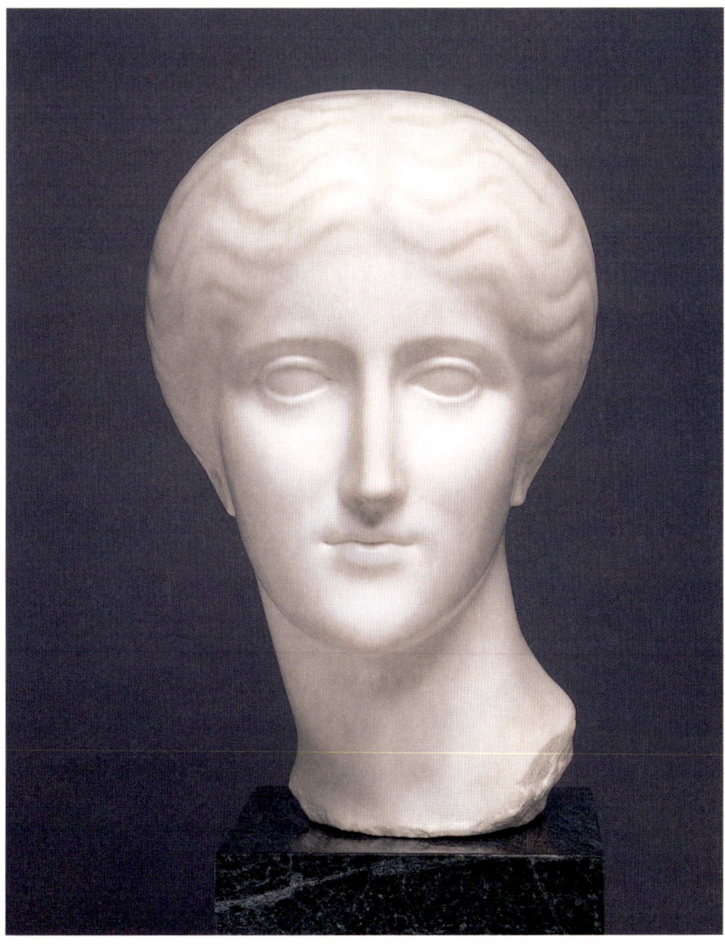
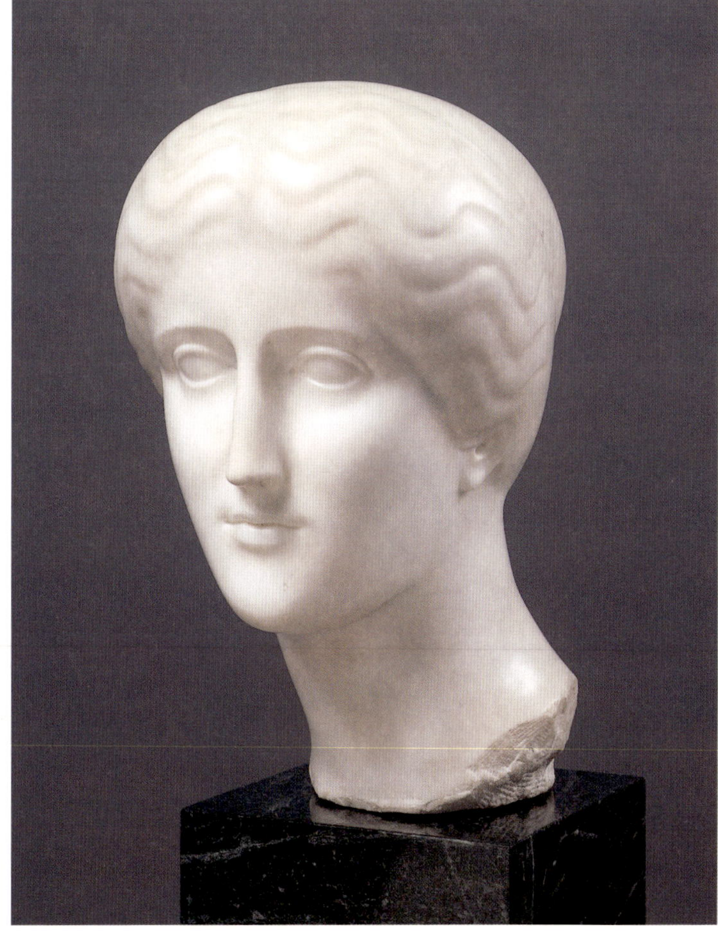

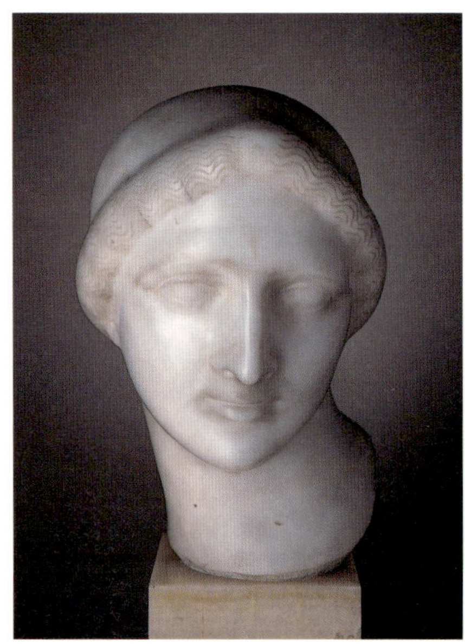

Fig. 36
Elie Nadelman
Ideal Head, c. 1910–11
Marble, 18 in. (45.7 cm) high
Museum of Art, Rhode Island School of Design,
Providence; Gift of Mrs. Gustav Radeke

Fig. 37
Elie Nadelman
Classical Figure, c. 1910–11
Marble, 34 3/4 x 15 3/8 x 13 5/8 in.
(88.3 x 39.1 x 34.6 cm)
Hirshhorn Museum and Sculpture Garden,
Smithsonian Institution; Gift of Joseph H.
Hirshhorn, 1966
Photography by Lee Stalsworth

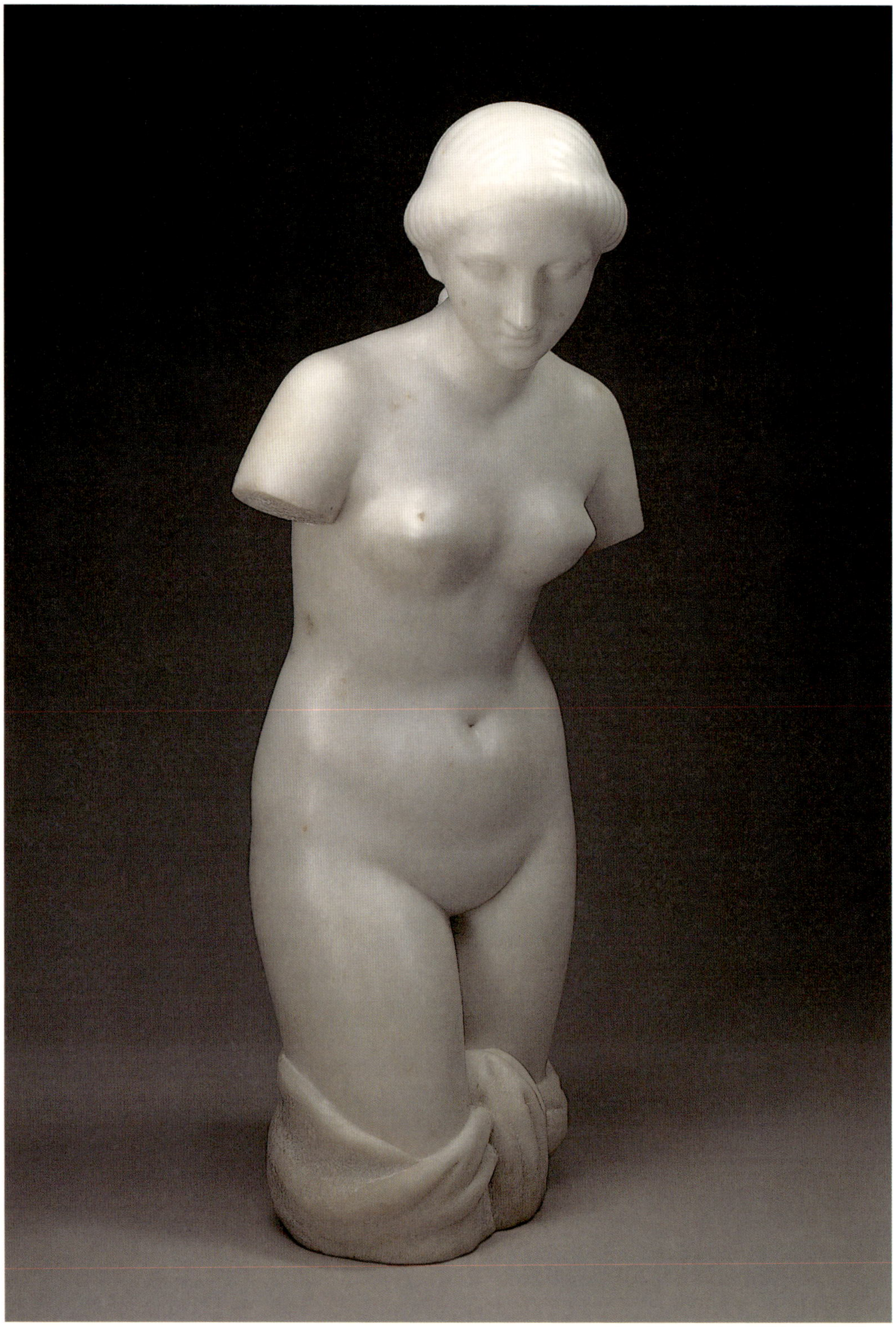

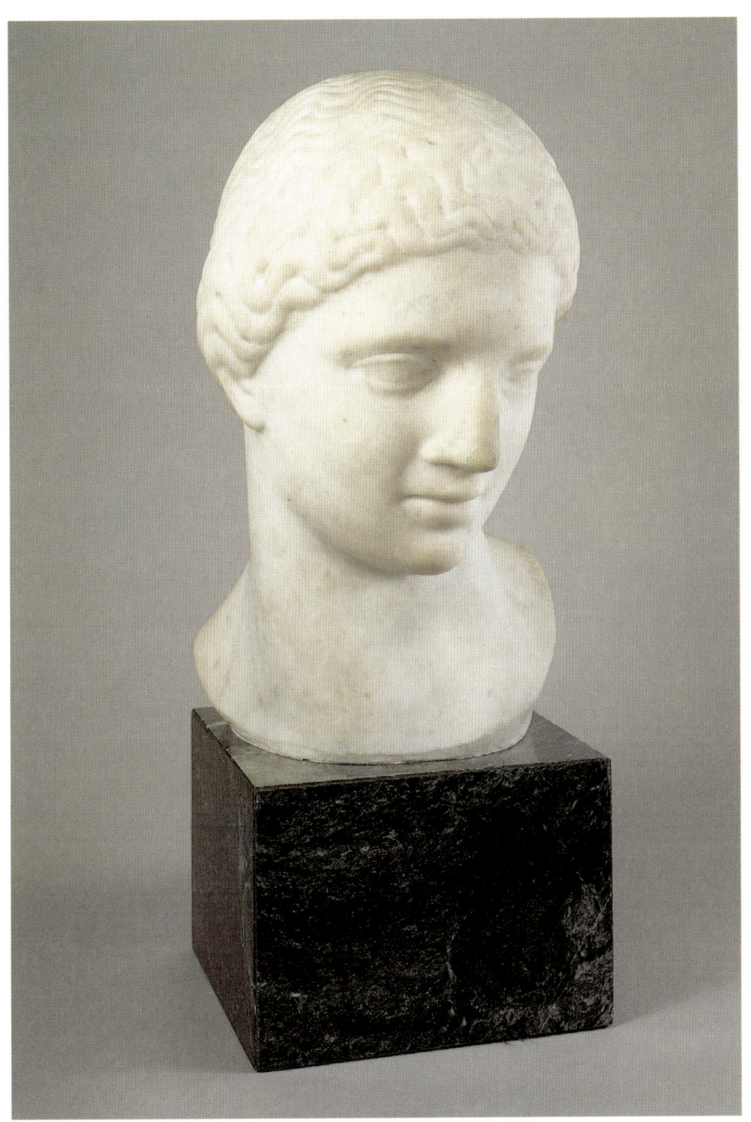 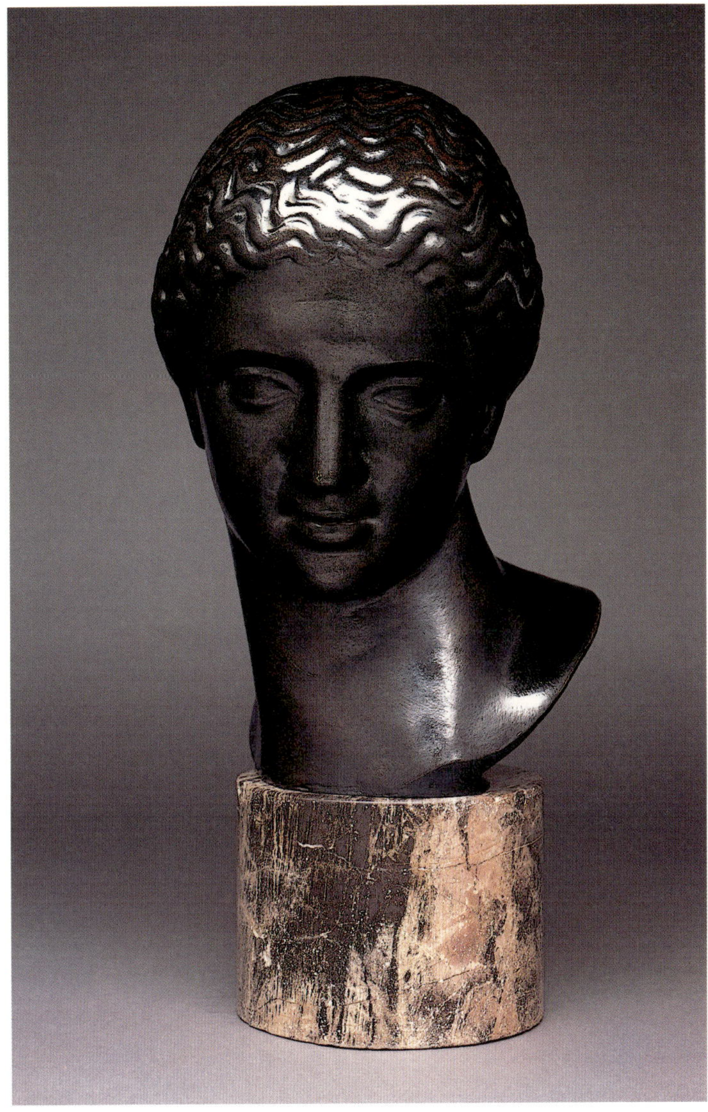

Fig. 38
Elie Nadelman
Classical Head, c. 1910–11
Marble, 15 1/2 in. (39.4 cm) high
The Charles Rand Penney Foundation,
courtesy The James Goodman Gallery

Fig. 39
Elie Nadelman
Female Head, c. 1910–11
Bronze with rich dark brown patina,
15 3/4 x 9 x 11 in. (40 x 22.9 x 28 cm)
Samuel P. Harn Museum of Art, University of
Florida; Museum purchase, funds provided by
the Caroline Julier and James G. Richardson
Acquisition Fund, Dr. and Mrs. David A. Cofrin
and Ruth Pruitt Phillips

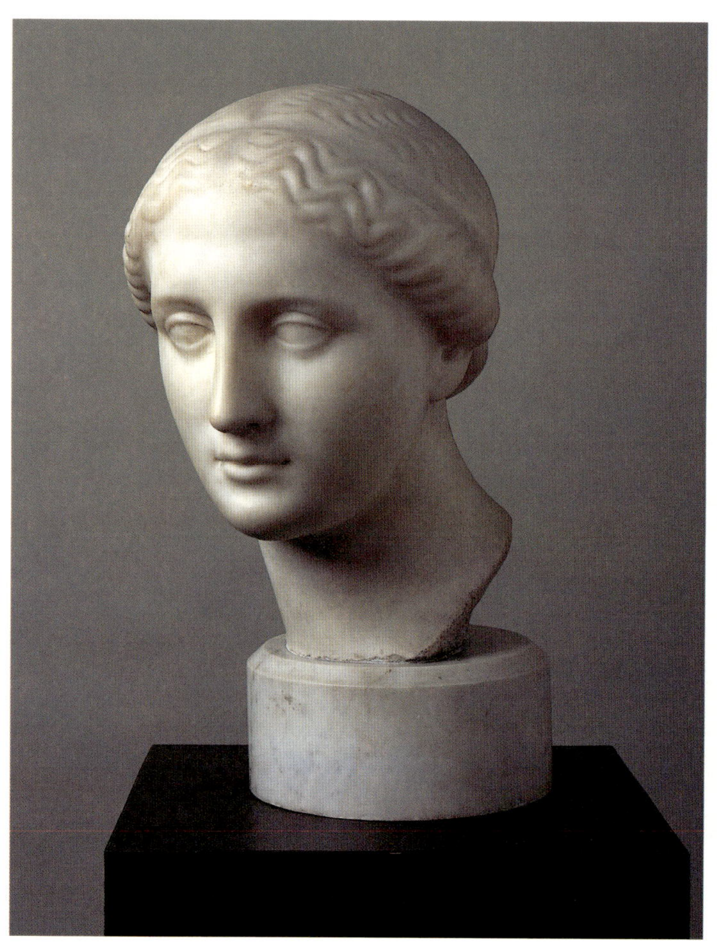 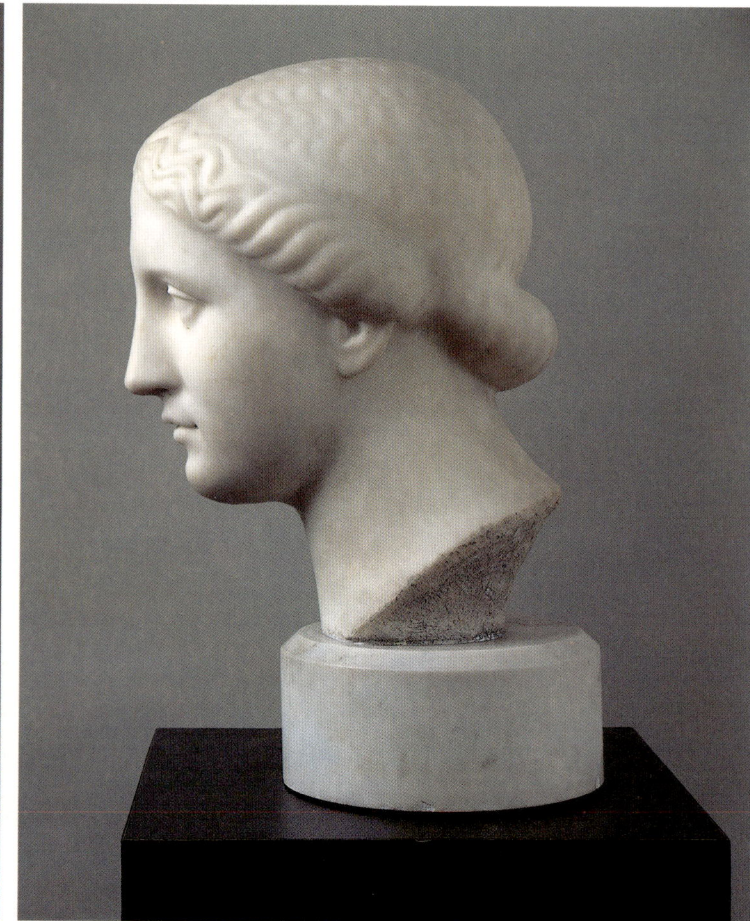

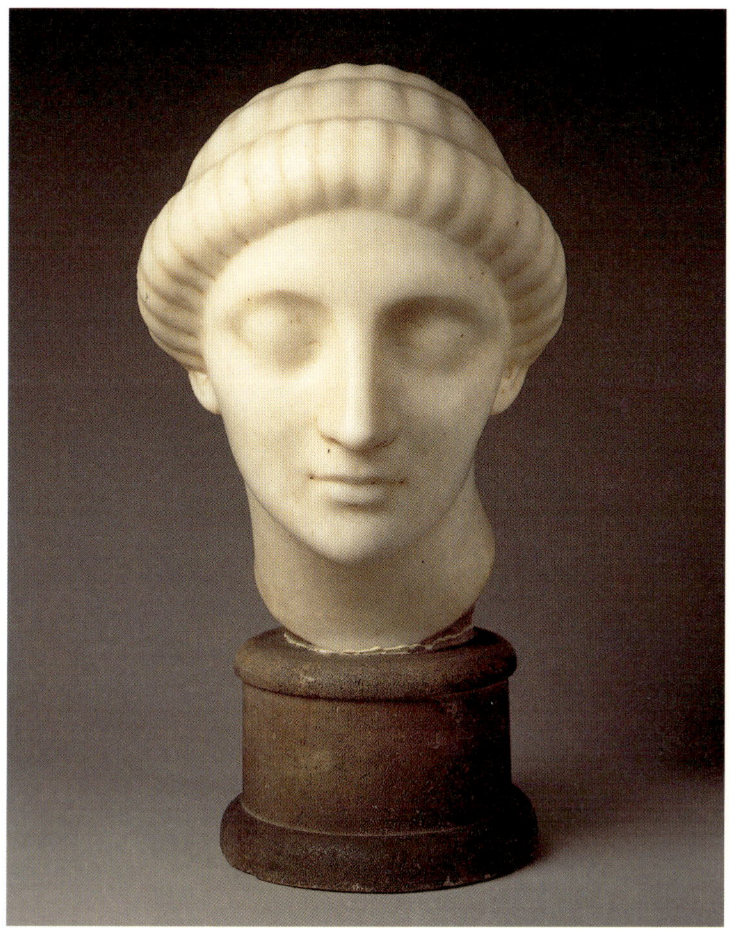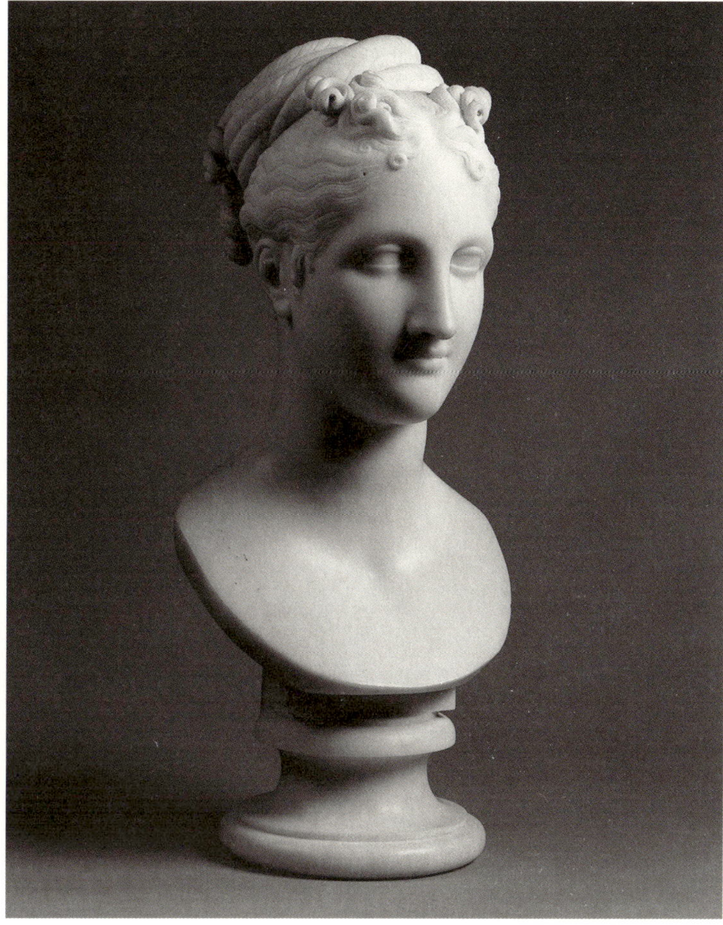

Fig. 41
Elie Nadelman
Female Head, c. 1910–11
Marble, 17 3/4 x 9 x 10 1/2 in.
(45.1 x 22.9 x 26.7 cm) including base
The Metropolitan Museum of Art, New York;
Gift of Mala Rubinstein Silson, 1992
©2002 The Metropolitan Museum of Art

Fig. 42
Antonio Canova
Idealized Head of a Woman, c. 1817
Marble, 22 1/4 x 9 1/2 x 9 3/4 in.
(56.5 x 24.1 x 24.8 cm)
Kimbell Art Museum, Fort Worth, Texas

Fig. 43
Elie Nadelman
Head of a Girl, c. 1910–11
Marble, 14 in. (35.6 cm) high
Erving and Joyce Wolf Collection
Photography by Jerry L. Thompson

Fig. 44
Elie Nadelman
The Four Seasons, 1911
Four terra-cotta sculptures, each 31 1/2 in.
(80 cm) high
Collection of The New-York Historical Society

Fig. 45
Unknown artist
Female Statuette, Boeotian, Tanagra,
c. 320 B.C.
Terra-cotta, 12 1/2 in. (32 cm) high
Musée du Louvre, Paris
Copyright Réunion des Musées Nationaux/
Art Resource, NY

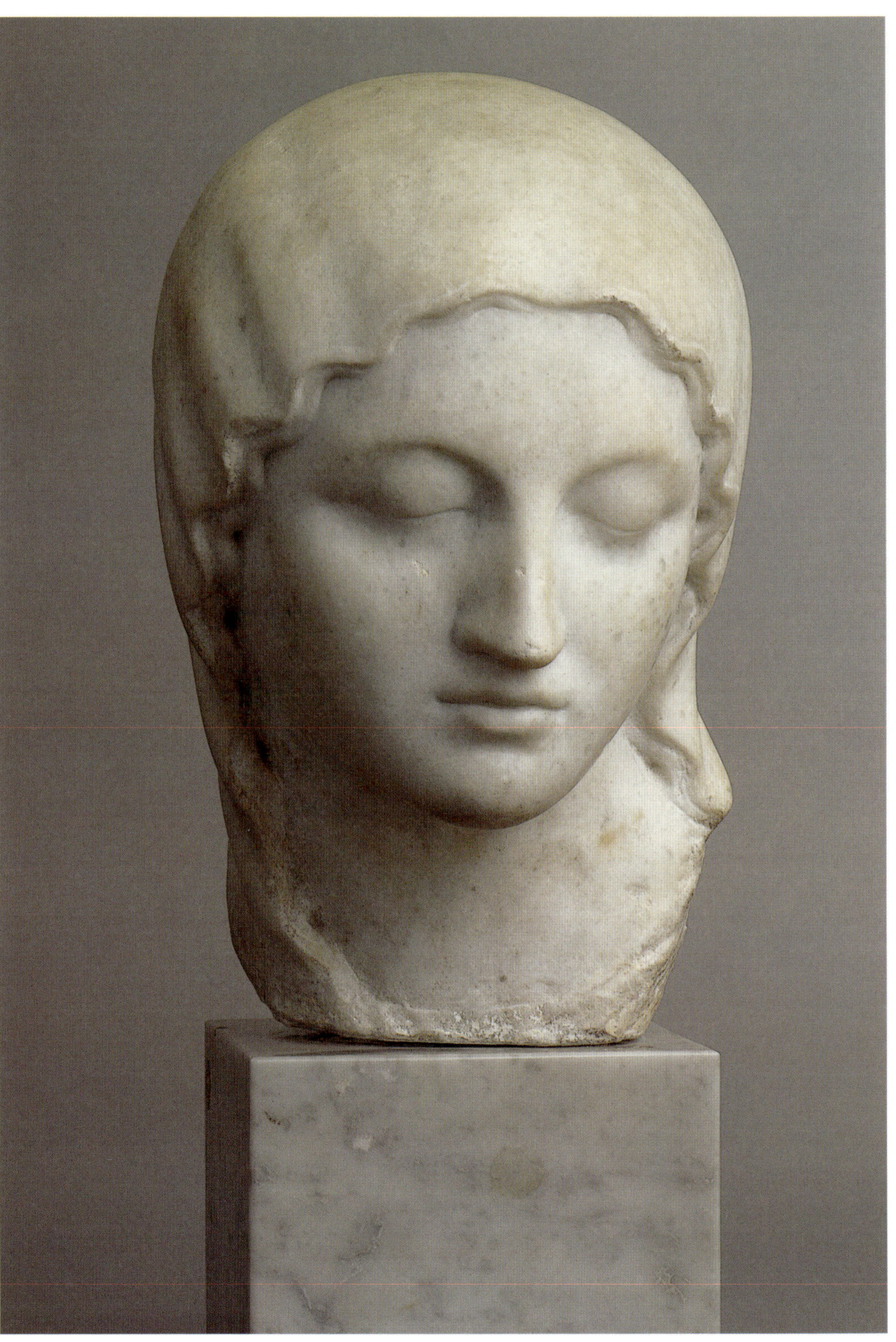

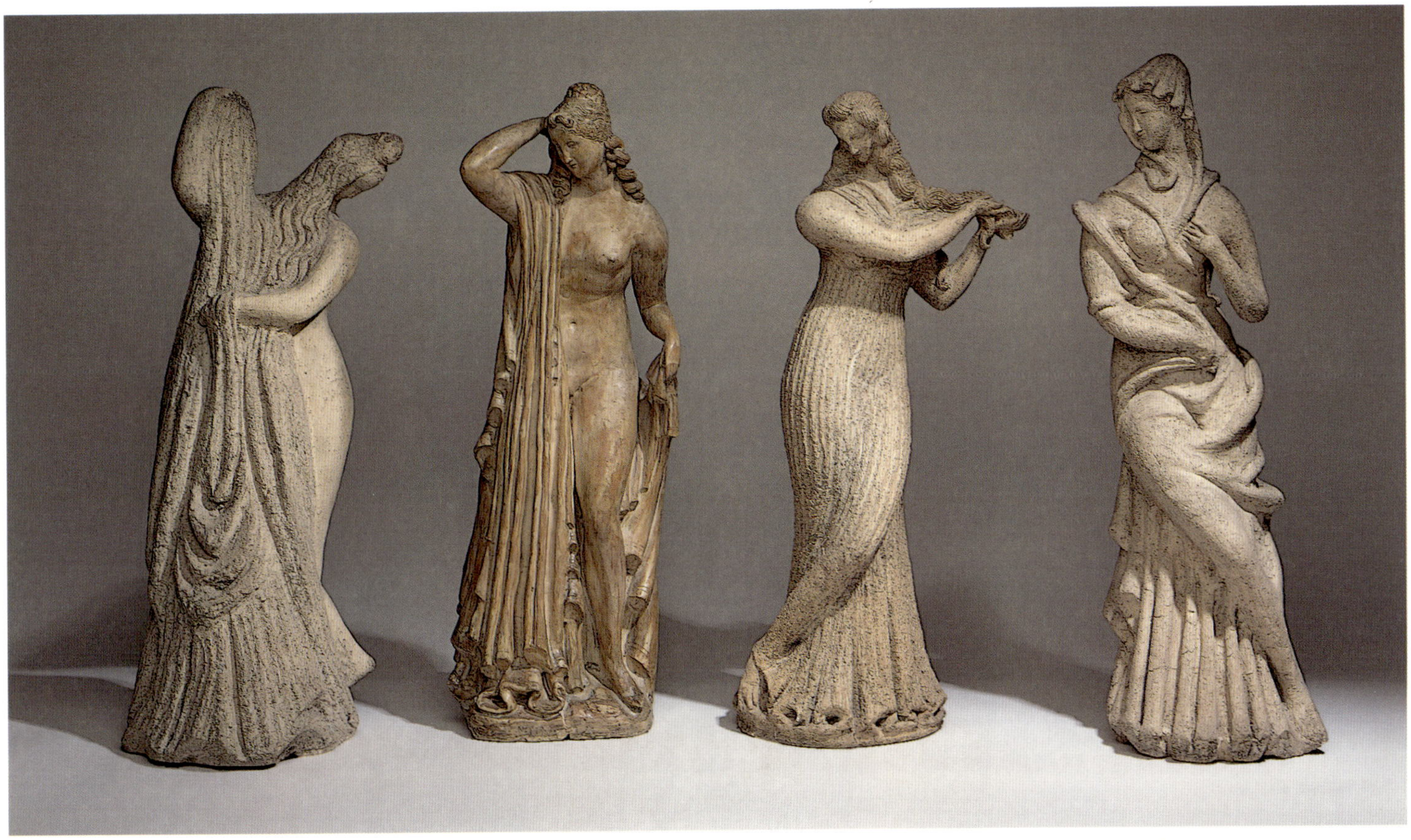

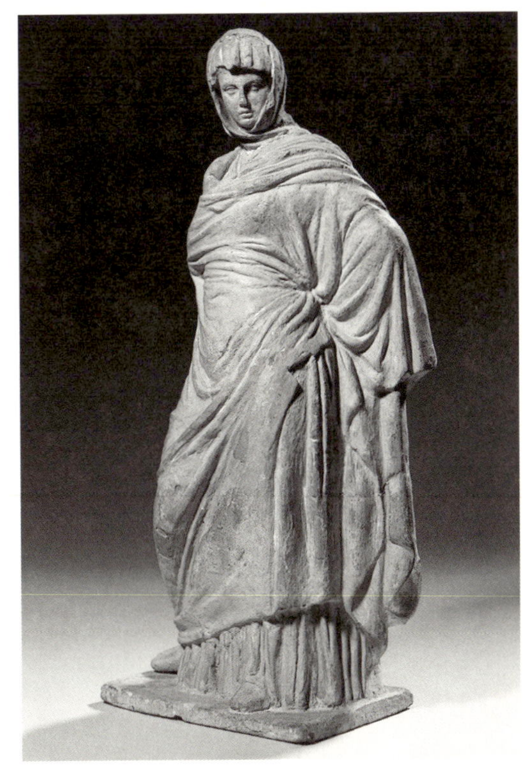

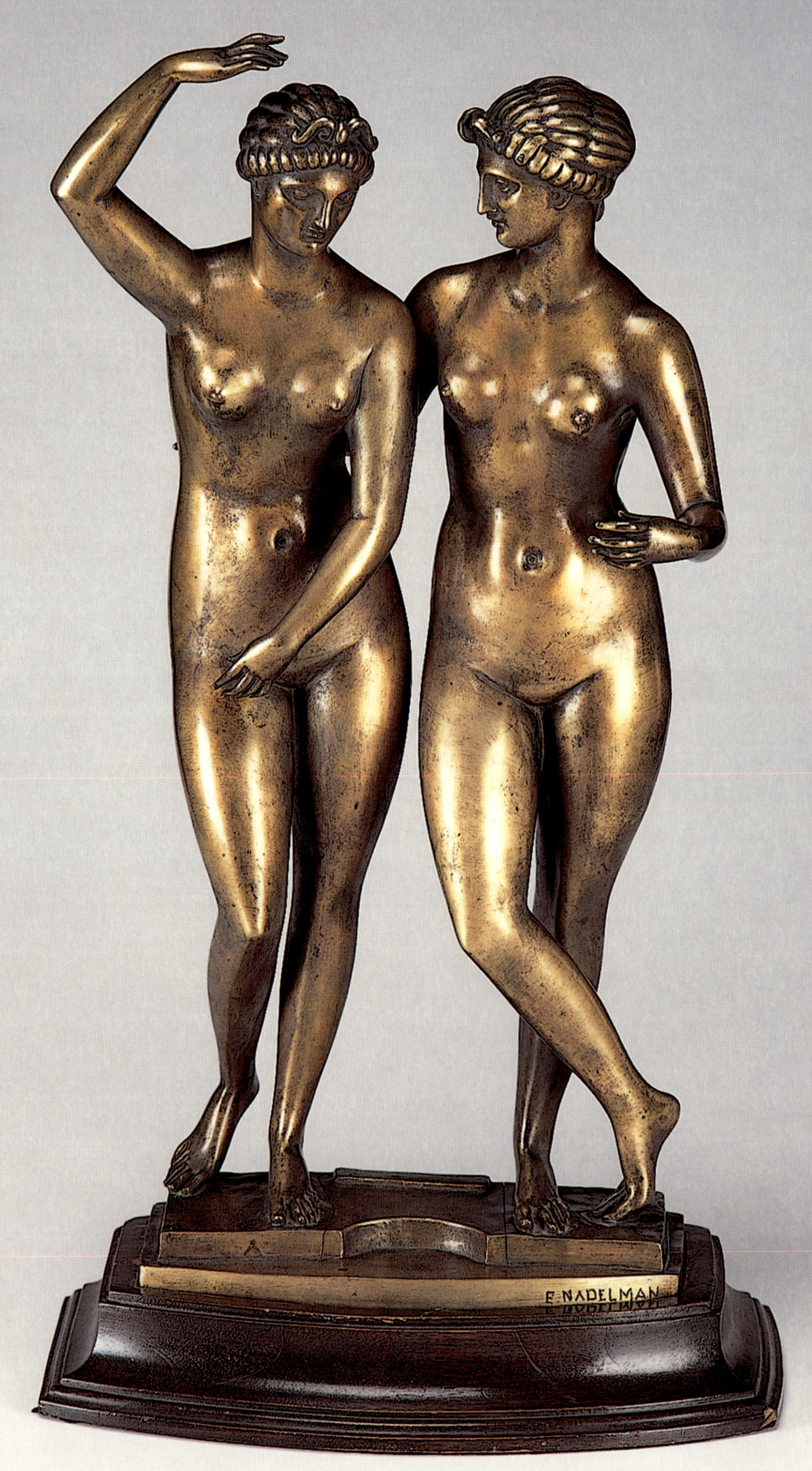
E. NADELMAN

Success Accelerates: Paris, 1912—14

Fig. 46
Elie Nadelman
Two Standing Nudes, c. 1912
Gilt bronze with wooden base
20 1/2 x 10 1/4 x 8 in. (52.1 x 26 x 20.3 cm)
The Joslyn Art Museum, Omaha, Nebraska
Gift of Martin Birnbaum

Fig. 47
Elie Nadelman's 1913 exhibition at
Galerie E. Druet, Paris, May–June 1913
Lincoln Kirstein Photograph Collection,
Jerome Robbins Dance Division, The New York
Public Library

Fig. 48
Giambologna
Architecture, c. 1570–80
Bronze, 14 in. (35.5 cm) high
Bayerisches Nationalmuseum, Munich

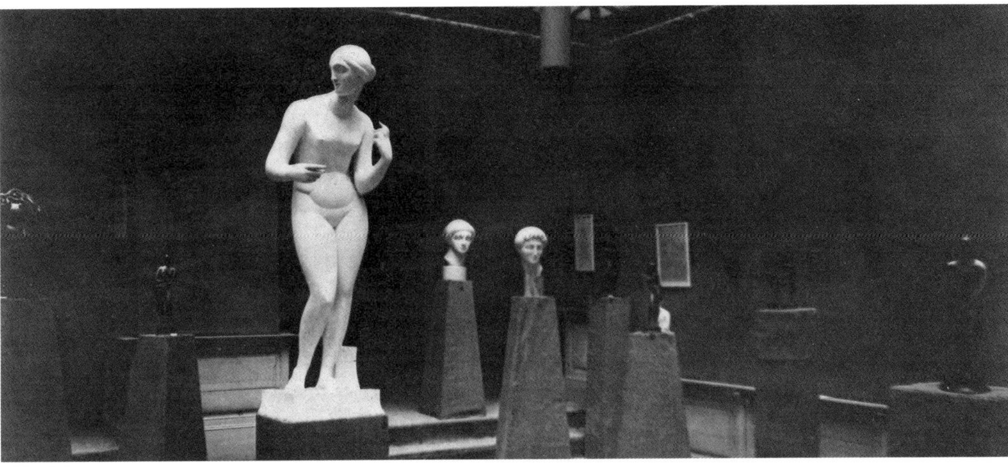

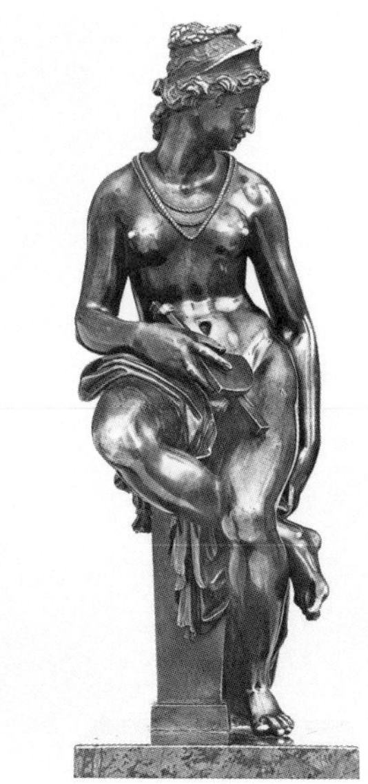

Back in Paris after the success of his Paterson Gallery show, Nadelman entered more actively into the Polish colony's bohemian life. No longer inhibited by lack of money, he now became a more frequent participant in café society, although he never formed deep friendships or dropped the reserve for which he was already known. Still, he was one of ten Polish artists living in Paris to found the Paris-based Society of Polish Artists.[75] In existence for only two years, from 1912 to 1914, the group nevertheless organized a number of exhibitions of its members' work, both in France and elsewhere, and staged public events, one of which was Nadelman's 1913 lecture on "new tendencies in modern art." In 1913 he was elected to Sztuka, the Kraków-based Society of Polish Artists, more than half of whose members now lived abroad.

During this period Nadelman worked primarily in bronze, translating the economically linear forms of his drawings into willowy figures with graceful, curvilinear gestures and lithe, adolescent bodies topped by coiffures of tight ringlets (FIGS. 46, 49–55). Gone from figures such as *Draped Female Figure* (FIG. 54) were the static, compact volumes and self-sufficient, static poses of his earlier plasters and marbles. In their place were elongated, sinuous forms whose rhythmic grace and supple, twisted torsos recalled Giambologna's *Architecture* (FIG. 48), which Nadelman had seen in Munich's Bayerisches Nationalmuseum, as well as the Mannerist conventions of Michelangelo, Primaticcio, and El Greco—a resemblance not lost on the press, which compared his work favorably with that of these progenitors.[76]

Fig. 49
Elie Nadelman
Standing Female Nude, c. 1912
Bronze with dark brown patina, 25 1/2 in.
(64.8 cm) high
Collection of Mr. and Mrs. Theodore C. Rogers
Photography by Jerry L. Thompson

Fig. 50
Elie Nadelman
Standing Male Nude, c. 1912–13
Bronze, 25 1/2 x 12 x 9 1/2 in.
(64.8 x 30.5 x 24.1 cm)
Private collection, New York
Photography by Matt Flynn

Fig. 51
Elie Nadelman
Standing Female Nude, c. 1912–13
Bronze, 21 3/4 x 8 5/8 x 7 1/4 in.
(55.2 x 21.9 x 18.4 cm) including base
The Museum of Modern Art, New York;
Aristide Maillol Fund
©The Museum of Modern Art/Licensed by
SCALA/Art Resource, NY

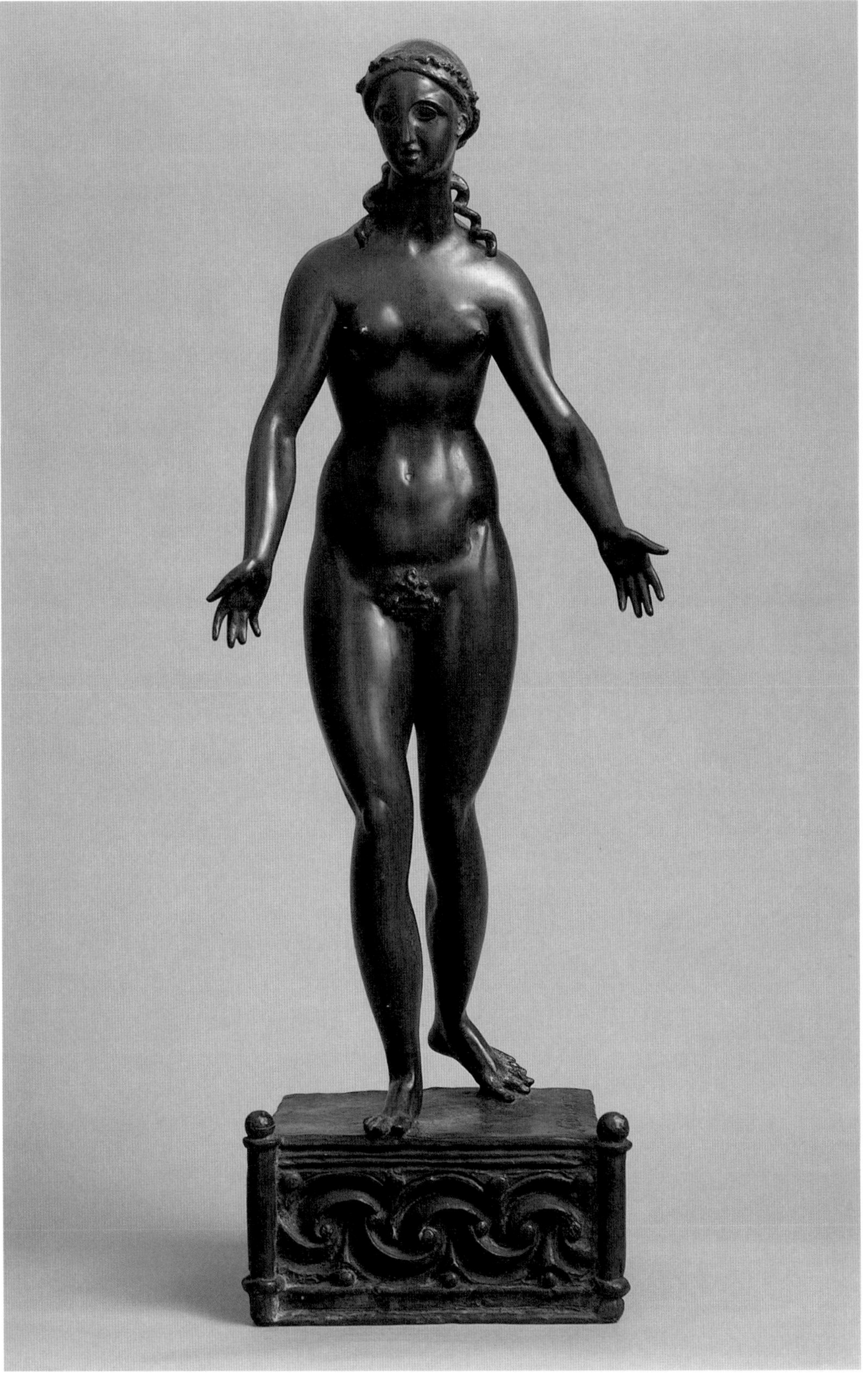

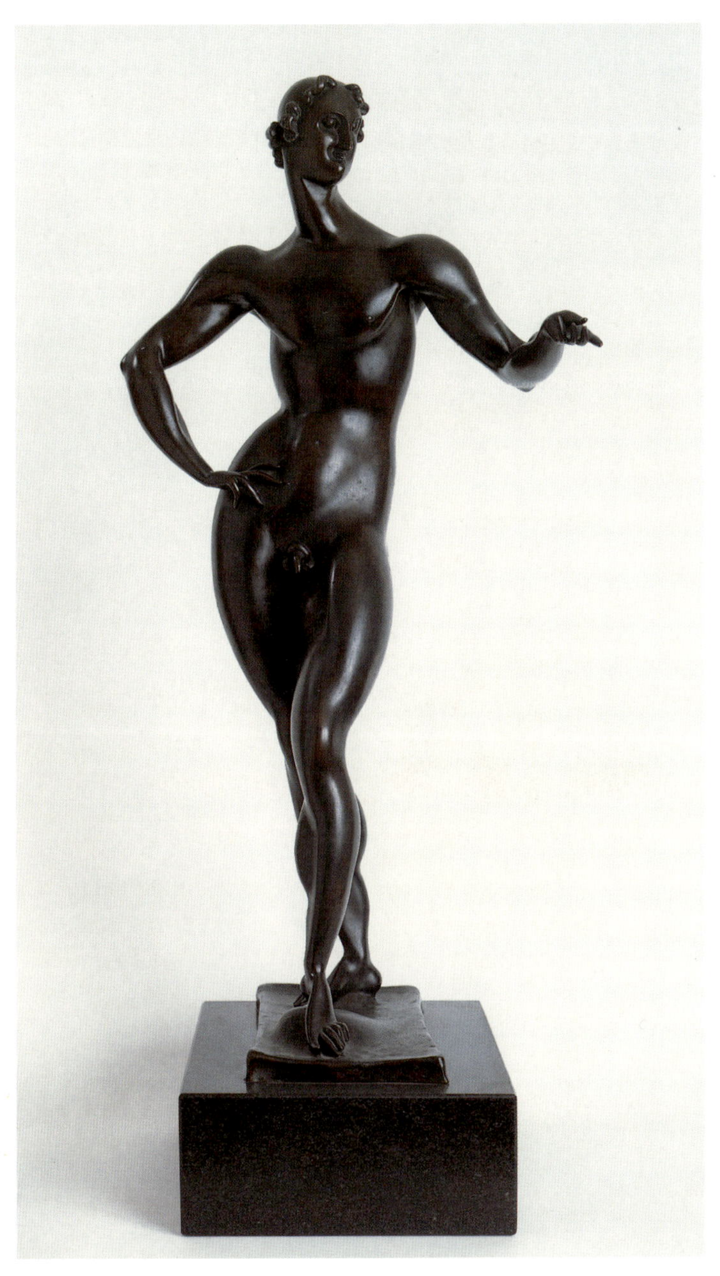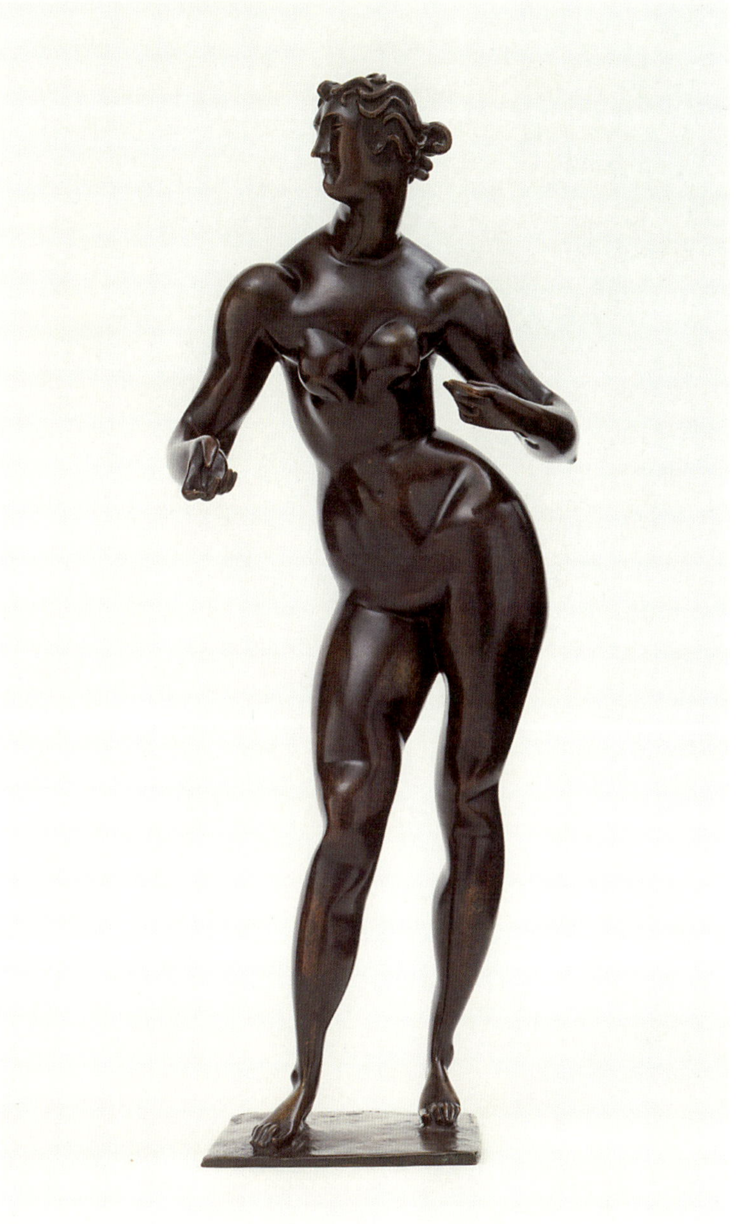

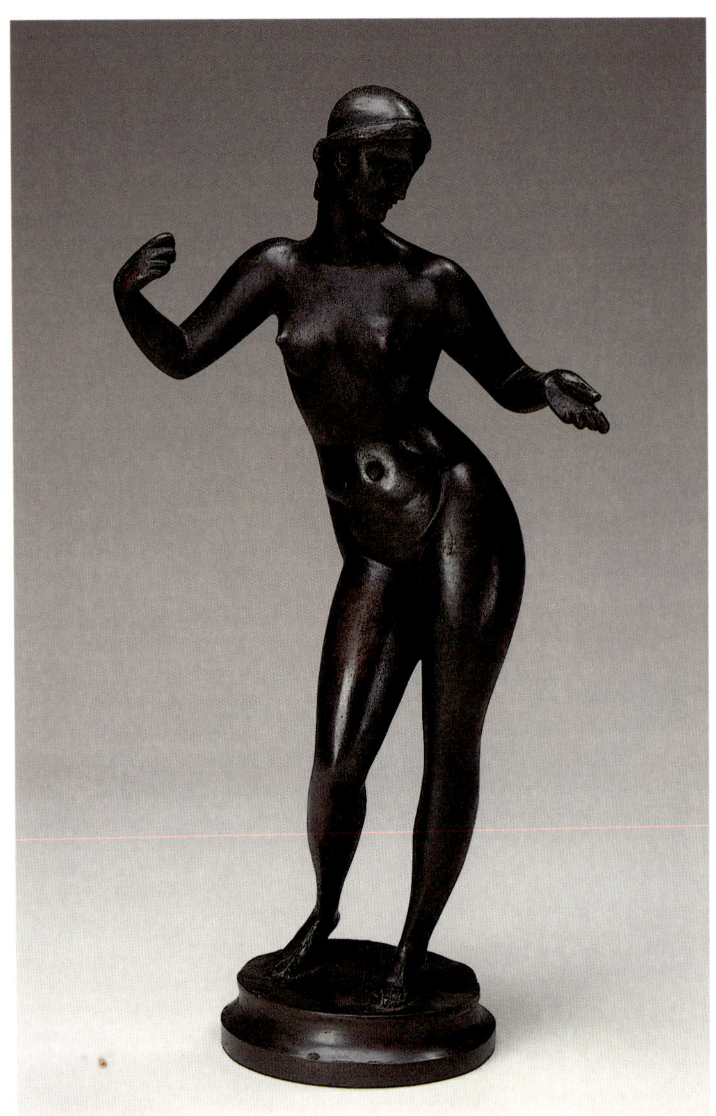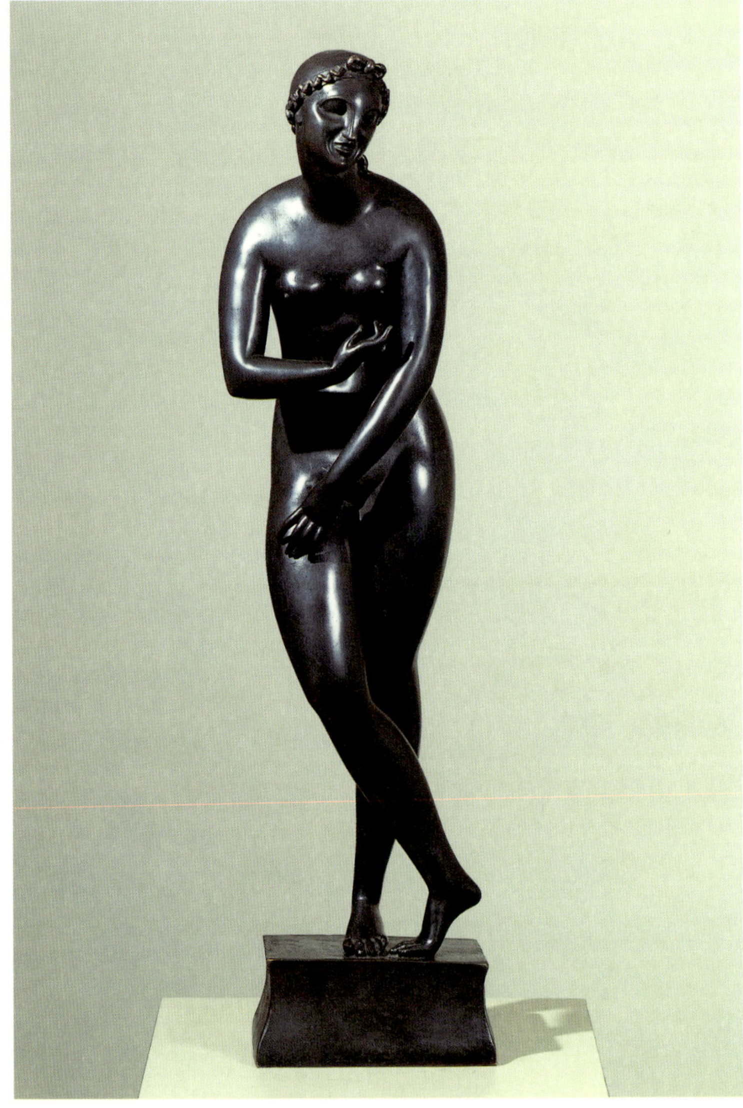

Fig. 52
Elie Nadelman
Standing Nude, c. 1912–13
Bronze, 15 3/4 x 7 7/8 x 5 1/8 in.
(40 x 20 x 13 cm)
Hirshhorn Museum and Sculpture Garden,
Smithsonian Institution; Gift of Joseph H.
Hirshhorn, 1966
Photography by Lee Stalsworth

Fig. 53
Elie Nadelman
Standing Woman, c. 1912–13
Bronze with black patina, 29 1/4 in.
(74.3 cm) high
Private collection, New York

Fig. 54
Elie Nadelman
Draped Female Figure, 1912–13
Bronze, 22 3/4 x 11 3/4 x 9 in.
(57.8 x 29.8 x 22.9 cm)
Norma B. Marin Collection; Promised
gift to Smith, Mount Holyoke, and Wellesley
College Art Museums
Photography by Jerry L. Thompson

Fig. 55
Elie Nadelman
Draped Standing Female Figure, 1912–13
(carved c. 1915)
Cherry wood, 23 in. (58.4 cm) high
Private collection

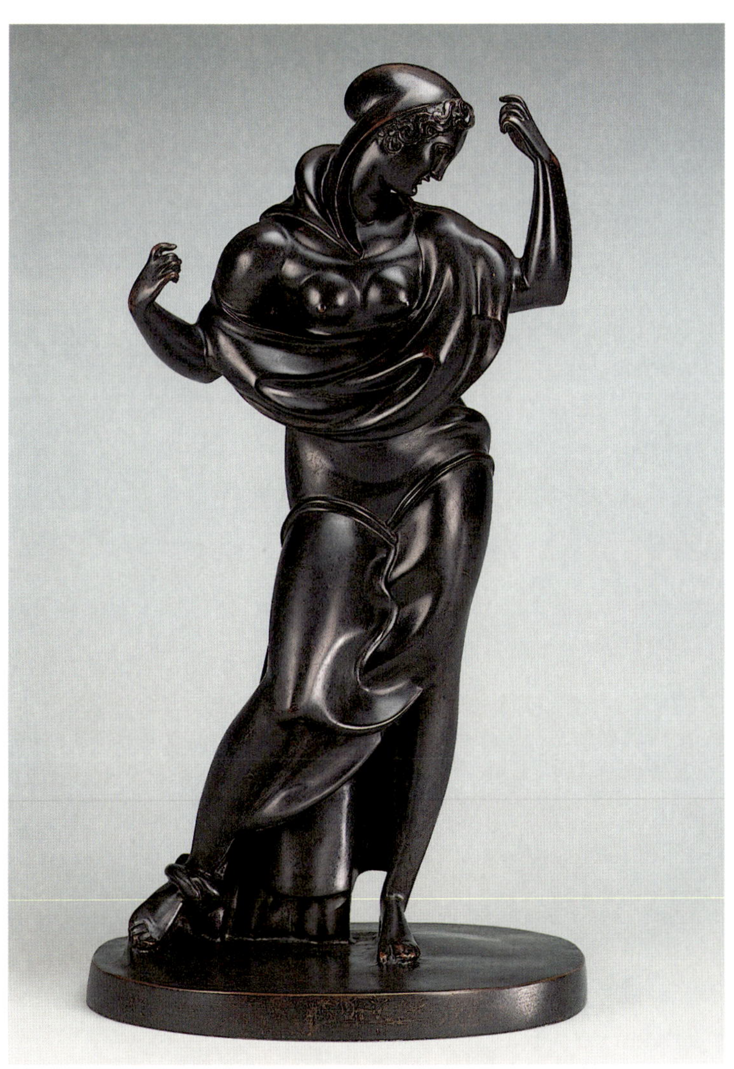

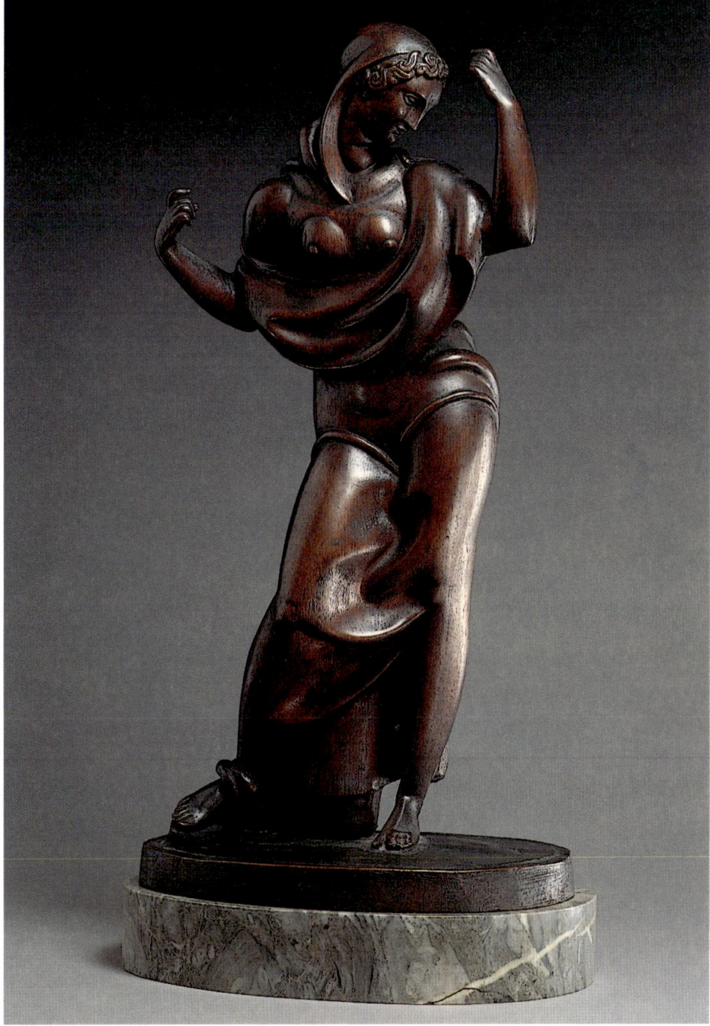

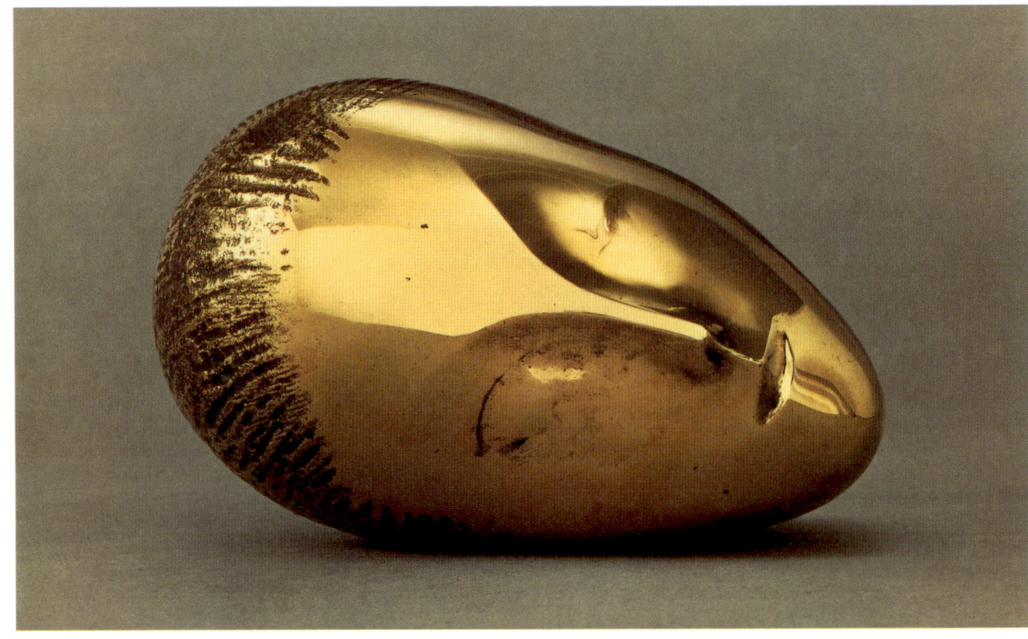

Inflected with the graceful rhythms and linear curves of Jugendstil, Nadelman's bronzes did not merely modernize the past. Drawing his subjects largely from the world of popular entertainment, he endowed sculptures such as *Juggler* (FIG. 57) with the fluid, sinuous movements of dancers and circus performers. The tubular necks and geometrically stylized facial features of these works (FIGS. 65–71) echoed the formal and conceptual simplicity of Constantin Brancusi's sculptures (FIG. 56). On loan to group shows in Germany in 1912, they were unfortunately not available for viewing when Arthur B. Davies and Walt Kuhn made their whirlwind trip through Paris to select work for New York City's 1913 International Exhibition of Modern Art, known as the Armory Show. As a result, Nadelman was represented in the exhibition exclusively by earlier work: twelve drawings and two plaster heads from his 1909 show at Galerie E. Druet. Nevertheless, with only two other Polish artists represented in the show—Gwozdecki and Eugene (Eugeniusz) Żak—Nadelman's participation secured his status as a premier exponent of modernism.

Success piled upon success for Nadelman in these years. His mannerist bronzes and marbles were showcased with enormous fanfare at the Druet gallery in May 1913 (FIG. 47), and a year later his novel synthesis of quotidian clothing and classical forms elicited Apollinaire's positive critical commentary. Up until 1914, all of Nadelman's figures, with the exception of *The Four Seasons*, had been nude. Like most modernists, he had shied away from clothing his

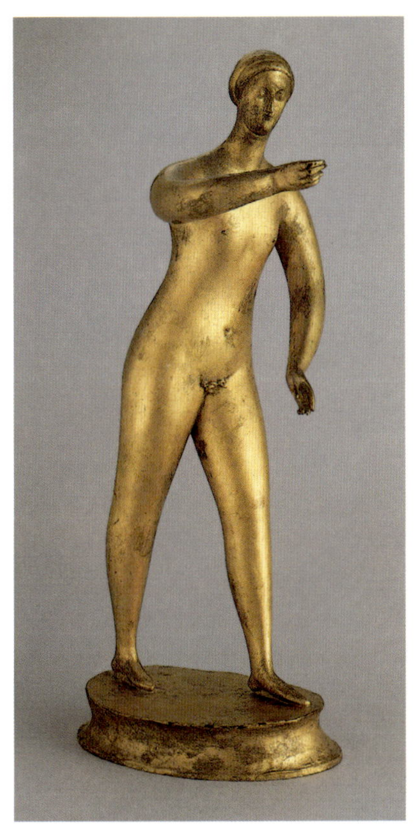

figures because it seemed to militate against the perception of abstract formal values. Sculptures of clothed figures had appeared in Parisian Salons since the late 1870s, but they were most often genre subjects representing the virtues of the poor and the nobility of labor. Exceptions existed, most notably Edgar Degas's wax figurines of dancers adorned with real cotton and silk costumes, but few of these had been exhibited.

By late 1914 Nadelman had found his own way to dissociate contemporary clothing from anecdote and social commentary. Already in several marble heads, his proclivity for reducing objects to generalized geometric shapes and his fascination with the recurrence of these shapes throughout art history had precipitated his playful equation between Mercury's helmet and a bowler hat (FIGS. 72, 73). Having taken this first step, he next made modern clothing—a top hat and an unmistakably contemporary bowler—more prominent (FIGS. 74, 75). Doing so was unprecedented. In Apollinaire's review of the 1914 Salon des Indépendants, the critic acknowledged that Nadelman's two plaster heads were the "first works in which a piece of modern clothing has been treated in an artistic manner."[77]

That summer, while on vacation at the seaside resort of Ostend, Belgium, Nadelman extended his involvement with contemporary subject matter by sketching the denizens of his boarding house as they went about their daily activities. His foray into genre was cut short by the onset of World War I that August. As a reservist in the Russian army, Nadelman was legally obligated to notify the consulate of his whereabouts. With a mixture of patriotism and a moralistic sense of duty, he presented himself to the Russian consulate in Brussels for service.[78] The authorities, however, advised against his attempting to travel through Germany to the Russian front and issued him a visa to go to England. Helena Rubinstein, then living in Paris, may have encouraged him to leave even England—having herself been persuaded by her American-born husband, Edward Titus, to move to the United States before the end of the year for the sake of their sons. Responsive to Nadelman's expressed desire to escape a war in which he had no country to fight for, Rubinstein commissioned him to create a large plaster relief for the salon she planned to open in New York later that spring (FIG. 76).[79] Nadelman accepted the commission and, on October 24, 1914, sailed on the *Lusitania* from Southampton, England, to New York for what he assumed would be a stay of several months.[80]

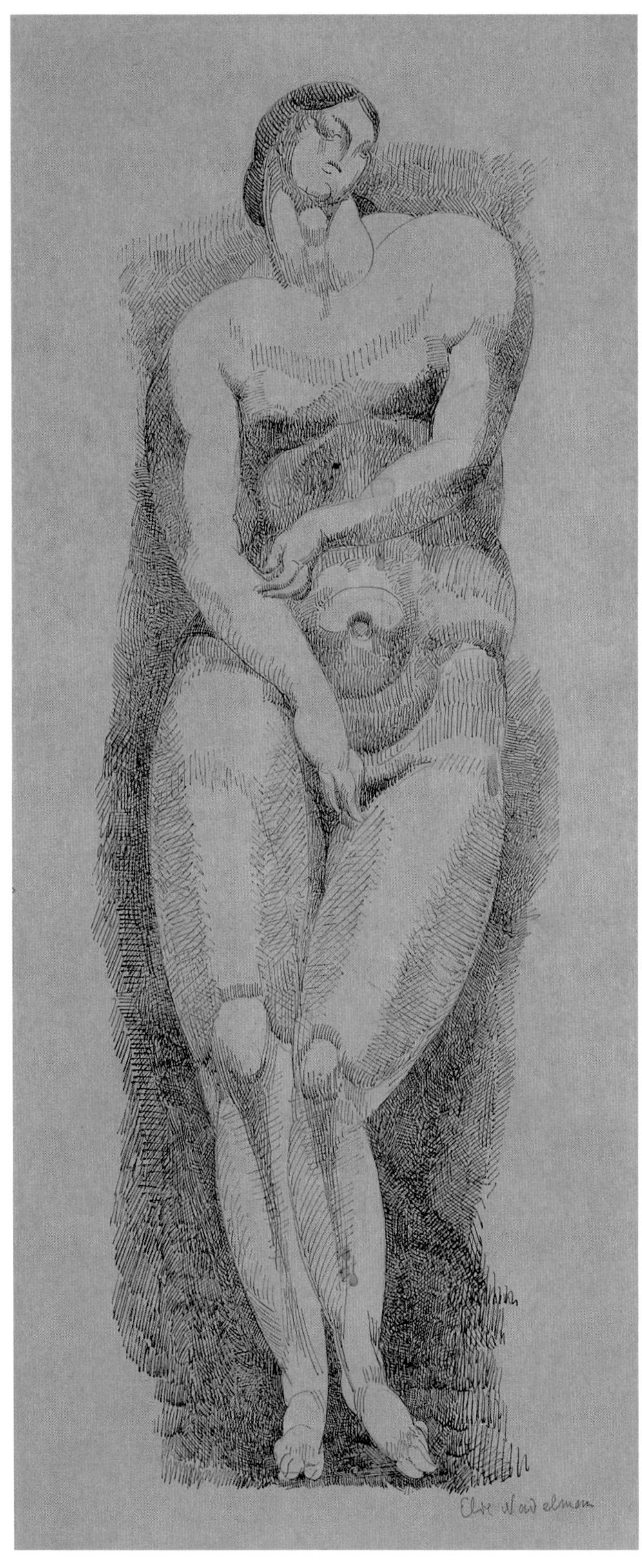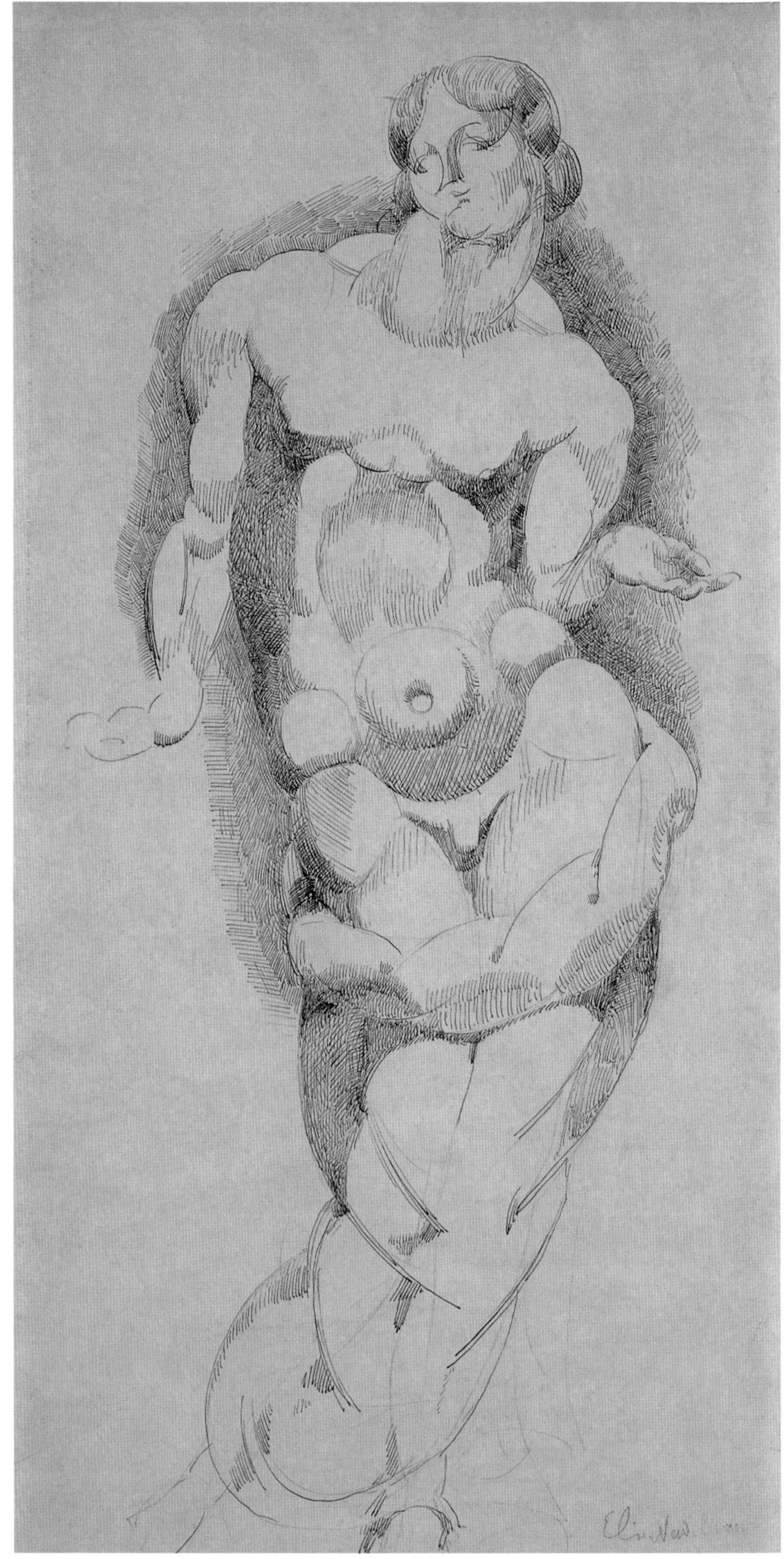

Fig. 58
Elie Nadelman
Standing Female Nude, c. 1912
Ink and pencil on paper, 22 x 9 in.
(55.9 x 22.8 cm)
Hirshhorn Museum and Sculpture Garden,
Smithsonian Institution; Gift of Joseph H.
Hirshhorn, 1966
Photography by Lee Stalsworth

Fig. 59
Elie Nadelman
Standing Male Nude, c. 1912
Ink and pencil on paper, 21 13/16 x 10 3/4 in.
(55.4 x 27.3 cm)
Hirshhorn Museum and Sculpture Garden,
Smithsonian Institution; Gift of Joseph H.
Hirshhorn, 1966
Photography by Lee Stalsworth

Fig. 60
Elie Nadelman
Decorative Figure (Woman), c. 1912
Sepia ink on paper, 19 1/4 x 8 3/8 in.
(48.9 x 21.3 cm)
Slong & Midas Properties, Inc., New York

Fig. 61
Elie Nadelman
Figure Study, 1913
Gilded bronze, 12 1/2 in. (31.8 cm) high
Hirshhorn Museum and Sculpture Garden,
Smithsonian Institution; Gift of Joseph H.
Hirshhorn, 1966
Photography by Lee Stalsworth

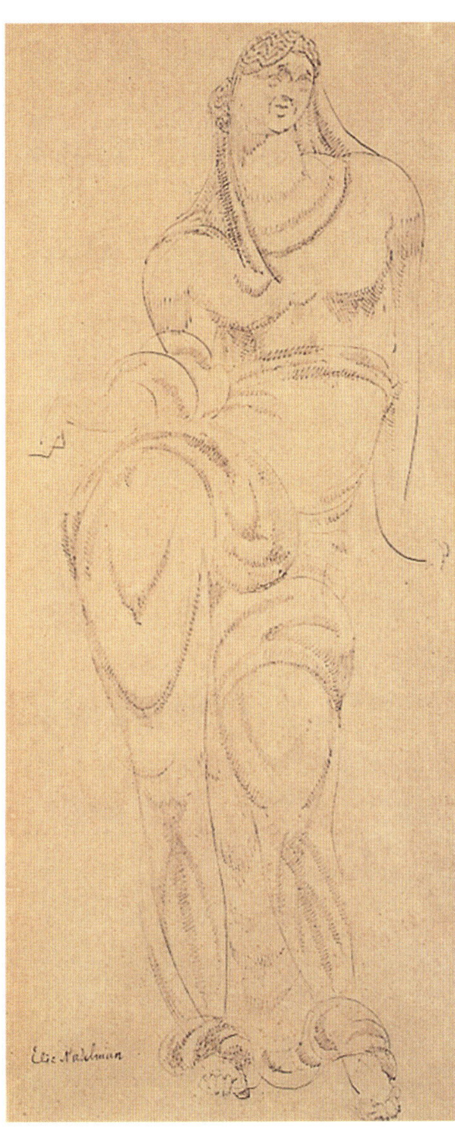

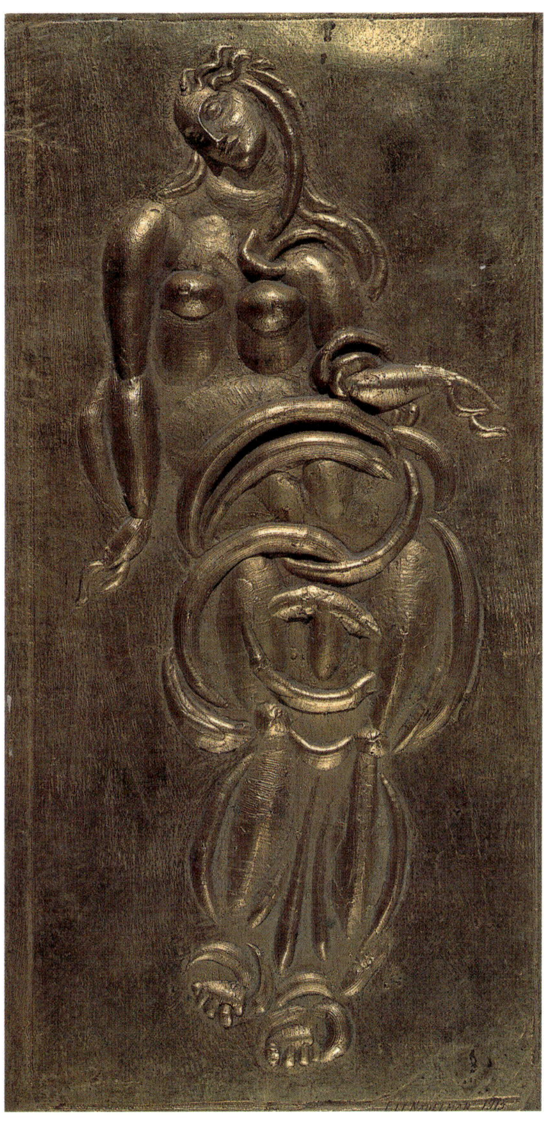

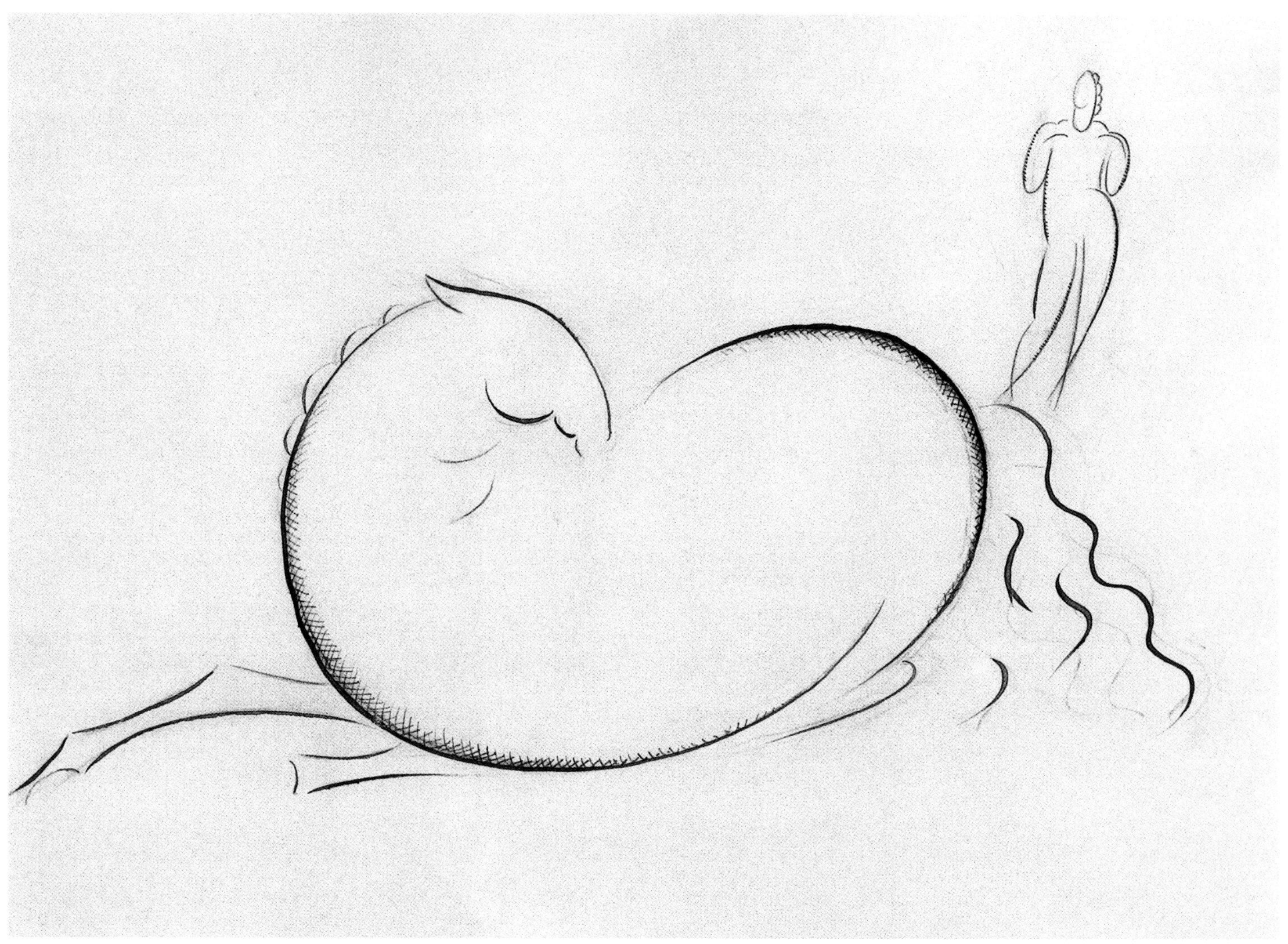

Fig. 62
Elie Nadelman
Reclining Horse, c. 1912
Ink on paper, 8 1/4 x 10 1/4 in.
(21 x 26 cm)
Private collection, New York

Fig. 63
Elie Nadelman
Woman on a Horse, c. 1912
Bronze relief, 7 x 7 1/2 x 1/4 in.
(17.8 x 19.1 x .6 cm)
The Metropolitan Museum of Art, New York;
Bequest of Schofield Thayer, 1982
©2002 The Metropolitan Museum of Art

Fig. 64
Elie Nadelman
Horse and Figure, c. 1912
Bronze relief, 7 3/4 x 10 3/4 x 3/8 in.
(19.7 x 27.3 x 1 cm)
The Metropolitan Museum of Art, New York;
Bequest of Schofield Thayer, 1982
©2002 The Metropolitan Museum of Art

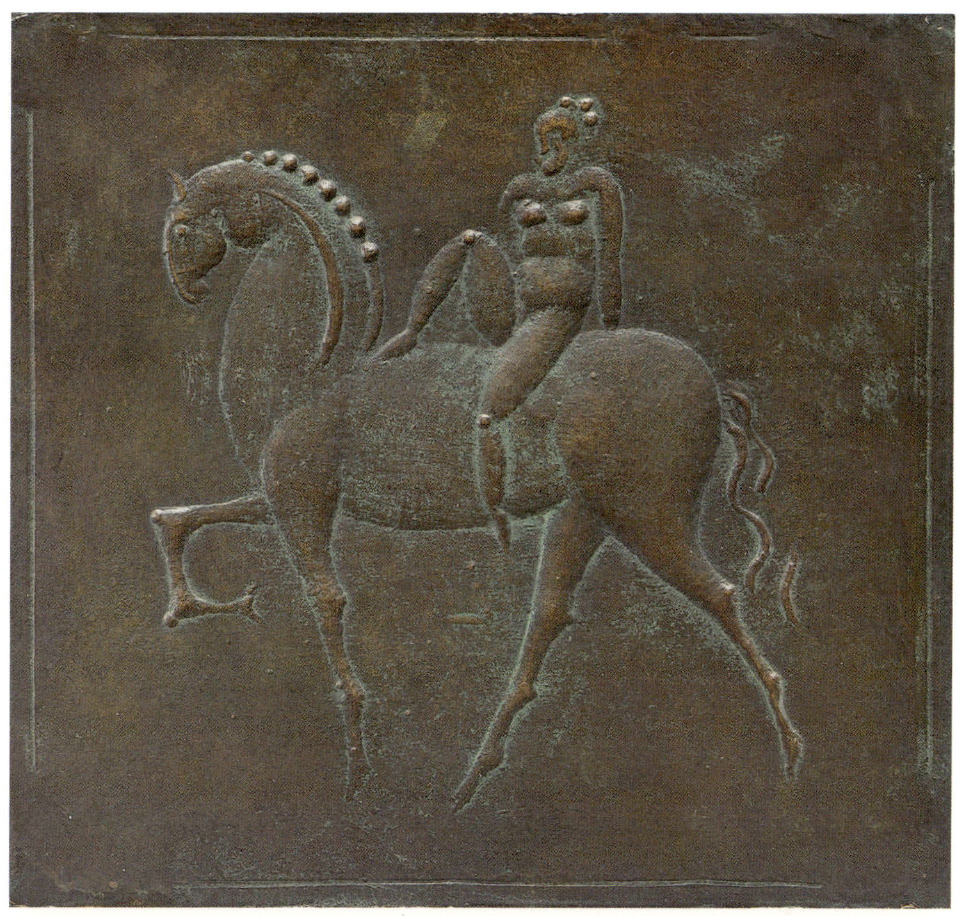

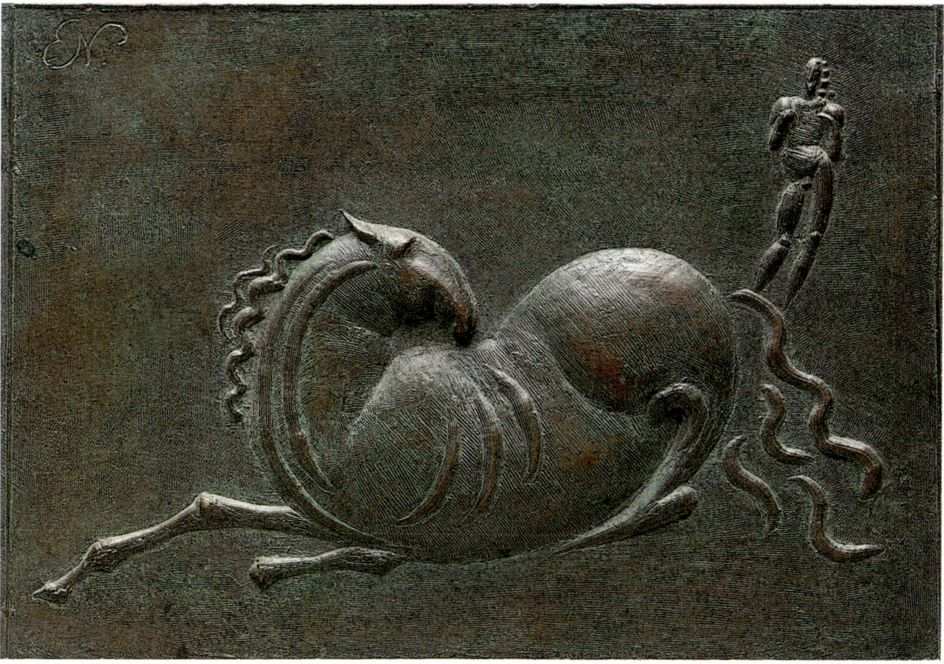

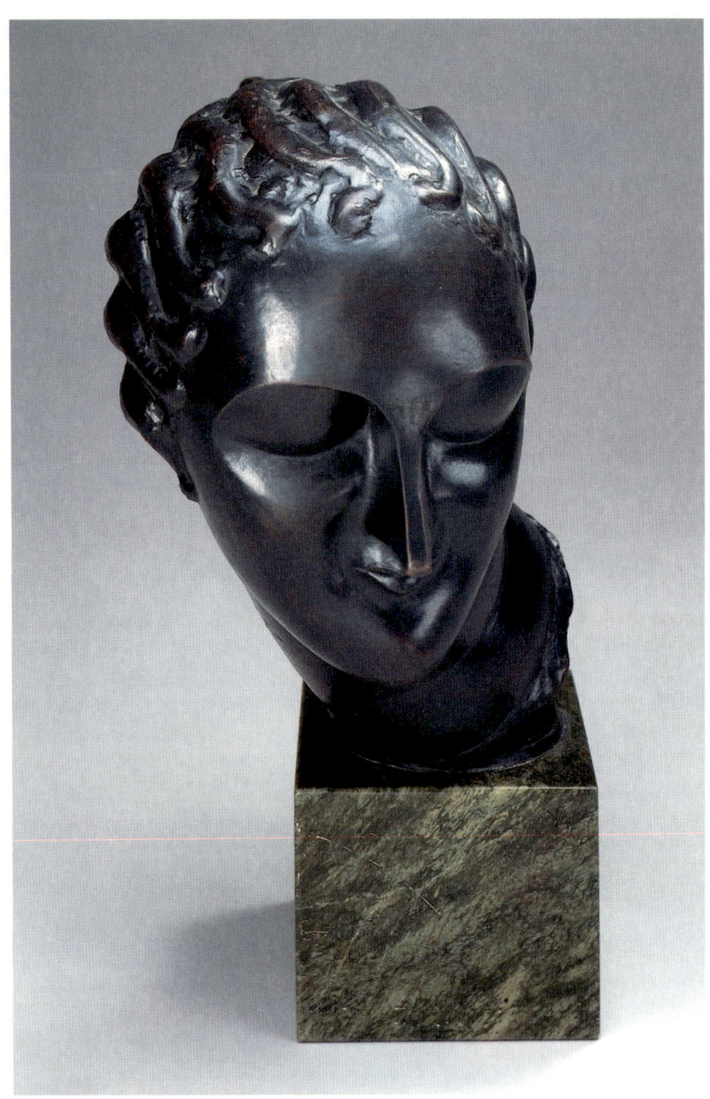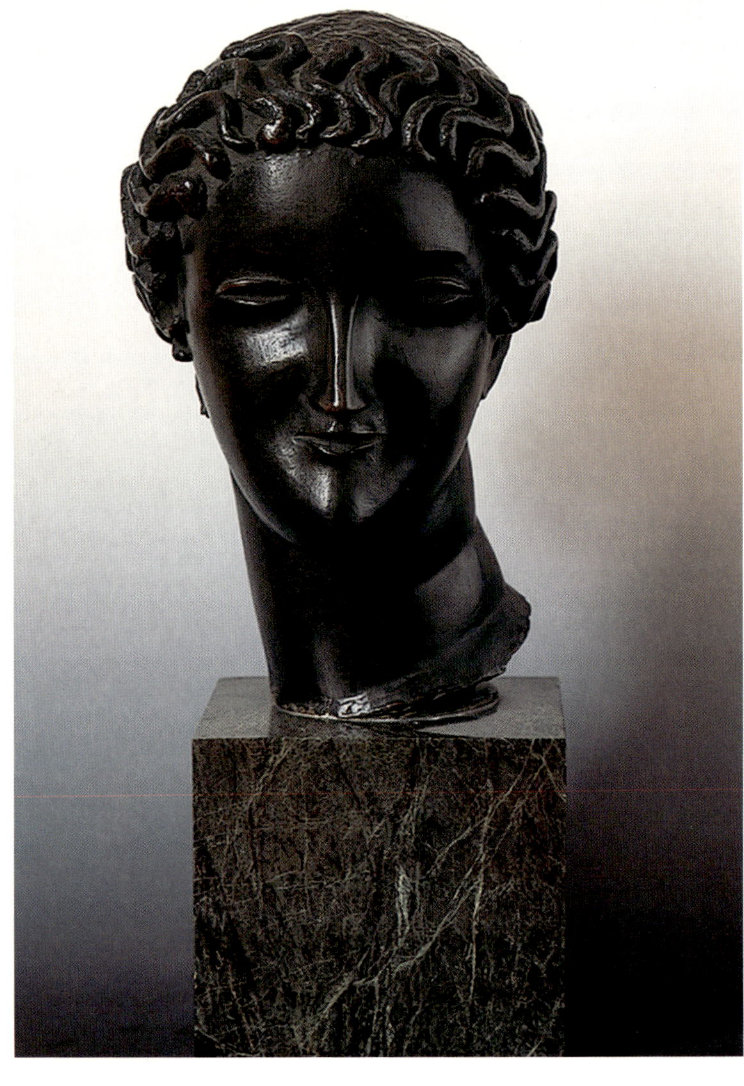

Fig. 65
Elie Nadelman
Head of a Woman, c. 1912–13
Bronze, 13 1/2 x 8 1/8 x 11 in.
(34.3 x 20.6 x 27.9 cm)
Hirshhorn Museum and Sculpture Garden,
Smithsonian Institution; Gift of Joseph H.
Hirshhorn, 1966
Photography by Lee Stalsworth

Fig. 66
Elie Nadelman
Head of a Woman, c. 1912–13
Bronze, 13 in. (33 cm) high
Private collection

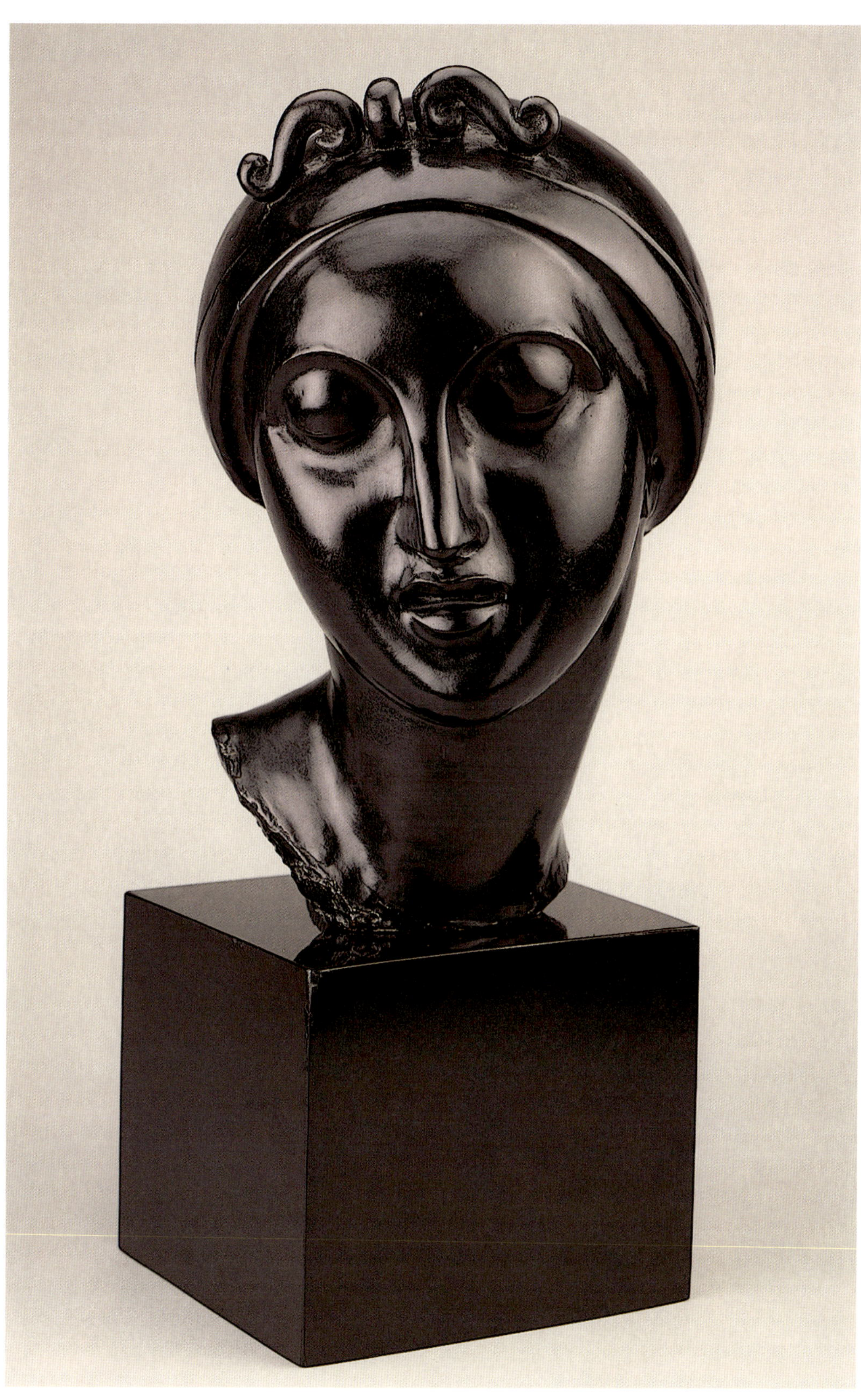

Fig. 67
Elie Nadelman
Ideal Head, c. 1912–13
Bronze, 13 in. (33 cm) high
Private collection

Fig. 68
Elie Nadelman
Head, c. 1912–13
Wood, 11 1/2 in. (29.2 cm) high, including base
Private collection, New York

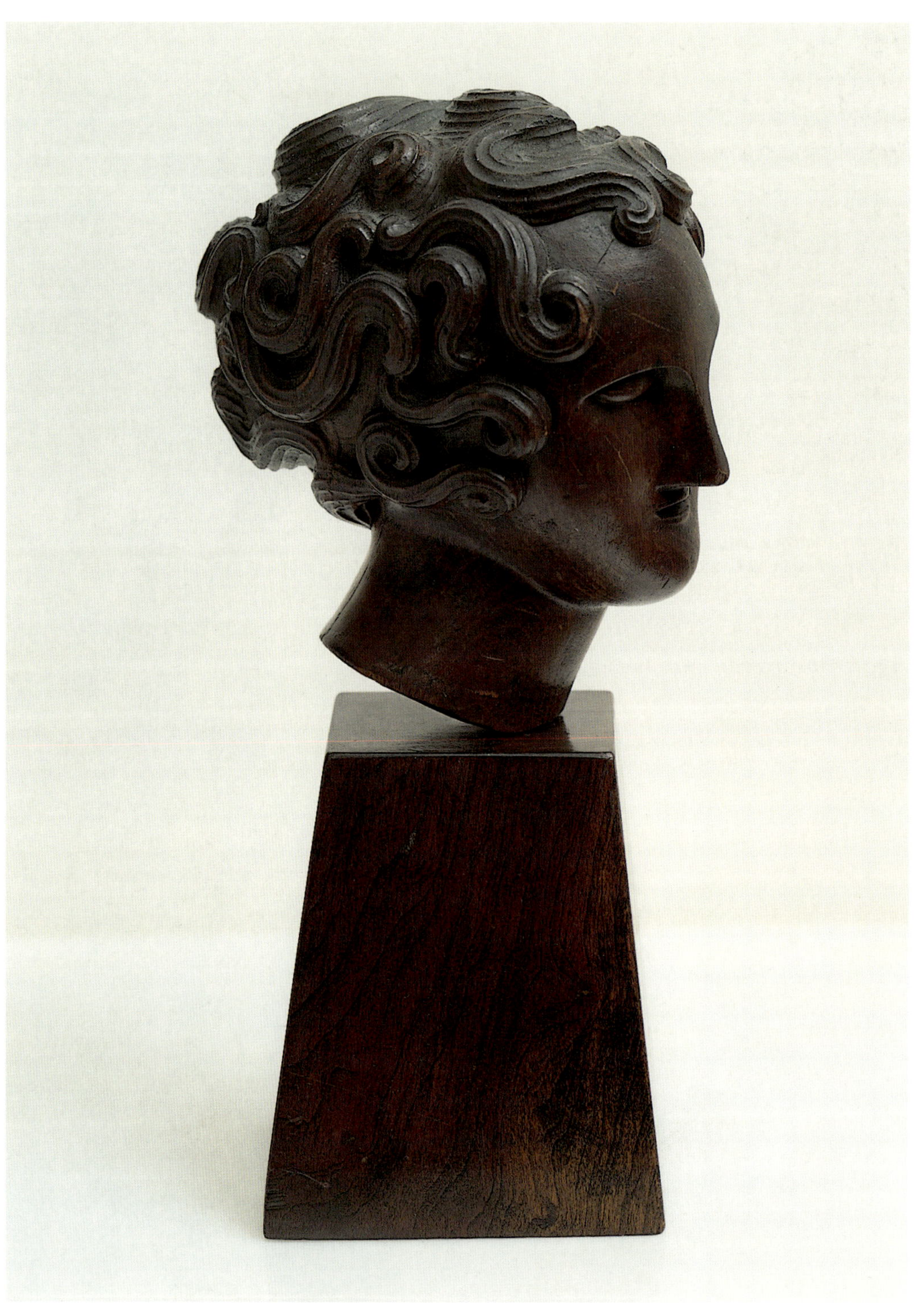

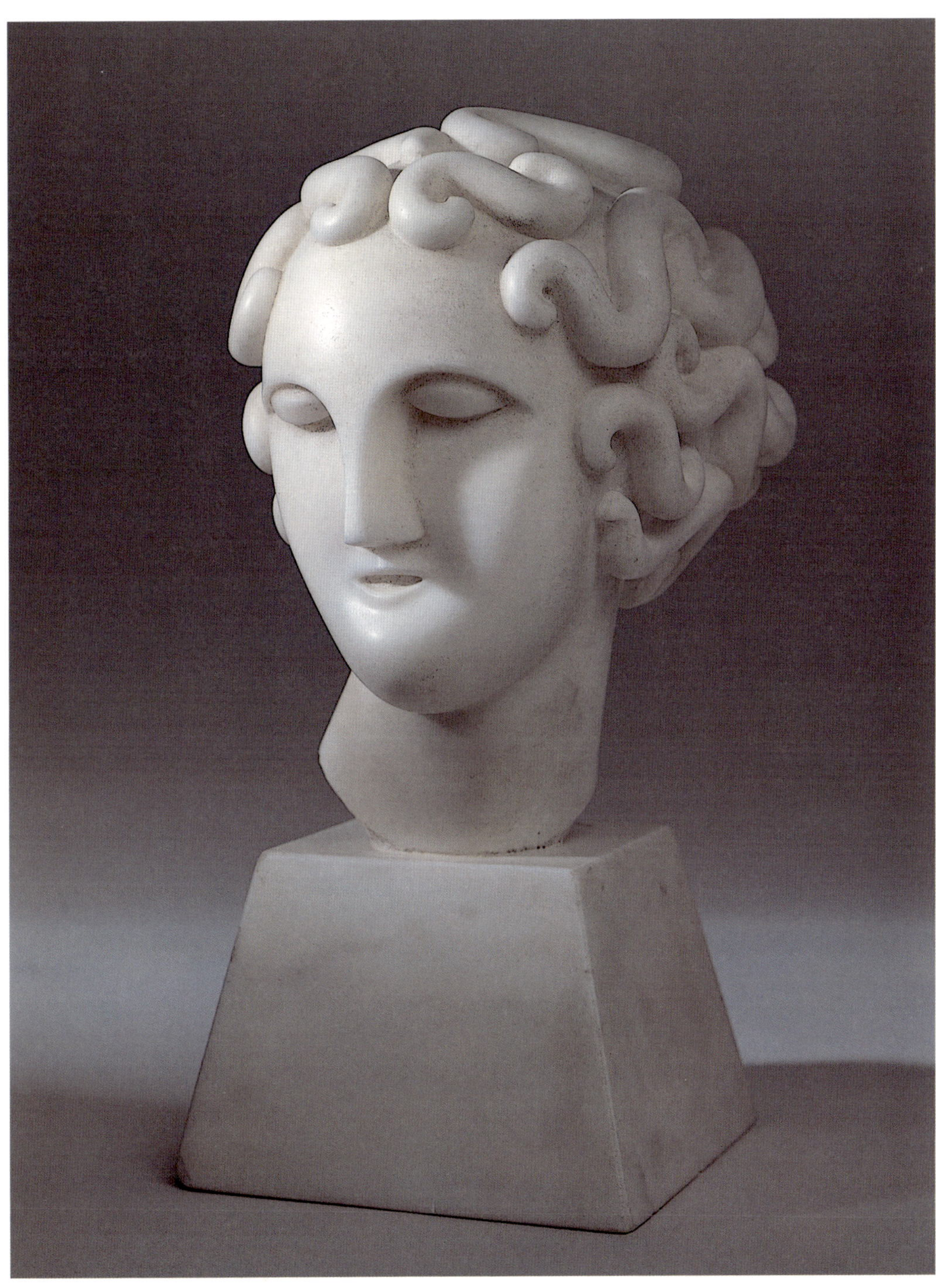

Fig. 69
Elie Nadelman
Head of a Woman, c. 1912–13
Marble, 8 in. (20.3 cm) high
Collection of Barbara and Pitt Hyde
Photography by David Nester

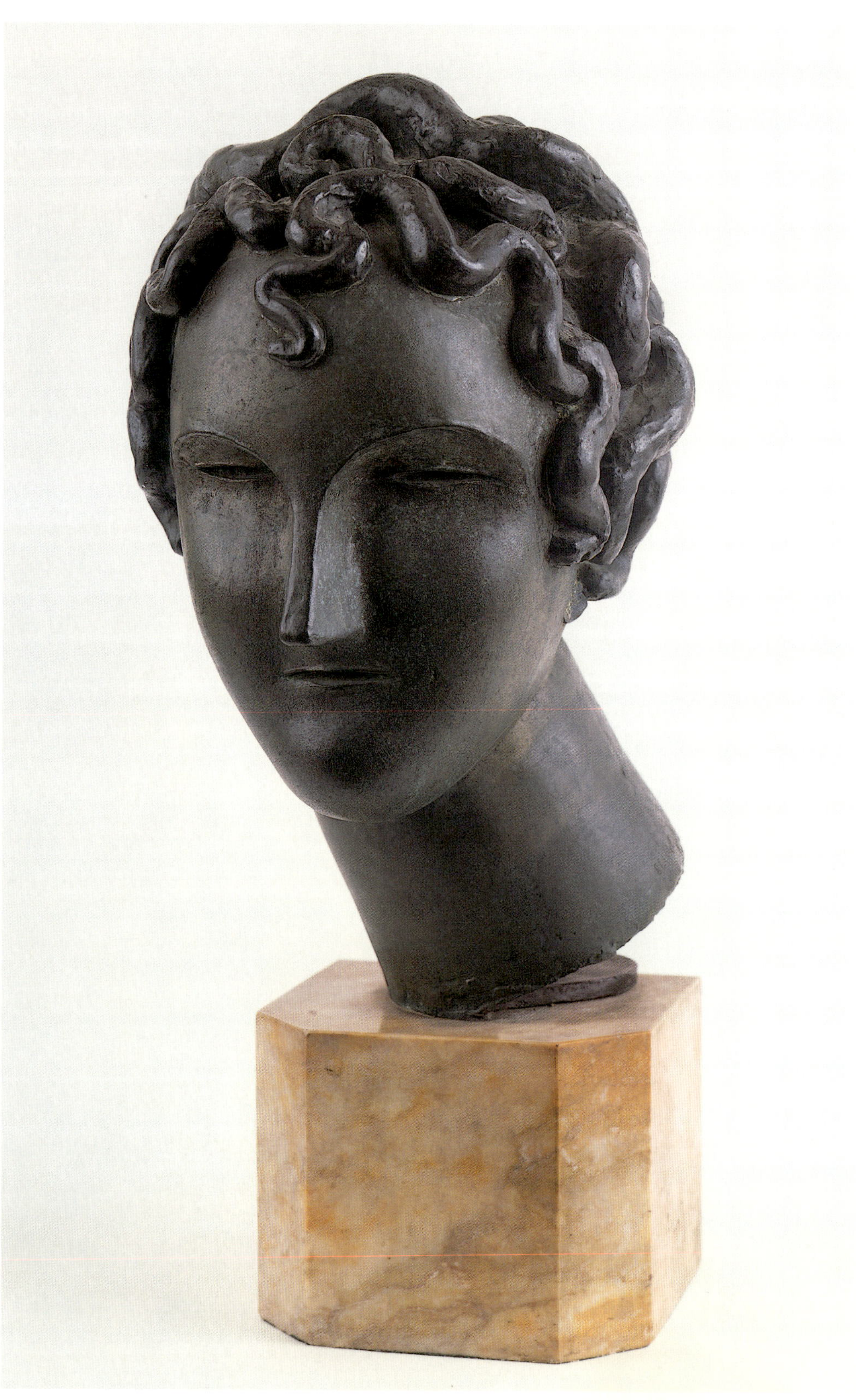

Fig. 70
Elie Nadelman
Head of a Boy, c. 1912–13
Bronze, 17 1/2 x 7 x 6 1/2 in.
(44.5 x 17.8 x 16.5 cm)
Private collection, courtesy Fraenkel Gallery,
San Francisco

Fig. 71
Elie Nadelman
Head of a Boy, c. 1912–13
Gilt bronze, 16 3/4 in. (42.5 cm) high
Private collection

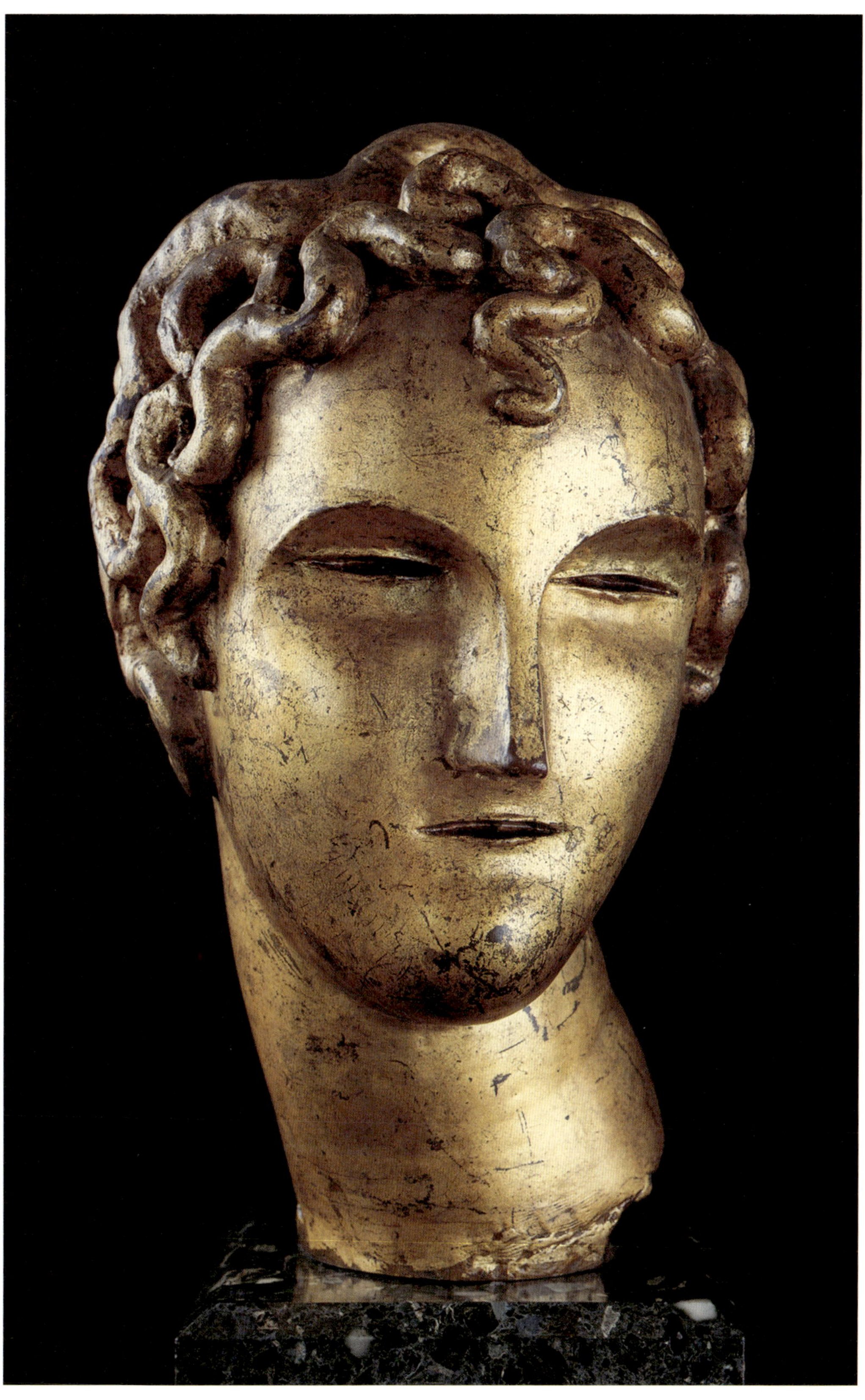

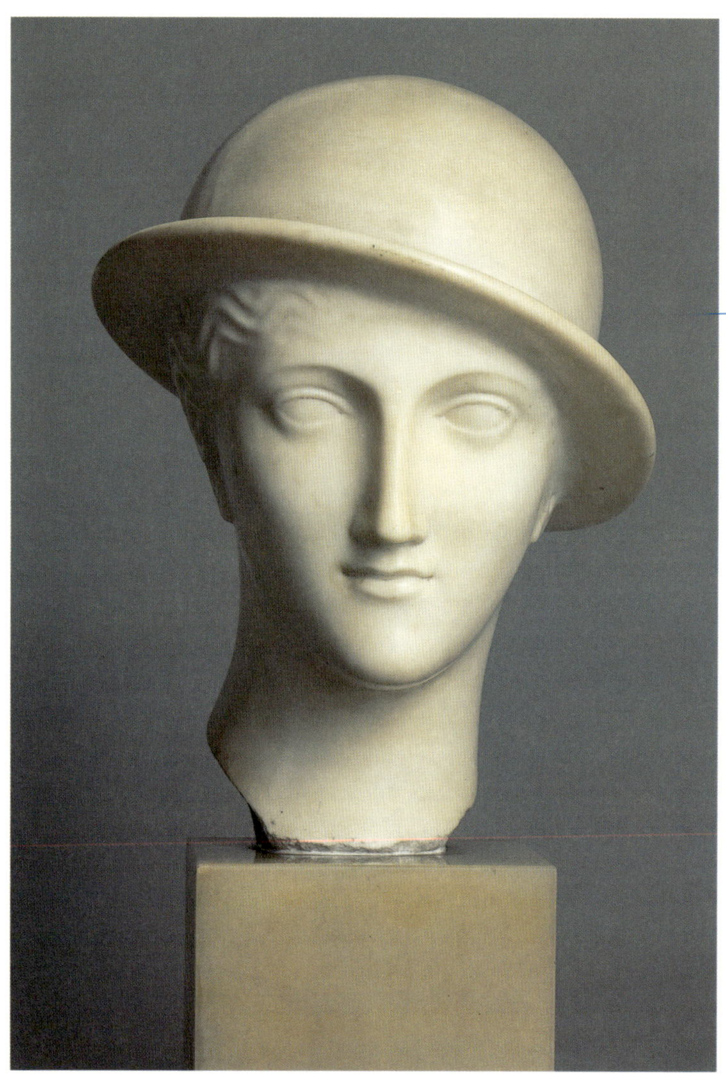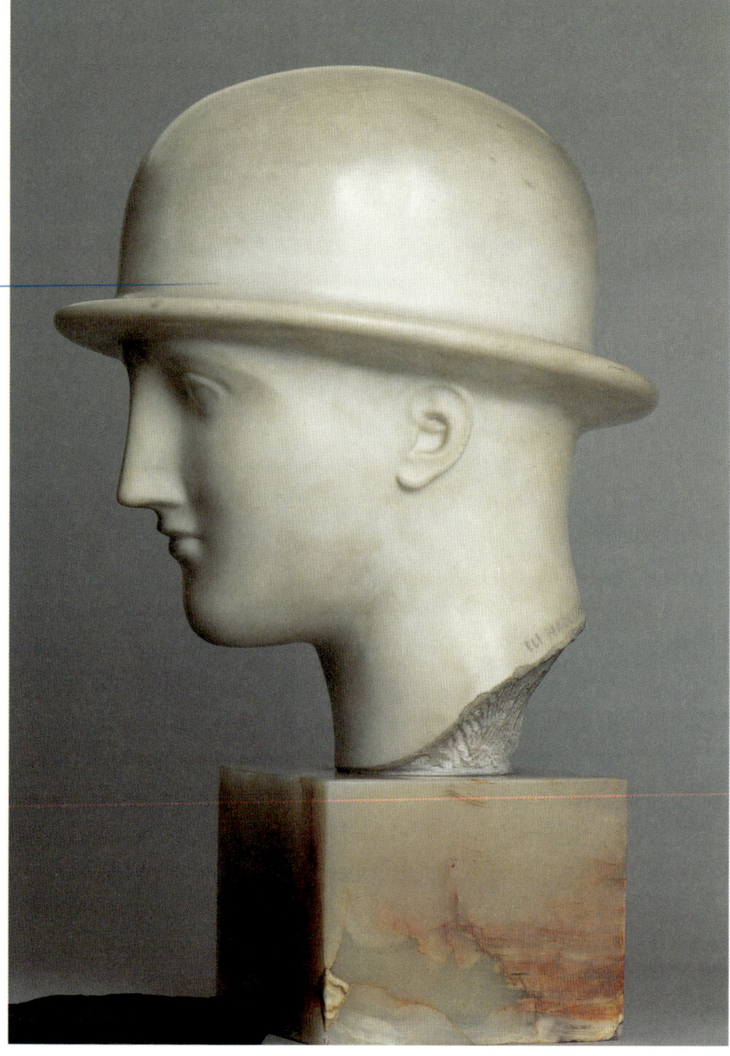

Fig. 72
Elie Nadelman
Mercury Petassos I, c. 1914
Marble, 16 in. (40.6 cm) high
Collection of Diane and Robert Moss
Photography by Jerry L. Thompson

Fig. 73
Elie Nadelman
Mercury Petassos II, c. 1914
Marble, 12 1/2 in. (31.8 cm) high
Collection of Diane and Robert Moss
Photography by Jerry L. Thompson

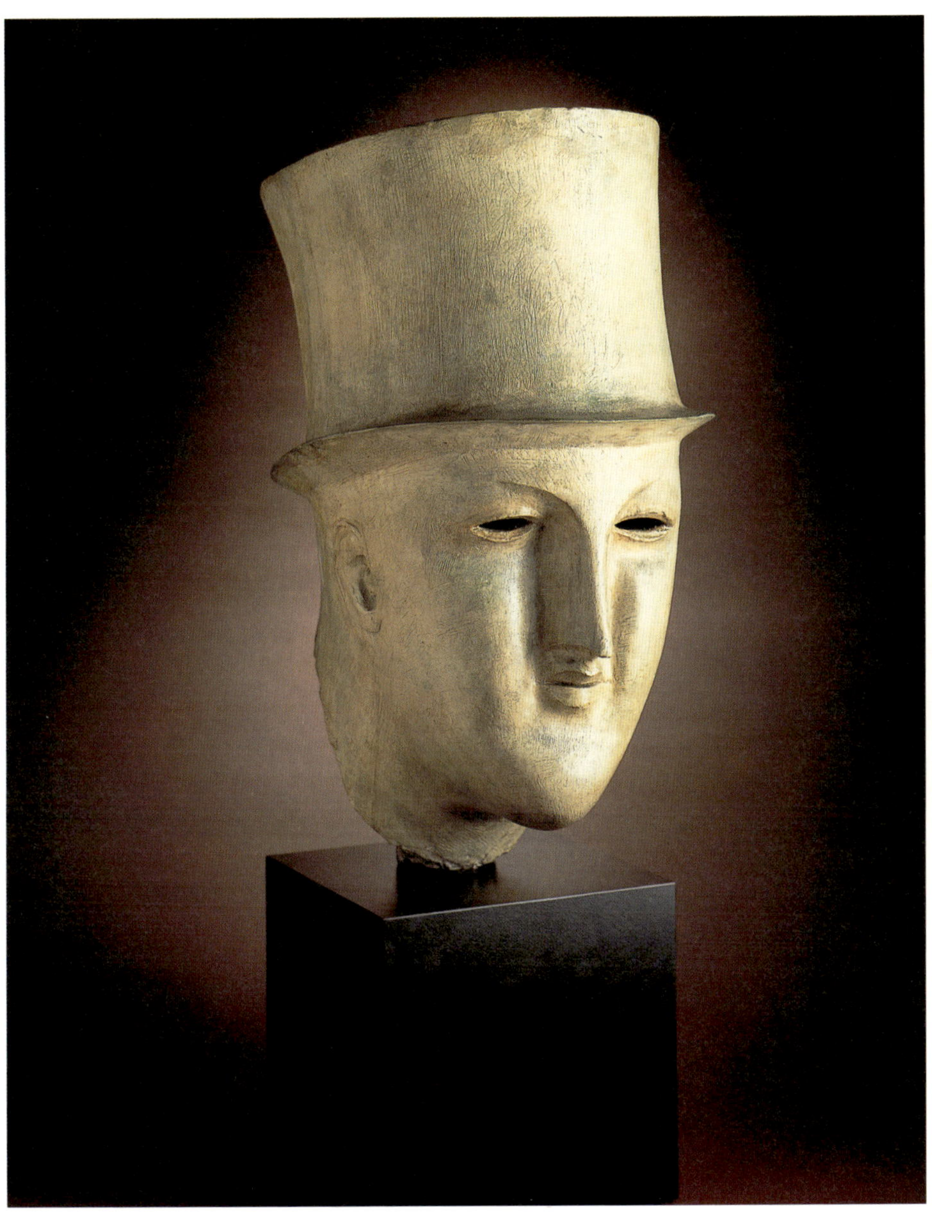

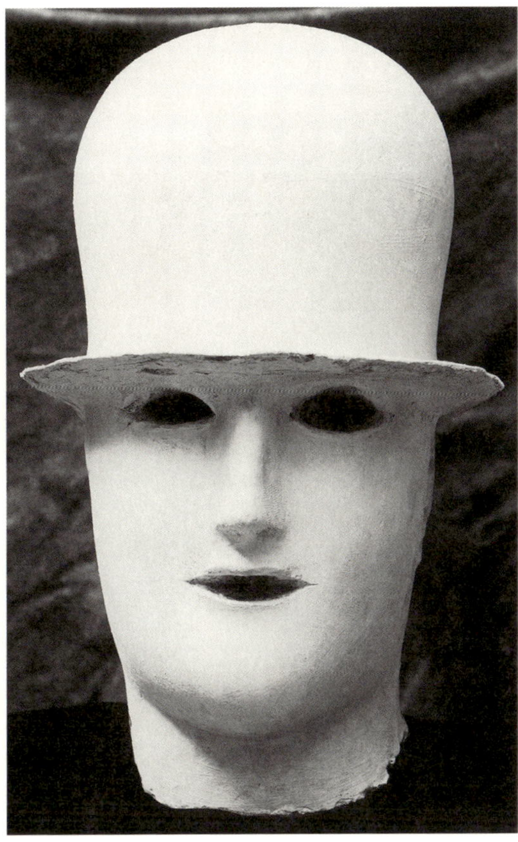

Fig. 74
Elie Nadelman
Le boulevardier, 1914
Plaster, 18 1/2 x 9 x 13 1/2 in.
(47 x 22.7 x 34.3 cm)
Los Angeles County Museum of Art;
Gift of Mr. and Mrs. Nathan Smooke
©2002 Museum Associates/LACMA

Fig. 75
Elie Nadelman
Head with Bowler Hat, c. 1915
Plaster, 15 in. (38.1 cm) high; destroyed
Photography by R. V./U. Smutny
Lincoln Kirstein Photograph Collection,
Jerome Robbins Dance Division, The New York
Public Library

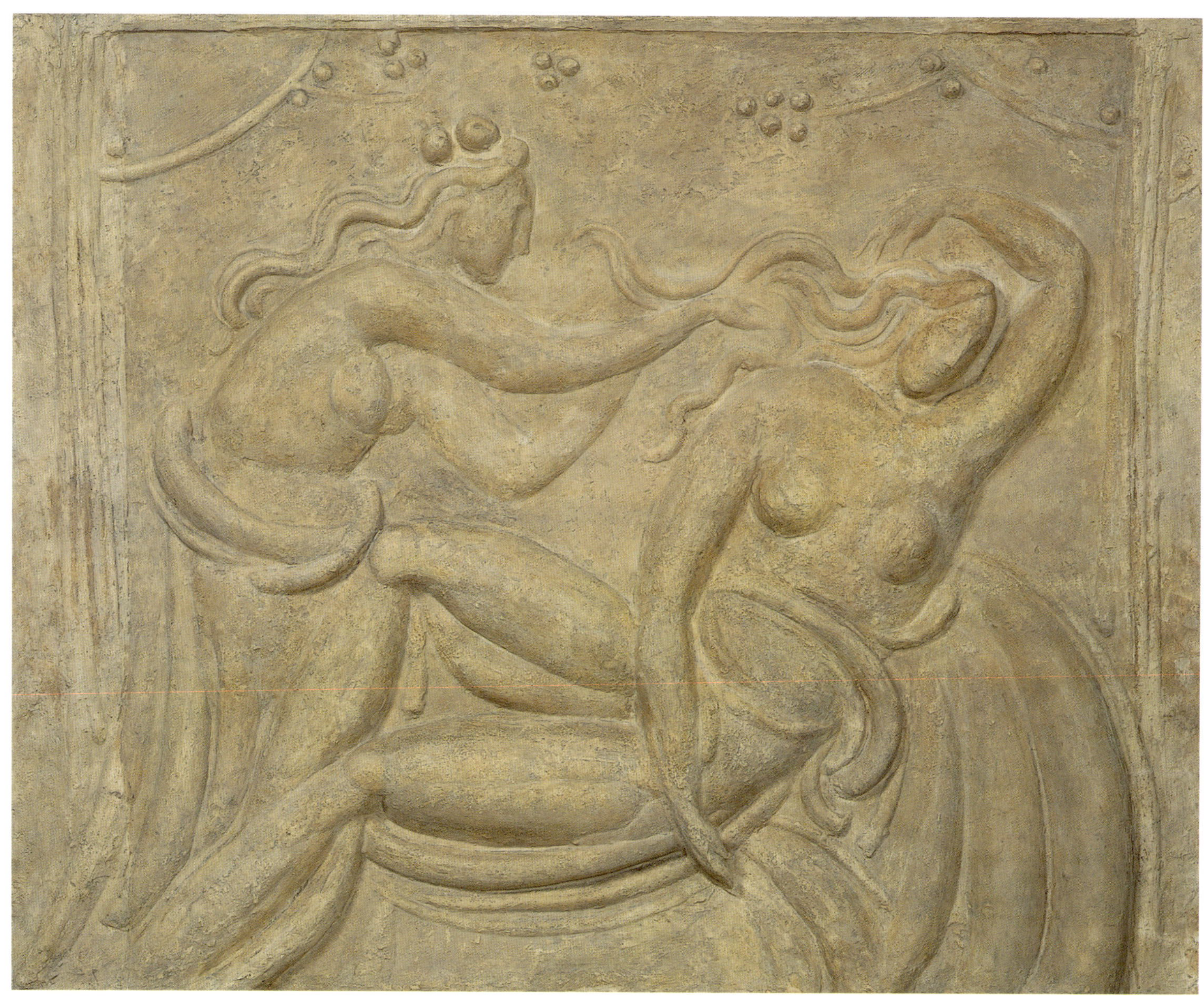

Fig. 76
Elie Nadelman
Two Nudes (originally titled ***Spring***), 1914–15
Plaster, 47 7/8 x 58 3/4 x 3 3/4 in.
(121.5 x 149.2 x 9.6 cm)
National Gallery of Art, Washington, D.C.;
Gift of Robert P. and Arlene R. Kogod
©2002 Board of Trustees, National Gallery
of Art, Washington

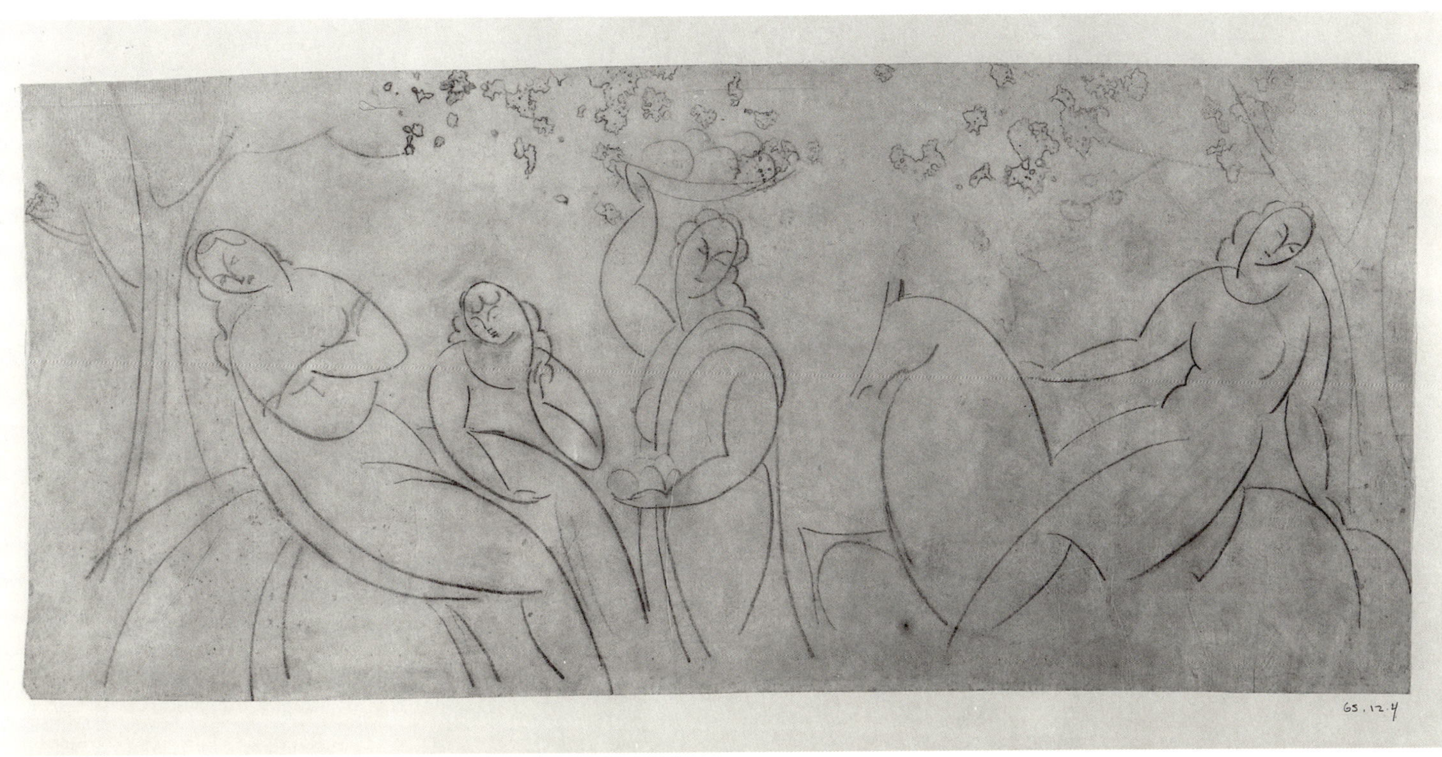

Fig. 77
Elie Nadelman
Study for "Autumn," c. 1914–15
Pencil on tracing paper, 8 1/4 x 18 1/2 in.
(21 x 47 cm)
The Metropolitan Museum of Art, New York;
Gift of Lincoln Kirstein, 1965
©2002 The Metropolitan Museum of Art

Fig. 78
Elie Nadelman
Woman with a Dog, c. 1914–15
Gilt-plaster relief, 11 1/4 x 14 1/4 in.
(28.6 x 36.2 cm)
The Cornell Fine Arts Museum, Rollins College,
Winter Park, Florida; Museum purchase:
Wally Findlay Acquisition Fund

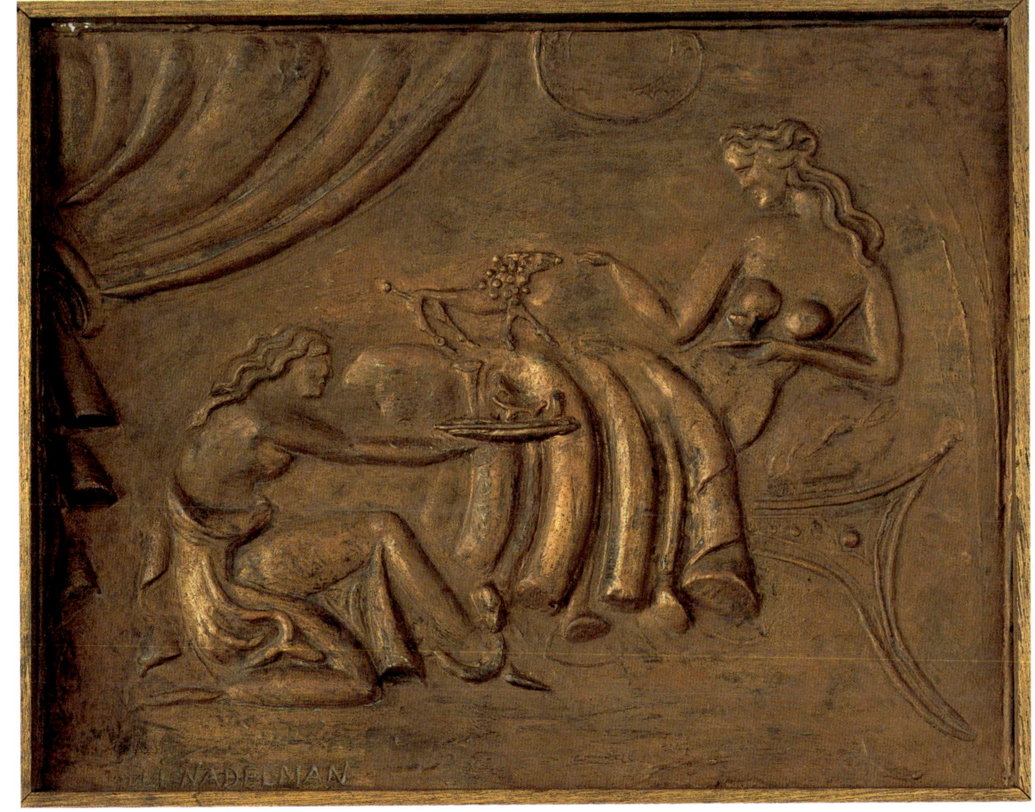

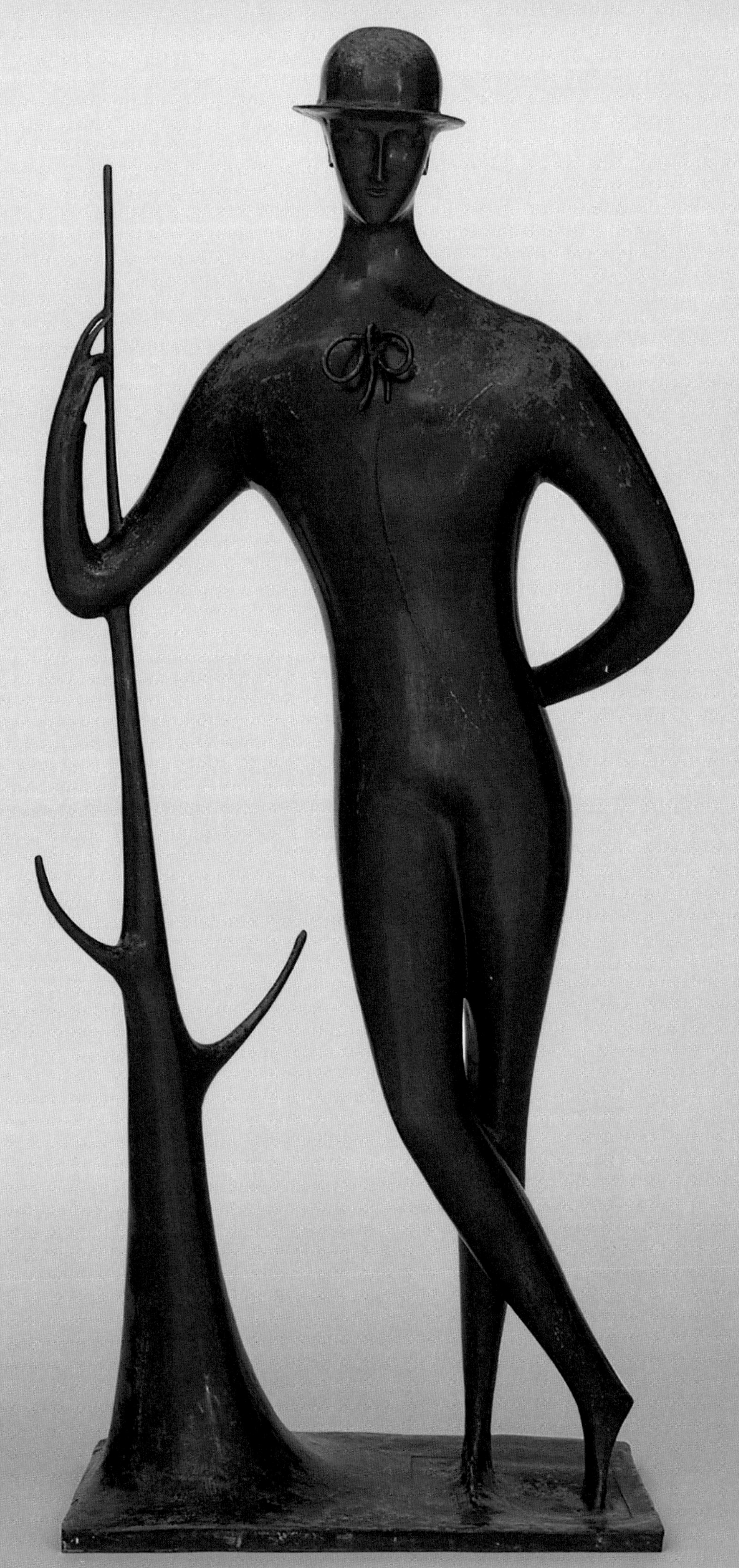

Unintentional Immigration and Meteoric Success
New York, 1914—17

Unaccustomed to speaking English and with few friends, Nadelman initially disliked America. In contrast to transplanted Europeans such as Marcel Duchamp, Albert Gleizes, and Francis Picabia, who exulted in America's exuberance, strength, and technological innovations, Nadelman bemoaned the country's materialism and lack of refinement. "There is nothing but money," he lamented in a letter of December 1914. "It is a country of bluffers and snobs and it is still quite wild (savage). Everything is disgraceful and brutal here. How far they are from Europe! I couldn't tell you how much I'd like to see Paris again!"[81]

The anti-Semitism Nadelman encountered within the mainstream Polish American community shocked him and dashed any hope he might have harbored of forging a connection with his countrymen.[82] Not until the spring of 1915, with the arrival of several Parisian friends, did he begin to widen his contacts. Through Jules Pascin, a painter he had known in Montparnasse, he became a member of the Penguin Club, an informal association of artists hospitable to recently arrived immigrants. Through it, he met John Weichsel, a fellow Polish Jew and founder of the People's Art Guild. The guild, located on New York's Lower East Side and dominated by Jewish immigrants and socialists, aimed to democratize art by displaying it in noncommercial, working-class settings where it presumably would have a salutary effect on people's daily lives.[83] Although Nadelman did not share Weichsel's view of art as a social tool for engendering humanistic understanding and sympathy, the two countrymen had similar views on aesthetics, which Nadelman affirmed by joining the guild and purchasing a watercolor from one of its exhibitions.[84] Weichsel, like Nadelman, believed that formal properties—line, color, and volume— rather than personal expression determined art's quality. In November 1913, a year before meeting Nadelman, he had written an article for *Camera Work* entitled "Cosmism or Amorphism," in which he had distinguished between artists for whom art's physical properties were primary—Cosmists, he called them—and Amorphists, who followed Kandinsky in giving preeminence to the expression of inner experiences.[85] Weichsel implicitly identified Nadelman as a "Cosmic" artist in an August 1915 article he wrote on the artist's work for the

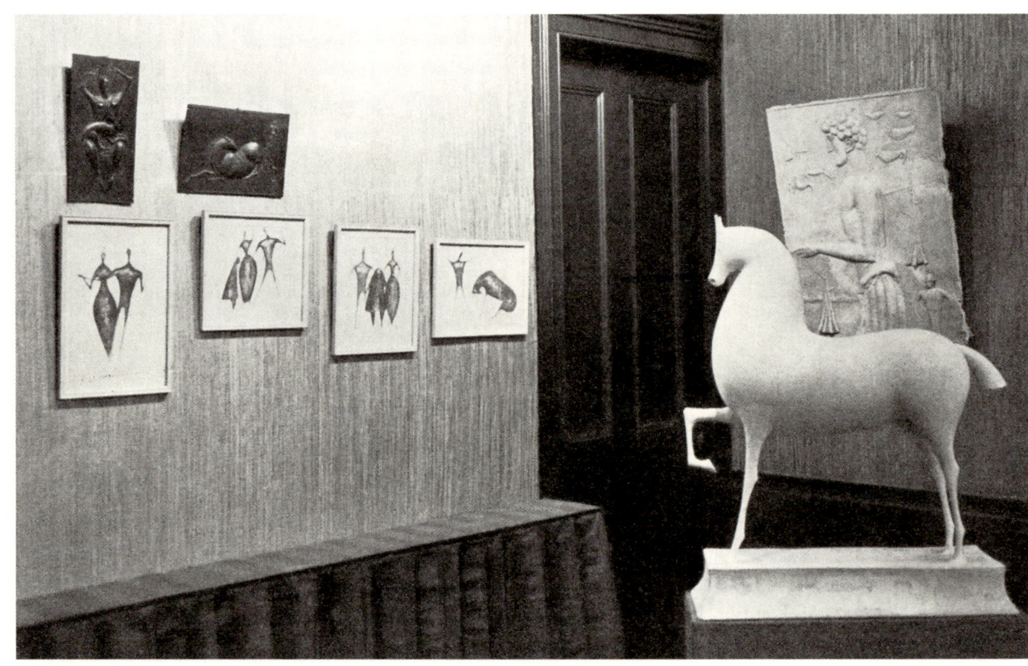

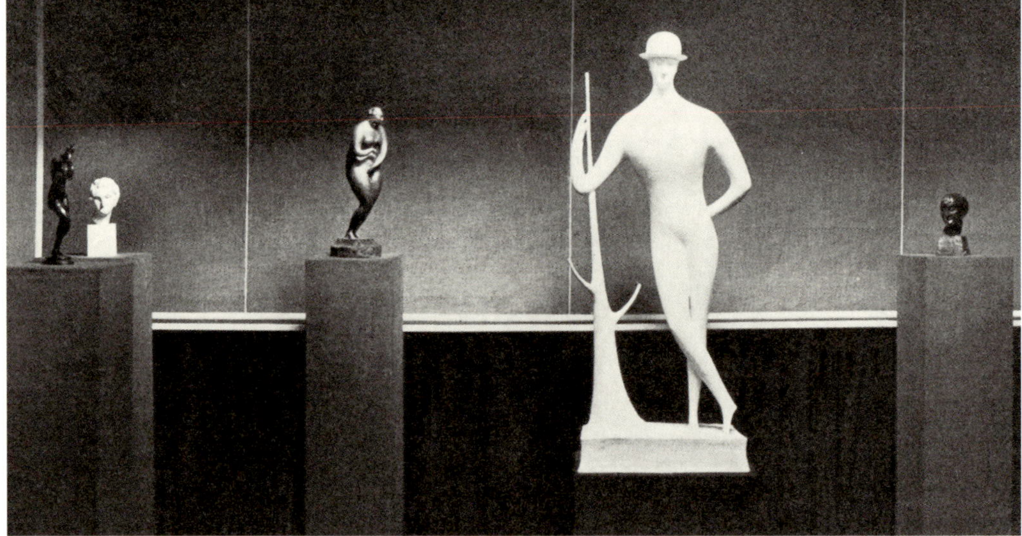

short-lived Jewish cultural periodical *East and West*. Four months later, in the text that accompanied his "291" show, Nadelman echoed Weichsel in condemning those who ignored art's physical properties in favor of "the abstract." Each art object and each subject, Nadelman explained, had an individual will, or "plastic life." Successful art captured the subject's inner physical forces—its "plastic life"—while simultaneously respecting the materials used to make it, which likewise had a will, or "plastic life." "A stone will refuse all the positions we may wish to give it if these are unsuited to it,"

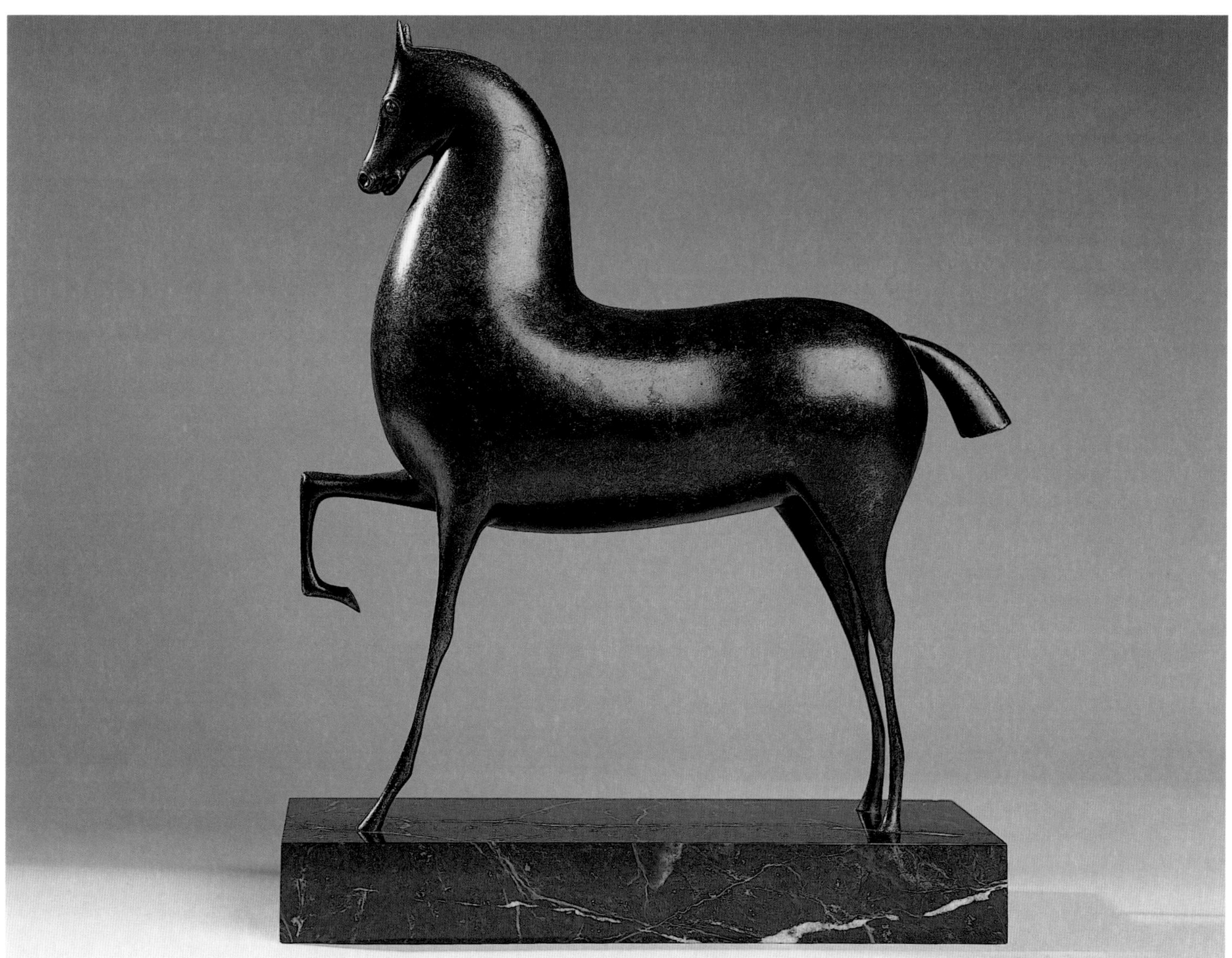

Nadelman reiterated. "By its own will it will fall back into the position that its shape in conjunction with its mass demands."[86] Only if artists respected the plastic will of their subjects and materials could their art transmit a sense of satisfaction and pleasure.

During his first months in New York, Nadelman contacted Martin Birnbaum, the proprietor of the Berlin-Photographic Gallery, to whom the visiting Polish critic Basler had spoken enthusiastically about Nadelman's work.[87] Birnbaum visited the artist in his studio on Fourteenth Street that spring and immediately offered to debut his work a few months later at his gallery. As part of his effort to promote the exhibition by establishing Nadelman as an "unheralded

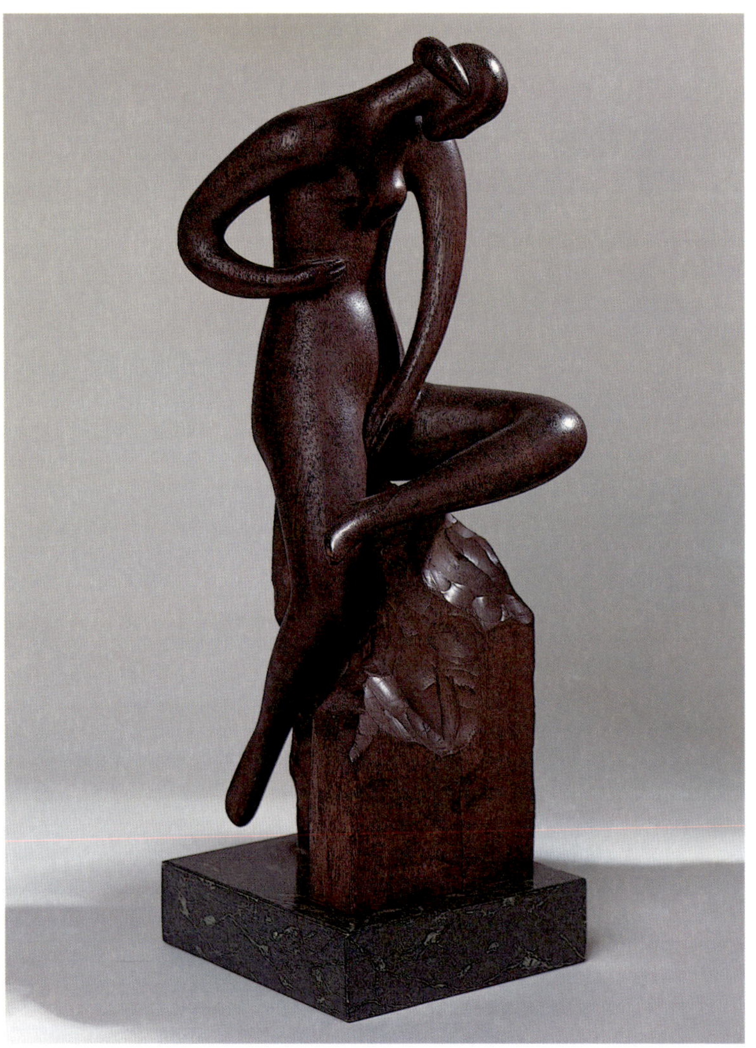

Fig. 83
Elie Nadelman
Seated Tubular Nude, c. 1915
Wood, 16 in. (40.6 cm) high
Collection of Barbara and Pitt Hyde
Photography by David Nester

Fig. 84
Elie Nadelman
Seated Female Nude, c. 1915
Bronze, 16 in. (40.6 cm) high
The Baltimore Museum of Art; The Cone
Collection, formed by Dr. Claribel Cone and
Miss Etta Cone of Baltimore, Maryland

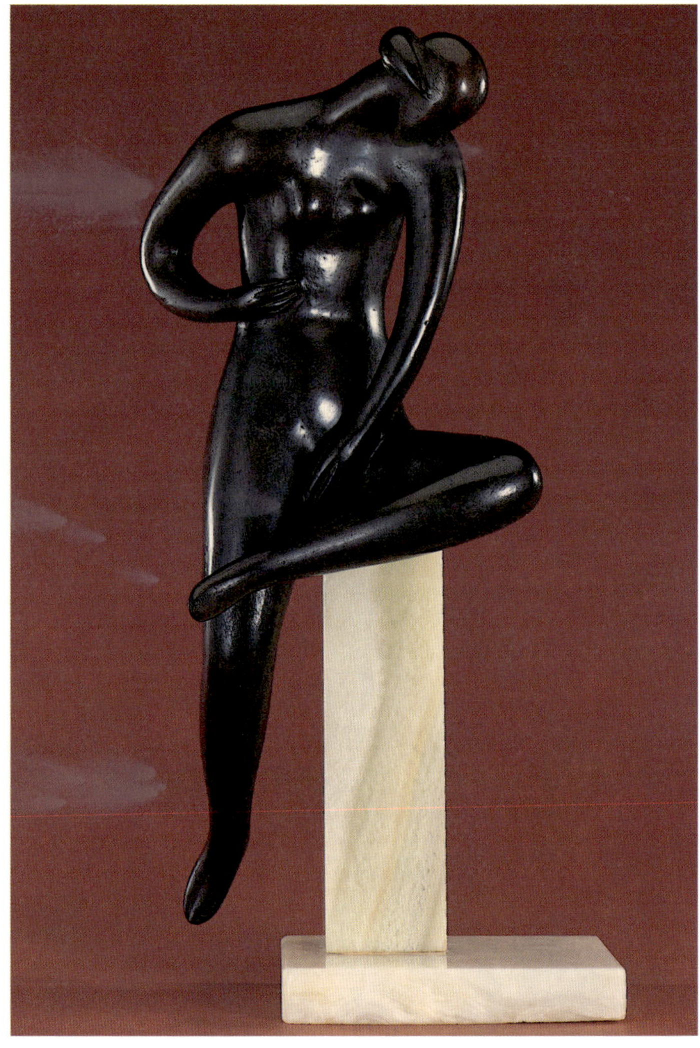

and unnamed genius," Birnbaum wrote an article on his work for the December 1915 issue of *International Studio*.[88] To finance the artist until the show opened, he sold one of Nadelman's marble heads to his primary client, the president of the Rhode Island School of Design (FIG. 36). Birnbaum's only demand of Nadelman was that the artist not show his work to anyone else in order to ensure that the exhibition would hit New York "like a bursting bomb."[89] Several months later, Birnbaum returned from a brief vacation to find an announcement of Nadelman's forthcoming show in December 1915 at Stieglitz's "291" gallery. Furious at Nadelman's apparent betrayal, Birnbaum canceled his show at the Berlin-Photographic Gallery. When questioned by Birnbaum about his defection, Nadelman downplayed its importance, saying that the "291" show would garner little attention.[90]

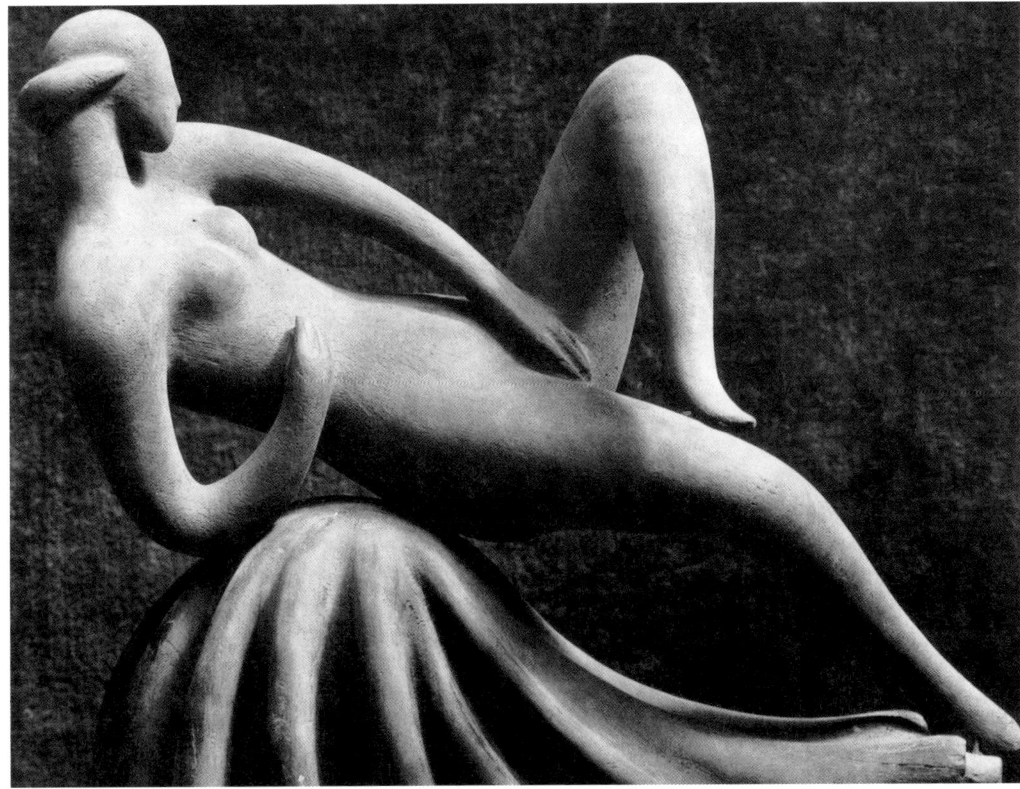

Stieglitz had, of course, known Nadelman's drawings from his Paris period, but the impetus to show the artist's sculpture may have come from Rubinstein, as she later claimed.[91] Since his arrival in America, Nadelman had completed the commissioned plaster relief for her salon as well as a large white plaster horse she would install in her New York apartment. The latter piece, along with another plaster work called *Young Man in Hat*—which depicted a young man, wearing a bowler hat and a string tie, leaning against a tree— dominated the "291" show (FIGS. 80, 81). Both freestanding plasters revealed Nadelman's continued emphasis on linear grace and simplicity and his burgeoning fascination with subjects drawn from everyday life. The elegant, crisp outlines and simplified compositions of these two sculptures announced the style with which he would become most associated. By uniting the smooth surfaces, distinct outlines, and volumetrically simplified forms that Hildebrand had advocated with the sensuous, flowing line of Jugendstil, Nadelman created images at once grave and insouciant. What was most striking about them and what distinguished them most from the work of Paul Manship and Gaston Lachaise—with which they shared a sinuous, linear elegance and streamlining of shapes—was their union of modernist simplification with genre subjects.

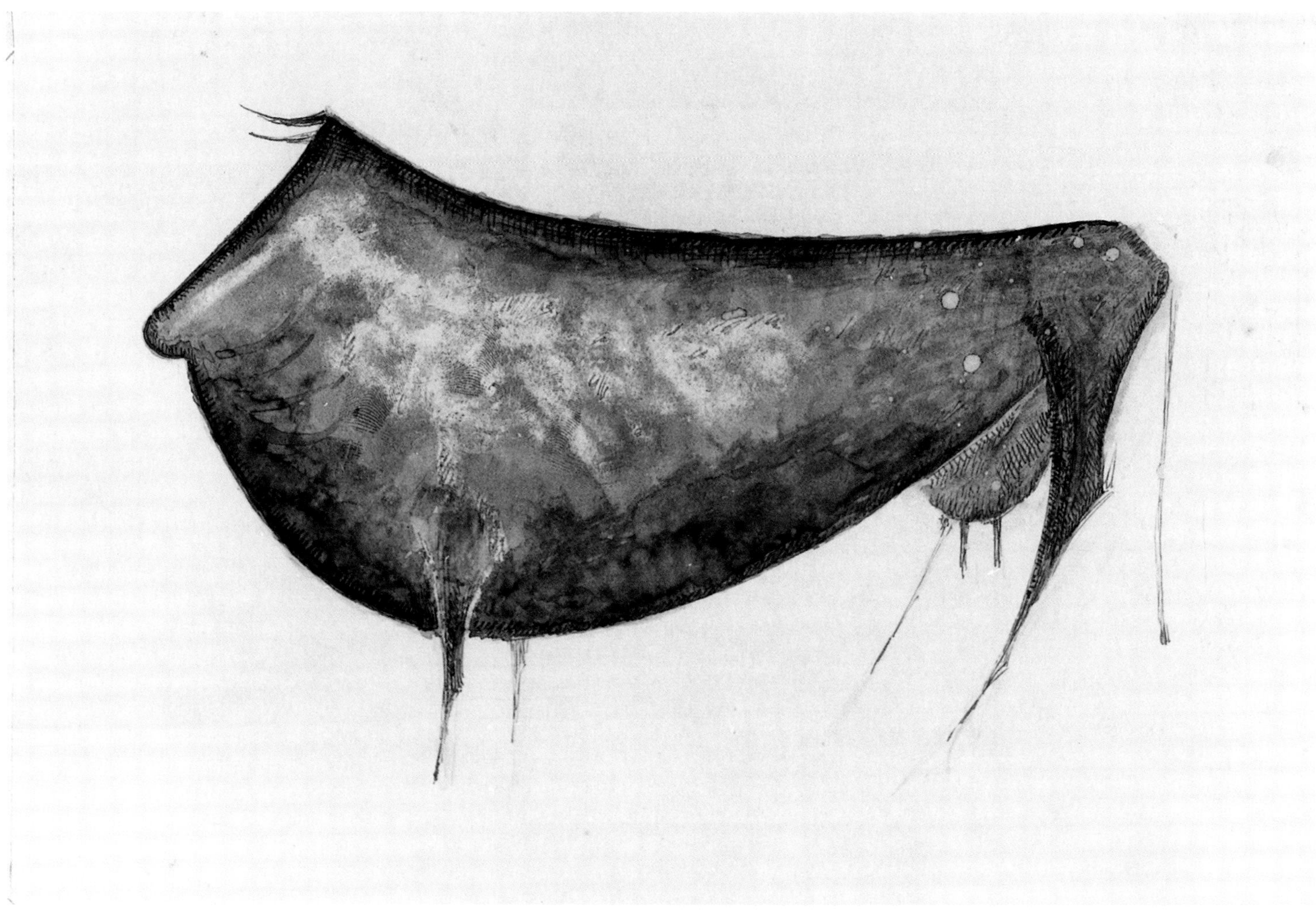

Fig. 86
Elie Nadelman
Cow, c. 1915
Ink wash, and pencil on paper,
7 3/4 x 10 1/8 in. (19.7 x 25.7 cm)
The Metropolitan Museum of Art, New York;
Gift of Lincoln Kirstein, 1965
©2002 The Metropolitan Museum of Art

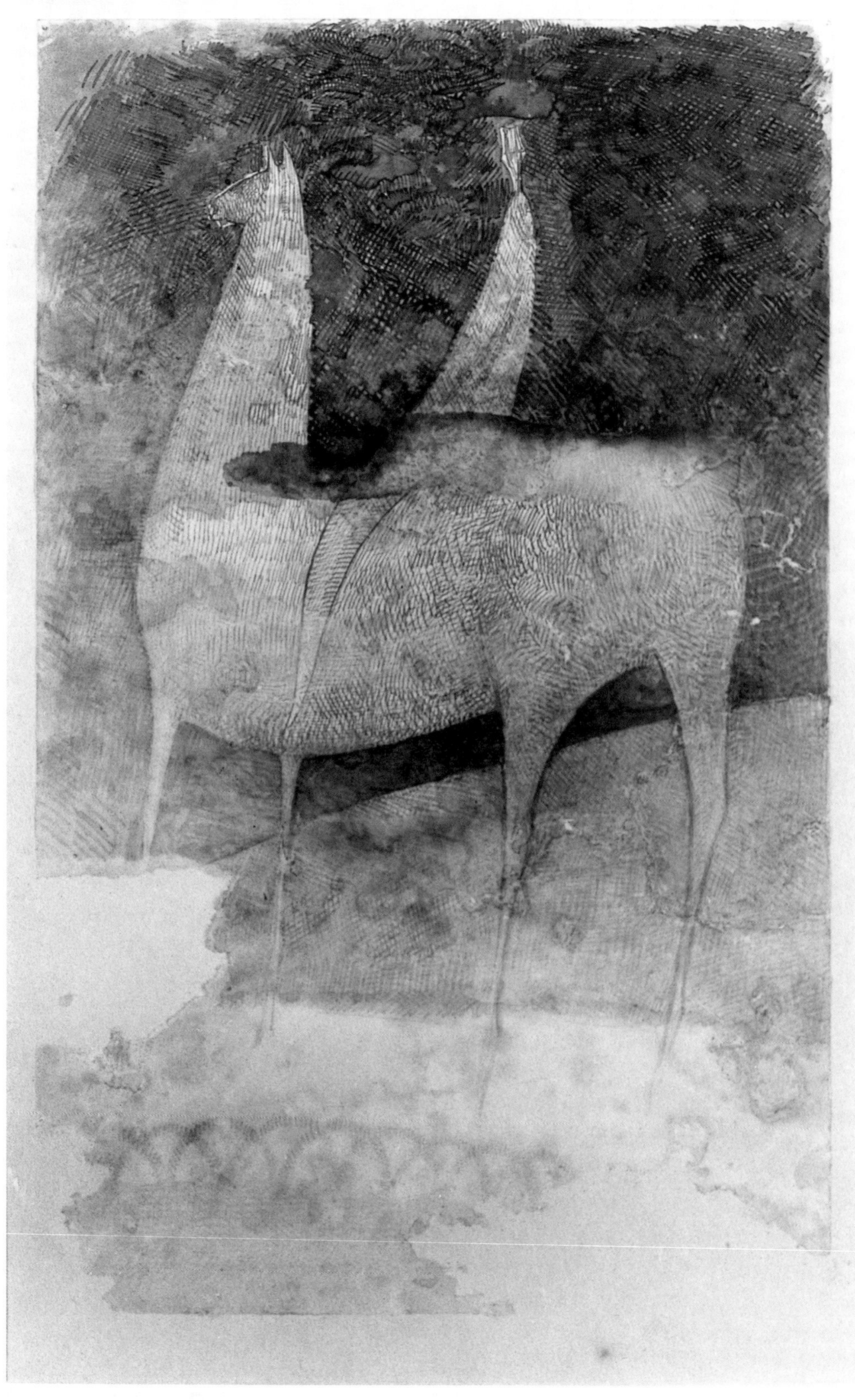

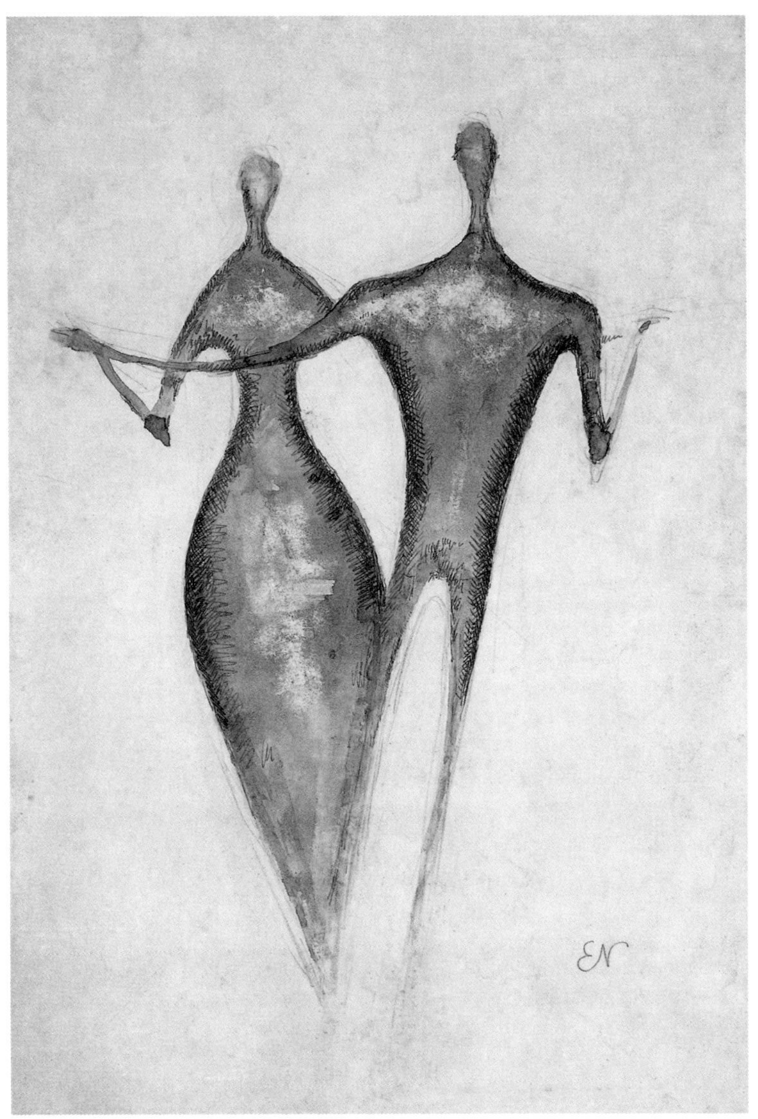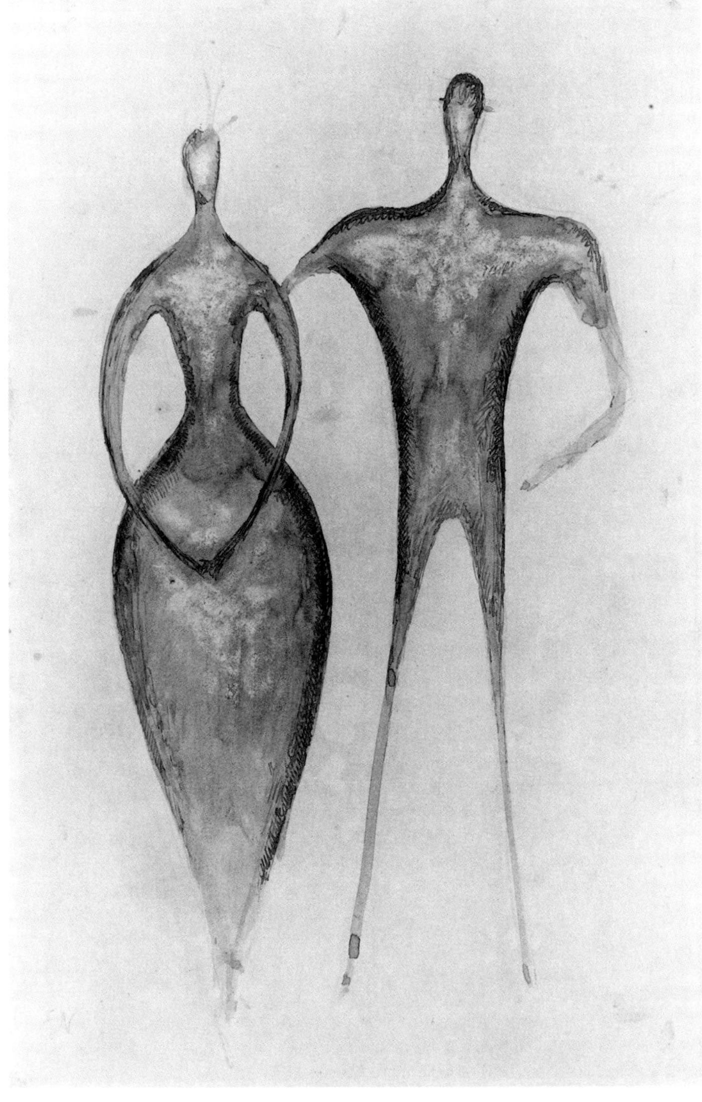

Fig. 88
Elie Nadelman
Tango, 1914–15
Brown ink and brown watercolor over pencil on
wove paper, 12 3/16 x 8 1/4 in. (31 x 21 cm)
The Art Institute of Chicago;
Sanford Schwartz gift

Fig. 89
Elie Nadelman
Woman and Man with Derby Hat, c. 1915
Brown ink and brownish watercolor over pencil
on wove paper, 12 3/16 x 7 9/16 in.
(30.9 x 19.2 cm)
The Art Museum, Princeton University;
Gift of Harry A. Brooks, Class of 1935
Photography by Clem Fiori

Fig. 90
Elie Nadelman
Poodle, c. 1915
Ink wash on wove paper, 6 1/16 x 6 3/16 in.
(15.4 x 15.7 cm)
Addison Gallery of American Art, Phillips
Academy, Andover, Massachusetts;
Gift of Martin Birnbaum

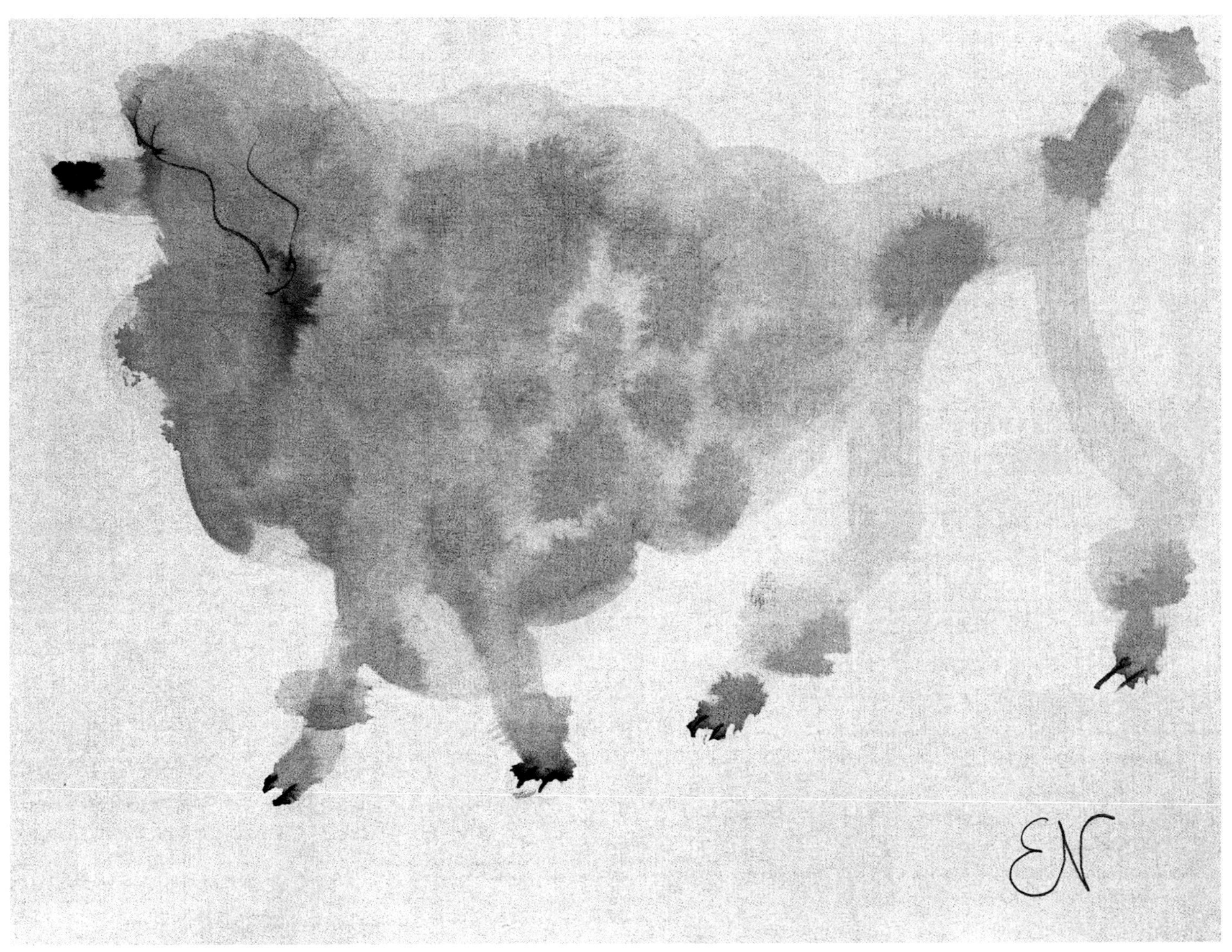

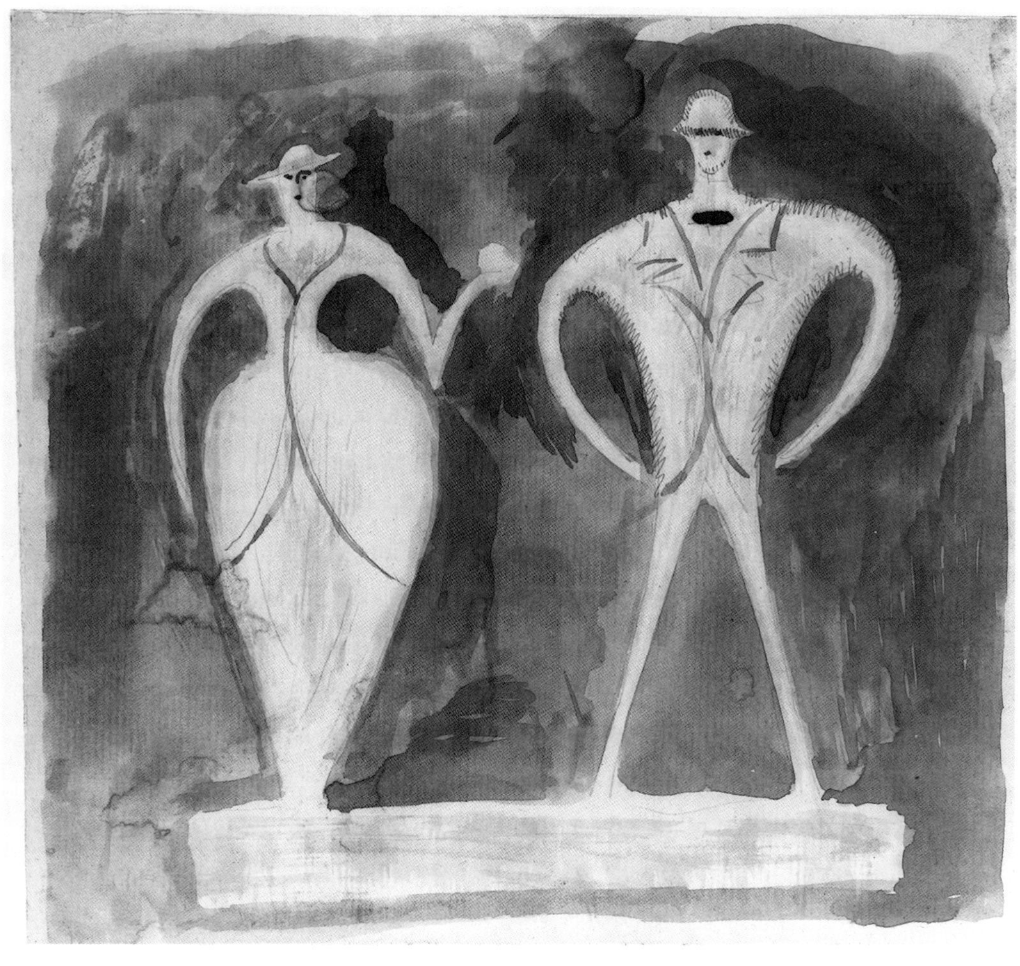

Fig. 92
Elie Nadelman
Horse, c. 1914–15
Blue and gray wash over pencil on wove paper,
7 13/16 x 10 3/8 in. (19.8 x 26.4 cm)
The Baltimore Museum of Art; Blanche Adler
Memorial Fund, by exchange

Fig. 93
Elie Nadelman
Poodle, c. 1915
Ink, wash, and pencil on paper,
8 x 10 1/4 in. (20.3 x 26 cm)
The Metropolitan Museum of Art, New York;
Gift of Lincoln Kirstein, 1965
©2002 The Metropolitan Museum of Art

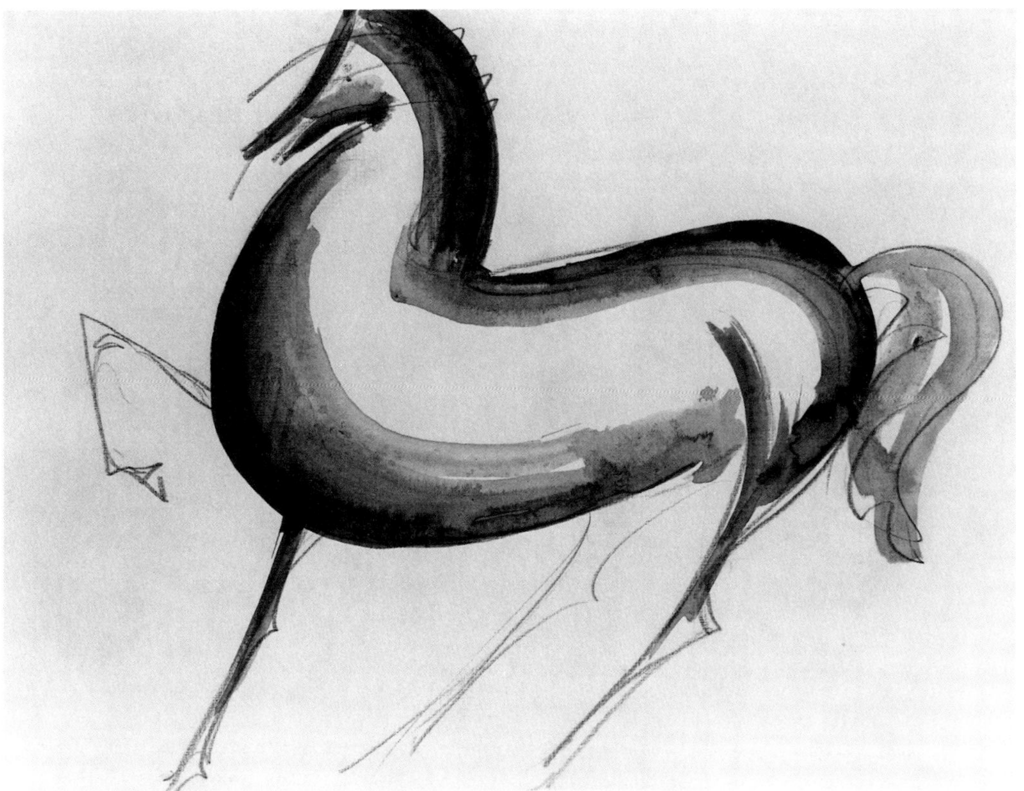

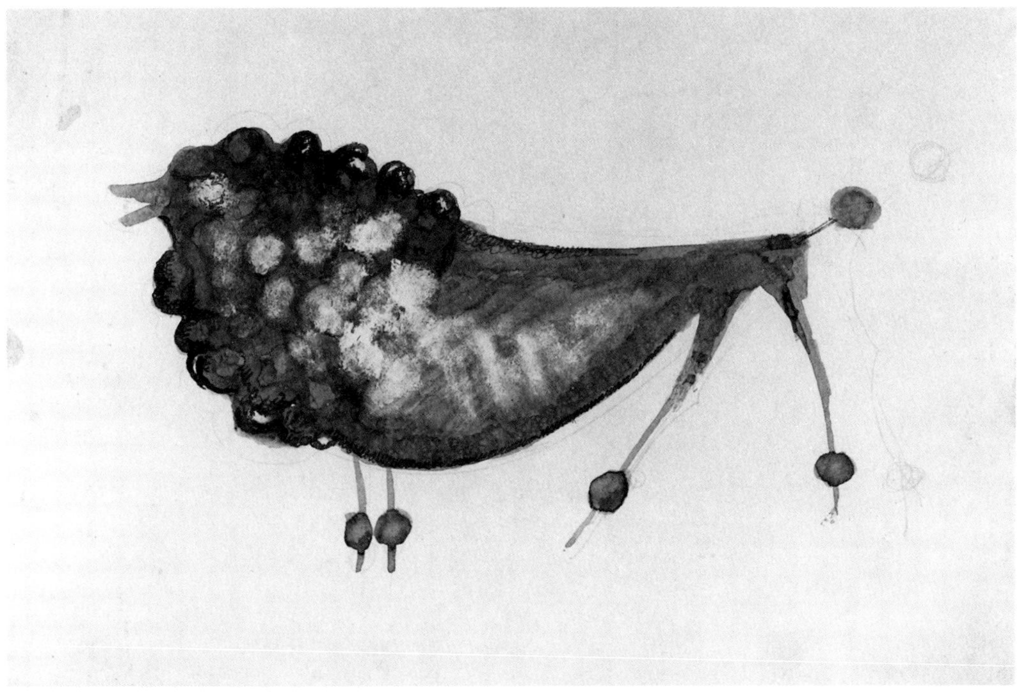

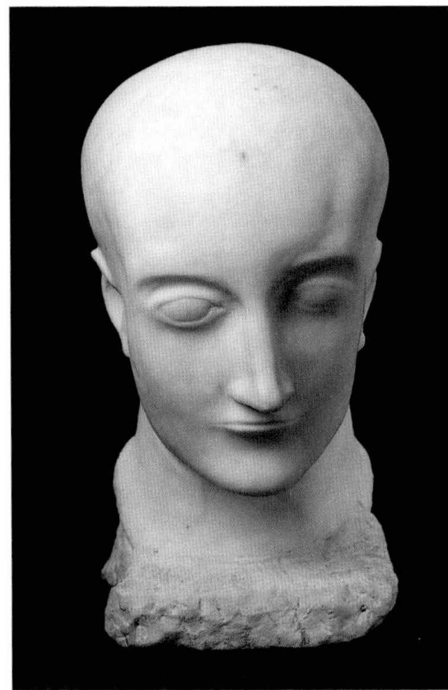

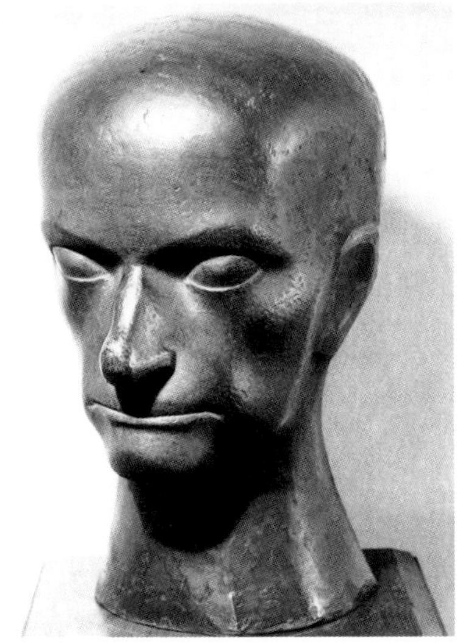

Nadelman's credentials as a classicist were well established by this time, and it seems puzzling that he would risk losing that imprimatur by dabbling in genre subjects. The impulse behind his new direction may have been his close reading of Charles Baudelaire's 1863 essay "The Painter of Modern Life." Nadelman's respect for the French poet-critic was profound; Baudelaire's was the only noncommissioned portrait he ever sculpted (FIG. 94), an homage that had earlier been paid to the poet by French modernist sculptor Raymond Duchamp-Villon (FIG. 95). In his essay Baudelaire called for an art that would interpret the age to itself on its own unique terms. Cautioning artists not to neglect the charm of everyday circumstances and contemporary manners, he alleged that beauty consisted of two elements: the eternal and the transitory. Without both together, beauty could not exist. "The true painter we're looking for," Baudelaire wrote, "will be the one who can snatch from the life of today its epic quality and make us feel how great and poetic we are in our cravats and our patent-leather boots."[92] Nadelman would heed these prescriptions in creating his stylized depictions of dandified men and fashionable women. For the first time in sculpture, the figurative and the contingent would be joined with the eternal and the immutable. His introduction of this new style in his "291" show entranced the New York press, and Stieglitz vouchsafed that his gallery "has not been so alive in quite some time."[93]

Soon after the opening, Nadelman met Judith Bernays, a Barnard College graduate, former Sorbonne student, and daughter of Ely Bernays, a wealthy financier. According to newspaper accounts of their engagement in February 1917, the two were brought together by their mutual interest in Sigmund Freud, Judith's uncle.[94] Most likely Nadelman was equally impressed by Judith's social pedigree and her father's financial connections. Indeed, Ely Bernays worked to secure Nadelman's economic independence by buying the artist's work (FIG. 96) and trying to place it in galleries. In October 1916, for example, he sent clippings to Roland Knoedler of M. Knoedler & Company and thanked him for visiting Nadelman's studio.[95] When Knoedler demurred from mounting an exhibition, Bernays turned to Nadelman's estranged former dealer, Martin Birnbaum, who had closed his Berlin-Photographic Gallery and become a junior partner at Scott & Fowles. Bernays effected a reconciliation between Nadelman and Birnbaum, who agreed to mount a show.

Nadelman's show at Scott & Fowles opened in February 1917. Consisting primarily of marbles and bronzes shown on gray pedestals in a

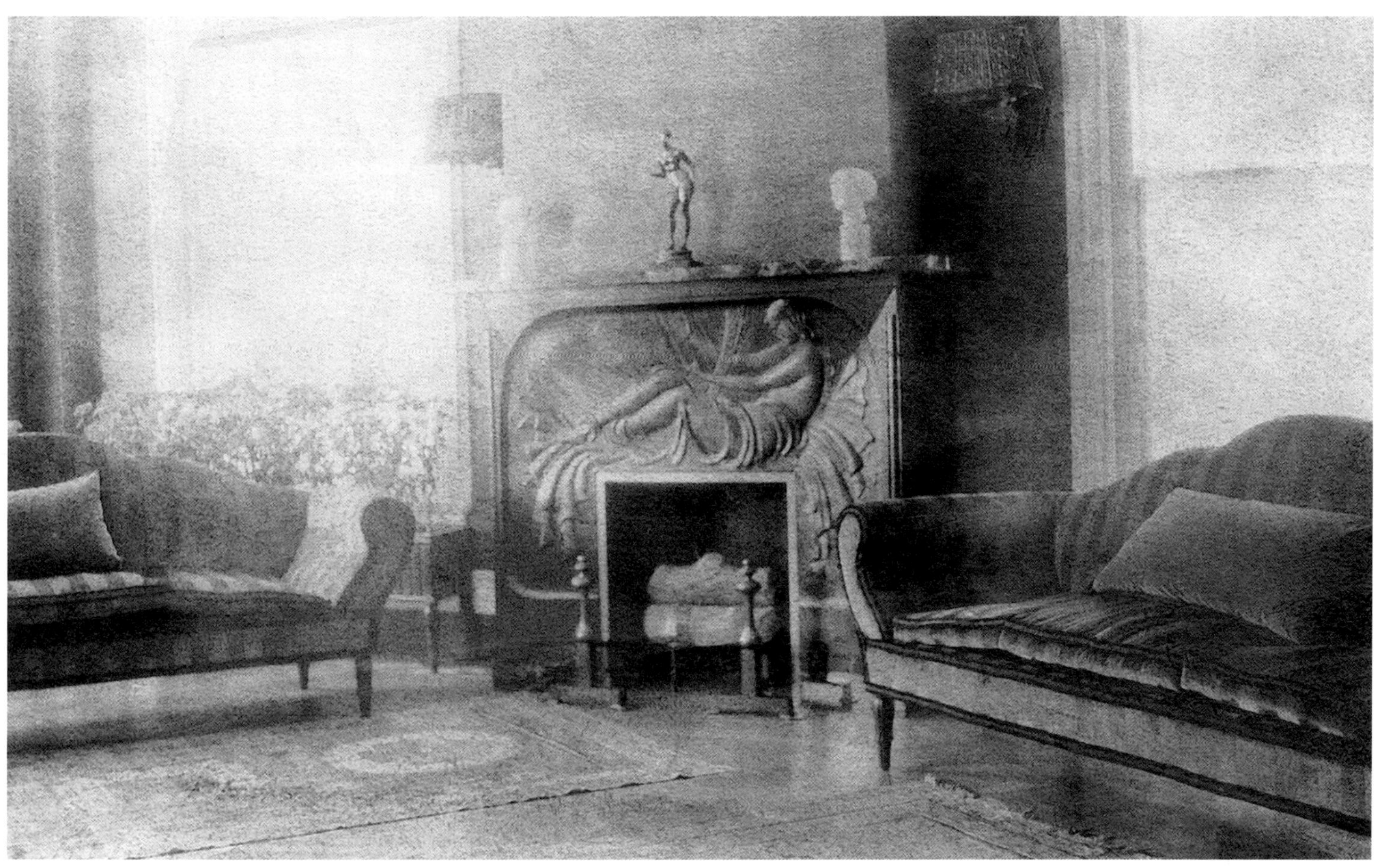

room whose walls were covered with dark blue satin, it was an instantaneous success, catapulting Nadelman from the small, elite enclave of "291" to the larger "uptown" art world. Even the presence in the show of bronze versions of *Young Man in a Hat* (initially entitled *Le promeneur*; now called *Man in Open Air*, FIG. 79) and *Horse* (FIG. 82) testified to what one critic called Nadelman's "sky rocket ascension" into "the empyrean blue of success."[96] Lauded as one of the important exhibitions of the season by senior *New York Sun* art critic Henry McBride, it all but sold out, generating enough money for Nadelman to invest eight thousand dollars in the stock market and leaving him swamped with orders for versions of the exhibited works in different materials and sizes and for commissioned portraits in marble.[97] By March 1917, less than a month after the show opened, the entire edition of *Le jeune cerf* (*Fawn*) had been sold (FIG. 98). The pace at which collectors acquired the work was so singularly rapid that critic Forbes Watson likened it to the sale of "hot cakes."[98] When it was over, Nadelman was ensconced as one of the stars of the art world.

Fig. 97
Elie Nadelman
Standing Buck, 1916–17
Bronze with brown patina, 27 15/16 in.
(71 cm) high
Collection of Jan and Frederick Mayer

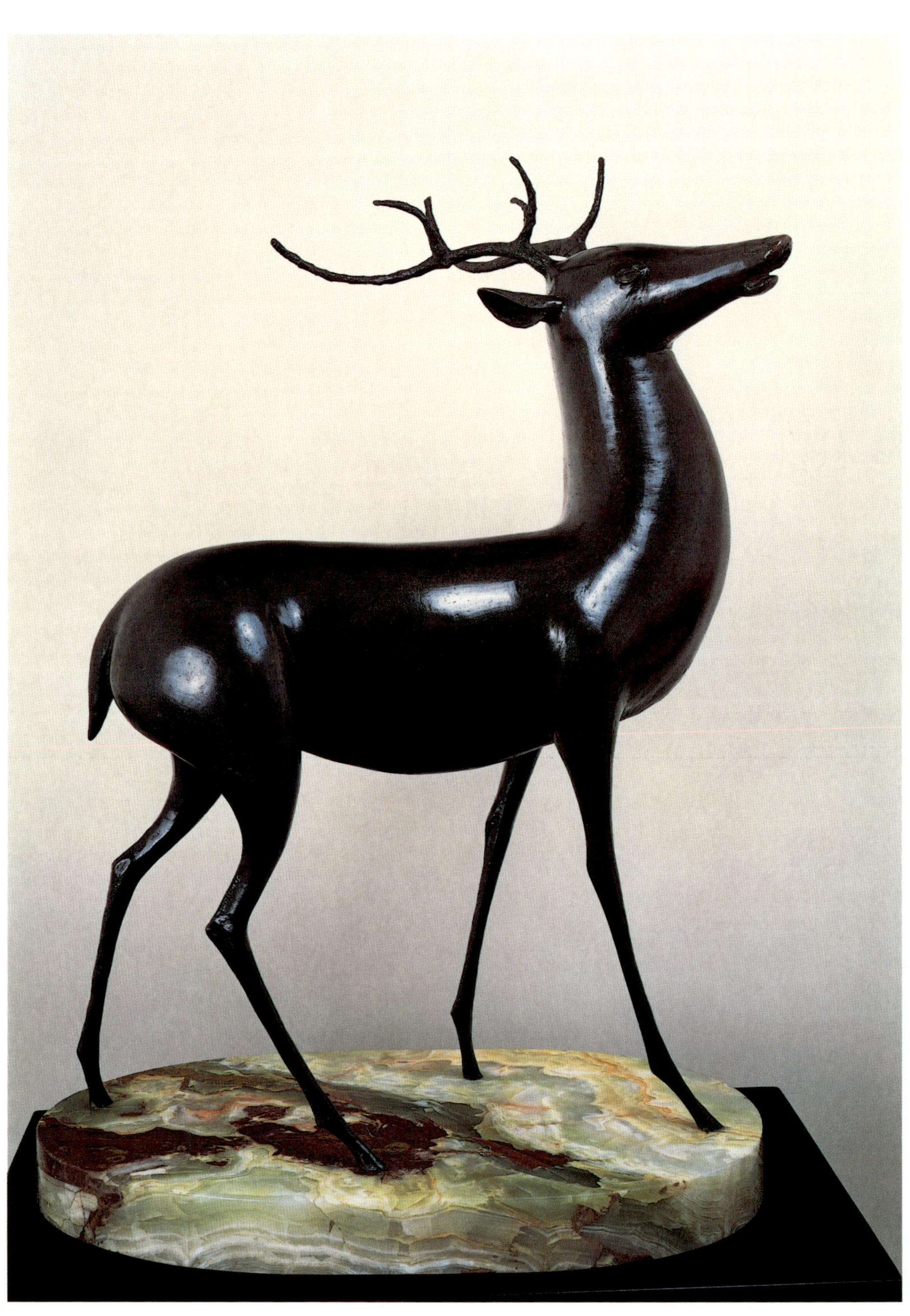

Fig. 98
Elie Nadelman
Fawn (originally called **Le jeune cerf**), 1916–17
Bronze, 18 1/2 x 17 x 9 1/2 in.
(47 x 43.2 x 24.1 cm)
The Corcoran Gallery of Art; Gift of Mildred
(Mrs. John B.) Hayward

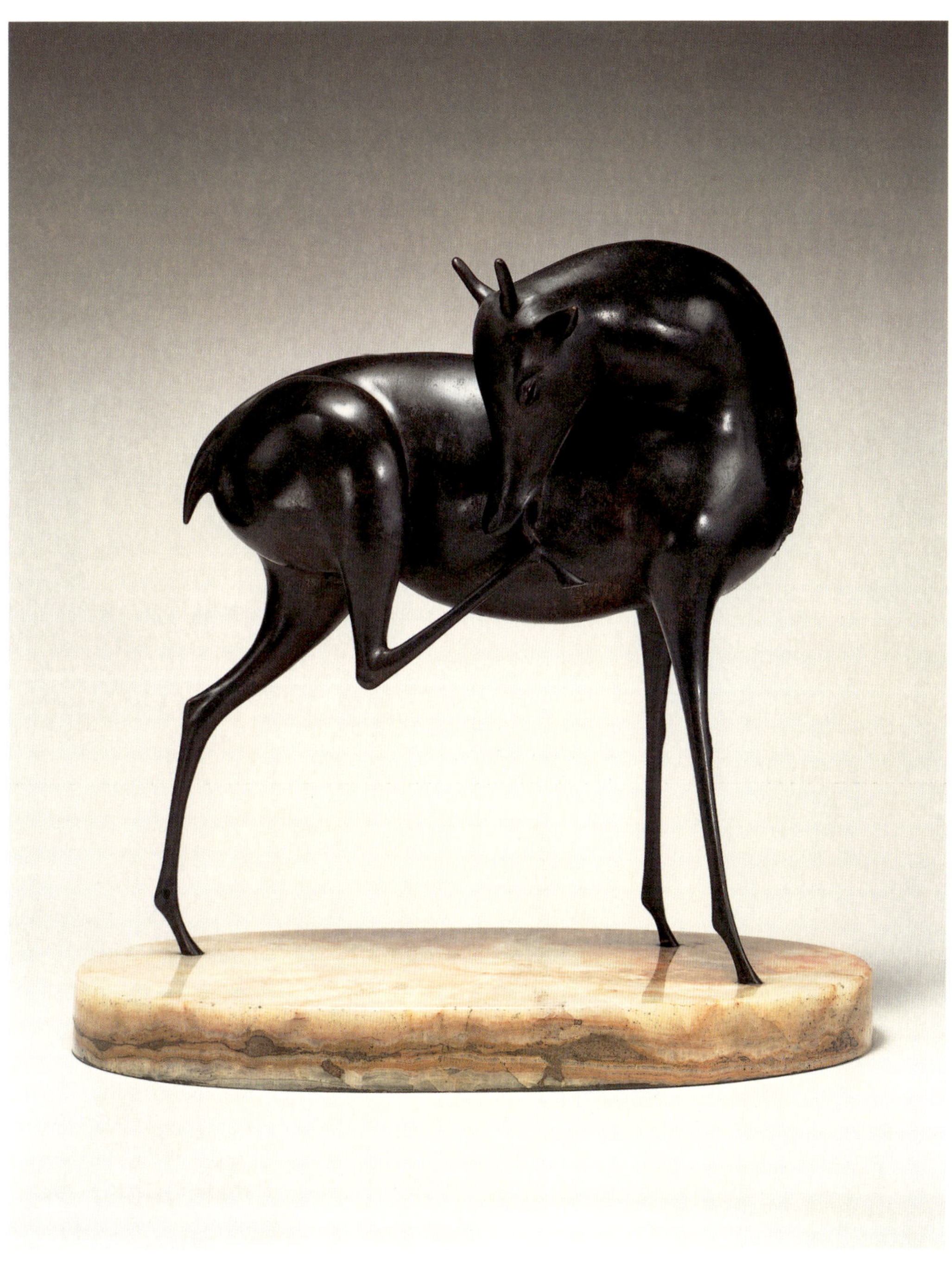

Fig. 99
Elie Nadelman
Resting Stag, 1916–17
Bronze, mounted on original onyx base,
18 x 21 x 10 1/2 in. (45.7 x 53.3 x 26.7 cm)
including base
Museum of Fine Arts, Boston; Museum purchase
with funds donated by Frank B. Bernis Fund,
Barbara L. and Theodore B. Alfond, anonymous
donor, Edwin E. Jack Fund, Arthur Mason Knapp
Fund, Ernest Kahn Fund, Arthur Tracy Cabot
Fund, Frederick Brown Fund, Morris and Louise
Rosenthal Fund, Samuel Putnam Avery Fund,
and Joyce Arnold Rusoff Fund

Fig. 100
Elie Nadelman
Wounded Stag, 1916–17
Bronze with natural gold patina
13 3/8 x 20 3/4 x 7 1/4 in.
(34 x 52.7 x 18.4 cm)
Private collection
Photography by Joshua Nefsky

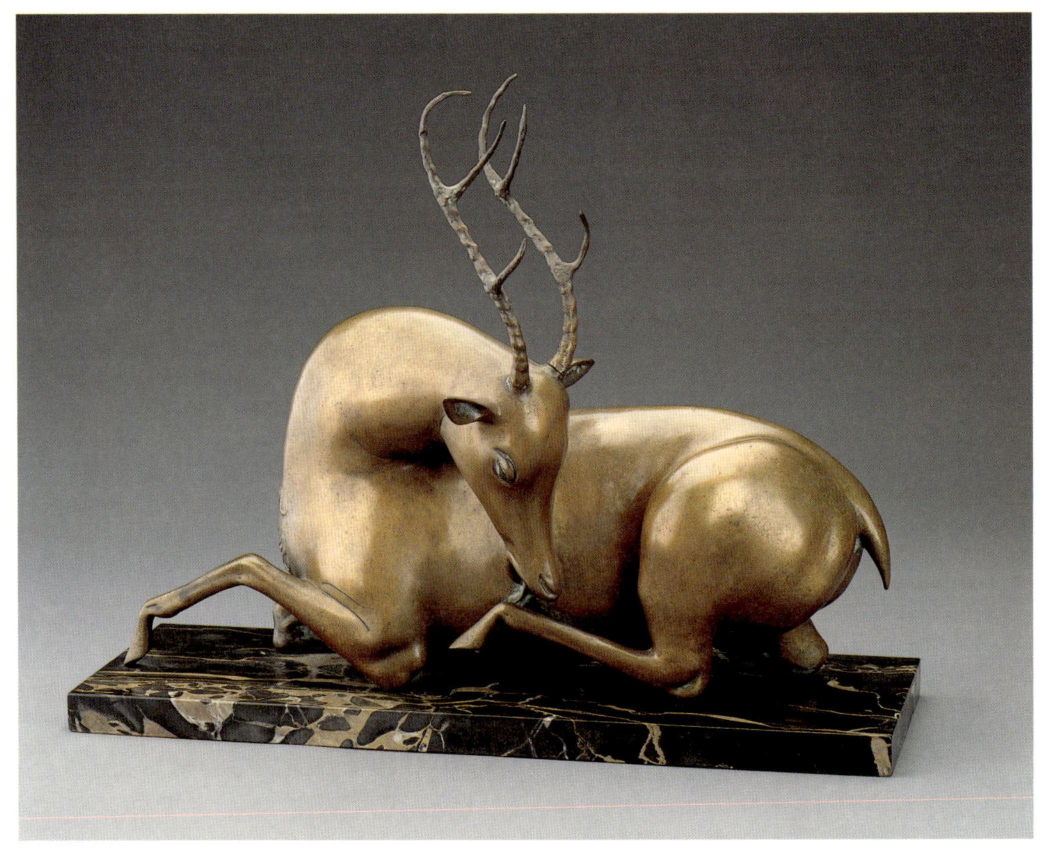

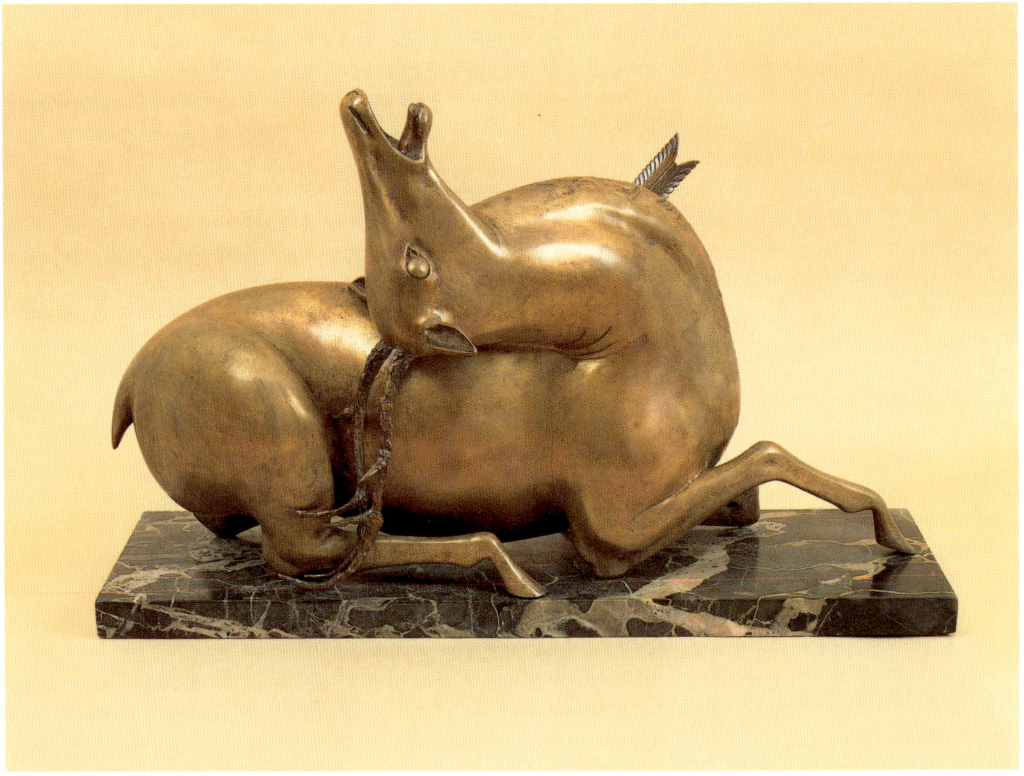

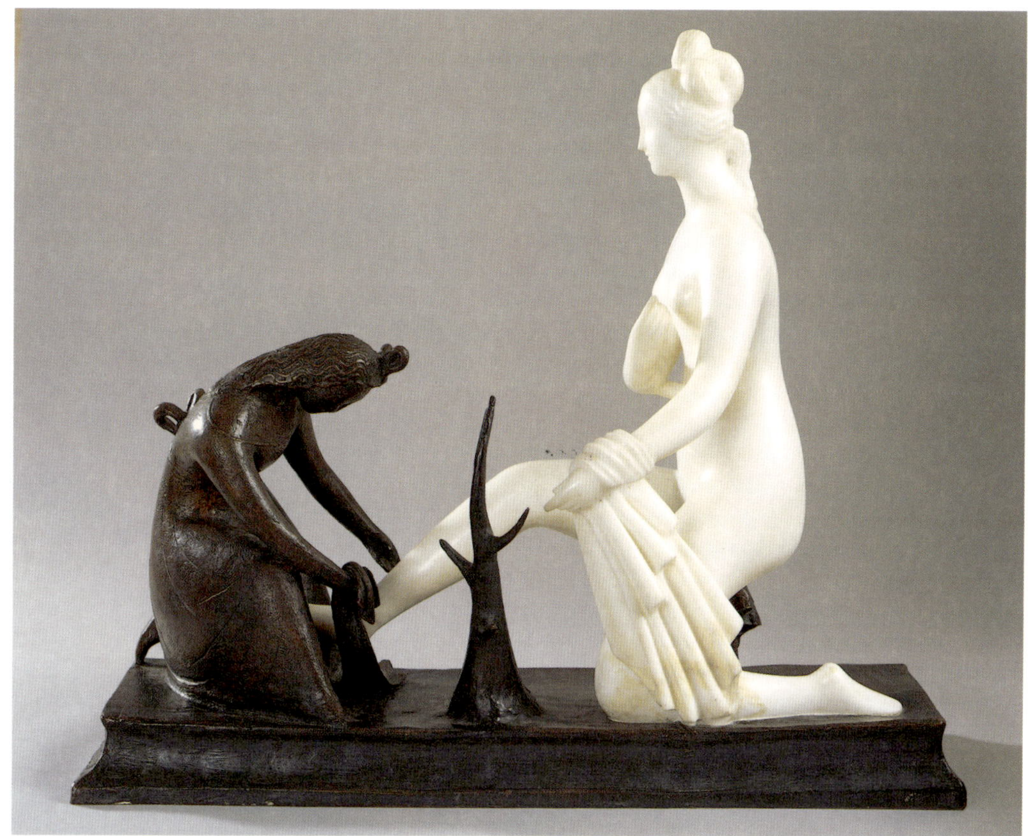

The show consisted of three parts: lyrically stylized animals in bronze (FIGS. 97–100); commissioned portraits (FIG. 163); and idealized heads and figures in marble, bronze, and wood (FIGS. 101, 103–106). All built on the marriage of volume and line that Nadelman had announced earlier in Paris. Infused with a stylized elegance and sinuous linearity, the work seemed to answer the needs of a country poised on the brink of war. At once gracefully animated and self-contained, it suggested a world of timeless harmony impervious to the vicissitudes of circumstance. No other artist, with the exception of Paul Manship (FIG. 102), achieved the elegance of shape, clarity of outline, and streamlined decorative stylization that marked Nadelman's bronzes. Singular too were his marbles, which he polished to such a high satin finish that they resembled glass or glazed porcelain.[99] Although Nadelman attributed their glistening surfaces to his desire to protect the marbles against deterioration, it would not be the last time that he experimented with one material emulating the look of another. With their features more delicate and modern than those in his earlier classical heads, these marbles exuded a warmth and psychological depth that caused at least one commentator to regard them as the greatest of Nadelman's triumphs.[100]

Fig. 102
Paul Manship
Dancer and Gazelles, 1916
Bronze, 69 3/4 x 73 x 19 in.
(177.2 x 185.4 x 48.2 cm)
Collection of The Corcoran Gallery of Art,
Washington D.C.; Museum purchase

Fig. 103
Elie Nadelman
Dancing Figure, 1916–17
Bronze, 29 1/2 x 12 x 11 1/2 in.
(74.9 x 30.5 x 29.2 cm)
Whitney Museum of American Art, New York;
Gift of an anonymous donor
Photography by Jerry L. Thompson

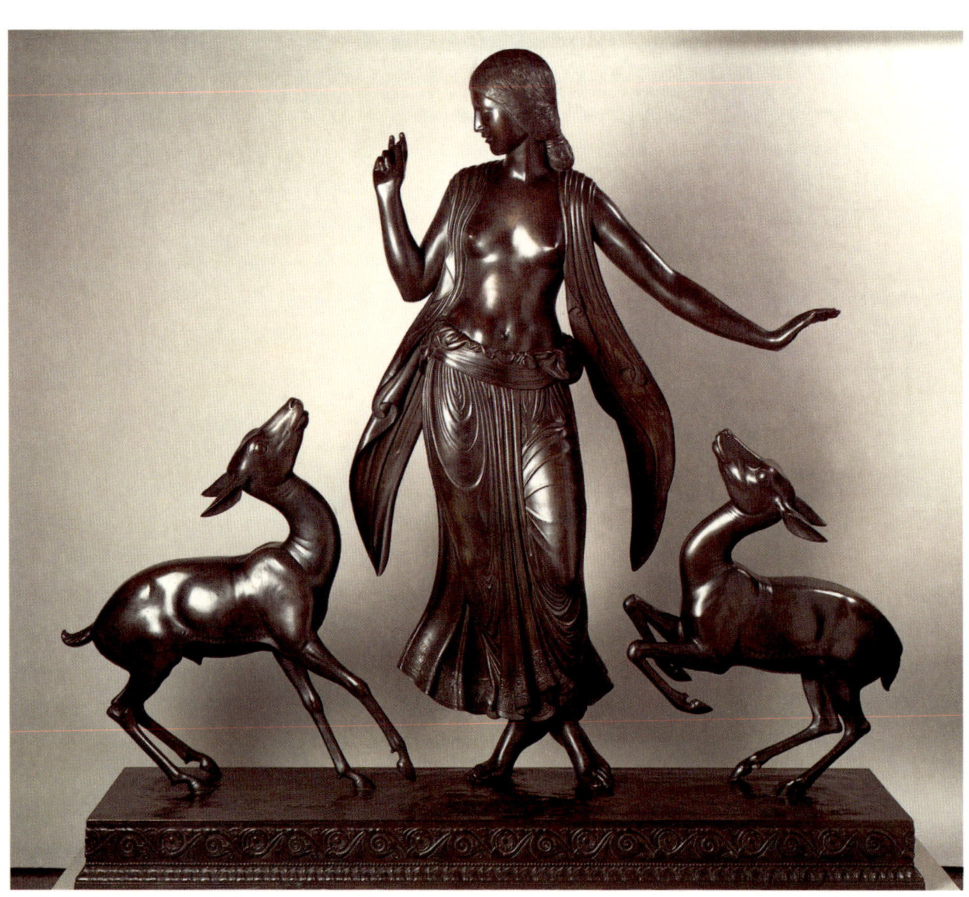

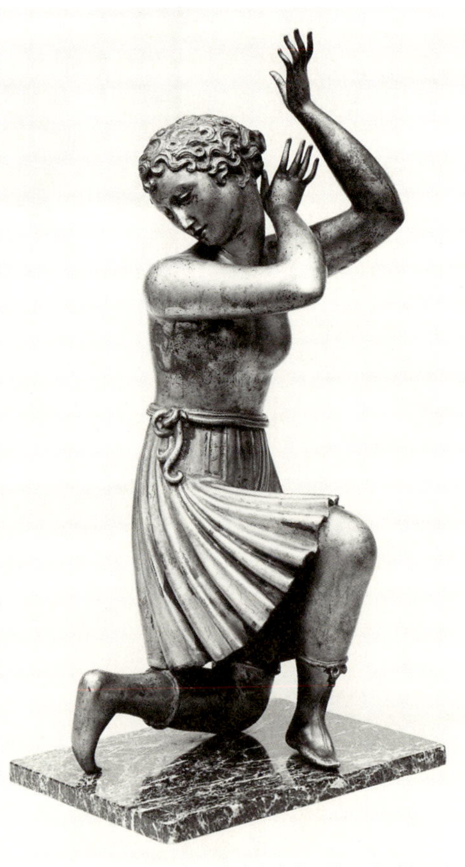

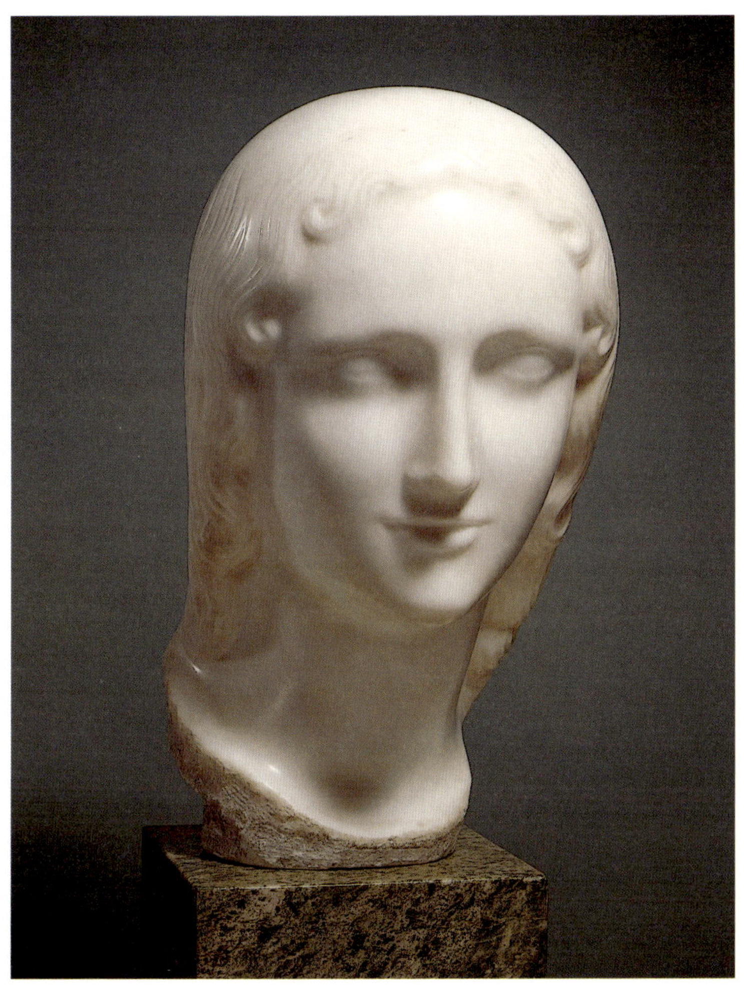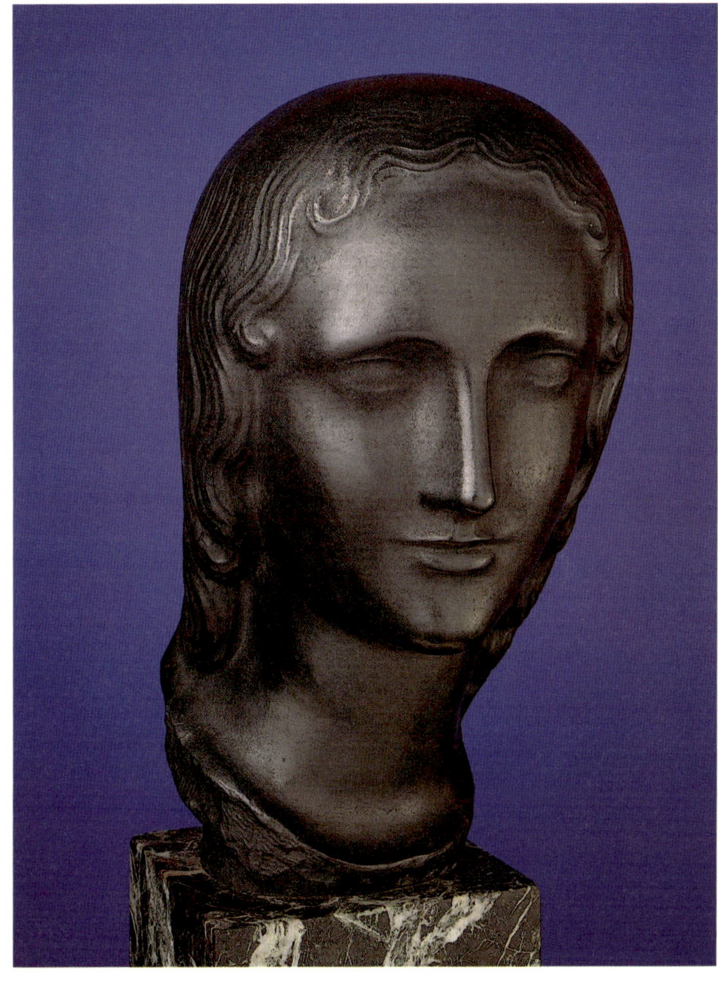

Fig. 104
Elie Nadelman
Ideal Head of a Girl with Long Hair, 1916–17
Marble, 14 3/4 x 8 1/2 x 10 in.
(37.5 x 21.6 x 25.4 cm)
Museum of Fine Arts, Springfield,
Massachusetts; Gift of Charles and Mary
Magriel, supplemented by a gift from the Fine
Arts Council and Museum Purchase Funds

Fig. 105
Elie Nadelman
Ideal Female Head, c. 1916–17
Bronze, 14 x 10 x 11 in. (35.6 x 25.4 x 27.9 cm)
Estate of Elie Nadelman, courtesy
Salander-O'Reilly Galleries, New York
Photography by Paul Waldman

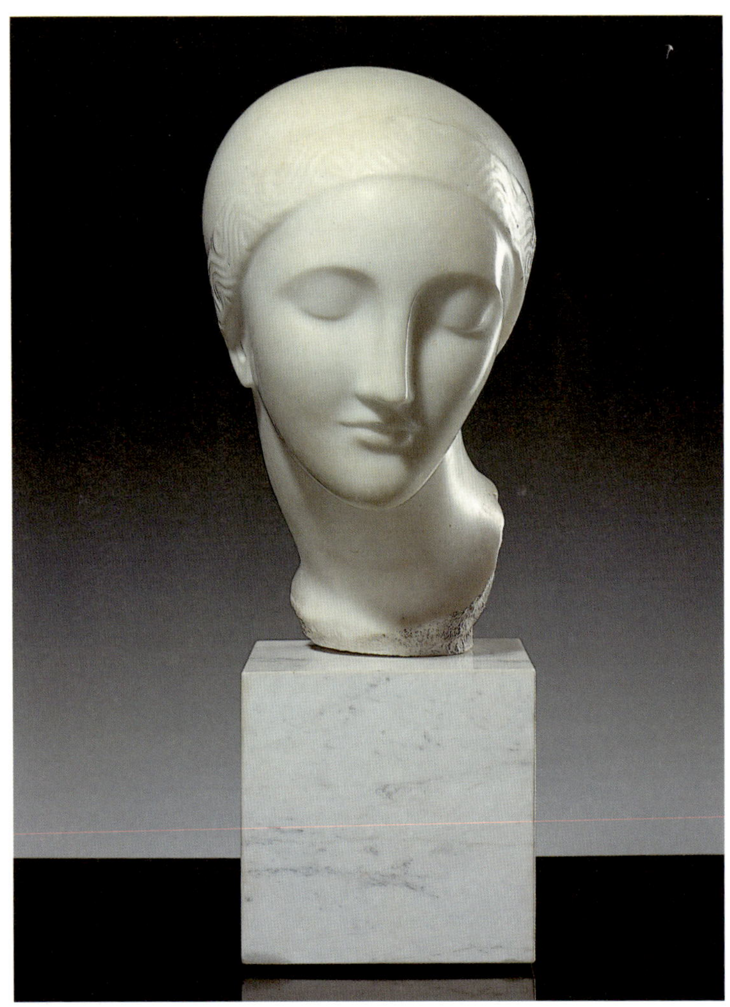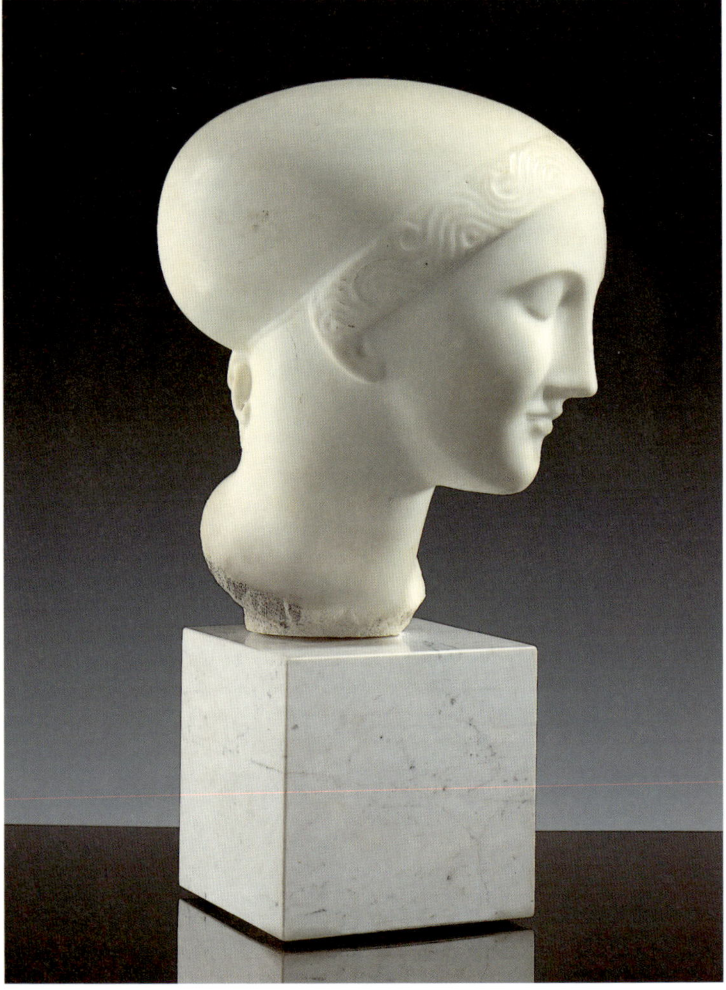

Fig. 106
Elie Nadelman
Early Ideal Head, c. 1916–17 (two views)
Marble, 17 in. (43.2 cm) high
Collection of Max Palevsky
Photography by Douglas M. Parker Studio

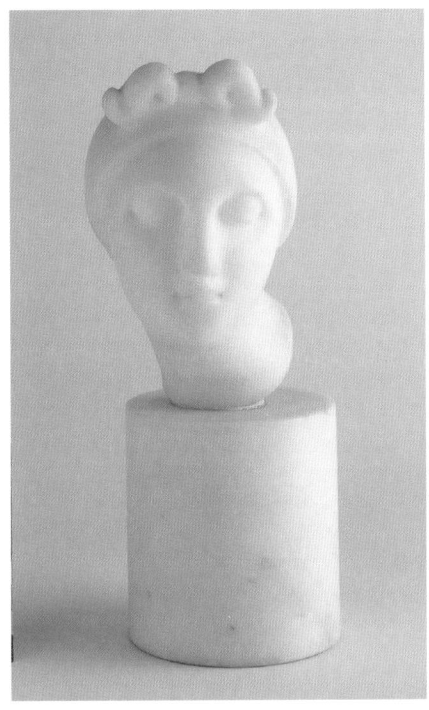

Fig. 107
Elie Nadelman
Classical Head with Headdress, c. 1910–11
Marble, 8 in. (20.3 cm) high
Slong & Midas Properties, Inc., New York
Photography by Matt Flynn

Fig. 108
Elie Nadelman
Female Head, c. 1925–30
Marble, 14 1/4 x 8 x 11 1/4 in.
(36.2 x 20.3 x 28.6 cm)
Estate of Elie Nadelman, courtesy
Salander-O'Reilly Galleries, New York
Photography by Paul Waldman

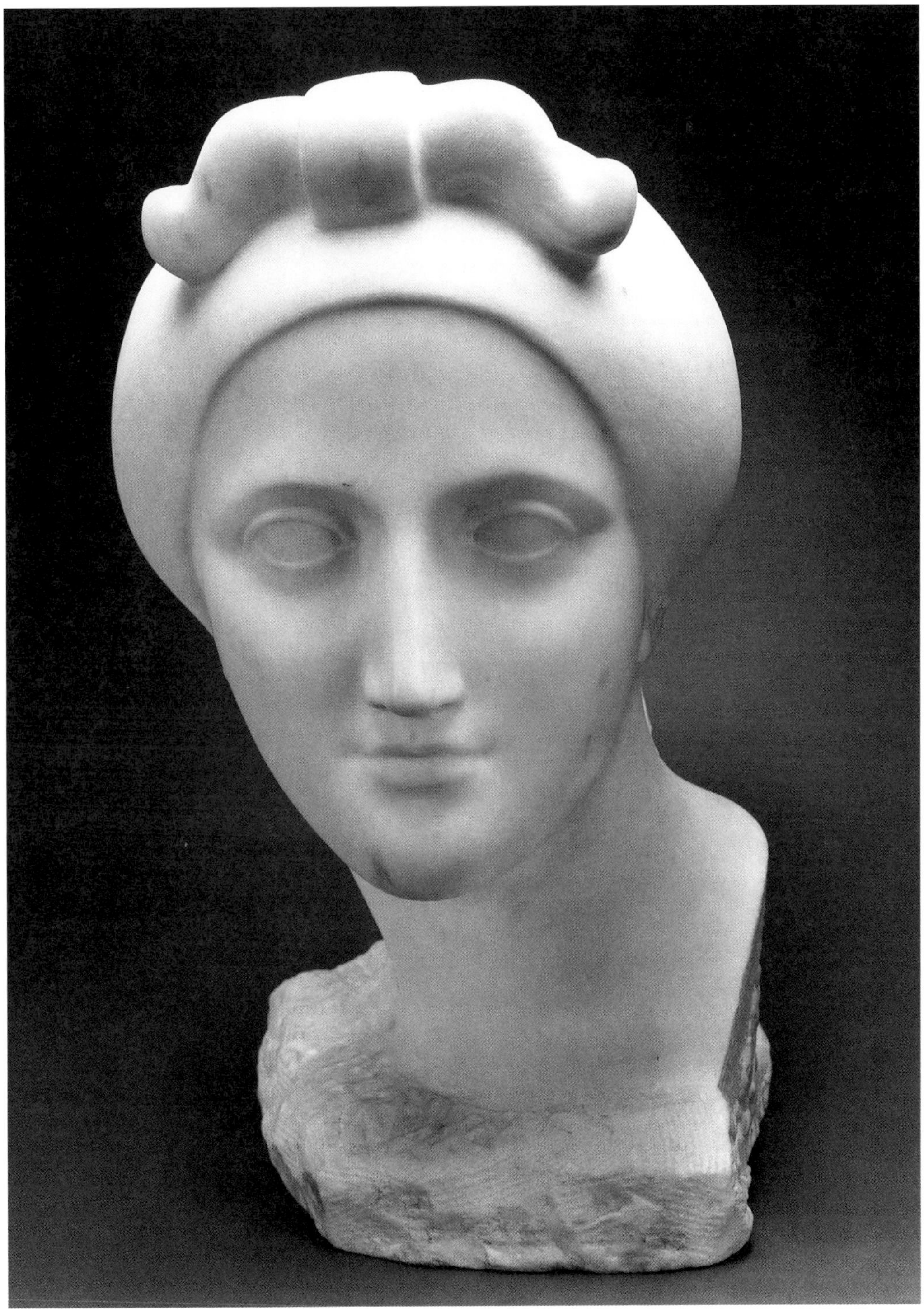

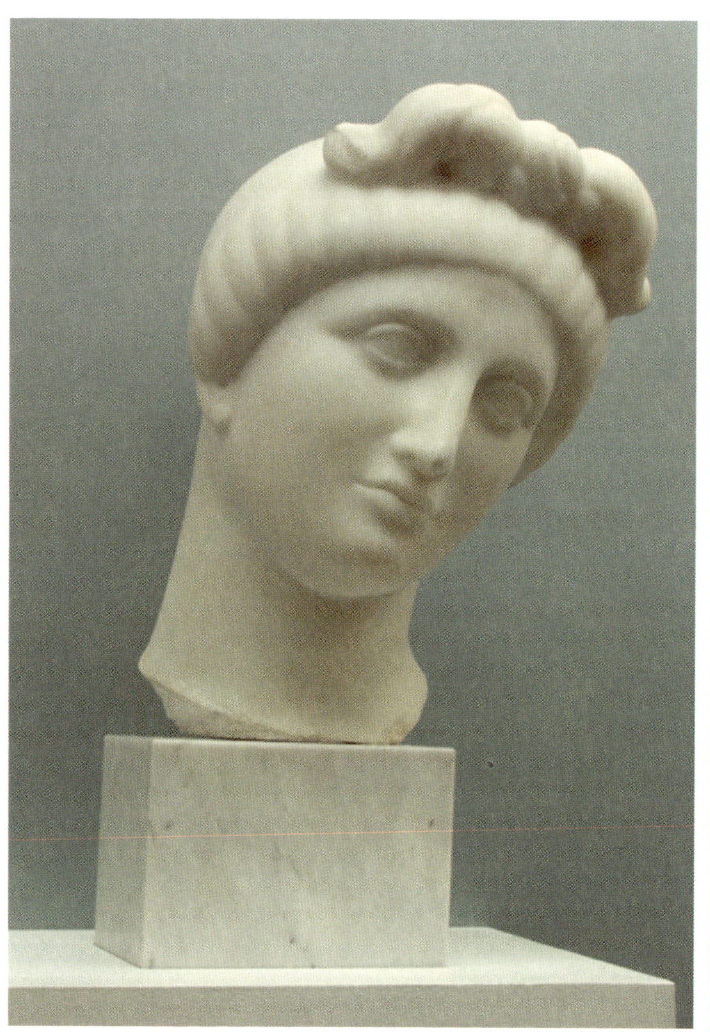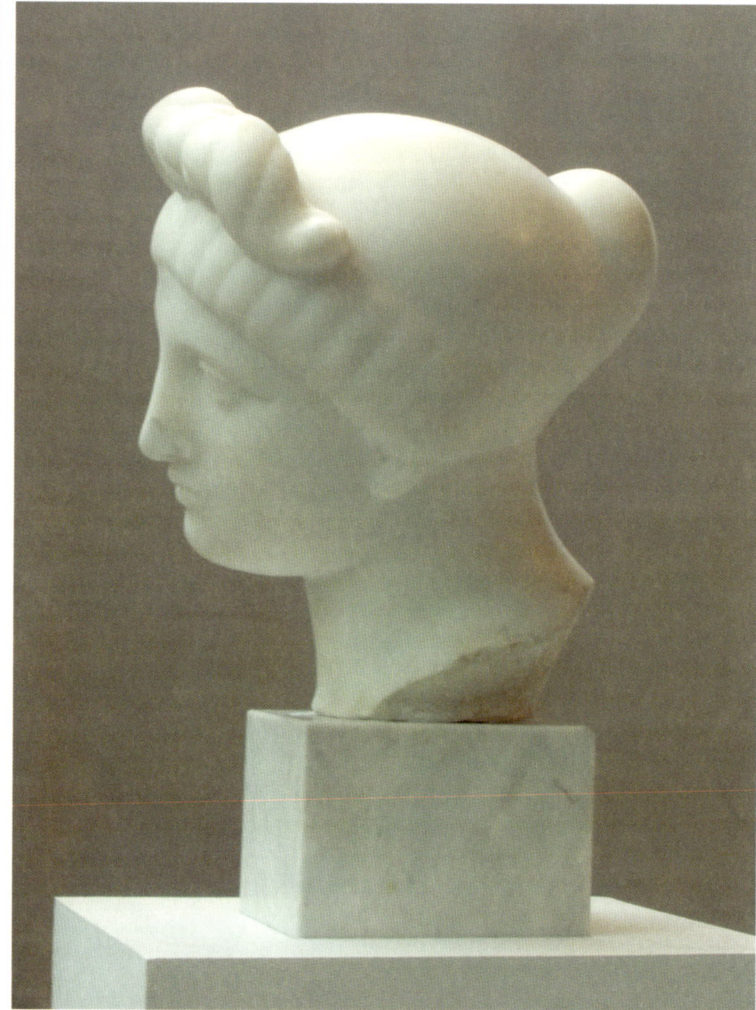

Fig. 109
Elie Nadelman
Classical Head with Headdress,
c. 1910–11 (two views)
Marble, 14 x 8 x 12 in. (35.6 x 20.3 x 30.5 cm)
Milwaukee Art Museum; Purchase, Virginia
Booth Vogel Acquisition Fund

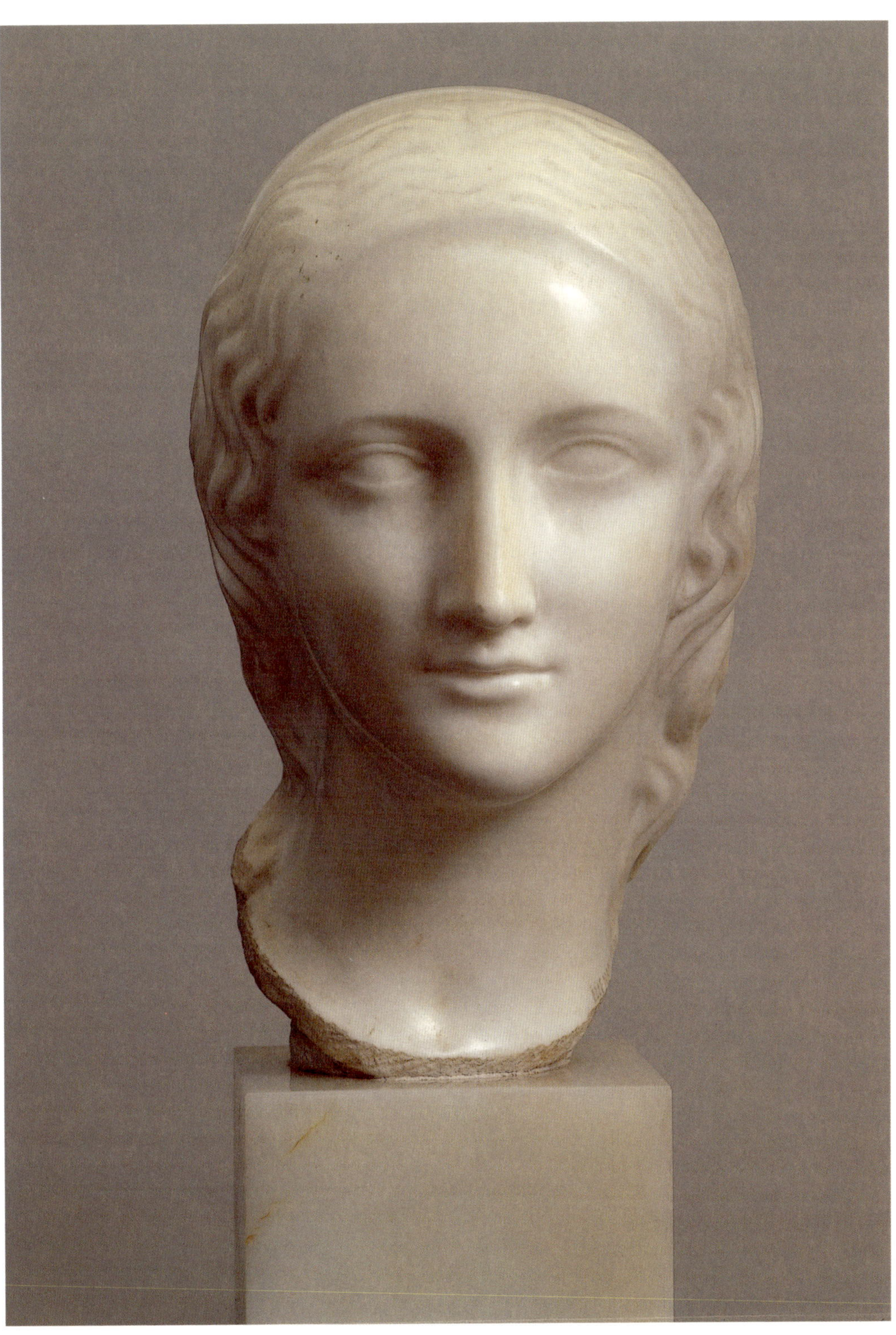

Fig. 110
Elie Nadelman
Classical Head, c. 1916–17
Marble, 14 in. (35.6 cm) high
Erving and Joyce Wolf Collection
Photography by Jerry L. Thompson

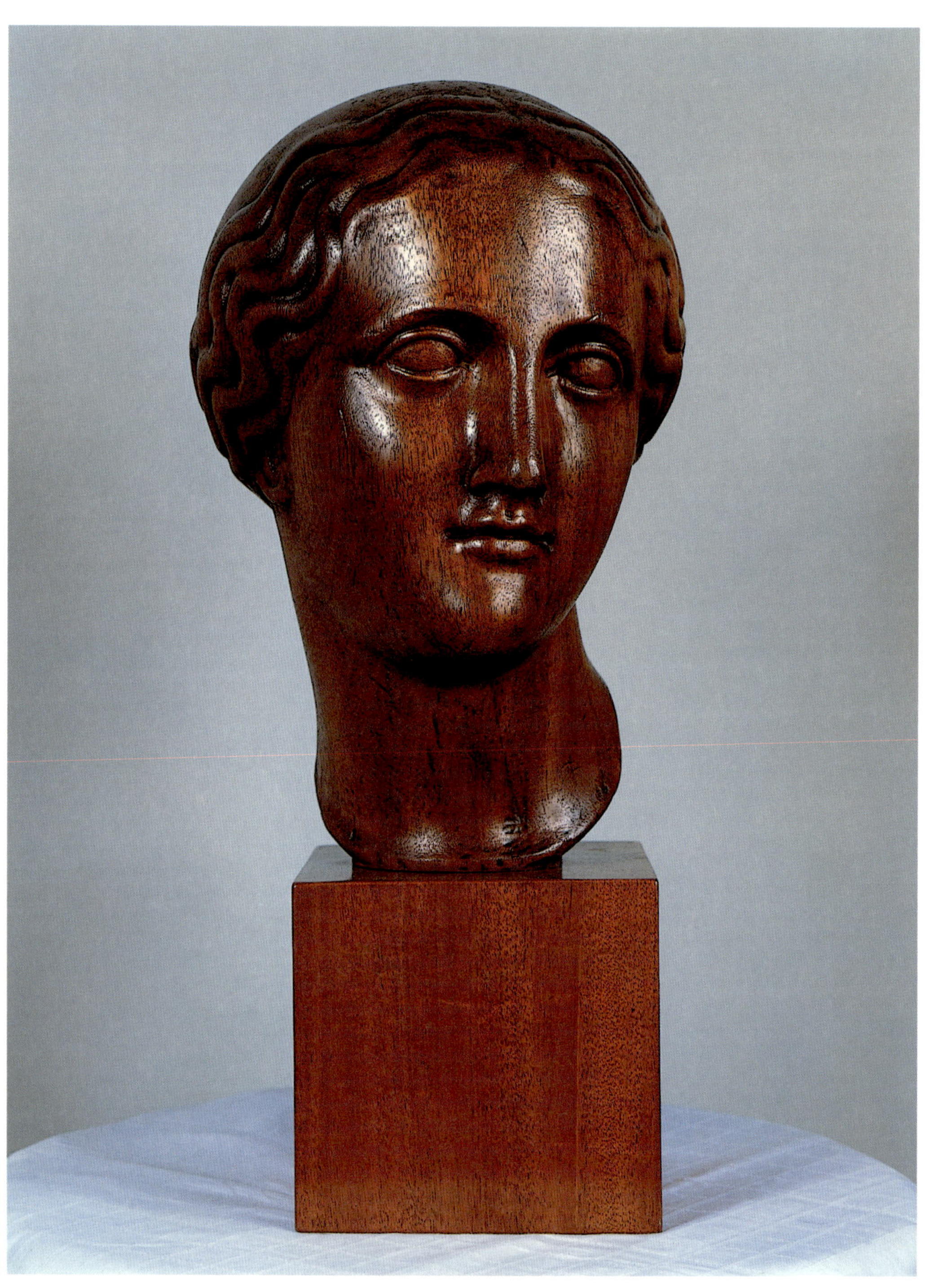

Fig. 111
Elie Nadelman
Small Head, c. 1916–17
Wood, 12 1/2 in. (31.8 cm) high
Collection of Suzanne Slesin and
Michael Steinberg

Fig. 112
Elie Nadelman
Classical Head, c. 1916–17
Marble, 14 1/2 x 9 1/2 x 10 3/4 in.
(36.8 x 24.1 x 27.3 cm)
Yale University Art Gallery; Gift of
Mrs. Francis P. Garvan

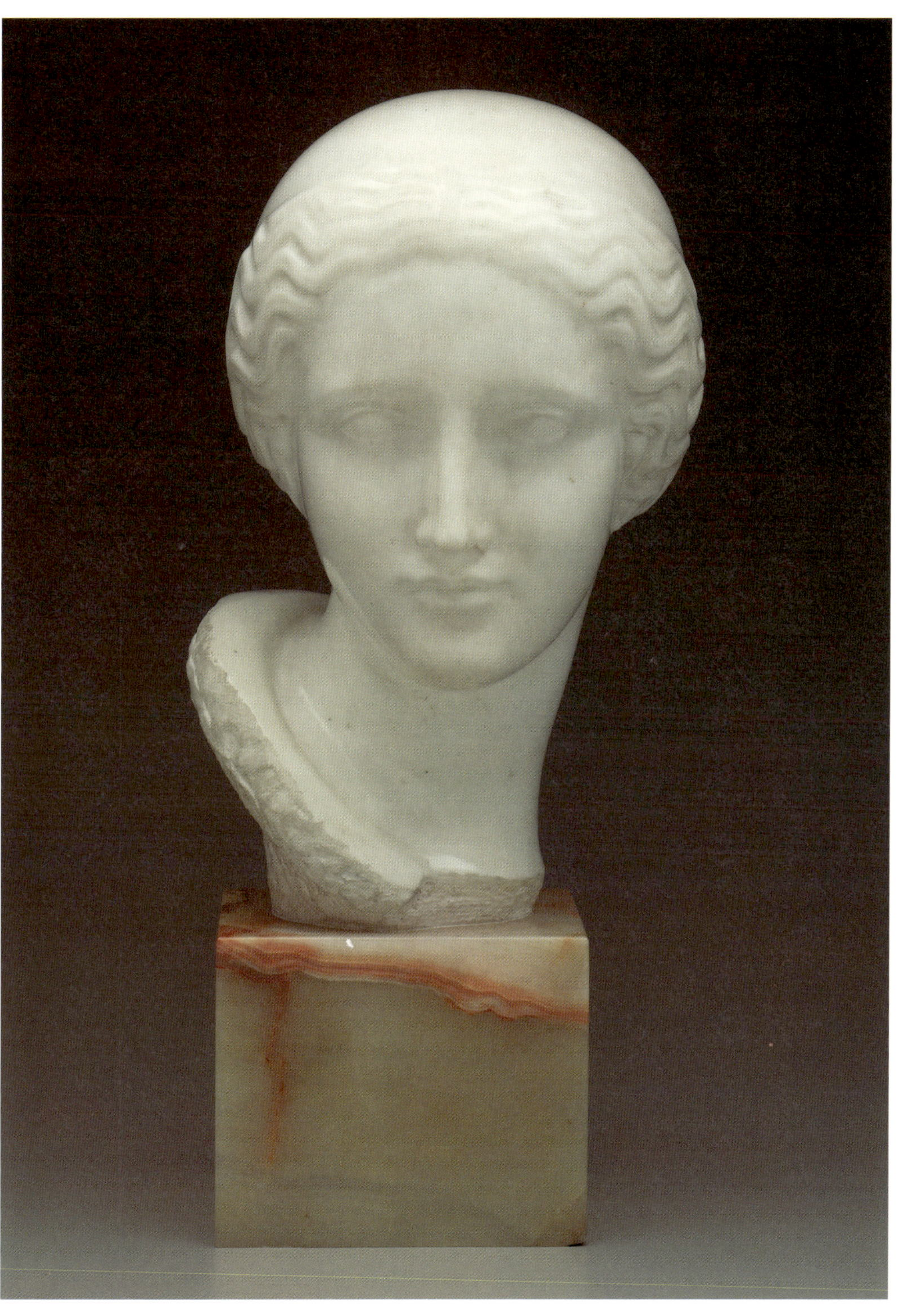

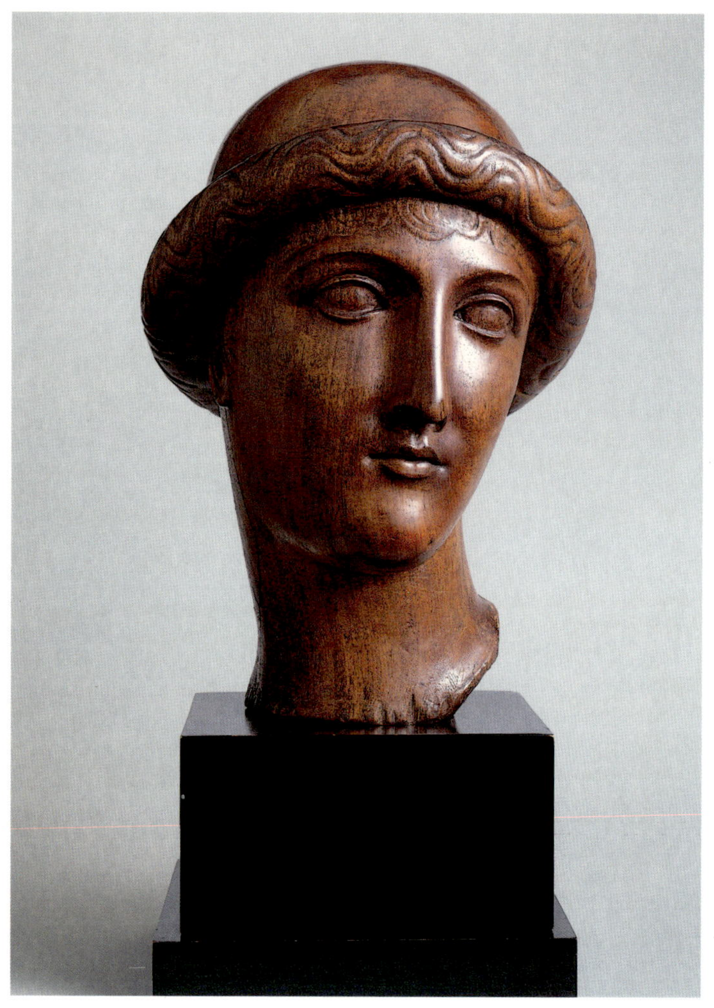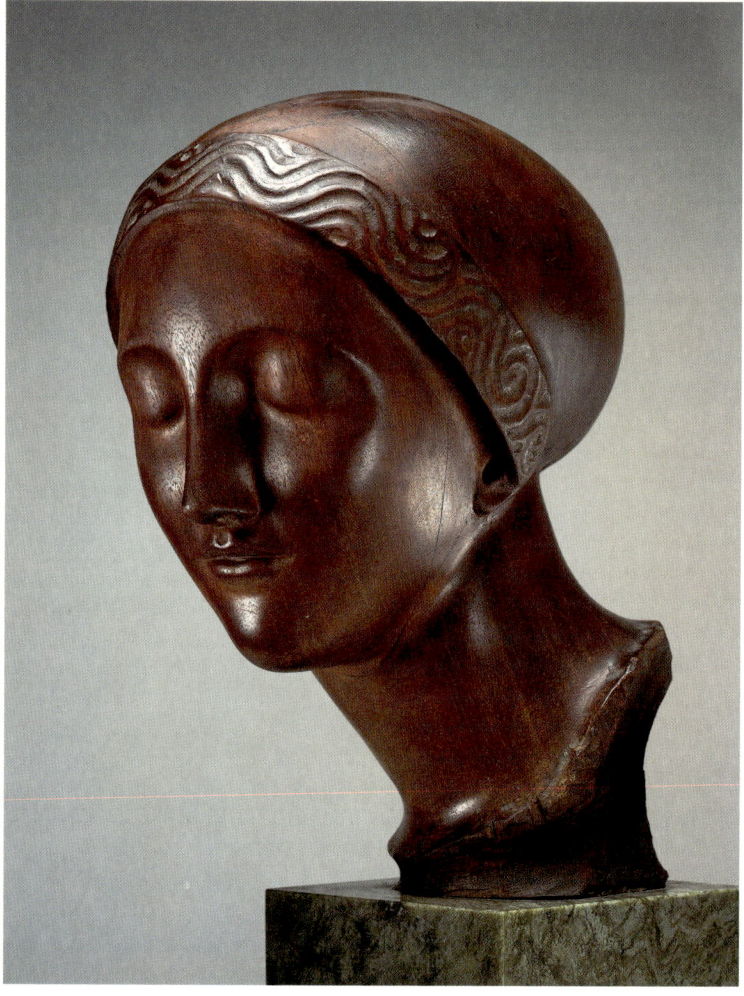

Fig. 113
Elie Nadelman
Ideal Head, c. 1916–17
Wood, 15 in. (38.1 cm) high
Private collection

Fig. 114
Elie Nadelman
Female Head, c. 1916–17
Cherry wood, 16 x 8 1/4 x 14 in.
(40.6 x 20 x 35.5 cm)
Estate of Elie Nadelman, courtesy
Salander-O'Reilly Galleries, New York
Photography by Paul Waldman

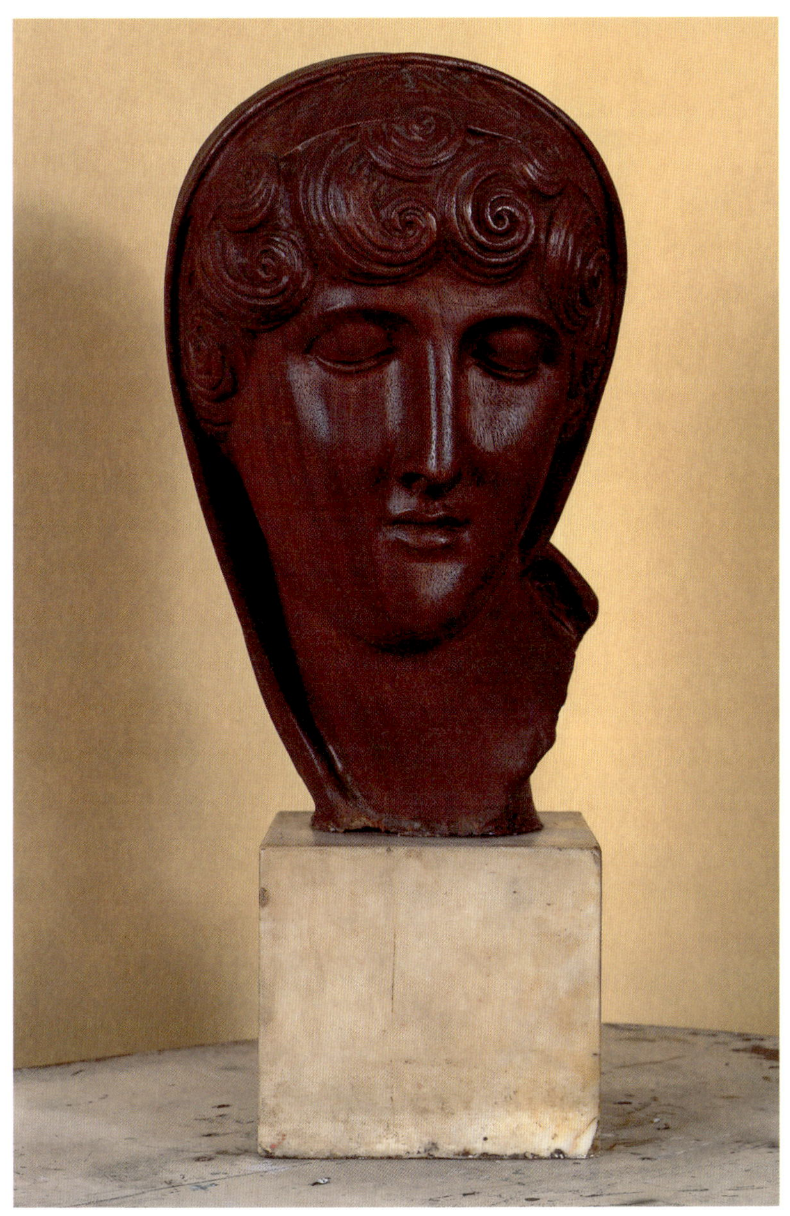
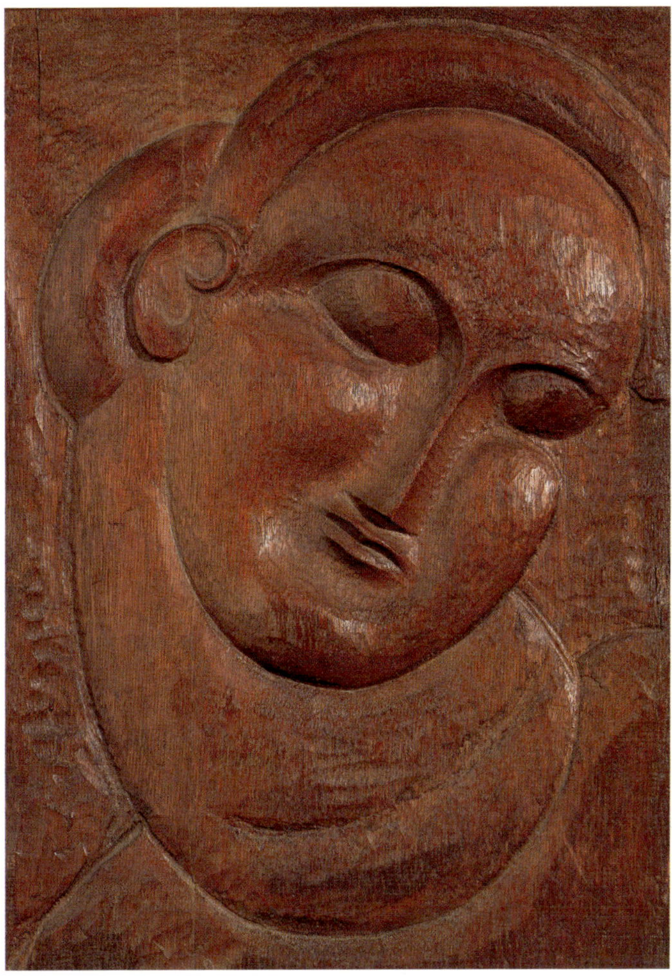

Fig. 115
Elie Nadelman
Hooded Head of a Woman, c. 1916–17
Wood, 15 1/2 in. (39.3 cm) high
Collection of Suzanne Slesin and
Michael Steinberg

Fig. 116
Elie Nadelman
Female Head, c. 1915
Cherry wood, 14 1/2 x 9 1/2 in. (36.8 x 24.1 cm)
Private collection, New York

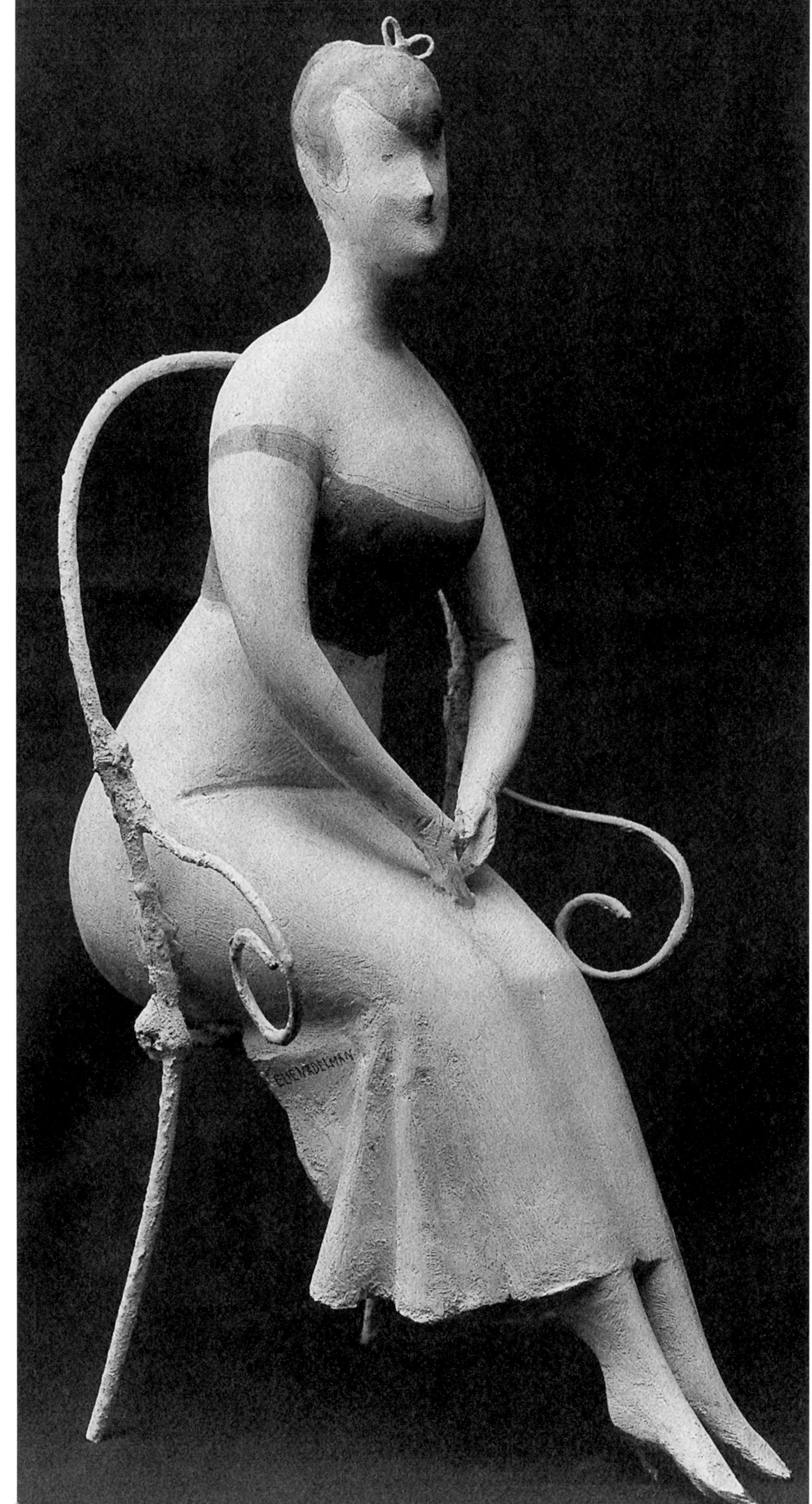
ELIE NADELMAN

Whimsical Insouciance: Plaster Genre Figures, 1917–19

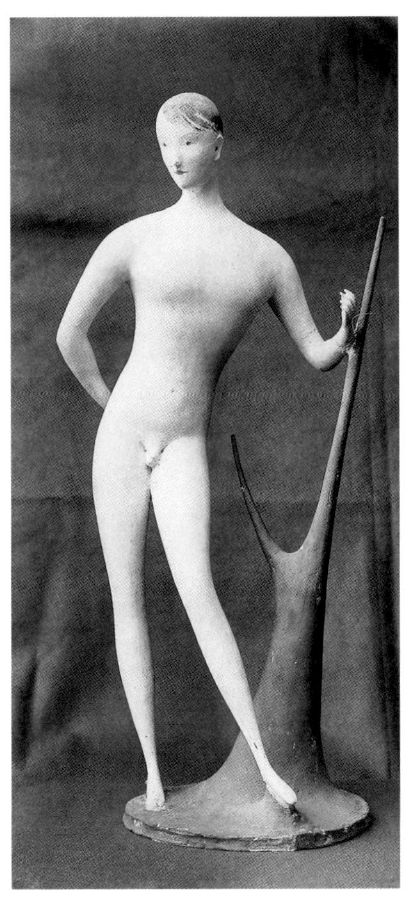

Fig. 117
Elie Nadelman
Femme assise, 1917
Painted plaster, 30 in. (76.2 cm) high;
destroyed
Photography by M. E. Hewitt Studio
Lincoln Kirstein Photograph Collection,
Jerome Robbins Dance Division, The New York
Public Library

Fig. 118
Elie Nadelman
Adolescent, 1917
Painted plaster, 40 in. (101.6 cm) high;
destroyed
Photography by M. E. Hewitt Studio
Lincoln Kirstein Photograph Collection,
Jerome Robbins Dance Division, The New York
Public Library

Nadelman's success in conjoining the eternal and the transitory was tested by the work he included in the December 1917 exhibition *Allies of Sculpture*, presented on the roof garden of the Ritz-Carlton Hotel for the benefit of various war relief committees. The invitation to participate had been based on his Scott & Fowles show; according to the exhibition's checklist, he initially intended to oblige the organizers with a selection of already exhibited work.[101] At the very last moment, however, he decided to premiere three new plaster pieces and include only one older work, his popular *Resting Stag* (FIG. 99). The new pieces depicted contemporary upper-class archetypes: an adolescent boy leaning against a tree, a female singer, and a woman seated on a chair (FIGS. 117–119).

Apart from the descriptive details of face and clothing, which Nadelman delineated with blue paint, these plaster figures conformed to modernist demands for simplification and clarity. To the art public, however, they seemed blatantly provocative, their playfulness and contemporaneity an assault on the seriousness of art. Embarrassed by the works' whimsical depiction of members of their social class, the show's all-female organizers relocated *Femme assise* (*Seated Woman*) (FIG. 117) and *Adolescent* (FIG. 118) to the farthest corner of the exhibition space, dangerously close to the open edge of the roof garden, which overlooked the street. Inexplicably, *Concert Singer* (FIG. 119) remained where it was. Several days later, under pressure, the organizers returned the two other works to their original positions—a futile recompense given that *Femme assise* (*Seated Woman*) was subsequently knocked off its pedestal and shattered. The press's coverage of the incident gave all three pieces a notoriety enjoyed by few other artworks, endowing them with the imprimatur of aesthetic radicality previously reserved for Duchamp's *Nude Descending a Staircase*. In a satirical feature article they were singled out, along with work of Brancusi and Henri Matisse, as avatars of modern art's preposterous incomprehensibility.[102]

Nadelman seemed to have genuinely been caught off guard by the tempestuousness of the response. His 1914 inclusions in the Salon des Indépendants had depicted men in contemporary hats, and only ten months

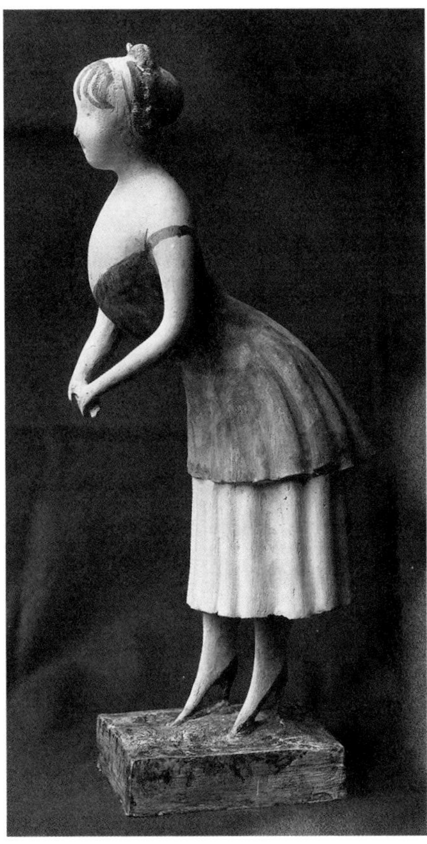
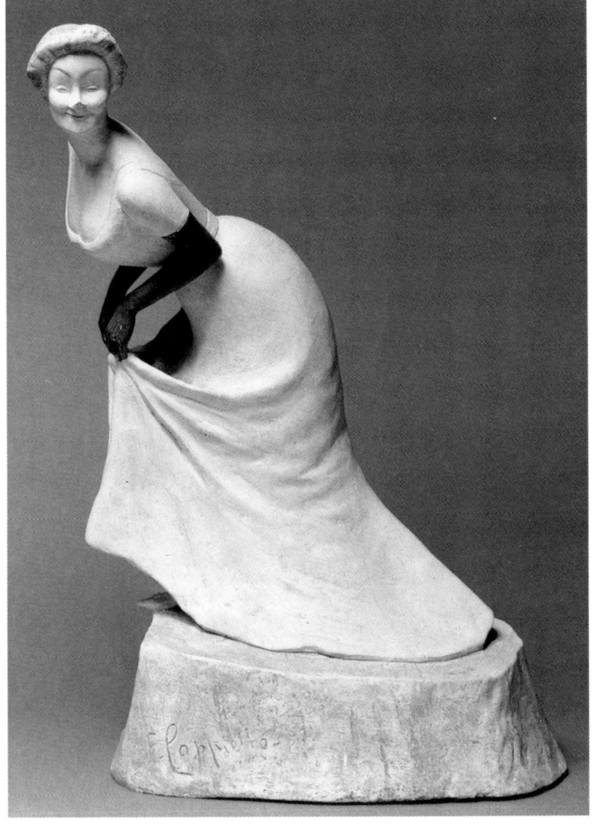

earlier, his bronze figure of a young man in a top hat, *Le promeneur* (FIG. 79), had elicited praise, not condemnation. Still, he could only imagine that his statuettes had created a furor because he had dressed them in contemporary costumes.[103] Contemporary clothing was not the problem, however; it had been employed in European and American public monuments and statues since the late nineteenth century as a way to transform classical prototypes into democratic and palpably nationalist images. Several sculptures in the Ritz-Carlton exhibition used the technique, including Daniel Chester French's *Standing Lincoln* (FIG. 121), which was purchased before the show's close by one of its organizers, Gertrude Vanderbilt Whitney.

Applied color was likewise not unprecedented. The end of the nineteenth century had seen the widespread reintroduction of color into statuary in both the United States and Europe as a way to enhance verisimilitude. Its use by artists such as Herbert Adams, Leonetto Capiello (FIG. 120), and Pierre-Auguste Renoir (FIG. 123), with whom Nadelman claimed to have been friendly in Paris, had provided him with firsthand appreciation of color's effectiveness as a tool in allying sculpture with contemporary life.[104] Yet it was not

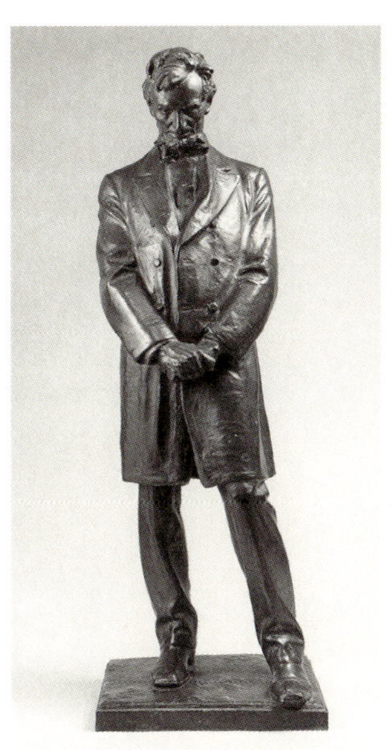 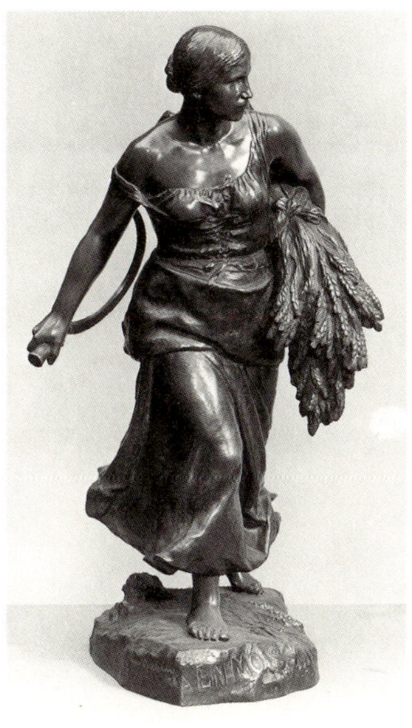 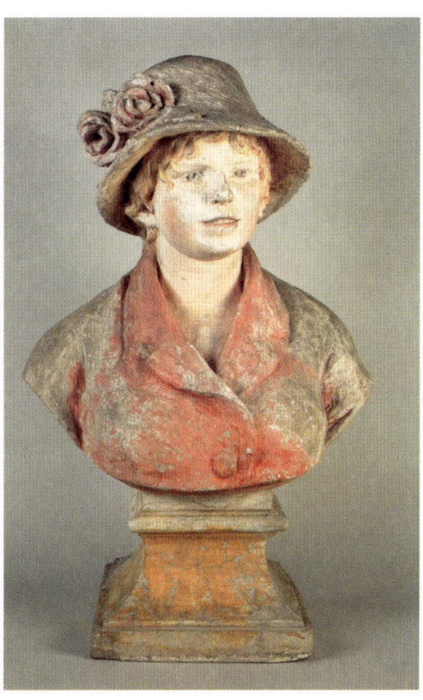

realism, but a desire for greater formal clarity that Nadelman cited as his reason for painting his figures. Once again, his mentor was Hildebrand, who credited color with establishing the light and dark contrasts upon which the perception of a composition's formal architecture depended. European abstract sculptors Henri Laurens, Alexander Archipenko, and Jacques Lipchitz had used color in this way to eradicate the structural ambiguities caused by variations of light. These precedents gave Nadelman confidence to affirm that his application of color was "perfectly consistent in thus defining the light-and-shade relations of hair and beard to the flesh quality of the face."[105]

Discounting color and contemporary costume as explanations, we are left wondering what triggered the public outrage over Nadelman's painted statuettes. Unlike modernists whose abstractions the public found incomprehensible, he had kept the outer physical appearance of his subjects inviolate, treating it neither as an occasion for subjective rumination nor as an opportunity for autonomous formal invention, both of which he abhorred. His malefaction seems to have been his marriage of illustrative realism and classical simplification, which confounded expectations and assumptions and endowed his work with satirical implications. Nadelman had conflated these apparent dichotomies out of a desire to keep the classical tradition alive by infusing it with the vitality of the present. In the process, he achieved a nuanced portrait that both celebrated and satirized American upper-class society—and mirrored his ambivalence toward a social world he was fast entering.

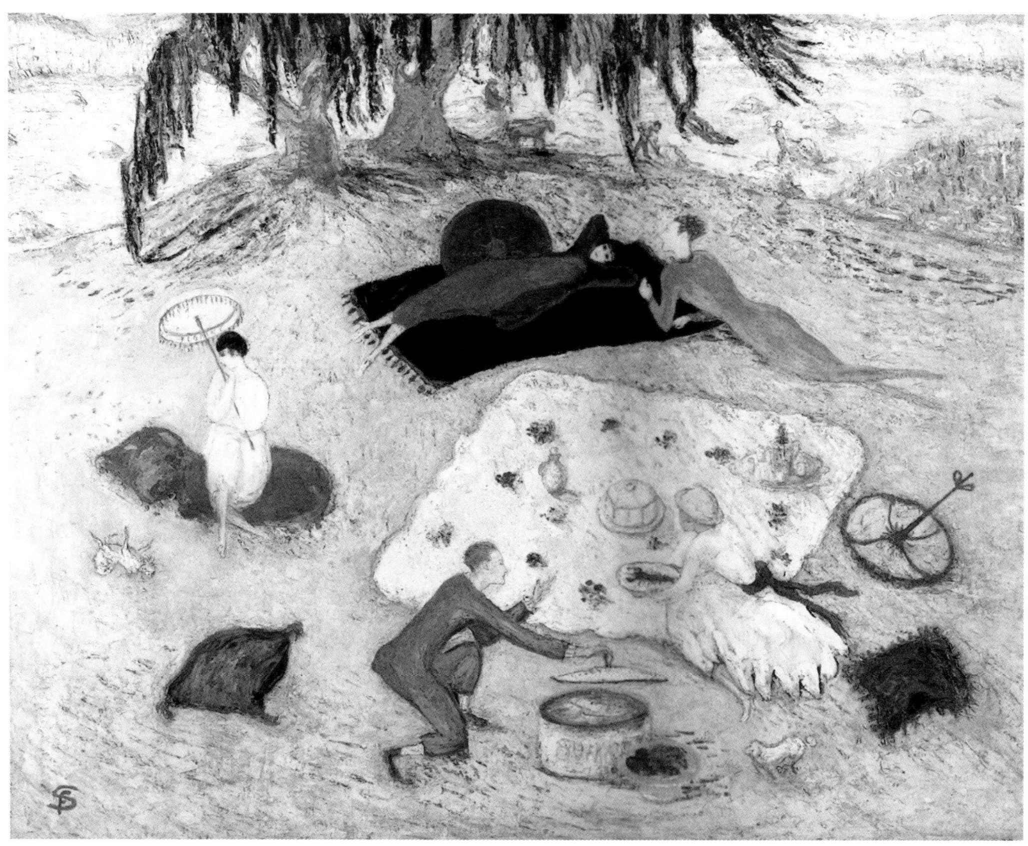

Nadelman's invention of a new sculptural vocabulary coincided with a shift in his social circumstances. Birnbaum had terminated his relationship with him in early 1917 after discovering that Nadelman was again violating his oral agreement of exclusivity by allowing M. Knoedler & Company to offer his work to its clients. At the same time, his engagement to Judith Bernays had broken off, apparently due—according to one source—to Nadelman's mistaken belief that the marriage would be accompanied by a dowry.[106] Shortly thereafter he became part of the circle around the wealthy, unmarried Stettheimer sisters: Florine, Henrietta (Ettie), and Caroline (Carrie). Florine's inclusion of him in her paintings *Picnic at Bedford Hills* (FIG. 124) and *Lake Placid* testify both to his membership in this elite group and to his flirtatious affair with Ettie. Seven years Nadelman's senior and the most intellectual of the Stettheimer sisters, Ettie had earned a bachelor's degree from Barnard College and a Ph.D. in psychology from Albert-Ludwig University in Freiburg, Germany. For her, the romance with Nadelman was relatively serious; she later portrayed him as her husband in her novel, *Love Days*, a thinly disguised autobiography written under the pseudonym Henrie Waste. Her depiction of

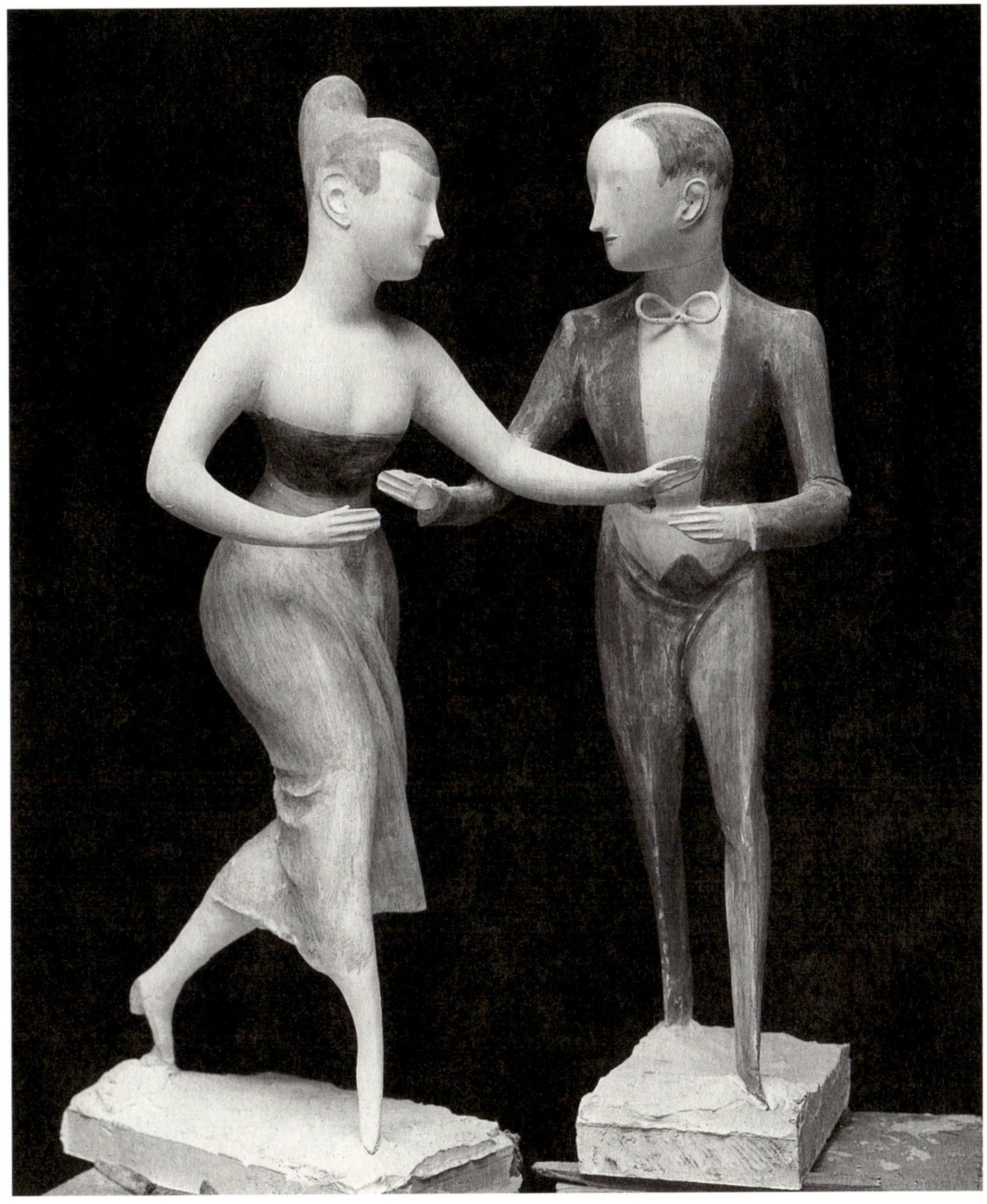

Fig. 125
Elie Nadelman
Tango, 1918
Painted plaster, 30 in. (76.2 cm) high;
destroyed
Photography by M. E. Hewitt Studio
Lincoln Kirstein Photograph Collection,
Jerome Robbins Dance Division, The New York
Public Library

the classically inspired artist Pol Grodz, newly arrived from Europe—beautiful, intense, a great talent but ultimately self-absorbed, friendless, colorless, and cold—mirrored the trajectory of her romance with Nadelman. In the end the relationship left her with nothing but disappointment, although it may have provided Nadelman with an introduction to his future wife, with whom Ettie had studied as a young girl in Stuttgart, Germany.[107]

Notwithstanding the termination of Nadelman's romance with Ettie, his participation in the Stettheimer milieu proved immensely important to his

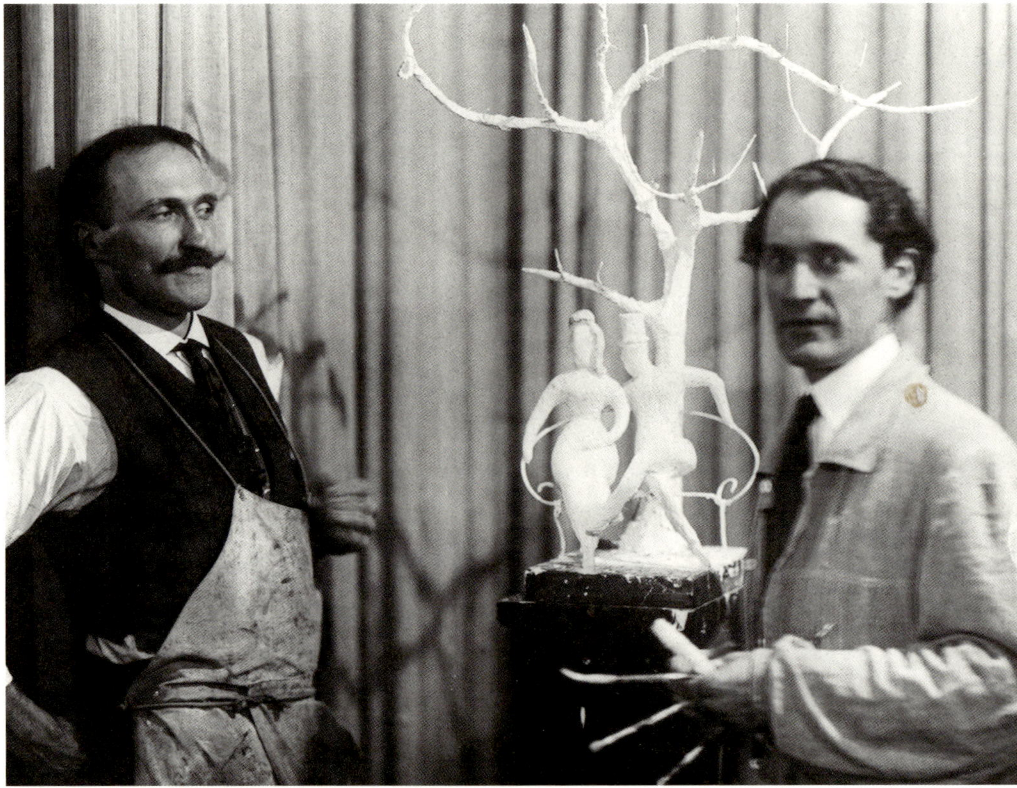

aesthetic development by exposing him to a sensibility that mocked both the pomposity of high culture and the self-righteous moralism of the avant-garde. Carrie's dollhouse, which she spent her life creating, and Florine's paintings combined the serious with the lightheartedly outrageous. Florine's paintings, in particular, exploited artifice and decorative excess to both celebrate and criticize American culture. In her depictions of department store sales, parades, beauty contests, circus performances, amusement parks, theater, and upper-class society, she combined a glowing admiration for American institutions and personae with a satirical critique of American social life.

Emboldened by this self-mocking yet reverent milieu, Nadelman ignored the public outrage his plaster genre sculptures had engendered. By the end of March 1918 he had finished two multifigure compositions: a couple dancing the tango and a pair of lovers seated on a park bench. *Tango* (FIG. 125)was shown at the Penguin Club that month; *Tree of Life*, as the seated lovers were called, was shown in the Whitney Studio Club's exhibition *Indigenous Sculpture*, so called because the twenty invited sculptors worked on site (FIG. 126).[108] A year and a half later, on October 27, 1919, a one-person exhibition of his work opened at M. Knoedler & Company, where Stettheimer's work had hung three

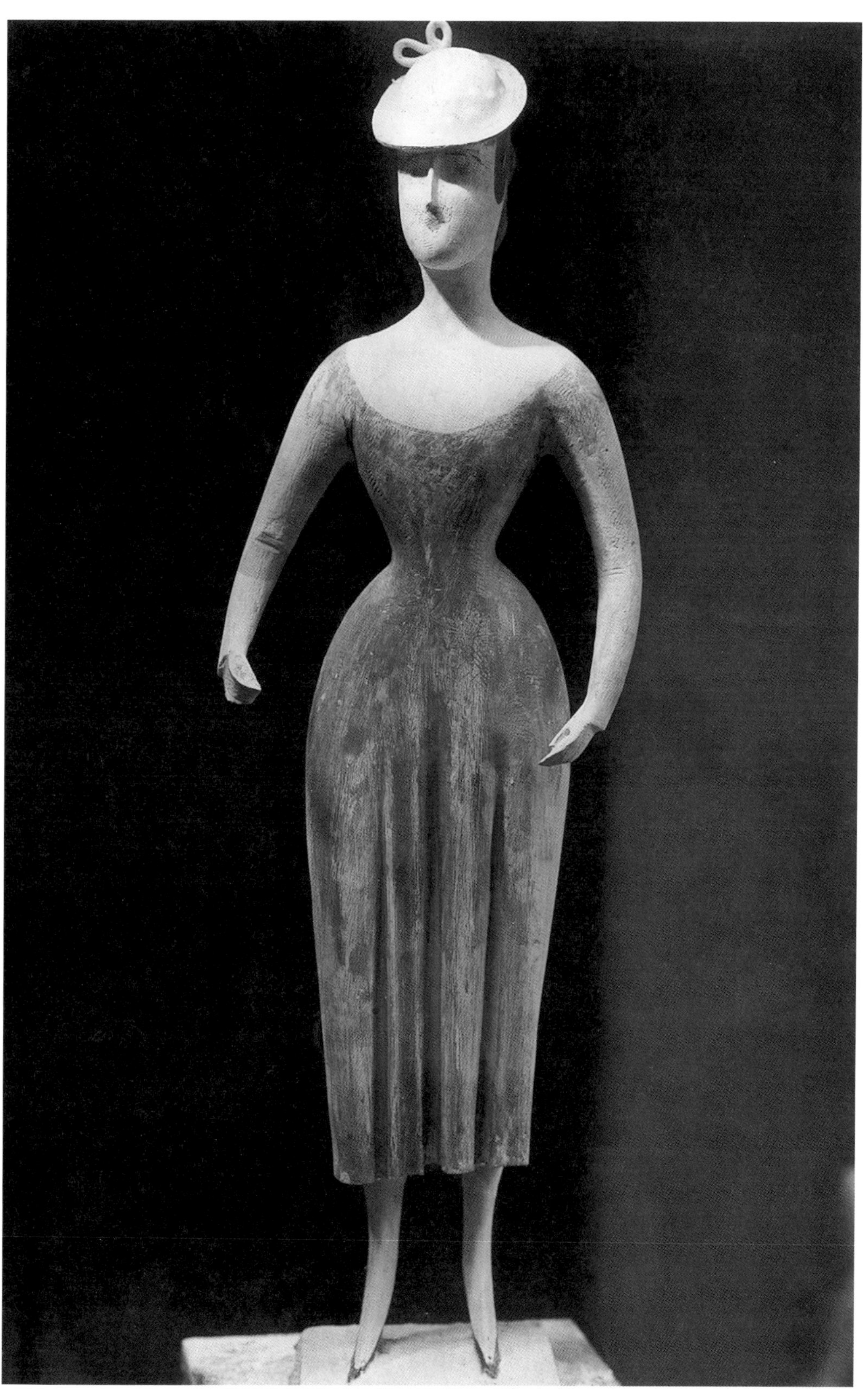

Fig. 127
Elie Nadelman
Standing Woman in Hat, 1918–19
Painted plaster, 30 in. (76.2 cm) high;
destroyed
Photography by M. E. Hewitt Studio
Lincoln Kirstein Photograph Collection,
Jerome Robbins Dance Division, The New York
Public Library

Fig. 128
Elie Nadelman
Circus Girl with Hoop, 1918–19
Painted plaster and wire, 30 in. (76.2 cm) high;
destroyed
Photography by M. E. Hewitt Studio
Lincoln Kirstein Photograph Collection,
Jerome Robbins Dance Division, The New York
Public Library

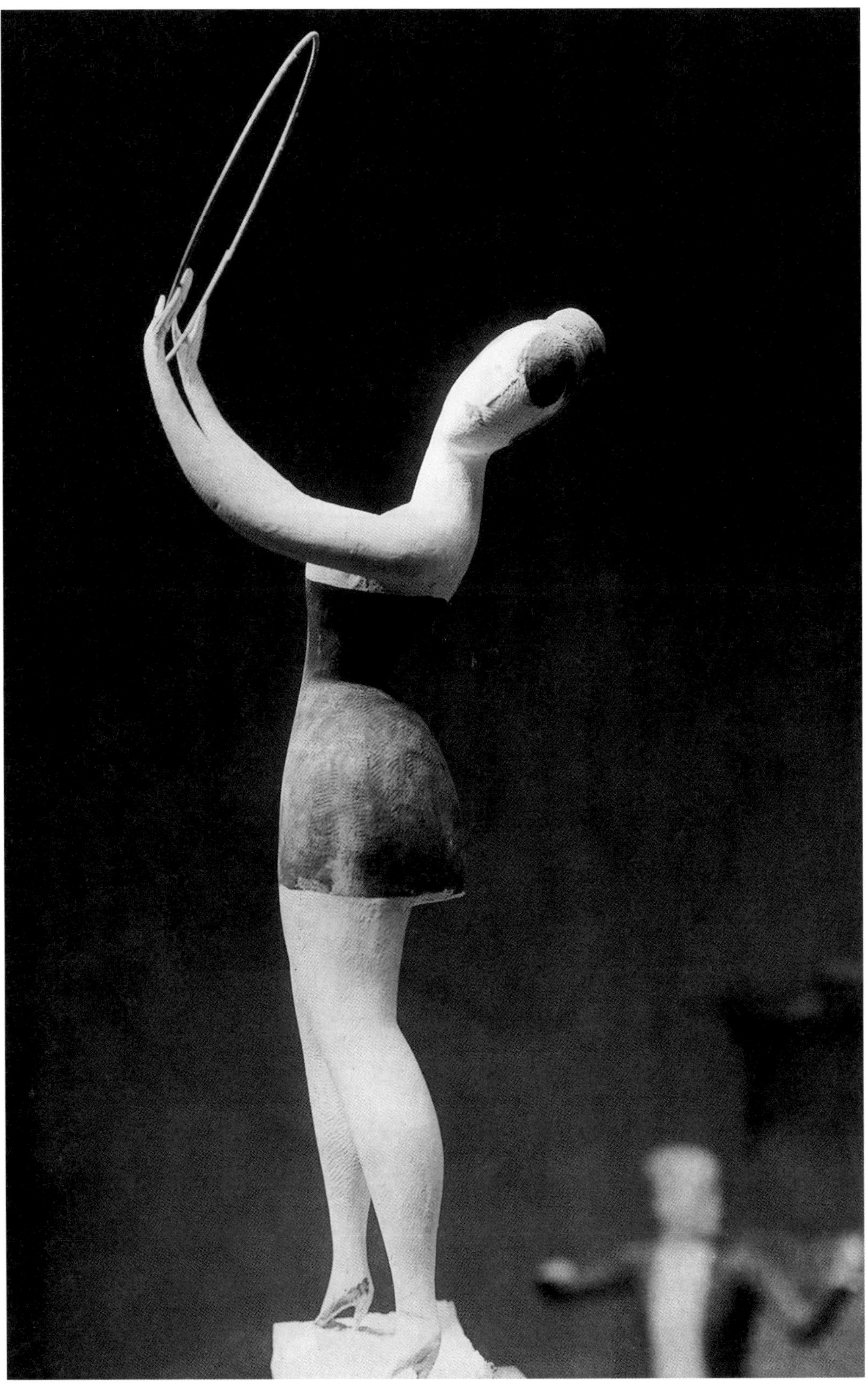

Fig. 129
Elie Nadelman
Top-Hatted Man, c. 1918–19
Painted plaster, 30 in. (76.2 cm) high;
destroyed
Photography by M. E. Hewitt Studio
Lincoln Kirstein Photograph Collection,
Jerome Robbins Dance Division, The New York
Public Library

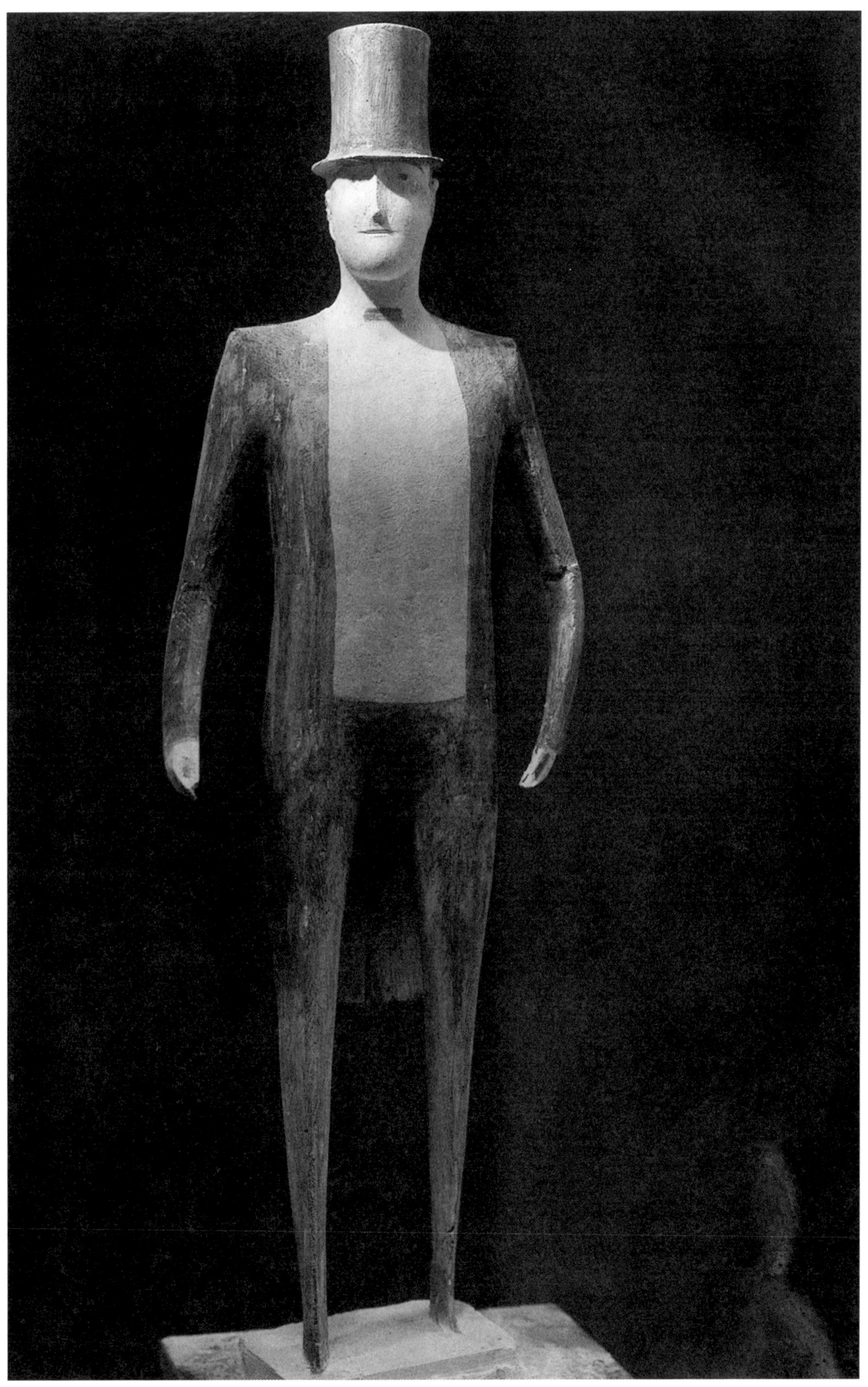

Fig. 130
Elie Nadelman
Standing Circus Girl, 1918–19
Plaster; destroyed
Photography by M.E. Hewitt Studio
Lincoln Kirstein Photograph Collection,
Jerome Robbins Dance Division, The New York
Public Library

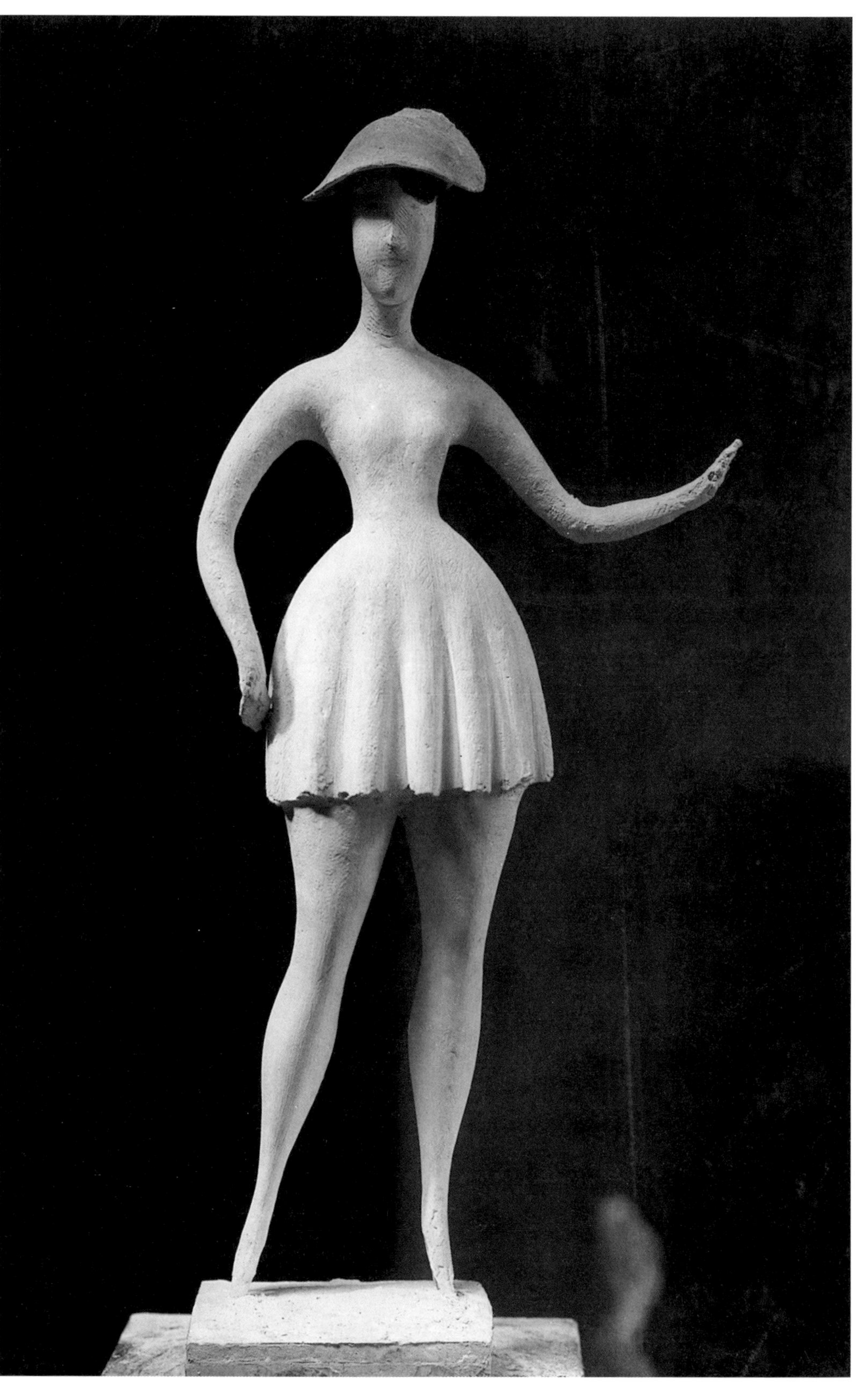

years earlier. In this exhibition Nadelman showcased a full panoply of painted plaster figures drawn from the worlds of popular entertainment and society. In accordance with the academic practice followed in French Salons, he presented them both as self-sufficient objects available for sale and as models for works that clients could order in wood or bronze.[109] Neither option materialized; when the show closed two weeks later, nothing had sold or been ordered.

Critical reception to the show was predominantly negative. The same conservative press that had castigated Ashcan realism less than a decade earlier for its overly frank and vulgar subject matter accused Nadelman's painted figures of being frivolous, insolent, and degenerate.[110] Even their advocates viewed them as permeated chiefly by humor and caricature. What elicited the most favorable response from commentators was Nadelman's installation. The artist had dotted his sixteen plaster sculptures around a darkened, olive-hued room in what McBride called "a sublime indifference to the conventions of art exhibitions."[111] To accentuate the works' ghostlike quality, he had illuminated them only with blue spotlights—an effect one commentator likened to "flashes of lightning" and another to the "Elysian fields of Orpheus."[112]

Only a few critics noticed the works' formal beauty and their epigrammatic treatment of character. To them, Nadelman had proved that the laws of harmonious proportion could be applied to figures in skirts and trousers as easily as to those in togas. The painter Agnes Pelton went so far as to connect Nadelman's plasters to specific Greek antecedents. To her, the works' iconic gestures and portrayal of casual human acts rendered them modern equivalents of Tanagra figurines.[113] Like these painted clay precedents, plasters such as *Standing Woman in Hat*, *Circus Girl with Hoop*, *Top-Hatted Man*, and *Standing Circus Girl* (FIGS. 127–130), with their coy charm and mannered prettiness, seemed purposely to eschew the heroic ambitions and grandeur of monumental public sculpture.

Whatever disappointment Nadelman may have felt at the show's lack of financial and critical success was more than mitigated by his marriage on December 31, 1919, to Viola Spiess Flannery, the elegant, wealthy widow of Joseph Flannery. The marriage gave Nadelman financial independence and an enviable position within upper-class society owing to Viola's family connections and the remarriage, years earlier, of her widowed mother to Count Naselli, the former Italian consul general in New York.[114] Four years Nadelman's senior, and the mother of two grown daughters, German-educated Viola was at ease with European culture and languages and, according to Thadée Natanson, willing to devote her fortune and her time to Nadelman.[115] The two became a golden couple.[116] Supported by a retinue of servants—cooks, gardeners, care-takers, butlers, ladies' maids, housekeepers, and a chauffeur—they lived a privileged existence of lavish entertainment and extended European sojourns. "Daylong bridge parties interrupted only by luxurious meals" was how Natanson described their 1927 trip to Paris.[117] In Paris in the early years of the century, Nadelman had kept primarily to himself, apart from romantic involvements and occasional interactions with artists and people of wealth—the Steins, the Natansons, and Helena Rubinstein, for example. In New York he now took out memberships in artists' groups and joined a host of gentlemen's clubs—the City Club, the Knickerbocker Whist Club, and the Cavendish Club—where he ate lunch, smoked cigars, and played cards. "The world was at Nadelman's to lunch yesterday," Marsden Hartley reported to Stieglitz after visiting the couple one summer in Gloucester, Massachusetts.[118] The artist who had lamented to Leo Stein in 1909 that social life and artistic creation were antithetical suddenly found himself managing both.[119]

For the first year and a half of the Nadelmans' marriage, they rented their residences, as Viola had earlier promised the Flannery family home on Fifth Avenue to her daughter, who had been married less than a week after she was. Initially they lived in suites in Manhattan's Hotel Savoy. This six-month idyll was followed by summer at the Beauport estate in Gloucester and winter and spring at the Delafield estate in Riverdale-on-Hudson, just north of Manhattan. Finding the idea of a country estate appealing, they purchased Alderbrook—a sixteen-acre nineteenth-century estate overlooking the Hudson River, not far from the Delafield property. Unoccupied for twenty-five years, Alderbrook was in ruins. The couple modernized the mansion, restoring it to its original gabled appearance and converting the existing carriage house into a studio for Nadelman.[120] To heighten the estate's rural atmosphere, they planted orchards and grape arbors; acquired horses, geese, chickens, and sheep to graze in the fields; and created a man-made lake for swimming and ice-skating. Simultaneously, they purchased and began renovating a townhouse at 6 East Ninety-third Street. Two years later, in January 1923, the townhouse was ready for occupancy, complete with a newly installed elevator and large top-floor, sky-lit studio for Nadelman. They celebrated its completion with a banquet for one hundred guests. "At home" Sunday soirees followed every week thereafter.

Fig. 131
Elie Nadelman
Head of a Woman in Profile, c. 1920–25
Collection of Michael Hall, Esquire
Photography by Jerry L. Thompson

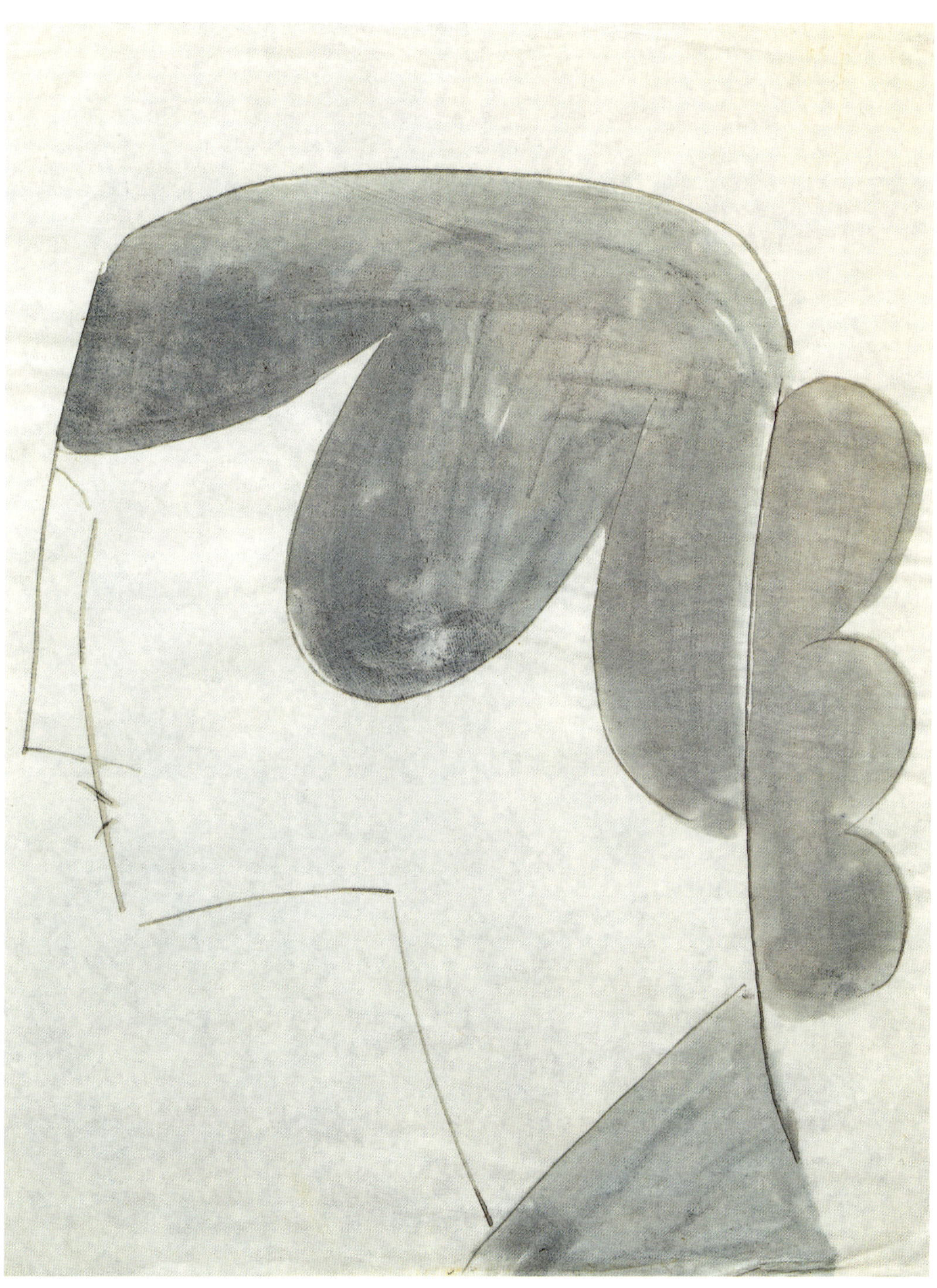

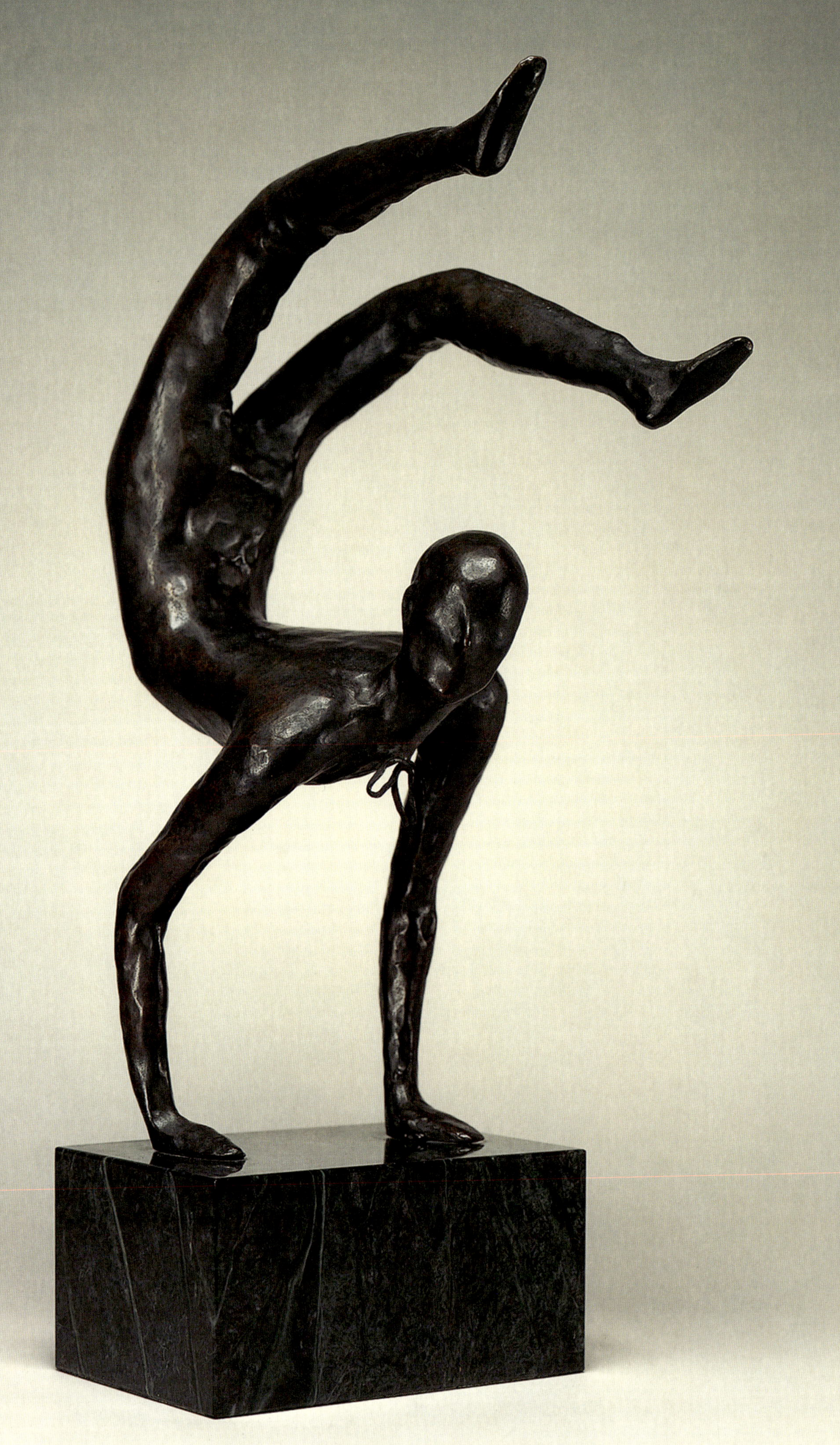

...ular Modernity: Wood and Bronze Genre Figures, ...0—25

...elman had forgone studio work for the first six months of his marriage in ...r to stay in the Hotel Savoy with Viola, whose weakness from a lingering ...ss left her confined to their rooms.[121] To avoid boredom, he bought a hand ...ting press for use in the hotel room and began to make etchings, primarily ...mages he had drawn earlier in Paris. Long intrigued by the idea that repli-...ing works in different sizes and materials produces unique but related ...ces, he saw in printmaking a ready-made way to experiment with slight ...iations in images. By eliminating hatching lines, adding a bun or multiple ...ns to a head of hair, altering the amount of ink on the press, or printing on ...fferently textured papers, he could modify an image each time he pulled a ...oof (FIG. 133). More interested in the permutation of images than in creat-ing flawless prints, Nadelman was content with inferior proofs that were more like "the work of a gifted amateur," as Lincoln Kirstein described them, than the finished artwork of a meticulous craftsman.[122] Not until 1951, six years after his death, were his plates professionally pulled by a master printer.

Renewed contact with his early drawings ignited Nadelman's interest in publishing a new portfolio edition of his *Vers l'unité plastique*. He spent most of 1920 and 1921 contacting publishers—Hamilton Easter Field (the Brooklyn-based arts patron and founder of *The Arts*), Scribner's, *Art in America*—without success.[123] Negotiations with Field went the farthest but fell apart over Field's conviction that more than eleven drawings in the publication would fatigue the public—like "a huge beer stein filled with champagne," as he put it.[124] Finally, in late 1921, E. Weyhe agreed to publish the book, now called *Vers la beauté plastique*, with thirty-two of the fifty-one reproductions that had been included in the earlier Paris edition.[125] Two years later, seventeen drawings were included—as an accompaniment to Nadelman's sculpture—in a monograph on his work pub-lished by William M. Fisher as part of William Murrell's Young Artists Series.[126]

Both *Vers la beauté plastique* and the Murrell monograph included the same short statement by Nadelman, in which he asserted that his drawings had "completely revolutionized the art of our time" by introducing abstract form into art—an aesthetic breakthrough he claimed Cubism had imperfectly imitated. In 1925 he repeated his attack on Cubism in response to a questionnaire

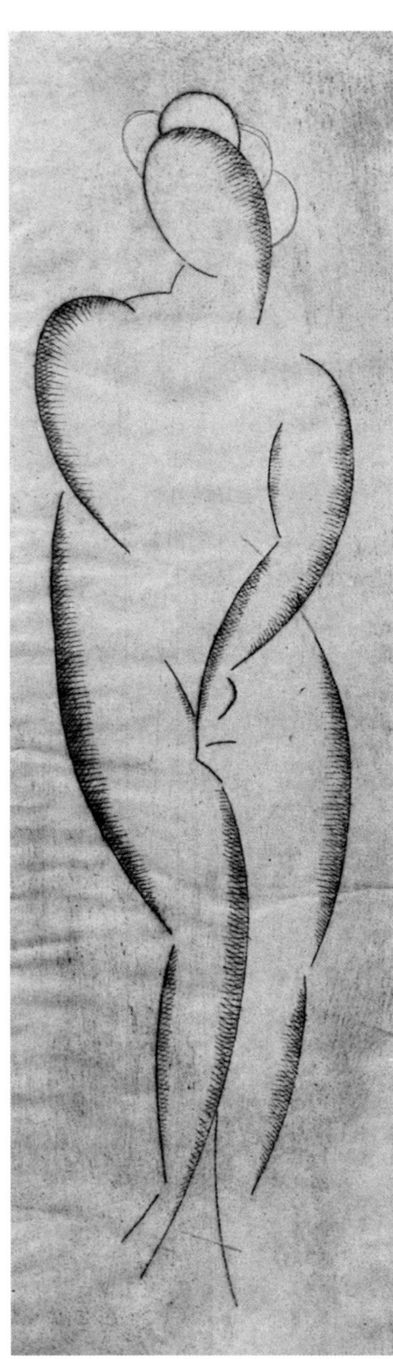

from *The Forum* on whether Cubism was "pure art or pure nonsense," asserting even more emphatically his primacy over Picasso as the originator of abstraction.[127] Even granting that his analytical drawings clarified and prodded Picasso's 1909 Cubism, Nadelman's claim to have invented abstract form was false. Whatever his reason for doing so, his attempt to award himself a more seminal role in the history of modernism than that which he had actually achieved paralleled the efforts by a subset of others within the immigrant community to elevate the stature they had attained in Europe. Coming to America made the reinvention of self and the aggrandizement of one's past possible. Distinguished professionals such as Bruno Bettelheim and artists such as John Graham and Arshile Gorky, for example, fabricated entirely new biographies for themselves upon arriving in the United States.[128]

By the mid-1920s it may have become psychologically important for Nadelman to elevate his earlier stature in Europe since his work, though financially rewarding, was fast being critically eclipsed by that of American sculptors such as Manship and Lachaise. By 1925 it had been almost five years since Nadelman had exhibited. "Small talk agreed," Kirstein reported, "he'd married rich and given up 'creating.'"[129] Indeed, while Joseph Brummer was hosting one-person shows of the work of Lachaise and Brancusi, Nadelman was purchasing Roman glass and antiquities from the prestigious dealer. One way for him to compensate for the perceived shift in his role from artist to collector was to exaggerate his earlier centrality to European modern art—a centrality he may have emphasized all the more out of a lingering belief in the superiority of European over American culture. This may have accounted for his otherwise inexplicable insistence on giving French titles to his works as late as 1925 and on presenting himself in that year as a Polish artist only temporarily making his home in America. In 1922 he named his son Jagiełło (soon changed to Jan), after the Polish royal dynasty. As late as 1944 he would describe Europe as his home: "It is the place where I was born, lived my youth, was inspired to dream my dreams of achievement; and it is the land that was good to me and helped me achieve my first success. It is in a real sense my closest friend."[130]

Nadelman's lingering affection for Europe, combined with his entrance into an American social elite, provided him with a unique vantage point from which to view American culture, specifically the circus and vaudeville, which were considered by many to be the nation's indigenous forms of expression. Fondness for these "lively arts," as they were called, and enthusiastic attendance at performances were widespread among artists, Nadelman included.[131]

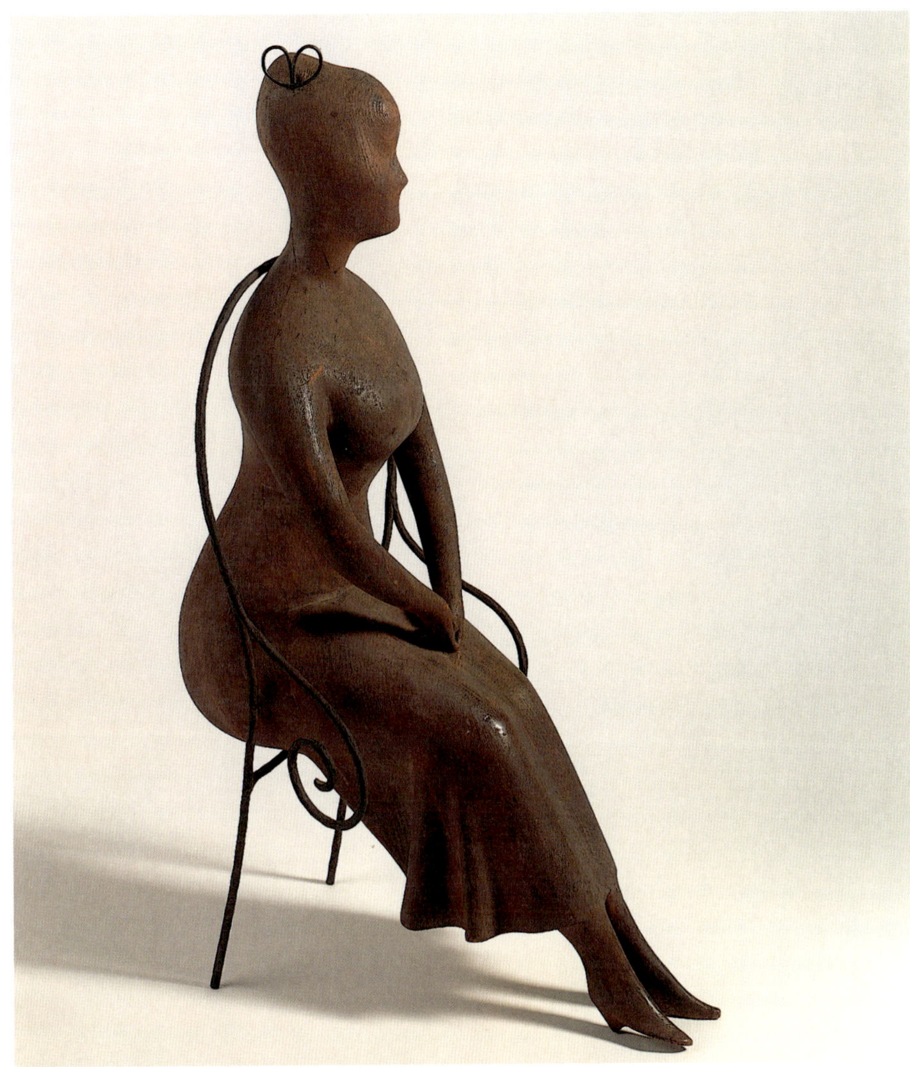

Fig. 134
Elie Nadelman
Seated Woman, c. 1920
Cherry wood and iron, 31 3/4 x 12 3/4 x 18 in.
(80.7 x 32.4 x 45.7 cm)
Addison Gallery of American Art, Phillips
Academy, Andover, Massachusetts;
museum purchase

He had tried in his 1917–19 plaster statuettes to transform the ephemeral and
fleeting gestures of society, vaudeville, and circus performers into idealized,
timeless images. His acknowledgment of the beauty that could be extracted from
everyday life had not, however, blinded him to the foibles of modern society or
the dichotomy of freedom and estrangement inherent in popular entertainment.
His skill in recording the dual aspects of modern leisure and mass culture—its
tawdry vulgarity as well as its infectious and unrestrained pleasure—would increase
with the translation of his plasters into bronze and wood. He had offered to
execute bronze and wood versions of his plasters at the time of his 1919 Knoedler
show, but with no orders forthcoming, it was not until the following November
that he exhibited any: an unpainted bronze cast of *Acrobat* (FIG. 132) and an
unpainted wood figure entitled *Seated Woman* (FIG. 134).

Fig. 135
Elie Nadelman
Dancer, c. 1920–22
Cherry wood, 28 1/4 in. (71.8 cm) high
The Jewish Museum, New York; Gift in memory
of Muriel Rand by her husband William Rand
© The Jewish Museum of New York/Art
Resource, NY

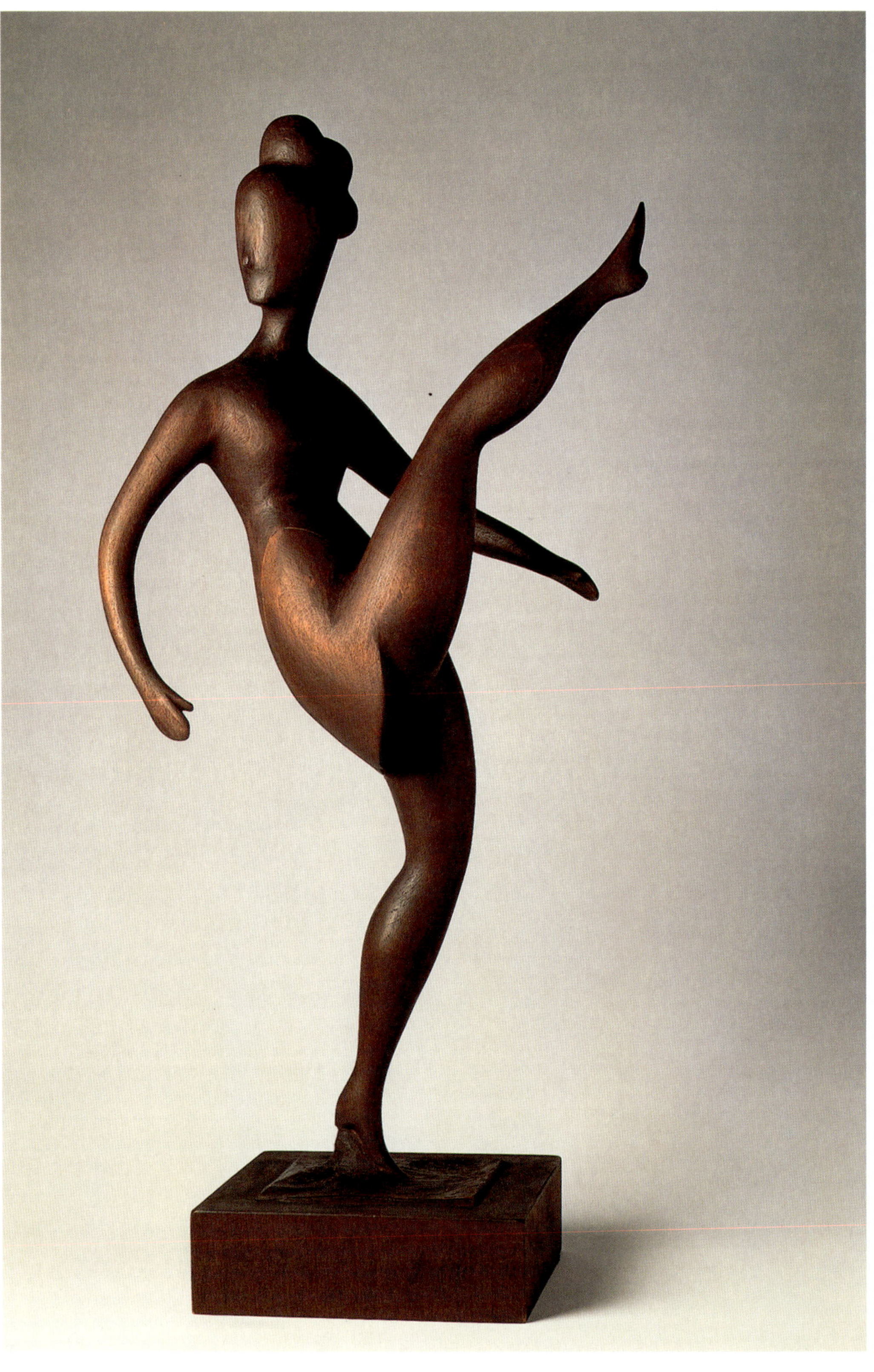

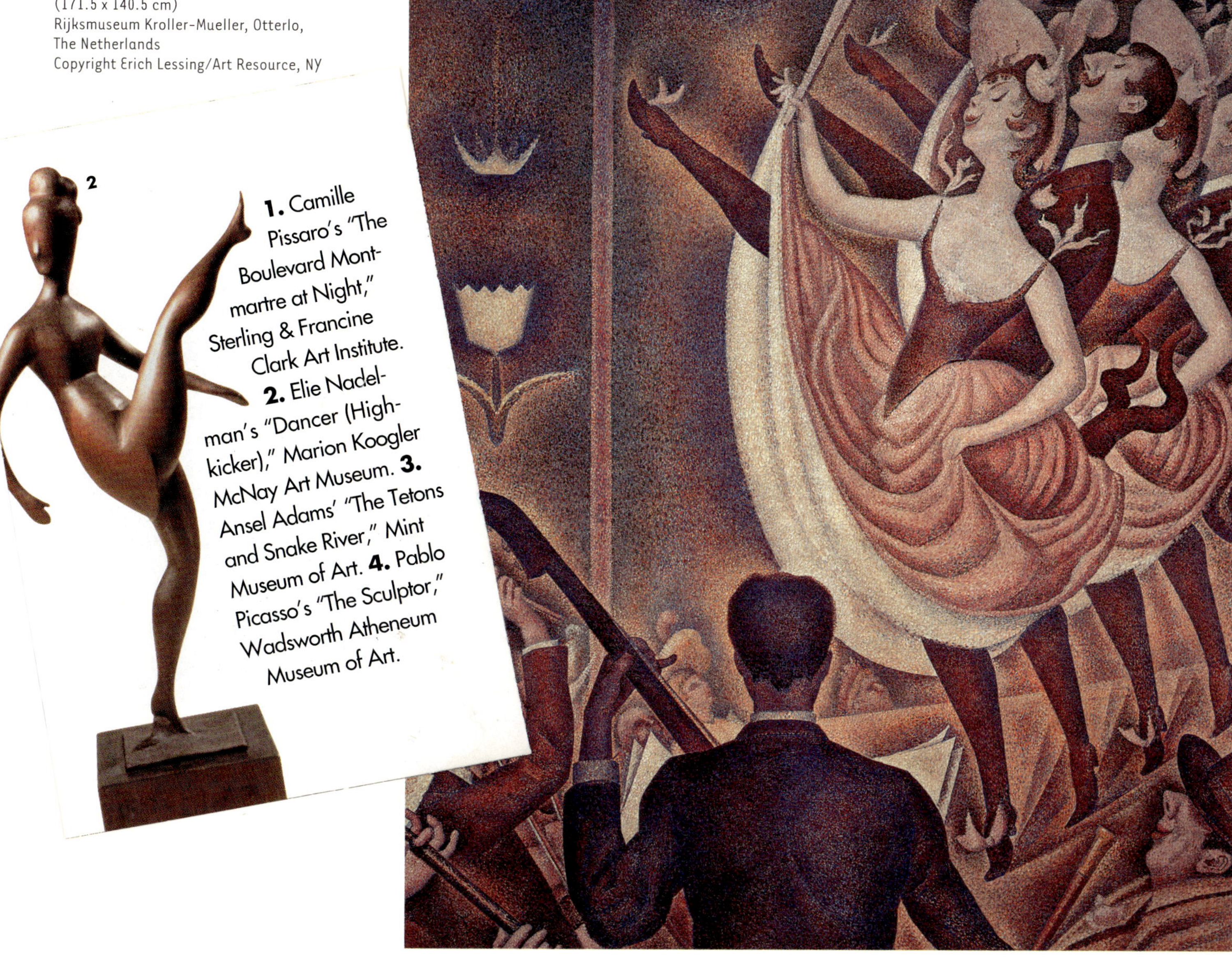

1. Camille Pissaro's "The Boulevard Montmartre at Night," Sterling & Francine Clark Art Institute. **2.** Elie Nadelman's "Dancer (High-kicker)," Marion Koogler McNay Art Museum. **3.** Ansel Adams' "The Tetons and Snake River," Mint Museum of Art. **4.** Pablo Picasso's "The Sculptor," Wadsworth Atheneum Museum of Art.

Fig. 137
Elie Nadelman
Hostess, c. 1920–24
Stained, gessoed, and painted cherry wood,
32 1/2 x 9 1/4 x 13 1/2 in. (82.6 x 23.5 x 34.3 cm)
Hirshhorn Museum and Sculpture Garden,
Smithsonian Institution, Gift of Joseph H.
Hirshhorn, 1966
Photography by Lee Stalsworth

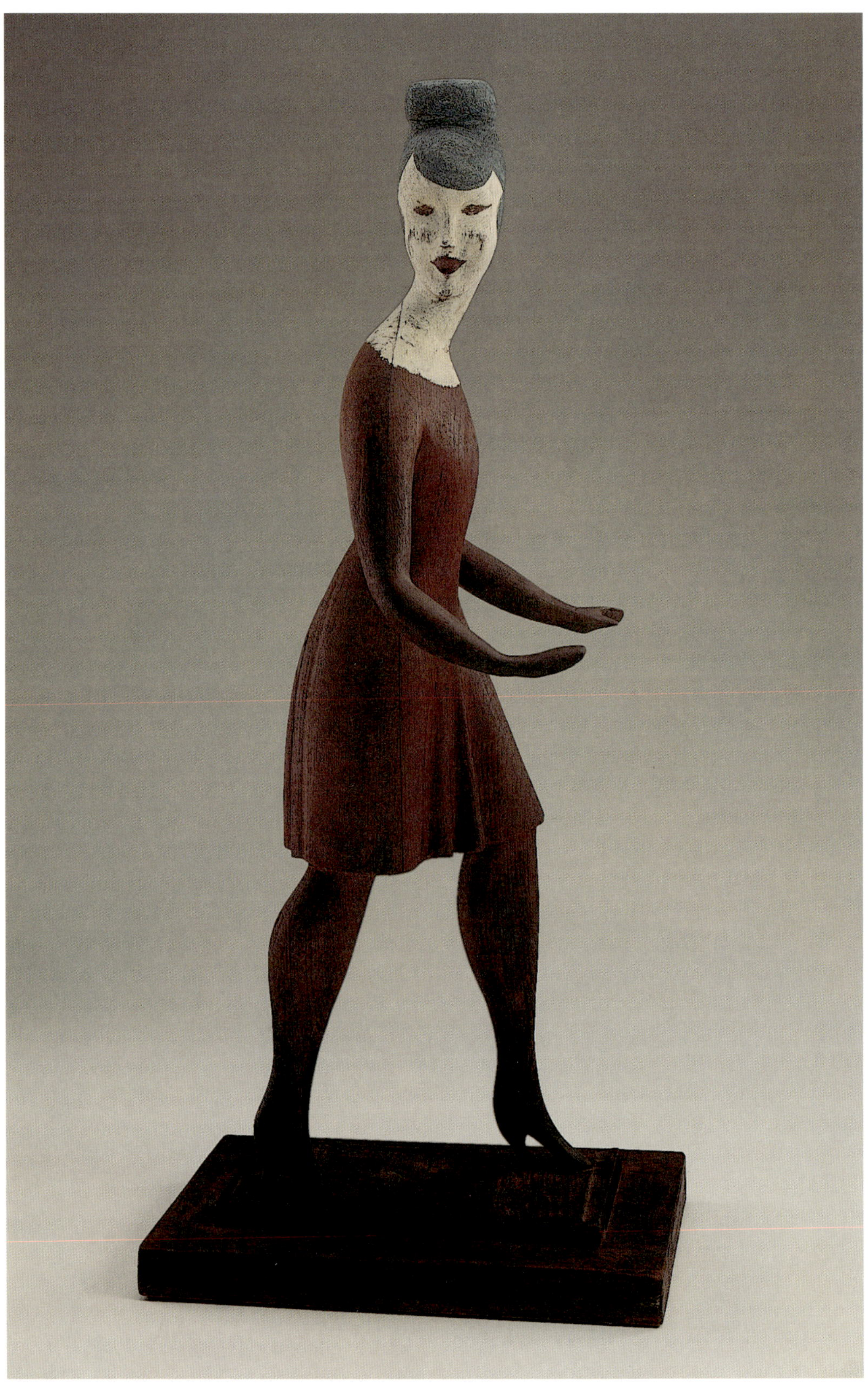

Fig. 138
Elie Nadelman
Chanteuse, c. 1920–24
Stained, gessoed, and painted cherry wood,
36 3/4 in. (93.3 cm) high
Private collection
Photography by Joshua Nefsky

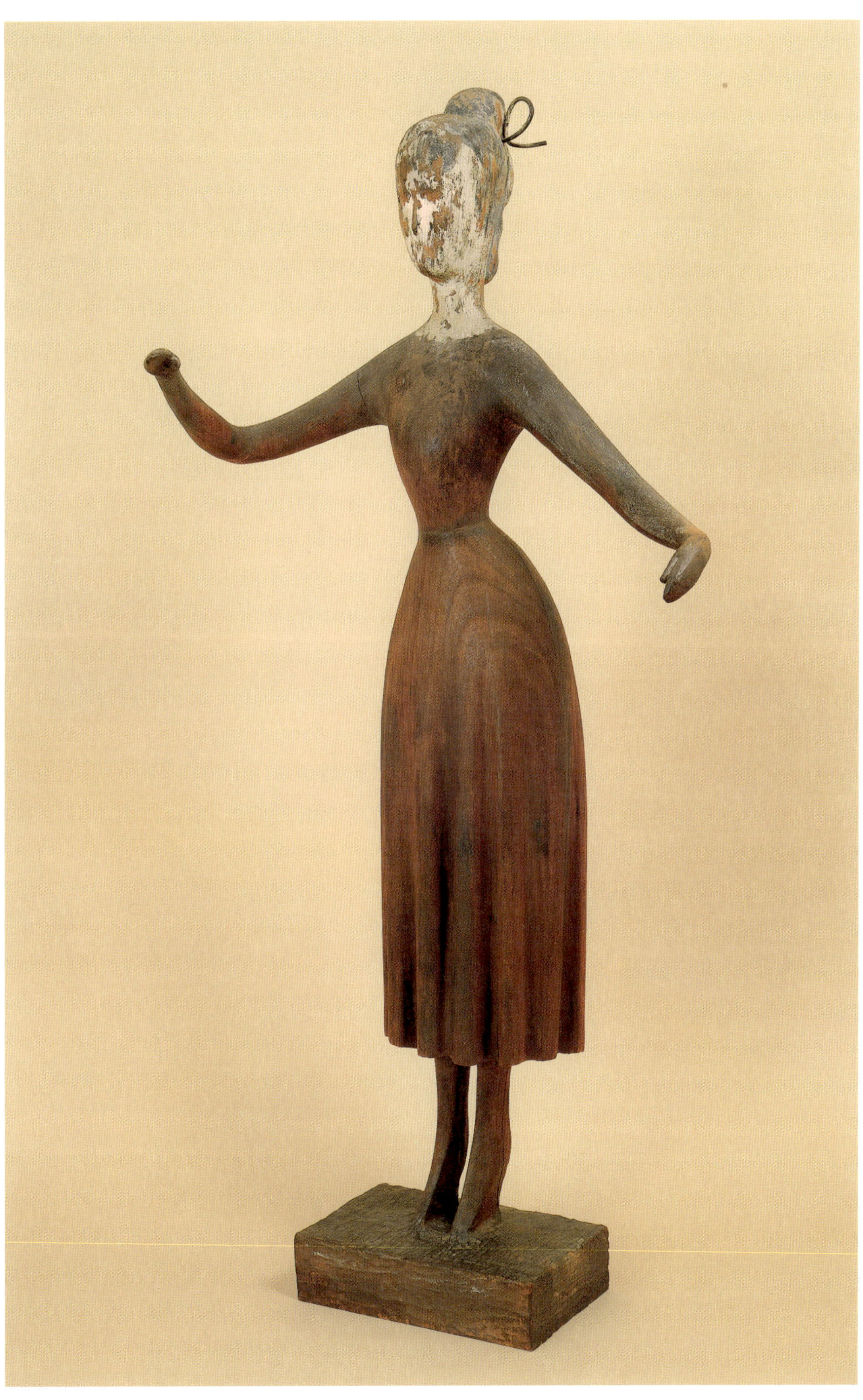

Fig. 139
Elie Nadelman
Dancer (originally titled *High Kicker*)
c. 1920–24
Stained, gessoed, and painted mahogany,
28 1/4 in. (71.8 cm) high
The Wadsworth Atheneum Museum of Art,
Hartford, Connecticut; Gift of James L.
Goodwin and Henry Sage Goodwin from the
Estate of Philip L. Goodwin

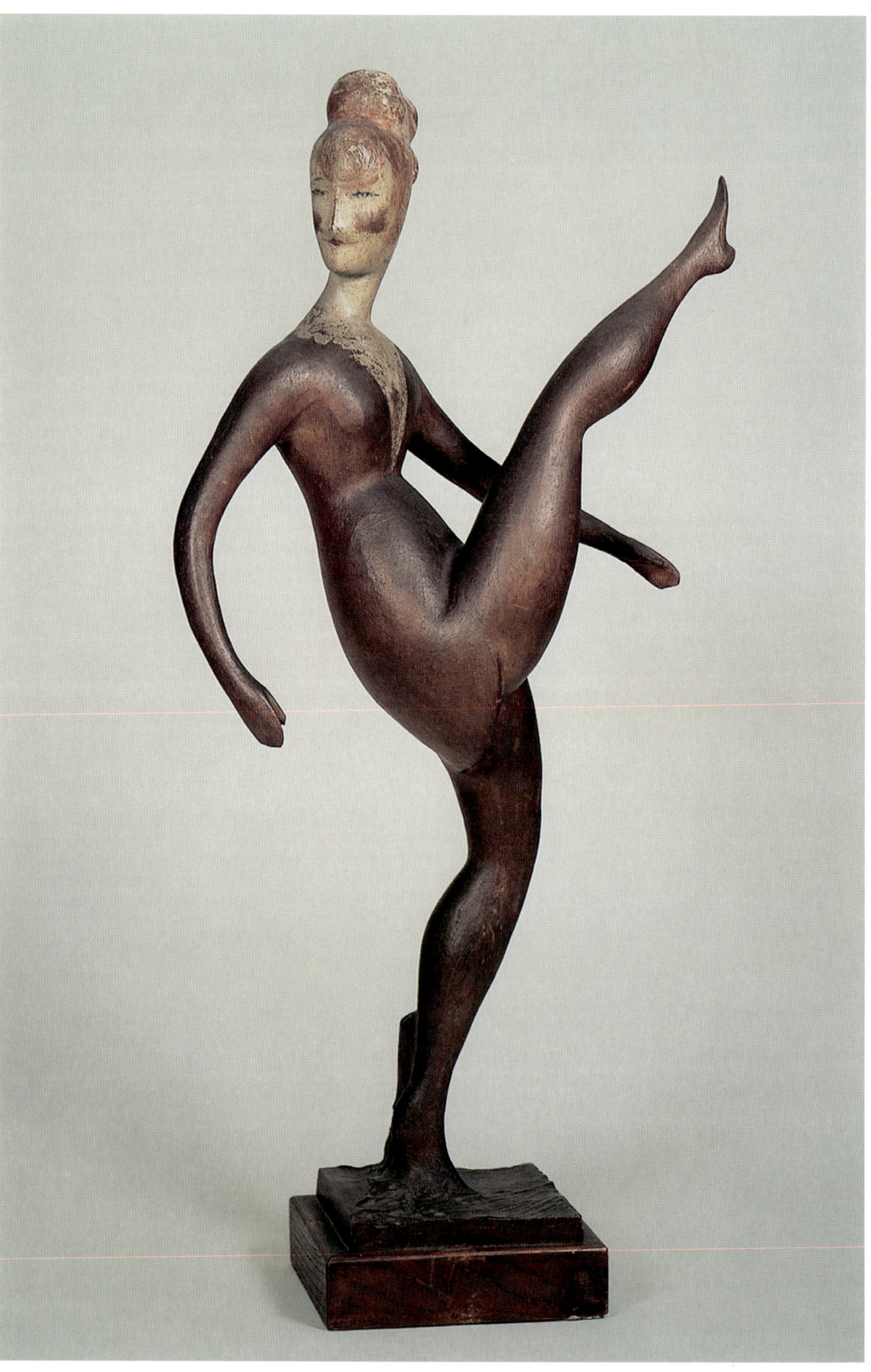

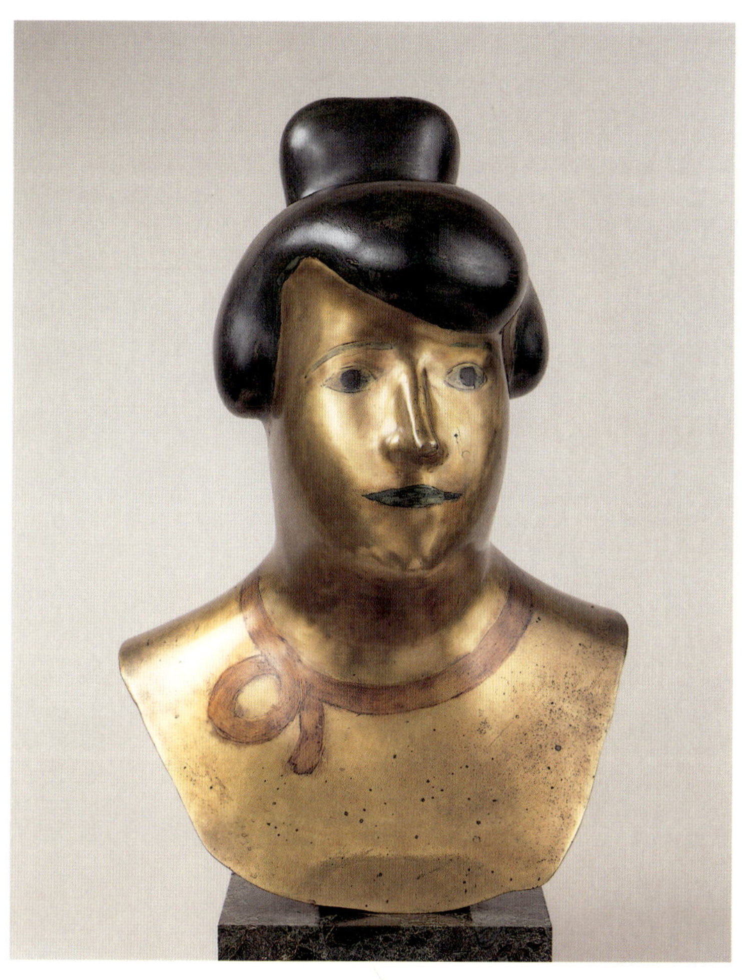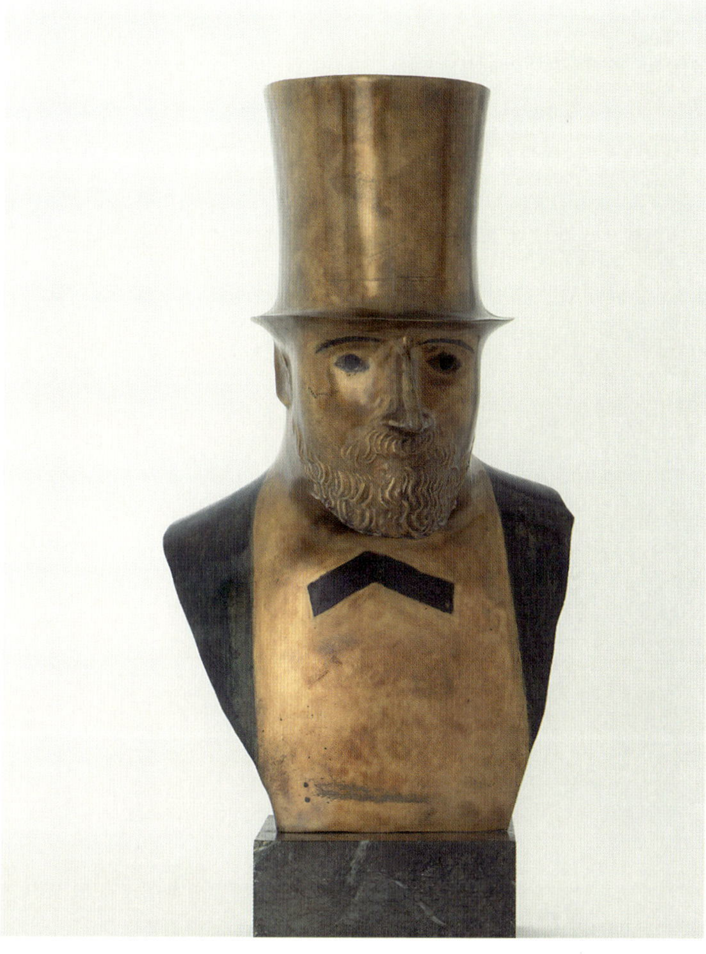

Fig. 140
Elie Nadelman
Bust of a Woman, c. 1920–24
Painted bronze, 23 5/8 in. (60 cm) high
Collection of Mr. Fayez Sarofim

Fig. 141
Elie Nadelman
Man in a Top Hat, c. 1920–24
Painted bronze, 26 x 14 7/8 x 13 1/4 in.
(66 x 37.8 x 33.7 cm)
The Museum of Modern Art, New York;
Abby Aldrich Rockefeller Fund
©The Museum of Modern Art/Licensed by
SCALA/Art Resource, NY

Fig. 142
Elie Nadelman
Circus Performer, c. 1920–24
Stained, gessoed, and painted wood,
33 3/4 in. (85.7 cm) high
Private collection, courtesy Berry-Hill
Galleries, Inc.

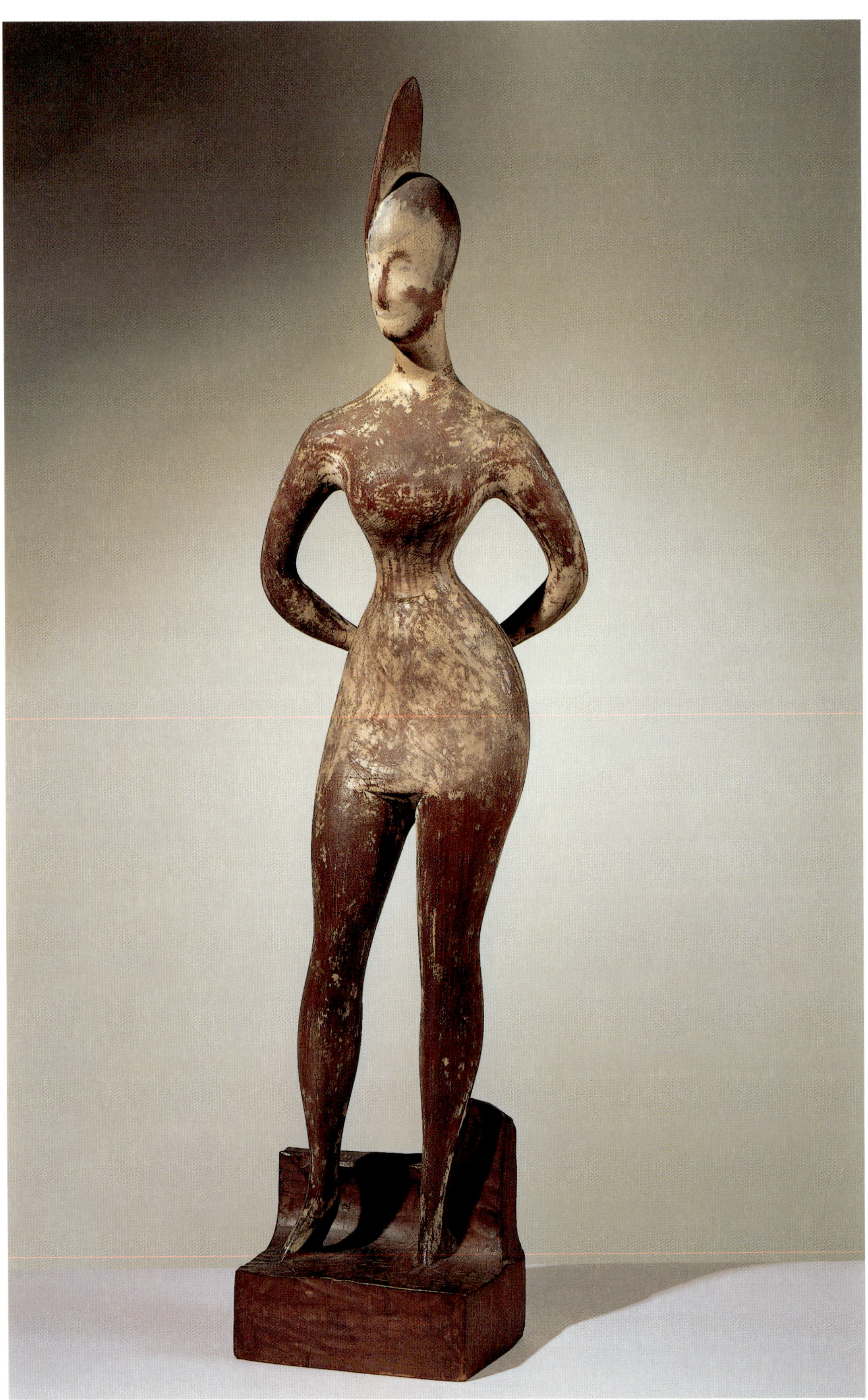

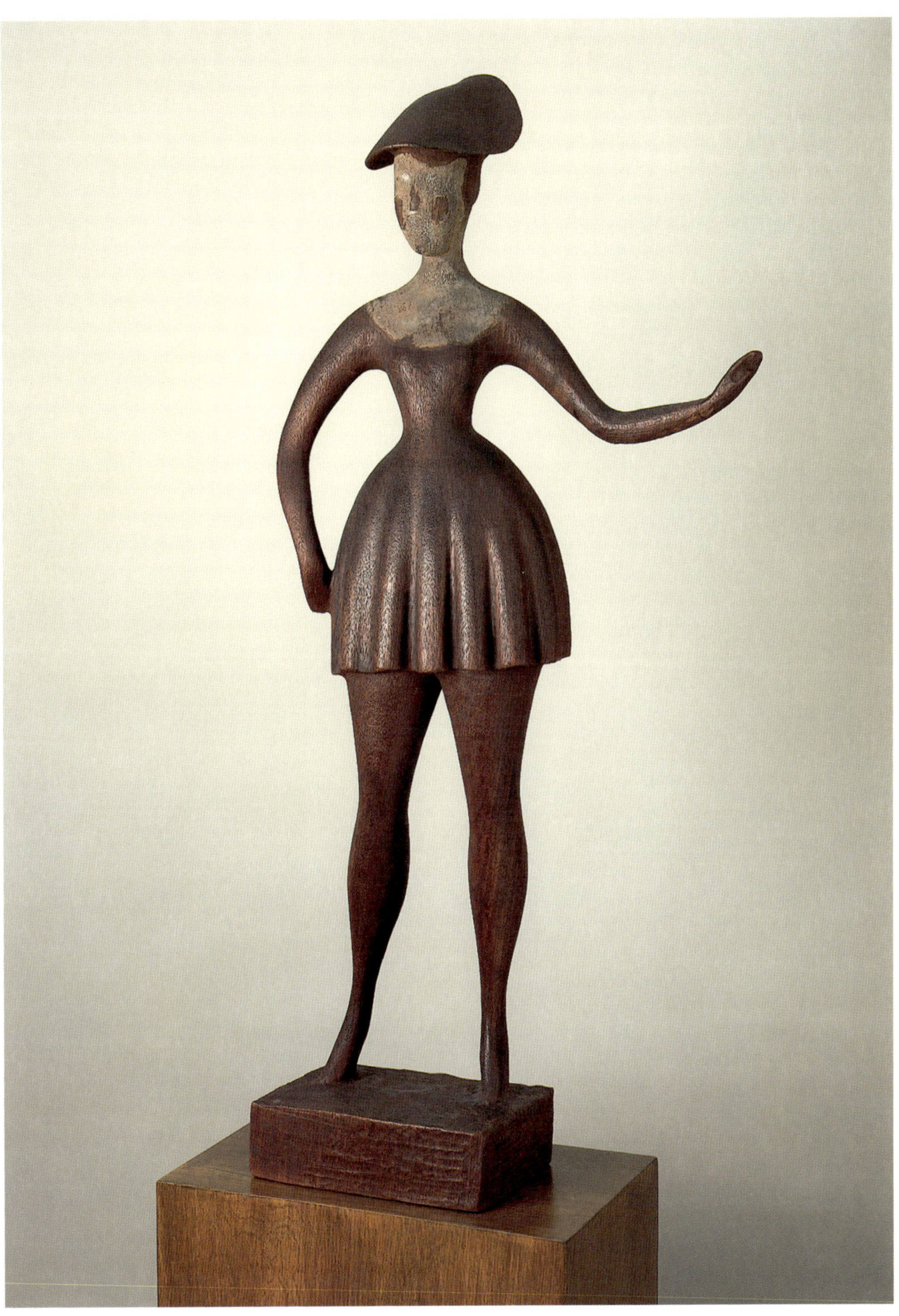

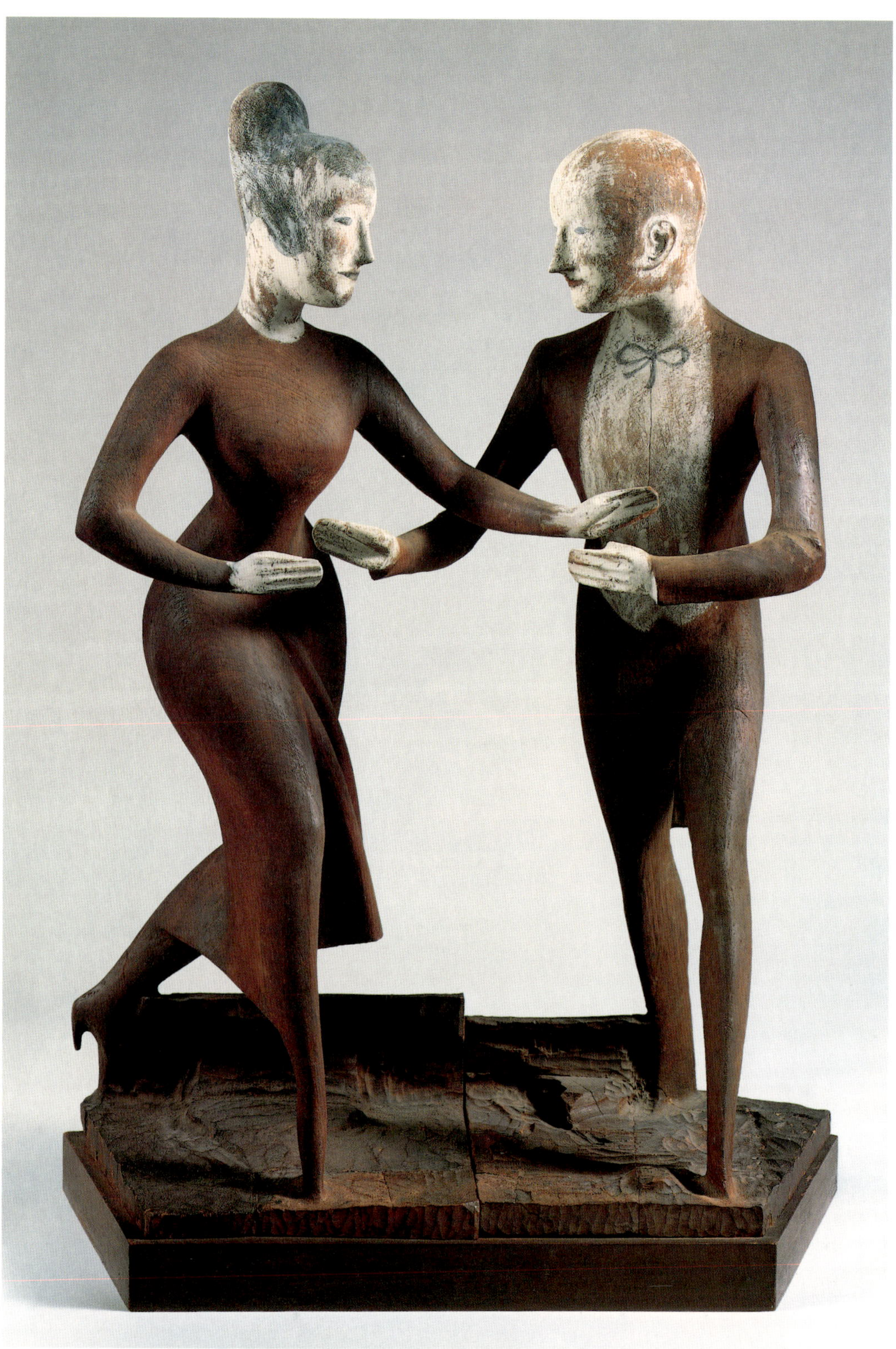

Fig. 144
Elie Nadelman
Tango, c. 1920–24
Stained, gessoed, and painted cherry wood,
3 units, 35 7/8 x 26 x 13 7/8 in.
(91.1 x 66 x 35.2 cm) overall
Whitney Museum of American Art, New York;
Purchase, with funds from the Mr. and Mrs.
Arthur G. Altschul Purchase Fund, the Joan and
Lester Avnet Purchase Fund, the Edgar William
and Bernice Chrysler Garbisch Purchase Fund,
the Mrs. Robert C. Graham Purchase Fund in
honor of John I. H. Baur, the Mrs. Percy Uris
Purchase Fund, and the Henry Schnakenberg
Purchase Fund in honor of Juliana Force
Photography by Jerry L. Thompson

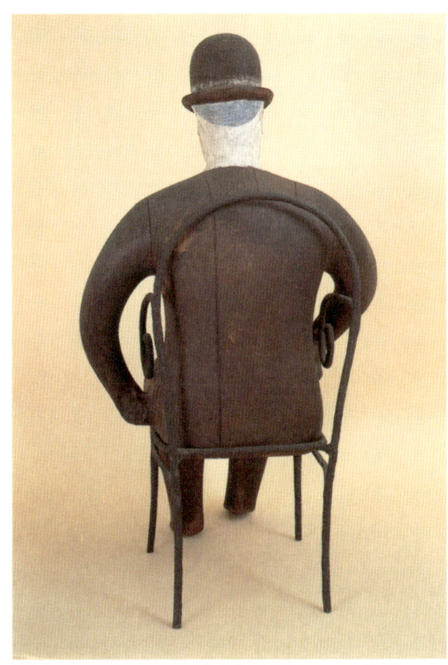

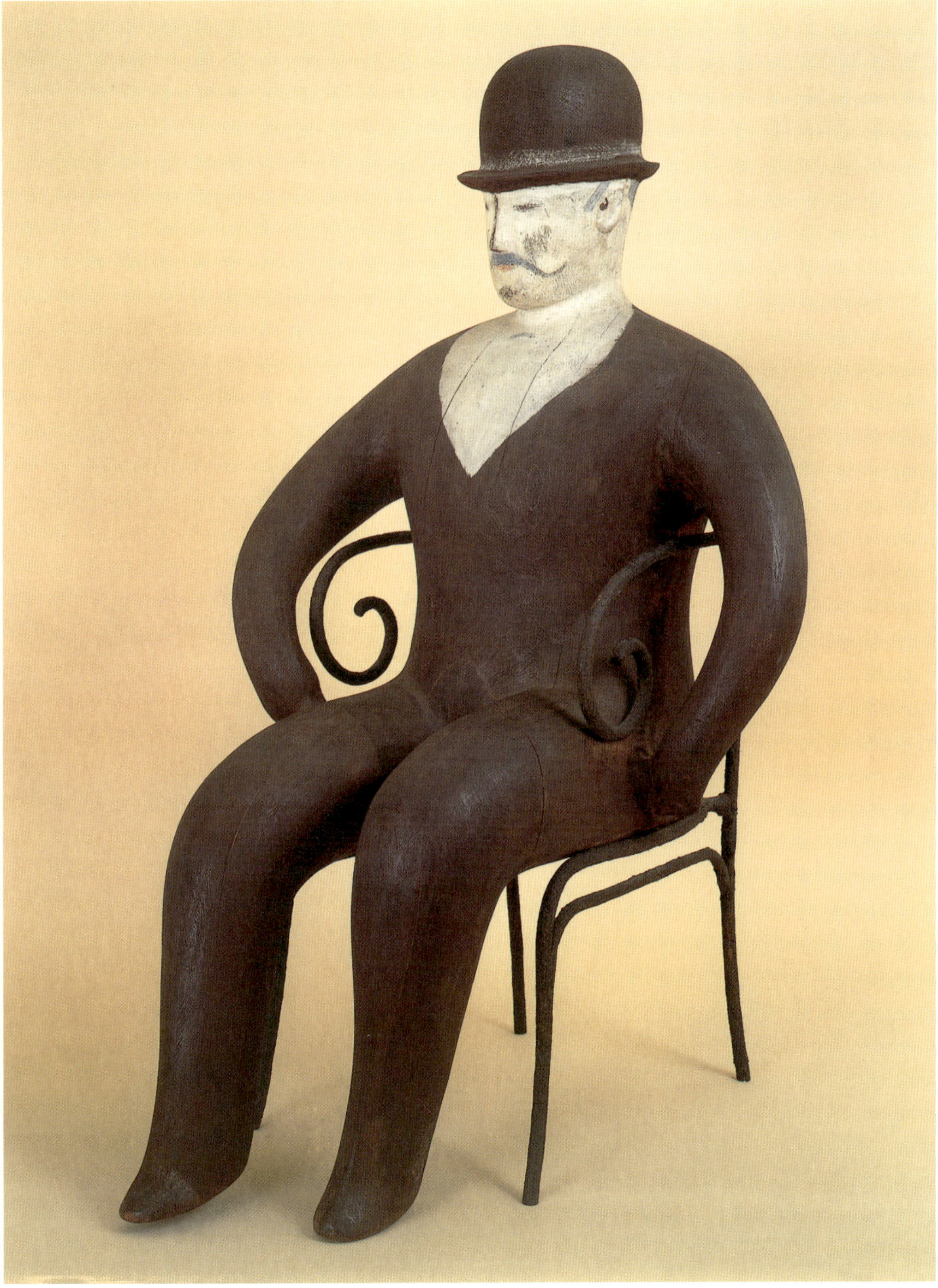

Fig. 145
Elie Nadelman
Host, c. 1920–24 (two views)
Stained, gessoed, and painted wood and iron,
28 1/2 in. (72.4 cm) high
Columbus Museum of Art, Ohio; Museum
purchase, Derby Fund and funds from the
Sessions and Schumacher Collections

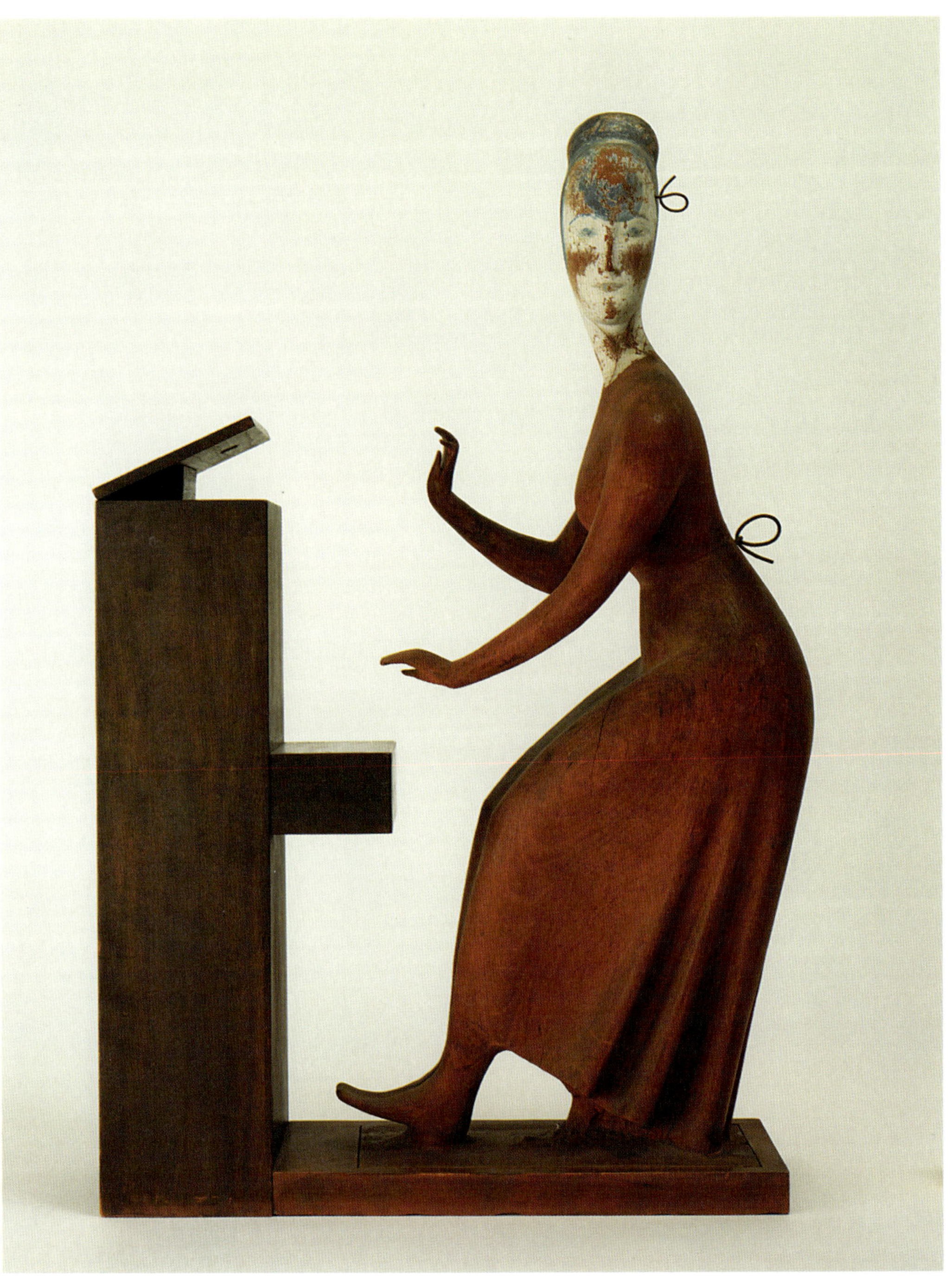

Fig. 147
Elie Nadelman
Orchestra Conductor (Chef d'orchestre),
c. 1920–24
Stained, gessoed, and painted cherry wood,
38 1/2 x 21 1/4 x 11 3/4 in.
(97.8 x 54 x 29.8 cm)
Hirshhorn Museum and Sculpture Garden;
Smithsonian Institution, Gift of Joseph H.
Hirshhorn, 1966
Photography by Lee Stalsworth

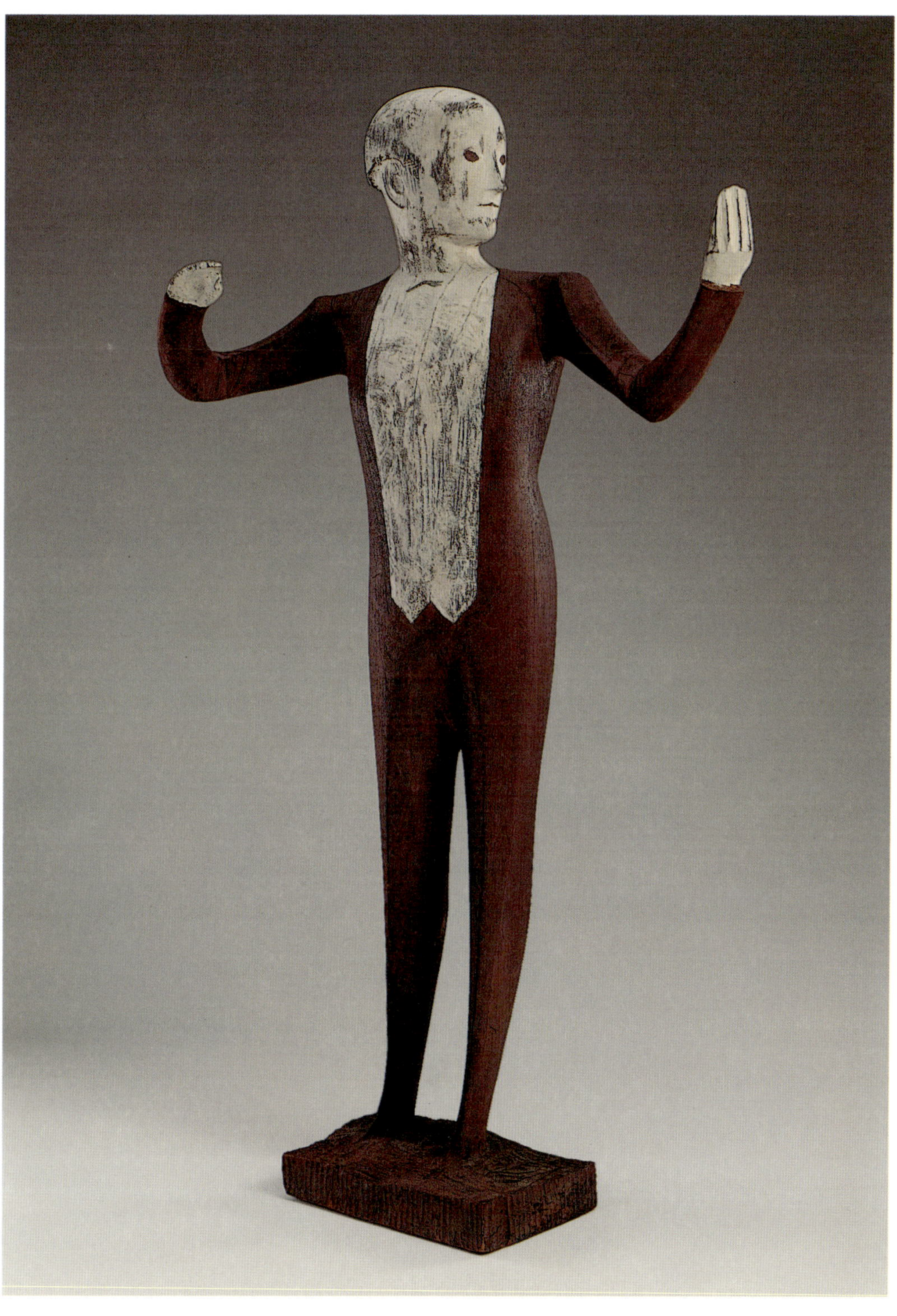

During this period Nadelman had become friendly with Stevenson Scott, co-owner of Scott & Fowles, who eventually persuaded Birnbaum to exhibit Nadelman's work once more at the gallery.[132] In March 1925 Birnbaum unveiled Nadelman's series of bronze and wood genre figures—now all painted (FIGS. 137–147)—along with commissioned portraits (FIGS. 161–162, 164–165) and his classical marble heads and torsos, again all highly polished to a porcelain-like shine (FIGS. 166–171). Birnbaum installed each category of work in a separate room of the gallery, with the portraits set within velvet-hung recesses in one room and the classical marbles arranged along the walls of another, much to the displeasure of Nadelman, who tried to have them moved into the middle of the room. Despite differing opinions among critics at the time about which aspect of the show they preferred, there has been little doubt since then that the elegantly stylized genre figures Nadelman showed in 1925 are among the masterpieces of twentieth-century American sculpture.

Cast in bronze or constructed from pieces of cherry wood glued together and covered with a reddish brown stain—over which Nadelman applied gesso and Prussian blue and red-orange paint to demarcate clothing, hair, and facial features—these pieces radiated an insistent classicism that recalled the lessons he had learned in Munich and Paris. With their solid forms and clearly defined volumes, works such as *Orchestra Conductor* (FIG. 147) resonated with an archaic simplicity and solemn monumentality absent from their more whimsical plaster prototypes. Taking his cue from Hildebrand, Nadelman had let neither expressively modeled surfaces nor descriptive details dilute the perceptual clarity and immediacy of his figures' architecture. He had reduced shape to elemental, readily grasped geometries, but unlike artists such as Maillol and Brancusi, whose work conveyed a sense of static repose, Nadelman had emphasized gesture by freezing actions at their most iconic, expressive point. As a result, the gestures of his figures became as hieratic and eternal as those immortalized by the sculptor of Munich's Aegina temple pediments and by the painter Giotto, whose work Nadelman had praised to Leo Stein in 1909.[133]

As Nadelman began these aesthetic excursions, he may have had Georges Seurat's work in mind, especially the French artist's paintings *Le cirque* and *Le chahut* (FIG. 136), whose depiction of the provocative and acrobatic dance popular in Parisian cafés at the turn of the century provided a compelling precedent for his own *Dancer* (FIG. 135). Nadelman had seen

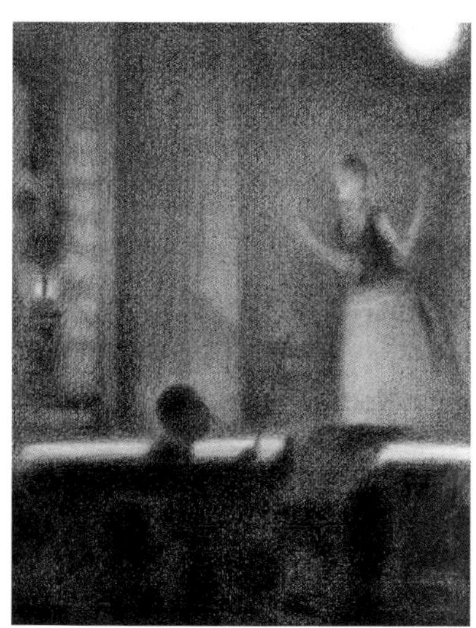

Seurat's retrospective exhibitions in Paris in 1905 at the Salon des Indépendants and in 1908–09 at the Galerie Bernheim-Jeune. The French Neoimpressionist's paintings had been particularly lauded by the artists and critics in Nadelman's Polish circle, and photographs of his works—including *Le cirque* and *Le chahut*—had been made and offered for sale by Nadelman's dealer Druet. Nadelman shared with Seurat a passion for formal simplicity and elemental gestures. Like Seurat, he depicted immobile figures with stiff, fixed postures whose ritualized solemnity contrasted markedly with the relaxed, joyous abandon of the figures in works by American urban realists such as John Sloan and William Glackens. Both Seurat and Nadelman described the spirited, carefree grace offered by commercialized popular entertainment, but both also infused their art with a wit that recognized the alienation engendered by this world of artifice and contrived pleasure.

The formal solemnity with which Nadelman portrayed the performers and entertainers of modern American life was unique in sculpture; his use of painted and unpainted wood was not. Wood had long been accepted as a fine art material. American sculptor Robert Laurent used it exclusively during this period, and Nadelman had already rendered several classical works from his Paris period in the medium. By 1920 his translation into wood of his plaster statuettes seemed so apt that critic McBride took credit in print for having earlier suggested it to him.[134] Likewise, Nadelman's application of paint to his wood figures, far from being idiosyncratic, was a natural extension of the painted wood altarpieces of Veit Stoss and Tilman Riemenschneider that had so powerfully impressed him in Kraków and Munich. Nadelman emulated the mottled quality of these fifteenth-century Gothic carvings by diluting his gesso and rubbing it away to reveal portions of the reddish brown understain.

Unusual, modulated surfaces had long intrigued Nadelman. Before 1913 he had radically variegated the patina on certain of his bronze works and was already contrasting smooth and rough marble in his portraits; by 1917 he had developed a technique for mottling bronze and was playing with the juxtaposition of dappled and flecked surface patterns by placing these mottled bronze pieces on marbled onyx bases (FIGS. 97–100). As he began his wood figures, he may also have subliminally called upon memories of the shimmering, uneven surfaces of Seurat's Conté crayon drawings (FIG. 148), which had been featured in a 1914 article in *L'art décoratif* in which his own work had appeared.

Sadly, many of Nadelman's wood statues were left unfinished or were damaged, and little is known for certain about exactly how he wanted his painted and gessoed surfaces to appear. He had hired specialized wood craftsmen to construct two or three duplicates of each of his wood figures, just as he had hired marble and bronze specialists to make his work in those materials. Following his practice of creating families of related but varied images, he intended to differentiate each wood piece through his treatment of its surface. During his lifetime only one piece sold: *High Kicker* (FIG. 139), to Stevenson Scott. Storage of the remaining figures in the basement and attic of the Riverdale house under less-than-ideal conditions may have damaged their surfaces. With few extant period photographs of painted wood figures, it is difficult to determine with accuracy how they were originally painted.[135] Yet because of Nadelman's essential classicism, it hardly matters. He had not intended to represent specific individuals, but rather the ideas or types of which individuals were tokens. By reducing form to tubular, simplified volumes, he had gained for his painted and unpainted genre sculptures access to the realm of the timeless and eternal and, in the process, presented contemporary life with the epic authority of the classical past.

Fig. 149
Élie Nadelman
Tango, c. 1917–19
Ink and wash on paper, 9 1/2 x 6 3/8 in.
(24.1 x 16.2 cm)
The Metropolitan Museum of Art, New York;
Gift of Lincoln Kirstein, 1965
©2002 The Metropolitan Museum of Art

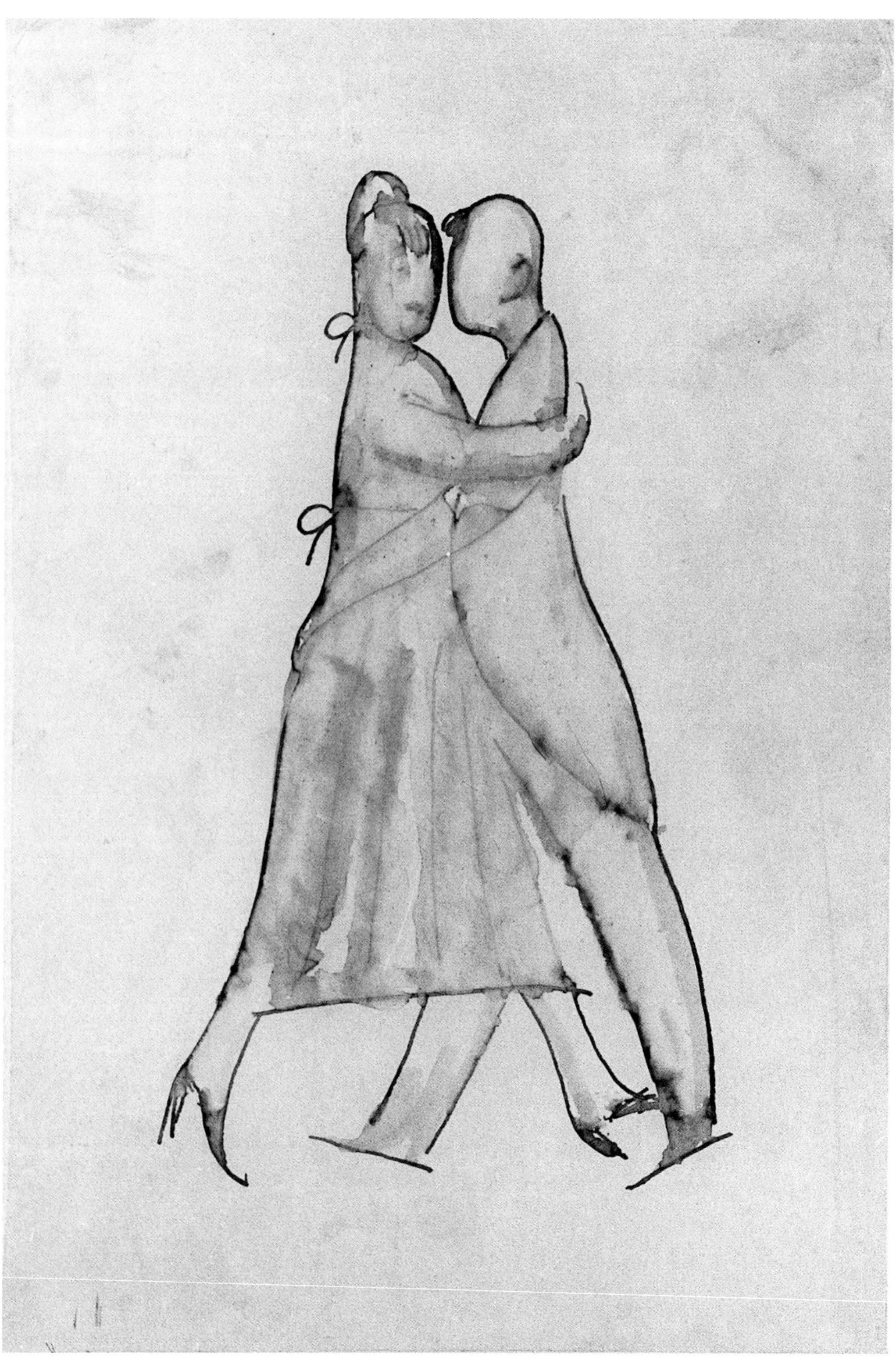

Fig. 150
Elie Nadelman
Two Figures, c. 1920
Ink on paper, 10 1/4 x 8 3/4 in. (26 x 22.2 cm)
Private collection, New York
Photography by Jerry L. Thompson

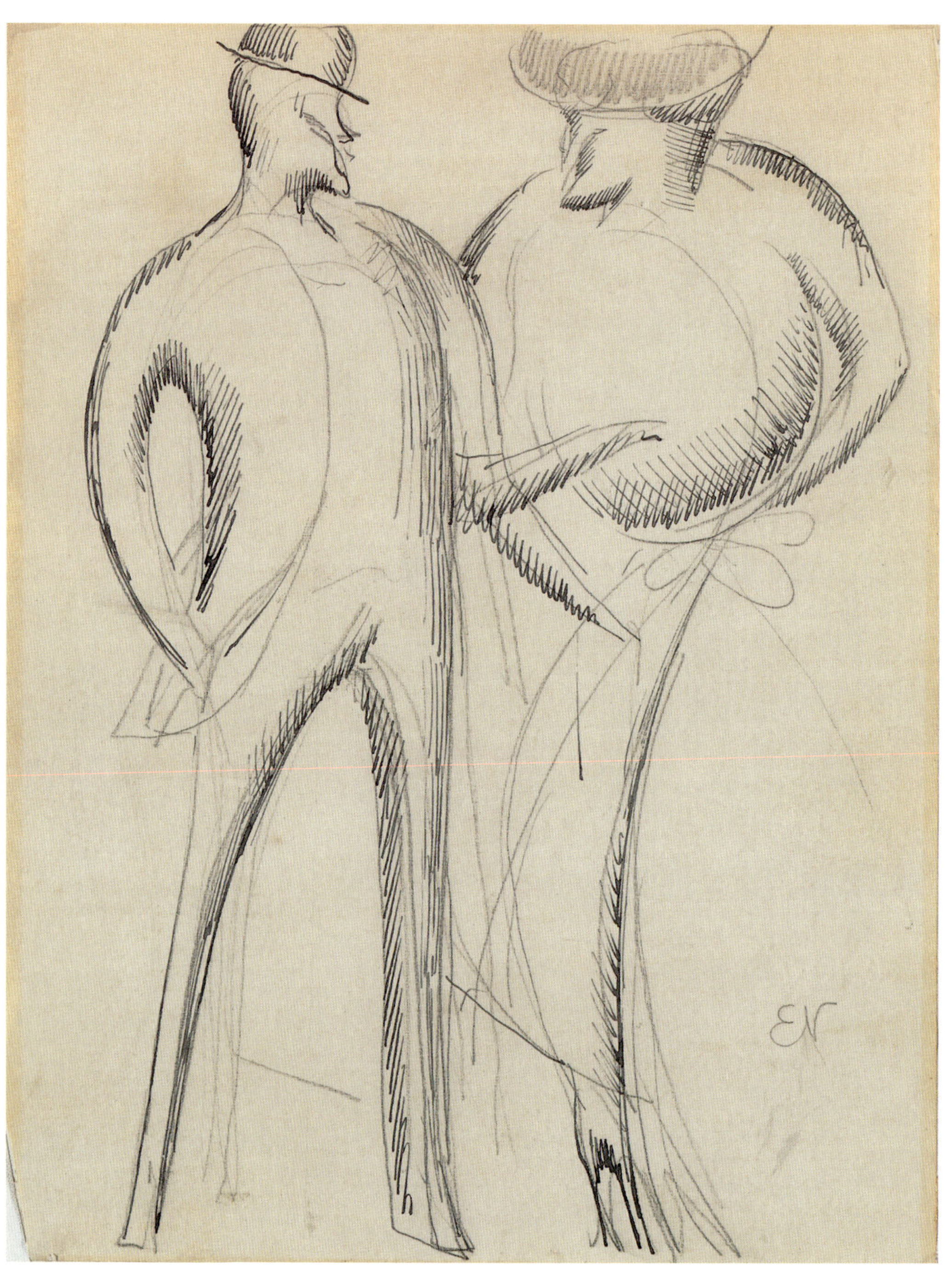

Fig. 151
Elie Nadelman
Untitled (Man on a Horse), c. 1915
Ink wash on paper, 7 1/2 x 8 1/4 in.
(19.1 x 21 cm)
Slong & Midas Properties, Inc., New York

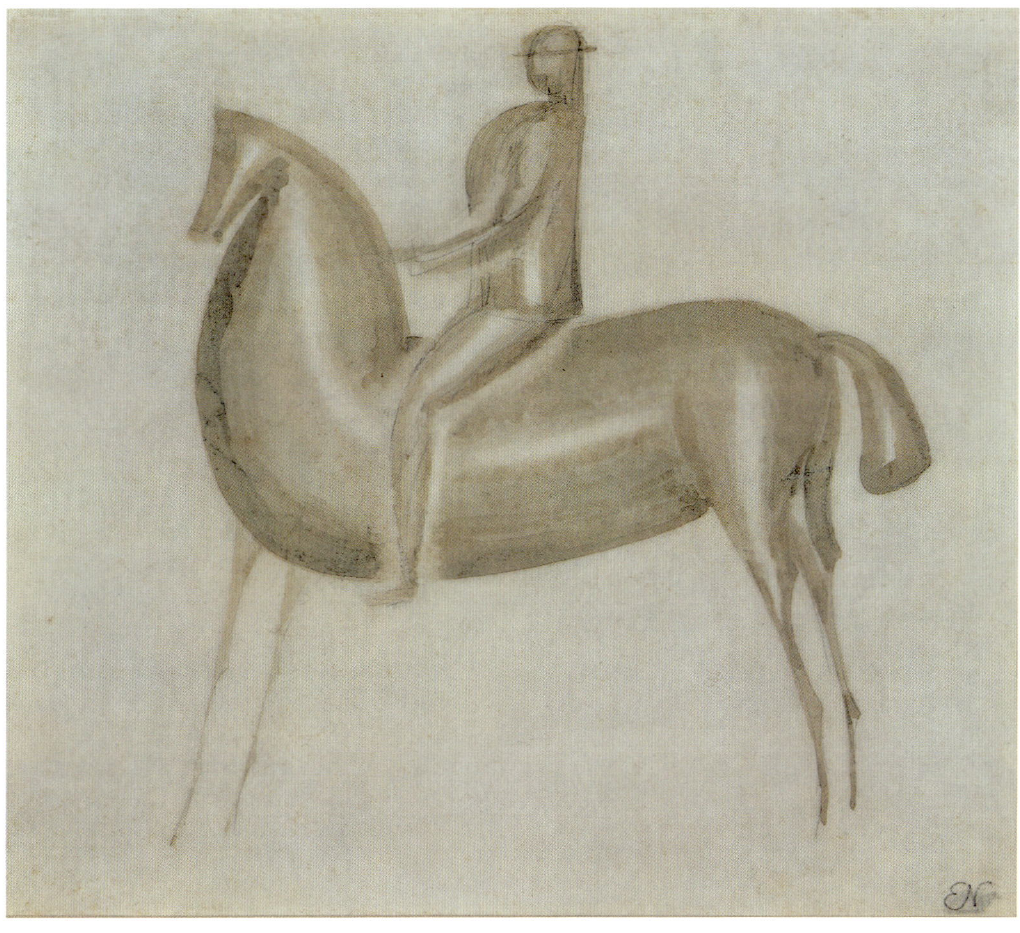

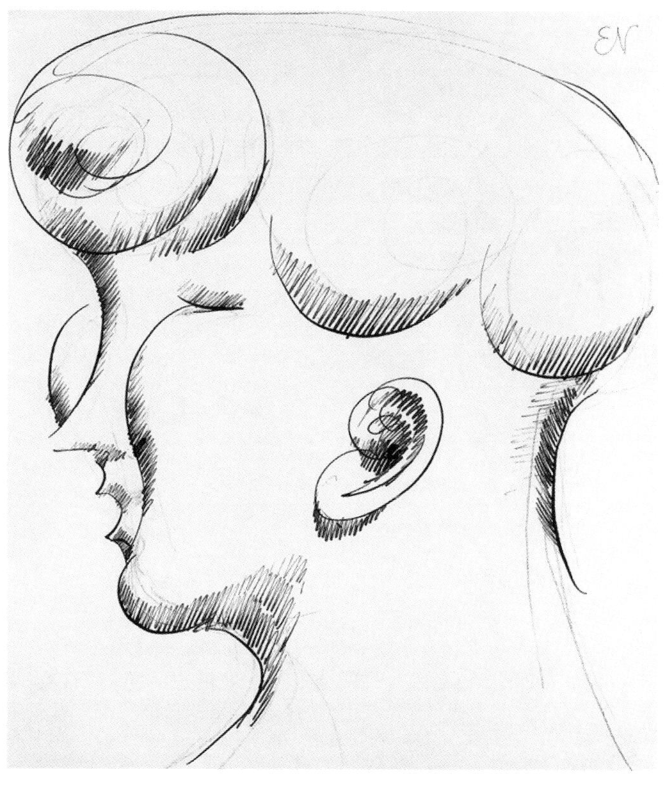

Fig. 152
Elie Nadelman
Woman's Head in Profile, Facing Left,
c. 1920–25
Ink over pencil on wove paper,
9 1/16 x 7 13/16 in. (23 x 19.8 cm)
National Gallery of Art, Washington, D.C.;
Gift of David E. Rust
©2002 Board of Trustees, National Gallery
of Art, Washington

Fig. 153
Elie Nadelman
Head of a Woman, c. 1920
Watercolor on paper, 12 x 7 1/2 in.
(30.5 x 19.1 cm)
Collection of Catherine and Michael Podell

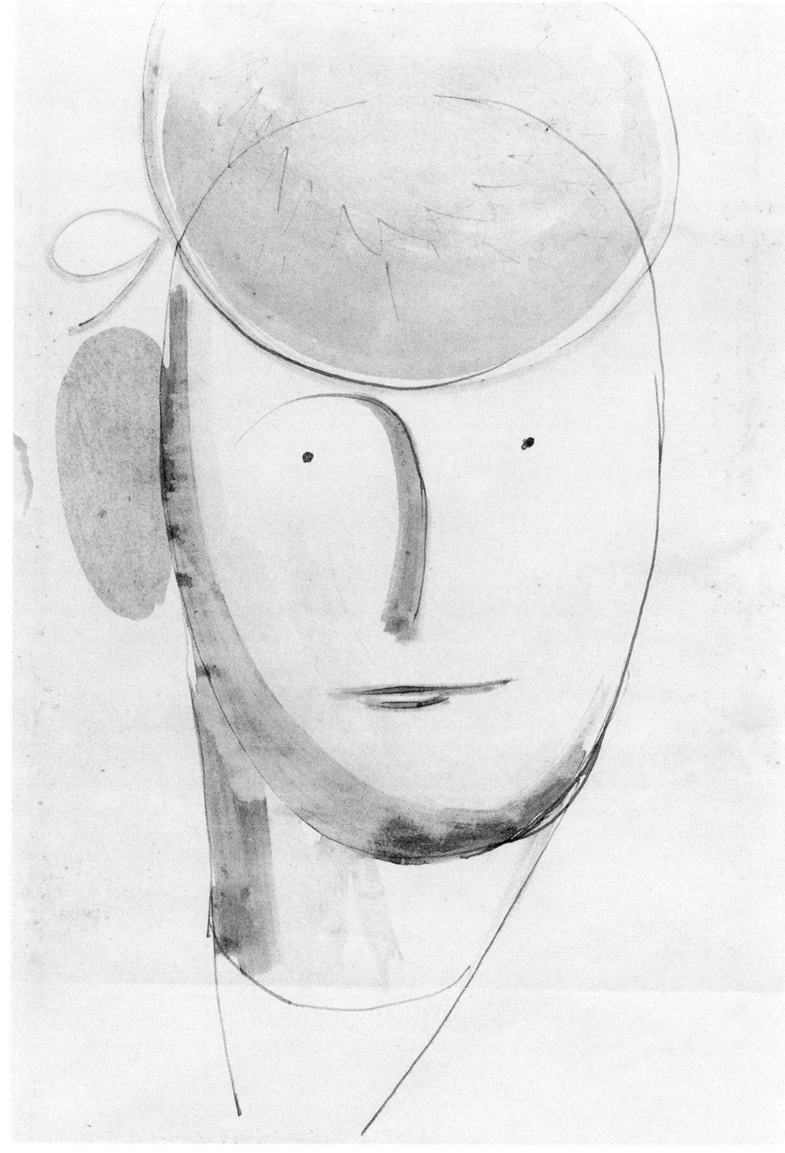

Fig. 154
Elie Nadelman
Head of a Woman with Hat, c. 1920–25
Pencil on tracing vellum, 16 1/2 x 10 3/4 in.
(41.9 x 27.3 cm)
Whitney Museum of American Art, New York;
Purchase, with funds from the Lily Auchincloss
Foundation, Vivian Horan, The List Purchase
Fund, the Neysa McMein Purchase Award, Mr.
and Mrs. William A. Marsteller, the Richard and
Dorothy Rodgers Fund, and the Drawing
Committee
Photography by Jerry L. Thompson

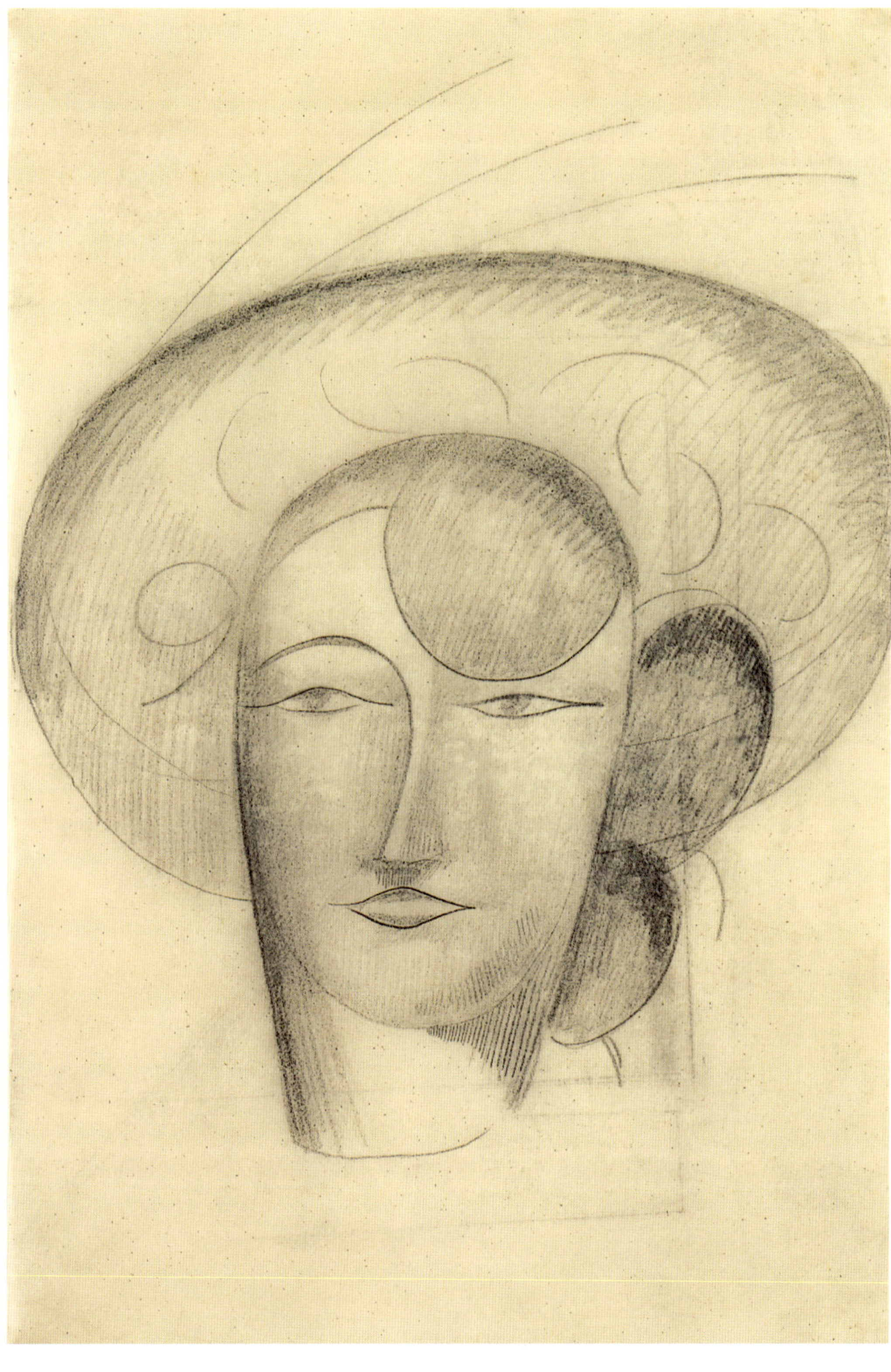

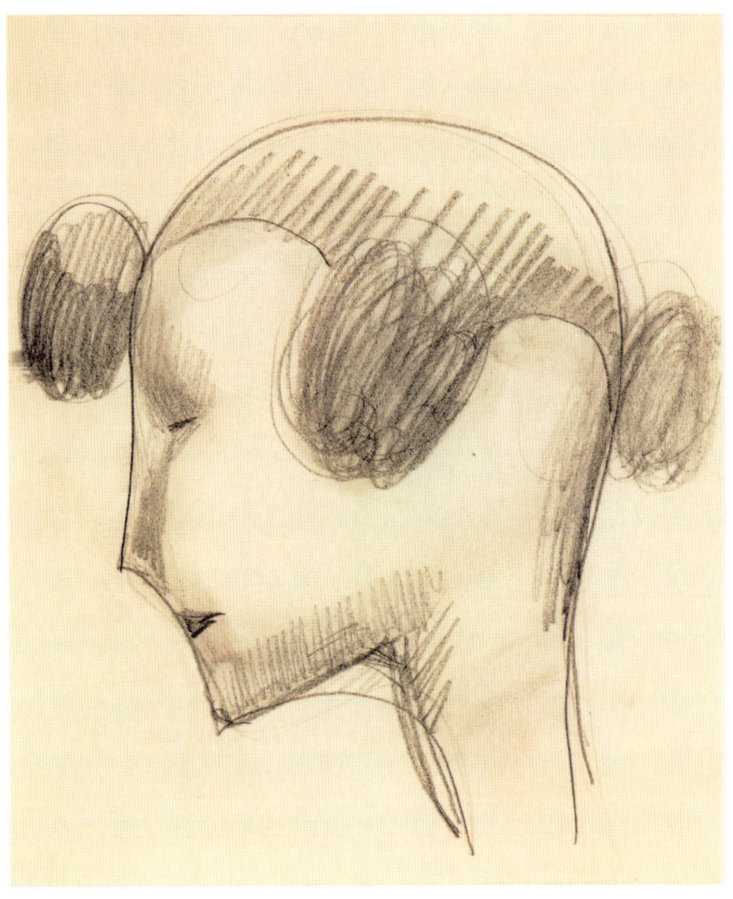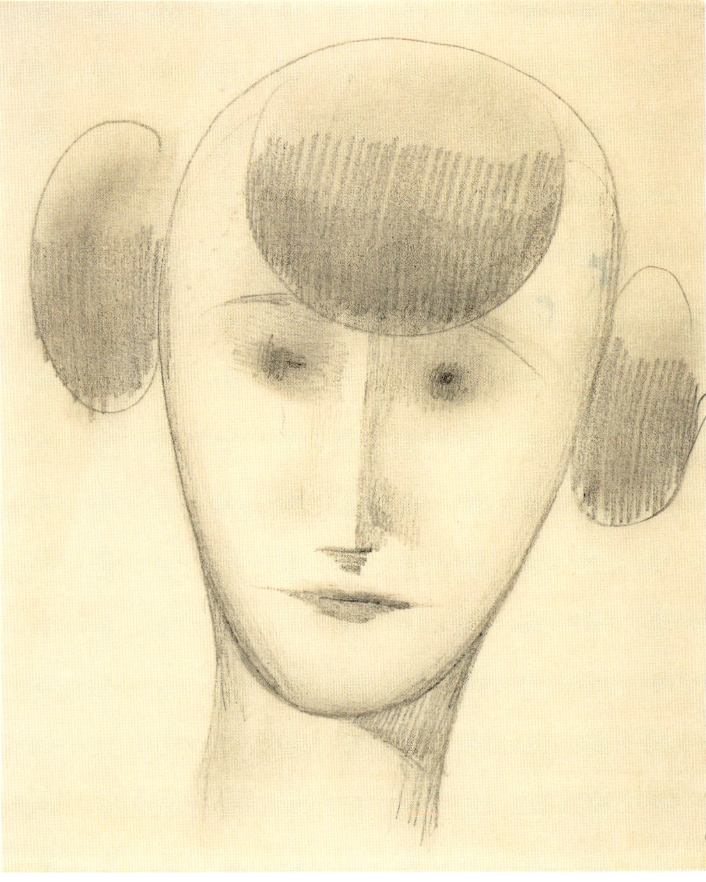

Fig. 155
Elie Nadelman
Female Head in Profile, c. 1920
Pencil on paper, 10 x 8 in. (25.4 x 20.3 cm)
Estate of Elie Nadelman, courtesy
Salander-O'Reilly Galleries, New York
Photography by Paul Waldman

Fig. 156
Elie Nadelman
Head of a Woman, c. 1920
Pencil on paper, 9 3/4 x 7 7/8 in.
(24.8 x 20 cm)
Estate of Elie Nadelman, courtesy
Salander-O'Reilly Galleries, New York
Photography by Paul Waldman

Fig. 157
Elie Nadelman
Profile of a Man's Head, c. 1915—20
Pencil and sepia ink wash on paper,
10 x 8 in. (25.4 x 20.3 cm)
Hirshhorn Museum and Sculpture Garden,
Smithsonian Institution, Gift of Joseph H.
Hirshhorn, 1966
Photography by Lee Stalsworth

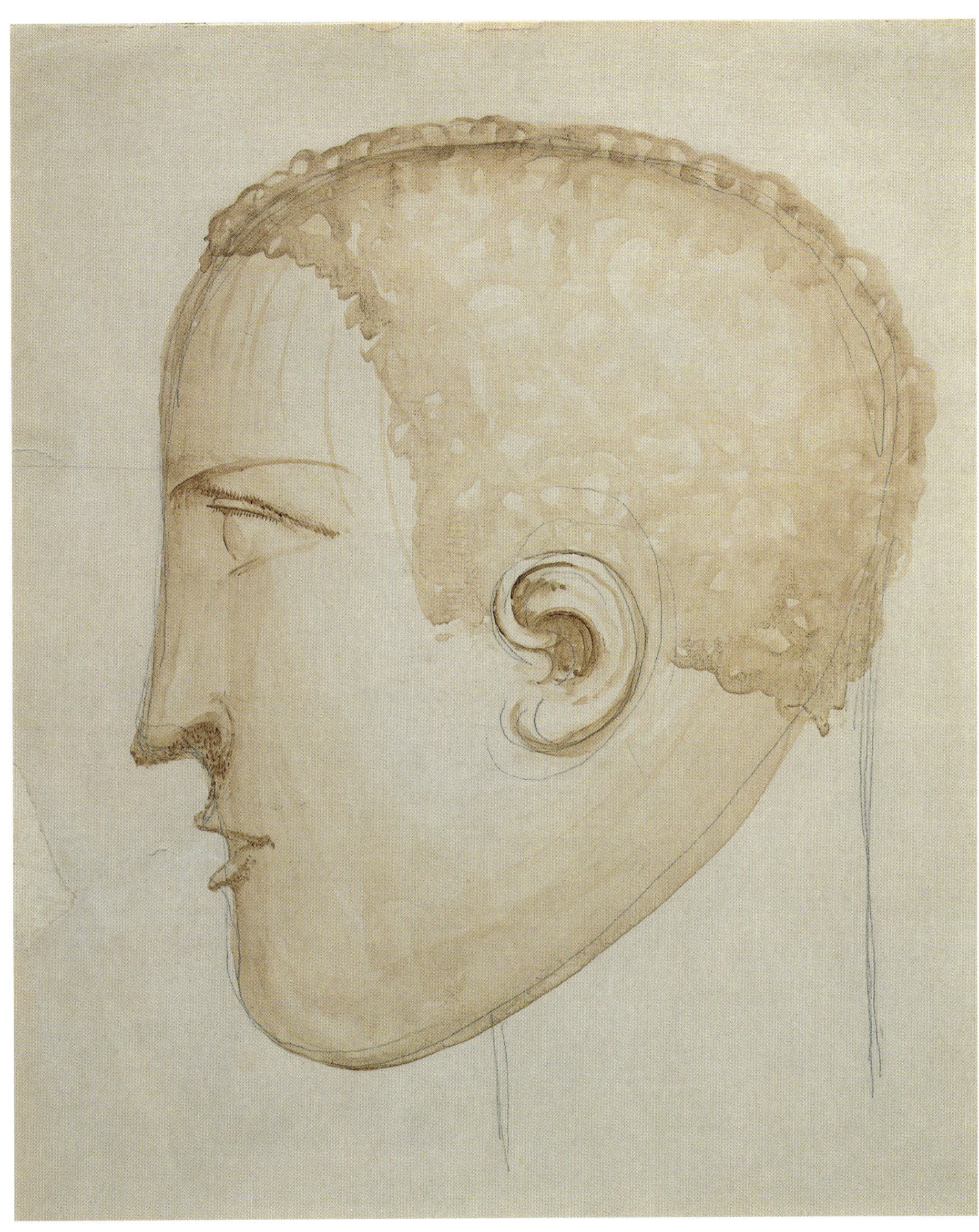

Fig. 158
Elie Nadelman
Profile of a Woman, c. 1925
Ink and ink wash on paper, 11 1/4 x 7 1/8 in.
(28.6 x 18.1 cm)
Private collection
Photography by Paul Waldman

Fig. 159
Elie Nadelman
Head of a Woman in Profile, 1920
Drypoint etching, 3 3/4 x 2 1/2 in. (9.5 x 6.4 cm)
Estate of Elie Nadelman, courtesy
Salander-O'Reilly Galleries, New York
Photography by Paul Waldman

Fig. 160
Elie Nadelman
Female Head, 1920
Drypoint etching, 4 1/4 x 2 3/4 in.
(10.8 x 7 cm)
Estate of Elie Nadelman, courtesy
Salander-O'Reilly Galleries, New York
Photography by Paul Waldman

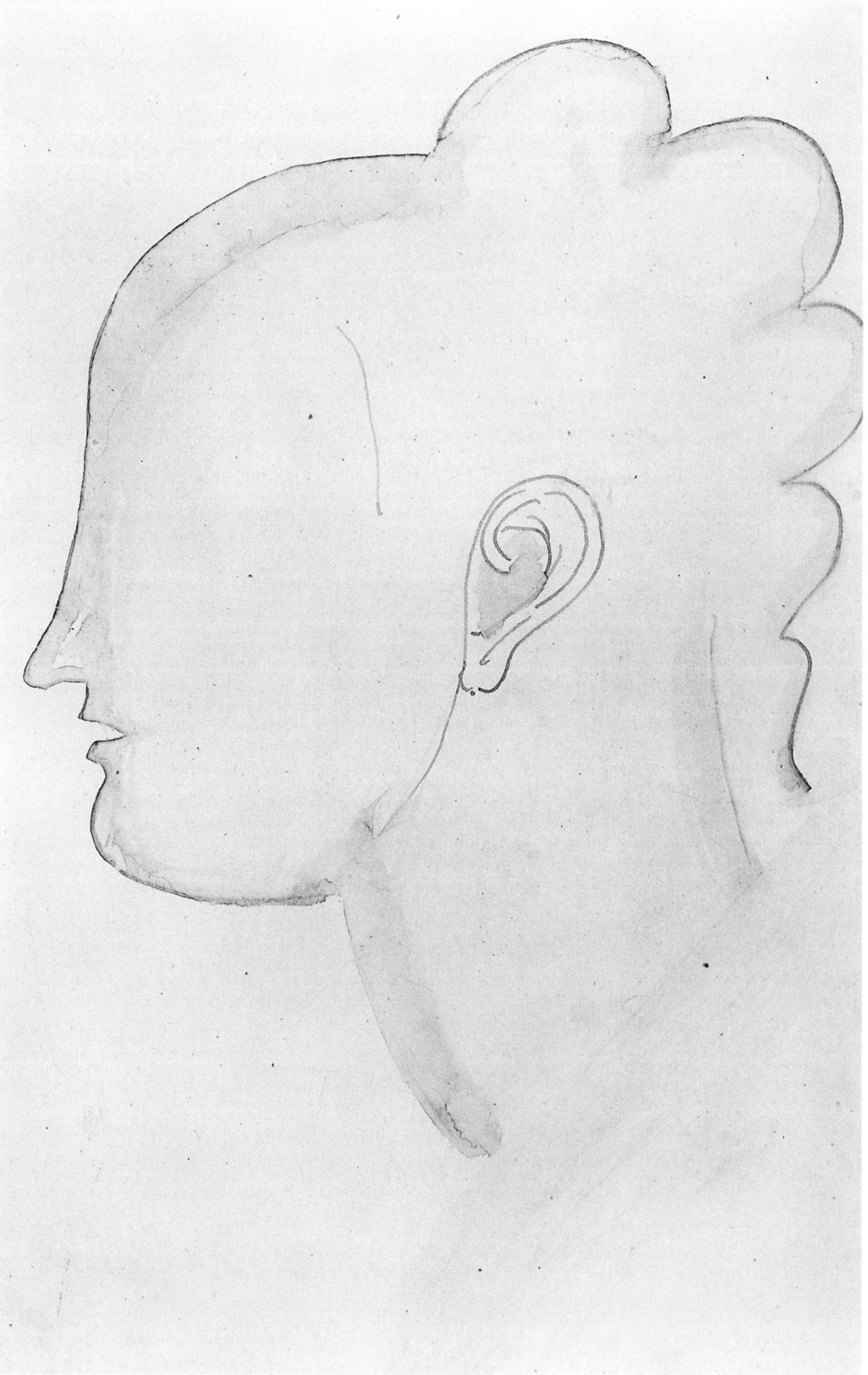

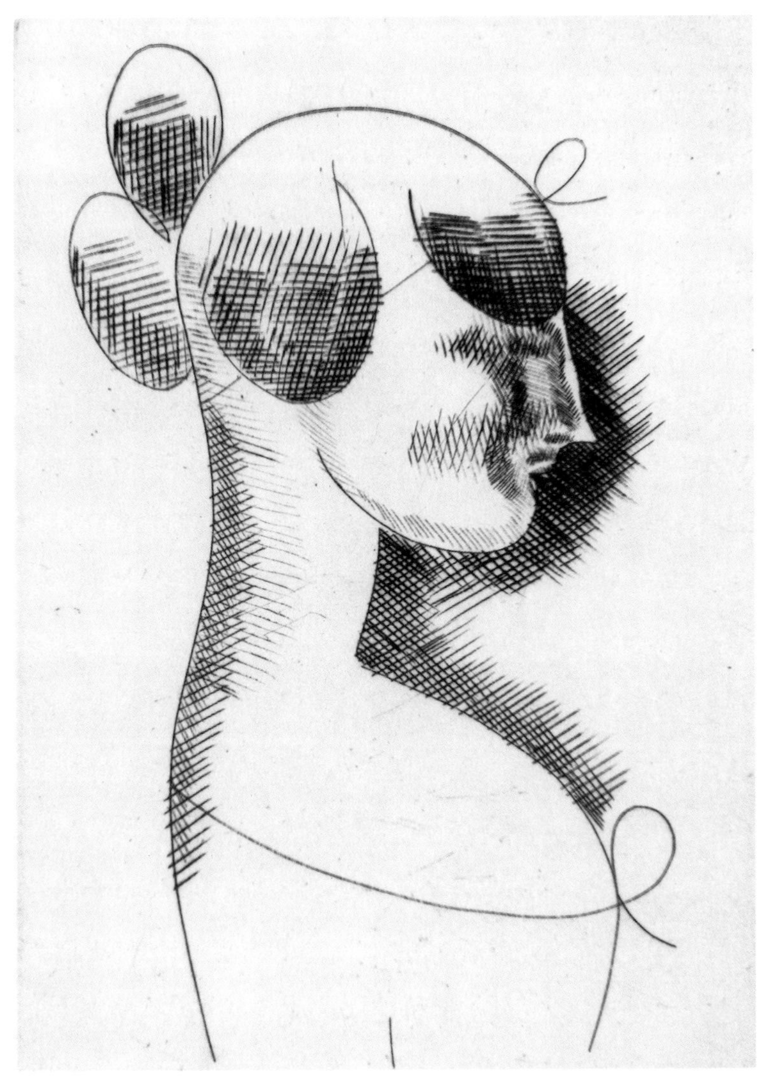 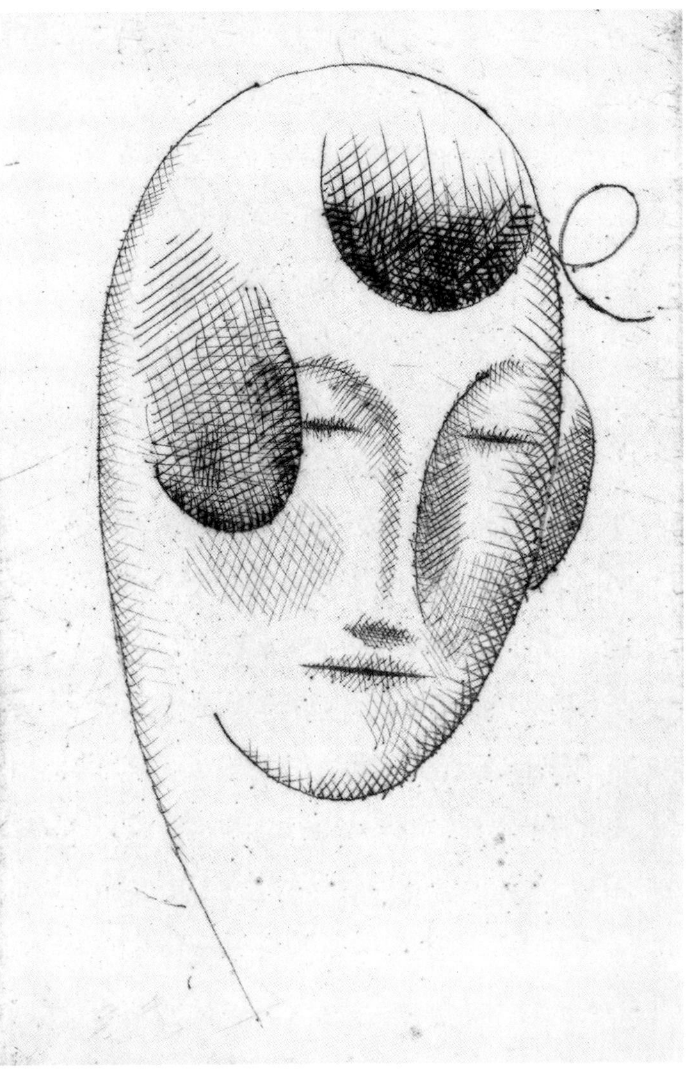

Fig. 161
Elie Nadelman
Portrait of Francis P. Garvan, Jr., c. 1920
Marble, 20 x 14 1/2 x 8 1/4 in.
(50.8 x 36.8 x 21 cm)
Yale University Art Gallery;
Gift of Mabel Brady Garvan

Fig. 162
Elie Nadelman
Portrait of Patricia Garvan, c. 1920
Marble, 21 1/2 x 16 in. (54.6 x 40.6 cm)
Philadelphia Museum of Art;
Gift of Beatrice B. Garvan

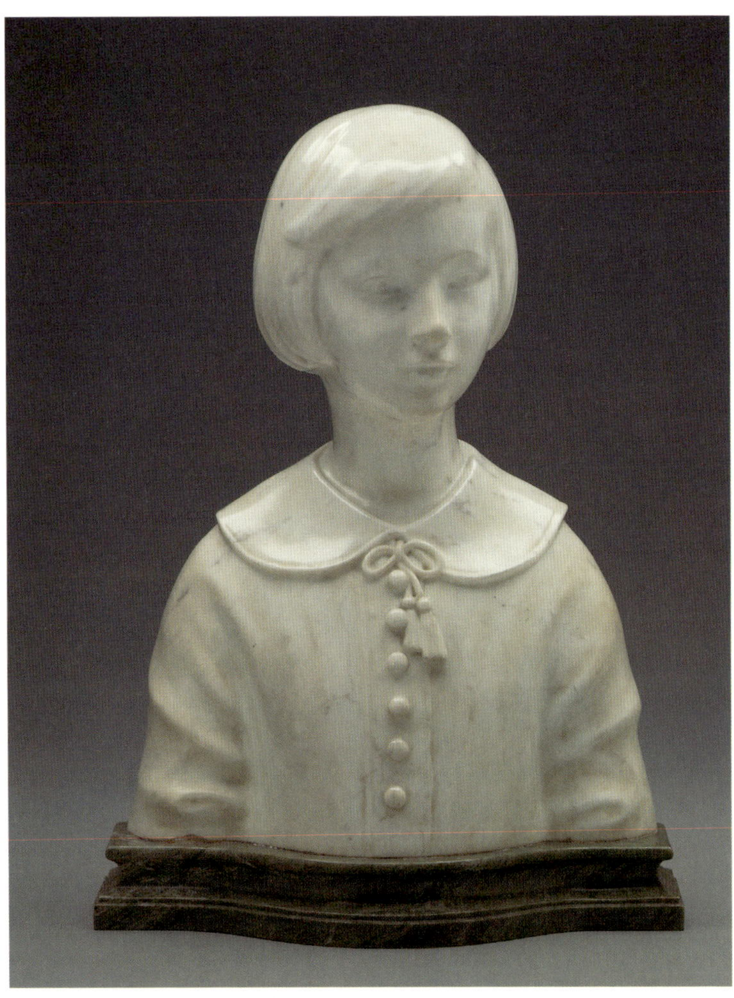

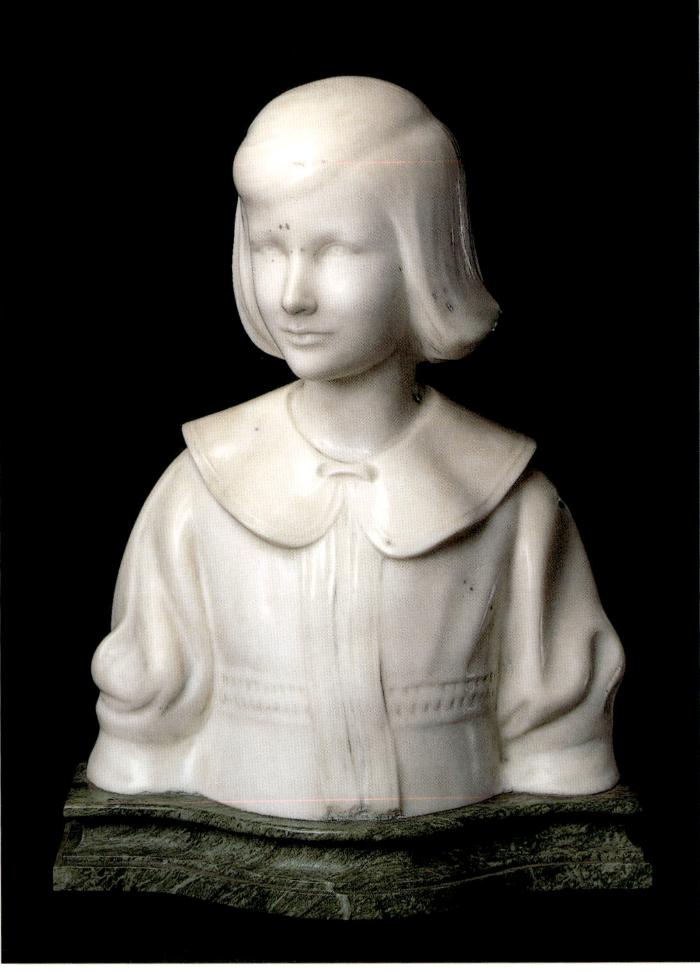

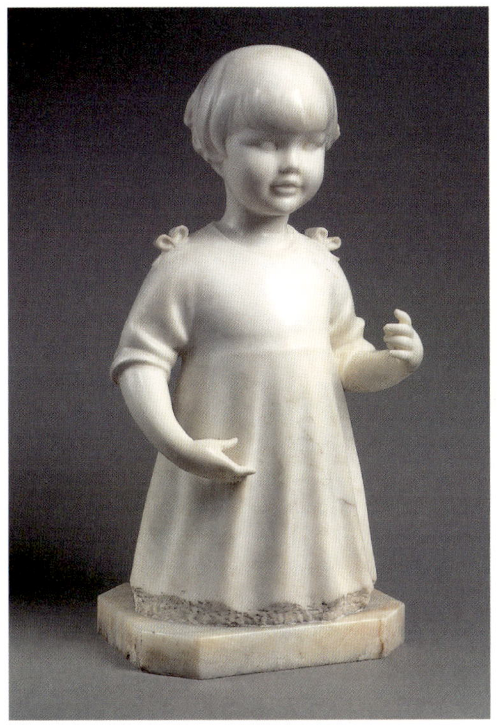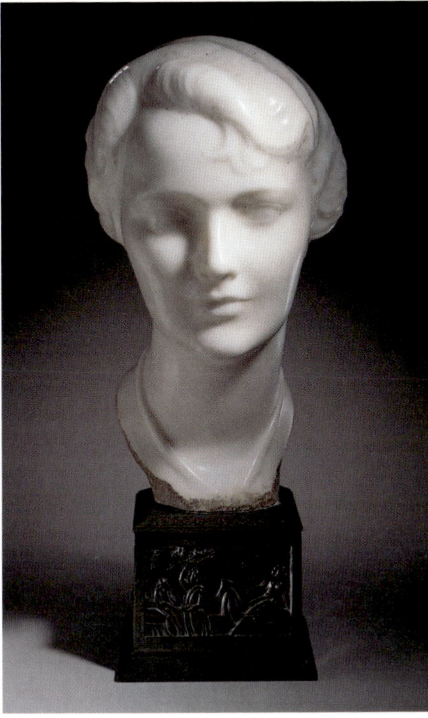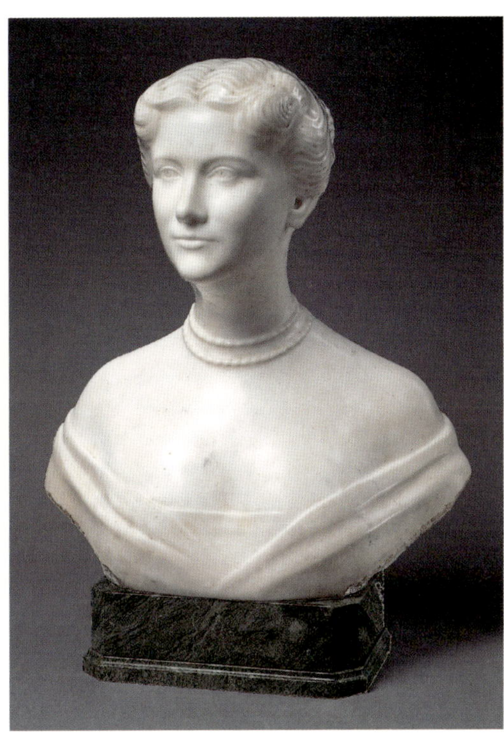

Fig. 163
Elie Nadelman
Portrait of a Young Girl (originally titled
Portrait of Marie), 1916–17
Marble, 30 x 14 x 14 1/2 in.
(76.2 x 35.6 x 36.8 cm)
The Metropolitan Museum of Art, New York;
Gift of Mrs. Stevenson Scott, 1946
©2002 The Metropolitan Museum of Art

Fig. 164
Elie Nadelman
Marie Scott, 1919
Marble with original bronze base,
20 1/4 x 8 1/2 x 10 in. (51.4 x 21.6 x 25.4 cm)
including base
Los Angeles County Museum of Art;
Gift of Mrs. Stevenson Scott
Photograph ©2002 Museum Associates/LACMA

Fig. 165
Elie Nadelman
Julia Gardiner Gayley, c. 1925
Marble, 23 3/8 x 19 1/2 in. (59.3 x 49.5 cm)
The Metropolitan Museum of Art, New York;
Gift of Mrs. Francis G. Coleman and
Mrs. Charles H. Erhart, Jr., 1980
©2002 The Metropolitan Museum of Art

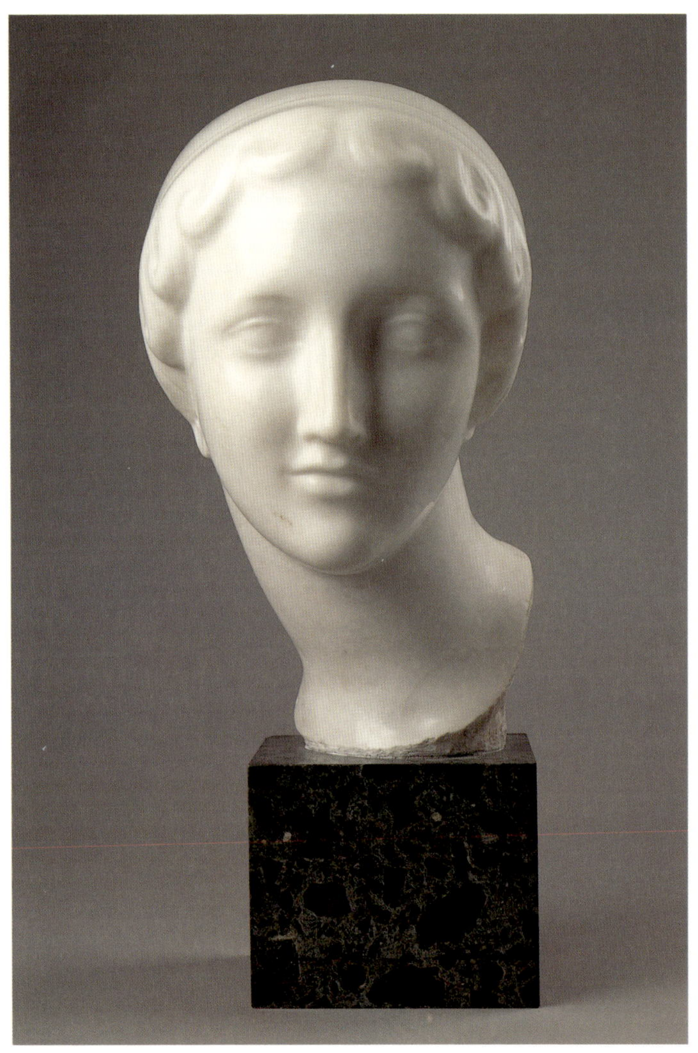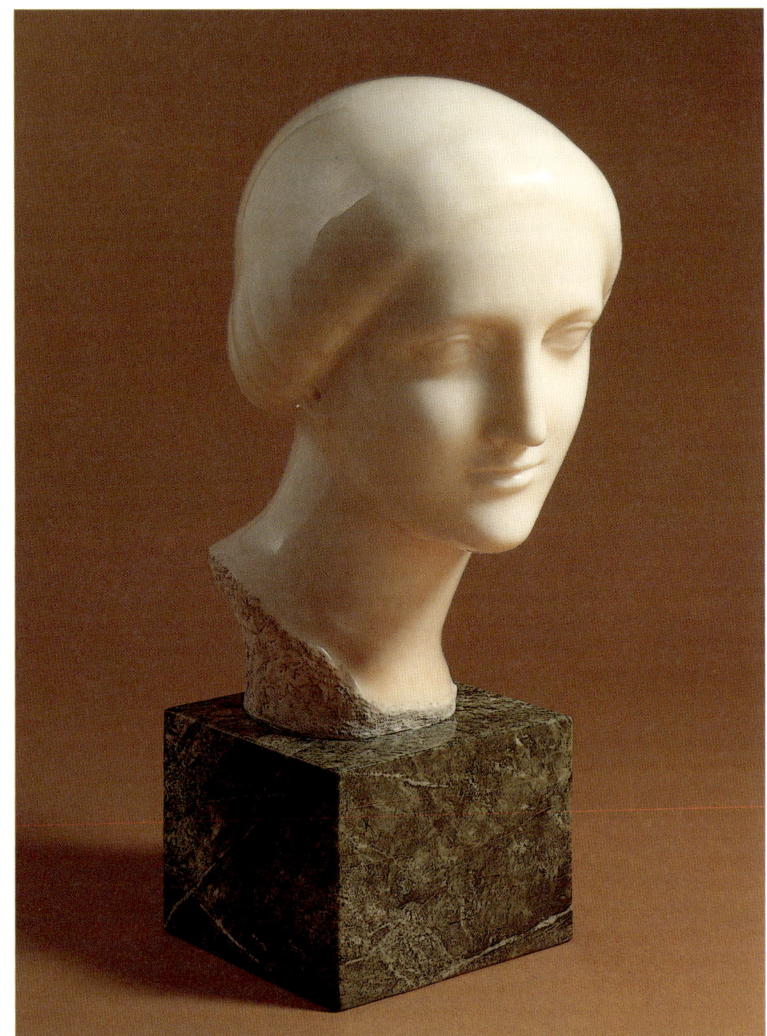

Fig. 166
Elie Nadelman
Idealized Female Head, c. 1920–24
Marble, 16 x 8 3/16 x 13 1/4 in.
(40.6 x 20.8 x 33.7 cm)
Collection of Hackett-Freedman Gallery,
San Francisco

Fig. 167
Elie Nadelman
Head of a Woman, c. 1920–24
Marble, 14 1/4 in. (36.2 cm) high
The Saint Louis Art Museum;
Gift of J. Lionberger Davis

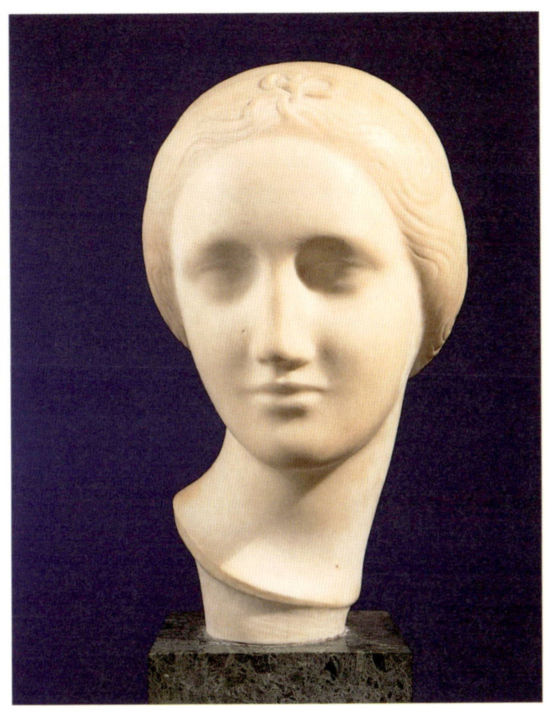

Fig. 168
Elie Nadelman
Female Head, c. 1925–30
Marble, 14 3/4 x 6 3/4 x 9 in.
(37.5 x 17.1 x 22.9 cm)
Estate of Elie Nadelman, courtesy
Salander-O'Reilly Galleries, New York
Photography by Paul Waldman

Fig. 169
Elie Nadelman
Goddess, c. 1920–24
Marble, 22 7/8 x 9 1/4 x 14 1/4 in.
(58.1 x 23.5 x 36.2 cm)
The Cleveland Museum of Art; Bequest
of James Parmelee
©The Cleveland Museum of Art, 2002

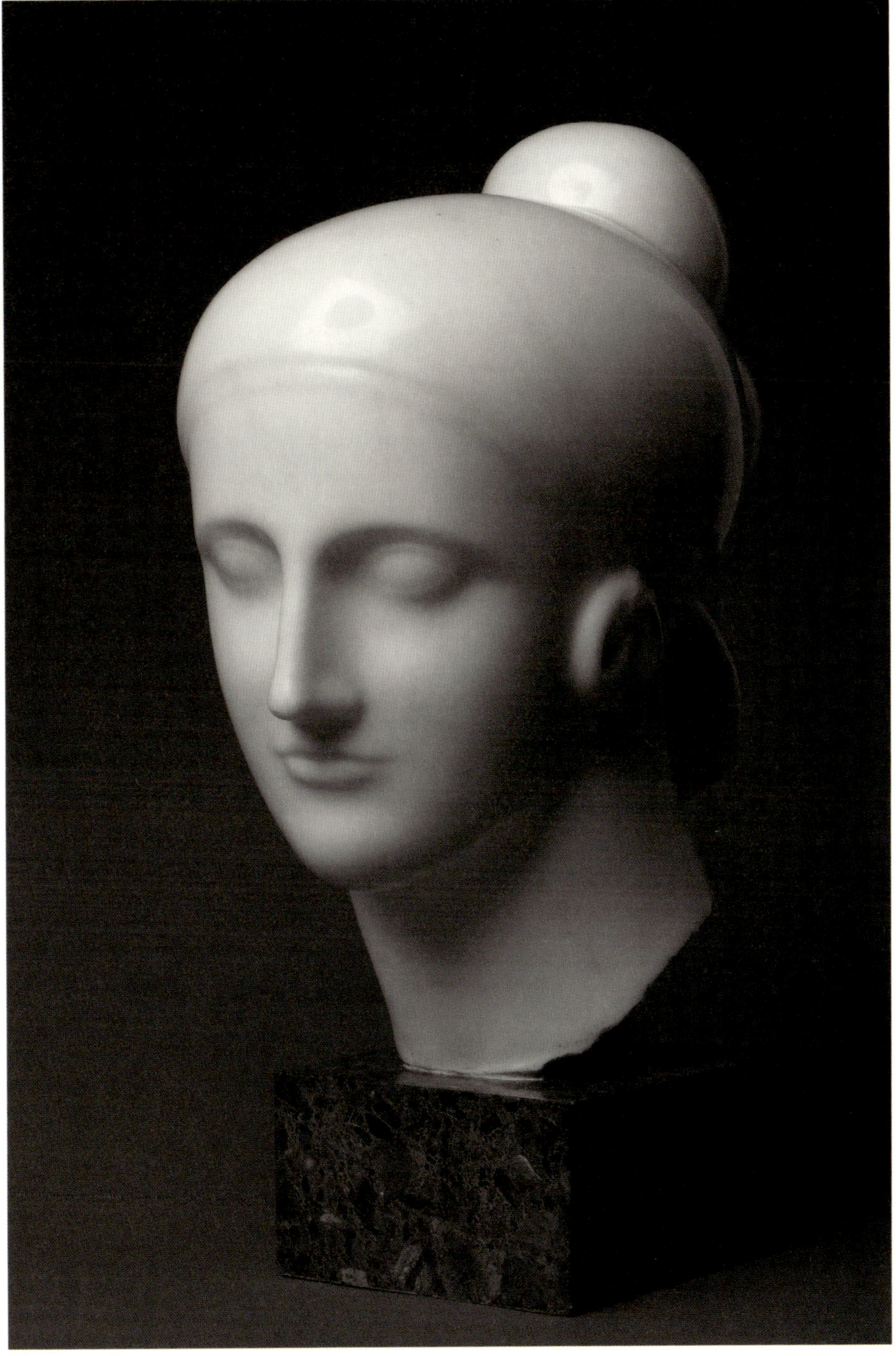

Fig. 170
Elie Nadelman
Standing Figure, c. 1920–24 (two views)
Marble, 37 3/8 x 10 9/16 x 11 7/8 in.
(94.9 x 26.8 x 30.2 cm) overall
Walker Art Center, Minneapolis;
Gift of the T. B. Walker Foundation, 1955

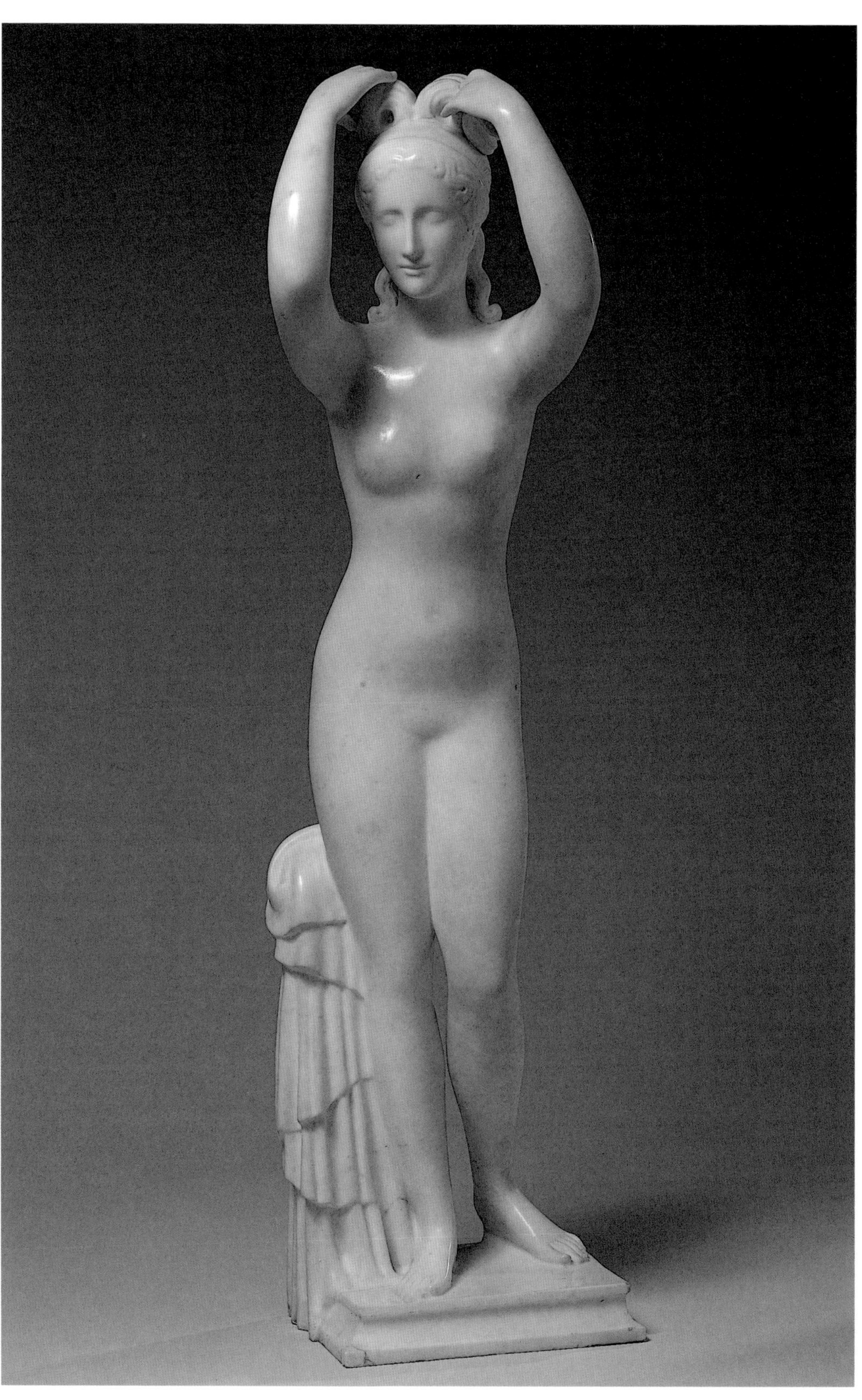

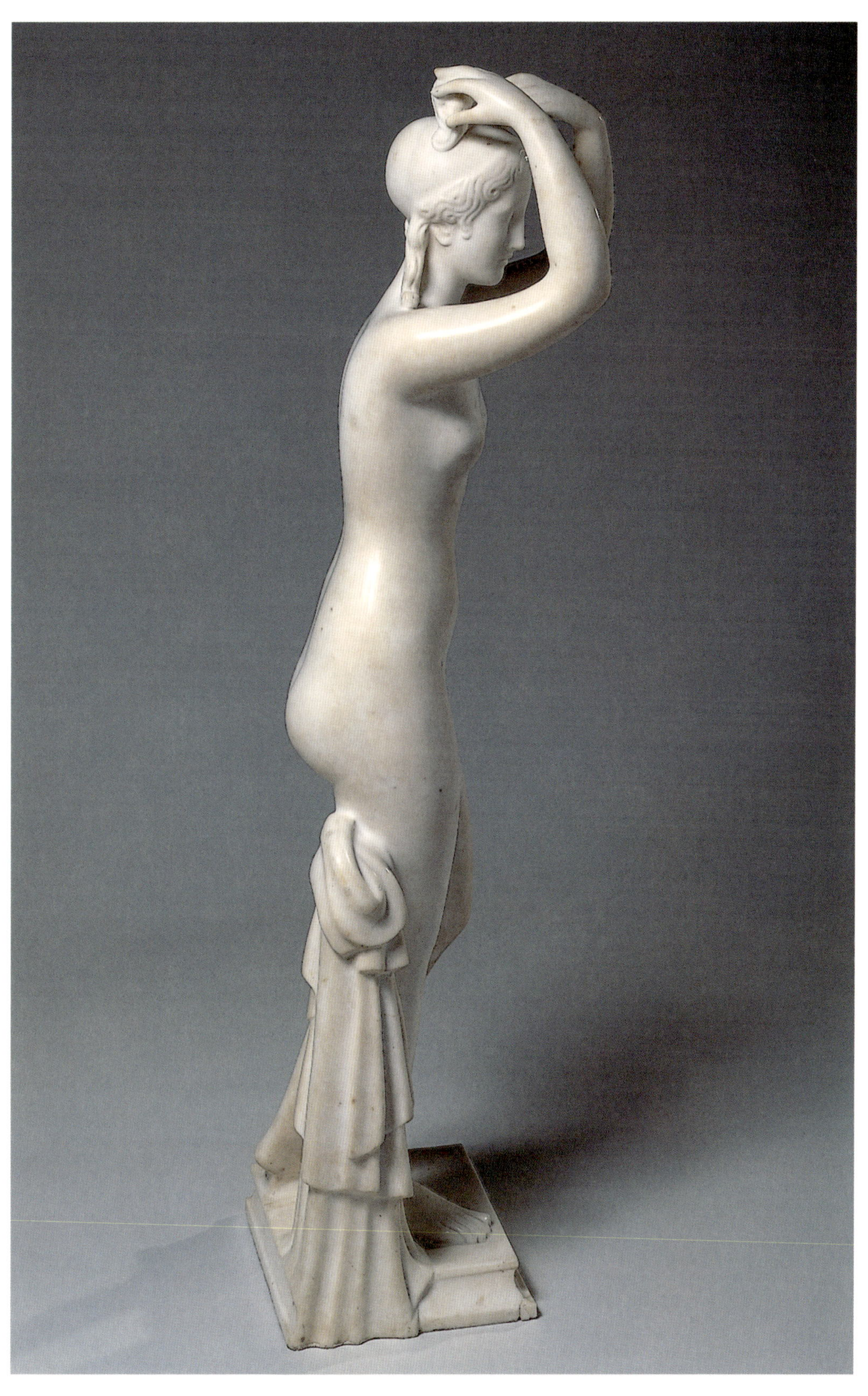

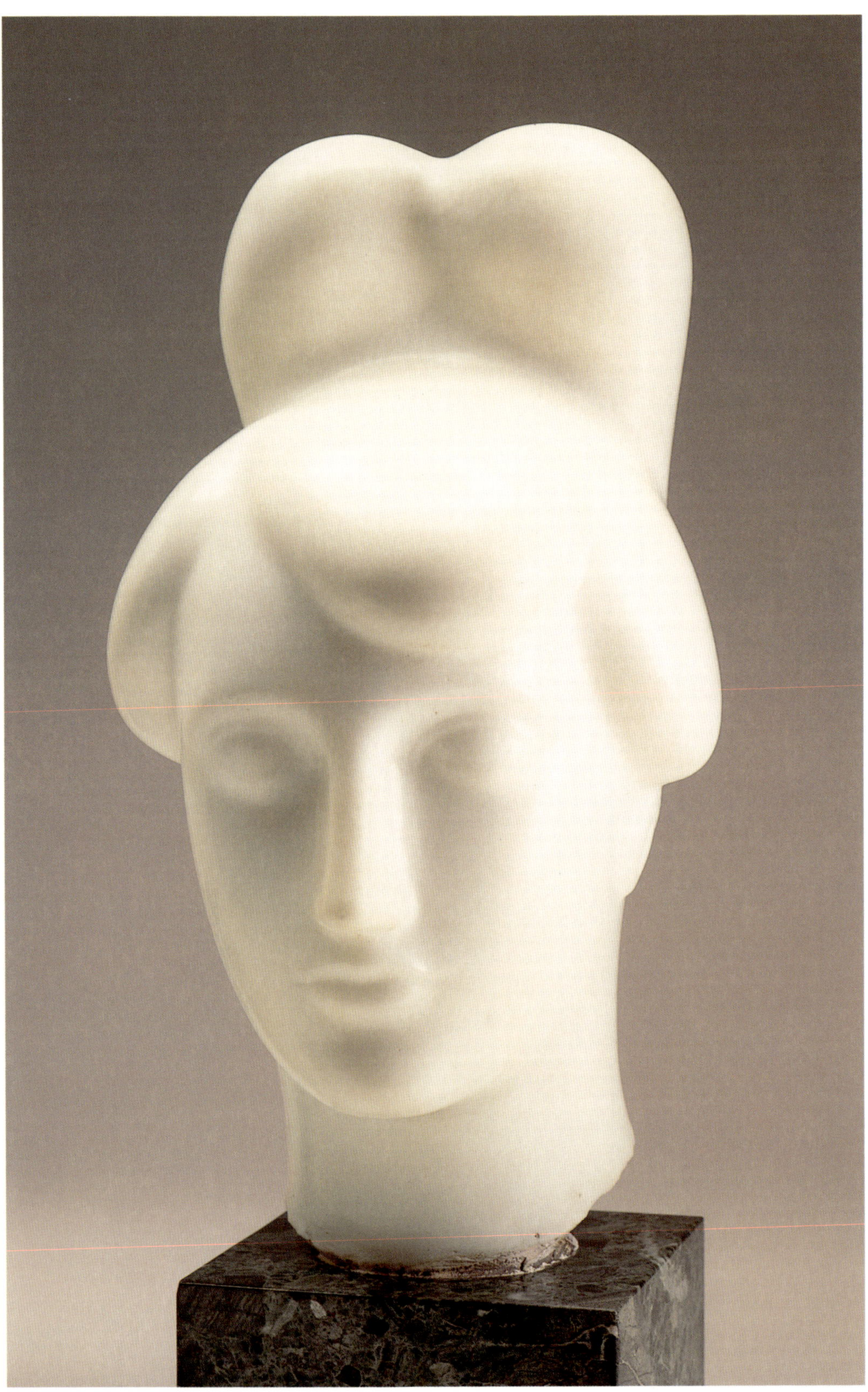

Fig. 171
Elie Nadelman
Untitled (Head of a Woman), c. 1920–24
Marble on onyx base, 23 x 10 x 11 1/2 in.
(58.4 x 25.4 x 29.2 cm)
Memorial Art Gallery, University of Rochester;
Gift of a friend of the Gallery in memory of
Hildegarde Lasell Watson

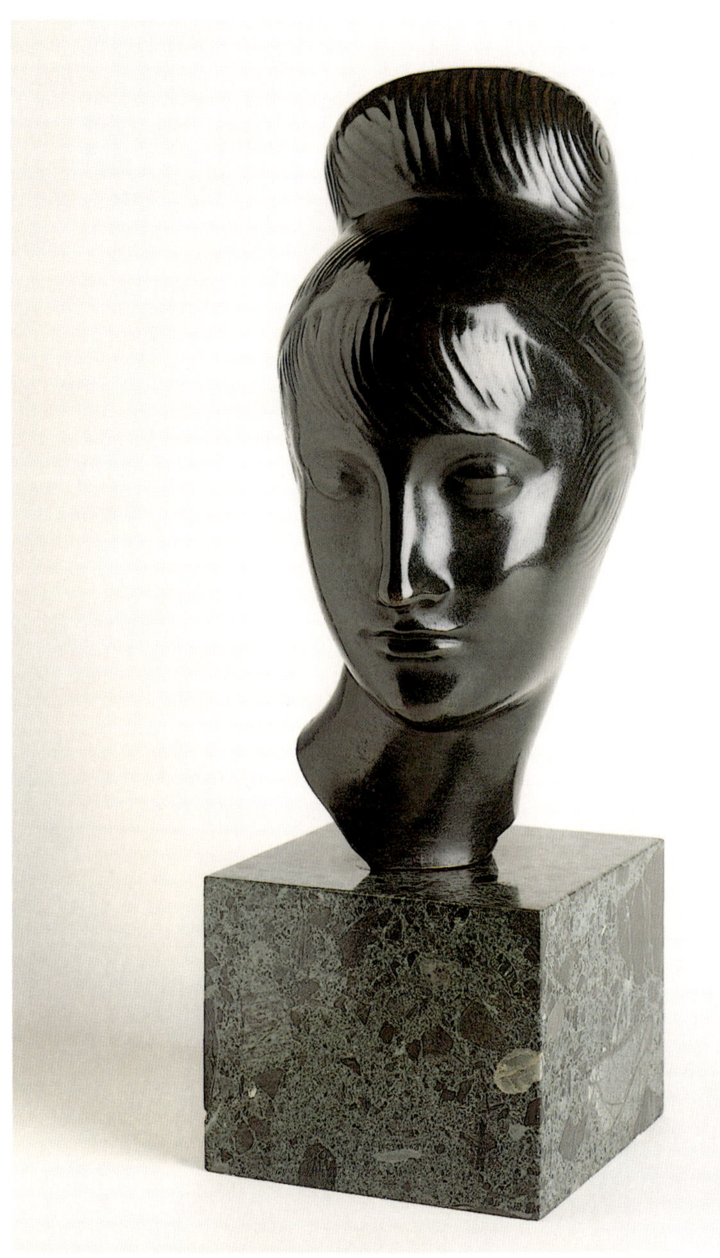

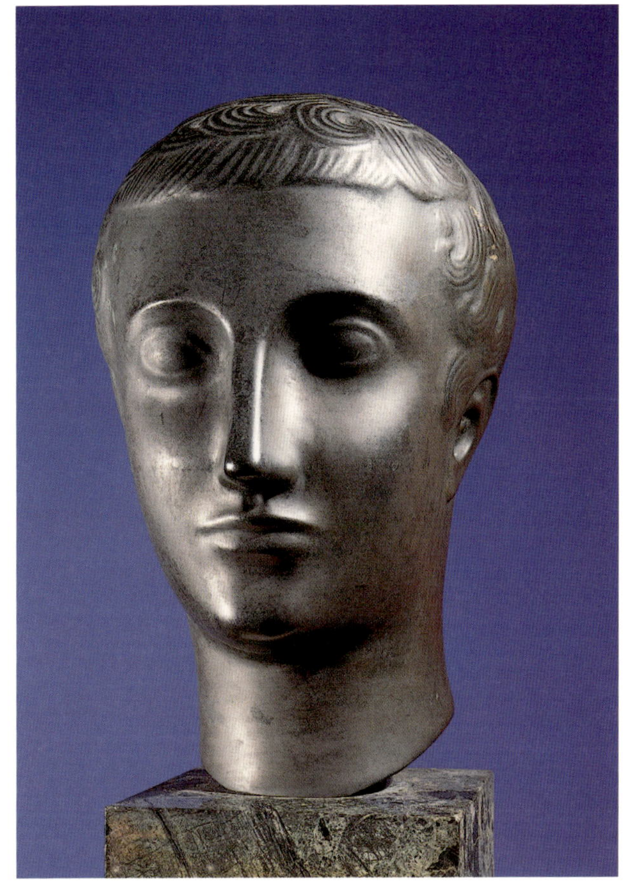

Fig. 172
Elie Nadelman
Head, c. 1920–24
Bronze, 18 1/2 x 5 3/4 x 9 1/2 in.
(47 x 14.6 x 24.1 cm)
Munson-Williams-Proctor Arts Institute,
Museum of Art, Utica, New York

Fig. 173
Elie Nadelman
Ideal Male Head, c. 1916–17
Bronze, 14 in. (35.6 cm) high
Estate of Elie Nadelman, courtesy
Salander-O'Reilly Galleries, New York
Photography by Paul Waldman

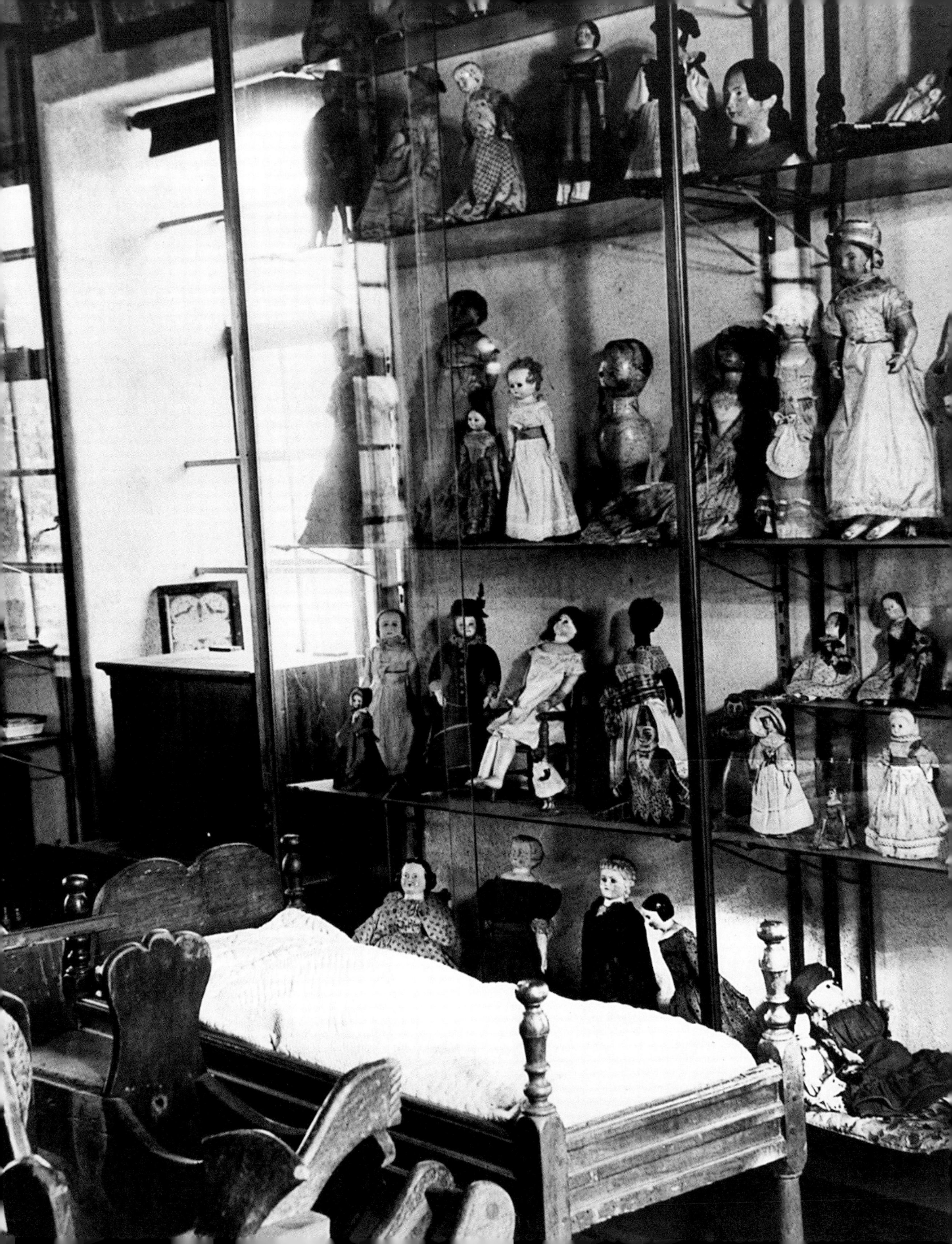

Nadelman as Collector: The Museum of Folk Arts

Nadelman's appreciation of populist materials and commonplace subjects found a parallel expression in the folk art objects that he and Viola began to collect shortly after their marriage. At the time of their marriage Viola was already an ardent collector of laces, embroideries, fabrics, and headdresses dating from ancient times to the present and from countries as far-flung as China, Japan, Italy, England, Persia, Egypt, and Greece.[136] When she and Nadelman moved into their townhouse, they had installed her extensive collection of ancient and contemporary glass decanters from all over the world, most of them in the shape of birds or animals, in specially designed glass cases built into the walls of their dining room. With its recurrence of similar shapes from different countries and epochs, the menagerie embodied the belief Nadelman had held since encountering the writings of Mecislas Golberg that objects from different times and cultures shared formal characteristics. Golberg's dismissal of aesthetic judgments based on style, nationality, and chronology had earlier encouraged Nadelman to draw artistic inspiration from across the whole spectrum of art history. It now provided the basis for his consideration of objects made by anonymous, unskilled craftsmen as equal to those made by trained artists.

Not surprisingly, Nadelman became as engaged in collecting vernacular art as Viola was. Guided by a shared instinct for gathering and classifying, the couple eventually assembled one of the most geographically and chronologically diverse collections of folk and applied art anywhere in the world.[137] As their collection grew, it increasingly became the focus of their lives. By the mid-1920s they were organizing their schedules around collecting excursions in Europe and America in chauffeured touring cars, stopping at roadside farms, barns, and antique shops to purchase objects. On these trips they never wavered from the theory they had gleaned from their earliest researches into glass decanters: the works of unschooled and anonymous craftsmen the world over shared formal characteristics whose roots could be found in ancient art.

One of the seminal experiences that encouraged the Nadelmans to break with the conservative collecting habits of most other members of their social class was the summer they spent in 1920 in Beauport, the seaside house in Gloucester owned by Boston socialite Henry Davis Sleeper. Sleeper had transformed an existing shingled waterfront house into a sequence of exotic, sumptuously decorated period rooms. Although the Nadelmans did not share Sleeper's taste for antique-filled interiors featuring Chinese wallpaper, crimson morocco bindings, and scarlet tulle lamps, the summer taught the couple that compelling interior decoration need not be accomplished exclusively through high-style artifacts. When they opened their townhouse in 1923, the living spaces featured uncluttered expanses and stark white walls intended to show-case their ever-expanding collection of handcrafted furniture and decorative arts. Already by 1924 the Nadelmans' holdings had reached a size substantial enough to warrant construction of a three-story building on their Riverdale property dedicated to displaying folk and applied art. By the time the building was completed two years later, they had decided to open their collection, by appointment, to art institutions, schools, and "individuals interested in art."[138] Initially called the Museum of Folk and Peasant Arts, it included close to fifteen thousand artworks from the United States, Hungary, Yugoslavia, Spain, France, Germany, Switzerland, Austria, and Russia.[139]

Blessed by relatively expansive finances and a passion for accumula-tion, the Nadelmans assembled the largest collection of vernacular and applied art in the country. They were not the first to appreciate or collect the material, however. Hamilton Easter Field, who had earlier expressed interest in publishing Nadelman's *Vers la beauté plastique*, had become interested in folk art early in the century; by the time he opened his Ogunquit School of Painting and Sculpture in Maine in 1913, he had purchased enough early American painting and furniture to furnish each of the colony's seaside cabins with it. This decor inspired visiting artists Alexander Brook, Bernard Karfiol, Yasuo Kuniyoshi, Robert Laurent, Charles Sheeler, Eugene Speicher, Maurice Sterne, and William Zorach to inaugurate their own collections of American vernacular art. By 1924 interest in folk art among artists was so intense that the Whitney Studio Club mounted an exhibition of artist-owned folk art. Entitled *Early American Art*, it included forty-five objects lent by approxi-mately eleven artists.[140] Three years later the Studio Club exhibited Isabel Wilde's folk art collection, and in 1929 Edith Halpert, director of the vanguard Downtown Gallery, opened the American Folk Art Gallery with Holger Cahill.[141] Cahill's exhibitions in 1932 and 1933 of American folk sculpture and painting at the Newark Museum and The Museum of Modern Art signaled the art establishment's recognition of the material.

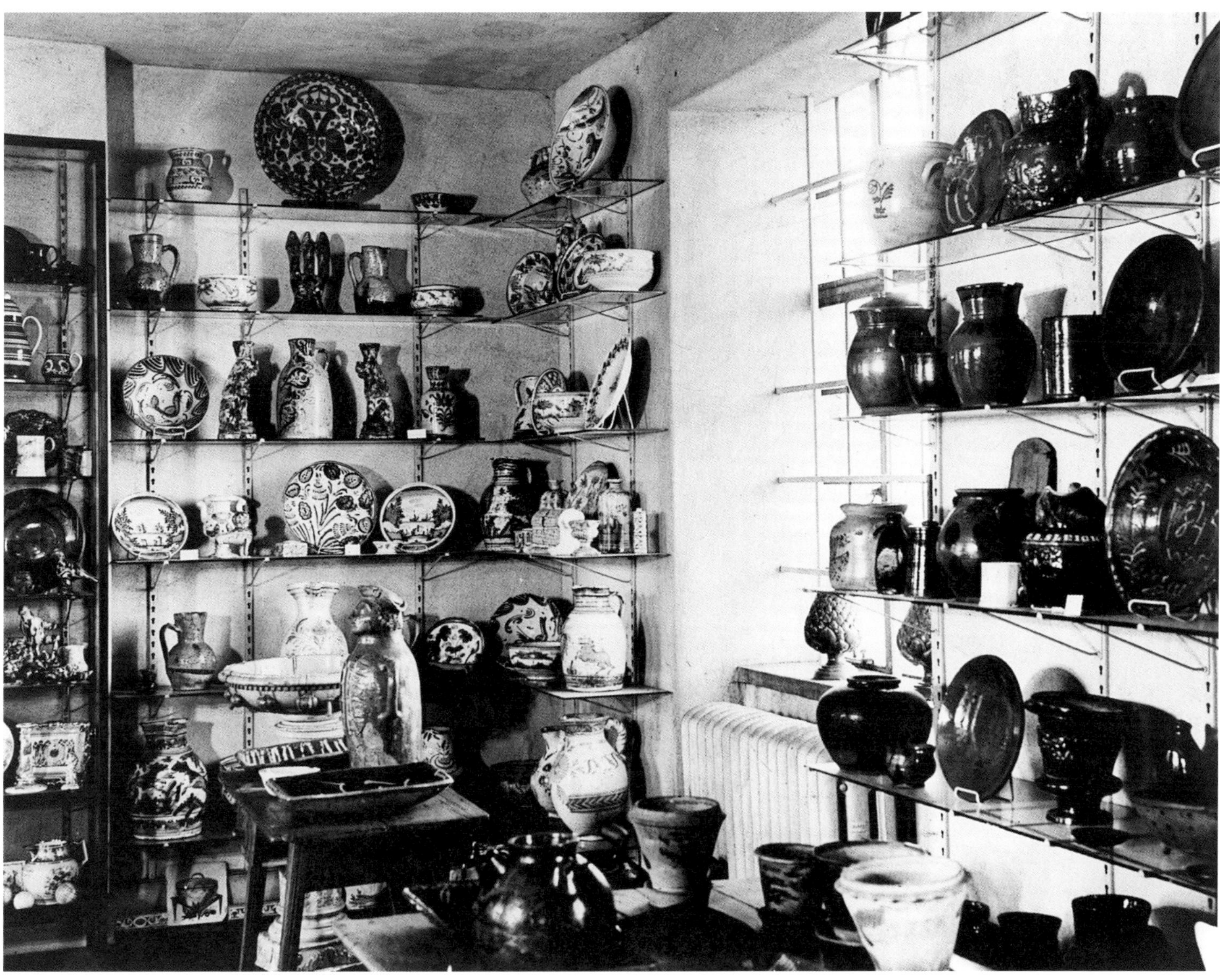

The Nadelmans' collection differed from that of these other folk art enthusiasts in two important respects. First—and not surprisingly, given Nadelman's European background and Viola's European education—they collected European as well as American folk art. Second, whereas most collectors selected folk art objects possessing the formal simplicity and expressive authenticity associated with modern "high" art, the Nadelmans' criterion was taxonomic. Their stated aim was to demonstrate the formal correlations between objects from different countries and epochs having common functions and mediums and to show the evolution of forms and manufacturing processes over time.[142] Because American folk objects were often of more

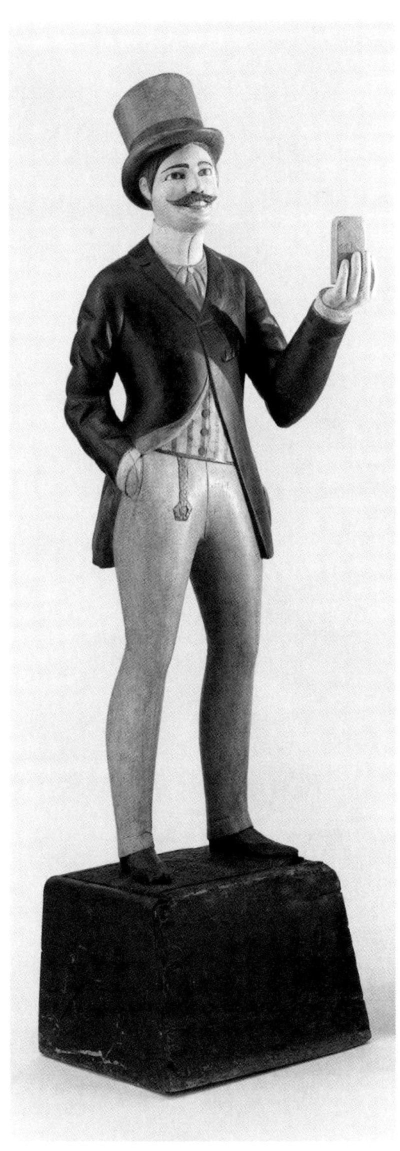

recent vintage than their European counterparts, this practice underscored the European roots of American vernacular products.[143] At the very least, it reinforced the commonalities between the two.

To communicate their ideas visually, the Nadelmans arranged objects in the museum's fourteen galleries didactically, according to function and medium (FIGS. 174, 176). To support their thesis that formal similarities existed between temporally and geographically unrelated objects, they collected not only applied art objects but also those with more ethnographic than aesthetic interest. Thus, in addition to objects normally associated with folk art—textiles, toys, furniture, wrought-iron work, pottery, hooked rugs, and wood carvings— they collected a wide range of utilitarian objects and furnishings: the interior of a Pennsylvania Dutch house and the corner of a Normandy cottage with built-in bed and cupboards; French and American eighteenth-century apothecary shops stocked with scales, mixing bowls, and jars filled with colored liquids and leeches; fire-fighting equipment; cockroach traps; American Revolutionary posters and broadsides; household and farm implements. To make the "original manner of using [objects] perfectly understood," the Nadelmans often juxtaposed products and tools.[144] Textiles, for example, were placed alongside looms and needles; candle molds and a candle-drying wheel were displayed next to candlesticks and candleholders. The couple even went so far as to make pressed-dough cakes from cake molds they owned in order to indicate the molds' function.

In their effort to illustrate the function of objects and the existence of formal correspondences across art's full spectrum, the Nadelmans occasionally sacrificed quality. It was not that their collection lacked exquisite examples of vernacular art; it was simply that their purchases were guided as much by intellectual and pedagogical impulses as by aesthetic ones. Contradicting the widely held belief that the couple collected only objects with "aesthetic significance," historians who have researched their folk art collection have concluded that "they gathered up every specimen they encountered of a specific category, taking the mediocre along with the good and great," and that one half of collecting for them consisted in saving everything.[145]

The Nadelmans' relative lack of concern with the preciousness of the individual object may account for the paltry acknowledgment their collection received in the writings of Cahill and Halpert, upon which most studies of American folk art have depended. In looking at utilitarian, everyday objects

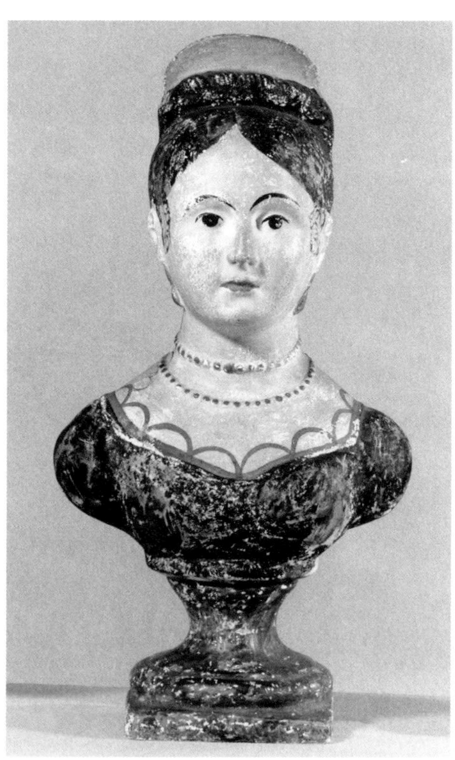
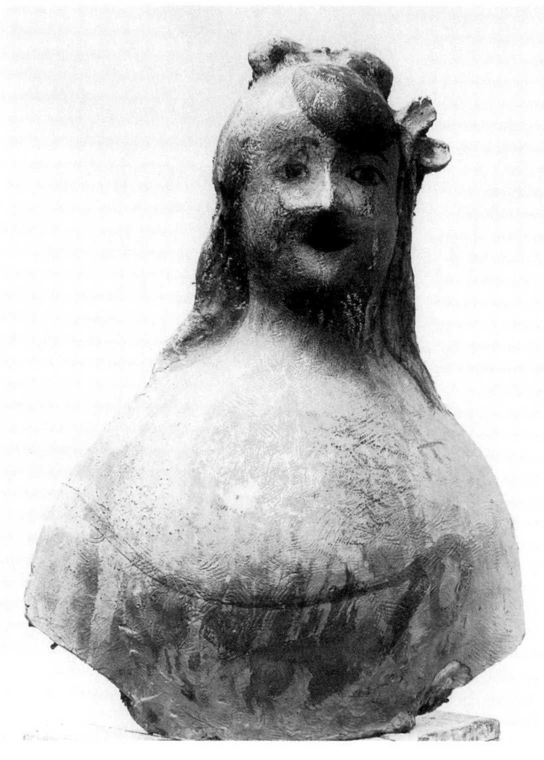

Fig. 177
Unknown artist
Bust of a Woman, c. 1850–90
Painted plaster of paris, 13 1/2 x 74 1/4 in.
(34.3 x 188.6 cm)
Collection of the New-York Historical
Society. Formerly in the Museum of Folk
and Peasant Arts

Fig. 178
Elie Nadelman
Girl's Half-Length Torso, 1925–27
Painted galvano-plastique, 30 in.
(76.2 cm) high
Estate of Elie Nadelman
Photography by R. V./U. Smutny
Lincoln Kirstein Photograph Collection,
Jerome Robbins Dance Division, The New York
Public Library

formally—without regard to chronology or national affiliation—the Nadelmans were ahead of their time. Not until the 1960s, with the advent of Pop art and formalist criticism, would this idea gain wide currency.

Although critics have tended to view Nadelman's iconic wood figurines as influenced by his exposure to folk art, the objects he collected in fact bore little visual resemblance to his sculpture. In those few instances where discernible formal similarities exist between his sculpture and his folk objects—as in the case of his Pennsylvania Dutch chalkware bust (FIG. 177) and one of his galvano-plastiques (FIG. 178)—his sculpture generally preceded his ownership of the folk object. Nor did Nadelman collect out of a feeling of kinship with those who handcrafted their art; most of his work was made with the help of studio assistants and skilled technicians. There is, however, one common denominator between his art and his folk collection: an ideological conviction that all art—high and low, ancient and modern, European and Asian—shares formal characteristics that define its aesthetic merit. This ability to see significant form in art from a wide array of epochs and styles would serve him well as he began his next group of sculptures.

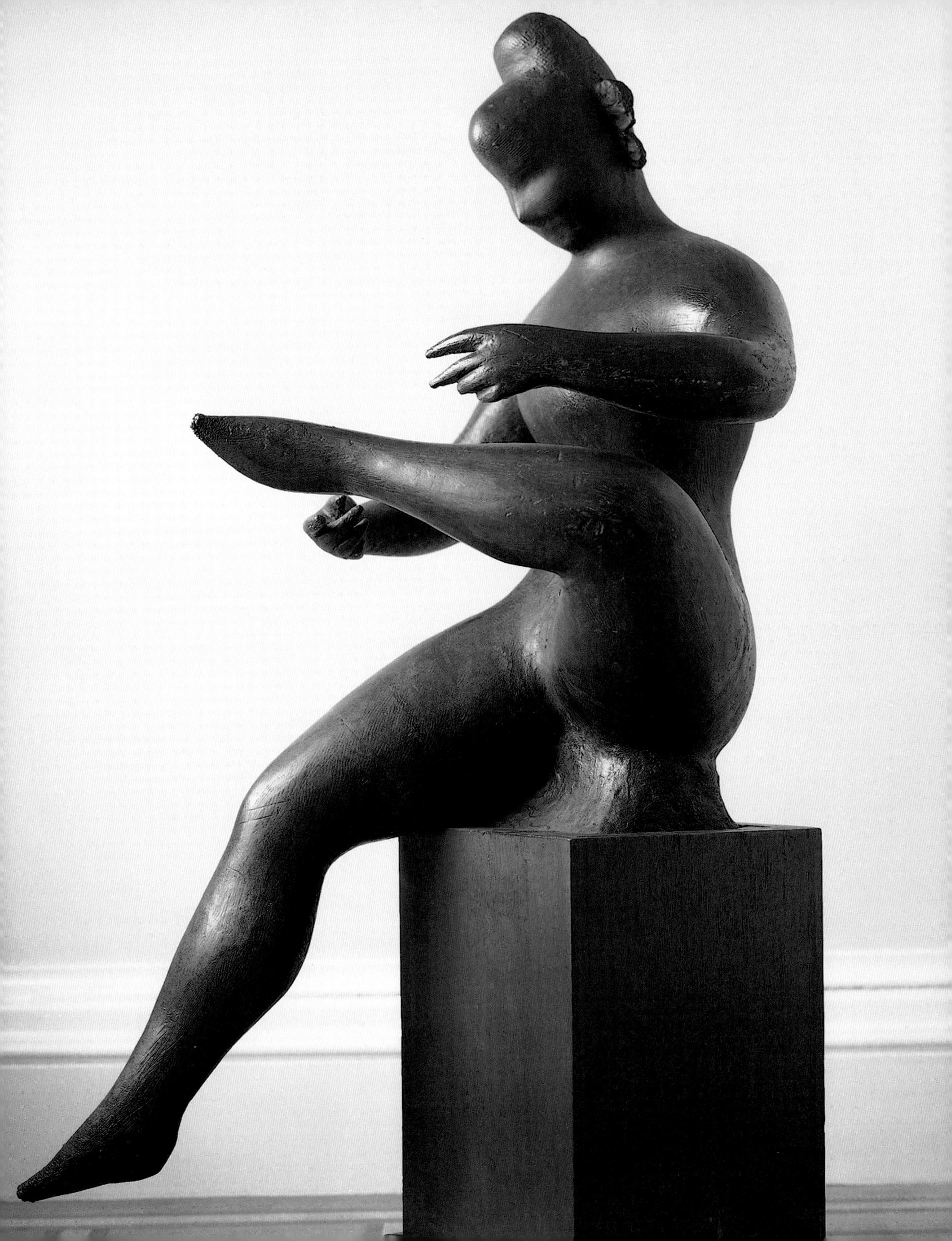

Galvano-Plastiques, 1925–27

Fig. 179
Elie Nadelman
Seated Woman with Raised Leg, c. 1925–26
Galvano-plastique, 50 1/2 x 25 x 27 in.
(128.3 x 63.5 x 68.6 cm)
Estate of Elie Nadelman, courtesy
Salander-O'Reilly Galleries, New York
Photography by Paul Waldman

By the fall of 1925 Nadelman had already embarked on a new constellation of figures that pushed cross-fertilizations between epochs to a new plateau.[146] As he had done in 1917 with his first genre figures, he began in plaster; but rather than paint the figures, as he had done then, he electroplated their surfaces with a thin veneer of metal.[147] The technique—which Nadelman called by its French name, *galvano-plastique*—was an industrialized variant of the French academic practice of tinting plaster to simulate other materials. Widely used in the applied arts, it had found only limited success in the fine arts. The medium appealed to Nadelman because of its potential for unusual finishes and its ability to replicate bronze, which allowed him to make art that was populist and affordable without being condescending—an issue that increased in importance to him as he became more committed to folk art.

Nadelman first experimented with electroplating plaster in a group of busts that he painted much as he had his 1920–24 bronze ones. The difference was that he deliberately left the surfaces rough and applied his paint with brushy, gestural flourishes rather than with crisp, precise demarcations (FIGS. 180, 181). Intrigued by electroplating's potential to create rich, mysterious surfaces, he dipped his next group of works—near life-size, full-length figures and busts—into different metal alloys, thereby eliciting a variety of dark-colored finishes, from green to tawny and gold.[148] He scratched these mottled, alchemical surfaces with a file to evoke the weathered appearance of antiquities and to create an allover surface shimmer (FIGS. 182, 183). Only occasionally did he add touches of blue to indicate hair, eyes, waistbands, and bodysuits.[149] What resulted was a flickering, modulated opalescence. Over time, the painted details have faded, and the metallic finishes have darkened so that the original effect is lost. Even period photographs, however, show that the areas of applied paint were faint, suggesting that Nadelman intended to strip these figures of all evident temporal references and thereby gain for them a timeless universality uncompromised by the humor and caricature that were imputed to his painted wood and bronze subjects. Their softened contours and indistinct facial demarcations—so different from the crisp, painted geometries of his earlier genre subjects—lent these life-size electroplated figures a muted, mysterious quality. With their poses less spirited and public than those of their

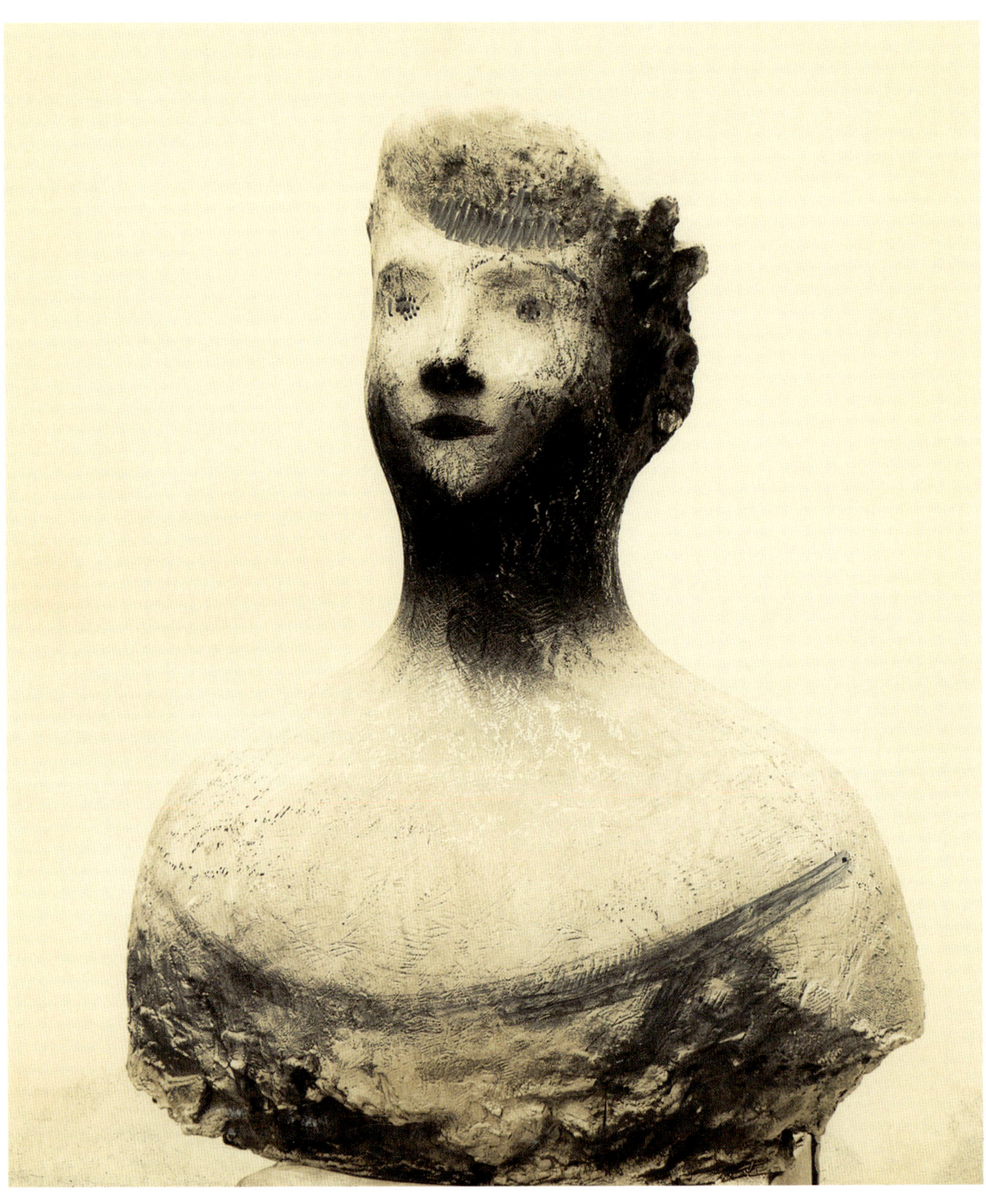

wood predecessors, these figures appear to have been caught in moments of private self-absorption, oblivious to the world outside themselves.

Nadelman's models likewise changed, as he shifted his gaze from the effervescent, lithe young women of post–World War I America to their more matronly predecessors. He still drew from the world of popular culture, but now his female stars of circus and vaudeville no longer evoked the stylized linearity of Irene Castle, avatar of the tango and fox-trot, but rather the full-bodied muscularity of music hall artists of the Edwardian era. Much of the

Fig. 181
Elie Nadelman
Man in Top Hat, 1925–26
Painted galvano-plastique,
27 x 22 1/2 x 10 in. (68.6 x 57.2 x 25.4 cm)
overall
Whitney Museum of American Art, New York;
Purchase, with funds from The Lauder
Foundation, Evelyn and Leonard Lauder Fund

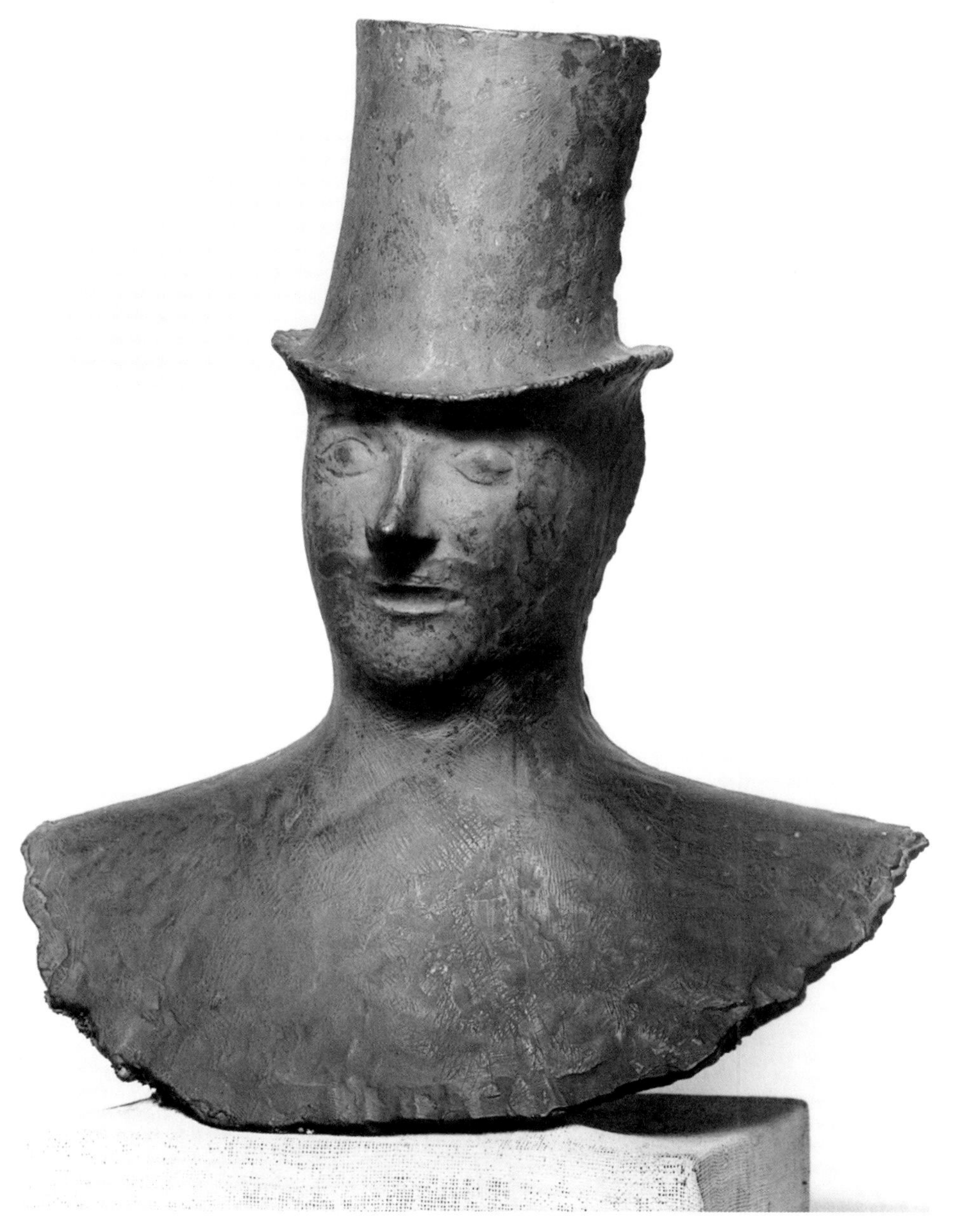

change can be attributed to Nadelman's new domestic lifestyle, which militated against attendance at circus and vaudeville performances until his son was old enough to take along as a companion. Just as his move to America had forced him to study antiquities primarily through two-dimensional reproductions, so now did he substitute newspaper and glossy photographs for direct observation of burlesque and vaudeville artists. The process licensed him to draw on related images from disparate epochs and with different functions. Indeed, his scrapbooks were full of publicity photos of tightly corseted burlesque queens

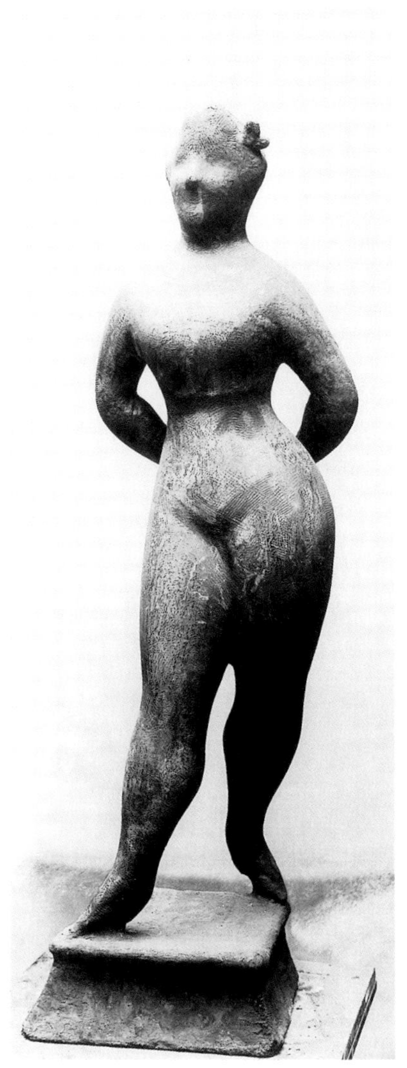

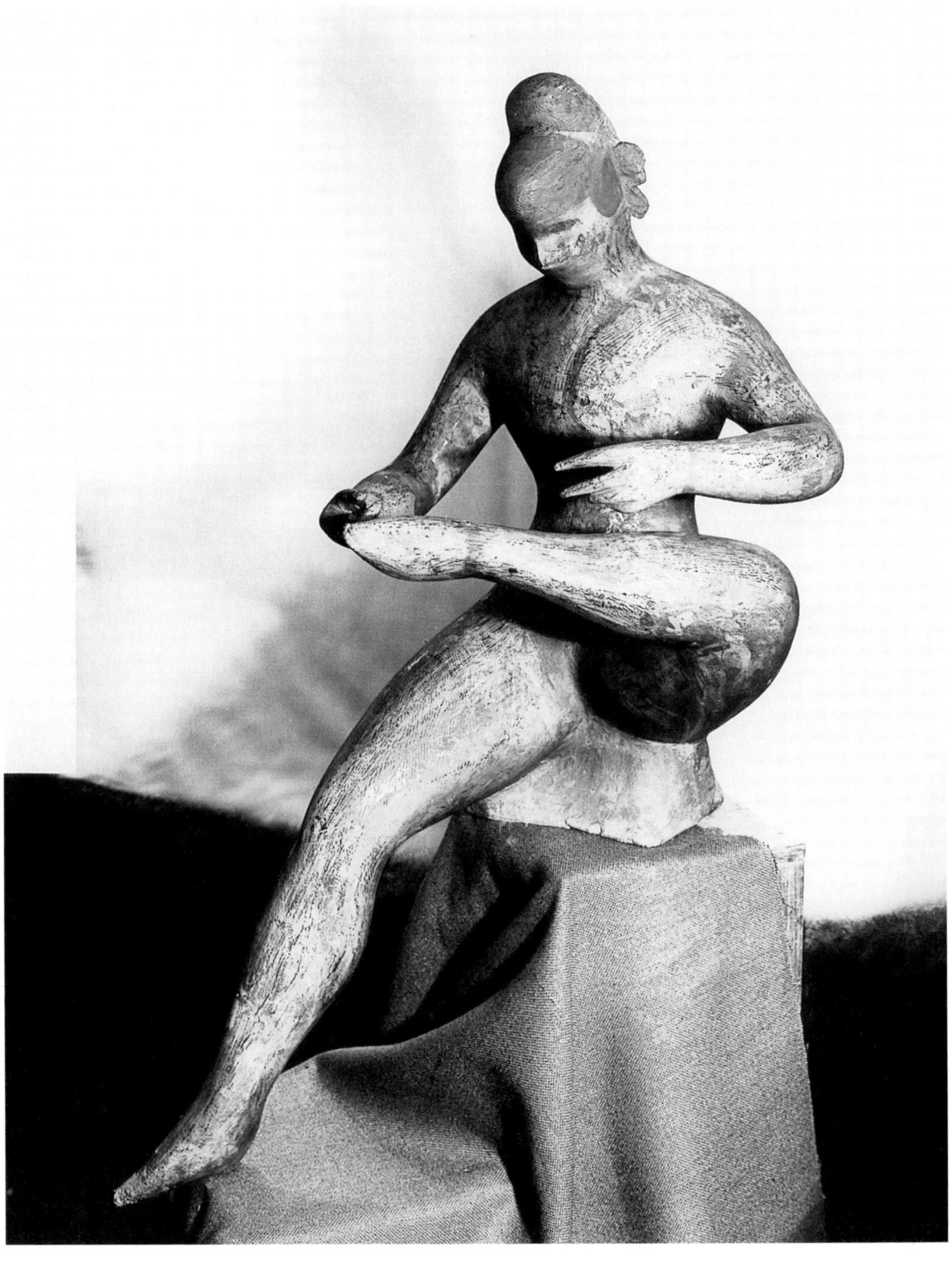

from the 1890s, their waists drawn in and their sturdy legs encased in tights, alongside postcards of classical statuary and advertisements showing women in bathing suits and corsets. Nadelman paid respect to the plump delicacy of these varied models, especially those from the American stage, by giving his figures a weightless buoyancy that counteracted their ample, pneumatic volumes. With their great, strong thighs and exaggeratedly small feet, they project a monumentality at once vulnerable and self-contained.

Nadelman exhibited ten of his galvano-plastiques in January 1927 at M. Knoedler & Company. Priced at one thousand dollars for full figures and five hundred for busts, they were vastly less expensive than his marble and bronze commissioned portraits, which the gallery offered at eight thousand and five thousand dollars, respectively. That Nadelman did not consider the electroplated pieces at Knoedler's to be prototypes for later translations into marble or bronze is confirmed by the gallery's price list and its letter to various museum directors offering them for sale.[150] Two years later, however, in declining a request from Juliana Force, director of the Whitney Studio Club, to lend one of his "spirited figures" to a show on the circus, he claimed they were "at present at the foundry to be cast in bronze."[151] Whether this was an excuse for turning down an institution that had not supported his work since 1917 or whether he had, in fact, begun to cast the work is unclear. Whatever the explanation, the precipitous loss of his financial independence following the 1929 stock market crash precluded any such effort; no bronze versions of these sculptures were ever made during his lifetime.

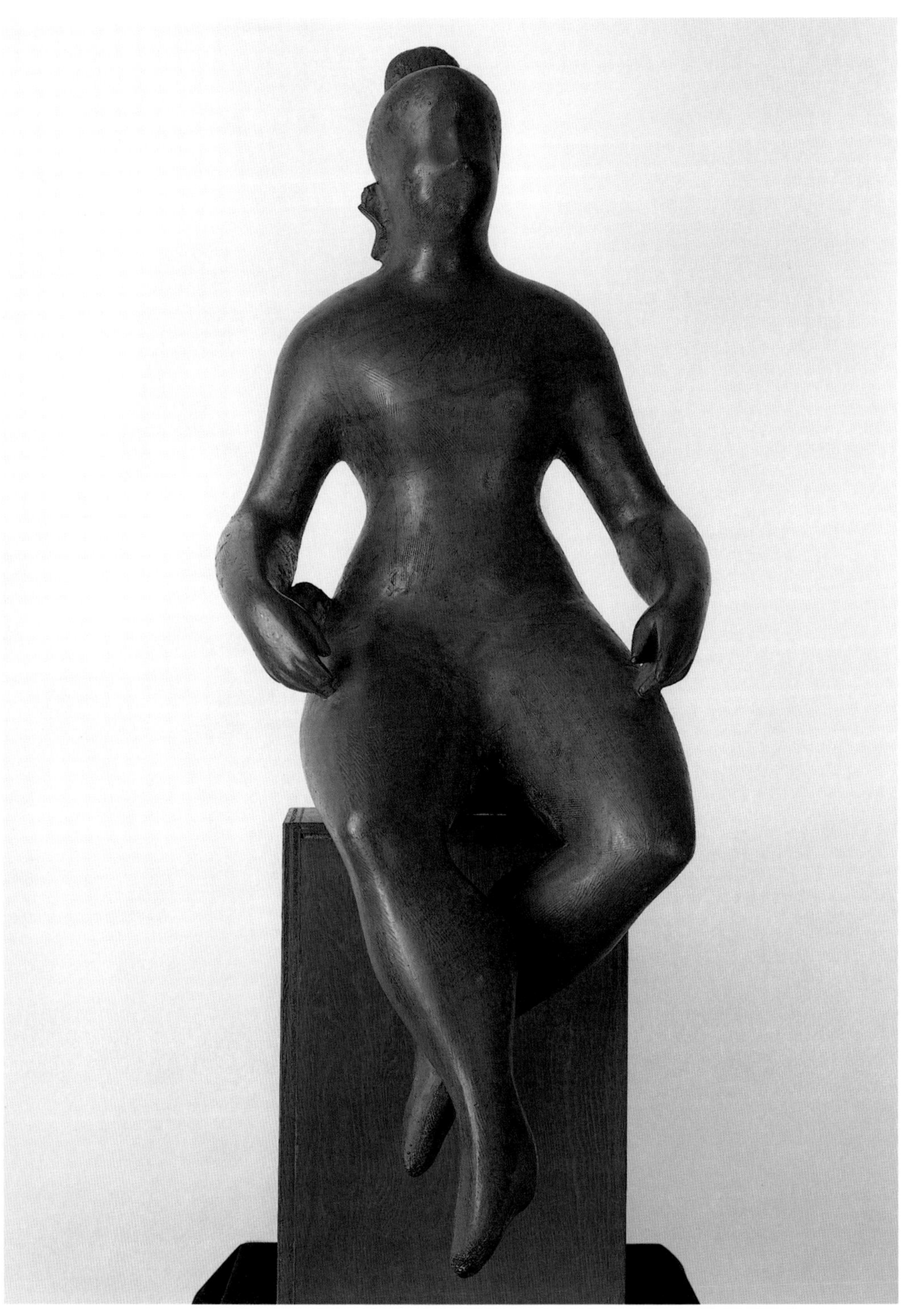

Fig. 184
Elie Nadelman
Seated Woman, c. 1925–26
Galvano-plastique, 48 x 20 3/4 x 23 1/2 in.
(121.9 x 52.7 x 59.7 cm)
Estate of Elie Nadelman, courtesy
Salander-O'Reilly Galleries, New York
Photography by Paul Waldman

Fig. 185
Elie Nadelman
Standing Female Figure, c. 1925–26
Galvano-plastique, 60 1/2 x 32 x 21 in.
(153.7 x 81.3 x 53.3 cm)
Whitney Museum of American Art, New York;
Purchase, with funds from The Lauder
Foundation, Evelyn and Leonard Lauder Fund
Photography by Jerry L. Thompson

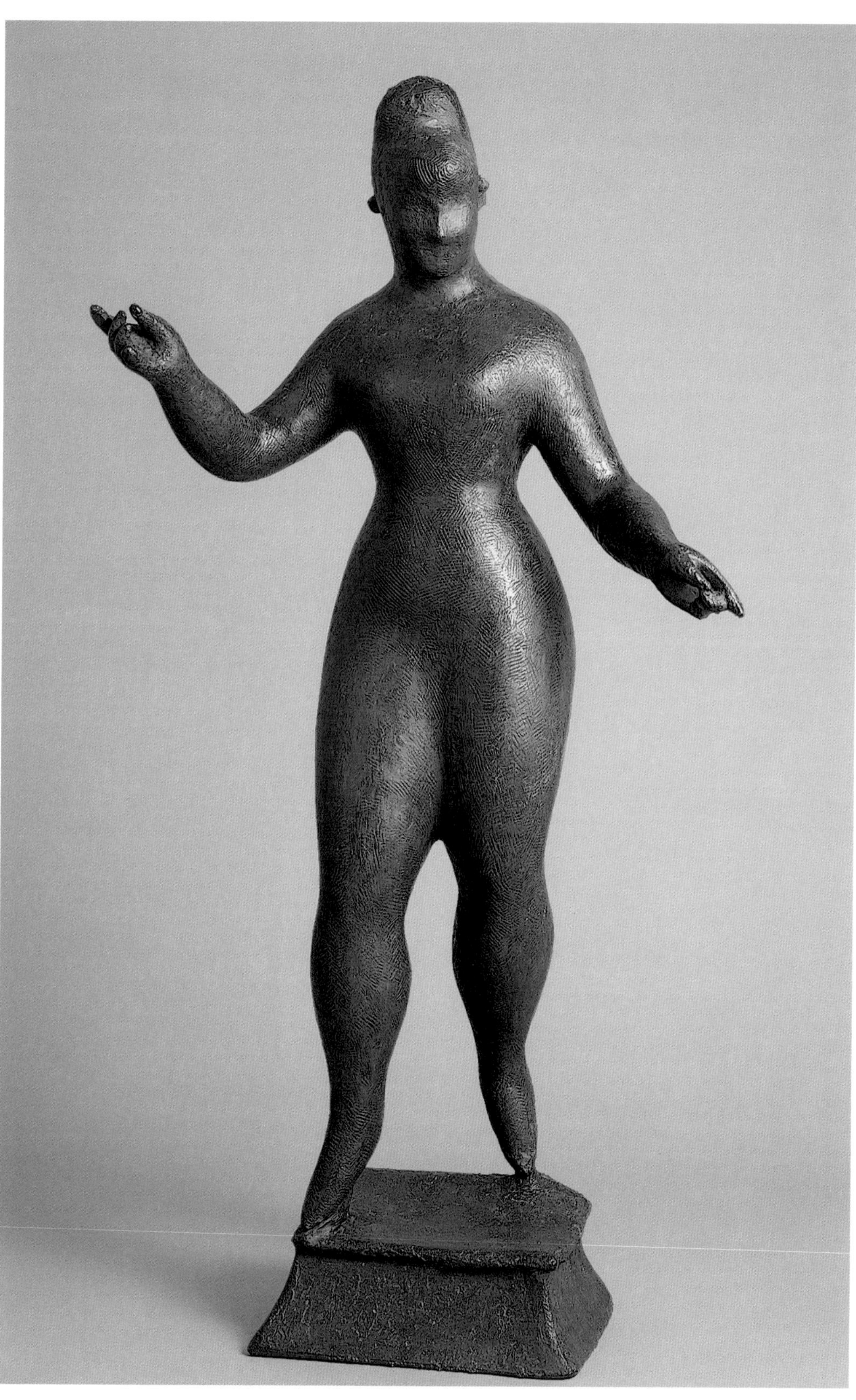

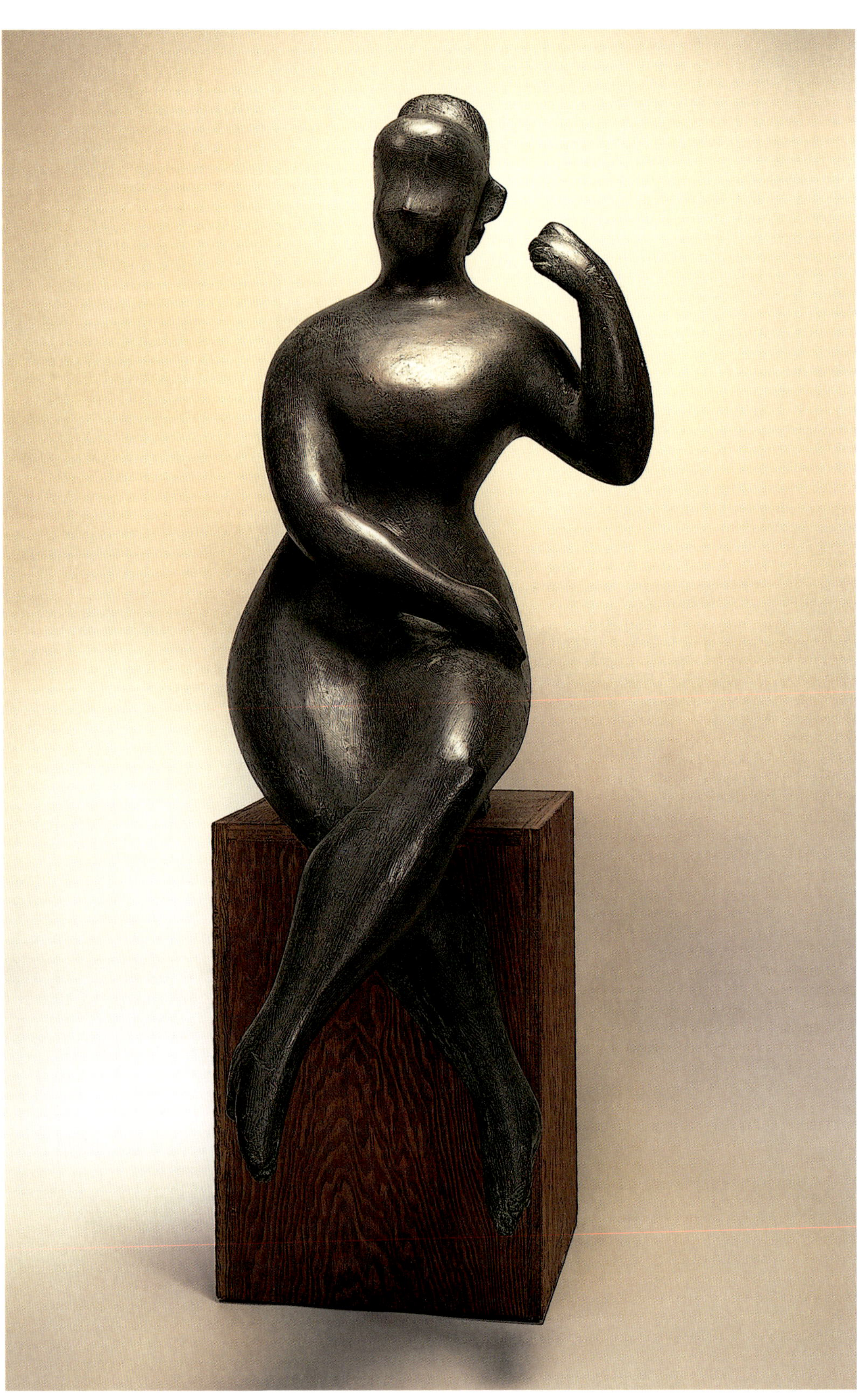

Fig. 186
Elie Nadelman
Seated Woman with Raised Arm, c. 1925–26
Galvano-plastique, 49 x 19 1/2 x 24 in.
(124.5 x 49.5 x 61 cm)
Estate of Elie Nadelman, courtesy
Salander-O'Reilly Galleries, New York
Photography by Paul Waldman

Fig. 187
Élie Nadelman
Standing Female Figure, c. 1925–26
Galvano-plastique, 61 x 30 x 19 1/4 in.
(154.9 x 76.2 x 48.9 cm) overall
Whitney Museum of American Art, New York;
Purchase, with funds from The Lauder
Foundation, Evelyn and Leonard Lauder Fund
Photography by Jerry L. Thompson

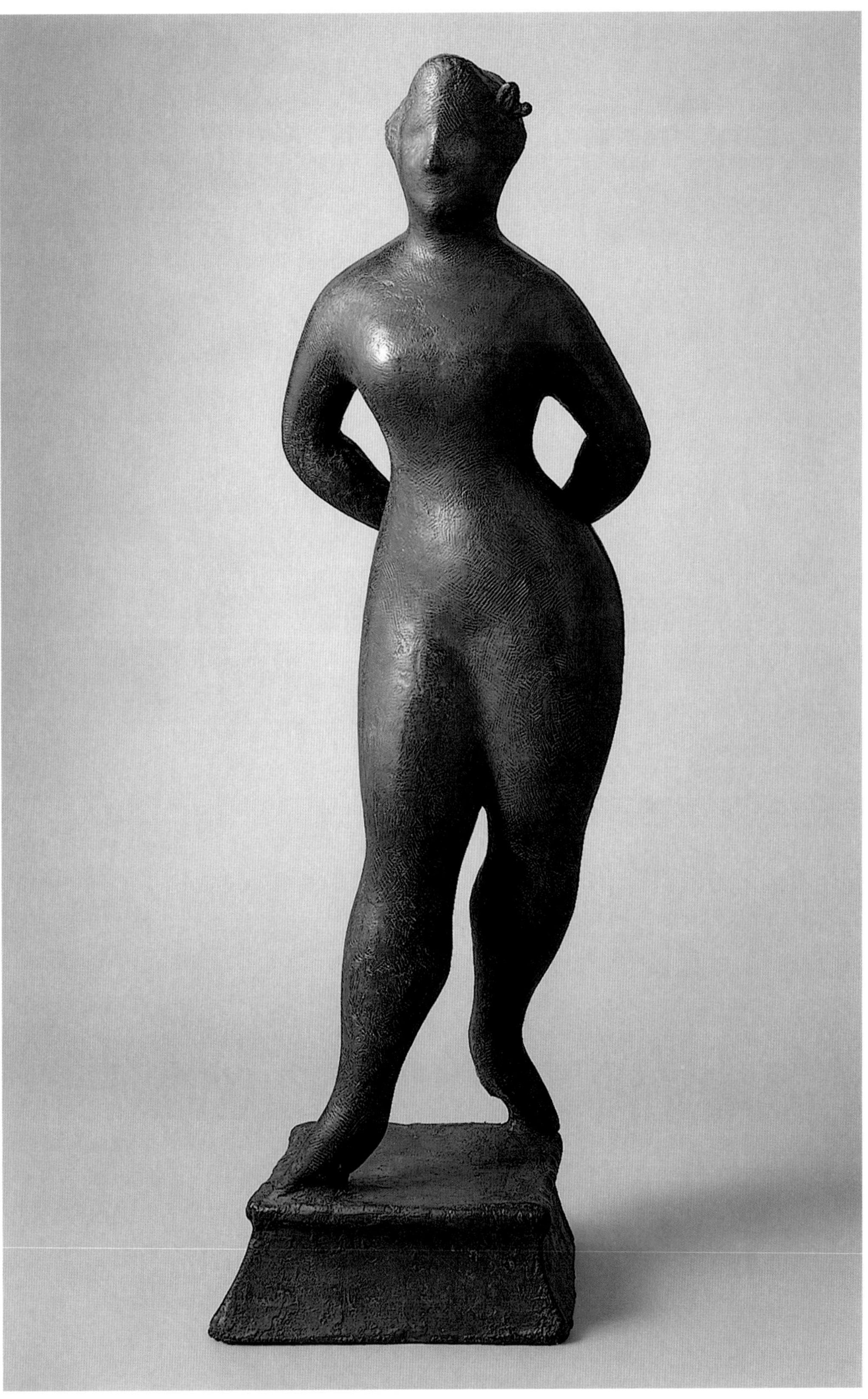

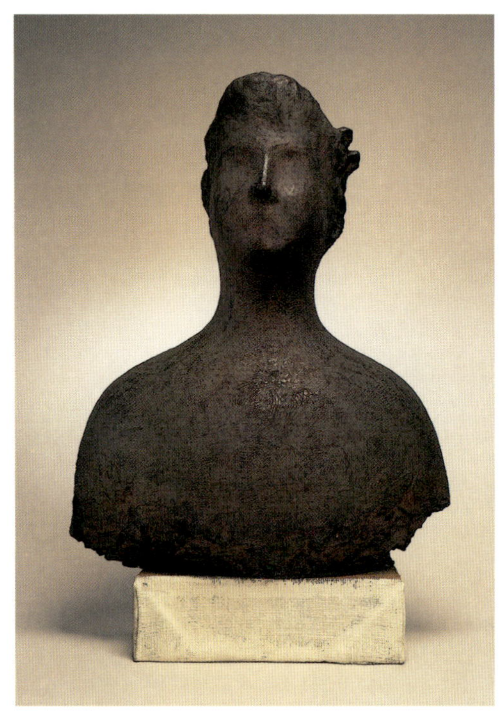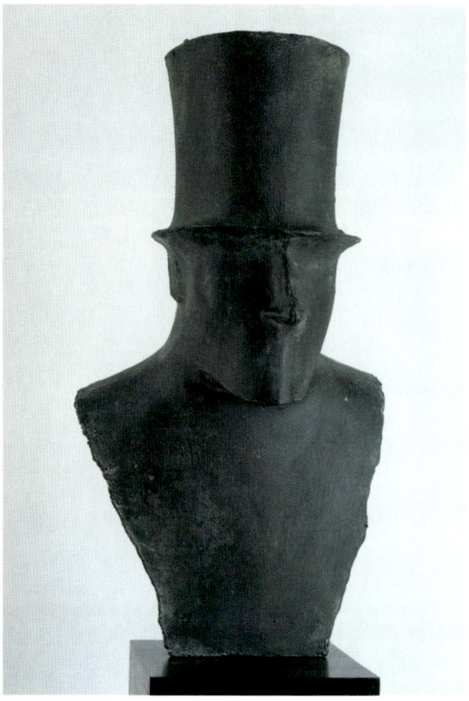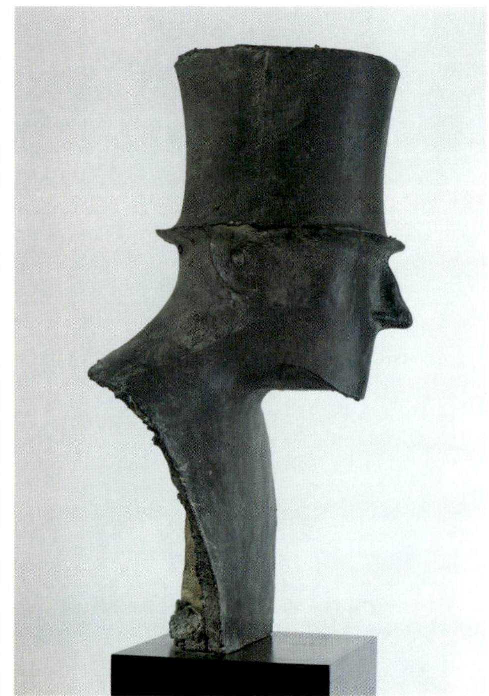

Fig. 188
Elie Nadelman
Female Bust, c. 1925–26
Galvano-plastique, 25 1/2 x 20 1/2 x 8 1/2 in.
(64.8 x 52.1 x 21.6 cm)
Estate of Elie Nadelman, courtesy
Salander-O'Reilly Galleries, New York
Photography by Paul Waldman

Fig. 189
Elie Nadelman
Man with Top Hat, c. 1925–26 (two views)
Galvano-plastique, 27 1/2 x 15 x 13 1/2 in.
(69.9 x 38.1 x 34.3 cm)
Collection of Richard and Camila Lippe

Fig. 190
Elie Nadelman
Bust of a Woman, c. 1925–26
Galvano-plastique, 32 1/2 x 17 x 12 in.
(82.6 x 43.2 x 30.5 cm)
Estate of Elie Nadelman, courtesy
Salander-O'Reilly Galleries, New York
Photography by Paul Waldman

Fig. 191
Elie Nadelman
Bust of a Woman, c. 1925–26
Galvano-plastique, 30 1/4 x 20 1/2 x 11 in.
(76.8 x 52.1 x 27.9 cm)
Estate of Elie Nadelman, courtesy
Salander-O'Reilly Galleries, New York
Photography by Paul Waldman

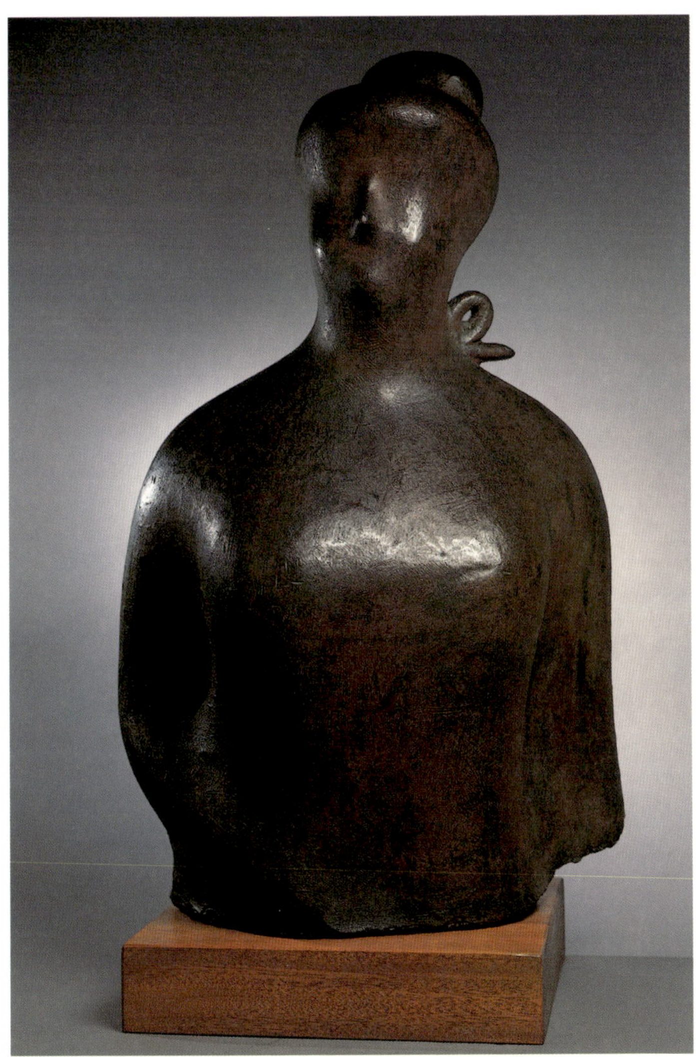

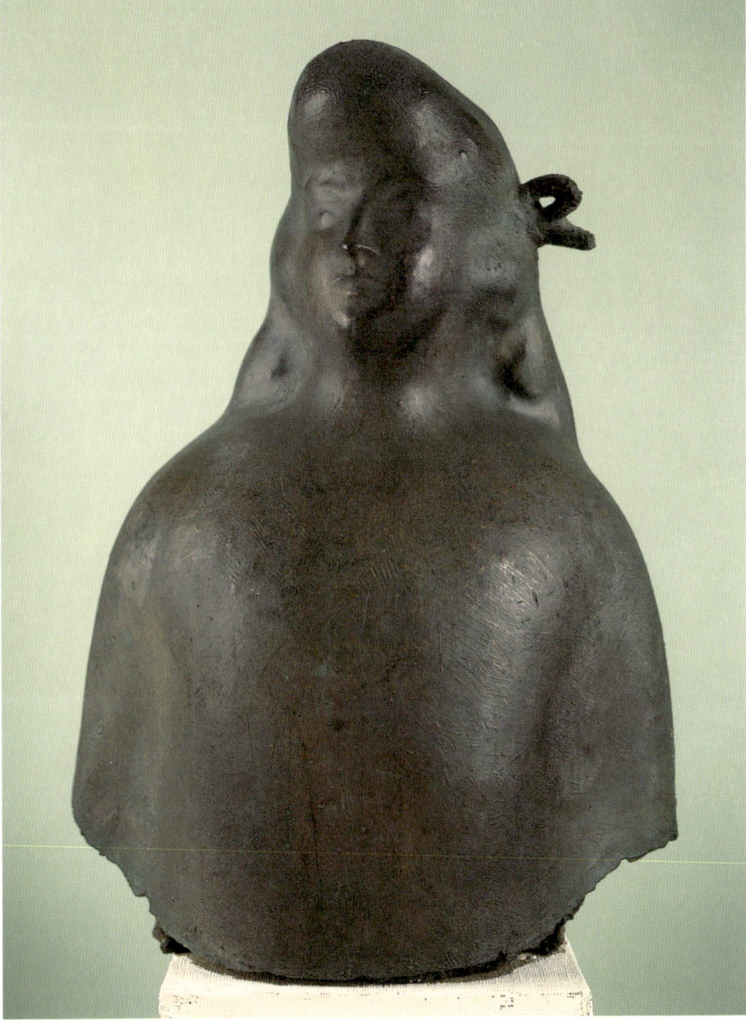

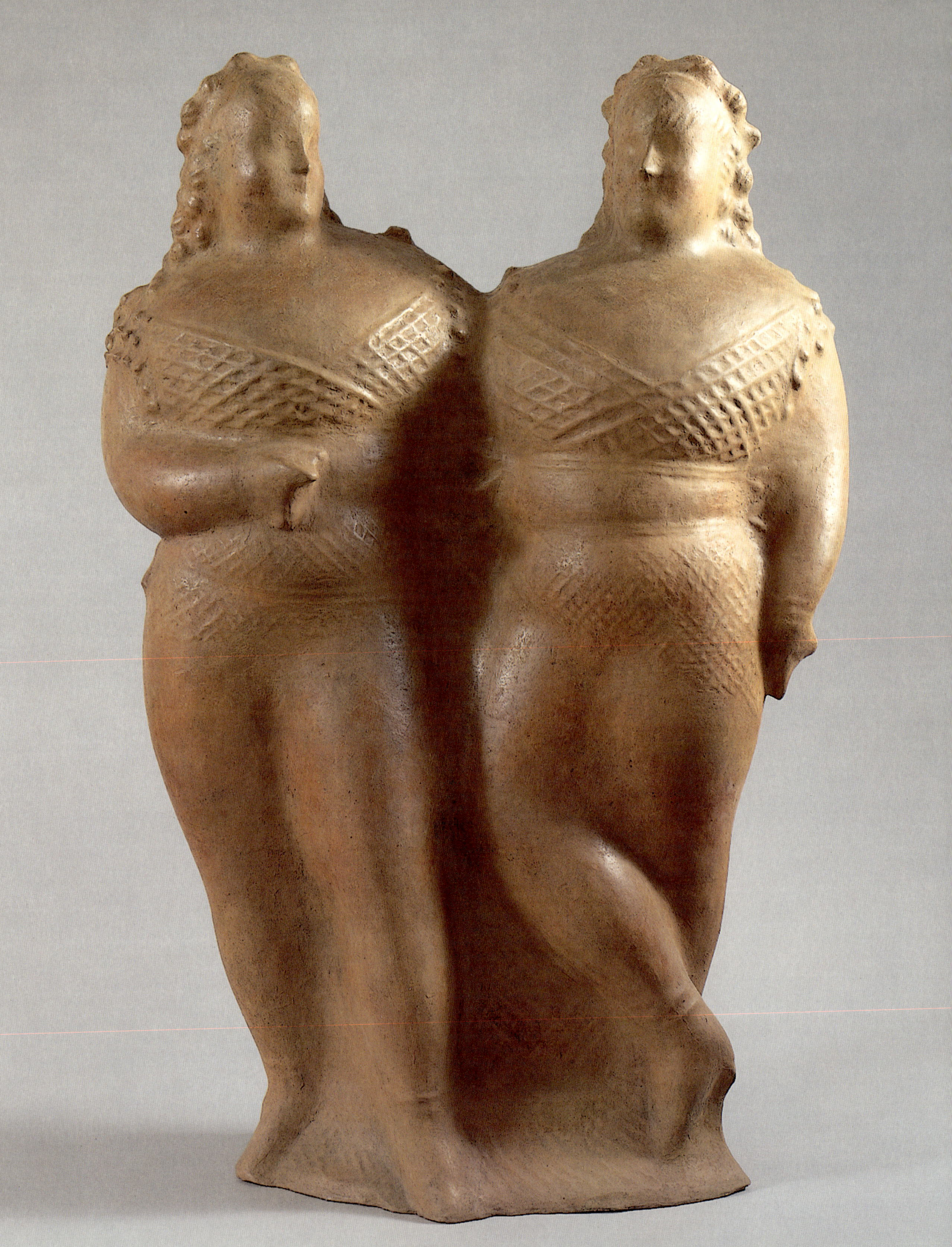

Toward a Domestic Market: Small-Scale Papier-mâchés and Terra-cottas, 1928–35

Nadelman's fascination with muted facial features and fugitive contours was even more pronounced in the three over-life-size sculptures of paired female circus performers that he executed in 1928 and 1929 (FIGS. 192, 196). As with his galvano-plastiques, he created them first as hollow-core plaster shapes, apparently from molds, judging from the existence of duplicate images. But rather than covering them with a thin coating of metal, he laminated two of them with brownish orange papier-mâché to give them the modulated coloration and delicate sensuality of unglazed terra-cotta. Combined with their melting contours and veiled facial features, these shimmering, luminous surfaces suggested a delicate weightlessness that contradicted the figures' massive, Amazonian proportions.

Joined in a single contour, these figures radiated a serene equanimity and detachment from the world, evincing unquestioned trust in each other and imperviousness to the anxieties of the outside world. Uninterrupted by surface detail, their seamless, fluid curvilinearity endowed them with an elusive mystery, more psychologically nuanced than in any of Nadelman's previous work. Coupled in poses of gentle intimacy and private communication, these paired figures display an idealized stillness and secular grace that is totally human without being individualized. No longer was Nadelman striving to create types or essences; the timeless and eternal realm of perfection for which he now aimed was not one of roles—circus performer, acrobat, or dancer—but one of relationships.

Nadelman had treated paired figures only four times before: *Two Standing Nudes, Sur la plage, Tree of Life,* and *Tango.* Apart from *Two Standing Nudes* (FIG. 46), however, those figures had been physically unconnected; they had shared an activity, but not a psychological closeness. To find models of coupled intimacy, Nadelman culled from a vast array of heterogeneous sources, splicing together layers of popular culture references with memories of ancient art. As he undertook *Two Circus Women,* he anachronistically combined images of Johann Gottfried Schadow's double portrait of Princesses Luise and Friederike of Prussia (FIG. 194)—famous in Germany during Nadelman's stay there as the country's greatest Neoclassical sculpture—with those of Tanagra

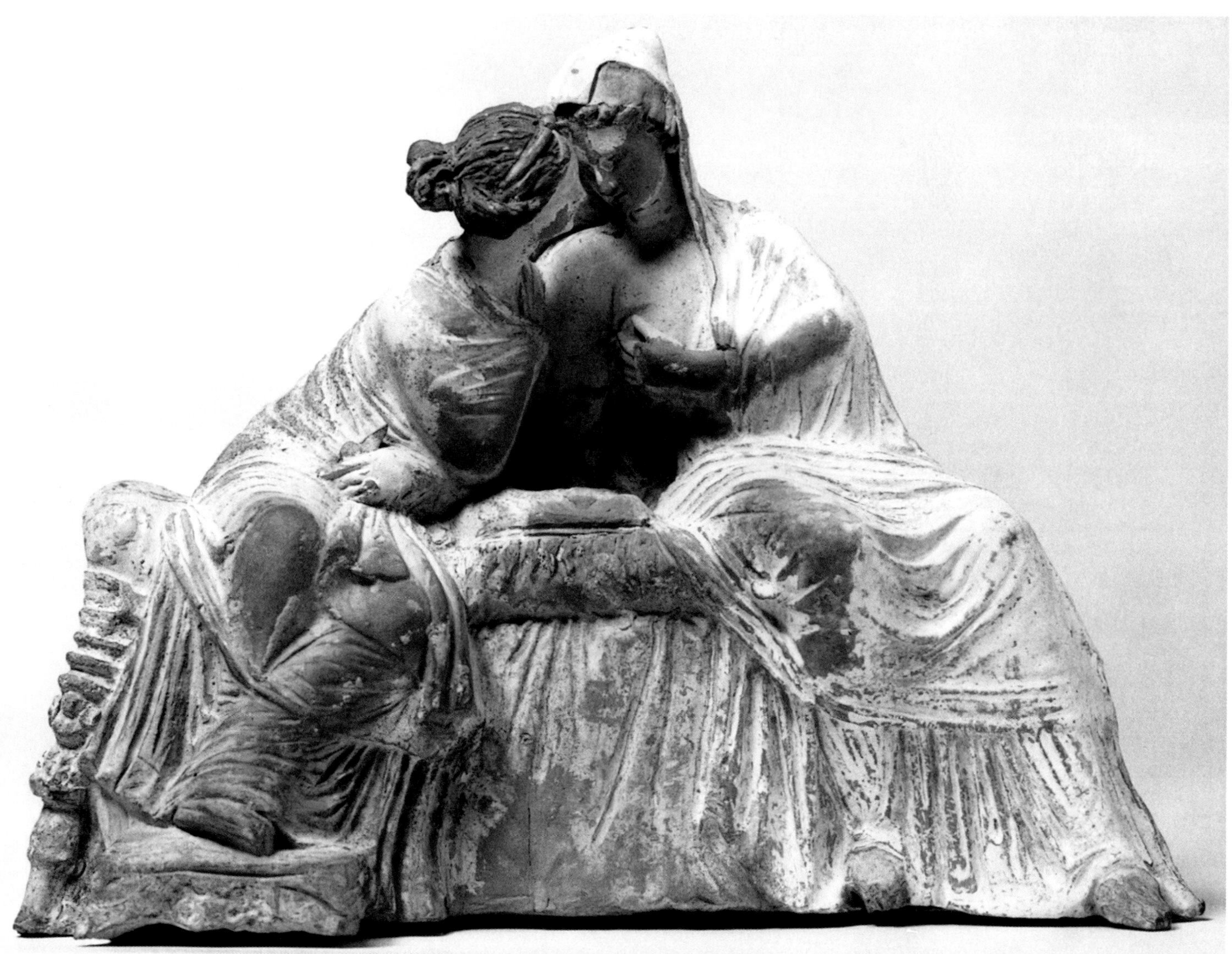

and Myrina terra-cottas (FIG. 193) from the late fourth to the first centuries
B.C. Indeed, these miniature figurines were so identified with the depiction of
women in close proximity posing with poetic gentility that Bessie Potter
Vonnoh's turn-of-the-century sculptures of females lounging on couches were
equated with Tanagra figurines in the American press (FIG. 195).[152] Tanagra and
Myrina figurines had not been central to Nadelman's thoughts since his Paris
days. What had rekindled his interest in them now was their kinship with the
gaily colored Pennsylvania Dutch chalkware ornaments in which his folk art
collection abounded. The similarities between these two disparate folk expressions perfectly illustrated his thesis about the parallels between ancient art
and American folk art. Both art forms imitated high-style prototypes; Tanagra

170

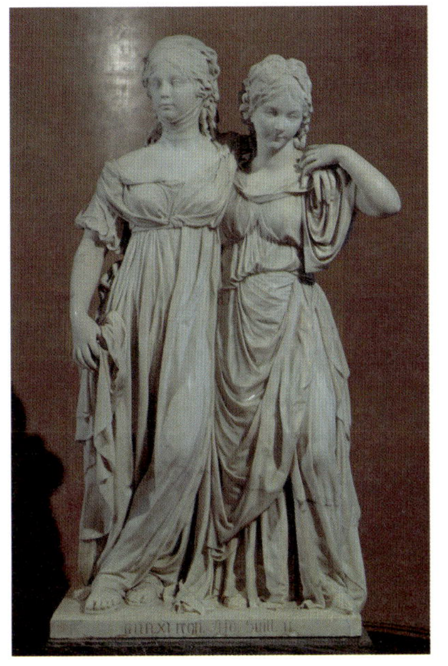

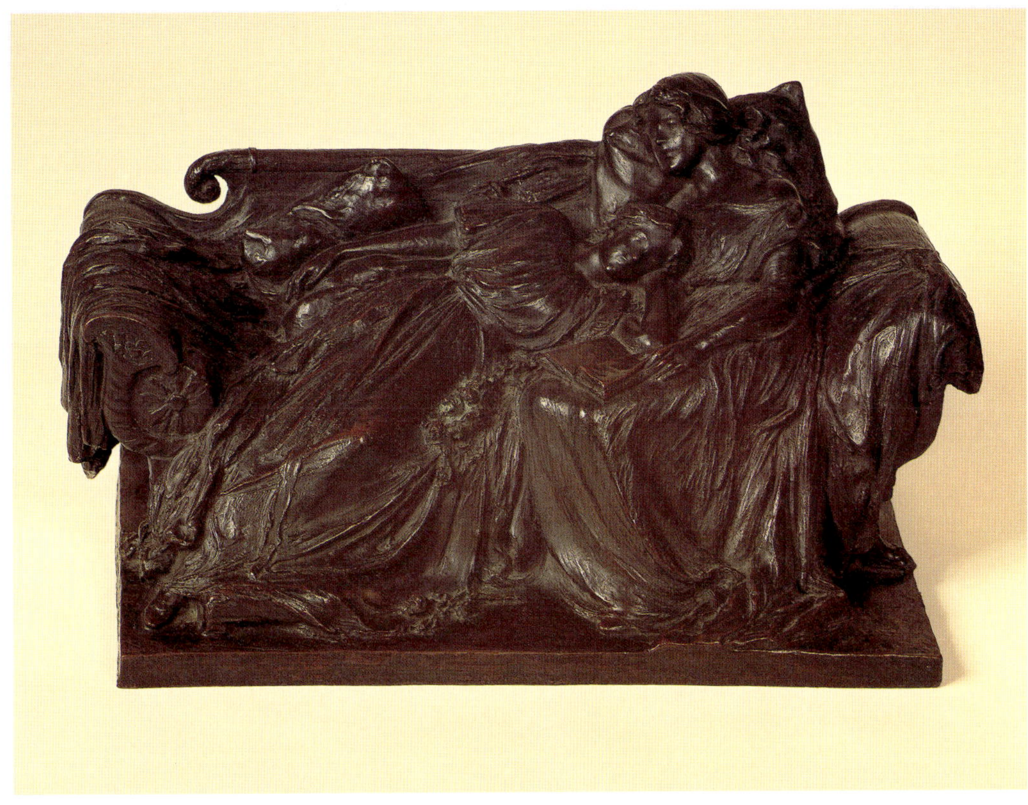

and Myrina figurines were inexpensive domestic versions of larger-scale temple statuary, while Pennsylvania Dutch chalkware ornaments were middle-class substitutes for high-end Staffordshire ceramics. Made in molds, both were deemed, in their time, to be at the low end of the aesthetic hierarchy. Both art forms were unpretentious in their subject matter and buoyant in their coloration, although the bright red, yellow, blue, and green tones in which the Tanagra and Myrina figurines were originally painted had significantly faded.

Nadelman's over-life-size paired circus women were related to these precursors in imagery but not in scale or coloration. Those aspects of Greek terra-cottas now caught his attention and led him to imagine small-scale painted versions of his own large-scale work. To this end, he installed a kiln in a specially built annex to his studio; by September 1930 he was firing multiple versions of small clay figurines identical in form to his larger sculptures (FIGS. 197–198). As he sought ways to individualize these ceramic multiples, he turned for guidance to Greek terra-cotta and Pennsylvania Dutch chalkware craftsmen. Greek craftsmen—or coroplasts, as they were called—had achieved variety by assembling their figurines from multiple casts. They transformed the identity and iconography of their figures by joining heads, arms, headdresses,

171

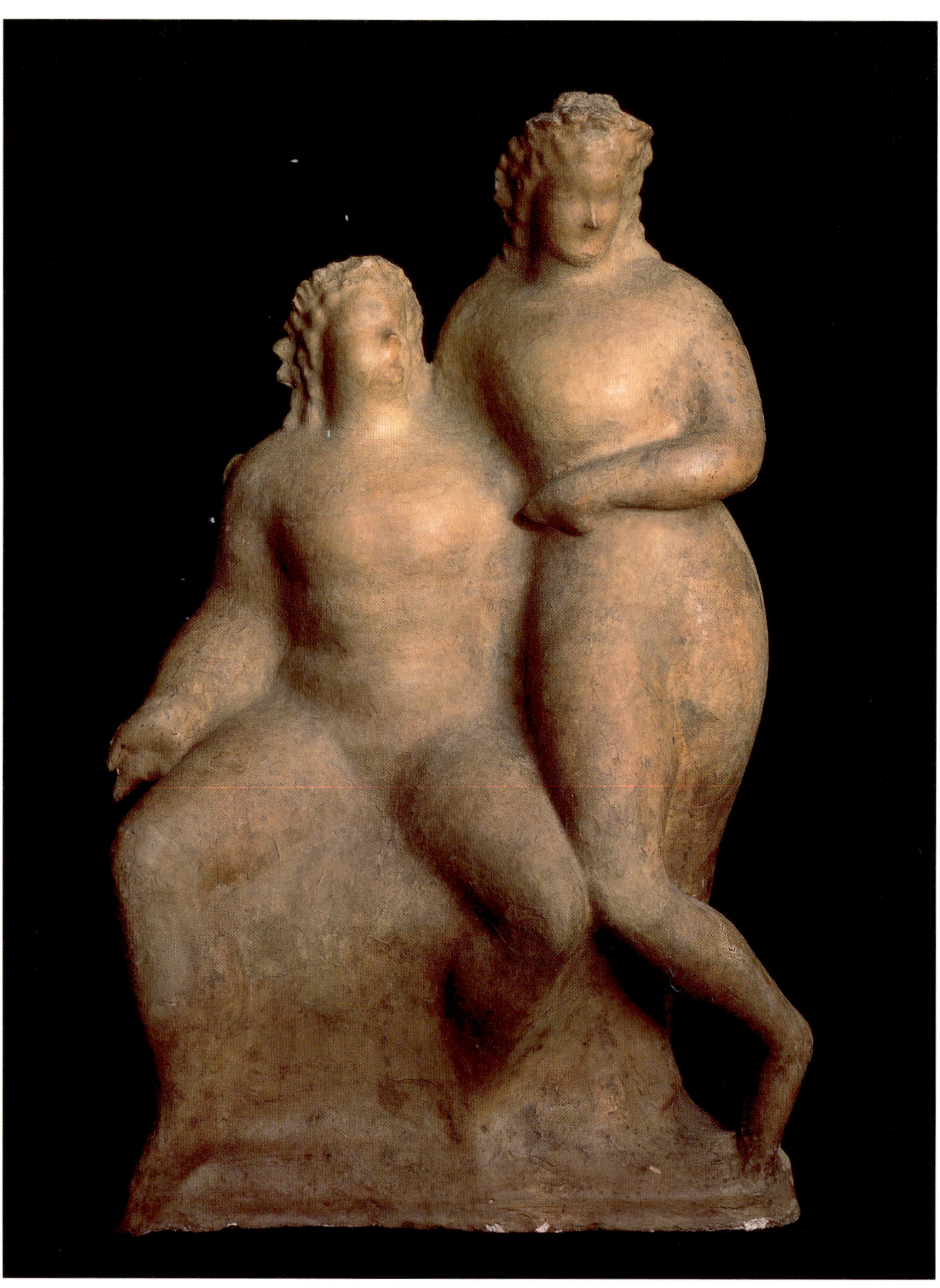

lyres, wings, or accessories to a standard body while the clay was still pliable. This method of achieving heterogeneity would appeal to Nadelman later; for now, he opted to differentiate each figure produced from the same mold by varying its color and surface treatment, just as chalkware craftsmen had done. These craftsmen had distinguished the figures and ornamental animals, birds,

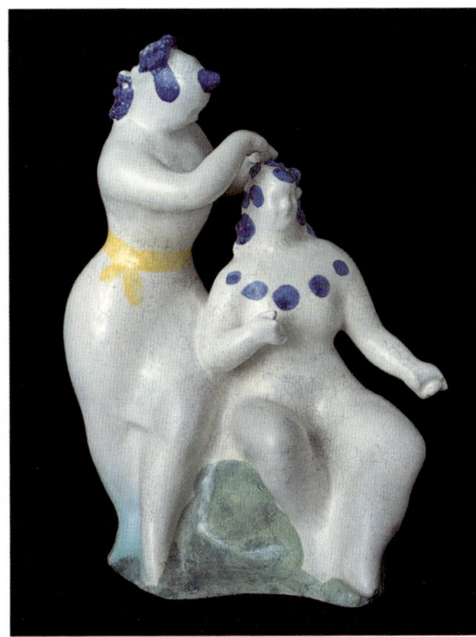

and bowls of fruit they produced from single molds by painting the unglazed surface of each form with differently pigmented watercolor or oil paint. Following their example, Nadelman produced duplicates of a handful of figures, each of whose hair, base, and clothing he painted differently. His wish was not to mass-produce identical pieces but to create familial sets of related works, each sharing a common shape but possessing unique features.

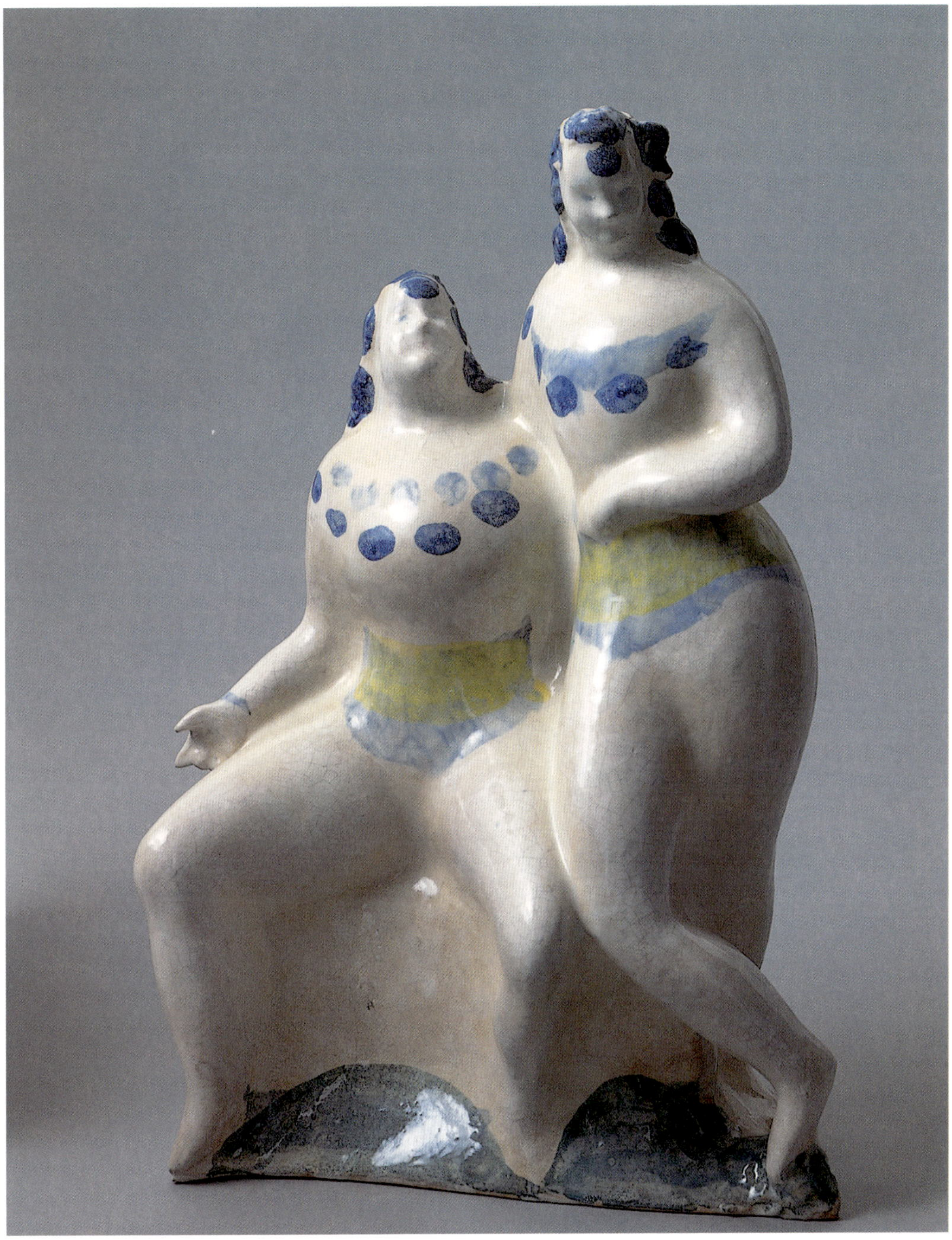

Fig. 199
Nadelman's figures arranged in the attic of Alderbrook after the artist's death, 1948
Photography by W. Eugene Smith/TimePix

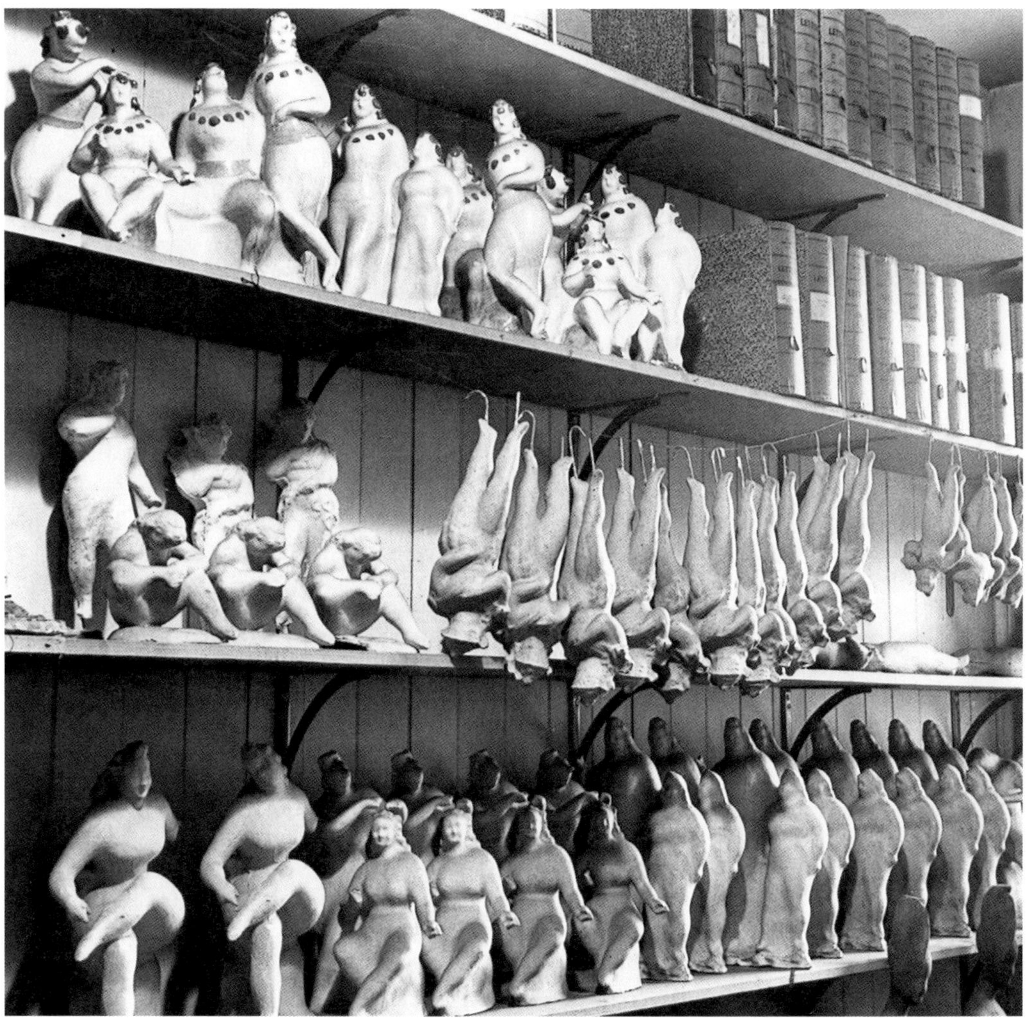

Fig. 200
Elie Nadelman
Standing Nude, c. 1930–35
Marble, 12 in. (30.5 cm) high
Erving and Joyce Wolf Collection
Photography by Jerry L. Thompson

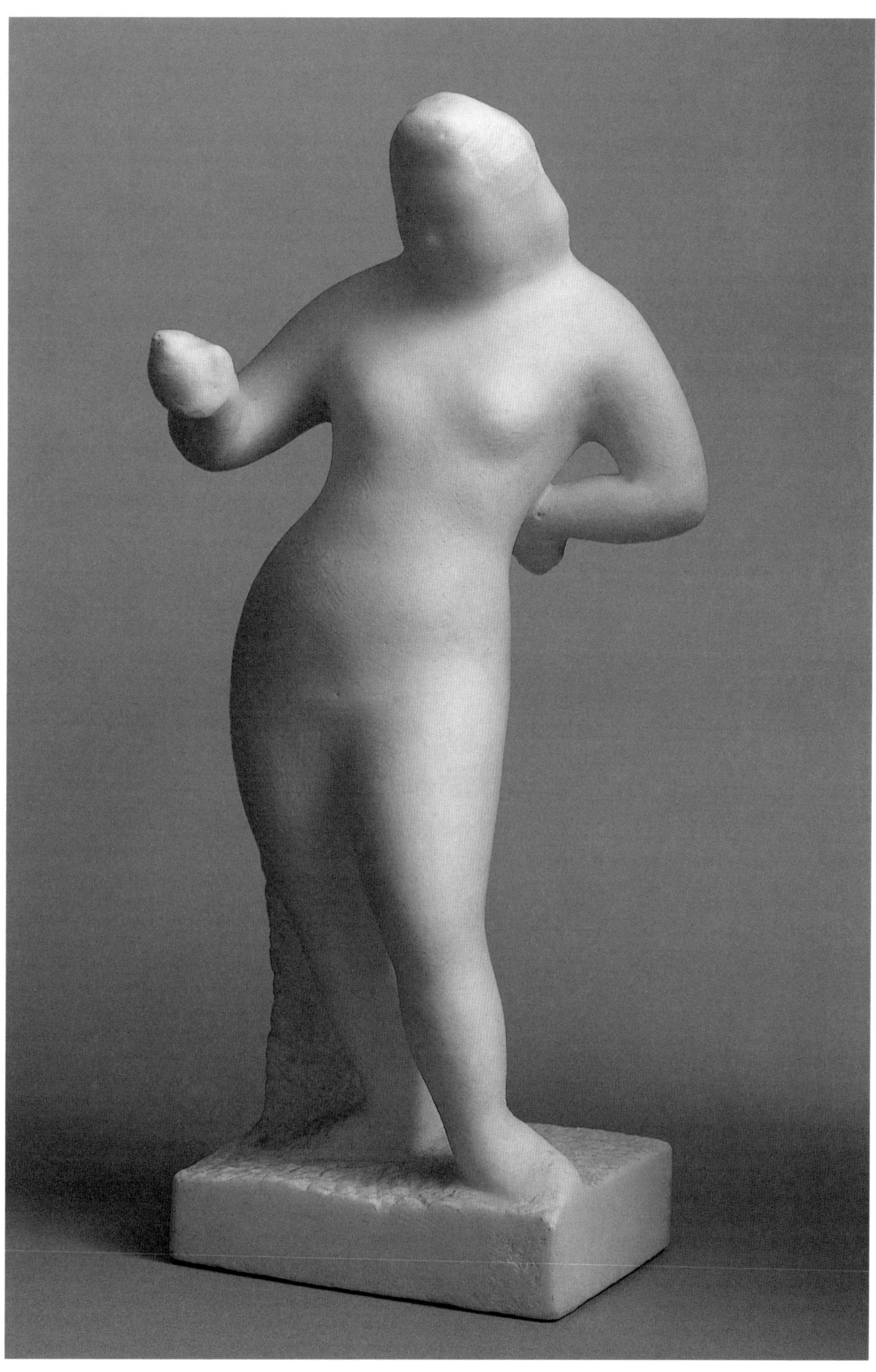

Fig. 201
Elie Nadelman
Standing Nude, c. 1930–35
Marble, 12 in. (30.5 cm) high
Erving and Joyce Wolf Collection
Photography by Jerry L. Thompson

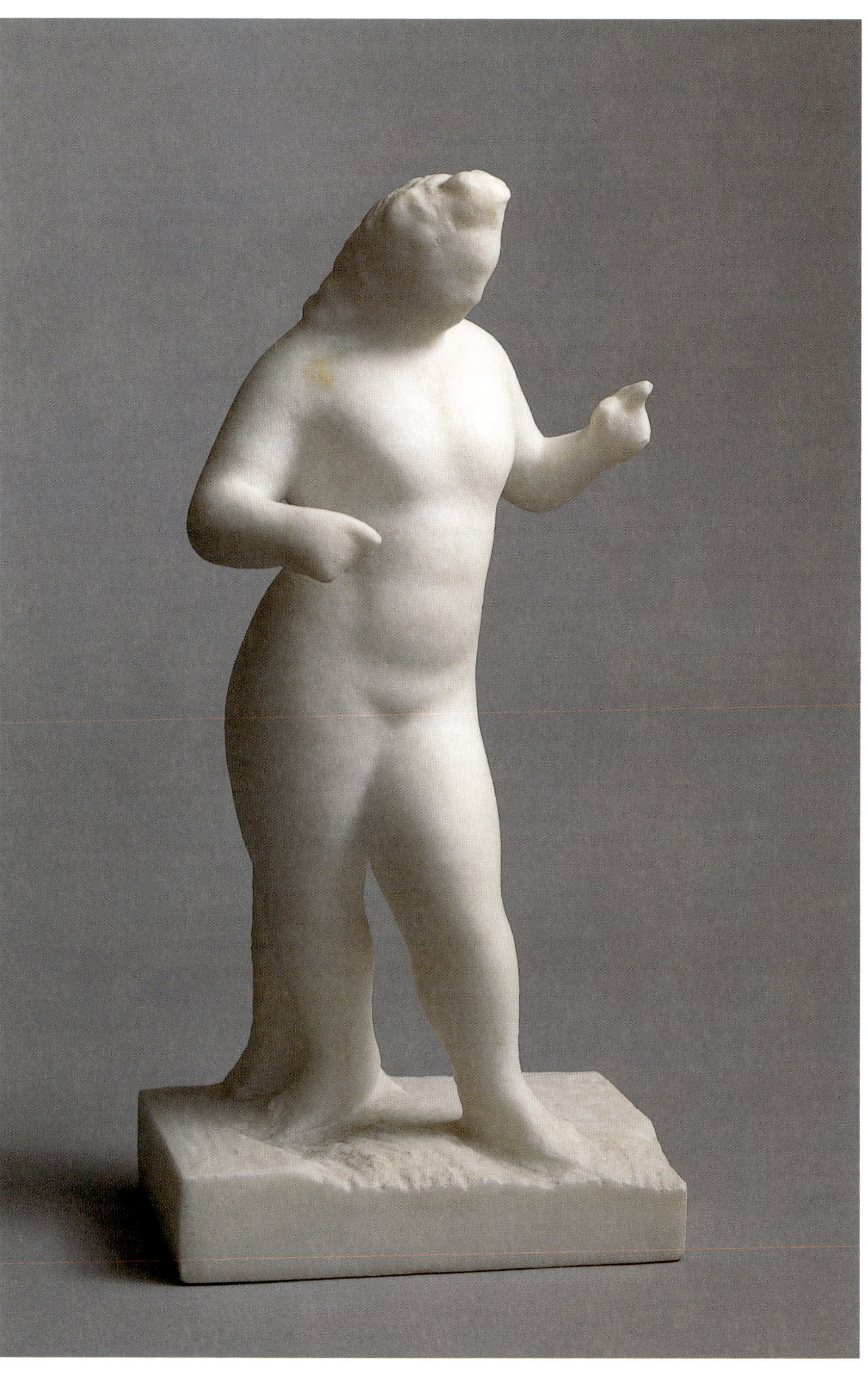

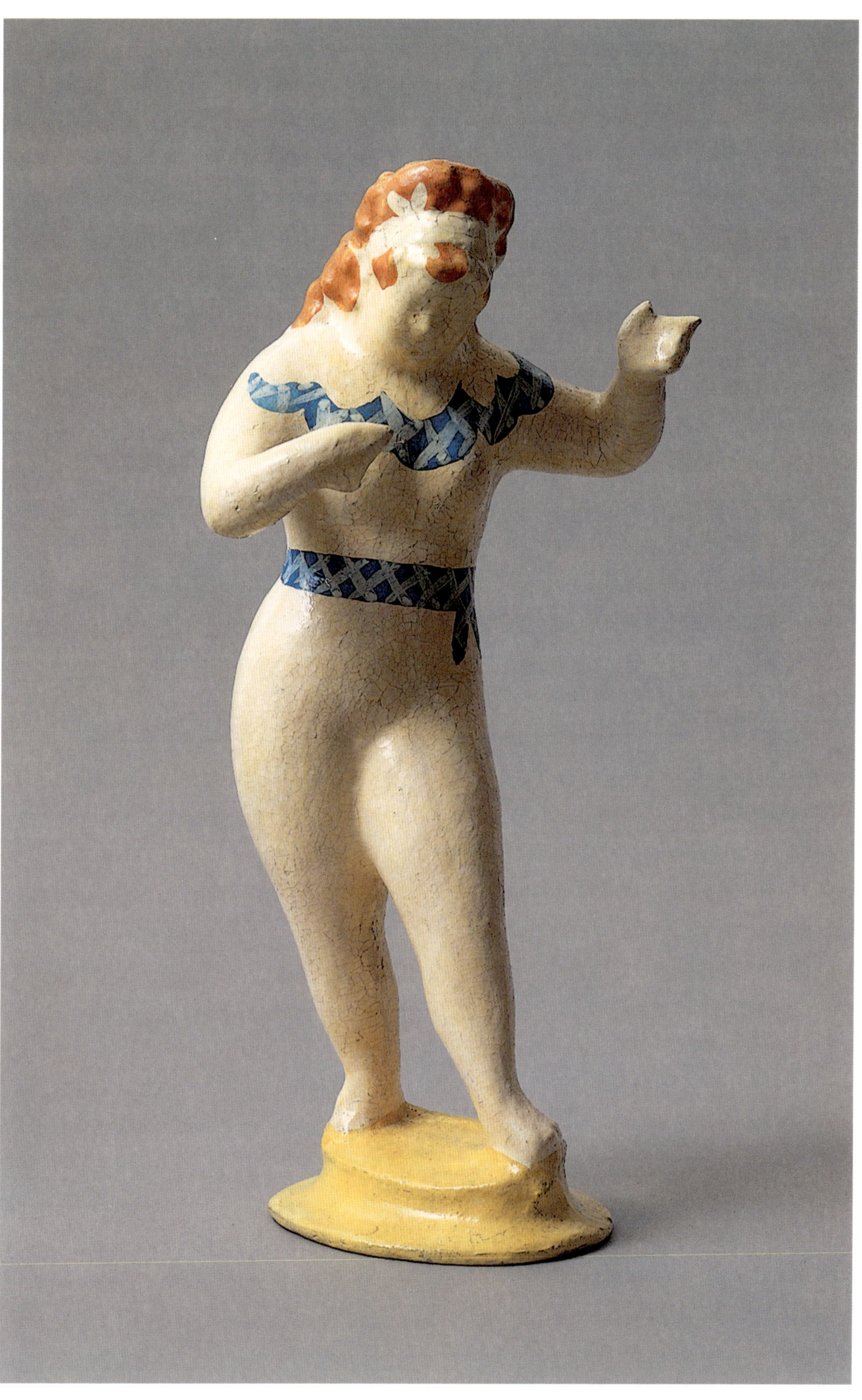

Fig. 202
Élie Nadelman
Untitled, c. 1930–35
Painted papier-mâché, 12 1/4 x 6 x 5 in.
(31.1 x 15.2 x 12.7 cm)
Whitney Museum of American Art, New York;
Purchase, with funds from The Lauder
Foundation, Evelyn and Leonard Lauder Fund
Photography by Jerry L. Thompson

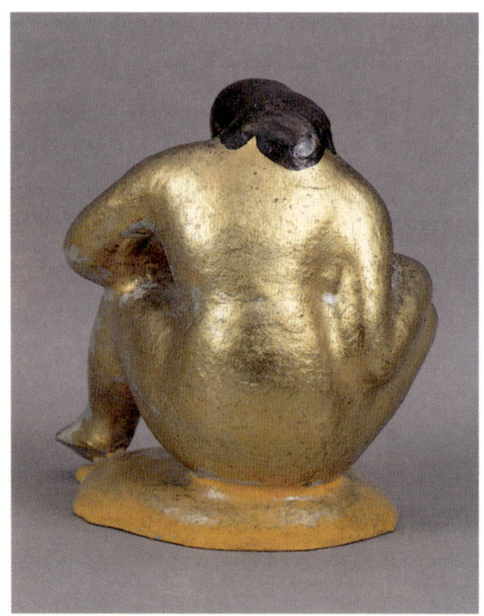

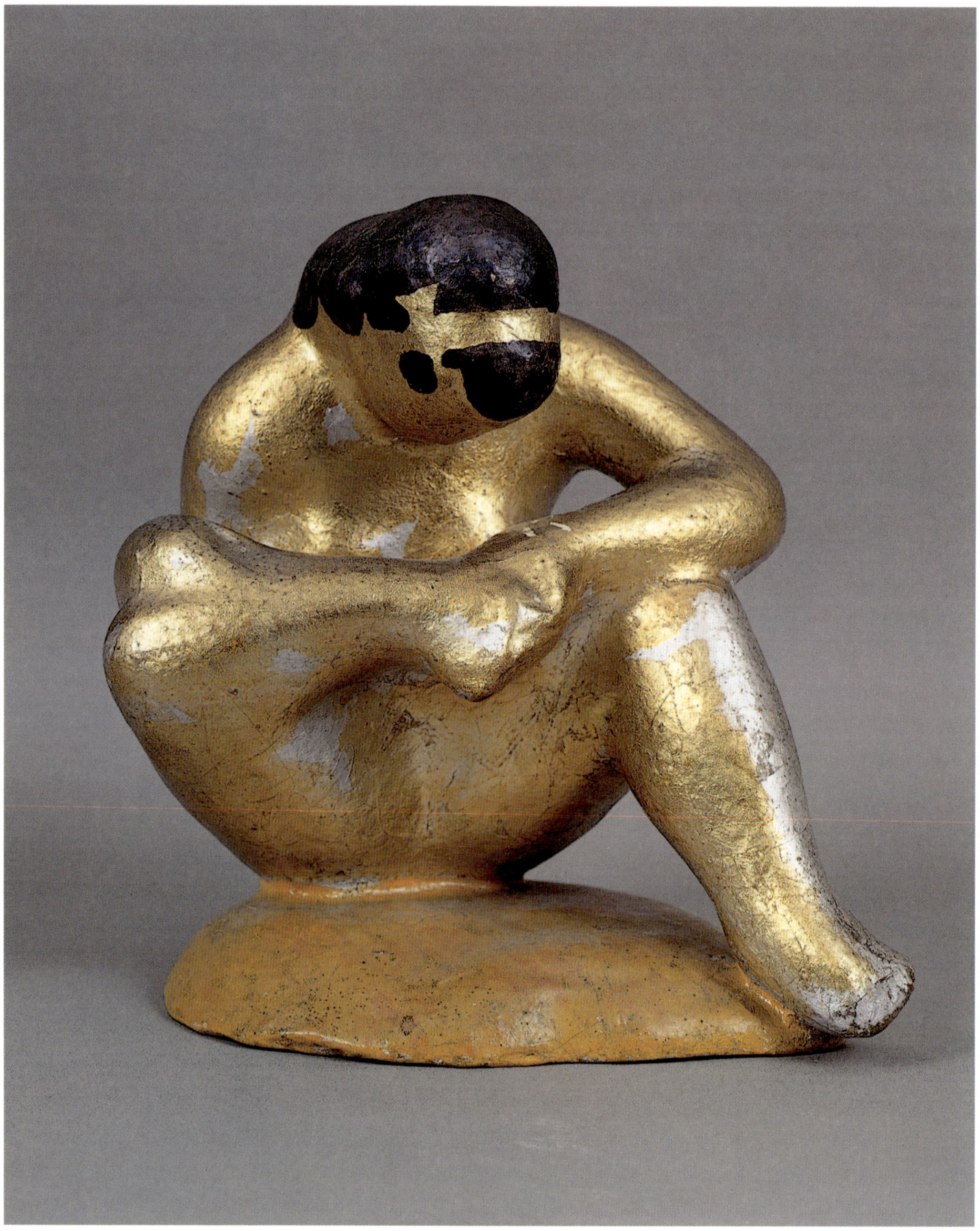

Fig. 203
Elie Nadelman
Untitled (Seated Woman), c. 1930–35
(two views)
Painted papier-mâché with gold leaf,
7 x 6 x 4 1/2 in. (17.8 x 15.2 x 11.4 cm)
Collection of halley k harrisburg and
Michael Rosenfeld

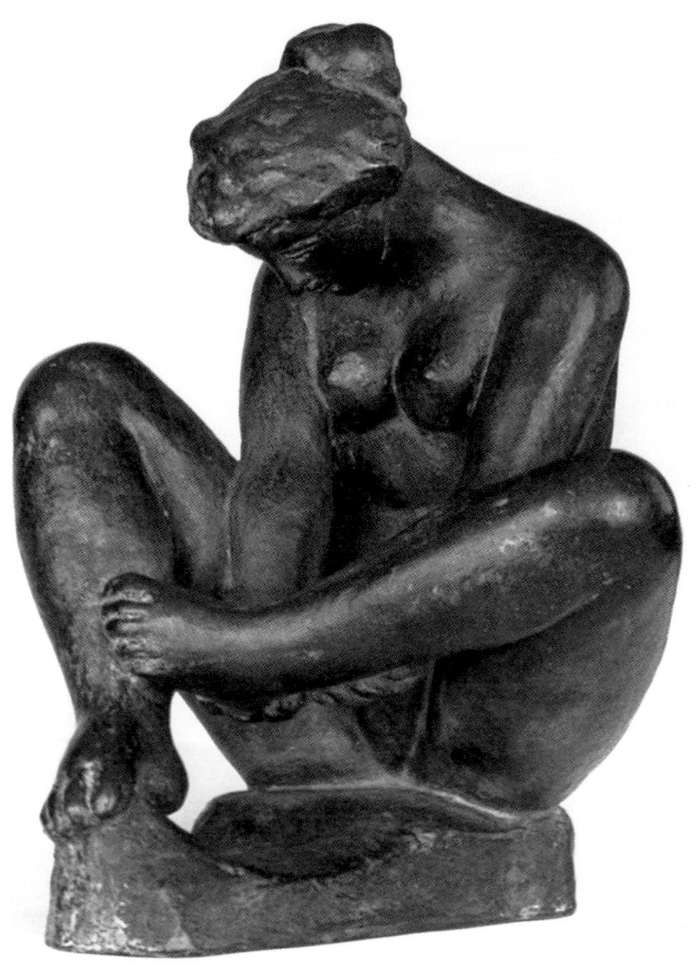

Nadelman's growing fascination with surface led him to glaze some pieces and leave others unglazed. He began to experiment with casting pieces in plaster and covering them with brown paper. Soon he had developed a special papier-mâché composite of boiled paper pulp, resins, and glue, which he cast in the same molds that he had used for his terra-cottas and plasters. He became so adept at simulating surfaces that it was almost impossible to tell whether a glossy patina was treated papier-mâché or glazed terra-cotta or whether a matte brown patina was unglazed terra-cotta, treated papier-mâché, or paper over plaster. Certain subjects predominated: paired females, females with a poodle, or seated females contemplating their feet—a subject that had earlier engaged artists such as Maillol (FIG. 204) and Edgar Degas.

The Depression and Its Consequences, 1929—35

Nadelman's reputation as a sculptor was secure enough in 1928 and 1929 to win him two major commissions for New York City buildings designed by the architectural firm of Walker and Gillette: a limestone frieze depicting construction workers on the facade of the Fuller Building (FIG. 207) and a pediment for the Bank of the Manhattan Company depicting the bank's seal, a reclining Aquarius pouring water from an urn (FIG. 205).[153] By this time, however, Nadelman's vocabulary had shifted from the crisply demarcated, idealized forms that had earlier won him renown to the amorphous contours and indistinct facial features of *Two Circus Women*. Correspondence between the architect and the bank's officers and differences between the maquette for the Fuller Building frieze and the final work (FIGS. 206, 207) indicate that Nadelman's clients were not receptive to his new style.[154] By the time the two buildings opened, Nadelman had accommodated their demands, and his Aquarius and Fuller Building workers matched the heroic style of American public art of the 1930s.

Nadelman had been well paid for his efforts: $10,500 for the Fuller Building's sculpture and $7,000 for the bank's. In October and November of 1929 he sent $8,000 of this income to his broker with the instructions to "buy 'on margin' because I understand the present market situation is favorable."[155] Twenty thousand dollars more followed in January and March of 1930. Sadly, Nadelman was no more immune to the consequences of the stock market crash than anyone else. His bank account plummeted, as did Viola's, which depended largely on rent from her real estate holdings. As more businesses went bankrupt and more commercial tenants defaulted on rent, the Nadelmans' bills mounted, and their taxes went unpaid. By the end of October 1930 they had begun to sell portions of their folk art and antiquities collections.[156] Efforts to raise money by taking out a second mortgage on their Ninety-third Street townhouse and building a freestanding rental unit on their Riverdale property proved fruitless. In April 1931—with sales of art all but nonexistent, their stocks nearly worthless, and their commercial rental properties generating little income—their realtor recommended that they liquidate their Riverdale property because of its high overhead and consolidate their belongings at their Ninety-third Street townhouse. Against his advice they rented the townhouse and moved full-time to Riverdale.[157]

Fig. 205
Elie Nadelman
Aquarius, 1930 (two views)
Bank of the Manhattan Company
40 Wall Street, New York
Bronze, 112 in. (284.5 cm); lost or destroyed
Photographs courtesy The Maddox Collection

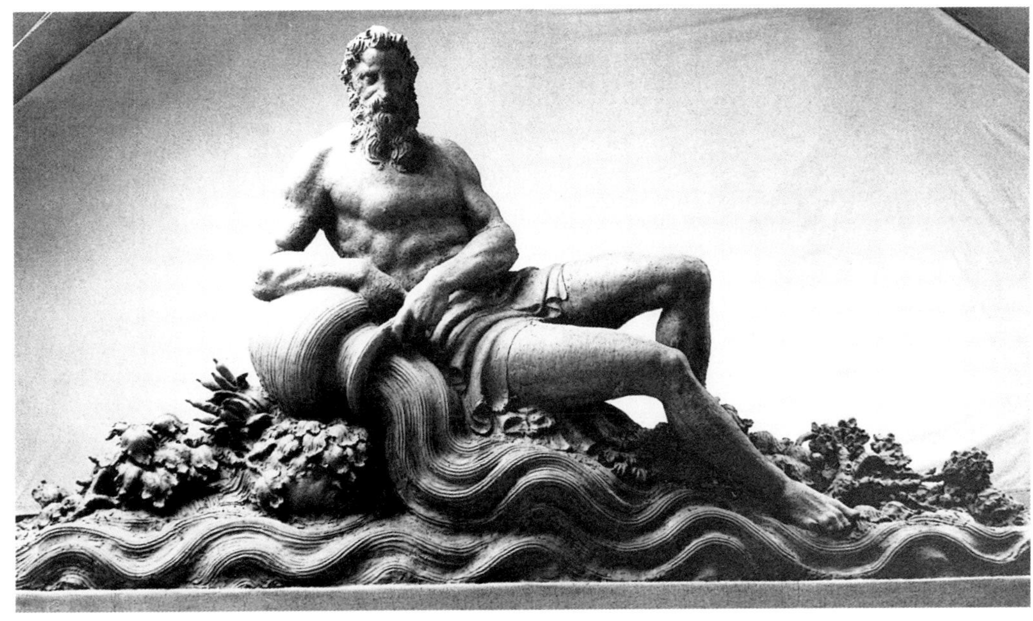

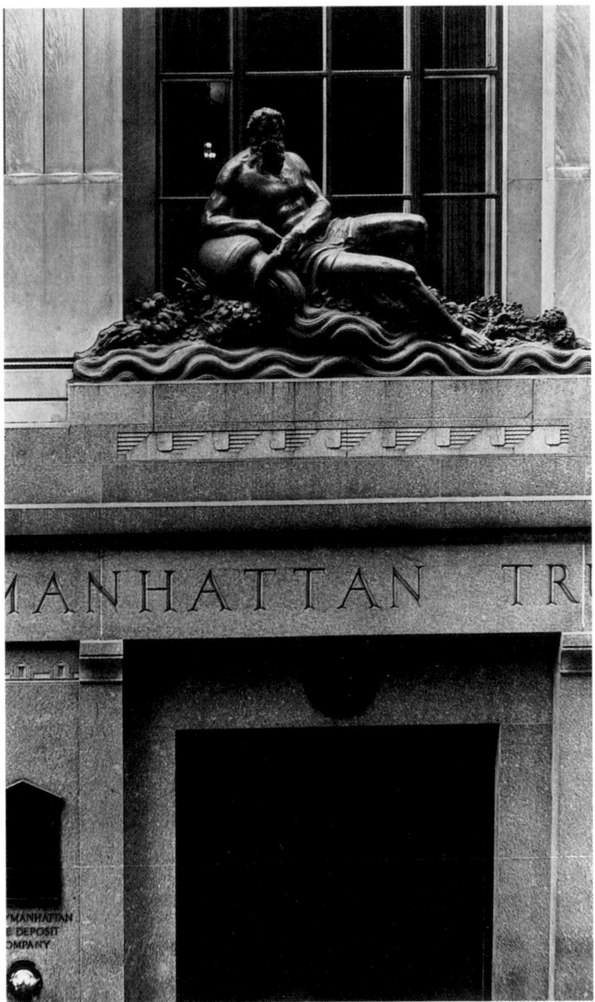

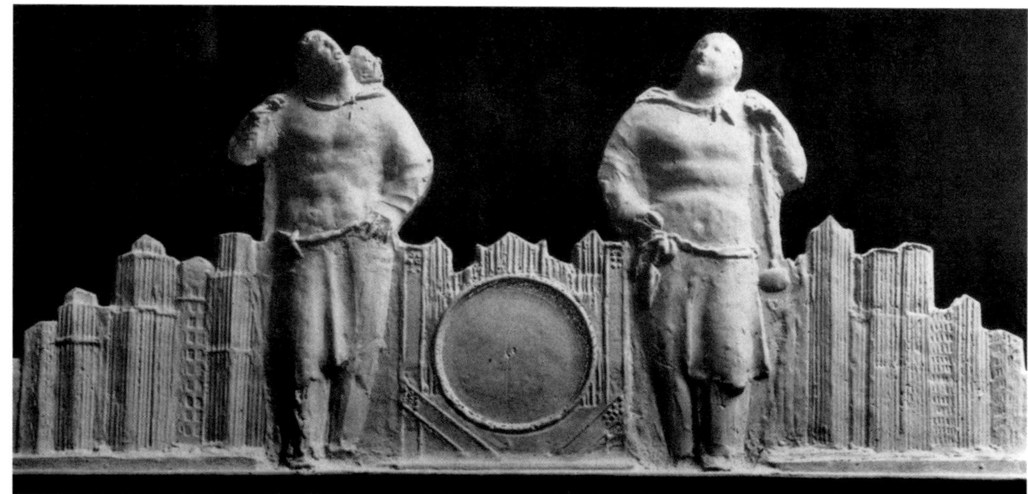

Fig. 206
Elie Nadelman
Maquette for Fuller Building frieze, 1929
Plaster, 20 in. (50.8 cm) high; destroyed
Lincoln Kirstein Photograph Collection,
Jerome Robbins Dance Division, The New York
Public Library

Fig. 207
Elie Nadelman
Frieze on Fuller Building facade, 1930–32
41 East Fifty-seventh Street, New York
Limestone, 144 in. (365.8 cm)
Photograph courtesy The Maddox Collection

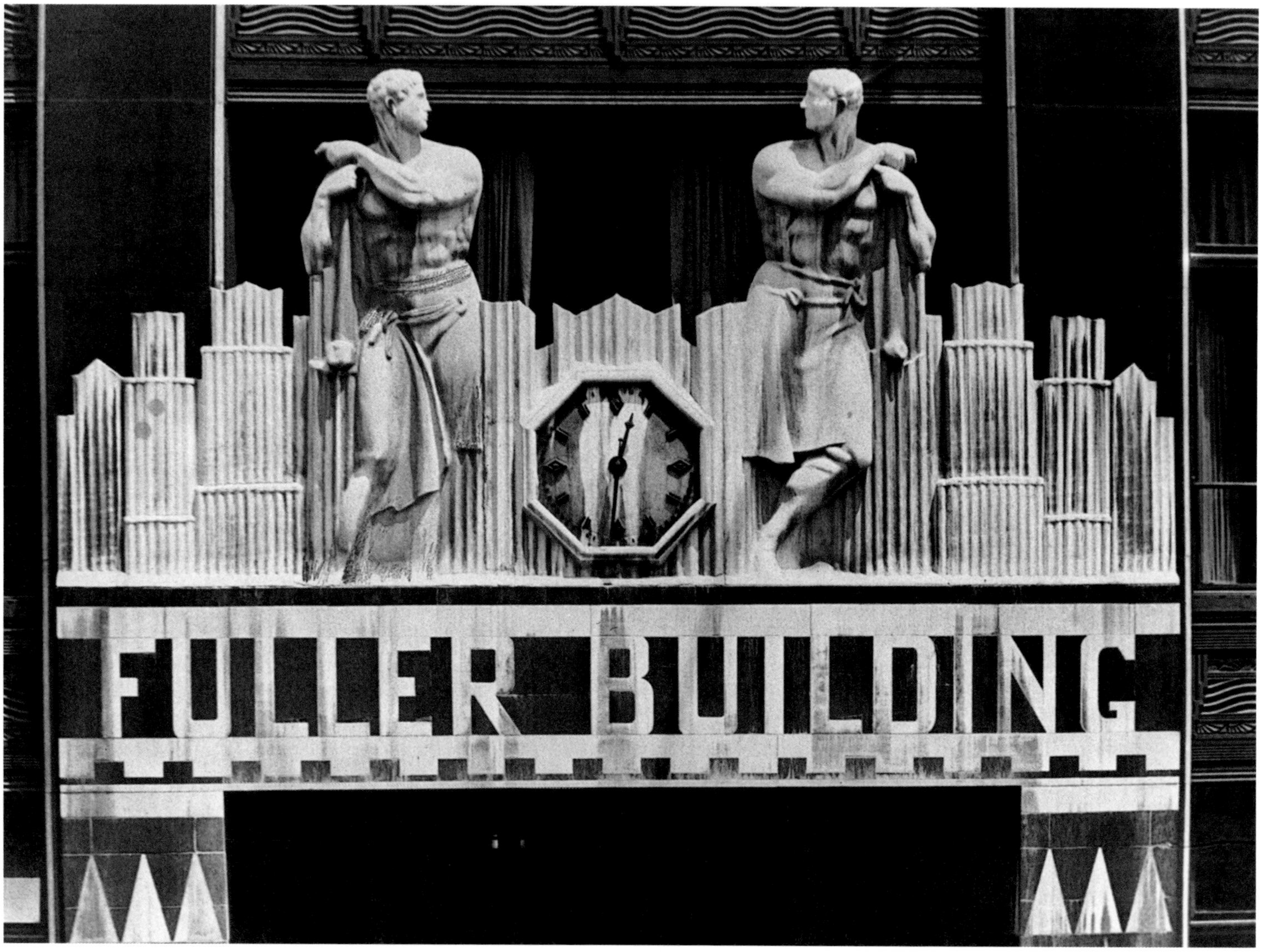

The Nadelmans' sale in October 1931 and July 1932 of another group of folk art objects to Henry F. du Pont and Abby Aldrich Rockefeller, respectively, kept the couple temporarily solvent, but in February 1933 the bank foreclosed on their townhouse and threatened to seize their other properties.[158] With no means of support, they exercised their only remaining option: to sell the land and buildings on their Riverdale estate to a neighborhood corporation with the resources to subdivide the property and build new homes. Inexplicably, the Nadelmans sailed for Europe that summer to visit Viola's ill daughter in an extravagant style, taking with them their son, Jan, one of his school friends, their chauffeur, and Viola's maid. Their retention of these employees and their continued acquisitions of folk art suggest that their resources, while depleted, were far from exhausted.

Still, the Nadelmans' life had changed irrevocably. Although they were allowed to live in their Riverdale house as renters until they could buy it back (which they did in 1936), Nadelman was forced to drop out of the private clubs to which he had belonged and to suffer the embarrassment of lawsuits brought against him by businesses he had earlier patronized.[159] More importantly, he lost the carriage house that had served as his studio for more than a decade. Its loss relegated him primarily to what had been the kitchen of the Riverdale house, shattering his sense of belonging to a grand atelier tradition. No longer was he surrounded by his earlier work, which was now stored in the attic and in a space he rented at the newly built Squibb Building on Fifth Avenue. Forced to work on a much smaller scale than before, he soon turned to imagery far more menacing and emotionally charged than any he had tackled before.

In the meantime, however, the Nadelmans put all their efforts into keeping their folk art museum open and their collection intact. Correspondence during this period is dominated by requests to former patrons for new commissions and by attempts to patent various inventions. Yet, for reasons of pride or arrogance, Nadelman failed to apply for any of the public commissions sponsored by the Roosevelt administration's various art programs. In 1933, for example, he had sailed to Europe without submitting an application for the City of Milwaukee's Abraham Lincoln memorial, about which he had earlier requested information. He would have been a seemingly ideal recipient of this or one of the sculptural commissions awarded under the aegis of the government's need-blind Section of Painting and Sculpture. Repeatedly, however, he failed to respond to the section's invitations to enter competitions yet was, at the same time, offended that it did not offer him work. Writing to section head Edward Bruce in 1936, he complained, "In all fairness, if achievement and reputation counted, I should not have been so entirely overlooked."[160]

That the Nadelmans had kept their museum open for as long as they did was a miracle given the economics of the 1930s. By 1934, however, they could no longer afford to pay their real estate taxes and were forced to close the museum. Deliverance came in the form of the Carnegie Corporation, whose art adviser, Roberta Fansler, had been enormously impressed the previous spring with what she described as "one of the really extraordinary collections in the country."[161] Her recommendation that the corporation financially assist the Nadelmans led to a four-thousand-dollar grant, which allowed the museum to reopen on April 17, 1935. In accordance with the corporation's requirement that the museum become more public, the Nadelmans accepted the imposition of a four-member advisory board and expanded their program to include a gallery guide and regular hours on Saturday and Sunday afternoons.[162] The museum remained open the following year despite the reduction of the corporation's support to two thousand dollars. In the meantime, its collection had begun to be documented by contemporary artists under the auspices of the Index of American Design, a subsidiary of the Works Progress Administration's Federal Arts Project set up to record American vernacular art.[163]

By 1937 both the museum's funding and its connection with the index had unraveled. Nadelman chafed at having to supervise artists assigned to draw and catalogue the collection, and he severed his relationship with the agency in July 1937, after slightly more than one hundred objects had been recorded. Meanwhile the Carnegie Corporation, which had never intended to provide the museum more than temporary support, refused to renew funding for a third year. Left without any means of paying its operating expenses, the museum closed.

Bereft of other options, the Nadelmans acknowledged that selling the collection was their only hope of keeping it intact. In February 1937 they consigned it to Edith Halpert for between $350,000 and $400,000. Despite their having given her one year to find a buyer, they began independently to contact prospects, one of them being Nelson Rockefeller, the son of Halpert's major folk art client. In May 1937 Nadelman wrote to Rockefeller suggesting that the philanthropist install the collection in Rockefeller Center and use profits from admission fees to purchase it over time.[164] Rockefeller demurred, and six months later Halpert bowed out in anger over Nadelman's undermining of her sales strategies.[165] In the meantime, Edna Little Greenwood had alerted the New-York Historical Society that the collection was for sale. On November 17, 1937, the society purchased it for $50,000, to be paid in installments over five years.[166] For Nadelman, it was a Pyrrhic victory. In response to a congratulatory letter from Greenwood, he lamented, "The dismantling of the Museum did also dismantle something in me."[167]

With the sale came Nadelman's appointment as curator of the collection, a position he apparently felt ensured his control over the material. Misunderstanding about his responsibilities to the museum created friction from the beginning. The museum rejected his requests that money be advanced for conservation and that the museum's largest exhibition hall be reserved for the collection's installation. In April 1939, little more than a year after receiving the collection, the museum dismissed Nadelman as curator because of what it viewed as his unwillingness to properly catalogue the collection or to adhere to a regular work schedule.[168] As a result, when the museum publicly unveiled the collection a year later in its newly created Folk Art Gallery, the objects no longer demonstrated the twin premises that had underscored the Nadelmans' acquisition of them: the European roots of American folk art and the formal continuities between the folk arts of different epochs and cultures.

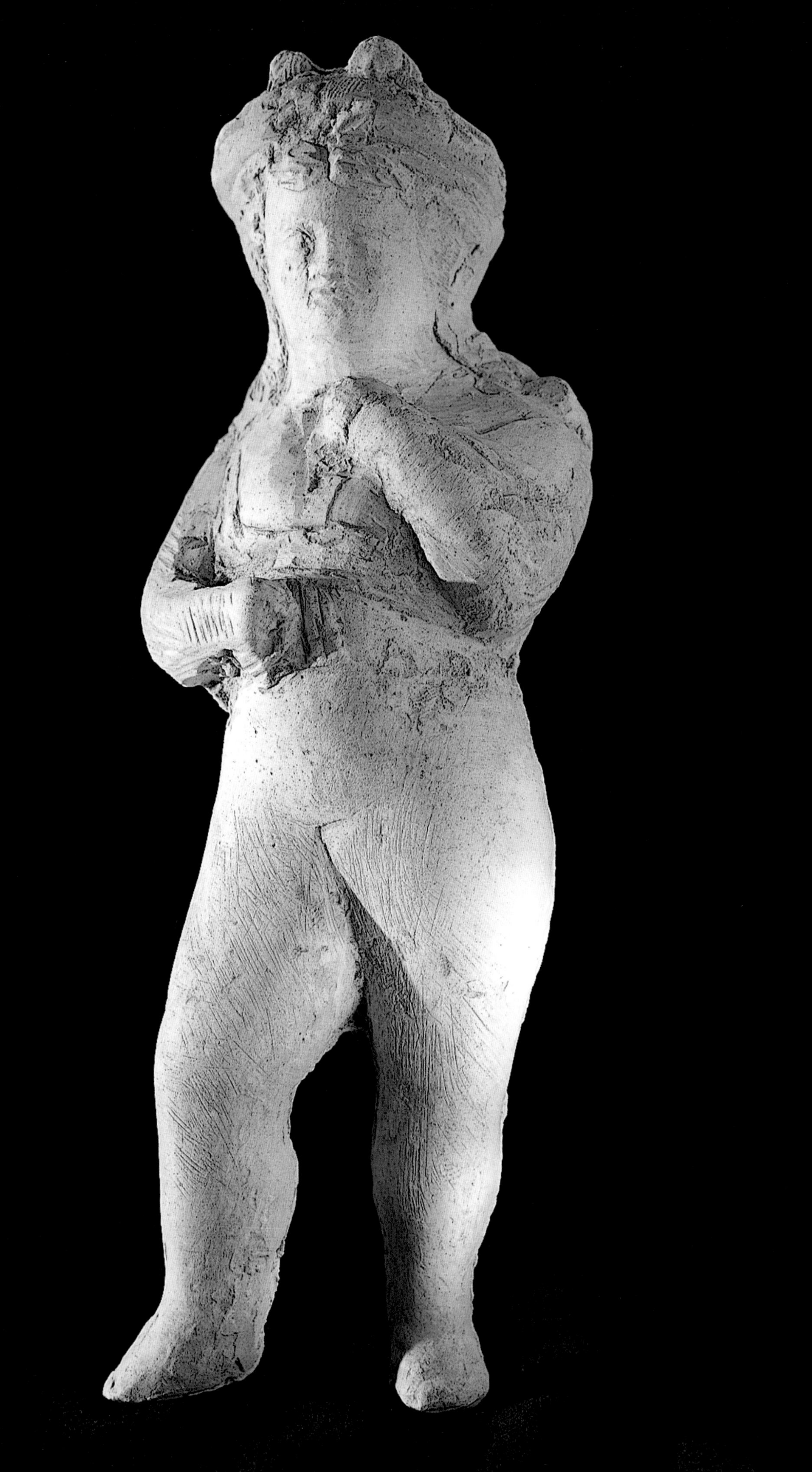

An Art of Flux, Anxiety, and Uncertainty
Miniature Figurines, 1938—46

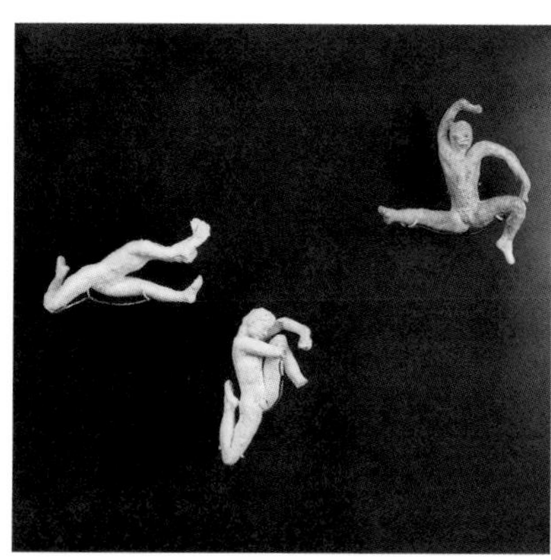

Fig. 208
Elie Nadelman
Figure, c. 1938—46
Plaster, 7 1/4 x 2 3/8 x 2 1/8 in.
(18.4 x 6 x 5.4 cm)
Estate of Elie Nadelman, courtesy
Salander-O'Reilly Galleries, New York
Photography by Paul Waldman

Fig. 209
Auguste Rodin
Mouvements de danse, c. 1910
Plaster, dimensions variable
Musée d'Orsay, Paris
Copyright Réunion des Musées Nationaux/
Art Resource, NY

The loss of Nadelman's folk art collection paralleled a decisive change in his art: from idealism and emotional restraint to flux, anxiety, and uncertainty. Upon his return to his studio after his dismissal from the museum, he began to cast single plaster figures so small they could be held in the hand and so numerous that they seem almost to have been created to fill the void left by the loss of his folk art collection (FIGS. 208, 212–213, 215–220). Laid out flat on tables in his studio like fragments from an archaeological excavation, these plaster figures bore witness to his fascination with familial groupings of related but different forms.[169]

In a dramatic reversal of his previous working methods, Nadelman adopted an improvisatory fabrication process. He began by sculpting miniature figures out of plastilene, a non-hardening clay, which he then cast in multiples. Rather than using paint to individualize multiple casts, as he had done earlier, he structurally reworked the casts after they had hardened. Sometimes he drew on them with pencil, but more often he carved them with a penknife, file, or kitchen fork. Sometimes the changes he made to their limbs, headwear, coiffures, and faces were modest; more often they were radical. He would eradicate whole limbs and faces in the course of modifying them and then carve totally new ones on the now-smaller mass of plaster. Occasionally he added pellets of plastilene to rebuild pieces, which he then recast, creating new forms upon which he carved further modifications. Sometimes he sanded away his file or knife markings, and sometimes he dipped the entire figure in liquid plaster to render its surface smooth. Mostly, however, he left the surfaces rough and scarred, which gave the figures an unfinished look, as if they had been caught in a state of metamorphosis. By abandoning smooth surfaces and idealized, geometric forms, Nadelman effectively liberated his art from overrefinement. Up to this time, his figures had been characterized by psychological withdrawal and reserved composure, undisturbed by psychic self-searching or spiritual tension. His new art gained from a sense of the mysterious and irrational in life.

In creating figures no more than five or six inches high, Nadelman followed the example set by vanguard artists in Paris in the early years of the century.[170] Rodin, Matisse, Picasso, Lipchitz, Henri Gaudier-Brzeska, and Manolo had all reacted to the tiny antiquities that flooded the market at the

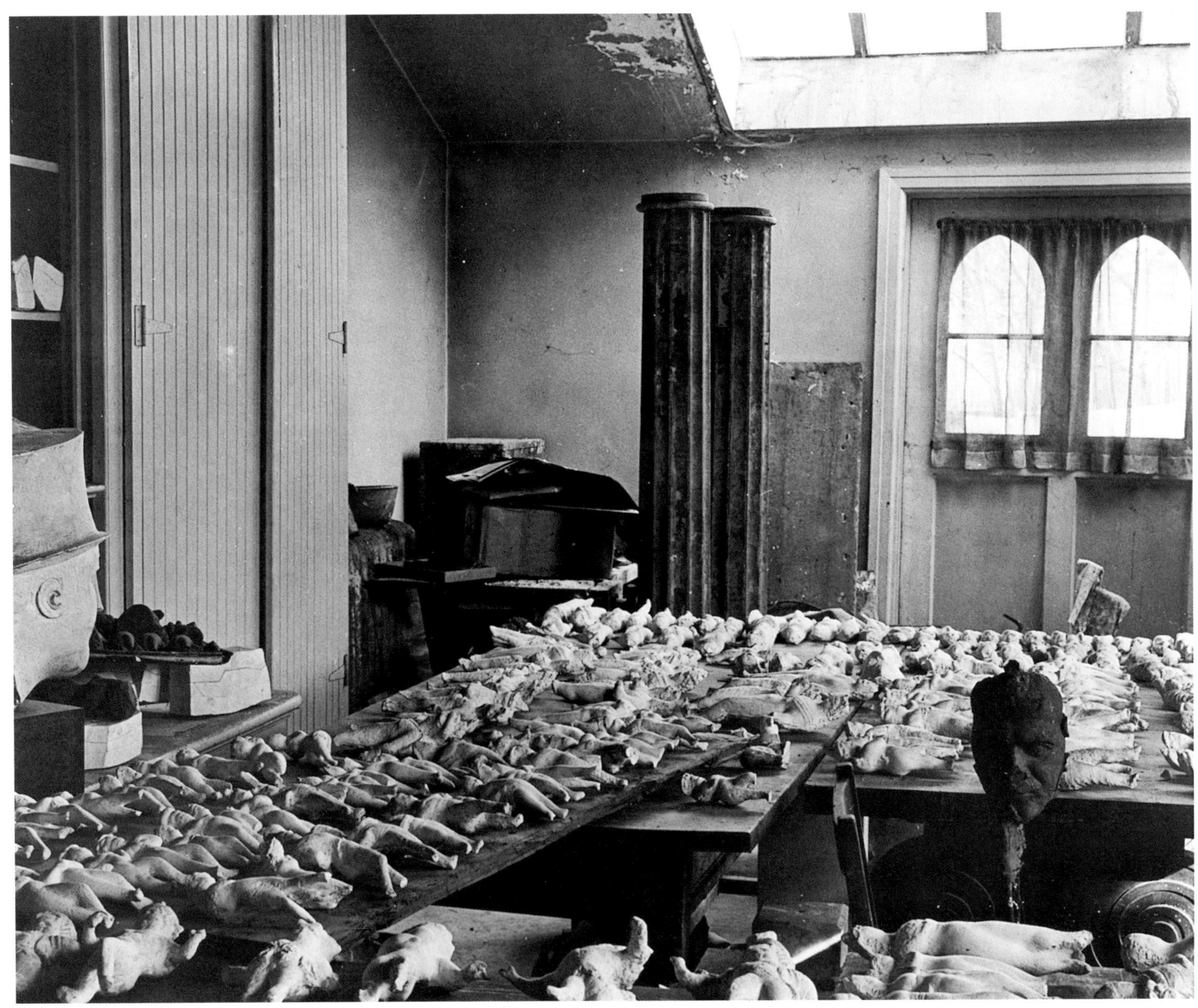

end of the nineteenth century by making works equally diminutive and transportable. Matisse, for example, had created a group of sculptures owned by Michael and Sarah Stein which measured an average of five inches in height, while Rodin had made hundreds of works so tiny they could fit into the palm of the hand (FIG. 209). Nadelman's miniatures, unfinished on their backs and unable to stand unassisted, bridged the fully three-dimensional work of these early twentieth-century sculptors with the shards and fragments of ancient art that typically had to lie flat or be mounted on bases.

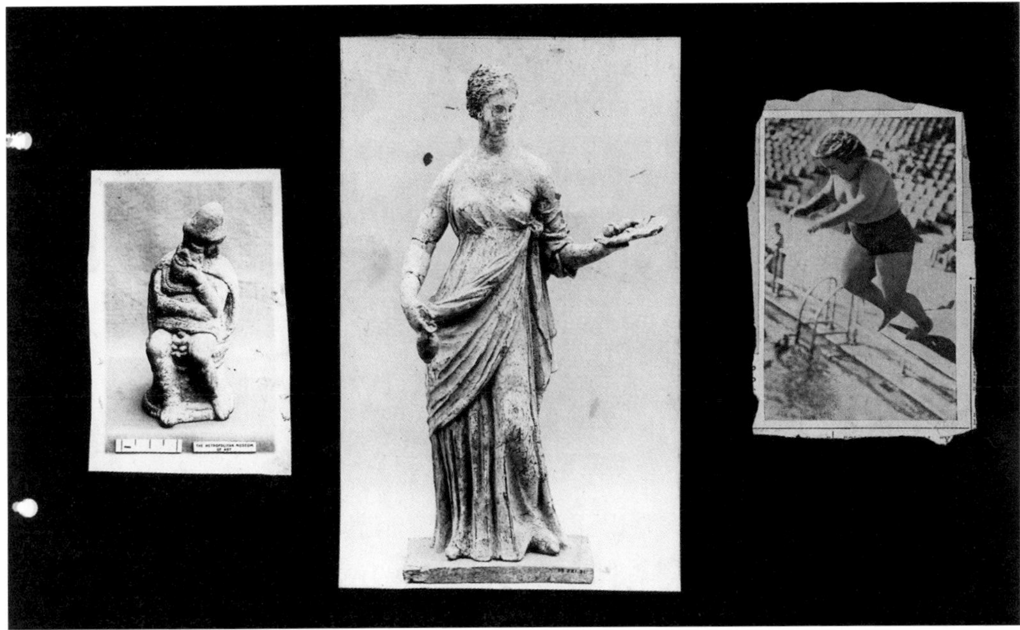

As before, Nadelman turned to Greek terra-cotta votives from Tanagra and Myrina as antecedents of his small-scale yet monumental sculpture. Yet now, instead of focusing on demure and statuesque peplos-clad women, he directed his gaze toward the figures of Eros that were popular in Tanagra in the third century B.C. Sold at fairs and temples for domestic use as toys and dolls, these small, ten- to twelve-inch-high terra-cottas offered a model for the portrayal of adolescent nudity and pubescent sexuality.

Nadelman had amassed an extensive library of illustrated catalogues and glossy photographs of Greek antiquities and terra-cottas, which he pasted into scrapbooks along with fashion and product advertisements and images of movie actresses, burlesque queens, and Kewpie dolls (FIG. 211). Classified and arranged taxonomically, these clippings and photographs became his source material. He propped them within arm's reach in the upstairs library where he worked so that he could constantly refer to them as he sculpturally amalgamated motifs from contemporary and ancient popular culture. Overlaying poses, gestures, and features from the ancient world with similar poses and gestures from contemporary times yielded forms that referred exclusively neither to the past nor to the present, but to both simultaneously. Just as his chronological references shifted indeterminately and fugitively between ancient times and the contemporary era, so too did his subject matter fluctuate between childlike innocence and brazen sexuality, with neither one gaining or relinquishing dominance.

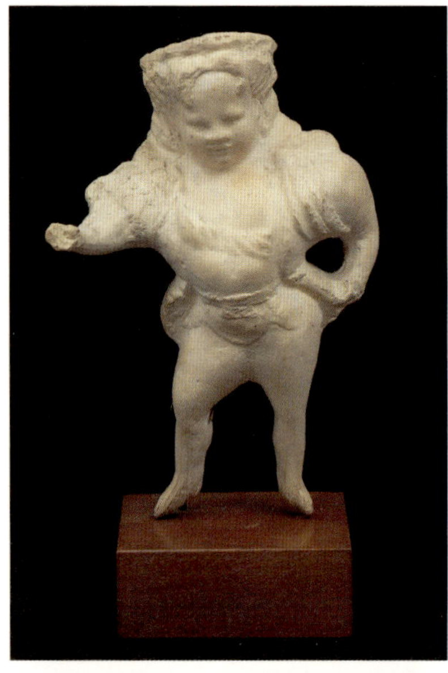

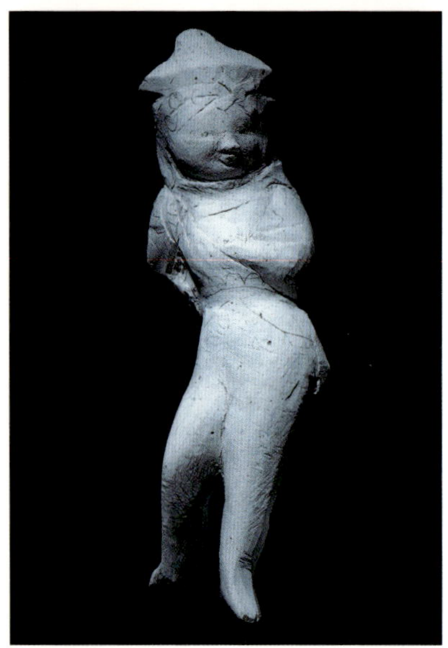

Never before had Nadelman's figures possessed the slightest degree of eroticism. They had appeared chaste rather than voluptuous, objects of neither passion nor desire. In contrast, his late fetishized plasters were overtly sexual, their demeanor oscillating disconcertingly between coy innocence and menacing carnality. Klaus Kertess wrote of them as inhabiting the taboo zone "where innocence and carnality meet"; Thomas Hess described them as being "so mired [in lust and sloth] that you can't tell whether an amply sexed divinity is about to lash into an orgasm of sacred charisma or spoon down another bowl of yogurt."[171] It is impossible to determine which parts of Nadelman's overripe child-women he derived from contemporary popular culture and which from antiquity, even though Brandt Junceau tellingly identified the ancient erotic terra-cottas in the collection of the Museum of Fine Arts, Boston, as the most "fondled" of Nadelman's source materials (FIG. 214).[172] What is clear is that Nadelman seized on sexual immodesty and animism as a way to strip his work of its impersonal idealism and invest it with an awareness of humanity's vulnerability. The magical objects that resulted mediated between man and the terrors of his environment.

The odd proportions and vampy poses of Nadelman's late plasters emerged against a backdrop of his increasing isolation from the art world. During the 1910s and 1920s he had joined various arts organizations and had taught sculpture at the Beaux-Arts Institute but had developed few close or lasting friendships with either dealers or other artists. This was due in part to a proclivity for privacy that he never relinquished, even with his wife, and in part to a distrust of others and a stubborn disregard for opinions that differed from his own.[173] In 1929, for example, he had requested that his work not be included in A. E. Gallatin's forthcoming book on art because, as he wrote to Gallatin, "I am sure you are not sufficiently acquainted with the nature and conception of my work. I don't know anyone who is. Time will reveal that."[174] His outspoken conviction that he was "the only man living" who understood his work and its display had repeatedly alienated Martin Birnbaum and eventually lost him a showcase for his work.[175] Nor did he spare the public his contempt. He responded to the rejection of one of his commissioned sculptures in 1935 by asserting: "The relationship between the artist and the public is not difficult, it is almost utterly impossible. It is the ignorant and presumptuous idea of the public that they may or should tell the artist what is right and wrong in his work. The public hates any trace of character, strength or life in a work of art."[176]

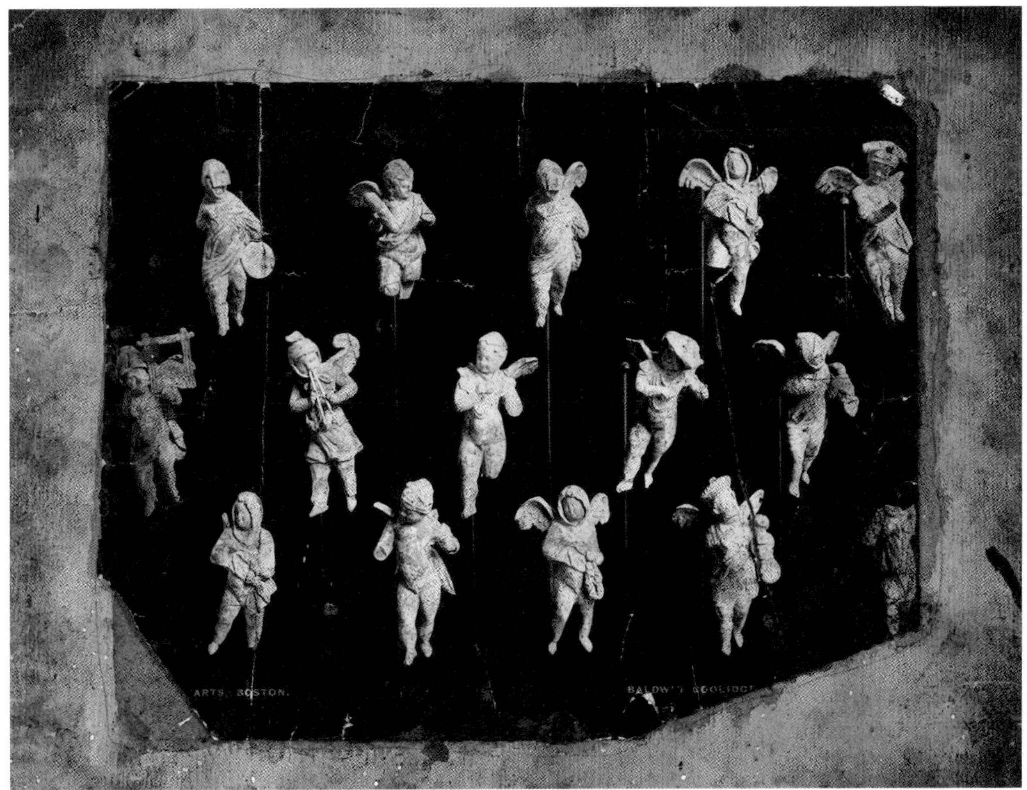

Fig. 214
Page from Nadelman's scrapbook containing
Greek "erotica" figurines from the Museum of
Fine Arts, Boston
Photograph courtesy Estate of Elie Nadelman

By 1940 Nadelman had not exhibited in New York for more than thirteen years. Notwithstanding his lack of dealer representation, he had declined the few requests made to him to participate in group shows on the basis that he had no available new work and did not wish to exhibit pieces he had shown previously. However right he may have been that the progress of his work depended on abstaining from exhibiting, the decision rendered him invisible in the eyes of the art world.[177] A new generation of artists, dealers, and collectors had emerged during the 1930s who had never seen his work and did not know he had ever existed—as McBride would later lament in the artist's obituary.[178] Even those who remembered him assumed he had stopped working. Those who trekked to Riverdale did so to discuss folk art; even they came away with eerie impressions. Jean Lipman, for example, described arriving by taxi in a violent storm and being greeted by Nadelman: "Tall, piercing black eyes, shabby dark suit, who in the first lightning-flash glimpse in the doorway of his great house looked to me like Heathcliff in *Wuthering Heights*. The house had been stripped of almost all the furniture and rugs and—storm or unpaid electric bills, I never knew—was lit only by a few candles."[179]

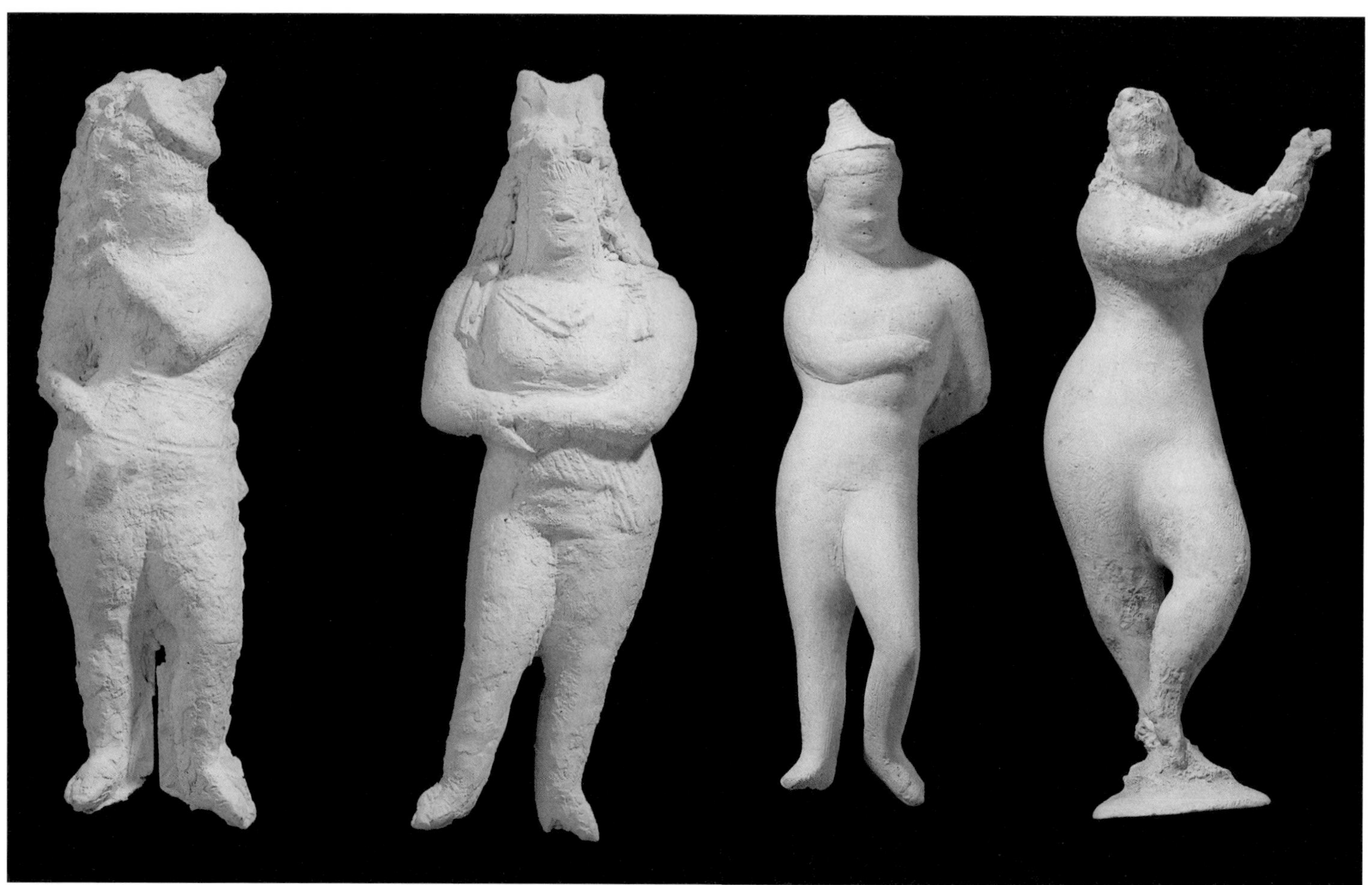

Figs. 215–218
Elie Nadelman
Untitled, c. 1938–46
Plaster
From 6 to 15 x 1 7/8 to 6 x 1 1/2 to 4 1/16 in.
(From 15.2 to 38.1 x 4.8 to 15.2 x 3.8 to 10.3 cm)
Whitney Museum of American Art, New York;
Purchase, with funds from The Lauder
Foundation, Evelyn and Leonard Lauder Fund
Photography by Jerry L. Thompson

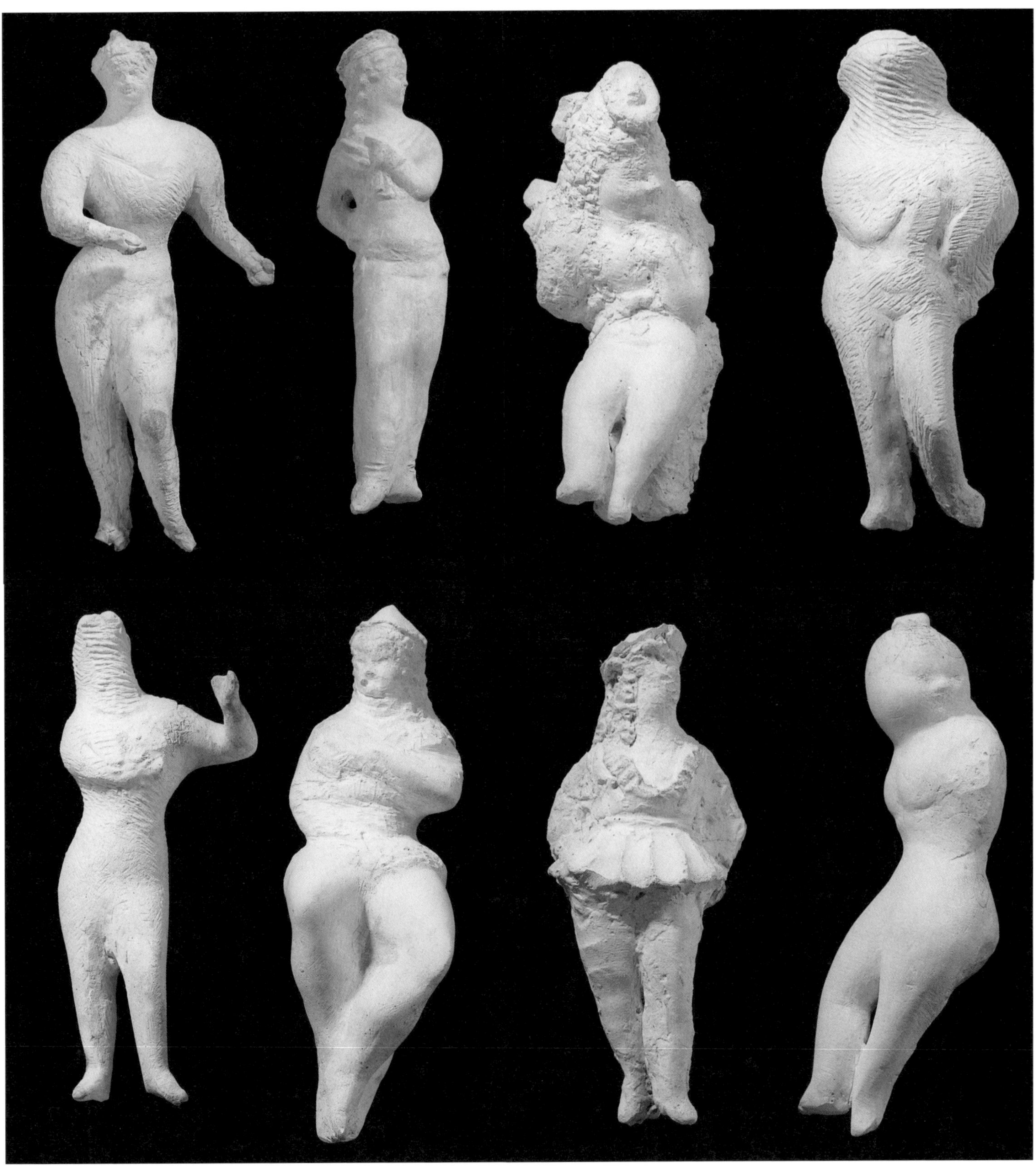

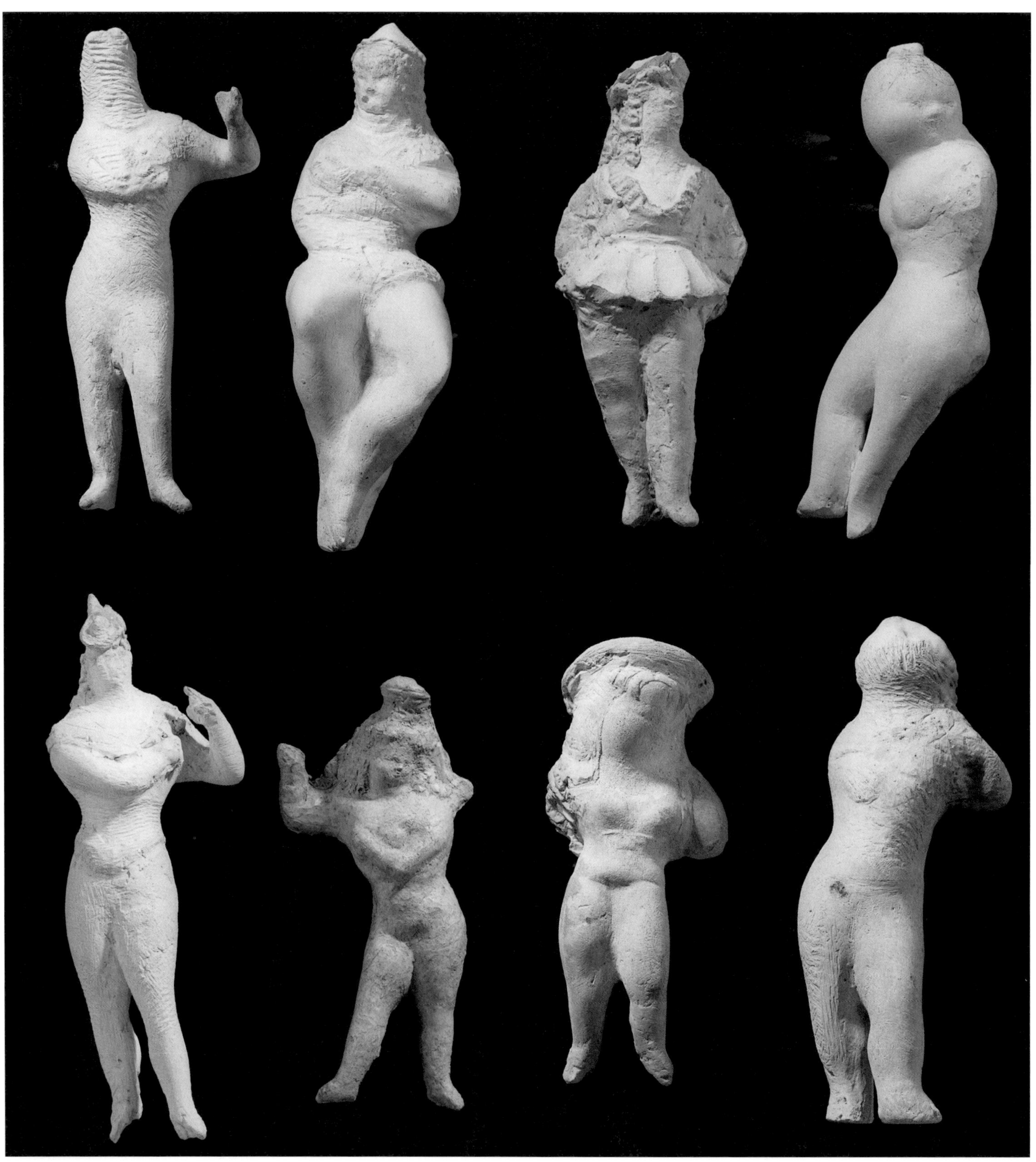

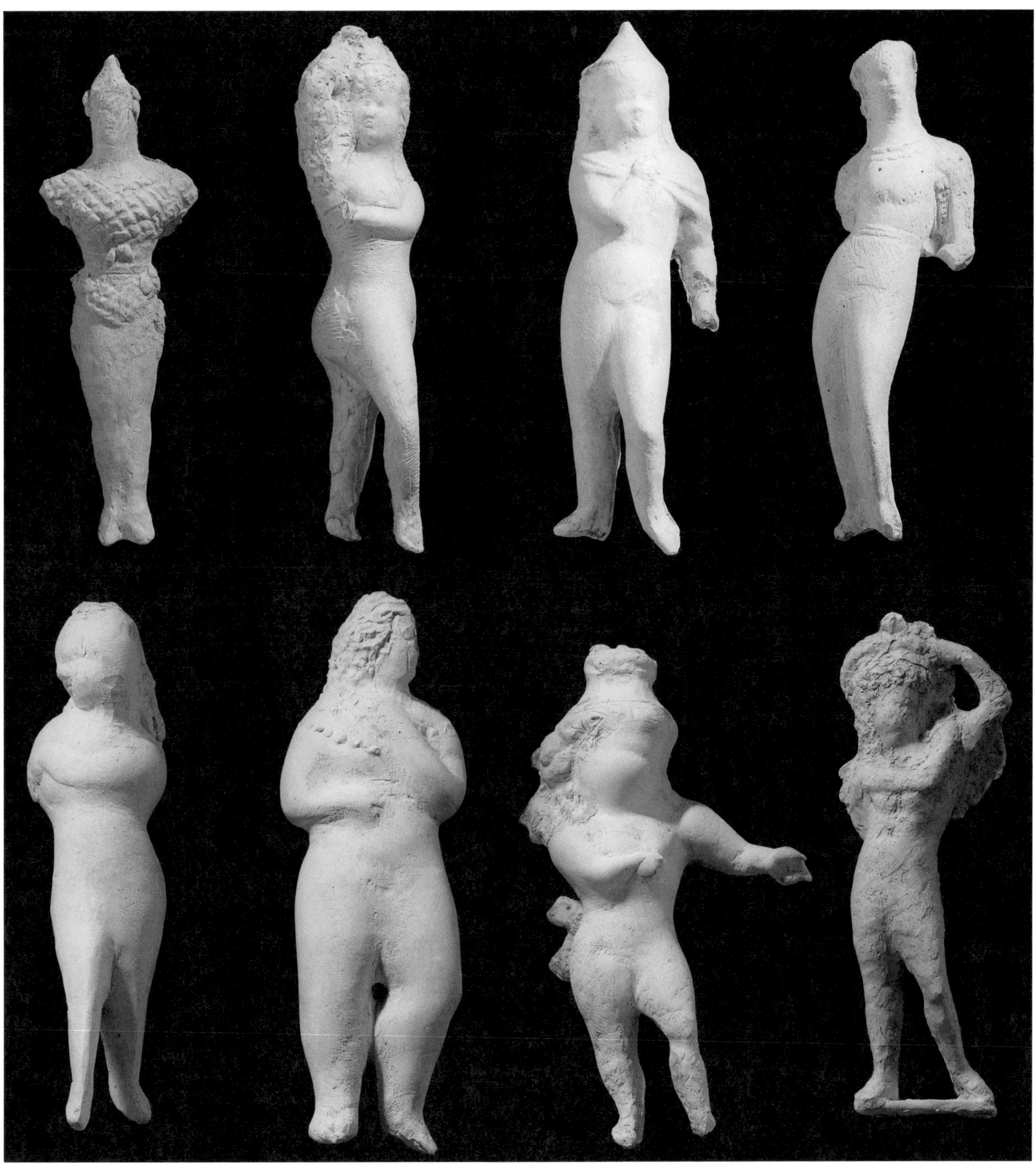

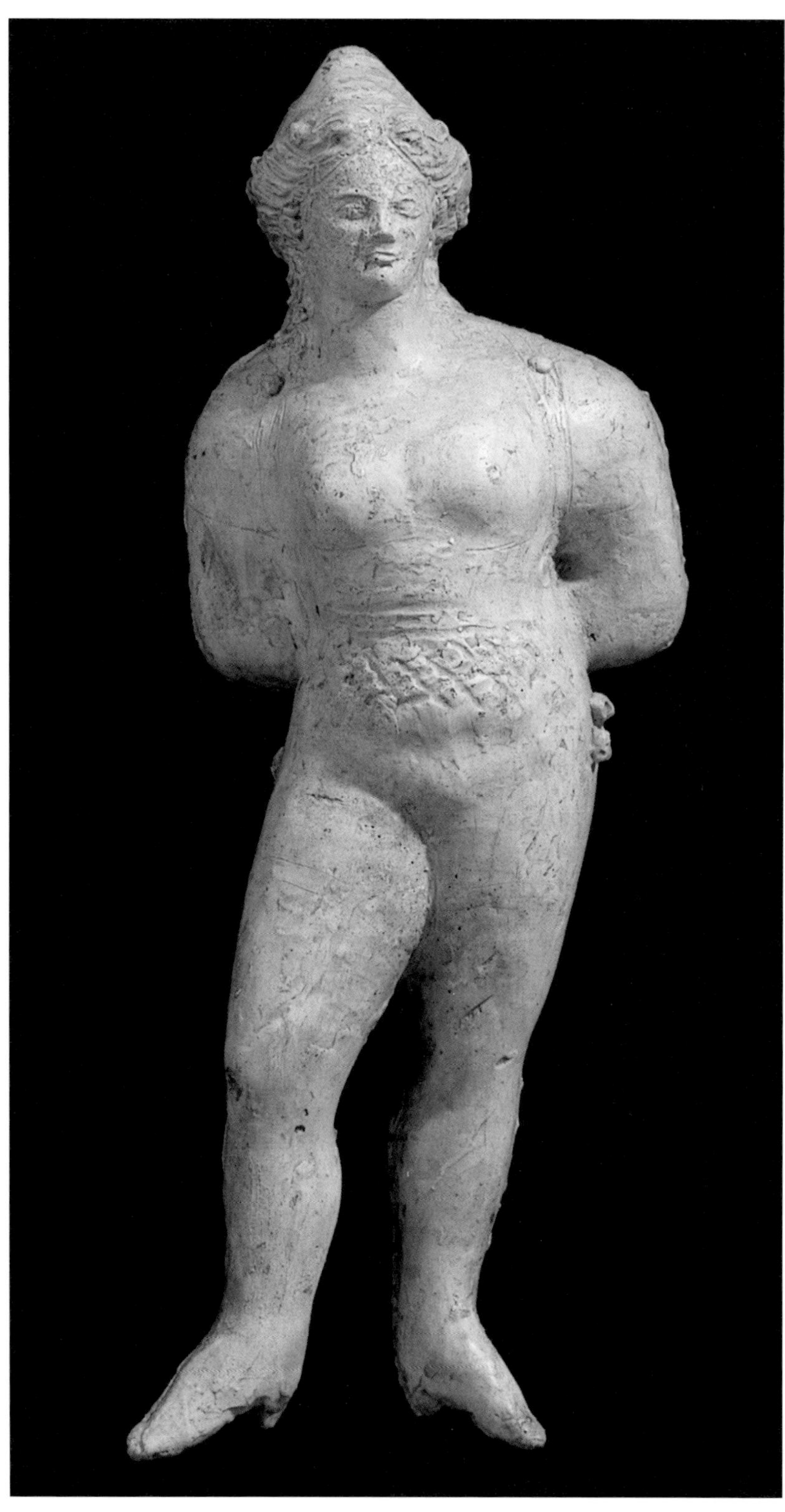
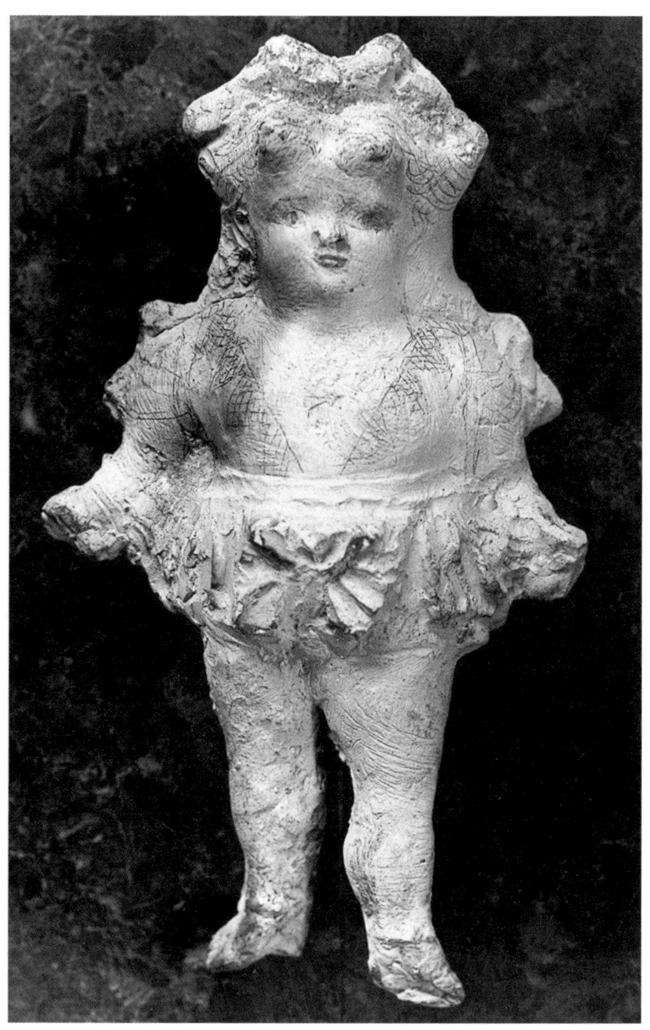

Paradoxically, by 1939 Nadelman was feverishly making art whose evocations of uncertainty and contingency resonated with that produced by a younger generation of artists who responded to the onset of World War II with a determination to bear witness to the unsettling realities of the time. During the Depression the country had wanted aesthetic testimonials to the enduring aspects of American life. With existence itself now thrown into question, art that once would have been unpopular was now accepted. Feelings of dislocation and anxiety elicited by the war spawned a desire among many young artists for styles that expressed the vulnerability and uncertainty they now perceived as inherent to the human condition. In step with artists such as Barnett Newman, Jackson Pollock, and Mark Rothko, Nadelman had developed an artistic language that conveyed the irrational forces in the human psyche. For him, however, its impetus had roots in a biography that was complicated by his Polish-Jewish identity, the psychological significance of which grew with the rise of Nazi Germany.

America had allowed Nadelman to ignore his Jewish heritage. He had married a Catholic, raised his son a Christian, and joined organizations whose members were predominantly non-Jewish.[180] Following Hitler's invasion of Poland in 1939 and his escalating campaign against its Jewish population, the veneer of ethnic neutrality became more difficult to maintain. Nevertheless, Nadelman's deep-seated emotional reticence and temperamental aversion to expressions of social, political, and ethnic difference led him to resist identifying solely with the plight of European Jews. In 1939 he declined an invitation to a dinner sponsored by the United Jewish Appeal to discuss the international threat to Jewish existence by writing: "I personally feel equally strongly for the victims of every race [and] feel that your organization which is concerned with one section of these victims has not the necessary appeal . . . (that appeal independent of race would have). . . . This is not an arbitrary statement; I am merely trying to be faithful to my own sense of duty to people whom all my life I have lived among."[181]

Two years later, when visited by Ilya and Resia Shor, Polish-Jewish artists who had recently escaped from Europe and sought his aid in securing a visa for his nephew Ludwik Nadelman, who had fled Poland for Marseilles, Nadelman exhibited little awareness of the dangers facing European Jews.[182] He had, in fact, attempted to intervene with the State Department on behalf of his nephew, just as, during the 1920s, he had aided his family financially by sending them monthly checks, sometimes in the thousands of dollars. Unhappily, his request for his nephew's visa proved insufficient; the Nazis arrested Ludwik in Marseilles and sent him to Auschwitz. Nadelman's later receipt of similar reports about other members of his family, most of whom would perish at the hands of the Nazis, could not have failed to undermine further his vision of an ordered, stable world grounded in reason and universal harmony—and concomitantly to accelerate the shift in his art toward images of vulnerability and uncertainty.[183]

After the United States entered the war, Nadelman actively threw himself into home-front service. He continued, however, to opt against participating in Jewish relief organizations and instead volunteered to chair Riverdale's Russian War Relief Committee. "Russian people," he declared, "have stood between our enemy and the democracies. . . . These brave people must be saved from starvation, disease and suffering to continue our battle against Hitler."[184] Deeply moralistic about duty and obligation, he joined the Riverdale Air Warden Service, volunteering, despite his age, to oversee the late night and early morning shifts no one else wanted. Members of the unit who put social engagements ahead of night duty received his harshest rebukes.[185] As wounded servicemen began to return home, Nadelman donated materials and his time to teach sculpture and drawing twice a week in the occupational therapy division of the Bronx Veterans Hospital, surreptitiously finishing the work of those unable to control their hand movements so as to save them embarrassment.[186]

During this period Nadelman's heart condition, which he had not disclosed to anyone, even Viola, began to worsen, leaving him with chronic fatigue, persistent coughing, and shortness of breath. Outwardly nonchalant about "my amusing pain," as he called it, he was forced to enter a Manhattan hospital for several overnight stays to allow his doctor to conduct tests.[187] Although he dismissed these confinements as unimportant, their occurrence at inopportune times—causing him on one occasion to miss seeing his son, Jan, who was home on a short leave from army service—suggests otherwise.

Virtually forgotten by the art world, relatively impoverished, and in constant pain, Nadelman lost his optimism about the future. Despite his disinclination to share his inner thoughts, he confided to Jan in 1946 that his "lifelong solitude and the fortitude needed to uphold it had become too difficult."[188] His death on December 28, 1946, has, until recently, been shrouded in mystery. Cynthia Nadelman has now made public that he took his own

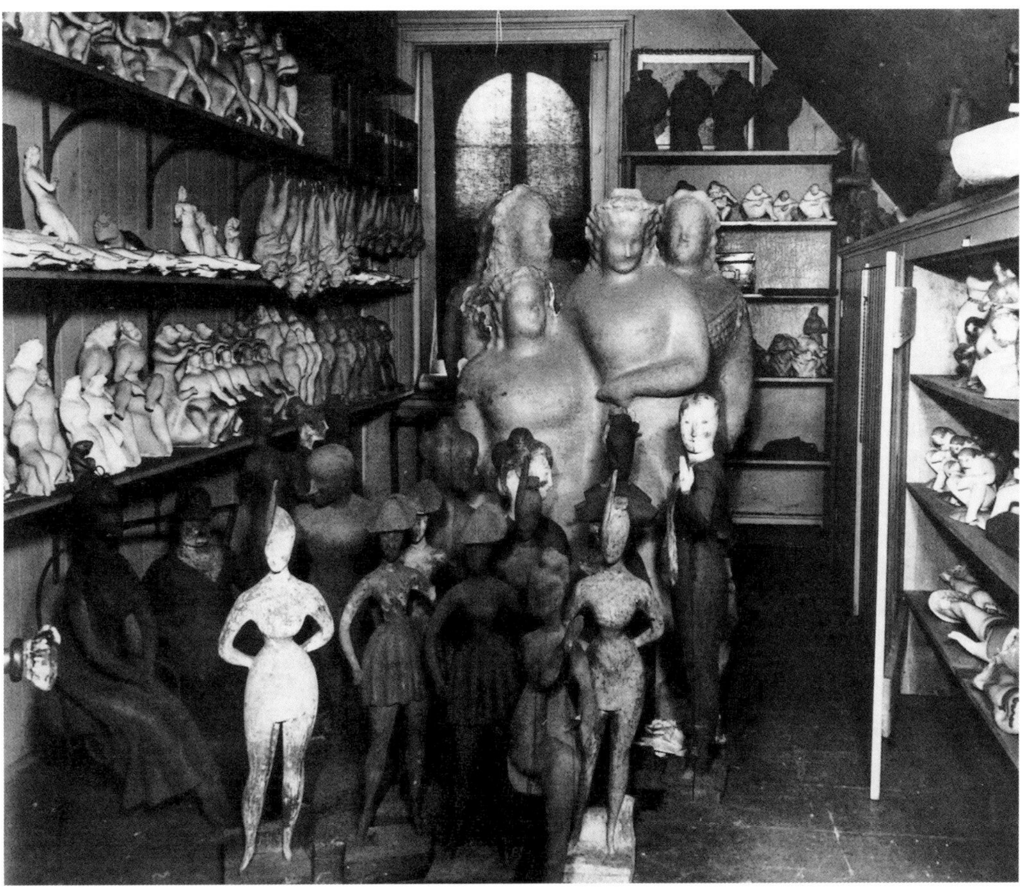

life.[189] Shortly before, he had told his wife that he felt he had achieved his goals as an artist. To his son he had earlier written: "I believe in the last analysis, things must be left in the hands of God, who has a way of settling life with a wisdom to us incomprehensible."[190]

Within a week of Nadelman's death, his work was sought out by Lincoln Kirstein, a respected writer on art and general director of the New York City Ballet. Kirstein had never met Nadelman but had known of his work since 1929, when he and two other Harvard University undergraduates had asked the artist to lend several of his sculptures to an exhibition they were preparing for the Harvard Society for Contemporary Art—a request Nadelman declined.[191] For more than twenty-five years after Nadelman's death, Kirstein studied, catalogued, and promoted the artist's work. He arranged for Nadelman's memorial exhibition at the Museum of Modern Art in 1948 and authored its catalogue, the first of many commentaries he would write on the work. In 1973 he published the most substantive monograph to date on Nadelman's life and work, which he based on extensive interviews with Viola, whom he saw several times a week and spoke with almost daily until her death in 1962, and on the artist's photographs, letters, books and sketches, to which she gave him unrestricted access. With enormous sensitivity to Nadelman's aesthetic, Kirstein repaired and refinished existing works and arranged for the casting of others in durable materials. While some of his decisions, particularly his approval of the gargantuan enlargement into marble of Nadelman's two papier-mâché circus women for the New York State Theater, have been questioned by scholars, there is no doubt that Kirstein's intention was to promote and extend the visibility of Nadelman's work.[192] New information has arisen in the years since Kirstein wrote his monograph that casts doubt on some of his accounts and interpretations, but not on his seminal importance to our knowledge of Nadelman; it is almost entirely due to his advocacy that Nadelman's reputation has flourished since his death.

Kirstein's efforts preserved for American art a body of sculpture that uniquely fused the language of abstraction with the subject matter of popular culture and everyday life. Using the formal correspondence between the arts of different times and places as a springboard, Nadelman created sculpture possessing both the authenticity and vitality of vernacular culture and the formal discipline and architectonic clarity of classicism. In so doing, he took the classicist quest for the timeless and the beautiful to a new plateau, creating out of the subject matter of contemporary popular culture an art that was outside the flow of time, uncontaminated by the contingencies and constraints of temporality.

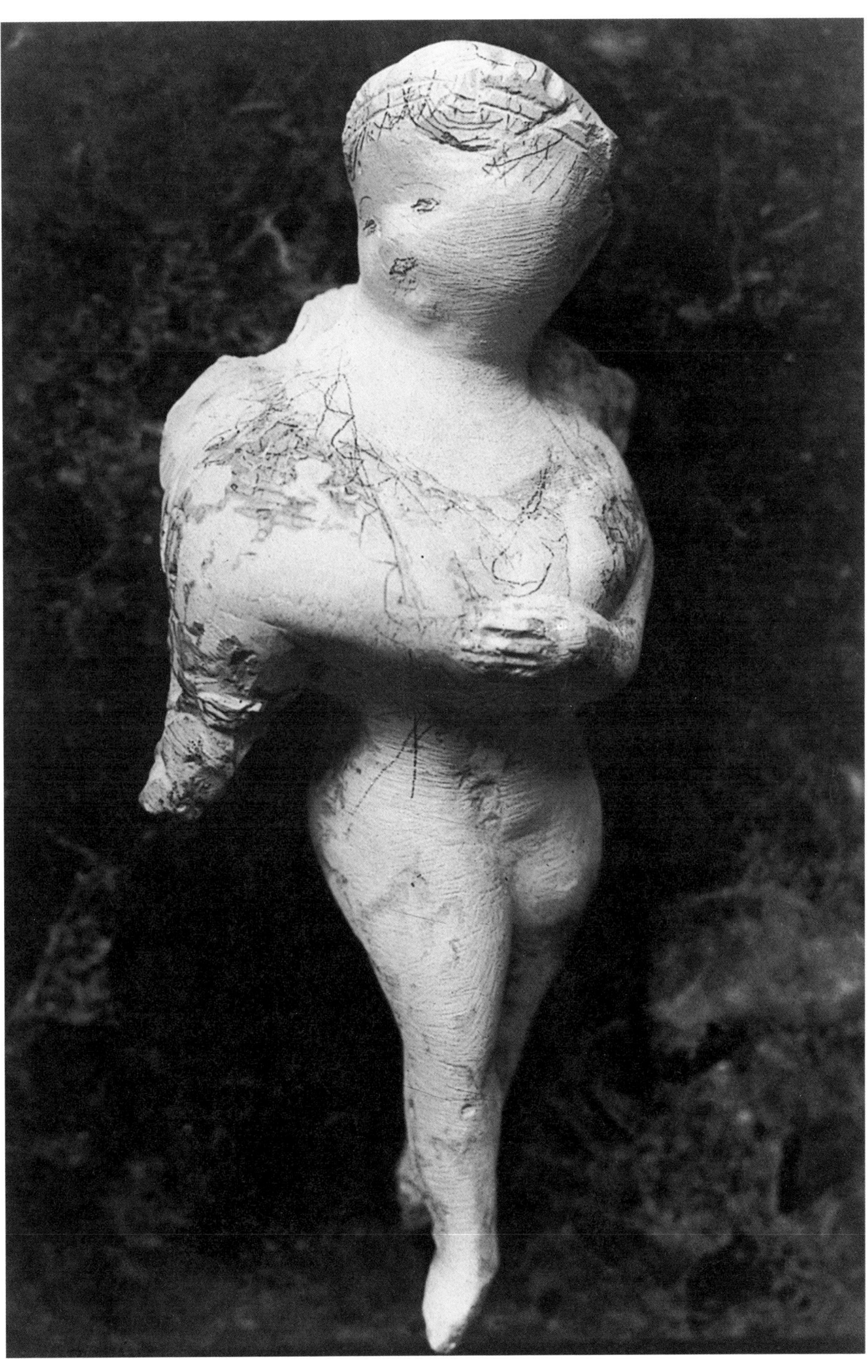

Fig. 222
Elie Nadelman
Figurine, 1938–46
Penciled plaster, 9 in. (22.9 cm) high
Estate of Elie Nadelman
Photograph courtesy The Maddox Collection

Notes

Originals of non-English texts, with translations by Anne Botstein, are in Nadelman Exhibition Files, Whitney Museum of American Art, New York.

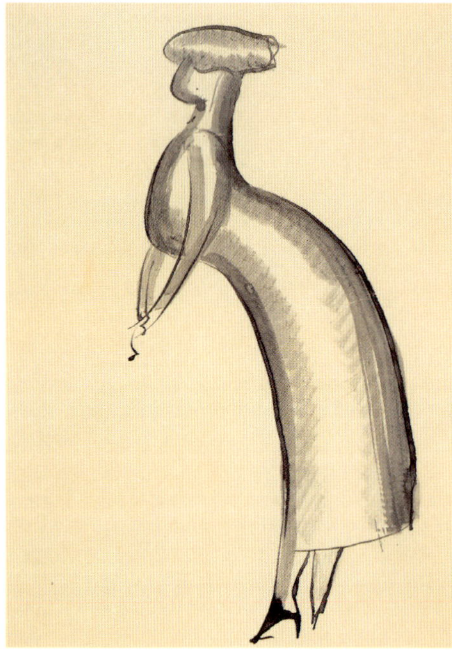

Elie Nadelman, **Concert Singer**, c. 1915–17. Ink and wash on paper, 10 1/4 x 7 3/4 in. (26.0 x 19.7 cm). Estate of Elie Nadelman, courtesy Salander-O'Reilly Galleries, New York
Photography by Paul Waldman

1. By the mid-eighteenth century Poland was being viewed as a buffer zone by Russia, Prussia, and Austria. In 1773 an alliance among Catherine the Great of Russia, Frederick II of Prussia, and Joseph II of Austria led to the country's first three-way partition. Further partitions followed in 1793. The Polish king abdicated in 1795, leaving what remained of the country to be divided among the three occupying powers. Several unsuccessful uprisings subsequently broke out, culminating in the January Insurrection of 1863–64, which took place in the Russian zone. Not until after World War I, with the Treaty of Versailles, did Poland regain its independence.

2. For information on the Jewish experience in Warsaw, see Alina Cala, "The Question of the Assimilation of Jews in the Polish Kingdom (1864–1897): An Interpretive Essay," *Polin* 1 (1986), pp. 130–50; Stephen D. Corrsin, *Warsaw before the First World War: Poles and Jews in the Third City of the Russian Empire, 1880–1914* (Boulder, Colo.: East European Monographs, 1989); Joseph Lichten, "Notes on the Assimilation and Acculturation of Jews in Poland, 1863–1943," in *The Jews in Poland*, ed. Chimen Abramsky, Maciej Jachimczyk, and Antony Polonsky (Oxford: Basil Blackwell, 1986), pp. 106–29; Ezra Mendelsohn, "A Note on Jewish Assimilation in the Polish Lands," in *Jewish Assimilation in Modern Times*, ed. Bela Vago (Boulder, Colo.: Westview Press, 1981), pp. 141–49. I am also extremely grateful to Marek Web, senior research scholar, Max Weinrich Center for Advanced Jewish Study at the YIVO Institute for Jewish Research, New York; and to Yale J. Reisner, director of research and archives, The Ronald S. Lauder Foundation at the Jewish Historical Institute, Warsaw, for their help with my research on the Jewish experience in turn-of-the-century Poland.

3. The Russian government's decree of 5 June 1862, partially emancipated the Jews within its zone, abolished most laws regulating Jewish residence and economic activity, and rescinded special taxes previously levied on Jews. Prior to this, restrictions on Jewish residency and economic activity had been severe, especially for those who spoke Yiddish and wore traditional Jewish clothing. See Corrsin, *Warsaw before the First World War*, p. 9.

4. By the last decades of the nineteenth century, Jews made up two-fifths of the total population of Warsaw. This population ratio fueled anti-Semitism throughout the Russian-controlled zone, as evidenced by the rise in popularity of the fervently anti-Semitic National Democrats, whose party slogan was "Stick to your own kind" (ibid., p. 101). In December 1881, two months before Nadelman's birth, a pogrom erupted in Warsaw: "The rioting began on Christmas Day, at the Church of the Holy Cross, and spread to other parts of the city in the next two days. It began with a sudden panic

during church services; twenty to thirty people were killed, someone shouted that a Jewish thief had started it, and soon a wave of looting and robbery by bands of youthful Poles began. . . . There were about a million rubles worth of property damage . . . several thousand Jewish families robbed or ruined, and several thousand arrests; the police and army remained generally passive until the third day of the pogrom" (ibid., p. 80). Violent anti-Jewish demonstrations continued to plague the city periodically thereafter, as did economic and social boycotts of Warsaw's Jews (see Mendelsohn, "A Note on Jewish Assimilation," pp. 144–45).

5. Ambivalence about ethnic identity was widespread among Warsaw's assimilated Jews. The assimilationist *kehile* board counseled Jews to list themselves as Poles in the 1882 census, and the October 21, 1881, issue of the popular assimilationist weekly *Izraelita* noted: "It should also be explained to the ignorant . . . that they are local inhabitants, that despite differences of faith and religious tradition . . . they belong to the people among whom they live" (see Corrsin, *Warsaw before the First World War*, p. 30). The latter phrase would be echoed by Nadelman in a 1939 letter to the United Jewish Appeal; see page 197, this volume.

6. In the early twentieth century Marszałkowska Street was Warsaw's main commercial artery, with the city's most beautiful parks and buildings and its wealthiest citizens located in the neighborhoods that bordered it. Aleksander Jankowski described the street as "the elegant world, the world of wealthy people. There are the palaces of the mighty and the homes of the rich, the seats of learning and art, monuments of love and praise, the temples of the refined world" (ibid., p. 42).

7. Most Warsaw Jews were not acculturated. According to the 1897 census, only 13.7 percent spoke Polish. More than 80 percent were religiously orthodox and limited in their formal education (ibid., p. 31).

8. Nadelman had four sisters—Cecilia, Rosa, Maria, and Helena—and two brothers: Robert—who had a dental practice at 14 Próżna, which he later moved to 2 Bolesława Prusa in Warsaw—and Maurycy, who took over the family jewelry business. For family names, see Cynthia Nadelman, "Chronology," in Suzanne Ramljak et al., *Elie Nadelman: Classical Folk* (New York: American Federation of the Arts, 2001), p. 111. I am grateful to Yale J. Reisner for locating family records in the Archives of the Jewish Historical Institute of Poland (correspondence with Patricia Hughes, 7 June 2001, Nadelman files, Whitney Museum).

9. The artist's son, Jan Nadelman, studied Polish at the University of Indiana under U.S. Army auspices in preparation for an assignment in intelligence after graduating from Princeton

University. In 1946 he joined the U.S. Foreign Service and was stationed as a vice consul in the American embassy in Warsaw. Viola Nadelman, Elie Nadelman's wife, reported that Nadelman subsequently mentioned to friends that he "little knew that when I left Poland that [*sic*] my son would go back to help my country" (unpublished Kirstein text, Nadelman Estate Papers).

10. No evidence exists that Nadelman ever returned to Poland to visit after he immigrated to America despite his frequent trips to Europe. Jan Nadelman believes that his father never did; Cynthia Nadelman, the artist's granddaughter, believes that he may have returned once (Cynthia Nadelman, conversation with the author, 11 March 2002).

11. Education among even non-Jewish Poles was limited; only 10 percent of Polish adults had a secondary-level education, according to the 1897 census (Corrsin, *Warsaw before the First World War*, p. 18).

12. For discussion of the relationship between Polish art and nationalism, see Jan Cavanaugh's *Out Looking In: Early Modern Polish Art, 1890–1918* (Berkeley, Los Angeles, and London: University of California Press, 2000).

13. *"Sztuka," 1897–1922* (Kraków: Sztuka, Society of Artists, 1922), pp. 25–26.

14. Stanisław Witkiewicz (1851–1915) was the first Polish critic to focus on the visual arts and the first to promote the "new art" in the press. See *The Witkiewicz Reader*, ed. and trans. Daniel Gerould (Evanston, Ill.: Northwestern University Press, 1992), and Cavanaugh, *Out Looking In*, pp. 25–27.

15. Stanisław Witkiewicz, "New Forms in Painting and the Misunderstandings Arising Therefrom" (1919), in *The Witkiewicz Reader*, p. 115.

16. Stanisław Przybyszewski (1868–1927) was one of the most influential Polish critics and intellectuals of the late nineteenth and early twentieth centuries. In *Life*, whose editor he became in October 1898, he argued repeatedly for a heritage for Polish artists distinct from nationalism. For more on Przybyszewski, see Cavanaugh, *Out Looking In*, pp. 27–36, and Czeslaw Miłosz, *The History of Polish Literature* (Berkeley and Los Angeles: University of California Press, 1983).

17. Przybyszewski regarded Satan as a manifestation of the "naked soul," that primal urge in man that drives the propagation of the species. Although he was twelve years younger than Sigmund Freud, his interpretation of art as a medium though which this "naked soul" could be revealed preceded Freud's similar theories. Przybyszewski's theories and his preoccupation with death permeated bohemian life in turn-of-

the-century Kraków. His unofficial anointment as high priest came to an end when a young, wealthy poet of the circle, Władysław Emeryk, invited Przybyszewski's wife, Dagny Jeull, to his family estate and shot her in the back of the head before turning the gun on himself. Emeryk explained in a letter to Przybysewski that he had done only what Przybyszewski himself should have done and what Dagny, overwrought by the knowledge of her husband's infidelities, wanted. A distraught Przybyszewski abandoned Kraków soon after and spent the remainder of his life in obscurity as a postal or railway clerk in Poland's Prussian zone. See Cavanaugh, *Out Looking In*, pp. 53, 55.

18. Salon Krywult, the only independent commercial gallery in Warsaw to exhibit contemporary art before 1906, was founded by Aleksander Krywult in 1880. For more information on the gallery, see Magdalena Płażewska, "Warszawski Salon Aleksandra Krywulta (1880–1906)," *Rocznik 10* (1966), pp. 297–422; Magdalena Płażewska, "Salon Krywulta," in *Polskie życie artystyczne w latach, 1890–1914*, ed. Aleksander Wojciechowski (Wrocław: Zakład Narodowy im. Ossolinskich, 1967), pp. 214–16.

19. For information on the Warsaw School of Drawing and the Warsaw School of Fine Arts, see Andrzej K. Olszewski, "Klasa Rysunkowa w Warszawie (Tzw. Szkola Gersona)," in Wojciechowski, ed., *Polskie życie artystyczne*, pp. 158–60.

20. *Pochód modernizmu*—variously translated as *The March of Modernism*, *Modernism on the March*, and *The Parade of Modernism*—portrayed Nadelman's classmates at the School of Drawing: Jan Rębowski, Adam Badowski, Jan Kauzik, Bolesław Kuźminuski, Karol Mondrała, Józef Gardecki, Leon Bigoziński, and Ludwik Lewandowski.

21. I am grateful to Bruce W. Menning, adjunct professor of history at the University of Kansas; Josh Sanborn, professor of history at Lafayette College; and Michael Stanisławski, professor of Jewish history at Columbia University, for sharing their expertise on the history of the Russian Imperial Army.

22. For discussion of Jews and effeminacy, see Sander L. Gilman, *The Jew's Body* (New York: Routledge, 1991), pp. 133–38.

23. Cavanaugh, *Out Looking In*, p. 226.

24. Nadelman's account of his Kraków experience was reported as early as 1915 by John Weichsel: "[Nadelman] tried the art-atmosphere of Kraków . . . and could endure it just two days" (Weichsel, "Eli Nadelman's Sculpture," *East and West* 1 [August 1915], pp. 144–48). Kirstein expanded upon this account (*The Sculpture of Elie Nadelman* [New York: Museum of Modern Art, 1948], p. 6).

25. The Academy of Fine Arts, Kraków, was the first full-fledged art academy in Poland. Initially a preparatory institution, it gained full status as an academy in 1900. From 1873 to 1893 it was led by Jan Matejko, the renowned Polish history painter and academician. In 1895 Julian Fałat, the modernist landscape painter, was elected chairman. Fałat replaced conservative professors with young modernists, reorganized the institution into three divisions—drawing, painting, and sculpture—and initiated reforms that transformed the school into one of the most progressive art academies in Europe. For more on the Academy of Fine Arts, Kraków, see Cavanaugh, *Out Looking In*, pp. 55–57; Piotr Krakowski, "Sculpture at the Academy of Fine Arts in Cracow," in *175 Years of Tuition in Painting, Sculpture, and Graphic Art at the Cracow Academy of Fine Arts* (Kraków, 1994), pp. 110–28.

26. On Dunikowski's importance, see Cavanaugh, *Out Looking In*, pp. 218–25.

27. Młoda Polska (Young Poland) sought to further Polish independence by bringing Polish art and literature to the world stage. The movement originated in Polish literature in the early 1890s and was christened Młoda Polska in an 1898 editorial in *Life*. The term originally referred to a secret society of Polish rebels who had been exiled to Switzerland following the November Insurrection of 1830–31.

28. Towarzystwo Artystów Polskich (Society of Polish Artists) or Sztuka, as it was called, was formalized on October 27, 1897. It played an important role in early Polish modernism by bringing together artists from occupied Poland with those living abroad through the exhibitions it organized inside and outside the country. Jan Stanisławski, the premier painter of Polish landscapes, was the group's driving force. After his death in 1907 Sztuka began to decline, finally disbanding in 1936. Membership in the group was highly selective and required the majority vote of its members. There were sixty-three members between 1897 and 1918. Nadelman joined the group in 1913 but stopped sending works for exhibition after 1914, when the outbreak of World War II forced the group to limit its exhibitions to Kraków. He was still listed as a member of the group in 1922 in its jubilee issue, *"Sztuka," 1897–1922* (p. 24). For more on Sztuka, see Cavanaugh, *Out Looking In*, pp. 59–76, 241–45, and *Stefania Krzysztofowicz-Kozakowska, Sztuka kręgu sztuki: Towarzystwo Artystów Polskich "Sztuka," 1897–1950*, exh. cat. (Kraków: Muzeum Narodowe w Krakowie, 1995), pp. 49–64.

29. For Polish students in Munich, see Halina Stępień, "Komentarz do katalogu wystawy 'Die Münchner Schule 1850–1914,'" *Biuletyn historii sztuki* 43, no. 1 (1981), pp. 74–88.

30. According to records of the Academy of Fine Arts, Munich, Nadelman did not enroll in courses. My thanks to B. Schultz for reviewing the academy's matriculation records on my behalf.

31. Following Lincoln Kirstein's lead, scholars have mistakenly assumed that Nadelman became familiar with Aubrey Beardsley's work during his stay in Munich. In fact, Beardsley's work was not published in Munich at the turn of the century, and it is unlikely that its decadent sexuality would have appealed to Nadelman. More likely, Nadelman encountered Jugendstil through the work of Thomas Theodor Heine (1867–1948) and Bruno Paul (1874–1968), the two artists most closely associated with *Jugend* and *Simplicissimus*.

32. Quoted in Kathryn Bloom Hiesinger, ed., *Art Nouveau in Munich: Masters of Jugendstil from the Stadtmuseum, Munich, and Other Public and Private Collections*, exh. cat. (Munich: Prestel, in association with the Philadelphia Museum of Art, 1988), p. 19.

33. Adolf von Hildebrand, *The Problem of Form in Painting and Sculpture*, trans. Max Meyer and Robert Morris Ogden (New York: Garland, 1978), p. 116.

34. For "Athens on the Isar," see Hiesinger, *Art Nouveau in Munich*, p. 11. The poster for the Munich Secession's 1892 inaugural exhibition, which featured a helmeted Athena, was designed by Franz von Stuck (1863–1928). Stuck used the same symbol in his poster for the Secession's 1897 exhibition.

35. For more on the Temple of Aphaia pedimental sculptures, see Dieter Ohly, *The Munich Glyptothek: Greek and Roman Sculpture: A Brief Guide*, trans. Helen Hughes-Brock (Munich: Beck, 1992), pp. 65–94, and J. J. Pollitt, *Art and Experience in Classical Greece* (Cambridge: Cambridge University Press, 1972), pp. 18–19.

36. Kirstein mistakenly assumed that the crèche figures in the Bayerisches National Museum were equivalent to American dolls: "In the Bavarian National Museum, there was a huge collection of Thuringian wood, china, and plastic dolls, with their clothes, carts, and animals. These miniatures, made by knowing adults for serious children, embodied that miniscule but monumental simplicity in contour which Nadelman later incarnated in notions of a mock-heroic commonplace" (*Elie Nadelman*, p. 161).

37. Three artists judged the competition: Olga Boznańska, Józef Pankiewicz, and August Sygietyński. Confusion has arisen over the prizes they gave. The magazine announced in its April 1904 issue that it would award three prizes, in the amounts of 750, 500, and 250 francs. When it announced the winners in August 1904, however, it gave only two names,

those of Gwozdecki and Nadelman. Some scholars have mistakenly assumed that no first prize was given and that Gwozdecki won second prize, Nadelman third prize. See, for example, Jerzy Malinowski, "Nadelman, Eli," in *Słownik artystów polskich i obcych w Polsce działajacych: Malarze, rzezbiarze, graficy* (Wrocław: Zakład Narodowy im. Ossolińskich, 1998), vol. 6, p. 3. Antoni Potocki's description of the second-place prize winner, however, confirms that it was Nadelman (see "O konkursie," *Sztuka*, no. 7 [August 1904], pp. 323–28). Nadelman's *Bemol* almost certainly refers to Chopin's best-known composition, his Piano Sonata in B Flat Minor (opus 35) from 1839. Known as the *Sonate funèbre* because of its funeral march, the composition is often construed as a patriotic expression of the failure of the Polish revolution of 1830.

38. Potocki wrote that Nadelman's drawing "predicted a sculptor with unusually strong treatment of the mass of material and perfect arrangement of figures" (ibid., pp. 323–28).

39. For information on the Polish colony (Kolonia Artystów Polskich [KAP]), see Elżbieta Grabska, *Autour de Bourdelle: Paris et les artistes polonais, 1900–1918*, exh. cat. (Paris: Paris-Musées, 1996), p. 13, and Antoni Potocki, "Kolonia paryska," *Sztuka*, no. 8–9 (1904), pp. 392–99.

40. Duchamp, quoted in Kenneth Eric Wayne, "The Role of Antiquity in the Development of Modern Sculpture in France, 1900–1914" (Ph.D. diss., Stanford University, 1994), p. 71.

41. Kenneth E. Silver and Romy Golan, *The Circle of Montparnasse: Jewish Artists in Paris, 1905–1945*, exh. cat. (New York: Jewish Museum and Universe Books, 1985), p. 11.

42. Guillaume Apollinaire (1880–1918) was one of French modernism's most important poets and art critics, known for, among other things, his essays on Cubism and his book *Cubist Painters* (1913). He was born Apolinary Kostrowicki in Rome, the illegitimate son of Angelica Kostrowicka, who was the daughter of a Polish papal chamberlain. Although Apollinaire did not speak Polish and kept his Polish ancestry secret, it undoubtedly contributed to his close association with the Polish colony. Polish-born Adolphe Basler (1876–1951) was an esteemed critic—and later dealer—of both French and Polish art. The numerous essays he wrote for Polish art journals are considered vital to understanding the Polish artistic tradition. André Salmon (1881–1969) was born in Paris. His extensive documentation of the Parisian social scene, especially that in Montparnasse, brought him in contact with the Polish colony. Cofounder, with Apollinaire and Max Jacob, of the review *Festin d'esope*, Salmon is credited with being the first Parisian art critic to recognize the importance of Cubism and the first to applaud Picasso's avant-garde canvases.

43. For descriptions of Nadelman's economic deprivation in Paris, see Thadée Natanson, *Peints à leur tour* (Paris: Editions Albin Michel, 1948), pp. 239–40, and André Beaunom "Ein Hellenist Eli Nadelman," *Das Zelt*, no. 3 (March 1924), p. 94.

44. Fauvist works had been included in the Salon des Indépendants five months earlier; dispersed throughout an exhibition of 4,269 pieces, however, they did not elicit attention as a group. Although Nadelman's inclusions in the 1905 Salon d'Automne were not mentioned in the press, the following year *Tygodnik Ilustrowany* noted in a review of that year's Salon that Nadelman's work was "known to us from last year's exhibit" (M. R., *Tygodnik ilustrowany*, no. 3 [1906], p. 50). For a history of the Salon d'Automne and the Salon des Indépendants, see Bruce Altshuler, *The Avant-garde in Exhibition: New Art in the Twentieth Century* (New York: Harry N. Abrams, 1994).

45. For thorough discussion of the relationship between twentieth-century sculpture and that of antiquity, see Wayne, "The Role of Antiquity."

46. Guillaume Apollinaire, "African and Oceanic Sculptures," in *Apollinaire on Art: Essays and Reviews, 1902–1918*, ed. Leroy C. Breunig, trans. Susan Suleiman (New York: Viking Press, 1972), p. 470.

47. André Salmon, "Elie Nadelman—chez Druet," *Gil Blas*, 1 June 1913, p. 3. "Eli Nadelman," *L'art décoratif* 16 [March 1914], p. 111.

48. Leo Stein and Thadée and Alexandre Natanson were the first to own Nadelman's work. They were listed as lenders in the exhibition catalogue of Nadelman's first solo show at Galerie E. Druet in 1909. Alexandre Natanson's collection, including his Nadelman pieces, was sold at auction on 16 May 1929, at Hôtel Drouot, Paris.

49. For more on Nadelman's attendance at Leo and Gertrude Stein's soirees, see Alice B. Toklas to Lincoln Kirstein, 1948, Nadelman Estate Papers, and Fernande Olivier, *Loving Picasso: The Private Journal of Fernande Olivier*, trans. Christine Baker and Michael Raeburn (New York: Harry N. Abrams, 2001), p. 255.

50. Alice B. Toklas to Lincoln Kirstein, 1948, Nadelman Estate Papers. For more on Nadelman's physical appearance, see Kirstein, *Elie Nadelman*, pp. 26, 191, 192, and Natanson, *Peints à leur tour*, p. 239.

51. Lipchitz, quoted in Kirstein, *Elie Nadelman*, p. 191; Gertrude Stein, "Elie Nadelman" (1911), published in *Larus: The Celestial Visitor* 1 (July 1927), p. 20; reprinted in *Portraits and Prayers* (New York: Modern Library, 1934), p. 52.

52. For Nadelman's polemics, see Salmon, "Eli Nadelman," p. 107, and Natanson, *Peints à leur tour*, p. 240.

53. Kineton Parkes described the fight between Nadelman and Marinetti: "In 1912 at the Galerie Bernheim Jeune, the manifesto of futurism at that time connoting progress was promulgated by Marinetti in his famous speech. . . . In Futurism was the salvation of art. This was the notable occasion when the destruction of all museums and monuments of the past was demanded—all artistic culture of the past derided. Nadelman was present in the gallery, and asked to be allowed to speak; the moment had a certain tenseness. He mounted the tribune and began 'If M. Marinetti says he will demolish all the art of the past, he shows that he does not understand the art of the past!' Marinetti, with a bound across the tribune, sprang at Nadelman and slapped him in the face. Nadelman repeated with a right jab on the nose; a supporter of Marinetti attacked Nadelman in the rear, and knocked him from the tribune into a group of screaming women. Someone turned out the light, and the public stormed out of the doors and made for the nearest cafés" ("After Futurism Comes 'Significant Form': A Polish Sculptor, Elie Nadelman, Introduces the Newest Phase in Sculptured Art," *The Sphere*, 2 October 1926, p. 18).

54. For Druet and the Armory Show, see Milton W. Brown, *The Story of the Armory Show* (New York: Abbeville Press, 1988), p. 72.

55. Identification of the work that Nadelman exhibited in his 1909 Druet show has been complicated by the existence of two photographs of Nadelman's work installed in this gallery (figs. 18, 47). Kirstein mistakenly assumed that both photographs were taken in 1909, and he dated the works in the photographs accordingly in preparing his catalogue raisonné. In fact, closer analysis reveals that the photographs, both of which depict the same corner of the gallery, were taken in different years. One depicts Nadelman's 1909 show; the other, his 1913 show. Reviews of the two shows and stylistic analyses of the depicted works support this assertion.

56. Adolphe Basler, "Amadeo [sic] Modigliani," *Modigliani*, special issue of *Paris-Montparnasse*, no. 13 (February 1930), unpaginated.

57. André Gide, 25 or 26 April 1909, in *Journal I: 1887–1925* (Paris: Gallimard, 1996), p. 609. Following Kirstein, scholars have mistakenly assumed that the head to which Gide referred was the abstract plaster study for *Reclining Nude* (fig. 85), which, in fact, was from a much later date; see Athena Spear, "Elie Nadelman's Early Heads (1905–1911)," *Allen Memorial Art Museum Bulletin* 28 (spring 1971), pp. 201–22. Based on stylistic analyses of Nadelman's 1909 show, the work Gide derided for its lack of detail resembled *Head of a Young Man* (fig. 26).

58. For an early example of a critic allying Nadelman's art with that of Primaticcio, see

Jean-Louis Vaudoyer, "Petites expositions," *La chronique des arts et de la curiosité*, no. 19 (8 May 1909), p. 151.

59. La Belle Edition issued a prospectus for a portfolio of Nadelman's drawings entitled *Quarante dessins de Elie Nadelman* in 1913. A year later it published the portfolio, which now included fifty-one of Nadelman's drawings, under the title *Vers l'unité plastique*. In 1921 thirty-two of these drawings were published by E. Weyhe as *Vers la beauté plastique*.

60. See André Salmon, "La sculpture vivante," *L'art vivant* 2 (1 April 1926), p. 260, and Basler, "Modigliani," unpaginated.

61. Alfred H. Barr, Jr., director of The Museum of Modern Art, wrote in 1948 of Nadelman's claim to have inspired Picasso's Cubism: "Cubism is a far richer and more complex affair than Nadelman admits, confining his attention to one brief phase which, I agree, he influenced. Rather than a 'seminal' influence upon cubism, I would say N.'s analytic drawings seem to have had a modifying and clarifying effect upon Picasso's cubism in 1909, the third year of its development." Quoted in Kirstein, *Elie Nadelman*, pp. 183–84. Kirstein likewise confirmed that "Nadelman's effect on Picasso was scarcely as important as he was later to claim," ibid. p. 184. Nadelman's claim to have invented Cubism particularly alienated contemporary critics. Jonathan Silver, for example, criticized Nadelman's "passionately self-justifying tone," arguing that the sculptor's assertion that Picasso stole the idea for Cubism from him was based on a misunderstanding: "Whatever the merits of his case for priority, and they are surely slight, his attitude shows that he misunderstood not only Cubism, but also the conditions, originating outside the history of art, which led to the development of Cubism and other advanced styles" ("Elie Nadelman: A Single Notion of Style," *Art News* 74 [November 1975], p. 70). Jed Perl's verdict was similar but more forgiving: "Only a flawed understanding of Cubism could give credence to Nadelman's foolish claim for a major role in that movement" ("Elie Nadelman," *Arts Magazine* [October 1978], p. 9).

62. Quoted in ibid., p. 16.

63. For Stieglitz's 1909 trip to Paris, see William Innes Homer, *Alfred Stieglitz and the American Avant-garde* (Boston: New York Graphic Society, 1977), p. 96.

64. The draft of Nadelman's text—written in longhand in English—is now in the Alfred Stieglitz/Georgia O'Keeffe Archive, Yale Collection of American Literature, Beinecke Rare Book and Manuscript Library, Yale University. It provides a less elegant, but in some ways clearer, version of Nadelman's ideas than the text that appeared in *Camera Work*, which was heavily edited by another hand.

65. Portions of Nadelman's text from the Paterson Gallery catalogue were translated into Polish and quoted in Adolphe Basler, "Eli Nadelman," *Sztuka*, no. 2 (1912), pp. 72, 74.

66. Nadelman included ten marble sculptures in his Paterson Gallery show, all of which Helena Rubinstein purchased. Kirstein mistakenly thought that she had purchased Nadelman's plaster horse from this exhibition as well, since it too was in her collection. The recent discovery of the catalogue and reviews of the Paterson Gallery show prove this incorrect.

67. Praksytelman is a Polonized spelling of Praxitelman. Kirstein attributed this sobriquet to Apollinaire. In fact, it was given to Nadelman by the Polish poet Bronisława Ostrowska, who authored the cabaret in which this character (played by Nadelman) appeared. Ostrowska and her husband, Stanisław K. Ostrowski, were among Nadelman's earliest friends and supporters in Paris. The cabaret was presented in conjunction with the inaugural exhibition of the Paris-based Society of Polish Artists in 1912. I am grateful to Elżbieta Grabska for providing this and other information on the Polish colony in Paris (correspondence with Patricia Hughes, Nadelman files, Whitney Museum, June 2001); see also Grabska, *Autour de Bourdelle*.

68. Helena Rubinstein was born in Kraków in 1870, the eldest of eight girls. Her cosmetics company grew from a small mail-order business in Australia to a global network of salons. By late 1914 she had moved with her husband, Edward Titus, and their two sons to Greenwich, Connecticut. In 1915 she opened her first New York salon. She would later marry Prince Gourielli Tchkonia, becoming Princess Gourielli.

69. Identification of the work Rubinstein commissioned from Nadelman in 1911 is difficult. Lincoln Kirstein, through conversations with Viola Nadelman, determined that Rubinstein commissioned two pieces from Nadelman soon after his 1911 show in London: a large plaster relief entitled *Spring* (fig. 76) and the quartet of statuettes now known as *The Four Seasons* (fig. 44). Kirstein identified the relief as the piece Rubinstein commissioned immediately after Nadelman's Paterson Gallery show and claimed that the artist made it for the billiard room of Rubinstein's London residence. However, published photographs, unknown to Kirstein, from early 1915 of this piece installed above the fireplace of Rubinstein's New York salon suggest that Nadelman made the relief after he came to America. This leaves *The Four Seasons* as the work Nadelman executed for Rubinstein in London, a supposition borne out by the suite's style, which bridges the curvilinear quality of his 1912–13 series and the more compact volumes and facial attributes of his 1908–11 series. Rubinstein brought these four statuettes to New York when she moved, along with the rest of her Nadelman collection, which she installed

in the main room of her New York salon. Magazine accounts from 1915 describe four Nadelman statuettes displayed in alcoves in the small waiting room of this salon. Given Rubinstein's collection of Nadelman pieces, these must be *The Four Seasons*, a conclusion confirmed by a photograph from the 1930s (now in the collection of the New-York Historical Society) showing the statuettes installed on separate shelves in the salon's oval waiting room. For descriptions of Rubinstein's salon, see "On Her Dressing Table," *Vogue*, 1 May 1915, p. 82, and Grace Hegger, "Beauty Bought and Paid For," *Vogue*, 15 November 1915, pp. 68–69, 116.

70. For more information on Tanagra, see R. A. Higgins, *Catalogue of the Terracottas in the Department of Greek and Roman Antiquities, British Museum*, 3 vols. (London: British Museum, 1954–2001); idem, *Tanagra and the Figurines* (London: Trefoil Books, 1986); and idem, *Greek Terracotta Figures* (London: Trustees of the British Museum, 1969).

71. For more on early-twentieth-century artists and Tanagra figurines, see Wayne, "The Role of Antiquity," p. 108.

72. See Claude Roger-Marx, "Les danses de Loïe Fuller et d'Isadora Duncan," *Comoedia illustré* 4 (1 February 1912), pp. 320–21, and Wayne, "The Role of Antiquity," p. 68.

73. Rubinstein described Nadelman as having "great charm," noting that he "expressed in his art what I was trying to say in my advertising to women all over the world. To me, Nadelman's purity of line and his feeling for form say 'beauty' better than all the fancy words coined for the beauty industry by Madison Avenue" (Helena Rubinstein, *My Life for Beauty* [New York: Simon and Schuster, 1966], p. 95). Following Rubinstein's death, her extensive collection of Nadelman works was sold at auction at Parke-Bernet Galleries, Inc., New York (20 and 27 April 1966).

74. Misia Natanson (1872–1950) was the wife of Thadée Natanson. She later married the Spanish artist José Maria Sert. For information on her Parisian salon, see Arthur Gold and Robert Fizdale, *Misia: The Life of Misia Sert* (New York: Alfred A. Knopf, 1980).

75. The Paris-based Society of Polish Artists (Sztuka)—not to be confused with the Kraków-based society of the same name or the magazine *Sztuka*, founded by Antoni Potocki—was founded in 1912 by Stanisław K. Ostrowski, who served as its president, and by Nadelman, Olga Boznańska, Gustaw Gwozdecki, Włodzimierz Konieczny, Józef Pankiewicz, Jan Rubczak, Władystaw Ślewiński, Edward Wittig, and Eugeniusz Żak. See Cavanaugh, *Out Looking In*, p. 43.

76. For comparison of Nadelman's art with that of Primaticcio, El Greco, and Michelangelo, see

Vaudoyer, "Petites expositions"; "Elie Nadelman—chez Druet," p. 3; Guillaume Apollinaire, "The Salon d'Automne," in Breunig, ed., *Apollinaire on Art*, p. 334; Dr. J. von Bülow, "Paris auf der Juryfreien Kunstschau in Berlin," *Kunstchronik*, n.s., 24 (31 January 1913), pp. 249–54; "Wystawa 'Sztuki' w Towarzystwo Zachęty Sztuk Pięknych w Warszawie," *Świat*, no. 48 (30 November 1912), p. 8; and *Sztuka* 3 (31 January 1913).

77. Guillaume Apollinaire, "March 5, 1914," in Breunig, ed., *Apollinaire on Art*, p. 358.

78. Nadelman's attempt to reenlist in the Russian army was highly unusual for anyone, particularly for someone of Jewish or Polish origin. Many Polish artists living in Paris, such as Moise Kisling and Simon Mondzain, joined the foreign legion of the French army; others chose to stay in Paris during the war. Nadelman described his action to a friend: "I presented myself at the Russian consulate to ask what I was supposed to do to get to Warsaw (as I am in the reserve). I was told they received an order not to send reservists from foreign countries to Russia. I went to London, where I could work a little" (Elie Nadelman to Henri-Pierre Roché, 29 December 1914, Henri-Pierre Roché Papers, Harry Ransom Humanities Research Center at The University of Texas at Austin).

79. According to an article from 1917, Nadelman "left Paris because as a Pole he had no country to fight for" (*The New York Evening Globe*, 4 February 1917, clipping in Elie Nadelman/Lincoln Kirstein files, Museum of Modern Art, New York). Rubinstein's New York salon was designed by Paul Frankl, to whom Nadelman introduced her after arriving in America. In his memoir Frankl recalled Nadelman's concern that Rubinstein would start collecting paintings. To prevent this, Frankl designed all of the salon's main rooms as round or oval spaces and installed niches in the walls (Paul T. Frankl, unpublished autobiography, c. 1954, p. 22, collection Paulette Frankl). I am grateful to Christopher Long for bringing this memoir to my attention.

80. "List or Manifest of Alien Passengers for the United States Immigration Officer at the Port of Arrival," SS *Lusitania*, New York, 31 October 1914, National Archives, Washington, D.C., microfilm T715, roll 2381.

81. Elie Nadelman to Henri-Pierre Roché, 29 December 1914, Henri-Pierre Roché Papers, Harry Ransom Humanities Research Center at The University of Texas at Austin.

82. Nadelman wrote to John Weichsel about the Polish American community: "I spoke to Osostowicz about the Polish meeting. He tells me it can't be done without difficulties. He is outraged about the anti-Semitism of the Poles here—all connection with Jews is almost impos-

sible here (Zanwaryh noticed too.) Therefore let's forget about it *forever*, that is my opinion" (Nadelman to Weichsel, 22 July 1915, John Weichsel Papers, 1905–1922, Archives of American Art/Smithsonian Institution, microfilm N60-1).

83. For Weichsel and the People's Art Guild, see Allan Antliff, "Cosmic Modernism: Elie Nadelman, Adolf Wolff, and the Materialist Aesthetics of John Weichsel," *Archives of American Art Journal* 38, no. 3–4 (1998), pp. 20–29; idem, *Anarchist Modernism: Art, Politics, and the First American Avant-garde* (Chicago: University of Chicago Press, 2001); and Gail Stavitsky, "John Weichsel and the People's Art Guild," *Archives of American Art Journal* 31, no. 4 (1991), pp. 12–19.

84. Nadelman purchased a watercolor by Ben Benn from the People's Art Guild in December 1915; Nadelman to Weichsel, December 1915, Nadelman Estate Papers.

85. John Weichsel, "Cosmism or Amorphism?" *Camera Work*, no. 42–43 (April–July 1913), p. 79.

86. Elie Nadelman, leaflet text which accompanied Nadelman's "291" exhibition, reprinted as "Eli Nadelman, of Paris," *Camera Work*, no. 48 (October 1916), p. 10.

87. In January 1915, shortly after introducing Nadelman to Birnbaum, Basler borrowed three hundred dollars from Alfred Stieglitz to finance his return to Europe. By April, he and Stieglitz were engaged in a bitter exchange of letters over the loan's repayment (Alfred Stieglitz/Georgia O'Keeffe Archive, box 4, folder 82). In 1927 Basler wrote to Nadelman reminding him of his role in introducing Nadelman to Birnbaum and asking for a percentage of the money Scott & Fowles earned from the sale of Nadelman's work as payment for the favor (Basler to Nadelman, August 1927, Nadelman Estate Papers).

88. Martin Birnbaum, *The Last Romantic: The Story of More than a Half-Century in the World of Art* (New York: Twayne, 1960), p. 86. Birnbaum's article—"Eli Nadelman," *International Studio* 57 (December 1915), pp. 53–55—would be the first of four he would publish on the artist's work, the three later versions essentially modifications of his 1915 text.

89. Birbaum, *The Last Romantic*, p. 85.

90. Birnbaum described the incident in his autobiography: "When I returned from a brief vacation, my mind full of plans for making [Nadelman's] exhibition a great success, I was bowled over by a little news item. It announced the first exhibition of Nadelman's work at Alfred Stieglitz's gallery at 291 Fifth Avenue. I was not merely surprised; I was enraged and outraged. When I faced Nadelman, however, he merely

smiled blandly and insisted that Stieglitz would show only drawings and a few unimportant experimental works that would not attract many people, whereas mine would really be his first important American exhibition. . . . I notified Nadelman, in no uncertain terms, that I was not playing second fiddle, and that there would be no further relations between us" (ibid., p. 86).

91. Rubinstein's claim cited in Hegger, "Beauty Bought and Paid For," and *My Life for Beauty*, p. 95.

92. Baudelaire, quoted in Stephen F. Eisenman et al., *Nineteenth-Century Art: A Critical History* (London: Thames and Hudson, 1994), p. 304.

93. Stieglitz wrote to Weichsel: "The Nadelman show opens today. It is very beautiful. And I am very glad that Nadelman has given me the priviledge [*sic*] to show his work. Nowhere could it have been shown to such advantage. If you can, do get a glimpse of the little room. It once more lives. It has not been so alive in quite some time. Whether New York will avail itself of sharing my privilege [*sic*], I do not know. In fact I feel that it will not. But it does not matter. Nadelman is prepared for the worst. So anything better than the worst will come as a surprise to him. And for his sake as a delight to me. Personally I do not care a rap whether New York turns up or not" (Alfred Stieglitz to John Weichsel, 8 November 1915, Weichsel Papers, microfilm N60-1).

94. *The New York Evening Globe*, 4 February 1917.

95. See Cynthia Nadelman, "Chronology," p. 115.

96. Henry McBride, "News and Comment in the World of Art: Nadelman and Pascin at Scott and Fowles," *The New York Sun*, 18 November 1917, sec. 5.

97. Ibid. For the show's financial success, see Henry McBride, "Exhibitions at the New York Galleries: Elie Nadelman's Sculptures," *Fine Art Journal* 3 (March 1917), pp. 227–28, *The Spur*, 15 February 1917, and Forbes Watson, *The New York Evening Post*, February 1917.

98. Ibid.

99. For period discussion of surface polish on Nadelman's marbles, see "Sculpture by Nadelman at Scott and Fowles," *The Brooklyn Daily Eagle*, 4 February 1917, sec. 3; Frederick W. Eddy, "News of the Art World," *The New York World*, 11 February 1917; "Exhibit of Sculpture," *The New York Evening Globe*, February 1917; and McBride, "News and Comment."

100. "Art Notes: The Sculpture of Nadelman Now on View," *The New York Times*, 2 February 1917.

101. The *Allies of Sculpture* catalogue checklist lists the following works by Nadelman: *Resting Deer*, *L'homme au chapeau*, *Femme assise*, and *Nude* (*Carved Wood*).

102. "Early Morning Offensive Saves Elie Nadelman Art from Suicide," *The New York Herald*, 16 December 1917.

103. *The New York World* published the letter that Nadelman wrote and sent to the press about the incident: "When the public does not find nude women in sculpture, they wonder whether the works are artistic or not. When one represents women in their dresses or men wearing hats, the public, not being accustomed to this, do not know whether there is art or solid insolence. Instead of trying to decide about the question the public revolts" ("His 'Modest' Art Offends Exhibit," *The New York World*, 19 December 1917, p. 9). Two years later Nadelman was more flippant: "Oh, it is a trifle—as though some one should throw charcoal dust on this marble. I blow it off, pouf! it is gone. As for the New York public, it is the same as that of Paris, London, or anywhere. They are all alike, and they all balk at any changed or novel viewpoint, in art especially. . . . Now we have all been accustomed, in sculpture shows, to seeing figures of women represented nude, and portraits of men fully clothed, even to realistic buttons on their coats and creases in their trousers. For reasons of my own—and I have at least 156 of them—I show the ladies dressed as we always see them, and the men with their hats on. Consequently, people jump at the idea that there must be something wrong" (quoted in Henry Tyrell, "At a Musical Tea with Nadelman," *The World Magazine*, 30 November 1919).

104. For Nadelman's claim of friendship with Renoir, see ibid.

105. "Ah, the blue hair!" Nadelman was reported as saying in 1919. "You, too, question that blue, though you never think of questioning the glaring white of plaster or marble, nor the metallic glitter of bronze, in a piece of portrait sculpture. The one is just as un-life-like as the other. Therefore, you are inconsistent. But I am perfectly consistent in thus defining the light-and-shade relation of hair and beard to the flesh quality of the face; because, remember, I am not making an image-copy of a man, but only expressing the essential proportions of a man's form, architecturally, as you might say" (ibid.).

106. Edward Bernays to Lincoln Kirstein, 1948, Nadelman Estate Papers.

107. Duchamp later remarked of Nadelman's affair with Ettie Stettheimer that it may have been "more serious on both sides than either imagined of his partner; that is, it was somewhat like a movie plot except that, in this plot,

nothing happened" (quoted in Cynthia Nadelman, "Chronology," p. 116). See also Parker Tyler, *Florine Stettheimer: A Life in Art* (New York: Farrar, Straus, & Co., 1963). Nadelman and Stettheimer remained in contact until his death. In 1926 Nadelman wrote to her thanking her for giving him a childhood photograph of his wife, Viola, who had been a close childhood friend of Ettie's in Stuttgart: "My dear Miss Stettheimer, Your present is the most precious and dearest thing I possess. I do not know how to thank you for it. I love you, Elie Nadelman" (Nadelman to Ettie Stettheimer, 17 February 1926, Florine and Ettie Stettheimer Papers, Yale Collection of American Literature, Beinecke Rare Book and Manuscript Library, Yale University). Two years later Nadelman gave Ettie one of his etchings, about which she apparently was unenthusiastic. "I should have thought," she wrote, "of a gay, light thing flaming with strength or with beauty and singing a 'yes' to the world" (Stettheimer to Nadelman, 1928, Nadelman Estate Papers). Nadelman wrote to Ettie after the death of her sister, Florine, in 1944: "Darling Ettie, I would like very much to see you. Will call soon again. All my love, Elie" (Nadelman to Stettheimer, 1945/46, Stettheimer Papers).

108. In January 1918 the Whitney Studio Club invited twenty painters to the club to create paintings. Their only instructions were to paint from memory, without any models. The club provided paint, brushes, palettes, turpentine, cigarettes, cigars, and whiskey. After the success of *Indigenous Paintings*, as the show was called, the club hosted a similar exhibition for sculptors. Gaston Lachaise and Elie Nadelman were the standout sculptors of the second show. See Avis Berman, *Rebels on Eighth Street: Juliana Force and the Whitney Museum of American Art* (New York: Atheneum, 1990), pp. 150–54, and idem, "Juliana Force and Folk Art," *Antiques* (September 1981), pp. 542–53.

109. According to handwritten notes in the catalogue of the Knoedler gallery show, prices for Nadelman's wood pieces ranged from six hundred to two thousand dollars; those for bronzes ranged from four hundred to eight hundred dollars (M. Knoedler & Co. Archives, New York).

110. One critic asked in his review, "Is Nadelman serious? Are these things art, or only insolence? Where does plastic beauty end, and decadence begin? Difficult questions, in view even of the small group on this page. How much more complicated in a fashionable Fifth Avenue gallery filled with a score or more of similar freakish presentments, and thronged with the very people supposed to be the originals of the types pilloried in plaster! Views concerning Nadelman and his works are nothing if not contradictory. Such epithets as 'outrageous,' 'degenerate,' 'neurotic,' 'unwholesome,' 'morbid,' 'effete,' 'gruesome,' 'sexless,' and even 'indecent,' are freely bandied" (Tyrell, "At a Musical Tea").

111. Henry McBride, "News and Comment in the World of Art," *The New York Sun*, 16 November 1919, magazine sec.

112. Charles Daniel, quoted in ibid.; Hamilton Easter Field, "Art New and Old in Current Shows," *Arts and Decoration* 12 (December 1919), p. 108.

113. Agnes Pelton, "Her Crowning Moment in Evening Dress," *The New York Sun*, 16 November 1919.

114. Viola came from a wealthy, elegant New York family. She spent her childhood in Stuttgart and was fluent in German as well as French, the language in which she and Nadelman initially corresponded. Following the death of her father, Louis Spiess, her mother settled in Rome, where she converted to Catholicism and married Count Naselli. In addition to her mother's estate, Viola inherited a fortune estimated at between one and three million dollars from her first husband, Joseph Flannery. Flannery died in 1915 at the age of forty, three years after being disbarred and convicted on charges of deceit and gross misconduct because of his involvement in a number of dubious real estate transactions with the city ("Joseph A. Flannery Dies," *The New York Times*, 21 September 1915, and "Flannery Disbarred for Realty Juggling," *The New York Times*, 18 May 1912). See "To Wed Polish Sculptor: Mrs. Viola Flannery Engaged to Elie Nadelman," *The New York Times*, 25 December 1919; "Wed Sculptor Nadelman: Mrs. Flannery a Bride a Week When Her Daughter Married," *The New York Times*, 7 January 1920.

115. Natanson, *Peints à leur tour*, p. 242.

116. Alice B. Toklas described the couple as having "that radiant beauty and happiness that makes one afraid for them" (Toklas to Lincoln Kirstein, 1948, Nadelman Estate Papers). Jan Nadelman, the couple's son, described his mother as a "cosmopolitan" who "embodied the best traditions of patrician upbringing. . . . " (quoted in Cynthia Jaffee McCabe, *The Golden Door: Artist-Immigrants of America, 1876–1976*, exh. cat. [Washington, D.C.: Hirshhorn Museum and Sculpture Garden, Smithsonian Institution, 1976], pp. 184–86). Since coming to America, Nadelman had been content to have his birth date listed as 1885. After his marriage to Viola, he corrected the error, perhaps owing to the age difference between the two of them.

117. Natanson, *Peints à leur tour*, p. 242.

118. Marsden Hartley, quoted in Cynthia Nadelman, "Chronology," p. 117.

119. Nadelman wrote to Leo Stein in July 1909: "For two weeks, I am having a great time—theater, concerts, visits—but I have to abandon all that for sculpture—both at the same time are not

possible" (Gertrude Stein and Alice B. Toklas Papers, Yale Collection of American Literature, Beinecke Rare Book and Manuscript Library, Yale University).

120. When the Nadelmans bought Alderbrook, as the Riverdale estate was called, the house had no gas, no heating, and no plumbing. Gaping holes in the ceilings made it possible to look through three stories.

121. According to newspaper accounts, Viola had been so ill for the two years before her marriage to Nadelman and had so rarely been seen in society that friends thought she had become a confirmed invalid. A week after her marriage, when her daughter wed, Viola was carried from her sickbed into the drawing room to attend the ceremony and did not stay for the reception ("To Wed Polish Sculptor"; "Wed Sculptor Nadelman").

122. Lincoln Kirstein, "The Prints of Elie Nadelman," in *The Dry Points of Elie Nadelman* (New York: Curt Valentin, 1952), unpaginated. Kirstein arranged in December 1951 to have the master printer Charles S. White pull prints from two dozen copper and zinc plates that Nadelman had left at his death. He published twenty-two of these prints in the 1952 volume.

123. Scribner's turned down Nadelman's book proposal as financially unpromising, and *Art in America* declined it in a letter addressed to "Mrs. Elsie Nadelman" (Scribner's to Nadelman, 1921, Nadelman Estate Papers; *Art in America* to Nadelman, 1920, Nadelman Estate Papers).

124. Hamilton Easter Field to Nadelman, 1921, Nadelman Estate Papers.

125. The 1921 publication of *Vers la beauté plastique* followed by one year Nadelman's purchase, through Henri-Pierre Roché, of artwork—much of it damaged—from his Paris period that had been kept by his Parisian landlady. Several months after the purchase, in February 1921, four crates arrived in New York, containing linoleum cuts Nadelman had made in Paris and bronze and plaster pieces, some of which had been at the Druet gallery.

126. *Elie Nadelman* was the sixth in the Younger Artists Series, following volumes on Ernest Fiene, Alexander Brook, Peggy Bacon, Yasuo Kuniyoshi, and Gus Mager. Based on a letter to Nadelman, it was published in December 1923; by February 1924, only thirty-five copies had been sold (William Fisher to Nadelman, February 1924, Nadelman Estate Papers).

127. *The Forum* solicited responses from selected artists to the question "Is Cubism Pure Art?" The magazine printed nine responses in its July 1925 issue under the heading, "Pure Art? Or Pure 'Nonsense'?" For response to Nadelman's

claim to have invented Cubism, see footnote no. 61.

128. Arshile Gorky was born Vosdanik Manuk Adoian in Armenia in 1904. He adopted the name Gorky and claimed that he and Maxim Gorky were cousins and had spent much time together. He further claimed to have attended the Rhode Island School of Design and to have studied under Wassily Kandinsky in Paris despite his never having been to Paris. John Graham, who was born Ivan Gratianovitch Dombrowski in 1865, repeatedly lied about his age, his background, and his education and variously claimed to have been a judge, diplomat, librarian, college professor, and writer.

129. Kirstein, *Elie Nadelman*, p. 224.

130. Elie Nadelman to Jan Nadelman, 27 September 1944, Nadelman Estate Papers.

131. See Michael G. Kammen, *The Lively Arts: Gilbert Seldes and the Transformation of Cultural Criticism in the United States* (New York: Oxford University Press, 1996).

132. For Birnbaum's embittered and perhaps distorted description of Nadelman "carefully cultivat[ing] Scott's society" and of the artist's relationship to the Scott & Fowles gallery during his 1925 exhibition there, see Birnbaum, *Last Romantic*, pp. 89–90.

133. Nadelman to Leo Stein, June or July 1909, Gertrude Stein and Alice B. Toklas Papers, Yale Collection of American Literature, Beinecke Rare Book and Manuscript Library, Yale University.

134. Henry McBride, *The New York Herald*, 14 November 1920.

135. After Nadelman's death the artist Bill King, among others, conserved and "completed" many of Nadelman's wood pieces under the supervision of Lincoln Kirstein (Bill King, correspondence with the author, 7 June 2001, Nadelman Exhibition Files, Whitney Museum). More recently, several wood pieces owned by the Hirshhorn Museum were extensively refurbished. For a full description of the Hirshhorn restoration, see Valerie J. Fletcher, "Elie Nadelman: Art and Craft in Context," in Ramljak et al., *Classical Folk*, pp. 80–95.

136. According to magazine accounts, Viola had begun collecting laces, embroideries, and costume accessories as a young girl ("Hobby Becomes a Museum of Folk Art," *Gas Logic* 58 [November 1935], pp. 8–9). Her collection of antique headdresses was exhibited in 1921 at a New York City private school; her collection of fabrics was presented at the Colony Club in March 1926 (unidentified clippings, Elie Nadelman/Lincoln Kirstein Papers, Museum of Modern Art, New York).

137. For in-depth discussion of the Nadelmans'
folk art collection, see Christine I. Oaklander,
"Elie and Viola Nadelman: Pioneers in Folk Art
Collecting," *Folk Art* 17 (fall 1992), pp. 48–55;
and Elizabeth Stillinger, "Elie and Viola
Nadelman's Unprecedented Museum of Folk
Arts," *Antiques* 146 (October 1994), pp. 516–25.

138. Mimeographed sheet describing the collection; cited in Stillinger, "Elie and Viola
Nadelman's Unprecedented Museum," p. 171.

139. The number of objects in the Nadelmans'
collection has been variously reported. One
source stated its holdings at approximately sev-
enty thousand objects. The mimeographed
sheet on the collection prepared by the
Nadelmans in 1935, however, gives the number
as approximately thirty thousand. That year the
New York Times reported the collection to con-
sist of "more than 10,000 objects of folk art."
When the New-York Historical Society purchased the collection in 1937, it recorded the
number of objects at 14,492. Discounting the
few pieces the Nadelmans had sold prior to this
date, this number most accurately reflects the
extent of their holdings (Oaklander, "Pioneers
in Folk Art Collecting," p. 48; Nadelman Estate
Papers; "Folk Art Museum to Be Opened Here:
Nadelman Collection, Including European and
American Types, Will Be Shown," *The New York
Times*, 16 April 1935; and *Annual Report of the
New-York Historical Society*, 1938, p. 17).

140. Organized by artist Henry Schnakenberg,
Early American Art included work lent by
Schnakenberg, Juliana Force, Charles Demuth,
Robert Locher, Charles Sheeler, Alexander
Brook, Peggy Bacon, Dorothy Varian, Katherine
Schmidt, Yasuo Kuniyoshi, and Elinor Wylie.
For more information on the show, see Berman,
Rebels on Eighth Street, pp. 201–2, and Berman,
"Juliana Force and Folk Art," pp. 543–54.

141. Cahill was a silent partner in Halpert's Folk
Art Gallery, owning a large block of its shares
and half of its inventory; see Stillinger, "Elie
and Viola Nadelman's Unprecedented
Museum," p. 516, and Oaklander, "Pioneers in
Folk Art Collecting," p. 55.

142. The Nadelmans stated their goal as collectors in the mimeographed sheet they prepared
for visiting members of the Brooklyn Institute
of Arts and Sciences, 19 October 1935; see
Stillinger, "Elie and Viola Nadelman's
Unprecedented Museum," pp. 520, 524

143. In a letter written after Nadelman's death,
Viola was more explicit: "the whole purpose of
our Museum, [was] the showing of the deriva-
tion of the American folk arts from the
European" (Viola Nadelman to Mr. Jaeger, 21
January 1949; quoted ibid., p. 523).

144. Stillinger, "Elie and Viola Nadelman's
Unprecedented Museum," p. 520.

145. Ibid., p. 521.

146. Nadelman began electroplating his plaster
figures in November 1925, according to bills
received from S. C. Tarrant Company
(Nadelman Estate Papers).

147. Electroplating involves dipping a plaster
form into a bath containing a bar of metal.
When an electrical current is applied, the metal
adheres to the plaster and coats it. It was a
process used by only a few fine artists, among
them Rodin and Alexander Archipenko. For
Nadelman's electroplating process, see Cynthia
Nadelman, "Plastiques Fantastiques," in *Elie
Nadelman: Galvano-Plastiques* (New York:
Salander-O'Reilly Galleries, 2001), unpaginated.

148. Critics variously described the color of
Nadelman's electroplated figures as "a golden-
colored bronze," as varying from "pale greens"
to "tawny," and as "pinkish copper" ("Elie
Nadelman," *The New York Evening Post*, 5
February 1927; "Novel Figures by Nadelman
Entertain," *The New York World*, 6 February
1927; and Helen Appleton Read, "Sculptured
Caricatures by Nadelman Are Shown," *The
Brooklyn Daily Eagle*, 6 February 1927, sec. E).

149. Some scholars have suggested that
Nadelman's galvano-plastiques resembled his
1920–24 painted bronzes, with their shiny, highly painted surfaces (Fletcher, "Art and Craft in
Context," pp. 80–95). In period photographs,
however, the finish appears matte; critics who
reviewed the exhibition described the sculptures
as having only "a touch of color" (see McBride,
"Nadelman's Defiant Art"; Read, "Sculptured
Caricatures"; "Novel Figures by Nadelman
Entertain").

150. For gallery price list and letter to museum
directors, see Cynthia Nadelman, "Plastiques
Fantastiques," unpaginated, and M. Knoedler &
Company Archives.

151. Nadelman to Juliana Force, March 1929,
Nadelman Estate Papers; quoted in Cynthia
Nadelman, "Chronology," p. 119. Following
Cynthia Nadelman, scholars have assumed that
Juliana Force's 1929 request to Nadelman to
borrow one of his "spirited figures" referred to
the artist's galvano-plastiques; however, given
Force's description of Nadelman's figures, she
could well have had the artist's wood genre
figures in mind.

152. William Dean Howells compared Bessie
Potter Vonnoh's work to Greek Tanagra
figurines (quoted in Ilene Susan Fort, "'Mere
Beauty No Longer Suffices': The Response of
Genre Sculpture," in Ilene Susan Fort et al.,
*The Figure in American Sculpture: A Question
of Modernity* [Los Angeles: Los Angeles County
Museum of Art in association with the
University of Washington Press, 1995], p. 77).

153. Nadelman signed the contract for the
Fuller Building limestone frieze on October 24,
1928; plans were not approved and work did not
begin until 1929. Plans for the Bank of the
Manhattan Company's Aquarius were approved
in August 1929. The Fuller Building frieze still
stands; the Aquarius was probably destroyed
when the Bank of the Manhattan Company's
building at 40 Wall Street was demolished.

154. According to correspondence between the
Bank of the Manhattan Company and the
architectural firm, the bank demanded that
Nadelman conform explicitly to an image of
Aquarius that showed the god "sitting in a
reclining posture on rising ground puring [*sic*]
water from an urn which forms a river and ter-
minates in lake." The bank asked Nadelman to
change his design to show Aquarius looking
from left to right, with his left hand in a down-
ward position touching an urn rather than
being posed over his head with water flowing
from a cornucopia, as Nadelman had proposed.
They further specified that the flowers and fruit
be made less prominent and the water enlarged
so as to indicate a lake (Bank of the Manhattan
Company to L. N. Gillette, Esquire, 10
September 1929, Nadelman Estate Papers).

155. Quoted in Cynthia Nadelman,
"Chronology," p. 119.

156. A truck arrived on October 31, 1930, to pick
up the material du Pont had purchased from
Nadelman (du Pont to Nadelman, Nadelman
Estate Papers).

157. Alliance Realty Company to Nadelman, 4
May 1931, Nadelman Estate Papers. By
February 1932 the dancers, to whom the
Nadelmans had rented their Ninety-third Street
townhouse, had stopped paying rent. In June
the realty company notified Viola Nadelman
that the tenants had pawned a number of books
from the Nadelman library (Alliance Realty
Company to Elie Nadelman, 8 February 1932,
and Auchincloss & Duncan to Mrs. Elie
Nadelman, June 1932, Nadelman Estate
Papers).

158. Viola Nadelman wrote to Henry F. du Pont
in January 1932 and again in January 1933 offering to sell additional folk art objects from the
couple's collection; he declined (Nadelman
files, Winterthur Museum, Delaware).

159. In 1936 the Nadelmans regained title of
their house from Alderbrook Inc. for $19,800
with mortgages of $60,000. Their finances, how-
ever, remained shaky: in 1940 Nadelman stated
that his primary income consisted of the four
thousand dollars a year he received from rental
of his commercial property at 222 East Fifty-
fifth Street, which Viola had sold to him for one
dollar. Viola, he wrote, had "not a penny to her
name" (Nadelman to U.S. Trust, 11 October
1940, Nadelman Estate Papers).

160. Nadelman to Edward Bruce, 1936, Nadelman Estate Papers. Ed Rowan, associate director of the section, responded by reminding Nadelman that he had been invited to participate in the Milwaukee competition but had never responded to the invitation, nor had he ever entered any of the section's open competitions (Nadelman Estate Papers).

161. Fansler, quoted in Stillinger, "Elie and Viola Nadelman's Unprecedented Museum," p. 521.

162. The Museum of Folk Arts' advisory board consisted of Holger Cahill, director of the Works Progress Administration/Federal Arts Project (WPA/FAP); Florence Levy, director of the American Federation of the Arts; René d'Harnoncourt, assistant to the president of the American Federation of the Arts; and Alfred H. Barr, Jr., director of The Museum of Modern Art.

163. Nadelman wrote to Holger Cahill, who was both a board member of the Nadelmans' Museum of Folk Arts and director of the WPA/FAP: "The museum is unique. Anyone who has the means to give the museum permanency should consider it a duty and a privilege" (Nadelman to Cahill, 1936, Nadelman Estate Papers).

164. "You would be saving [the museum] for all times as I no longer have means to support it, having given to it all I possessed" (Nadelman to Nelson Rockefeller, 27 May 1937; quoted in Oaklander, "Pioneers in Folk Art Collecting," p. 51).

165. A strongly worded letter from Halpert on November 27, 1937, to the Nadelmans suggests that friction between herself and the couple may have led her to break her contract just two months before its expiration: "You undoubtedly appreciate the obstacles which confront me and which I must surmount to succeed. I cannot stress too much, therefore, the importance of your cooperation and strict compliance with this understanding, for in the event you frustrate my efforts and negotiations with people I have in mind, I will be seriously damaged in an amount difficult of ascertainment" (Downtown Gallery Papers, box 129, quoted in ibid., p. 55 n. 23).

166. According to Cynthia Nadelman's research, Edna Little Greenwood initiated the New-York Historical Society's purchase of the Nadelmans' collection. An avid collector of early American household arts and crafts, Mrs. Greenwood had visited the Nadelmans' museum but was not a personal friend of theirs, as she was of Alexander J. Wall, director of the society. She also knew Juliana Force, to whom she likewise wrote in an effort to help the Nadelmans sell their collection (Stillinger, "Elie and Viola Nadelman's Unprecedented Museum," p. 525 n. 21; Oaklander, "Pioneers in Folk Art Collecting,"

p. 55 n. 24; and Greenwood to Juliana Force, October 1937, Nadelman Estate Papers).

167. Nadelman to Edna Greenwood, draft of November 1937 letter, Nadelman Estate Papers. In the same letter Nadelman affirmed that it was "always in my mind that to achieve what we planned it would be best to work through some organization." Indeed, in the beginning, the Nadelmans intended to have their collection eventually become the property of the City of New York ("City Will Receive Prized Collection of Primitive Art," New York Herald Tribune, 30 October 1931).

168. Alexander J. Wall, director of the New-York Historical Society, wrote to Nadelman of the museum's decision to dismiss him: "I am requested to say that unless you can give your full time each day, as the other curators do, the work of completing the proper cataloguing and recording of the history of each object cannot go forward. I told the Committee of our talk in which you stated that you could not make such a catalogue, and that you could not work specified hours but wanted to be free to come and go as you felt it necessary. Of course, that is not museum practice, especially when there is so much to be done here, and we feel that we must engage the services of one who can devote his time to the work as stated." Nadelman responded bitterly in a reply to George Zabriskie, president of the society: "It is regrettable that I was not given a hearing when my case was discussed at a meeting of the Committee. From a letter, which Mr. Wall has sent me I see that my case was entirely misrepresented" (Wall to Nadelman, 17 April 1939, and Nadelman to Zabriskie, 19 April 1939, Elie Nadelman Papers, New-York Historical Society Archives, New York City; reprinted in Oaklander, "Pioneers in Folk Art Collecting," p. 52). Nadelman had, in fact, offered a year earlier to forfeit his salary if his plans for the collection's installation proved unsatisfactory: "I am perfectly willing to give two years of my services free so as to partly meet expenses which the society will incur in making the transfer to another room if my work turns out to be unsatisfactory" (Nadelman, telegram to Alexander Wall, 15 September 1938, New-York Historical Society Archives).

169. For discussion of Nadelman's late plasters, see Brandt Junceau, "Late Nadelman," M/E/A/N/I/N/G 6 (November 1989), pp. 28–34; Klaus Kertess, "Child's Play: The Late Work of Elie Nadelman," Artforum 23 (March 1985), pp. 64–67; and idem, "Clay Acting: The Late Works of Elie Nadelman," in Ramljak et al., Classical Folk, pp. 96–109.

170. For discussion of the relationship between small-scale vanguard sculptures of the early twentieth century and small-scale antiquities, see Wayne, "The Role of Antiquity," pp. 164–66.

171. Kertess, "Clay Acting," p. 105; Thomas Hess, "Nadelman and Lotusland," New York, 3 November 1975, pp. 77–79.

172. Junceau, "Late Nadelman," p. 18.

173. In an interview after Nadelman's death, Viola described him as a profoundly private person who never revealed his innermost thoughts and feelings, even to her (in Jean Evans, "A Sculptor Passes but His Marble Lives On," The New York Star, 31 July 1948, magazine sec., pp. 4–5).

174. Nadelman to A. E. Gallatin, October 1929, Nadelman Estate Papers. Four years earlier, in 1925, the sculptor sent photographs of his work to Colour magazine with the request that the magazine not show them to other artists should they not be published, presumably because he feared his aesthetic ideas might be stolen (Nadelman to editor of Colour, 21 September 1925, Nadelman Estate Papers).

175. Birnbaum, Last Romantic, p. 90.

176. Nadelman to Mrs. Stewart Walker, 1935, Nadelman Estate Papers.

177. Nadelman expressed his rationale for not exhibiting in a letter to Alfred H. Barr, Jr., stating that it was "absolutely necessary for me, that is, for the progress of my work, to entirely abstain from exhibiting at this time" (Nadelman to Barr, 4 March 1939, Nadelman Estate Papers).

178. Henry McBride, "Neglected Sculpture: The Odd Story of a Brilliant Artist Who Escaped Critical Attention," The New York Sun, 28 February 1947.

179. Jean Lipman, "American Folk: Six Decades of Discovery," in American Folk Painters of Three Centuries, ed. Jean Lipman and Tom Armstrong (New York: Hudson Hills Press, 1980), p. 221.

180. For example, the Knickerbocker Whist Club, of which Nadelman was a member, included few Jews among its members (see Bylaws and membership list of the Knickerbocker Whist Club, 1927, The New York Public Library).

181. Draft of letter from Nadelman to the United Jewish Appeal, April 1939, Nadelman Estate Papers.

182. Resia Shor, interview with the author, 21 February 2002.

183. One of Nadelman's nephews identified himself in a letter to Jan Nadelman after the war as "one of the last members of the once large family of Nadelmans. . . . All the others were murdered by Germans in Poland during the war" (M. Zimmerman to Jan Nadelman, January 1947, Nadelman Estate Papers).

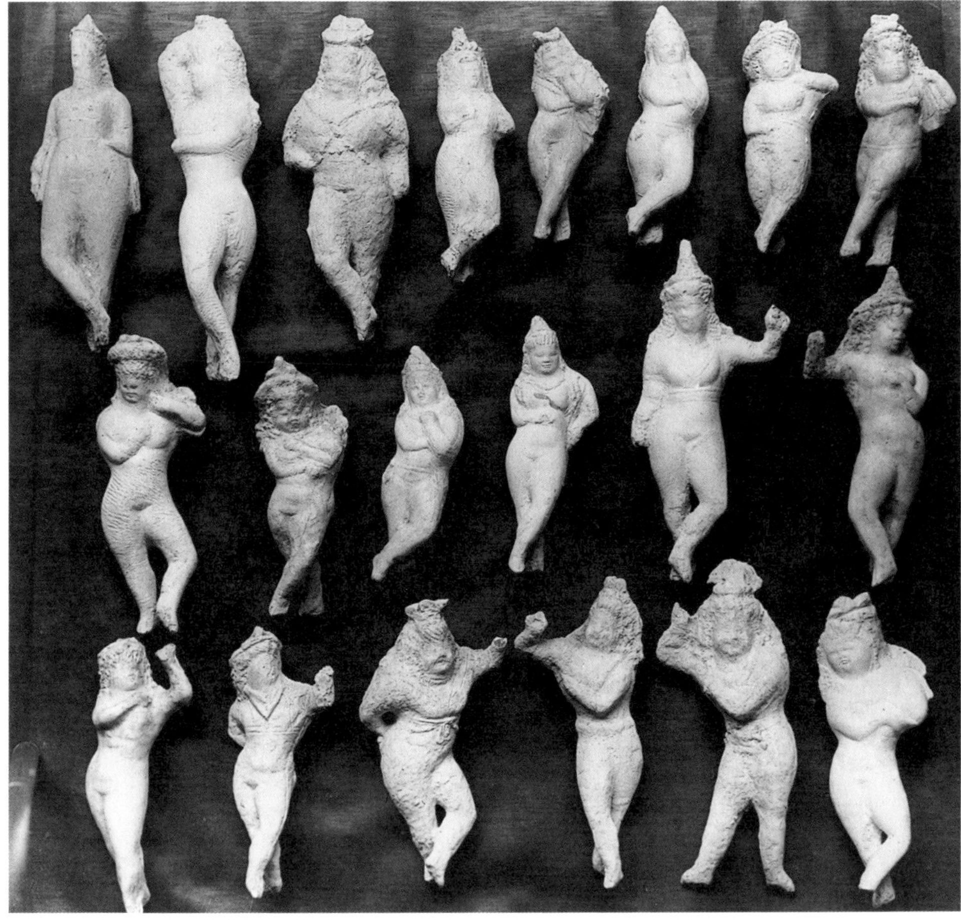

Elie Nadelman, ***Plaster figurines***, c. 1938–46. Plaster, dimensions variable. Photograph courtesy The Maddox Collection

184. Draft of letter, October 1942, Nadelman Estate Papers.

185. Kirstein, *Elie Nadelman*, p. 242.

186. The administrator of the Bronx Veterans Administration Hospital expressed his gratitude for Nadelman's generosity in a letter to Viola: "In bringing his highly developed skill in sculpture and ceramics to the disabled boys, twice weekly for two years, he brought much beauty and inspiration to their lives. His bright enthusiastic personality did much to combat their suffering and fatigue" (ibid., 58).

187. Nadelman, quoted in ibid., p. 20.

188. Elie Nadelman to Jan Nadelman, 27 September 1946, Nadelman Estate Papers.

189. Cynthia Nadelman, "Chronology," p. 122.

190. Elie Nadelman to Jan Nadelman, undated letter, Nadelman Estate Papers.

191. Kirstein identified this exhibition as a survey of progressive sculpture (*Elie Nadelman*, p. 342). Wanda Corn, however, wrote of it as a show on folk art, stating that Kirstein had requested Nadelman's sculptures so that the relationship between folk art and modern art could be demonstrated (*The Great American Thing: Modern Art and National Identity, 1915–1935* [Berkeley and Los Angeles: University of California Press, 1999], p. 396).

192. John Walker, Harvard Society for Contemporary Art, to Elie Nadelman, 5 October 1929, Nadelman Estate Papers. Kirstein oversaw the posthumous casting in bronze and terracotta of many of Nadelman's works, especially his late ones. His most questionable intervention was his decision to posthumously cast in bronze Nadelman's two paper-over-plaster circus women (figs. 192, 196) for Nelson Rockefeller and to approve their threefold enlargement in marble for the Philip Johnson–designed New York State Theatre at Lincoln Center. Both posthumous versions

voided the delicate sensuality and graceful intimacy of the originals and raised questions about posthumous re-creations of work in materials not designated by the artist. The pieces were cited as examples of the "unethical and pernicious practice" of enlargement at a conference organized by the College Art Association (reported on by Sylvia Hochfield, in "Problems in the Reproduction of Sculpture," *Art News* 73 [November 1974], pp. 20–29). While it is true that Nadelman routinely both enlarged and reduced work and also experimented with translating images into different materials, he was always sensitive to the interrelationship among form, size, and material and to the way sculpture interacted with its environment. Responding to a benefactor who had requested a wall sculpture for her pool, he asked to see the site in order to make a piece that accorded with its spirit, character, and size. "To place something that has been made previously and not for this particular purpose will never be satisfactory," he wrote to Mrs. Taylor (17 March 1942, Nadelman Estate Papers).

Exhibition History

Bold indicates one-artist exhibitions. Catalogues and brochures are cited within data on individual exhibitions; exhibition reviews mentioning Nadelman are indented following each exhibition.

The research papers compiled for this catalogue and exhibition, which contain photocopies of exhibition catalogues, brochures, announcements, reviews, and articles, including foreign periodicals and newspapers translated by Anne Botstein, are preserved in the Whitney Museum archives.

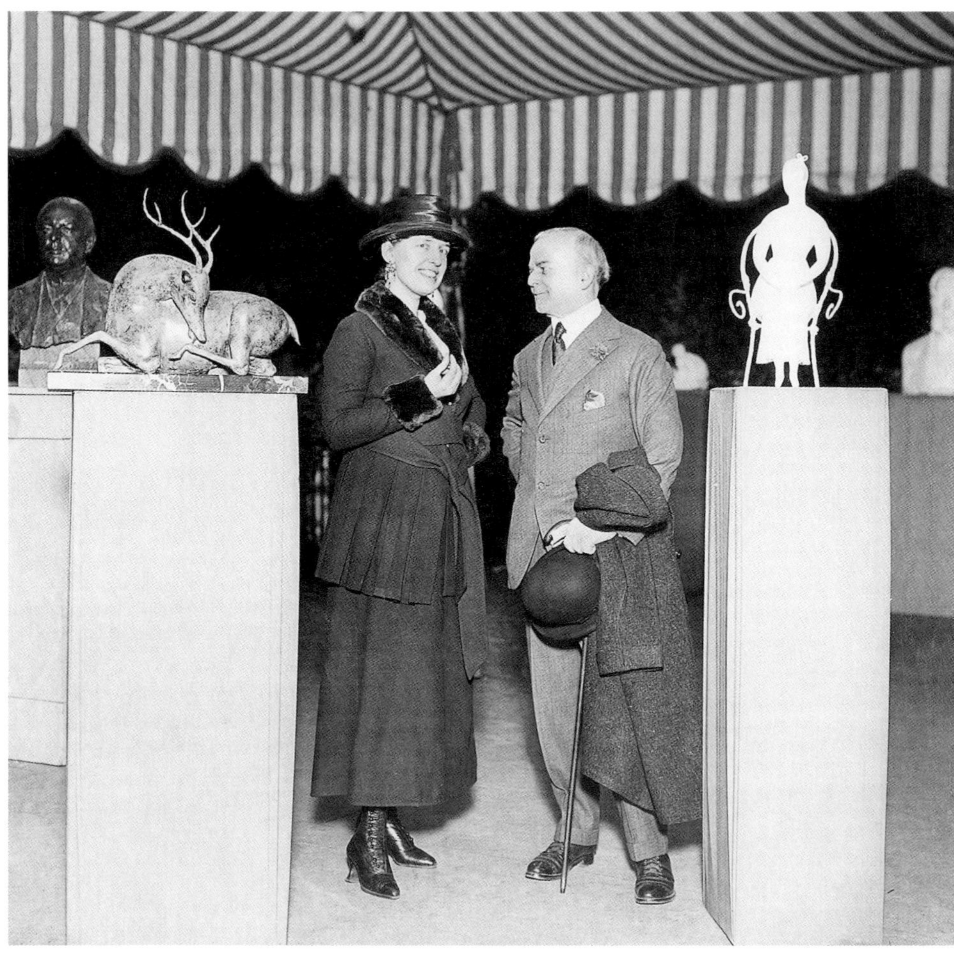

Muriel Draper and Christian Brinton with Elie Nadelman's *Resting Stag* and *Femme assise* at the *Allies of Sculpture* exhibition, Ritz-Carlton Hotel, New York, December 1917. Lincoln Kirstein Photograph Collection, Jerome Robbins Dance Division, The New York Public Library

1902

Salon Aleksandra Krywult, Warsaw, *Humor w sztuka*, 1 January–15 February 1902 (checklist).

> Nadelman, Elie, and Witold Wojtkiewicz. "Pochód modernizmu." *Tygodnik Ilustrowany*, no. 35 (30 August 1902), p. 699.

1905

Salon d'Automne, Grand Palais, Paris, *Troisième exposition*, 18 October–25 November 1905 (catalogue).

1906

Salon d'Automne, Grand Palais, Paris, *Quatrième exposition*, 6 October–15 November 1906 (checklist).

1907

Société des artistes indépendants, Serres du Cours-la-Reine, Paris, *Vingt-troisième exposition*, 20 March–30 April 1907 (catalogue).

1909

Galerie E. Druet, Paris, *Exposition Elie Nadelman*, 26 April–8 May 1909 (catalogue).

> Vaudoyer, Jean-Louis. "Petites expositions: M. Nadelman (Galerie Druet)." *La chronique des arts et de la curiosité* (supplement to *Gazette des beaux-arts*), no. 19 (8 May 1909), pp. 150–51.

1910

Bernheim-Jeune et Cie, Paris, *Nus*, 17–28 May 1910 (checklist).

Société artistique et littéraire russe, Impasse Ronsin, Paris, 1910.

Apollinaire, Guillaume. "The Art World: The Russian Painters in the Impasse Ronsin—The Truth about the Steinhil Case." In *Apollinaire on Art: Essays and Reviews, 1902–1918*. Edited by Leroy C. Breunig, pp. 115–16. Translated by Susan Suleiman. 1972. Reprint, New York: Da Capo Press, 1988.

1911

Towarzystwo przyjacióę sztuk pięknych Kraków, Poland, *Sztuka*, 9 February–14 March 1911 (checklist).

"Wystawa Rzeźby w Krakowie," *Krakowski Miesięcznik artystyczny*, 11 February 1911, pp. 22–23.

Wm. B. Paterson, London, *Exhibition of Sculpture by Eli Nadelman*, April 1911 (catalogue).

"Exhibitions: Mr. Nadelman's Sculpture." *Art News* 2 (15 April 1911), p. 51.

"'La Mysterieuse,' by the New Polish Sculptor, Elie Nadelman." *The New York Times*, 16 April 1911.

"A New Sculptor: Two Examples of the Work of Elie Nadelman." *Black and White*, 1 April 1911, p. 25.

"A Polish Sculptor." *Art Chronicle* 5 (15 April 1911), p. 208.

Société normande de peinture moderne, Galerie d'art ancien et d'art contemporain, Paris, *Première exposition*, 20 November–16 December 1911 (checklist).

1912

Towarzystwo przyjaciół sztuk pięknych, Lvov, Poland, *Sztuka*, 1912 (checklist).

Towarzystwo przyjaciół sztuk pięknych, Kraków, Poland, *Sztuka*, 18 February–31 March 1912 (checklist).

Galeríes J. Dalmau, Barcelona, *L'exposició d'art polonès: Grupu d'artistes polonesos residents a París*, May–June 1912 (catalogue).

Salon d'Automne, Grand Palais, Paris, *Dixième exposition*, 1 October–8 November 1912 (catalogue).

Apollinaire, Guillaume. "The Opening: October 2." In *Apollinaire on Art*, pp. 248–51.

"Artyści polscy w 'Salonie' paryskim." *Tygodnik Ilustrowany*, no. 3 (1912), pp. 49–50.

"Polacy w paryskim Salonie jesiennym." *Świat*, no. 46 (1912), pp. 3–5.

Towarzystwa Zachęty Sztuk Pięknych w Królestwie Polskiem, Salon Lachet, Warsaw, *Sztuka*, November 1912 (catalogue).

"Wystawa 'Sztuki' w Tow. Zachęty sztuk Pięknych w Warszawie." *Świat*, no. 48 (November 1912), pp. 7–9.

Kunsthaus Lepke, Berlin, *Juryfreie Kunstschau*, 26 November–31 December 1912 (checklist).

Bülow, Dr. J. V. "Paris auf der Juryfreien Kunstschau in Berlin." *Kunstchronik*, n.s., 24 (31 January 1913), pp. 249–54.

1913

Towarzystwo przyjaciół sztuk pięknych Kraków, Poland, *Towarzystwo artystów polskich "Sztuka,"* 1913 (checklist).

Akademischer Verband für Literatur und Musik in Wien, Vienna, *Internationale Schwarz-Weiss-Ausstellung*, 1913 (catalogue, with texts by Paul Stefan, Emil Alphons Rheinhardt, Paris von Guetersloh, and Peter Altenberg).

Galerie Miethke, Vienna, *Die neue Kunst*, January–February 1913 (catalogue, with an introduction by Adolphe Basler).

Gil Blas, 7 February 1913, p. 4.

Rathe, Kurt. "Wien." *Der Cicerone* (Leipzig) 4 (February 1913), pp. 149–50.

Roessler, Arthur. "Expressionistenausstellung (Galerie Miethke)." *Arbeiter Zeitung* (Vienna) 20 (1913).

Towarzystwo pryjaciót szutk pięknych, Poznan, Poland, *Sztuka*, 1913 (catalogue).

Société des artistes polonais à Paris, Pavilion de la Société des artistes polonais à Paris, *Les artistes polonais*, 20–29 January 1913 (checklist).

"L'évolution nouvelle." *Gil Blas*, 28 January 1913, p. 4.

Association of American Painters and Sculptors, Armory of the Sixty-ninth Infantry, New York, *International Exhibition of Modern Art*, 17 February–15 March 1913 (catalogue). Traveled to The Art Institute of Chicago and Copley Hall, Copley Society of Boston.

Künstlerhaus-Ausstellung, Berlin, *LIX. Ausstellung der Krakauer Künstler-Vereinigung "Sztuka,"* March 1913 (catalogue).

Société des artistes indépendants, Quai d'Orsay, Paris, *Vingt-neuvième exposition*, 19 March–18 May 1913 (catalogue).

Galerie E. Druet, Paris, *Exposition d'art plastique de Eli Nadelman*, 26 May–7 June 1913 (catalogue).

Apollinaire, Guillaume. "The Art World." In *Apollinaire on Art*, pp. 319–20.

"Elie Nadelman—Chez Druet." *Gil Blas*, 1 June 1913, p. 3.

Jean, René. "Petites expositions: Exposition Eli Nadelman (Galerie Druet)." *La chronique des arts et de la curiosité* (supplement to *Gazette des beaux-arts*), no. 23 (7 June 1913), p. 179.

Neue Kunst Hans Goltz, Munich, *Neue Kunst*, August–September 1913 (catalogue, with text by Wilhelm Hausenstein, preface by André Salmon).

"L'évolution nouvelle." *Gil Blas*, 18 July 1913, p. 4.

Ausstellungshaus am Kurfürstendamm, Berlin, *Herbst-Ausstellung*, 1913 (catalogue).

Salon d'Automne, Grand Palais, Paris, *Onzième exposition*, 15 November 1913–15 January 1914 (catalogue).

Apollinaire, Guillaume. "The Opening: November 19, Sculpture." In *Apollinaire on Art*, pp. 328–29.

———. "The Salon d'Automne: November 15, Boussingault." In *Apollinaire on Art*, pp. 333–34.

Salmon, André. "Le Salon d'Automne." *Montjoie!* no. 11–12 (November–December 1913), pp. 1–7, 11.

1914

Société des artistes indépendants, Champs de Mars, Paris, *Trentième exposition*, 1 March–30 April 1914 (catalogue).

Apollinaire, Guillaume. "The Salon des Indépendants: March 5." In *Apollinaire on Art*, pp. 358–59.

Whitechapel Art Gallery, London, *Twentieth-Century Art: A Review of Modern Movements*, 8 May–20 June 1914 (catalogue).

Galerie Georges Giroux, Brussels, *Salon des artistes indépendants de Paris*, 16 May–7 June 1914 (checklist).

1915

Little Galleries of the Photo-Secession, New York, *Sculpture and Drawings by Elie Nadelman*, 8 December–19 January 1915.

Britton, James. "Exhibitions Now On: Nadelman at the Secession." *American Art News* 14 (11 December 1915), p. 6.

Caffin, Charles. *The New York American*, December 1915.

Carey, Elizabeth Luther. "Art Notes: Elie Nadelman's Sculpture on View." *The New York Times*, 17 December 1915.

McBride, Henry. "Current News of Art and the Exhibitions." *The New York Sun*, 12 December 1915.

Nadelman, Elie. "Eli Nadelman of Paris." *Camera Work* 48 (October 1916), p. 10.

———. *The Springfield Republican*, December 1915.

Stieglitz, Alfred. "Nadelman Exhibition, Two Rooms, December 1915." *Camera Work* 48 (October 1916), p. 68. Reprinted in Marianne Margolis, *Camera Work: A Pictorial Guide* (New York: Dover Publications, 1978), p. 137.

Watson, Forbes. *The New York Evening Post*, December 1915.

Wright, Willard Huntington. "The Aesthetic Struggle in America." *The Forum* 2 (February 1916), pp. 201–20.

Montross Gallery, New York, *Contemporary Group Exhibition*, 12–30 December 1915 (checklist).

1916

Cabaret Voltaire, Zurich, *Ausstellung Cabaret Voltaire*, February 1916 (catalogue).

1917

Rhode Island School of Design, Providence, *Contemporary Group Exhibition*, 9–27 January 1917 (checklist).

Scott & Fowles, New York, *An Exhibition of Sculpture and Drawings by Elie Nadelman*, February 1917 (catalogue, with introduction by Martin Birnbaum).

"Art and Artists: Nadelman at Scott and Fowles." *The New York Globe*, 1917.

"Art Notes: The Sculpture of Nadelman Now on View." *The New York Times*, 2 February 1917.

Eddy, Frederick W. "News of the Art World: Classic Sculpture by Elie Nadelman." *The New York World*, 11 February 1917.

McBride, Henry. "News and Comment in the World of Art." *The New York Sun*, 4 February 1917. Reprinted in Henri McBride, *The Flow of Art: Essays and Criticisms of Henri McBride* (New York: Atheneum Publishers, 1975), ed. Lincoln Kirstein, pp. 107–09.

———. "Exhibitions at the New York Galleries: Elie Nadelman's Sculptures." *Fine Art Journal* (Chicago) 3 (March 1917), pp. 227–28.

H. C. N. "Exhibit of Sculpture." *New York American*, 1917.

The New York Evening World, 15 February 1917.

The Philadelphia Record, 11 February 1917.

"Sculpture by Nadelman." *American Art News* 15 (3 February 1917), p. 3.

"Sculpture by Nadelman at Scott and Fowles." *The Brooklyn Daily Eagle*, 4 February 1917.

The Spur, 15 February 1917.

Watson, Forbes. "At the Art Galleries." *The New York Evening Post Saturday Magazine*, 3 February 1917.

Scott & Fowles, New York, *Exhibition of Nadelman and Pascin*, November 1917.

"American Contemporary Art Display." *American Art News* 16 (17 November 1917), p. 3.

Caffin, Charles H. "New and Important Things in Art: Nadelman and Manship." *New York American*, 26 November 1917.

Crowninshield, Frank. "Sculpture at a New York Salon: The Work of a Triumvirate of Modern Sculptors." *Vanity Fair*, January 1918, p. 54.

Eddy, Frederick W. "News of the Art World." *The New York World*, 18 November 1917.

Kobbe, Gustav. "Ancient Greece and Fifth Avenue Rub Elbows with 'Utah Copper' during Busy Week in World of Art." *The New York Herald*, 18 November 1917.

McBride, Henry. "News and Comment in the World of Art: Nadelman and Pascin at Scott and Fowles." *The New York Sun*, 18 November 1917.

———. "Exhibitions at New York Galleries: Nadelman, Demuth, and Other Modern Artists." *Fine Art Journal* (Chicago) 12 (December 1917), pp. 46, 51–52.

H. C. N. "Art and Artists: Contemporary American Art Exhibition at Scott & Fowles." *The Globe and Commercial Advertiser*, 12 November 1917.

Roof Garden of the Hotel Ritz-Carlton, New York, *Allies of Sculpture*, 5–25 December 1917 (catalogue, with foreword by Gertrude Atherton).

"Blue-Haired Figures Out in Light Again: Nadelman's Statuettes Back to Their Original Place in Ritz-Carlton Sculpture Show." *The New York World*, 20 December 1917.

Crowninshield, Frank. "Elie Nadelman, in a Modernist Mood." *Vanity Fair*, May 1918, p. 64.

"Early Morning Offensive Saves Nadelman Art from Suicide." *The New York Herald*, December 1917.

"Freak Art Holds Attention at the New York Show." *The Buffalo Evening News*, 14 December 1917.

"His 'Modest' Art Offends Exhibit." *The New York World*, 19 December 1917.

"Nadelman Statuette Maimed; Spite, He Says." *The New York World*, 29 December 1917.

1918

Whitney Studio Club, New York, *Indigenous Sculpture*, March 1918.

"Sculptors Have Indigenous Test." *The New York Sun*, 10 March 1918.

Penguin Club, New York, *Contemporary Art*, March 1918.

Crowninshield, Frank. "Elie Nadelman, in a Modernist Mood." *Vanity Fair*, May 1918, p. 64.

McBride, Henry. "Views and Reviews in the World of Art." *The New York Sun*, 24 March 1918.

1919

New Society of Artists, New York, *First Annual Exhibition of the New Society of Artists*, October 1919.

M. Knoedler & Company, New York, *An Exhibition of Sculpture and Drawings by Elie Nadelman*, 27 October–8 November 1919 (catalogue).

Field, Hamilton Easter. "Modern Art Shown at Knoedler Gallery." *The Brooklyn Daily Eagle*, 2 November 1919.

———. "Art New and Old in Current Shows." *Arts and Decoration* 12 (December 1919), p. 108.

"McBride Not Satisfied." *American Art News* 18 (1 November 1919), p. 4.

McBride, Henry. "News and Comment in the World of Art." *The New York Sun*, 2 November 1919.

———. "News and Comment in the World of Art." *The New York Sun*, 16 November 1919, magazine sec.

"Notes on Current Art." *The New York Times*, 2 November 1919.

Pelton, Agnes. "Her Crowning Moment in Evening Dress." *The New York Sun*, 16 November 1919, magazine sec.

Tyrrell, Henry. "At a Musical Tea with Nadelman." *The New York World Magazine*, 30 November 1919. Reprinted in Lincoln Kirstein, *Elie Nadelman* (New York: Eakins Press, 1973), pp. 276–78.

E. Gimpel and Wildenstein, New York, *First Annual Exhibition of the American Painters, Sculptors, and Gravers*, 3–22 November 1919 (catalogue).

"Exhibitions Opening This Week: Art at Home and Abroad." *The New York Times*, 2 November 1919, sec. 4.

McBride, Henry. "News and Comment in the World of Art." *The New York Sun*, 26 October 1919.

Dallas Art Association, Adolphus Hotel Junior Ballroom, Dallas, *First Annual Exhibition of Contemporary International Art*, 19–27 November 1919.

"Dallas Art Association." *American Art News* 18 (22 November 1919), p. 2.

1920

Albright Art Gallery, Buffalo, *Fourteenth Annual Exhibition of Selected Paintings by American Artists and a Group of Small Selected Bronzes by American Sculptors*, 29 May–7 September 1920.

Bernheim-Jeune et Cie, Paris, *Exposition Nadelman: Sculpture et dessins*, 23 September–13 October 1920 (catalogue).

"Les arts." *Intransigeant*, 13 October 1920.

"Bernheim-Jeune et Cie." *Petit messager*, 11 October 1920.

M. C. "Paris Letter: Sculpture by Nadelman." *American Art News* 19 (13 November 1920), p. 3.

The Chicago Tribune, 1 October 1920.

"Divers." *Carnet de la semaine*, 9 October 1920.

"Exposition Nadelman." *Opinion!* 8 October 1920.

L'oeuvre, 29 September 1920.

"Petites expositions." *La chronique des arts et de la curiosité* (supplement to *Gazette des beaux-arts*) 20 (31 October 1920), p. 144.

"Les petites expositions." *Comoedia*, 2 October 1920.

Victoire, 1 October 1920.

New Society of Artists, E. Gimpel and Wildenstein, New York, *Second Annual Exhibition of the New Society of Artists*, 8–27 November 1920 (catalogue).

"Exhibitions Now On: The Little Academy." *American Art News* 19 (13 November 1920), p. 4.

McBride, Henry. "Sculptors Take Precedence in Exhibition of the New Society of Artists." *The New York Herald*, 14 November 1920.

1922

Colony Club, New York, April 1922.

"Art: The First of the April Exhibitions." *The New York Times*, 9 April 1922.

Lloyd, David. "This Week in the World of Art and Artists: Modernists of Various Kinds in Three Shows." *The New York Evening Post*, 8 April 1922.

1923

New Society of Artists, Anderson Galleries, New York, *New Society of Artists: Fourth Exhibition*, 2–27 January 1923.

Galerie Flechtheim, Berlin, March 1923.

"Berliner Ausstellungen: Galerie Flechtheim." *Kunstchronik und Kunstmarkt*, n.s., 34 (23 March 1923), p. 497.

"Die Galerie Alfred Flechtheim." *Der Sammler* 17, no. 11 (1923), p. 83.

Modern Artists of America, Joseph Brummer Galleries, New York, *Second Annual Exhibition of Modern Artists of America*, April 1923.

Read, Helen Appleton. "News and Views on Current Art." *The Brooklyn Daily Eagle*, 29 April 1923.

1924

New Society of Artists, Anderson Galleries, New York, *The New Society of Artists Fifth Exhibition*, 2–31 January 1924.

Albright Art Gallery, Buffalo, *Eighteenth Annual Exhibition of Selected Paintings and Small Bronzes by American Artists*, 20 April–30 June 1924.

"Elie Nadelman: Tête de Femme." *Academy Notes* 19 (July–December 1924), p. 67.

1925

Artists' Gallery, under the auspices of Himebaugh & Brown, New York, January 1925.

"The Artists' Gallery," *The New York Evening Post*, 24 January 1925.

Scott & Fowles, New York, *Sculpture by Elie Nadelman*, March 1925.

"Art: Exhibitions of the Week: Sculpture." *The New York Times*, 15 March 1925.

Cortissoz, Royal. "A Spring Interlude in the World of Art Shows: Reversions—Henri Matisse and Elie Nadelman in a Normal Mood." *New York Herald Tribune*, 15 March 1925.

F[lint], R[alph]. "Nadelman Exhibits in Triple Capacity." *The Art News* 23 (14 March 1925), pp. 1–2.

R. F. "New York Gallery Findings," *The Christian Science Monitor* (Boston), 18 March 1925.

McBride, Henry. "Modern Art: Elie Nadelman Sculptures." *The Dial* 78 (June 1925), pp. 527–29.

———. "Neo-Greek Sculptures Shown." *The New York Sun*, 14 March 1925.

Patterson, Augusta Owen. "Arts and Decoration." *Town and Country*, 1 April 1925, pp. 54, 95.

Read, Helen Appleton. "New York Exhibitions: Eli Nadelman." *The Arts* 7 (April 1925), pp. 228–29.

Arts Club at the Art Institute of Chicago, Chicago, *Sculpture by Elie Nadelman*, 1 May–4 June 1925 (catalogue).

Bulliet, C. J. "Jugoslav to Work for a While in U.S." *The Chicago Evening Post*, 5 May 1925.

"Chicago Critic Hits Foreign Sculpture." *The Art News* 23 (13 June 1925), p. 8.

1926

New Society of Artists, Anderson Galleries, New York, *The New Society of Artists: Seventh Exhibition*, 6–30 January 1926 (catalogue).

"The New Society of Artists." *The Connoisseur* 74 (February 1926), p. 127.

New Society of Artits, Grand Central Galleries, New York, *Eighth Annual Exhibition of the New Society of Artists*, 15 November–4 December 1926.

"Hundreds Visit New Artists' Show." *The New York Times*, 28 November 1926, sec. 1.

1927

M. Knoedler & Company, New York, *Sculpture by Elie Nadelman*, 31 January–12 February 1927 (catalogue).

"Around the Galleries of New York: Sculptural Figures by Elie Nadelman." *The New York Times*, 6 February 1927, sec. 7.

"Current Events in Art: Novel Figures by Nadelman Entertain." *The New York World*, 6 February 1927, Metro sec.

Kalonyme, Louis. "Art's Spring Song: Modern and Ultra-Modern American Art in the New York Galleries." *Arts and Decoration* 6 (April 1927), pp. 67, 102, 104.

McBride, Henry. "Nadelman's Defiant Art: Sculptures at Knoedler Galleries Another Test for the Liberal Mind." *The New York Sun*, 5 February 1927. Reprinted in *Creative Art* (May 1932), pp. 393–95

———. "Modern Art." *The Dial* 4 (April 1927), pp. 353–55.

"Midwinter Finds Art Season Crowded with Exhibitions: Elie Nadelman." *The New York Evening Post*, 5 February 1927.

Read, Helen Appleton. "Sculptured Caricatures by Nadelman Are Shown." *The Brooklyn Daily Eagle*, 6 February 1927, sec. E.

National Academy, New York, *Spring Academy*, 1927.

Bernheim-Jeune et Cie, Paris, *Exposition Elie Nadelman*, 23 May–3 June 1927 (catalogue).

1929

California Palace of the Legion of Honor, San Francisco, in cooperation with the National Sculpture Society, New York, *Contemporary American Sculpture*, April–October 1929.

Quinton, Cornelia B. Sage, and William Warren Quinton. "Exhibition Contemporary American Sculpture: National Sculpture Society; California Palace of the Legion of Honor." *The American Magazine of Art* 20 (May 1929), pp. 251–54.

Municipal Art Gallery, Atlantic City Boardwalk, Atlantic City, N.J., *Contemporary American Art*, summer 1929.

Jewell, Edward Alden. "Contemporary American Art Joins Boardwalk Parade." *The New York Times*, 23 June 1929.

1930

Society of Independent Artists, Grand Central Palace, New York, *Fourteenth Annual Exhibition of the Society of Independent Artists*, 1–30 March 1930.

1931

Anderson Galleries, New York, in cooperation with the American Art Association, *Spring Salon 1931*, 20 April–9 May 1931 (catalogue, with foreword by Elsa Rogo).

Averell House, New York, *Art for the Garden*, November–December 1931.

Stewart, A. "Rare Sculpture for the Garden at Averell House." *The Art News* 10 (5 December 1931), p. 14.

1932

International Gallery, New York, *Sculpture from the Private Collection of Helena Rubinstein*, 16 April–6 May 1932 (catalogue, with introduction by Marie Sterner).

"Around the Galleries." *The Art News* 30 (23 April 1932), p. 10.

"Beauty Specialist Displays Her Nadelmans." *The Art Digest* 14 (15 April 1932), p. 15.

Breuning, Margaret. "Art Galleries Showing Spring Exhibits." *The New York Evening Post*, 23 April 1932, sec. 3.

[du] B[ois], G[uy] P[ène]. "Eli Nadelman." *Arts Weekly* (New York) 1 (30 April 1932), pp. 169, 174, 175.

Jewell, Edward Alden. "Art in Review: A Gallery Resembles One of the 'Classic' Corridors in the Louvre." *The New York Times*, 24 April 1932, sec. 2.

Nirdlinger, Virginia. "Eli Nadelman: International Gallery." *Parnassus* 4 (April 1932), pp. 13, 22.

Read, Helen Appleton. "In the Galleries." *The Brooklyn Daily Eagle*, 24 April 1932, sec. E.

Kraushaar Galleries, New York, 18 May–15 June 1932.

"Attractions in the Galleries." *The New York Sun*, 28 May 1932.

Burrows, Carlyle. "A French Draftsman Featured in Brooklyn; Varied Art Here." *New York Herald Tribune*, 29 May 1932.

McCormick, W. B. "Sculpture and Debut." *New York American*, 23 May 1932.

1933

M. Knoedler & Company, New York, *International Horse Show of Art*, 20 March–1 April 1933.

"Big Entry List Being Filled for Art Horse Show." *New York American*, 22 March 1933.

Reinhardt Galleries, New York, *Baby Show: Exhibition of Children's Portraits*, 1–13 May 1933 (catalogue).

Burrows, Carlyle. "Baby Show of Art a Winning Event of the Waning Season." *New York Herald Tribune*, 7 May 1933.

1937

Milch Galleries, New York, *Special Exhibition of Contemporary American Sculpture*, February 1937.

Karl Freund Gallery, New York, *Ducks and Geese in Art of the Ages*, April 1937.

Burrows, Carlyle. "Ducks and Geese in Art." *New York Herald Tribune*, 2 May 1937.

"Five New Group Shows." *The New York Times*, 25 April 1937.

1938

Carnegie Institute, Pittsburgh, *An Exhibition of American Sculpture*, 5 May–19 June 1938 (catalogue).

Musée du Jeu de Paume, Paris, *Trois siècles d'art aux États-Unis*, May–July 1938; exhibition organized in collaboration with The Museum of Modern Art, New York (catalogue, with essay by Alfred H. Barr, Jr.).

1944

Philadelphia Museum of Art, Philadelphia, *History of an American: Alfred Stieglitz, "291" and After*, 1 July–1 November 1944 (catalogue, with texts by Henry Clifford and Carl Zigrosser).

1948

The Museum of Modern Art, New York, *The Sculpture of Elie Nadelman*, 5 October–28 November 1948 (catalogue, with text by Lincoln Kirstein). Traveled to Institute of Contemporary Art, Boston; Baltimore Museum of Art.

"Art: Monumental Dolls." *Time*, 18 October 1948, p. 46.

B[reeskin], A[delyn] D. "Elie Nadelman." *The Baltimore Museum of Art News* 3 (December 1948), pp. 5–6.

———. "Elie Nadelman." *The Baltimore Museum of Art News* 5 (February 1949), pp. 6–7.

Burrows, Carlyle. "Nadelman Exhibit Open at Museum of Modern Art Today." *New York Herald Tribune*, 6 October 1948.

———. "Elie Nadelman Recalled—His Great Facility and Wit." *New York Herald Tribune*, 10 October 1948, sec. 5.

Coates, Robert M. "The Art Galleries: East and West." *The New Yorker*, 16 October 1948, pp. 89, 90–91.

Cox, Shelby Shackelford. "Elie Nadelman: A Sculpture Review." *Right Angle* (Washington, D.C.) 11 (February–March 1949), unpaginated.

Crawford, Peggy F. "Nadelman Revived." *The Art Digest* 23 (15 October 1948), pp. 15, 35.

Dame, Lawrence. "Regarding Boston." *The Art Digest* 23 (1 April 1949), p. 34.

Devree, Howard. "Sculptor's Work on Display Today." *The New York Times*, 6 October 1948.

———. "Prolific Sculptor." *The New York Times*, 10 October 1948, sec. 3.

Driscoll Jr., Edgar J. "This Week in the Art World: Nadelman's 'Dressmaker Art' Intrigues." *The Boston Sunday Globe*, 20 March 1949.

McBride, Henry. "Lyrical Sculpture." *The New York Sun*, 15 October 1948.

"Nadelman Rediscovered." *Newsweek*, 18 October 1948, p. 105.

Preston, Stuart. "The Nadelman Revival." *Art News* 47 (October 1948), pp. 22–24, 51.

1949

Yale University Art Gallery, New Haven, Conn., *Sculpture since Rodin*, 14 January–13 February 1949.

M. Knoedler Galleries, New York, *Elie Nadelman: Drawings*, 29 November–10 December 1949.

B[rian], D[oris]. "Howard and Nadelman." *The Art Digest* 24 (15 December 1949), p. 22.

C[ampbell], L[awrence]. "Elie Nadelman." *Art News* 48 (January 1950), pp. 45–46.

Preston, Stuart. "New West, Old East: Drawings." *The New York Times*, 4 December 1949, sec. 2.

M. Knoedler Galleries, New York, *To Honor Henry McBride: An Exhibition of Paintings, Drawings, and Water Colours*, 29 November–17 December 1949 (catalogue).

McBride, Henry. "A Critic Confesses." *The New York Sun*, 2 December 1949.

1950

Edwin Hewitt Gallery, New York, *Symbolic Realism*, 3–22 April 1950.

Albright Art Gallery, Buffalo Fine Arts Academy, Buffalo, *Dramatic Choice: The Theater Collects*, 4 November–1 December 1950 (catalogue).

Edwin Hewitt Gallery, New York, *Small Sculptures by Elie Nadelman*, 28 November–16 December 1950 (catalogue, with text by Lincoln Kirstein).

Bird, Paul. "Elie Nadelman." *The Art Digest* 25 (1 December 1950), p. 17.

McBride, Henry. "By Henry McBride." *Art News* 49 (January 1951), p. 50.

Preston, Stuart. "Religious Subjects: Mystery." *The New York Times*, 3 December 1950, sec. 2.

1951

Yale University Art Gallery, New Haven, Conn., *Pictures for a Picture: Of Gertrude Stein as a Collector and Writer on Art and Artists*, 11 February–11 March 1951 (catalogue). Traveled to Baltimore Museum of Art.

Feragil Gallery, New York, *Nadelman: Some Famous Papier-Mâché and Ceramics*, June 1951.

Edwin Hewitt Gallery, New York, *Wood Sculpture by Elie Nadelman*, 28 November–22 December 1957 (catalogue, with text by Lincoln Kirstein).

Fitzsimmons, James. "New York Gets a Spate of Sculpture Shows." *The Art Digest* 26 (1 December 1951), pp. 14, 34.

Porter, Fairfield. "Reviews and Previews." *Art News* 50 (December 1951), p. 46.

Preston, Stuart. "Diverse One-Man Shows: Dandy." *The New York Times*, 9 December 1951, sec. 2.

1953

Swetzoff Gallery, Boston, *Sculpture: Nadelman*, 28 September–17 October 1953.

1954

Art Studio, Deerfield Academy, Deerfield, Mass., January 1954.

Walker Art Center, Minneapolis, *Reality and Fantasy, 1900–54*, 23 May–2 July 1954.

1955

Edwin Hewitt Gallery, New York, *Elie Nadelman*, 28 March–16 April 1955.

M[unro], E[leanor] C. "Elie Nadelman." *Art News* 54 (April 1955), p. 47.

P[reston], S[tuart]. "About Art and Artists." *The New York Times*, 29 March 1955.

Preston, Stuart. "The Wide Range of New Shows: The Pursuit of Beauty." *The New York Times*, 31 April 1955, sec. 2.

R[osenblum], R[obert]. "Elie Nadelman." *Arts Digest* 29 (15 April 1955), p. 20.

Musée National d'Art Moderne, Paris, International Program of The Museum of Modern Art (organizer), *Cinquante ans d'art aux États-Unis: Collections du Museum of Modern Art de New York*, April–May 1955 (catalogue). Traveled to Tate Gallery, London (catalogue: *Modern Art in the United States: A Selection from the Collections of the Museum of Modern Art, New York*).

1956

Downtown Gallery, New York, *Spring 1956*, 29 May–29 June 1956 (checklist).

1957

Brooklyn Museum, Brooklyn, *Golden Years of American Drawings: 1905–1956*, 22 January–17 March 1957 (catalogue, with text by Una E. Johnson).

Edwin Hewitt Gallery, New York, *Elie Nadelman, 1882–1946*, 16 April–18 May 1957 (catalogue, with text by Lincoln Kirstein).

E. B. "Reviews and Previews." *Art News* 56 (April 1957), p. 10.

Preston, Stuart. "Gallery Variety: New Shows Offer Work by Nadelman, Ernst, Pascin, Gross, and Others." *The New York Times*, 21 April 1957, sec. 2.

Y[oung], V[ernon]. "In the Galleries: Elie Nadelman." *Arts* 31 (April 1957), p. 56.

1958

Edwin Hewitt Gallery, New York, *Elie Nadelman: Fifteen Small Bronzes and Drawings*, 7–30 April 1958.

C[ampbell], L[awrence]. "Elie Nadelman." *Art News* 57 (May 1958), p. 13.

Preston, Stuart. "Various Modern Veins." *The New York Times*, 20 April 1958, sec. 2.

Sawin, Martica. "Elie Nadelman." *Arts* 32 (May 1958), p. 55.

Schwartz, Marvin D. "News and Views from New York." *Apollo* 68 (June 1958), p. 241.

The Museum of Modern Art, New York, *The Philip L. Goodwin Collection*, 8 October– 9 November 1958.

Barr, Alfred H., Jr. "The Philip L. Goodwin Collection." *The Museum of Modern Art Bulletin* 26 (fall 1958), pp. 4–11.

Hewitt Gallery, New York, *Elie Nadelman: Figures and Figurines, 1930–1940*, 5–31 December 1958 (catalogue, with text by Lincoln Kirstein).

Grosser, Maurice. "Art: Elie Nadelman's Figurines." *The Nation* 22 (27 December 1958), p. 503.

M[ellow], J[ames] R. "In the Galleries: Elie Nadelman." *Arts* 3 (December 1958), pp. 52–53.

P[orter], F[airfield]. "Elie Nadelman." *Art News* 37 (December 1958), p. 15.

1959

Whitney Museum of American Art, New York, *The Collection of the Sara Roby Foundation*, 29 April–14 June 1959.

Detroit Institute of Arts, Detroit, *Sculpture in Our Time: Collected by Joseph H. Hirshhorn*, 5 May–23 August 1959 (catalogue). An abbreviated version of the exhibition traveled to Milwaukee Arts Center; Walker Art Center, Minneapolis; William Rockhill Nelson Gallery of Art, Kansas City, Mo.; Museum of Fine Arts, Houston; Los Angeles County Museum; De Young Memorial Museum, San Francisco; Colorado Springs Fine Arts Center; Art Gallery of Toronto.

Saltmarche, Kenneth. "Notes on Special Exhibitions: Sculpture in Our Time." *The Art Quarterly* 22 (winter 1959), pp. 350–55.

Sokolniki Park, Moscow, *American National Exhibition in Moscow (Modern Painting and Original Sculpture Exhibit—Moscow)*, 25 July– 5 September 1959.

Worcester Art Museum, Worcester, Mass., *The Dial and the Dial Collection*, 30 August– 8 September 1959.

Worcester Art Museum News Bulletin and Calendar 24 (May 1959), pp. 3–4.

1960

Corcoran Gallery of Art, Washington, D.C., *A Loan Exhibition from the Edith Gregor Halpert Collection*, 16 January–28 February 1960 (catalogue, with introduction by Hermann Warner Williams Jr.).

Munson Williams Proctor Institute, Utica, N.Y., *Art across America*, 15 October–31 December 1960.

Robert Isaacson Gallery, New York, *Elie Nadelman*, 18 October–19 November 1960.

Preston, Stuart. "Current and Forthcoming Exhibitions: New York." *The Burlington Magazine* 102 (December 1960), p. 549.

R[oskill], M[ark]. "Elie Nadelman." *Art News* 59 (December 1960), p. 15.

Sawin, M[artica]. "Elie Nadelman." *Arts* 35 (December 1960), p. 53.

The Museum of Modern Art, New York, *One Hundred Drawings from the Collection of the Museum of Modern Art*, 11 October 1960– 2 January 1961.

1961

Robert Isaacson Gallery, New York, *Drawings by Elie Nadelman*, 8 November–2 December 1961 (catalogue).

Burns, James T., Jr., ed. "Art: Relax and Enjoy." *Progressive Architecture* 42 (December 1961), p. 71.

C[ampbell], L[awrence]. "Elie Nadelman." *Art News* 60 (December 1961), p. 57.

1962

Rex Evans Gallery, Los Angeles, *Drawings by Elie Nadelman*, 8–27 January 1962.

Langsner, Jules. "Los Angeles Letter, Part II: February 1962." *Art International* 6 (March 1962), pp. 49–50.

Newark Museum, Newark, N.J., *A Survey of American Sculpture: Late Eighteenth Century to 1962*, 10 May–20 October 1962 (catalogue, with text by William H. Gerdts).

"American Sculpture." *American Artist* 26 (September 1962), pp. 40–47, 68–73.

Downtown Gallery, New York, *Thirty-sixth Spring Annual: The Figure*, 22 May– 15 June 1962.

American Federation of Arts (organizer), *Sculptors' Drawings from the Joseph H. Hirshhorn Collection*. Shown at Forum Gallery, New York, 1–20 October 1962. Traveled to Jewish Community Center, Washington, D.C.; Duke University, Durham, N.C.; New Britain Museum of American Art, New Britain, Conn.; Krannert Art Museum, University of Illinois, Urbana; Laguna Gloria Art Museum, Austin, Tex.; Lytton Center of the Visual Arts, Hollywood, Calif.; Des Moines Art Center (catalogue).

Gentlein, Frank. "Art and Artists: Jewish Center." *Washington Evening Star*, 19 May 1963, sec. F.

Solomon R. Guggenheim Museum, New York, *Modern Sculpture from the Joseph H. Hirshhorn Collection*, 3 October–6 January 1962.

Rudikoff, Sonya. "New York Letter." *Art International* 7 (25 November 1962), pp. 60, 62.

1963

Whitney Museum of American Art, New York, *The Decade of the Armory Show: New Directions in American Art, 1910–1920*, 27 February–14 April 1963. Traveled to City Art Museum, Saint Louis; Cleveland Museum of Art; Pennsylvania Academy of the Fine Arts, Philadelphia; Art Institute of Chicago; Albright-Knox Art Gallery, Buffalo.

Art Gallery of Toronto, *Baudelaire*, 4 April–2 May 1963.

American Federation of Arts Gallery, New York, *The Educational Alliance Art School: Retrospective Art Exhibit*, 29 April–18 May 1963 (catalogue, with texts by John I. H. Baur and Alexander Dobkin).

Sheldon Memorial Art Gallery, Lincoln, Nebr., *A Selection of Works from the Art Collections at the University of Nebraska*, May 1963.

1964

Rose Art Museum, Brandeis University, Waltham, Mass., *Boston Collects Modern Art: A Loan Exhibition from the Poses Institute of Fine Arts*, 24 May–14 June 1964.

Museum of Fine Art, Baltimore, *An Exhibition of Paintings, Drawings, and Sculpture*, 6 October –15 November 1964.

1965

Brooklyn Museum of Art, Brooklyn, *The Herbert A. Goldstone Collection of American Art*, 15 June–12 September 1965 (catalogue).

1966

Zabriskie Gallery, New York, *The American Sculptor, 1900–1930*, 5–30 April 1966.

Kramer, Hilton. "The American Sculptor, 1900–1930." *The New York Times*, 23 April 1966.

Perls Gallery, New York, in cooperation with the Public Education Association, *Seven Decades, 1895–1965: Crosscurrents in Modern Art*, 12 April–21 May 1966.

1967

Zabriskie Gallery, New York, *Elie Nadelman (1882–1946)*, 7 February–4 March 1967 (catalogue, with text by Alfred Werner).

J. B. "Elie Nadelman." *Arts Magazine* 41 (February 1967), p. 61.

C[ampbell], L[awrence]. "Elie Nadelman." *Art News* 65 (February 1967), pp. 17, 18.

J. G. "Elie Nadelman." *World Journal Tribune*, 10 February 1967.

Goldin, Amy. "New York: Elie Nadelman." *Artforum* 8 (April 1967), pp. 59–60.

Kramer, Hilton. "Nadelman's Achievement." *The New York Times*, 11 February 1967.

"Welt der Kunst: Elie Nadelman." *Aufbau* 33 (24 February 1967), p. 19.

Willard, Charlotte. "Galleries: Really and Truly." *The New York Post Saturday Magazine*, 11 February 1967, p. 14.

Albright-Knox Art Gallery, Buffalo, *Drawings and Watercolors from the Albright-Knox Art Gallery*, 18 December–31 January 1967.

1968

Stanford Museum, Stanford University, Stanford, Calif., *Modern Sculpture*, 29 October– 27 November 1968.

1970

Felix Landau Gallery, Los Angeles, *Modern Masters: Watercolors and Drawings*, 30 March–25 April 1970 (catalogue).

Nebraska Art Association, Lincoln, Nebr., *American Sculpture*, 11 September–15 November 1970 (organized to inaugurate the Sheldon Memorial Sculpture Garden, University of Nebraska).

The Museum of Modern Art, New York, *Four Americans in Paris: The Collections of Gertrude Stein and Her Family*, 19 December 1970– 1 March 1971 (catalogue, with texts by Margaret Potter et al.).

1971

Library and Museum of Performing Arts, Lincoln Center, New York, *Dance in Sculpture*, 1 February–30 April 1971.

Museum of Art, Rhode Island School of Design, Providence, *Selection I: American Watercolors and Drawings*, 30 December 1971– 23 January 1972.

Bulletin of Rhode Island School of Design: Museum Notes 57 (January 1972), pp. 47–49.

1974

Zabriskie Gallery, New York, *Elie Nadelman*, 5–30 March 1974 (catalogue, with text by Sanford Schwartz).

Brown, Gordon. "Elie Nadelman." *Arts Magazine* 48 (May 1974), p. 62.

Herrera, Hayden. "Elie Nadelman at Zabriskie." *Art in America* 62 (May–June 1974), pp. 103–4.

Kramer, Hilton. "For Nadelman, There Is No Lost Grandeur." *The New York Times*, 17 March 1974.

Schwartz, Barbara. "New York." *Craft Horizons* 34 (August 1974), p. 38.

Siegel, Jeanne. "Elie Nadelman (Zabriskie)." *Art News* 73 (May 1974), p. 102.

Smith, Roberta. "Elie Nadelman." *Artforum* 12 (June 1974), pp. 74–75.

Louis Newman Galleries, Beverly Hills, Calif., *Elie Nadelman: Selected Drawings and Etchings*, 10–23 June 1974 (catalogue).

Albright-Knox Art Gallery, Buffalo, *American Art in Upstate New York*, 12 July–25 August 1974.

1975

Delaware Art Museum, Wilmington, *Avant-garde Painting and Sculpture in America, 1910–25*, 4 April–18 May 1975 (catalogue), with text on Nadelman by Gilbert T. Vincent.

Whitney Museum of American Art, New York, *The Sculpture and Drawings of Elie Nadelman*, 23 September–30 November 1975 (catalogue, with text by John I. H. Baur). Traveled to Hirshhorn Museum and Sculpture Garden, Smithsonian Institution, Washington, D.C.

Bourdon, David. "Nadelman Pyramids to Fame Again." *The Village Voice*, 6 October 1975, pp. 98–99.

Butler, Joseph T. "America: The Sculpture and Drawings of Elie Nadelman." *The Connoisseur* 191 (February 1976), p. 307.

Hess, Thomas B. "Nadelman and Lotusland." *New York*, 3 November 1975, pp. 77–79.

Hobhouse, Janet. "Elie Nadelman at Zabriskie and the Whitney Museum." *Art in America* 64 (March 1976), pp. 104–5.

Hoesterey, Ingeborg. "New York." *Art International: The Art Spectrum* 19 (20 December 1975), p. 46.

Hughes, Robert. "Easy to Love." *Time*, 6 October 1975, p. 64.

Kramer, Hilton. "Sculptures at the Whitney Restore Nadelman to Glory." *The New York Times*, 24 September 1975.

Kroll, Jack. "Return of a Master." *Newsweek*, 6 October 1975, p. 82.

Kuh, Katharine. "Elie Nadelman Rediscovered." *Sculpture Review* 3 (29 November 1975), pp. 34–36.

Schwartz, Barbara. "Exhibitions: Letters: New York/Sculpture and Craft." *Craft Horizons* 35 (December 1975), pp. 16, 17.

Silver, Jonathan. "Elie Nadelman: A Single Notion of Style." *Art News* 74 (November 1975), pp. 70–72.

Smith, Roberta. "Reviews: Whitney Museum of American Art and Zabriskie Gallery." *Artforum* 14 (December 1975), pp. 65–66.

Zabriskie Gallery, New York, *Elie Nadelman (1882–1946): Paper, Plaster, and Ceramic Sculpture*, 7 October–8 November 1975 (catalogue).

Brown, Gordon. "Elie Nadelman." *Arts Magazine* 50 (December 1975), p. 25.

Zucker, Barbara. "Elie Nadelman (Zabriskie)." *Art News* 74 (November 1975), pp. 115–16.

1976

Whitney Museum of American Art, New York, *Two Hundred Years of American Sculpture*, 16 March–26 September 1976 (catalogue, with texts by Tom Armstrong et al.).

1977

Queens Museum, Flushing, N.Y., *American Sculpture: Folk and Modern*, 12 March–8 May 1977 (catalogue, with texts by Patricia Mainardi et al.).

Mainardi, Patricia. "American Sculpture: Folk and Modern." *Arts Magazine* 51 (March 1977), pp. 107–11.

1978

Forum Gallery, New York, *Sculpture (Early Works): Chaim Gross, Gaston Lachaise, Elie Nadelman, Hugo Robus*, March 1978 (catalogue, with text by Roberta K. Tarbell).

Wave Hill Environmental Center, Bronx, N.Y., *Figure in the Landscape*, 14 May–31 October 1978.

Robert Schoelkopf Gallery, New York, *Drawings: Elie Nadelman, Gaston Lachaise*, 16 September–14 October 1978.

Perl, Jed. "Elie Nadelman." *Arts Magazine* 53 (October 1978), p. 9.

Schwartz, Ellen. "Elie Nadelman, Gaston Lachaise." *Art News* 77 (December 1978), pp. 152–53.

Hirschl and Adler Galleries, New York, *The Eye of Stieglitz*, 7 October–2 November 1978 (catalogue, with introduction by Richard York).

O'Beil, Hedy. "The Eye of Stieglitz." *Arts Magazine* 53 (January 1979), pp. 27, 28.

1979

Everson Museum, Syracuse, N.Y., *A Century of American Ceramics, 1878–1978*, 5 May–23 September 1979 (catalogue, with texts by Garth Clark et al.). Traveled to Renwick Gallery, Washington, D.C.; Cooper-Hewitt Museum, New York; Philbrook Art Center, Tulsa; Chicago Public Library Cultural Center, Chicago; Allentown Art Museum, Allentown, Pa.; Toledo Museum of Art.

Kuspit, Donald B. "Elemental Realities." *Art in America* 69 (January 1981), pp. 79–87.

Baltimore Museum of Art and American Federation of Arts (organizers), *Master Drawings and Watercolors of the Nineteenth and Twentieth Centuries* (catalogue, with texts by Victor Carlson and Carl Hynning Smith). Shown at Solomon R. Guggenheim Museum, New York;

Des Moines Art Center; Art Museum of South Texas, Corpus Christi; Museum of Fine Arts, Houston; Denver Art Museum.

1980

Zabriskie Gallery, New York, *Elie Nadelman: Heads*, 29 April–24 May 1980 (catalogue), with text by Athena T. Spear.

Bass, Ruth. "Elie Nadelman." *Art News* 79 (October 1980), pp. 225, 228.

Kramer, Hilton. "Elie Nadelman." *The New York Times*, 16 May 1980.

Fogg Art Museum, Harvard University, Cambridge, *Three American Sculptors and the Female Nude: Lachaise, Nadelman, Archipenko*, 17 April–15 June 1980 (catalogue, with texts by Jeanne L. Wasserman and James B. Cuno). Traveled to Bowdoin College Museum of Art, Brunswick, Me.

1981

Max Hutchinson Gallery, New York, *Sculptors' Drawings and Maquettes*, January–February 1981.

Russell, John. "Sculptors' Drawings and Maquettes." *The New York Times*, 6 February 1981, sec. 3.

Worcester Art Museum, Worcester, Mass., *"The Dial": Arts and Letters in the 1920s*, 7 March–10 May 1981 (catalogue, with text by Michael True).

1982

Zabriskie Gallery, New York, *Flat and Figurative*, January–February 1982.

Cohen, Ronny. "Elie Nadelman: Zabriskie Gallery," *Artforum* 21 (October 1982), pp. 71–72.

Raynor, Vivien. "Art: Zabriskie Offers a Sculpture Twin Bill." *The New York Times*, 29 January 1982, sec. C.

Wave Hill Environmental Center, Bronx, N.Y., *Elie Nadelman*, March 1982.

Glueck. Grace. "Elie Nadelman." *The New York Times*, 5 February 1982.

Raynor, Vivien. "Sprightly Nadelman Show at Wave Hill." *The New York Times*, 7 March 1982.

Galerie Zabriskie, Paris, *Two Sculptors, the Paris Years: Alexander Archipenko, 1908–1921; Elie Nadelman, 1904–1914*, 16 March–8 May 1982.

Hirschl and Adler Galleries, New York, *Carved and Modeled: American Sculpture, 1810–1940*, 20 April–4 June 1982.

Zabriskie Gallery, New York, *Elie Nadelman: One Hundredth Anniversary Exhibition: Sculptures and Drawings*, 26 May–16 July 1982 (catalogue).

Cohen, Ronny. "Elie Nadelman." *Artforum* 21 (October 1982), pp. 71–72.

Fort, Ilene Susan. "Elie Nadelman." *Arts Magazine* 57 (October 1982), p. 20.

Glueck, Grace. "Art: Nadelman's Women, an Anniversary Tribute." *The New York Times*, 28 May 1982, sec. 3.

Smith, Roberta. "Several Happy Returns." *The Village Voice*, 6 July 1982, p. 78.

1984

Parrish Art Museum, Southampton, N.Y., *Forming*, 29 July–23 September 1984 (catalogue, with text by Klaus Kertess).

Russell, John. "Art: Just the Show for Summer in Hamptons." *The New York Times*, 3 August 1984, sec. C.

Fred L. Emerson Gallery, Hamilton College, Clinton, N.Y., *Nadelman as Guide: Elie Nadelman: Sculpture, Works on Paper*, 15 September–4 November 1984 (catalogue).

1985

Zabriskie Gallery, New York, *Elie Nadelman: Drawings*, 3 April–4 May 1985 (catalogue, with text by Virginia M. Zabriskie).

Russell, John. "Drawings by Elie Nadelman." *The New York Times*, 3 May 1985.

Parrish Art Museum, Southampton, N.Y., *Fauns and Fountains: American Garden Statuary, 1890–1930*, 14 April–2 June 1985 (catalogue).

Jewish Museum, New York, *The Circle of Montparnasse: Jewish Artists in Paris, 1905–1945*, 22 October 1985–2 February 1986 (catalogue, with texts by Kenneth E. Silver et al.).

Bass, Ruth. "The Circle of Montparnasse." *Art News* 85 (March 1986), pp. 144–45.

Brenson, Michael. "Modern Jewish Artists Wrestle with Tradition." *The New York Times*, 17 November 1985.

Fairweather Hardin Gallery, Chicago, *Nadelman: Drawings*, 5–30 November 1985.

1986

Edward Thorp Gallery, New York, *Elie Nadelman*, 8 March–5 April 1986.

Russell, John. "Elie Nadelman." *The New York Times*, 14 March 1986, sec. C.

H. S. "Elie Nadelman." *Art News* 85 (summer 1986), p. 146.

Zabriskie Gallery, New York, *Elie Nadelman: The Four Seasons*, 16 December 1986–17 January 1987.

1987

Sidney Janis Gallery, New York, *Sculpture by Elie Nadelman in Marble, Wood, and Bronze*, 28 September–31 October 1987 (catalogue, with text by E. Jan Nadelman).

R. B. "Elie Nadelman." *Art News* 86 (December 1987), pp. 146, 148.

Gibson, Eric. "Nadelman's World." *New Criterion* 6 (January 1988), pp. 56–59.

Russell, John. "Elie Nadelman." *The New York Times*, 23 October 1987, sec. C.

1989

Hirschl and Adler Galleries, New York, *Uncommon Spirit: Sculpture in America, 1800–1940*, 22 April–9 June 1989 (catalogue, with text by Susan E. Menconi).

1990

Sid Deutsch Gallery, New York, *Gertrude Stein: The American Connection*, 3 November–8 December 1990 (catalogue, with text by Gail Stavitsky). Traveled to Terra Museum of American Art, Chicago; University Art Museum, University of Minnesota, Minneapolis; Butler Institute of American Art, Youngstown, Ohio; Kalamazoo Institute of Arts, Kalamazoo, Mich.

1991

Edward Thorp Gallery, New York, *Elie Nadelman: Drawings and Sculpture*, 13 April–11 May 1991 (catalogue).

Hirschl and Adler Galleries, New York, *Six American Modernists*, 9 November 1991–4 January 1992 (catalogue).

1993

Whitney Museum of American Art, New York, *In a Classical Vein: Works from the Permanent Collection*, 18 October 1993–3 April 1994 (brochure, with text by David Freedberg).

1995

Zabriskie Gallery, New York, *Elie Nadelman (1882–1946)*, 5–30 December 1995 (checklist).

Kramer, Hilton. "Reintroducing Nadelman, a Man Curators Forgot." *The New York Observer*, 18 December 1995, pp. 1, 29.

1996

Salander-O'Reilly Galleries, New York, *Elie Nadelman*, 8 October–2 November 1996 (catalogue, with texts by Cynthia Nadelman and Hilton Kramer).

Esplund, Lance. "Elie Nadelman." *Modern Painters* 9 (winter 1996), pp. 102–4.

Glueck, Grace. "Elie Nadelman." *The New York Times*, 1 November 1996, sec. C.

H[aggerty], G[erald]. "Elie Nadelman: Salander-O'Reilly." *Art News* 96 (February 1997), pp. 114, 116.

1997

Salander-O'Reilly Galleries, New York, *Elie Nadelman, 1882–1946*, 13 November–13 December 1997 (catalogue, with texts by Gail Levin and John B. Van Sickle).

1998

Beth Urdang Gallery, Boston, *Elie Nadelman on Paper*, 14 March–11 April 1998.

Galerie Piltzer, Paris, *Elie Nadelman: Les années parisiennes, 1904–1914*, 7 October–7 December 1998 (catalogue, with text by Pick Keobandith).

Attias, Laurie. "International Reviews: Elie Nadelman (Galerie Piltzer)." *Art News* 98 (March 1999), p. 144.

1999

Salander-O'Reilly Galleries, New York, *Elie Nadelman: The Late Work*, 7 September–2 October 1999 (catalogue, with texts by Brandt Junceau, Klaus Kertess, Arlene Shechet, and Kiki Smith).

Esplund, Lance. "The More the Merrier." *Modern Painters* 12 (winter 1999), pp. 79–81.

2000

Whitney Museum of American Art at Fairfield County, Conn., *Talk of the Town: Guy Pène du Bois and Elie Nadelman*, 11 February–10 May 2000 (brochure, with text by Shamim Momin).

Jewish Museum, New York, *Paris in New York: French Jewish Artists in Private Collections*, 5 March–25 June 2000 (catalogue, with text by Romy Golan).

Gouveia, Georgette. "A Creative Hotbed for Jewish Artists." *The Journal News*, 9 March 2000, p. 2E

Harpaz, Beth J. "To Life!" *The Chicago Tribune*, 8 March 2000.

Mendelsohn, John. "Outsider Art." *Second Front*, 3 March 2000, pp. 37–38.

Russell, John. "Jewish Artists Who Made Paris Their Exuberant Garret." *The New York Times*, 10 March 2000, sec. E.

Hackett-Freedman Gallery, San Francisco, *Elie Nadelman: Sculpture and Drawings*, 4–27 May 2000 (catalogue).

Heckscher Museum of Art, Huntington, N.Y., *Aaron Copland's America: A Cultural Perspective*, 4 November 2000–21 January 2001 (catalogue, with texts by Gail Levin and Judith Tick).

2001

Salander-O'Reilly Galleries, New York, *Elie Nadelman: Galvano-Plastiques*, 6 February–3 March 2001 (catalogue, with text by Cynthia Nadelman).

Gallery Camino Real, Boca Raton, Fla., *Elie Nadelman*, 8 February–3 March 2001.

American Federation of the Arts (organizer), *Elie Nadelman: Classical Folk* (catalogue, with texts by Suzanne Ramljak et al.). Shown at Marion Koogler McNay Art Museum, San Antonio, Tex.; Frick Art and Historical Center, Pittsburgh.

Duncan, Michael. "A New Look at Nadelman." *Art in America* 90 (April 2002), pp. 132–39.

Goddard, Dan R. "Elie Nadelman." *Art News* 100 (September 2001), p. 181.

Kunstmuseum, Lucerne, Switzerland, *Atlas, Anatomie, Angst: Max von Moos (1903–1979)*, 15 December 2001–3 March 2002 (catalogue, with text by Roman Kurzmeyer).

Chronology

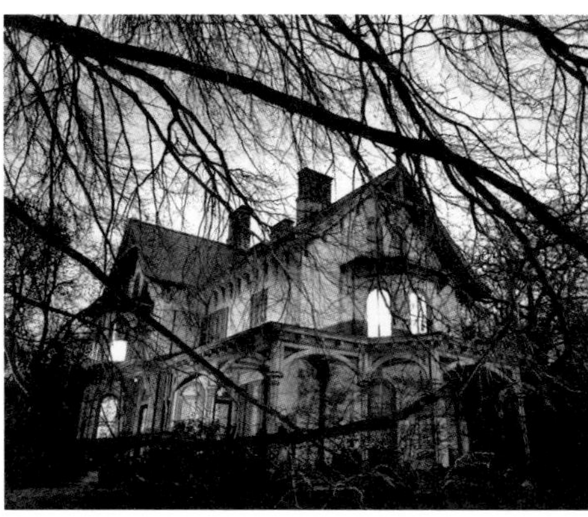

Alderbrook, 1948
Photography by W. Eugene Smith/TimePix

1882

February 20. Eliasz Nadelman, born in Warsaw, Poland, the youngest of seven children, to Hannah and Philip Nadelman, a jeweler. The family lives above their jewelry store at 143 Marszałkowska Street in the city's most elegant commercial and residential district.

1899

Spring. Graduates from a Warsaw Gymnasium.

Fall. Enters Warsaw's School of Drawing.

1900

Volunteers in the Russian imperial army, serving for one year as a noncommissioned trainee.

1902

January 1–February 15. Salon Krywult exhibits *The March of Modernism*, coauthored in 1900 with Witold Wojtkiewicz while both artists were at the School of Drawing.

Visits Kraków with the intention of enrolling in the city's Academy of Fine Arts; leaves after only two days.

1904

Travels to Munich, where he stays for six months.

August. Wins second prize for his drawing *Bemol* (B Minor) in a drawing competition sponsored by *Sztuka*, a Paris-based journal.

1905

Relocates to Paris with the five-hundred-franc prize money from *Sztuka*.

Takes a studio at 16, avenue du Maine, off the rue Vaugirard in Montparnasse; becomes part of Paris's Polish Colony.

October. Shows three drawings and a plaster figure in the Salon d'Automne; participates in subsequent Salons d'Automne and in Salons des Indépendants over the next nine years.

1907

Through Thadée Natanson, co-owner of *La revue blanche*, meets important critics, gallery owners, and collectors. Becomes a regular guest at the Saturday evening soirées hosted by Leo and Gertrude Stein.

1908

Moves into a studio at 15, rue Boissonade, Montparnasse.

1909

April 26–May 8. One-person exhibition at Galerie E. Druet, Paris; shows thirteen plaster models and one hundred drawings.

1910

October. *Camera Work* publishes the artist's statement on art.

1911

April. One-person exhibition at Wm. B. Paterson Gallery, London; shows ten marble heads. Helena Rubinstein purchases entire show.

1912

Joins with nine other Polish artists to found the Society of Polish Artists; society dissolves 12 years later, in 1924.

November. *Sztuka* publishes first article on his art by Adolphe Basler.

1913

February 17–March 15. Shows twelve drawings and two sculptures in the Armory Show, New York.

May 26–June 7. One-person exhibition at Galerie E. Druet, Paris; shows bronze and marble figures and heads, and drawings.

1914

La Belle Edition publishes *Vers l'unité plastique*, a portfolio of fifty-one reproductions of his drawings.

March. *L'Art décoratif* publishes first French-language article on his art by André Salmon.

August 11. Vacationing in Belgium when World War I breaks out. After attempt to re-enlist in Russian Army fails, travels to London.

Ocotober 24. Sails to America on the *Lusitania*; lands in New York City on October 31.

1915

Moves into a walk-up studio at 244 West Fourteenth Street.

December. *International Studio* publishes first English-language article on his art by Martin Birnbaum.

December 8–January 19, 1916. One-person exhibition at Alfred Stieglitz's Little Galleries of the Photo-Secession, known as "291"; includes plasters of *Young Boy with Hat* (fig. 79) and *Horse* (fig. 82).

1917

February. One-person exhibition at Scott & Fowles, New York; includes bronzes of figures and animals, marble heads, and commissioned portraits.

February. Engagement to Judith Bernays, daughter of financier Ely Bernays.

December. Includes four sculptures in *Allies of Sculpture* exhibition at the Ritz-Carlton Hotel, New York; his painted plaster figures arouse public controversy.

1919

October 27–November 8. One-person exhibition at M. Knoedler & Company, New York; shows painted plaster figures of contemporary archetypes.

December 31. Marries Viola Spiess Flannery.

1920

January–early June. Lives in the Hotel Savoy, New York City; makes drypoints with a hand press.

Mid-June–September. Rents Beauport, the seaside home in Gloucester, Massachusetts, belonging to Henry Sleeper.

September 23–October 13. One-person exhibition at Galerie Bernheim-Jeune, Paris; consists of a selection of his painted plaster figures shown at M. Knoedler & Company.

Fall. Begins renting the Delafield Estate, Riverdale-on-Hudson, New York.

1921

Purchases Alderbrook, a summer estate in Riverdale overlooking the Hudson River.

Purchases townhouse at 6 East 93rd Street, New York City.

December. E. Wehye publishes *Vers la beauté plastique*, a portfolio of thirty-two reproductions of his drawings.

1922

July 29. Birth of his son, whom he names Elie Jagiełł, after the Polish royal dynasty. Three years later, changes son's name to Elie Jan; son goes by the name Jan.

1923

January. Moves into New York City townhouse.

Begins collecting antiquities and folk art.

December. William Murrell publishes *Elie Nadelman* as part of Younger Artists Series.

1925

March. One-person exhibition at Scott & Fowles; includes marble heads and painted figures in bronze and wood of contemporary types. Show travels to the Arts Club at the Art Institute of Chicago from May to June.

1926

January. Naturalization.

November 28. Opening of the Museum of Folk and Peasant Arts in a three-story building on Riverdale property; collection shown by appointment.

1927

January 31–February 12. One-person exhibition of near-life-size galvano-plastique figures at M. Knoedler & Company, New York; show travels to Galerie Bernheim-Jeune, Paris.

Becomes a United States citizen.

1928

December 12. Signs contract to design and execute a limestone frieze for the Fuller Building, New York.

1929

August. Bank of the Manhattan Company, New York, approves design of his sculpture of Aquarius for the facade of its building.

1931

Precipitous decline in his fortune. Sells portions of his folk art and antiquities collections to raise cash.

1933

Bank forecloses on New York City townhouse.

Sells Alderbrook, his Riverdale estate, to a neighborhood corporation. Remains in his house as a renter.

1935

April 17. Funded by a grant from the Carnegie Corporation, folk art collection opens to the public; now called the Museum of Folk Arts.

1936

June 11. Buys back house on Alderbrook property.

1937

November 17. Sells folk art collection to the New-York Historical Society for $50,000; serves as curator of the collection until April 1939.

1942

Joins the Riverdale Air Warden Service.

1944

Teaches sculpture and drawing twice weekly to wounded servicemen in the occupational-therapy division of the Bronx Veterans Hospital.

1945

Develops heart condition.

1946

Heart condition worsens; enters hospital several times during October and November for stays of several days.

December 28. Takes his own life.

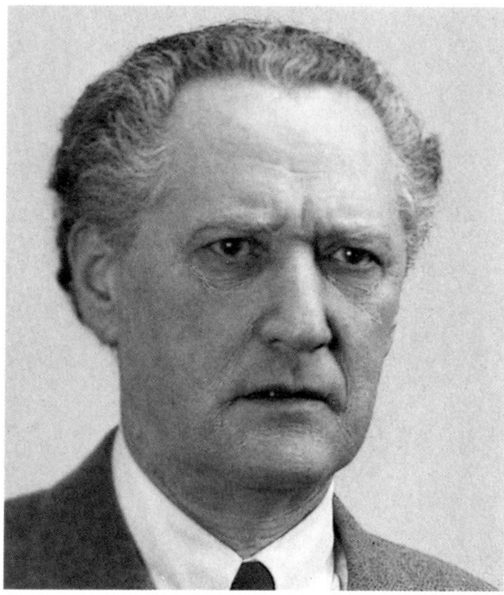

Passport photo, 1933. Courtesy Estate of Elie Nadelman

Selected Bibliography

For books and articles on subjects related to, but not specifically discussing Nadelman, see footnote references.

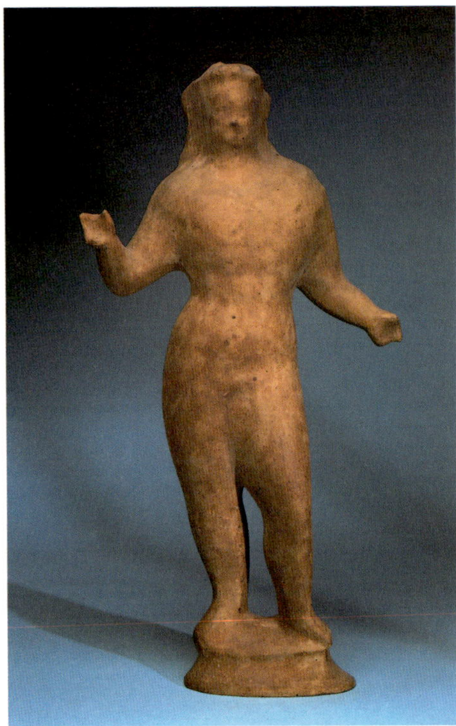

Elie Nadelman, **Standing Woman**, c. 1930–35. Papier-mâché, 19 1/2 x 9 1/8 x 5 1/4 in. (49.5 x 23.2 x 13.3 cm). Estate of Elie Nadelman, courtesy Salander-O'Reilly Galleries, New York
Photography by Paul Waldman

Antliff, Allan. *Anarchist Modernism: Art, Politics, and the First American Avant-garde.* Chicago: University of Chicago Press, 2001.

———. "Cosmic Modernism: Elie Nadelman, Adolf Wolff, and the Materialist Aesthetics of John Weichsel." *Archives of American Art Journal* 38, no. 3–4 (1998), pp. 20–29.

Aronson, Chil. *Art Polonais Moderne.* Paris: Éditions Bonaparte, 1929.

Basler, Adolphe. "Art français, art européen." *Montjoie!* 1 (29 March 1913), p. 6.

———. "Les arts plastiques." *Montjoie!* 1 (14–29 June 1913), p. 12.

———. "Eli Nadelman." *Sztuka* (Lvov), no. 2 (1912), pp. 72, 74.

———. *La sculpture moderne en France.* Paris: G. Crès, 1928.

Baur, John I. H. *The Sculpture and Drawings of Elie Nadelman.* Exhibition catalogue. New York: Whitney Museum of American Art, 1975.

Beaunom, André. "Ein Hellenist: Elie Nadelman." *Zelt* (Vienna) 1 (March 1924), pp. 94–95, 97.

Berman, Avis. "Sculptor in the Open Air: Elie Nadelman and the Folk and Popular Arts." In *Elie Nadelman: Classical Folk,* Exhibition catalogue. New York: American Federation of Arts, 2001, pp. 46–79.

Birnbaum, Martin. "Eli Nadelman." *International Studio* 57 (December 1915), pp. 53–55.

———. "Elie Nadelman." In *Introductions: Painters, Sculptors, and Graphic Artists.* New York: Frederic Fairchild Sherman, 1919. Reprinted in Lincoln Kirstein, *Elie Nadelman* (New York: Eakins Press, 1973), pp. 279–83.

———. "Elie Nadelman: An Introduction." In *Catalogue of an Exhibition of Sculpture and Drawings by Elie Nadelman.* Exhibition catalogue. New York: Scott & Fowles, 1917.

———. "Elie Nadelman: Sculptor." *Menorah Journal* (New York) 11 (October 1925), pp. 484–88.

———. *The Last Romantic: The Story of More than a Half-Century in the World of Art.* New York: Twayne, 1960.

Bourdon, David. "The Sleek, Witty, and Elegant Art of Elie Nadelman." *Smithsonian* 10 (January 1976), pp. 84–91.

"Breaking Loose from the Rodin Spell." *Current Opinion* 62 (March 1917), pp. 206–8.

Burroughs, C[lyde H.]. "The Sculpture of Elie Nadelman." *Bulletin of the Detroit Institute of Arts of the City of Detroit* 1 (February 1920), pp. 73–75.

Craven, Wayne. *Sculpture in America.* Rev. ed. Newark: University of Delaware Press; New York and London: Cornwall Books, 1968; reprinted 1984.

Crowninshield, Frank. "American Work of a Polish Sculptor." *Vanity Fair,* March 1917, p. 59.

———. "Sappho: A Statue, in African Marble, by Elie Nadelman." *Vanity Fair,* April 1918, 64.

———. "Sculpture at a New York Salon: The Work of a Triumvirate of Modern Sculptors." *Vanity Fair,* January 1918, p. 54.

———. "Sculpture of Mystery, by Elie Nadelman." *Vanity Fair,* September 1917, p. 58.

Davis, Virginia H. "Heads by Elie Nadelmann [sic]." *International Studio* 80 (March 1925), pp. 482–83.

"Eli Nadelman." *Tygodnik polski* (New York), 29 December 1946, p. 15.

Elsen, Albert E. *Origins of Modern Sculpture: Pioneers and Premises.* New York: George Braziller, 1974.

Fletcher, Valerie J. "Elie Nadelman: Art and Craft in Context." In *Elie Nadelman: Classical Folk,* pp. 80–95.

Fornaro, Carlo de. "Elie Nadelman: Vers la beauté plastique." *Social* (Havana) 14 (July 1929), pp. 37, 64–65.

———. "In the Art World: Elie Nadelman." *Tatler* (New York) (December 1929), p. 52.

Fort, Ilene Susan. *The Figure in American Sculpture: A Question of Modernity.* Exhibition catalogue. Los Angeles: Los Angeles County Museum of Art in association with University of Washington Press, 1995.

Gerdts, William H. "American Sculpture." *American Artist* 26 (September 1962), pp. 40–47, 68–73.

Gide, André. "24 décembre" and "Lundi, 25 ou 26 avril." *Journal I: 1887–1925.* Edited by Eric Marty, 604–5, 608–9. Paris: Gallimard, 1996. Also reprinted in Lincoln Kirstein, *Elie Nadelman,* pp. 273–74.

Goodman, Jonathan. "The Idealism of Elie Nadelman." *Arts Magazine* 63 (February 1989), pp. 54–59.

Grabska, Elżbieta. *Autour de Bourdelle: Paris et les artistes polonais, 1900–1918.* Exhibition catalogue. Paris: Paris-Musées, 1996.

Harper, [Russell Lynes]. "After Hours." *Harper's Magazine*, April 1948, pp. 381–84.

Herrera, Philip. "Indelible Impressions." *Town and Country*, October 1996, pp. 312–14.

Junceau, Brandt. "Late Nadelman." *M/E/A/N/I/N/G* 6 (November 1989), pp. 28–34.

Junceau, Brandt. "Make it Old, Make it New." In *Elie Nadelman (1882–1946): The Late Work*. Exhibition catalogue. New York: Salander O'Reilly Galleries, 1999, pp. 17–23.

Keobandith, Pick. *Elie Nadelman: Les années parisiennes, 1904–1914*. Exhibition catalogue. Paris: Galerie Piltzer and Au Même Titre, 1998.

Kertess, Klaus. "Child's Play: The Late Work of Elie Nadelman." *Artforum* 23 (March 1985), pp. 64–68.

―――――. "Clay Acting: The Late Works of Elie Nadelman." In *Elie Nadelman: Classical Folk*, pp. 96–109.

―――――. "Modeling" In *Elie Nadelman (1882–1946): The Late Work*, pp. 9–11.

[King, Frederick A.]. "A 'Hellenist' Sculptor Driven Here by the War." *Literary Digest*, 3 March 1917, pp. 550–51, 553.

Kirstein, Lincoln. *The Dry Points of Elie Nadelman*. New York: Curt Valentin, 1952.

―――――. *Elie Nadelman*. New York: Eakins Press, 1973.

―――――. *Elie Nadelman: Drawings*. New York: H. Bittner, 1949. Rev. ed. New York: Hacker Art Books, 1970.

―――――. "Elie Nadelman: 1882–1946." *Harper's Bazaar*, August 1948, pp. 132–35, 186.

―――――. "Elie Nadelman: Figures and Figurines, 1930–1940." In *Elie Nadelman: Figures and Figurines, 1930–1940*. Exhibition catalogue. New York: Edwin Hewitt Gallery, Robert Isaacson, 1958.

―――――. "Elie Nadelman: Sculptor of the Dance." *Dance Index* 7 (6 November 1948), pp. 130–51.

―――――. *The Sculpture of Elie Nadelman*. Exhibition catalogue. New York: Museum of Modern Art, 1948.

―――――. "Small Sculptures by Elie Nadelman." In *Small Sculptures by Elie Nadelman*. Exhibition catalogue. New York: Edwin Hewitt Gallery, 1950.

―――――. "Wood Sculpture by Elie Nadelman." In *Wood Sculpture by Elie Nadelman*. Exhibition catalogue. New York: Edwin Hewitt Gallery, 1951.

Kramer, Hilton. "Elie Nadelman." In *Elie Nadelman*. Exhibition catalogue. New York: Salander-O'Reilly Galleries, 1996.

―――――. "Reintroducing Nadelman, a Man Curators Forgot." *New York Observer*, 18 December 1995, 1, p. 29.

Levin, Gail, and John B. Van Sickle. "Elie Nadelman's New Classicism." In *Elie Nadelman, 1882–1946*. Exhibition catalogue. New York: Salander-O'Reilly Galleries, 1997. Reprinted in *Sculpture Review* 46 (spring 1998), pp. 8–15.

Malinowski, Jerzy. Entry on Nadelman in *Słownik artystów polskich i obcych w Polsce działagacych: Malarze, rzezbiarze, graficy*. Vol. 6. Wrocław: Zakład Narodowy im. Ossolińskich, 1998.

Markoff, Małgorzata. "Elie Nadelman rzeźbiarz z Warszawy," Special literary supplement to *Przegląd Polski*, 4 January 2002, pp. 6–7.

Marter, Joan M., Roberta K. Tarbell, and Jeffrey Wechsler. *Vanguard American Sculpture, 1913–1939*. Exhibition catalogue. New Brunswick, N.J.: Rutgers University Art Gallery, 1979.

McBride, Henri. "News and Comment in the World of Art." *The New York Sun*, 4 February 1917. Reprinted in Henri McBride, *The Flow of Art: Essays and Criticisms of Henri McBride*. (New York: Atheneum Publishers, 1975), p. 107.

McBride, Henri. "Modern Art: Elie Nadelman Sculptures." *The Dial* 78 (June 1925), pp. 527–29. Reprinted in Lincoln Kirstein, *Elie Nadelman*, pp. 278–79.

McBride, Henri. "Nadelman's Defiant Art: Sculptures at Knoedler Galleries Another Test for the Liberal Mind." *The New York Sun*, 5 February 1927. Reprinted in *Creative Art* (May 1932), pp. 393–95.

McBride, Henry. "Neglected Sculpture: The Odd Story of a Brilliant Artist Who Escaped Critical Attention." *The New York Sun*, 28 February 1947.

McCabe, Cynthia Jaffee. *The Golden Door: Artist-Immigrants of America, 1876–1976*. Exhibition catalogue. Washington, D.C.: Hirshhorn Museum and Sculpture Garden, Smithsonian Institution, 1976.

Mellow, James R. "Is This the 'Proper Time' for Elie Nadelman?" *Art News* 81 (summer 1982), pp. 104–06.

Mikocka-Rachubowa, Katarzyna. "Rzeżbiarze polscy w Paryużu 1830–1914," in "Między Polską a Światem". Warsaw: Instytut Sztuki PAN, 1993, pp. 171–99.

Montjoie! (Paris) 1 (29 March 1913): 4; (14–29 June 1913): 7; (November–December 1913): 1, p. 11.

Murrell, William, ed. *Elie Nadelman*. Younger Artists Series, no. 6. Woodstock, N.Y.: William M. Fisher, 1923.

Nadelman, Cynthia. "Elie Nadelman." *Biuletyn historii sztuki* (Warsaw) 56 (1994), pp. 1–13.

―――――. "Elie Nadelman: Galvano-Plastiques." In *Elie Nadelman: Galvano-Plastiques*. Exhibition catalogue. New York: Salander-O'Reilly Galleries, 2001.

―――――. "Elie Nadelman: Patents Pending." In *Elie Nadelman*. Exhibition catalogue. New York: Salander-O'Reilly Galleries, 1996.

―――――. "Elie Nadelman's Beauport Drawings." *Drawing* 7 (November–December 1985), pp. 75–78.

―――――. Entry for *Seated Woman* in *Addison Gallery of American Art: Sixty–five Years*. Exhibition catalogue. Andover, Mass.: Addison Gallery of American Art, Phillips Academy, 1996.

―――――. "The Shocking Blue Hair of Elie Nadelman." *American Heritage* 40 (March 1989), pp. 80–91.

Nadelman, E. Jan. "Carving Out a Life." *Art and Antiques* 7 (April 1990): 94–100.

Nathanson, Thadée. *Peints à leur tour*. Paris: Albin Michel, 1948.

Parkes, Kineton. "After Futurism Comes 'Significant' Form: A Polish Sculptor, Elie Nadelman, Introduces the Newest Phase in Sculptured Art." *The Sphere* (London) 107 (2 October 1926), p. 18.

―――――. *Sculpture of To-Day*. Universal Art Series, ed. Frederick Marriott. Vol. 2. New York: C. Scribner's Sons, 1921.

Pelton, Agnes. "Her Crowning Moment in Evening Dress." *The New York Sun*, 16 November 1919, magazine sec.

"Połonica: Eli Nadelman." *Wiadomosci tygodnik* (London), 28 November 1954.

Ramljak, Suzanne. "The Sculptor of Poise: Elie Nadelman and Classicism." In *Elie Nadelman: Classical Folk*, pp. 10–45.

"Rediscovered Genius." *Life*, 24 May 1948.

"'Reverie' by Elie Nadelman." *Bulletin of the Detroit Museum of Art* 12 (May 1918), pp. 54, 56–57.

Salmon, André. "Eli Nadelman." *L'Art décoratif* 16 (March 1914), pp. 107–114.

———. "Humanisme." In *La jeune sculpture française*. Paris: Société des Trente, 1919. An edited version of "Eli Nadelman" (1914).

———. "La sculpture vivant." *Art vivant* 2 (1 April 1926), pp. 258–260.

Schwartz, Sanford. "An Aristocrat of Life and Culture" (review of Lincoln Kirstein's *Elie Nadelman*). *The New Yorker*, 20 October 1975, pp. 154–69.

———. "Elie Nadelman." In *Elie Nadelman (1882–1946)*. Exhibition catalogue. New York: Zabriskie Gallery, 1974.

Shechet, Arlene and Kiki Smith. "Arlene Shechet and Kiki Smith Conversation." *Elie Nadelman (1882–1946): The Late Work*, pp. 13–15.

"'Significant Form' as It Progresses from 'Futurism.'" *Literary Digest*, 30 October 1926.

Spear, Athena Tacha. "An Early Marble Head by Nadelman at Oberlin." *Acquisitions of Modern Art by Museums*, supplement to *The Burlington Magazine* 114 (July 1972), p. 509.

———. "Elie Nadelman's Early Heads (1905–1911)" and "Accessions." *Allen Memorial Art Museum Bulletin* (Oberlin College) 28 (spring 1971), pp. 201–22, 238.

———. "The Multiple Styles of Elie Nadelman: Drawings and Figure Sculptures, ca. 1905–12." *Allen Memorial Art Museum Bulletin* (Oberlin College) 31 (1973–74), pp. 34–58.

Stein, Gertrude. "Elie Nadelman." *Larus* 1 (July 1927): 19–20. Reprinted in Lincoln Kirstein, *Elie Nadelman*, pp. 274–275.

Stieglitz, Alfred. Installation photographs of "Nadelman Exhibition, Two Rooms, December 1915." *Camera Work* 48 (October 1916): 68. Reproduced in Marianne Margolis, *Camera Work: A Pictorial Guide* (New York: Dover Publications, 1978), p. 137.

Tyrell, Henry. "At a Musical Tea with Nadelman." *The New York World Magazine*, 30 November 1919. Reprinted in Lincoln Kirstein, *Elie Nadelman*, pp. 276–78.

Vers la beauté plastique, New York: E. Wehye, 1921.

Vers l'unité plastique, Paris: La Belle Edition, 1914.

Watson, Katharine. "Sculpture: Hellenistic to the Twentieth Century." *Apollo* (London) (February 1976), pp. 98–105.

Wayne, Kenneth Eric. "The Role of Antiquity in the Development of Modern Sculpture in France, 1900–1914," Ph.D. diss., Stanford University, 1994.

Weichsel, John. "Eli Nadelman's Sculpture." *East and West* 1 (August 1915), pp. 144–48.

Werner, Alfred. "Nadelman: Recluse of Riverdale." *Commentary* 9 (June 1950), pp. 545–50.

———. "Nadelman: Redivivus." *Art and Artists* 10 (November 1975), pp. 4–11.

Nadelman Folk Art Collection Bibliography

"Bird's-eye View of European Peasant Types." *Antiques* 25 (June 1934), p. 222.

"City Will Receive Prized Collection of Primitive Art." *The New York Herald Tribune*, 30 October 1931.

"Fantasies in Glass: Nadelman Collection of Animals and Birds." *The Antiquarian* 3 (January 1925), 1, pp. 6–7.

"Folk Art Bought for Display Here." *The New York Times*, 24 January 1938.

"Folk Art Museum to Be Opened Here: Nadelman Collection, Including European and American Types, Will Be Shown." *The New York Times*, 16 April 1935.

Gould, Mr. and Mrs. G. Glen. "The Collector: The Nadelman Ship Figureheads." *International Studio* 94 (September 1929), pp. 51–53.

———. "Dolls for the Antiquarian." *International Studio* 91 (December 1928), pp. 50–51.

———. "Plaster Ornaments for Collectors." *House and Garden* 56 (August 1929), pp. 84–85, 122.

"Hobby Becomes a Museum of Folk Art." *Gas Logic* 58 (November 1935), pp. 8–9.

Jewell, Edward Alden. "Folk Arts Museum Opening to Public." *The New York Times*, 27 April 1935.

Lowe, Jeannette. "New York's New Historical Museum: Opening of the Enlarged Buildings of the Historical Society." *The Art News* 37 (8 April 1939), pp. 17, 20.

Morgenthal, James. "'Junk' Says Old Boy, but Visitor to Folk Arts Museum Disagrees." *Riverdale News*, September 1935, pp. 3–4.

"Museum of Folk Art Will Go to the Public: Elie Nadelman's Collection of Riverdale May Be Opened to Visitors within a Year." *The New York Times*, 1 November 1931, sec. 2.

"The Nadelman Folk Art Collection." *Antiques* 33 (March 1938), p. 152.

"Nadelman's Folk Art." *Art Digest* 12 (1 March 1938), p. 15.

"Nadelman's Museum." *Art Digest* 6 (15 November 1931), p. 8.

"New York: Folk Art Purchased by the New York Historical Society." *The Art News* 36 (5 February 1938), p. 17.

Oaklander, Christine I. "Pioneers in Folk Art Collecting: Elie and Viola Nadelman." *Folk Art* 17 (fall 1992), pp. 48–55.

"Riverdale Museum Opened to the Public." *The Museum News* (15 April 1935): 2.

Stillinger, Elizabeth. "Elie and Viola Nadelman's Unprecedented Museum of Folk Arts." *Antiques* 146 (October 1994), pp. 516–25.

Storey, Walter Rendell. "Folk Art Has Its Museum." *The New York Times*, 28 April 1935.

Watson, Forbes. "The Innocent Bystander: A Museum of the Folk Arts." *American Magazine of Art* 28 (May 1935), p. 312.

Published Writings by Nadelman

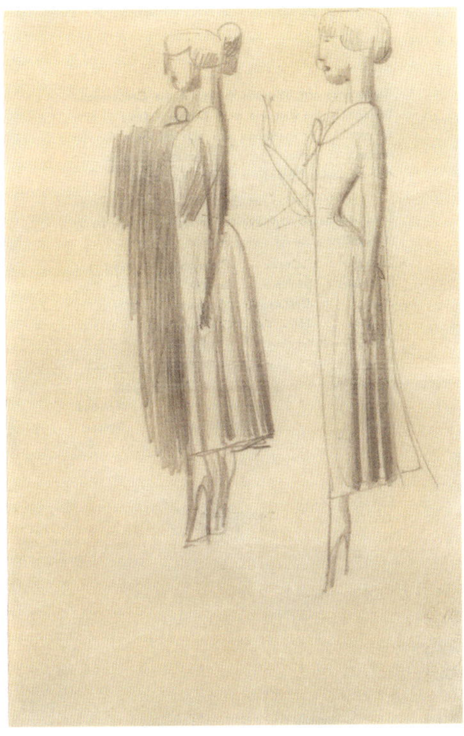

Elie Nadelman, **Two Women in Profile**, c. 1920–25.
Pencil on paper, 15 1/4 x 12 in. (38.7 x 30.5 cm).
Collection of Christopher English Walling, New York
Photography by Jerry L. Thompson

From "Photo-Secession Notes." *Camera Work*, no. 32 (October 1910), p. 41.

I am asked to explain my drawings. I will try to do so, although form cannot be described. Modern artists are ignorant of the *true forms* of art. They copy nature, try to imitate it by any possible means, and their works are *photographic reproductions*, not works of art. They are works without style and without unity.

It is form in itself, not resemblance to nature, which gives us pleasure in a work of art.

But what is this true form of art? It is significant and abstract, i.e., composed of geometrical elements.

Here is how I realize it. I employ no other line than the curve, which possesses freshness and force. I compose these curves so as to bring them in accord or in opposition to one another. In that way, I obtain the life of form, i.e., harmony. In that way I intend that the life of the work should come from within itself. The subject of any work of art is for me nothing but a pretext for creating a significant form, relations of forms which create a new life that has nothing to do with life in nature, a life from which art is born, and from which spring style and unity.

From significant form comes style, from relations of form, i.e., the necessity of playing one form against another, comes unity.

I leave it to others to judge of the importance of so radical a change in the means used to create a work of art.

(Signed) *Elie Nadelman*

Introduction to *An Exhibition of Sculpture by Elie Nadelman*. Exhibition catalogue. London: Wm. B. Paterson, 1911.

There should exist among Artists a common understanding about the aim and the means of Plastic Art.

No such understanding exists among the Artists of to-day, and it is owing to this lack of a common understanding that it is impossible for them to create such masterpieces as the Parthenon, which demand a collective effort.

The reason of this is that the Artist of to-day neither knows the proper means of true Art, nor his function in this Art.

I should like to say a few words on the Artist, and later, on Art itself.

One very characteristic trait of the contemporary Artist is that he is himself most pessimistic about the results of his Art. He feels that his works invariably fail to realize his ideals and his intentions (intentions which are often wrong, as we shall see). Hence comes his discouragement.

In the beginning he is still full of confidence in his Art and in his own power to realize his ideals. He sees and feels Beauty both in Nature and in himself. He wants to express it in his Art, and he realizes that the result of his effort is very far from his intention. But he is not discouraged. He returns to work with greater intensity, and again the result fails to give him satisfaction. He comes back to his work once more. He wants to surmount those difficulties at any cost, but the *means* which he employs do not allow him.

He then approaches the perfect works of Art which have been bequeathed to him by the Ancient Ages, and he marvels to see how there the Artist's power has matched his *intention*, producing that sureness, that perfection, that harmony in his work.

Where lies the mistake of the modern Artist? His mistake lies in this:—

First, he frequently believes that every kind of beauty can be employed as a subject for a work of Plastic Art, while actually only *plastic beauty* itself is translateable in terms of Plastic Art.

Secondly, he has a false idea of the part that thought and reasoning play in the creation of a work of Art. He believes that thought and reasoning are not only useless, but actually harmful to sentiment. He believes wrongly that sentiment itself is the creative element of the work of Art.

But the thing is in reality quite different. Sentiment is not the creative activity of the work of Art. All its activity is confined to stimulating thought, and it is reason that directs the making and the realisation of the work of Art.

* * * *

There are no different ways of understanding Plastic Art. There is only one way of understanding it. Whence then come these different tendencies in Art?

There are works of Art of a primitive kind, having but a faint resemblance to Nature; there are naturalistic works of Art, which are faithful copies, imitations of Nature; and again there are works of Art in which Nature is interpreted by Art-made Laws, proper to the Artist and independent of Nature. Let us see how these different works come into existence.

The beauty of Nature seduces man; he approaches it without understanding it, and he begins to imitate it. At first his results are naturally primitive, but little by little he succeeds in copying it more faithfully, until he arrives ultimately at works in which naturalism is pushed to its farthest limits.

The Art critics assert that these are different kinds of Art, and that the differences have arisen from the various needs and characters of the epochs that produced them. The assertion is wrong. These different works are only successive steps that man is obliged to trace, in order to arrive at true Art. When, in this progress, the Artist has reached to a naturalism pushed to its extreme possibilities, he realizes the futility of his effort. He sees that he is not a creator, in the true sense of the word, while he faithfully copies things already existing, and that in the work that he produces, he does not introduce any ideal capable of justifying them. He then addresses himself to his own reason, and asks:—

What is Art?

What is Beauty?

What is Perfection?

I cannot here show the whole process that his mind must follow before arriving at the only possible, the only true answer to these questions. But the answer, the result is this:

The Artist finally understands that the element that brings beauty in Plastic Art is logic, *logic in the construction of form.* All that is logical is beautiful, all that is illogical is inevitably ugly.

To give a very simple example, two straight lines placed in such a position that they balance one other ⁀ already contain beauty, inasmuch as they are logically built.

But if we break this balance so that the two lines no longer have a logical relation to one another, beauty disappears.

And in speaking of lines the question presents itself, what is Form? What is perfect Form? What is perfection in Art? The Artist finally understands that only the lines which have a significance are perfect, and that the lines without significance, of which he made use before, are incapable of perfection.

If a piece of string is thrown on the ground it will form each time a new sinuous line. Can we call these haphazard lines, these forms, perfect forms?

We cannot: since these forms have no meaning, they are incapable of perfection.

But if we take this same string and try to enclose as much space as possible within its length we obtain a circle. We have there a line *with a significance*, perfect that is, containing in itself the idea of perfection.

It is only *significant* forms, therefore, that are perfect forms.

And now the artist has a road open to him.

Possessing through logic the art of construction, possessing the idea of perfect Form, that is *significant* Form, he can build his work calmly and with the certitude that, having built it of perfect forms, having composed these forms in logical relation to one another, beauty will result of its own accord. He is no longer the slave of Nature, because even when he borrows from Nature an object as a motive for his work, he no longer *imitates* this object, but he *interprets* by his own proper means. And he can then even create objects that do not exist in Nature, such as Architecture. And even in this case he will be nearer to Nature than before, when he was copying it slavishly. He is now nearer Nature's *meaning*, because Nature itself among other elements, uses significant forms and logic in the construction of those forms.

He can now speak freely the language of Nature, while before he was vainly trying to repeat sounds of which he did not realize the meaning.

Eli Nadelman

"Eli Nadelman, of Paris." *Camera Work*, no. 48 (October 1916), p. 10.

We are flooded with pictures and sculptures, but are without plastic art. We seek, in painting and sculpture, all things save those which they could and should give to us. We have several ideals of art, but we lack the true one. At one time we imitate nature so closely that we make nothing but sterile copies of her. At another we separate ourselves from her completely and turn toward the abstract, where we float in the void and no longer find anything. We would like to possess a great art which, by its authority and clarity, would impose itself upon all; and we possess but vague attempts which change daily and fail to satisfy.

For a long while the true meanings of plastic art have escaped us. We do not recognize that essential quality which gives to this art its true value, and which permits it to develop in all its grandeur.

Neither an exact copy of nature, nor a geometrical abstract form, nor all the productions of painting and sculpture in our time that can be placed between these two extremes, possess that quality.

The ultimate quality of painting and sculpture is plasticity.

Matter has an individual will which is its life. A stone will refuse all the positions we may wish to give it if these are unsuited to it. By its own will it will fall back into the position that its shape in conjunction with its mass demands.

Here is a wonderful force, a life that plastic art should express. Here is a life which, cultivated, enriched by art, will reach a dazzling power of expression that will stir us.

It is this will of matter expressed in shapes and volume that I call plasticity. This power, this will, is not solely found imprisoned in matter itself. It is a natural force that corresponds to our own instinct. In looking at a tower whose height is too great a feeling of disquiet comes over us. We feel that the material labors under strain and does not find itself normally conditioned. In the same way any object in which the needs of the material have been respected transmits to us a sense of satisfaction. It is from this that contact between us and a work of plastic art derives. It is, therefore, the plasticity of the image that awakes sensations in us; and the most indifferent object reveals itself to us with an unfamiliar force and charm if this object is interpreted by a purely plastic means, independently of what a work of plastic art represents, it is solely by its plasticity that it speaks to us. Plasticity is the poetry of plastic art. It is its essence. To seek its poetry elsewhere is to draw it toward error.

Eli Nadelman

From *Vers la beauté plastique*, a portfolio of
thirty-two reproductions of Nadelman's
drawings. New York: E. Wehye, 1921.
Reprinted in *Elie Nadelman*, ed. William
Murrell, Younger Artists Series, no. 6.
(Woodstock, N.Y.: William M. Fisher, 1923).

These drawings, made sixteen years ago, have
completely revolutionized the art of our time.
They introduced into painting and sculpture
abstract form, until then wholly lacking.
Cubism was only an imitation of the abstract
forms of these drawings and did not attain their
plastic significance. Their influence will continue and will be felt more profoundly in the art of
the future.

Elie Nadelman

From "Pure Art? Or 'Pure Nonsense'?
Nine Selected Letters From Our Readers"
The Forum, 74 (July 1925), p. 148.

Editor of THE FORUM:—

Your projected symposium, "Is Cubism Pure
Art?", interests me exceedingly and for a special
reason. Before Picasso ever thought of Cubism,
I revealed in my work a new principle of Plastic
Art, previously unrevealed. This principle discovered by me was that of *Abstract Form*, but I
did not depart from nature, I merely interpreted
Nature through Abstract Form, which introduced into my sculpture and drawings *Plastic
Beauty* which before this discovery was entirely
lacking in the plastic arts of our time.

Picasso is not the originator of Abstract Form,
he merely exaggerated the abstract forms discovered by me, and not knowing their workings,
piled up pell-mell abstract forms, abandoning
nature more or less, and sometimes entirely,
with a result which is meaningless and
unsignificant from the point of view of plastic
art and is merely a sensational novelty.

Of this assertion I am in a position to give
convincing proof. It is manifest, however, that I
cannot do this in the form of a brief letter, nor
even in the compass of a formal article. I must
prove my point by divers illustrations interspersed
with explanations. In view of this fact, I make
the following proposal:—that you invite any
representative exponents of Cubism whom you
may choose to meet me at any time and place
you may select, with the object of giving me an
opportunity to answer your questions *à vive
voix.*

Such an exposition by me, combined with
the discussion to which it would give rise, could
not fail to be constructively valuable in the clar-
ification of what Cubism is, or rather is not, in
relation to Pure Plastic Art.

Stenographic notes could be taken of this
discussion and published in THE FORUM.

I believe the artistic world would be grateful
to you for bringing this about, as it would bring
a solution to a controversy which has lasted so
many years. I most sincerely hope that you will
take advantage of this offer.

Elie Nadelman
New York City

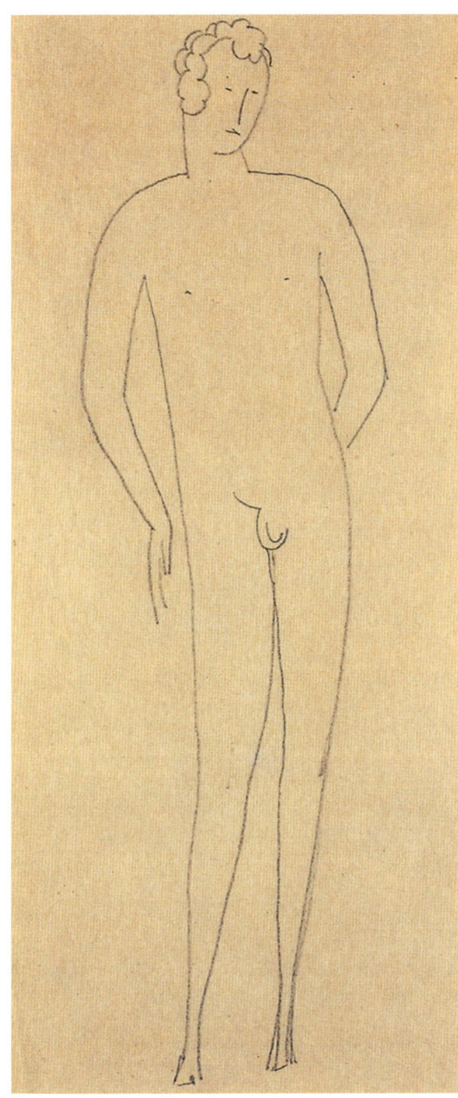

Elie Nadelman, **Classical Model—Male**, c. 1920. Pencil
on paper, 7 7/8 x 5 in. (20 x 12.7 cm). Slong & Midas
Properties, Inc., New York

Acknowledgments

All projects of this magnitude depend on the assistance and good will of many individuals. This one is no exception. I am extremely grateful to the many scholars who provided me with primary source documents, information, and insights into Elie Nadelman and his world. My thanks in particular go to Leon Botstein, Jan Cavanaugh, Elzbieta Grabska, Elizabeth Koszarski, Christopher Long, Jerzy Malinowski, Bruce W. Menning, Renata Piatkowska, Yale J. Reisner, Josh Sanborn, B. Schultz, Michael Stanislawski, and Marek Webb for their help in clarifying and extending my understanding of the environment and chronology of Nadelman's formative years. I am equally indebted to Avis Berman, Valerie Fletcher, Brandt Junceau, Klaus Kertess, Hilton Kramer, Christine Oaklander, Suzanne Ramljak, and Elizabeth Stillinger for their thoughtful writings on Nadelman's work. My own research was greatly facilitated by their efforts as well as by those of Cynthia Nadelman, who has written perceptively on her grandfather's work, and Lincoln Kirstein, whose extensive research and commentaries on Nadelman's life and art is the bedrock upon which all Nadelman scholarship has depended. I also wish to thank Larry Salander and his staff, in particular Leigh Morse and Eric Larsen, for their passionate advocacy of the project, their generous help in facilitating my search for works, and their support of my efforts to portray the relationship between Nadelman's life and the production and reception of his art. Finally, I owe a tremendous debt of gratitude to Anne Botstein for her translations of Polish-, German-, and French-language articles and books on Nadelman and his milieu. Her translations provided invaluable new perspectives and data on Nadelman's life and art prior to his arrival in America.

My colleagues at the Whitney, in particular Maxwell L. Anderson, Alice Pratt Brown Director, and Garrett White, Rachel de W. Wixom, and Makiko Ushiba in the Publications and New Media Department, extended themselves to an extraordinary degree to ensure the success of this project. It has also been my good fortune to have an exemplary team of project assistants to whose dedication, diligence, ingenuity, and attention to detail the success of this project is owed. Jennifer Palladino helped in all phases of the exhibition and catalogue preparation, including loan requests, manuscript preparation, the assembly of photographs for publication, and rights clearance. Patricia Hughes procured all of the initial primary research data and began the process of assembling the bibliography and verifying the footnotes, both of which Evelyn Hankins completed with tremendous skill and resourcefulness. I am deeply grateful to them as well to Anne Lampe for her help in the project's early stages, and to Karen Bookatz, Kerry Corrigan, Sarida D'Agostino, Erin Decker, Adrienne Goering, Heather Mackenzie, Andrew Scharf, Sarah Smith, Bridget Stoyko, and Mary Tinti for the countless hours they spent looking through books, periodicals, and microfilm for references to Nadelman. Particularly I wish to thank Matthew Yokobosky for devising an elegant and inspiring installation plan for the exhibition that respected Nadelman's debt to classicism as well as his modernity.

No exhibition of such an ambitious scale as this one can be mounted without an extraordinary level of generosity from private collectors and institutions. I am immensely beholden to the lenders who generously agreed to part with cherished and fragile objects in order that Nadelman's art be given its due. I also particularly wish to acknowledge the financial aid given by The National Endowment for the Arts, The Brown Foundation, Inc., Houston, Laurie Tisch Sussman, Shen Family Foundation, Susan R. Malloy, The Lunder Foundation, the J. M. Kaplan Fund, Dedalus Foundation, and the Whitney's American Fellows and Chairman's Council. Their support of this project and belief in the quality of early-twentieth-century American art made possible both the exhibition and catalogue.

Most of all, I would like to thank Jan, Laurelaine, and Cynthia Nadelman for their hospitality, their generosity as lenders, and their indulgence in allowing me unfettered access to the Nadelman archives. In attempting to place Nadelman's art in the context of his life experiences, I have developed interpretations and opinions that do not always mirror their own. That they accommodated the expression of these opinions testifies to their graciousness as individuals and to their faith in Elie Nadelman's achievement as an artist.

Barbara Haskell

Index

All works are by Elie Nadelman unless otherwise indicated.

Page numbers in italics refer to illustrations.

Parentheses following page numbers denote references to endnotes.

Elie Nadelman: Sculptor of Modern Life was organized by Barbara Haskell, Curator of Early Twentieth-Century Art, Whitney Museum of American Art, with the assistance of Jennifer Palladino, Senior Curatorial Assistant, Prewar Art, and Evelyn Hankins, Assistant Curator, Prewar Art and Special Projects.

This publication was produced by the Publications and New Media Department at the Whitney Museum of American Art:

Director: Garrett White

Editorial: Rachel de W. Wixom, Managing Editor
Thea Hetzner, Associate Editor
Libby Hruska, Associate Editor

Design: Makiko Ushiba, Senior Graphic Designer
Christine Knorr, Graphic Designer

Production: Vickie Leung, Production Manager

Rights and Reproductions: Anita Duquette, Manager, Rights and Reproductions
Jennifer Belt, Photographs and Permissions Coordinator

Assistant: Carolyn Ramo

Catalogue design: Makiko Ushiba
Editor: Karen Jacobson
Proofreader: David E. Brown
Indexer: Susan G. Burke
Polish proofreader: Monika Weiss

Printing and binding: Butler and Tanner Ltd, Frome, London, and New York
Color separations: Radstock Reproductions, England

Printed and bound in England